THE THOMPSON

CHAIN-REFERENCE

BIBLE

COMPANION

THE THOMPSON

CHAIN-REFERENCE

BIBLE

COMPANION

A Handbook For The
Classic Chain-Reference Bible

HOWARD A. HANKE

B. B. Kirkbride Bible Company, Inc.
Indianapolis, Indiana U.S.A.

The Thompson Chain-Reference Bible Companion

This book is a revised and expanded version of
The Thompson Chain-Reference Bible Survey,
Copyright © 1981 by B. B. Kirkbride Bible Co., Inc.

Copyright © 1989 by B. B. Kirkbride Bible Co., Inc.,
Indianapolis, Indiana 46206

ISBN 0–88707–174–0

Library of Congress catalog card number:
89-062998

Printed in the United States of America

Editor: June Gunden, Peachtree City, Georgia
Designer: Shelley Lowell, Atlanta, Georgia
Artist: Bob Russo, Atlanta, Georgia

Illustrations
Shelley Lowell: 27, 36-37, 44, 49, 51, 55, 61, 66, 78,
79, 84, 86, 93, 94, 104, 106, 108, 109, 111, 116, 124,
131, 132, 136, 156, 182, 190-191, 197, 203, 225, 240,
 254, 255, 257, 261, 270, 282, 284, 288, 292-293, 327,
376, 383, 400-401, 410, 411, 413, 415, 418, 425, 443,
444, 446, 447, 452, 461, 468, 472, 479, 482, 484, 489,
492, 498, 537, 541

Special Artwork
Bob Russo: 44-45, 52-53, 112, 144, 183, 192, 204, 535

Photographs
All photographs are by the author except:
Courtesy Doug L. Gunden: 54, 186, 194, 200-201,
212, 238, 260, 329, 361, 388
Courtesy Leonard M. Ward: 413, 425, 564-565

Dedicated to my wife, Hazel Kinlaw Hanke, and to our children,
George, Katherine, Ilka, and Raymond

Table of Contents

Contents:
Essays

Contents:
Major Maps, Charts, and Diagrams

Contents:
Photographs
(Listed by Geographical Location)

Photographs
(continued)

Contents:
Artwork and
Illustrations

Abbreviations

General	ch.,	chapter,	
	chs.	chapters	
	LXX	Septuagint	
	NT	New Testament	
	OT	Old Testament	
	v.,vv.	verse, verses	

Books of	Ge.	Genesis	Ezr.	Ezra
the Bible	Ex.	Exodus	Ne.	Nehemiah
	Le.	Leviticus	Est.	Esther
	Nu.	Numbers	Jb.	Job
	De.	Deuteronomy	Ps.	Psalms
	Jos.	Joshua	Pr.	Proverbs
	Jud.	Judges	Ec.	Ecclesiastes
	Ru.	Ruth	Song	Song of Solomon
	1 S.	1 Samuel	Is.	Isaiah
	2 S.	2 Samuel	Je.	Jeremiah
	1 K.	1 Kings	Lam.	Lamentations
	2 K.	2 Kings	Eze.	Ezekiel
	1 Chr.	1 Chronicles	Da.	Daniel
	2 Chr.	2 Chronicles		

Other Publications and Versions

ABC — *Abingdon Bible Commentary*. New York: Abingdon-Cokesbury, 1929.

Ant. — William Whiston, trans. *Josephus Complete Works*. Grand Rapids: Kregel Publications, 1963.

ASV — American Standard Version of the Bible

CBC — Adam Clarke. *Clarke's Bible Commentary*. New York: Abingdon-Cokesbury, n.d.

DDB — John D. Davis. *Davis Dictionary of the Bible*. Grand Rapids: Baker Book House, 1973.

EA — *Encyclopedia Americana*. New York: Americana Corporation, 1957.

EHB — *Eerdmans' Handbook of the Bible*. Ed. David Alexander and Pat Alexander. Grand Rapids: Wm. B. Eerdmans Co., 1973.

ER — *Encyclopedia of Religion*. Ed. Vergilius Ferm.

Ho.	Hosea	Mk.	Mark	1 Ti.	1 Timothy
Joel	Joel	Lu.	Luke	2 Ti.	2 Timothy
Am.	Amos	Jn.	John	Tit.	Titus
Obad.	Obadiah	Ac.	Acts	Phm.	Philemon
Jona.	Jonah	Ro.	Romans	He.	Hebrews
Mi.	Micah	1 Co.	1 Corinthians	Ja.	James
Na.	Nahum	2 Co.	2 Corinthians	1 Pe.	1 Peter
Hab.	Habakkuk	Ga.	Galatians	2 Pe.	2 Peter
Zep.	Zephaniah	Ep.	Ephesians	1 Jn.	1 John
Hag.	Haggai	Ph.	Philippians	2 Jn.	2 John
Zec.	Zechariah	Col.	Colossians	3 Jn.	3 John
Mal.	Malachi	1 Th.	1 Thessalonians	Jude	Jude
Mt.	Matthew	2 Th.	2 Thessalonians	Re.	Revelation

New York: The Philosophical Library, 1945.

HBD   Madeleine S. Miller and J. Lane Miller. *Harper's Bible Dictionary*. New York: Harper and Brothers, 1954.

HBH   Henry H. Halley. *Halley's Bible Handbook*. Grand Rapids:Zondervan Publishing House, 1962.

HCC   Kenneth Scott Latouratte, *History of the Christian Church*. New York: Harper and Row, 1953.

ISBE   *International Standard Bible Encyclopedia*. Grand Rapids: Wm. B. Eerdmans Co., 1959.

KJV   King James Version of the Bible

MAP   Charles W. Slemming, *Made According to Pattern*. London: Marshall Morgan & Sons, n.d.

NBC   *New Bible Commentary*. Ed. F. Davidson, A. M. Stibbs, and E. F. Kevan. Grand Rapids: Wm. B. Eerdmans Co., 1953.

NIV   New International Version of the Bible

RSV   Revised Standard Version of the Bible

SBD   William Smith. *Smith's Bible Dictionary*. Old

Other Publications and Versions
(continued)

	Tappan, N. J.: Fleming H. Revell, 1977.	printed Grand Rapids: Baker Book House, 1978.
TCRB	Thompson Chain-Reference Bible. 5th ed. Indianapolis: B. B. Kirkbride Bible Co., 1988.	TWBE *The World Book Encyclopedia,* 1975.
TMC	*The Modern Commentary.* New York: Grosset and Dunlop, 1935.	WBC *Wycliff Bible Commentary.* Chicago: Moody Press, 1962.
TSB	*The Story of the Bible.* New York: Wm. H. Wise and Co., 1952.	WBE *Wycliff Bible Encyclopedia.* Ed. Charles F. Pfeiffer and Everett F. Harrison. Chicago: Moody Press, 1975.
TWBC	*The Wesleyan Bible Commentary.* Grand Rapids: Wm. B. Eerdmans Co., 1967; re-	ZPEB *The Zondervan Pictorial Encyclopedia of the Bible.* Grand Rapids: Zondervan Publishing House, 1975.

Preface

If the Thompson Chain-Reference Bible has one primary focus, it is the interrelationship of the Holy Scriptures. All the years of Dr. Thompson's research were given to identifying the themes and thoughts that run like a continuum through the individual books of the Bible. By linking together the verses on a given subject, the Bible becomes its own infallible commentary, for the reader can understand one verse by receiving instruction from the others on that subject.

For that reason the chains of references in the Thompson Chain-Reference Bible are its backbone. True, there is a wealth of other information, but the greatest aid to the Bible student is still the placing of Scripture beside Scripture, allowing God's Holy Spirit to instruct by using the very Word of God.

The author of this Companion has the same goal as that of Dr. Thompson: that individual verses of Scripture be seen in the context of larger Biblical themes. However, this is an expansion of Dr. Thompson's work in one particular area. It takes the most important of the Biblical messages— God's plan of redemption—and shows how it has been given from Genesis to Revelation. To do this the author looks at particular verses throughout the Scriptures and comments on them in their context.

This book is not a Bible survey in that it does not undertake to provide general facts about every section of the Bible. Nor is it a standard commentary since it does not seek to expound on all passages of Scripture. Rather it is a unique combination of factual data and commentary on selected verses that contribute to the purpose of showing the interrelationships of Scripture.

A Bible scholar once said: "What is unfolded in Scripture is one great economy of salvation —*Unum Continuum Systema*— an organism of divine acts and testimonies, which, with the beginning of Genesis with creation, advances progressively to its completion in the person and work of Christ, and is to find its close in the new heaven and earth predicted in the Apocalypse; and it is only in connection with this whole that the details can be properly estimated."[1]

It is the purpose of this book to comment on the details of Scripture in a way that will deepen the reader's gratitude to God Almighty for his unspeakable gift—salvation through Jesus Christ our Lord.

The Practical Advantages of this Companion

This book will be of great value to all who love to study the Word of God in depth. Dr. Hanke's passion for the Scriptures is evident on every page.

For teachers of the Word. The book is structured by Biblical book so that it can be used side-by-side with any Scripture lesson. It provides succinct background information about the book being studied, including: (1) The Name of the book, (2) Authorship and Date of the book, and (3) its Background, Purpose and Content.

In addition to the background information about the Biblical book, the reader will find the following resources: commentary on specific verses, special essays on major subjects, maps, charts, diagrams, illustrations and photographs.

For reference help the teacher can refer to the Dictionary beginning on p. 583 of this Companion. This mini-dictionary lists the major people, places and themes of the Bible. In addition, for each entry there is a side margin reference to the Thompson Bible chains that apply to the subject. This is the only Bible dictionary available with this valuable asset for study. It combines both a brief, identifying definition of the subject as well as the chain-reference resource for deeper study.

Another reference aid to the teacher is the extensive Bibliography which begins on p. 651. Here are eighteen pages providing at a glance a list of some of the best-loved and most helpful publications available to the Bible student. It will be invaluable to those who are searching for additional resources for Bible study.

For serious Bible students. All of the richness of the Thompson Chain-Reference system is put to work in this Companion. Every page of commentary carries side margin references based on the same valuable topics and numbers that are found in the Thompson Bible.

If, for example, the subject at hand is the well-known verse in Is. 7:14, "...Behold a virgin shall conceive and bear a son, and shall call his name Immanuel," the student will turn to the book of Isaiah in this Companion and find the commentary for this verse on pp. 227-230. He will then notice that the side margins contain the topics and numbers which he can look up in his Thompson Bible and read extensively what the Bible has to say about the subject at hand.

In this case Dr. Hanke has discussed several main points: the virgin birth aspect of the verse, the prophetic nature of the verse, the fact that the one prophesied about is indeed the Christ, and the implications of the name Immanuel. For each of these points there are topics in the side margin that provide the reader with Biblical references that correlate. For example there is "Immanuel," "Christ's Divinity—Humanity," "Incarnation," "The Virgin Birth," "Messianic Prophecies,""Christ's Name," and so on.

In the special essay sections of this Companion the topics and numbers that refer the reader to the Thompson Bible are placed in small boxes adjacent to the text to which they apply.

The themes of the special essays are thus given depth because the reader can quickly locate all the Scriptures on the subject through the chain of references.

For students of Bible history and archaeology. Just as the Archaeological Supplement to the Thompson Bible provides the student with a vast reservoir of information about Biblical locations, this book is rich in additional historical and archaeological insights.

The author has had an "on the spot" acquaintance with almost every place in Europe and the Near East where Bible events took place. He has done extensive research and study at these locations in over a hundred study expeditions. Dr. Hanke brings a rich repertoire of lecture notes as well as numerous photographic windows through which the modern reader can visualize and better understand the unity of the Old and New Testaments, which "holy men of God" wrote as the Holy Ghost stimulated and directed their thinking.

A quick glance at the list of essays on pp. 8-9 will show the pages devoted to places of historical interest to the Bible student. Also, there are many insightful comments made throughout the text that can be readily found by checking the Subject Index at the back of the book.

For all who love the Word! One of the most fruitful methods of study is the placing of Scripture beside Scripture—comparing and contrasting the great themes and subjects, integrating one passage with another, outlining and organizing the events and message.

Accordingly, throughout this Companion Dr. Hanke has meticulously treated passages of Scripture in light of other Scripture. He is especially gifted in the area of illuminating the unity of the Biblical message, pointing out time and time again that there is nothing in the New Testament that does not have its roots in the Old Testament.

As in the Thompson Chain-Reference Bible, this book contains many charts and diagrams which visually compare one passage of Scripture with another in order to grasp Biblical truths. Often this results in a broader view of a subject. For example, on page 400-401 there is a diagram showing "The Progressive Development of the Church." Then on the next two pages a chart shows exactly how these worship centers developed from the earliest reference in Genesis to the present time. The chart provides descriptive information, Bible references, the location of in-depth commentary in the Companion, and reference to the place in the Thompson Bible where further study can be made. It should be noted that the Thompson Bible introduces this subject and the Companion provides additional tools for studying it. The Companion contains many such amplifications of subjects that are already a part of the Thompson Chain-Reference Bible.

This Companion is in essence a hand-in-glove edition prepared for use with the Thompson Chain-Reference Bible. The reader will want to keep them side by side on his bookshelf, for when he reaches for one the other will no doubt follow.

The Publisher

*Jesus Christ the same yesterday,
and to day, and for ever.*

Hebrews 13:8

THE THOMPSON

CHAIN-REFERENCE

BIBLE

COMPANION

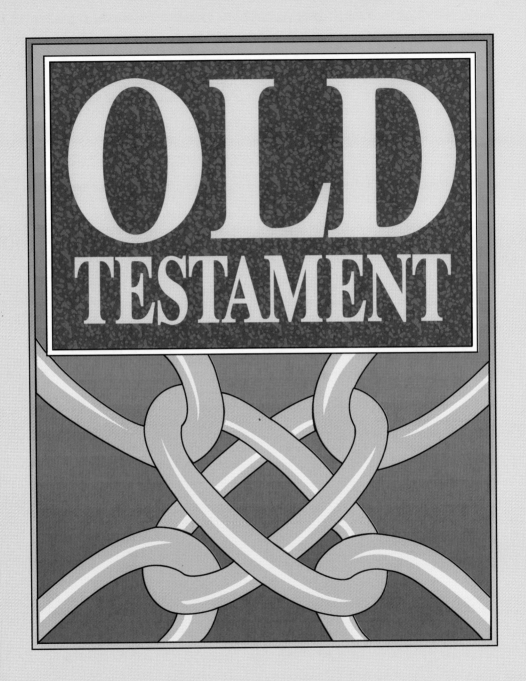

The Old Testament

The thirty-nine Old Testament books give an account of redemptive history from Genesis to Malachi.

OT Outline
4222a

On these pages we have reflections of love and hate in all their passions. We see the rise and fall of nations and the clash of armies marching across the stage of time. We see the good and the bad, the heroes and the villains on parade. The best and the worst of human nature is clearly portrayed. Problems of philosophy and theology are discussed in poetry and prose as well as dreams, religion and the law. All of these writings are designed to give understanding to future generations. Woven into the fabric of this literature is the redemptive drama leading to salvation from sin.

Redemption
2978-2979

Man is pictured as a free moral agent with power to choose good or evil. He has a free will to choose salvation or to reject it.

In this record we see how man became vain, conceited and engrossed in his selfish pursuits. In the flood under Noah, God made plain the harsh punishment for sin. Only righteous Noah, his wife, his three sons and their wives were preserved to perpetuate the human race.

In due time God chose Abraham, a Semite, to be the progenitor of the people who would produce the Messiah. The writers of the thirty-nine books, in concert, give a prophetic glimpse of this coming Messiah and his characteristics.

Messiah
695

God chose the Hebrews, a closely-knit people with a deep commitment to keeping their ethnic bloodstream pure, for his Messianic line. No other race of people has had a continuing geneal-

Chosen Ones
2725

ogy for 2000 years — from Abraham to the Advent of Jesus Christ, the Messiah. By maintaining their inter-family relationship, they were able to assimilate, accumulate and preserve the holy oracles over a period of 1500 years. These writings were eventually canonized and declared to be the authoritative Word of God, the Old Testament.

God's Word
Sacred
427

The Messiah historically depicted in the New Testament is the same Messiah that is prophetically portrayed in the Old Testament. This shows that God and Christ are eternally one and the same in all generations. The Savior in the Old Testament and the New Testament are one— the "same yesterday, today and forever."

One God
2649

How It Was Written

It is difficult to pinpoint a date when the Old Testament books were written and when they were first considered to be the Word of God. Scholars have agreed that the books were written during the space of about one thousand years. Tradition holds that the book of Job may be the oldest book in the OT, and that Moses may have had personal contact with Job when he was in Midian exile. Conservative Bible scholars assume that Moses compiled and wrote most of the materials in the Pentateuch (see discussion of this on page 36). Much of the OT was compiled by Ezra in about 536 B.C. Malachi is credited with writing his book about 400 B.C.

Bible, Origin
and Growth
4220

One Bible scholar remarks that "the Bible books are called inspired as the Divinely determined products of inspired men; the Bible writers are called in-

"Word"
Inspired
417

spired, as breathed into, by the Holy Spirit so that the product of their activities transcends human powers and becomes Divinely authoritative … Inspiration is, therefore, usually defined as supernatural influence exerted on the sacred writers by the Spirit of God, by virtue of which their writings are given Divine trustworthiness."[1]

The Old Testament books were written by men who were aware of this inspiration of the Scriptures, often expressing it by "thus saith the Lord." These authors were divinely possessed with the idea that their writings were to be preserved and handed down to future generations as norms of faith and conduct (cf. 2 S. 23:2; Ps. 49:1-4; Je. 36:27-32).

"Word" Endures
415

The figure of a scribe found in an ancient Egyptian tomb.

How It Was Preserved

The OT itself provides valuable hints as to how it was preserved. In Exodus 40:20 the "testimony" or the tablets of the law containing the Ten Commandments were placed in the ark of the covenant for safekeeping. The laws of Deuteronomy were delivered to the sons of Levi to be deposited beside the ark. In 1 Kings 8:9 the record states that when Solomon brought the ark up from the City of David to the temple, the tablets were still its sole contents.

Ark of the Covenant
216

Another possible means of preserving the Word came through Hezekiah whose men were credited with copying a large number of proverbs (Pr. 25:1). The scribes to whom the OT manuscripts were entrusted were trained in rabbinical and Mosaic Law and above all else, in accuracy. They were "letter of the law" scholars, who frequently discarded a manuscript on

Law Perfect
436

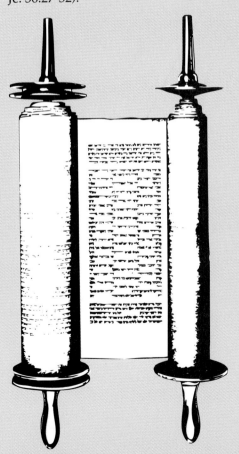

The Law of Moses.

which an error had been made. They were totally obsessed with the idea that they had the responsibility of transmitting and preserving the "Word of God" exactly, in every "jot" and "tittle," the two smallest consonantal forms in the Hebrew alphabet (cf. Mt. 5:18).

The rabbis considered the Old Testament books to be so sacred that, when worn out from use, they could not be destroyed or discarded as rubbish. These worn-out manuscripts were placed in a vault (called *genizah*) in some isolated part of the temple or synagogue. It is quite likely that King Josiah found a worn copy of the Law in the *genizah* following a wicked period of idolatry under Kings Manasseh and Amon (2 K. 22:8). Josiah then instituted a religious reform based on the

> God's Word
> Sacred
> **427**

parts of the Law (how much is unknown) that had been preserved. Thus, the words of the Lord were recognized as such (2 K. 22:13,18-19) long before there was mention of a Biblical canon.

How We Know It's Authentic

The finding of the Dead Sea Scrolls in 1947 has not only given scholars additional Hebrew Bible books which are much earlier than any extant manuscripts, it has also confirmed the validity of the previously found manuscripts. Comparing the Dead Sea Scrolls of Isaiah with the Masoretic (i.e., medieval) text reveals a 95 percent word for word identity. The remaining five percent of the variants deal mainly with a slip of the pen or spelling. The noted Yale professor,

> Dead Sea Scrolls
> **4362**

Millar Burrows, says that the Isaiah Scroll is very important for establishing the best possible text of the Old Testament. "Essentially it is the same as the book of Isaiah in our Bible, a voice from 2,000 years ago. Preserved in the wondrous providence of God, confirming the integrity of the Bible."[2]

*Pictures
Isaiah Scroll
4362*

The entire Bible has been checked and double checked by the test of time to such an extent that there is no longer any reasonable doubt about it. The noted scholar and archaeologist, Kathleen Kenyon, is assuring at this point:

> The Christian can take the whole Bible in his hand and say without fear or hesitation that he holds in it the True Word of God, handed without essential loss from generation to generation, throughout the centuries.[3]

Jesus himself confirmed the authenticity of the OT Scriptures. "Haven't you read this Scripture?" he asked forthrightly as he quoted Psalm 118:22 to show that the rejection of the Messiah by the people was already foretold in Scripture (Mk. 12:10, NIV). In another instance Jesus chided Nicodemus for his lack of spiritual understanding: "Art thou a master of Israel, and knowest not these things?" (Jn. 3:10). Jesus also referred to the new birth, a concept that had been taught in the Old Testament (Eze. 36:26). It must be remembered that the Synoptic period actually occurred in the OT period.

*New Birth
2154*

When the spiritually dead temple leaders criticized the common people, who, ignorant of the Scriptures (Jn. 7:49), uttered the hosannas, Jesus was asked, "Do you hear what these children are saying?" He responded with a quote from Psalm 8:2: "From the lips of children and infants you have ordained praise" (Mt. 21:16, NIV).

In his divine knowledge Jesus acknowledged the Scriptures to be true. They were the source of his authority. After his resurrection he reproved those foolish and "slow of heart" who did not believe all that was written in the Scriptures (Lu. 24:25). To Jesus, "thus it is written" was sufficient.

Another determining factor of authenticity rests on the sterling character of the writers and the belief that they were God's spokesmen. "Holy men of God spake as they were moved by the Holy Ghost" (2 Pe. 1:21). The spiritual benefit which the people received from the ensuing writings corresponded with and confirmed the people's belief in the divine origin of the words. Each individual book of a

*"Word" Inspired
417*

Qumran. The caves in which some of the Dead Sea Scrolls were found.

prophet of the Lord was accepted as the Word of God. The pragmatic results of these books verified their authority. Their concepts and precepts actually worked in everyday life (2 Ti. 3:16). This is what made the books authoritative even before the church had officially accepted them.

Power of "Word"
421

Most conclusive is the practical way in which Bible concepts and principles work in stabilizing society. No one can deny that the ideas expressed in the Great Commandment (Mt. 22:37-38) and in the Ten Commandments (Ex. 20:1-17), if applied, would solve the moral and ethical issues in the world of nations.

The Jews were people of the Book. Their unquestioned confidence in the authority of the sacred writings won many heathen people from their impotent and impoverished superstitions to the true and living God.

Love of "Word"
420

How It Became
The Official Canon

The step-by-step process of canonization is shrouded in the unknowable; the action was evidently so gradual that there was no awareness of it.

Bible, Origin and Growth
4220

However, we know that the idea of canonization existed long before there was a word to express it, because the early Hebrews assumed that the holy scrolls were written by holy men under the leadership of the Holy Spirit (2 Pe. 1:21). For many years they circulated the Old Testament scrolls as inspirational reading and as guidelines for ethical and moral conduct. At some time in history the Old Testament books were generally accepted as the authoritative Word of God (2 Ti. 3:16).

The New Testament furnishes important evidence that there existed a fixed canon to which authoritative appeal could be made. Most important are the Old Testament writings referred to by the authors of the New Testament. References to "the Scriptures," "the Holy Scriptures," "the Law and the Prophets," and so on are numerous: Matthew 5:17; 17:12; 22:29,40; Luke 16:16; 24:44; John 10:34-35; 12:34; 15:25; 19:36; Acts 13:15; 18:24; 28:23; Romans 1:2; 1 Corinthians 14:21; 2 Timothy 3:15; 2 Peter 1:20. These citations certainly assume that Jesus and the apostles had a great regard for the Old Testament, as separate and fixed. The frequent references in the New Testament to Old Testament books indicate that there was a closed OT canon before the New Testament was canonized.

The world-famous Rabbinical Council or Synod (A.D. 90-118) met in Jamnia for the purpose of placing the final seal of approval on the Old Testament books as the Word of God. Their action was not something new; they gave ecclesiastical approval to that which had been accepted as true for hundreds of years. The test of time had made its final pronouncement. The canon does not derive its authority from the church, whether Jewish or Christian. The office of the church is merely that of a custodian of the Scripture and a witness of its power.

How The Order
Of Books Developed

The Hebrews classified the Old Testament Scriptures into three main categories: the Torah or Law, the Nebhiim or Prophets, and the Kethubim or the Writings by the Sopherim (the wise).

Book of the Law
525

1. The Torah ("Law") included the first five books—the Pentateuch, or the Books of Moses. They were Genesis, Exodus, Leviticus, Numbers, and

Jamnia (Biblical Jabneel). The site where the Rabbinical Council of A.D. 90-118 met to place final approval on the Old Testament canon. The breaker in this picture indicates a submerged wall. Some masonry juts out of the cliff at the left. Much of the ancient city is now covered with sand.

Deuteronomy.

2. The Nebhiim ("Prophets") embraced (a) the four so-called former prophets: Joshua, Judges, 1 and 2 Samuel (counted as one book), 1 and 2 Kings (also counted as one book) and (b) the four so-called latter prophets: Isaiah, Jeremiah, Ezekiel, and the twelve minor prophets, which counted as one book.

Prophets
2065

3. The Kethubim ("Writings") included: Psalms, Proverbs, Job, and the Five Rolls—Songs, Ruth, Lamentations, Ecclesiastes, and Esther—plus the historical books, Daniel, Ezra and Nehemiah (counted as one book), and 1 and 2 Chronicles (counted as one book).

The New Testament gives clear evidence of this threefold division of the Old Testament canon (Lu. 24:44). Also,

Jesus suggested the final order and arrangement of the books of the Old Testament canon by saying, "From the blood of righteous Abel unto the blood of Zacharias" (Mt. 23:35; cf. Lu.11:51). This expression is used in the same sense in which one would say "from Genesis to Malachi."

History does not reveal why the books are grouped as they are. The arrangement was evidently based on content and the possibility that one section of the canon was closed before the other. However, the importance of classifying the books is secondary to the fact that they are a part of the canon.

How It Relates To The New Testament

The Old Testament contains a message that has blessed mankind throughout all generations. In reading it one soon finds evidence that it is a collection of holy writings, describing a unique religion. In these inspired words one discerns a God of mercy (Jona. 4:2) and love (Je. 31:3), as well as one of judgment (Is. 30:18). The religious system described in the OT had a priesthood (2 Chr. 11:13) directed by a high priest (Ex. 21:10).

> Bible
> 414-434

The spiritual well-being of the Hebrew people was supervised by a group of evangelists, called prophets (2 K. 5:8). The people of God were called the *qahal* — "the congregation" — the called out ones (Ps. 82:1; 89:5), corresponding to the *ekklesia* of the NT "church" (Mt. 18:17; Ac. 2:47). The worship centers manifested progressive development from the simple altar (Ge. 8:20) to the tabernacle (Ex. 26:1) followed by the temple (1 K. 7:50) or house of the Lord (2 S. 7:13; 1 K. 5:5), and finally the synagogue (Mt. 12:9). In these centers of worship the Holy Writings were presented to meet the moral, ethical, and religious needs of the people "for doctrine, for reproof, for correction, for instruction in righteousness" (2 Ti. 3:16b).

> Prophets
> 2065

> Places for Worship
> 4316

This raises the question: what religion is this? The traditional answer would be that it is Judaism, the religion of the Jews. But this is too simplistic. It is more than that. In a real sense OT religion was Christianity in embryonic form. It was a system by which people in the OT escaped the penalty for sin and

> Sin's Penalty
> 3352

gained fellowship with their Creator. In this system one sees all the aspects of the "church" as it was before the coming of Christ the Messiah.

> Messianic Hope
> 4186

The OT is the basic source for the concept of a monotheistic holy God (De. 4:3; 6:4), who is presented in three persons: Elohim, or "God" (Ge. 1:1); YHWH, or "LORD" (Ge. 3:23); and Ruach, or "Spirit" (Ge. 6:3; cf. Lu. 4:18), corresponding to the NT Father, Son and Holy Ghost or Spirit (Mt. 28:19).

Both the OT and the NT emphasize the teaching that the basic requirement is one's love for God and love for man.

> Love Preeminent
> 4182

When a lawyer asked Jesus, "Which is the great commandment in the law?" (Mt. 22:36), Jesus quoted God's words to Moses, "Thou shalt love the LORD thy God with all thine heart..." (De. 6:5) and "thou shalt love thy neighbor as thyself" (Le. 19:18; cf. Mt 22:37-39). This is perhaps the simplest statement of what Christianity is all about, and it puts OT religion on a lofty plane.

Jesus concluded his statement thus: "On these two commandments [love God; love man] hang all the law and the prophets" (Mt. 22:40). In the Good News Bible (American Bible Society) this passage reads: "The whole Law of Moses and the teachings of the prophets depend on these two commandments." In fact, Paul tells the Christians of Jewish origin in Galatia that "all the law is fulfilled in one word, even in this; Thou shalt love thy neighbor as thyself" (Ga. 5:14). John adds this test of discipleship, "By this we know that we love the children of God, when we love God, and keep his commandments" (1 Jn. 5:2; see also 1 Jn. 4:11-17). With this love in his heart,

> Brotherly Love
> 2200-2202

man will not disobey either the first four commandments, dealing with man-to-God obligations, or the other six, referring to man-to-man relationships (De. 5:6-21).

> Love to God
> 2207

The moral, ethical, and religious standards of the Christian faith were drawn from the OT legal code which God gave to Moses and the Israelites on Mount Sinai about fourteen hundred years before the advent of Christ.

At that time God placed upon Moses the responsibility of implementing and recording the plan whereby man could approach God and meet his requirements (Ex. 19:3; De. 4:14). The Decalogue (Ex. 20; Jn. 7:19) and carefully constructed rules governing sacrifices, offerings, and the treatment of community members and strangers were designed to make of the Israelites a holy nation, if they would be obedient (Ex. 19:5-6). The OT contained symbolism which expressed faith in God's promise of redemption and which was finally fulfilled in Christ. The law was only a shadow of the good things to come, but even a shadow presupposes an object and that object was Christ.

> Decalogue
> 949

Man in his sinful state is unable to achieve the high standard instituted by God through Moses, and later reemphasized by Jesus: to love God with his whole heart and his neighbor as himself. The enablement to fulfill the divine commandment of love must come from God, because he is love (1 Jn. 4:8). To this end he made provision by the promise of a Savior.

> Purpose of Law
> 4055

> God's Love
> 2206

Even in OT times, before the advent of Christ, believers were enabled to experience saving faith such as was referred to by Habakkuk, "The just shall live by his faith" (Hab. 2:4). This was reaffirmed by Paul (Ro. 1:17; Ga. 3:11) and the writer of Hebrews 10:38.

> Justification
> by Faith
> 1203

There is even evidence in the OT of experiencing "Sermon on the Mount" love as seen in the story of Jacob and Esau. In order to escape Esau's vengeance (Ge. 27:41) for stealing his birthright, Jacob fled to Paddan Aram in Haran (Ge. 28:6). Years later Jacob decided to return home but he fully expected his brother to vent his hostility upon him. Jacob's scouts told Jacob that his brother Esau was coming to meet him with 400 men (Ge. 32:6). Jacob, under conviction for his sin, probably imagined each man was fully armed and ready to do battle. Jacob was "greatly afraid" and organized his tribe into battle formation (Ge. 32:7-8). He put his fighting men in the front ranks and placed his wives and children in the rear (Ge. 33:1-3). Jacob rationalized that he could buy his brother off with gifts (Ge. 32:13-20).

> Enemies
> 3395

When Jacob came face to face with Esau, a miracle of love happened. Instead of Esau showing hostility and hate toward Jacob, he showed compassion and love. "Esau ran to meet him, and embraced him, and fell on his neck, and kissed him: and they wept" (Ge. 33:4). Instead of seeing the face of a vengeful brother, Jacob viewed his brother's face as though he "had seen the face of God" (Ge. 33:10b).

> Good for Evil
> 1437

Years later this love attitude was again expressed by Joseph when he confronted his brothers in Egypt (Ge. 45:1-5). Certainly this attitude of love expressed by Esau and Joseph gives rationale to the love commandment given by God through Moses (De. 6:5; Le. 19:18; cf. Mt. 22:37-40).

It is obvious that divine revelation, whether in the OT or in the NT, is substantially the same and manifests itself through common agencies and means. The basic principles of redemption are essentially the same regardless of the time or place, because God transcends time; he never changes. The bruis-

Immutability
2480

ing of the seed in Genesis refers to the divine sacrifice, already planned (Ge. 3:15). The sacrifice by Abel illustrated God's acceptance of the blood sacrifice (Ge. 4:4) and the blood ritual continued until Christ validated it by his own supreme sacrifice on the cross. Thus the sacrifice of blood portrayed in the OT was fulfilled in Christ, and the Holy Spirit witnesses to the fact in the believer's heart.

Christ's
Sacrifice
3366

Genesis

The Name

The word *genesis* does not appear in the Hebrew Bible, but is derived from the Hebrew *bereshith* as used in Ge. 1:1, "In the beginning God created the heaven and the earth."

The Greek word *genesis* means variously: "birth," "origin," "genealogy" or "generation." The translators of the Greek version of the Scripture, the Septuagint, used the word *genesis* as the name for the first book in the Bible. The term is most appropriately used in this connection because the book of Genesis answers "the question of how the world originated, how sin came into the world, how man fell from grace, how God gave hope of redemption to fallen man, how sin spread, how a great judgment was visited upon the sinful world in the Flood, how a remnant of the human race was providentially saved, how the human race again spread abroad still proudly asserting itself."[1]

Thus the name "Genesis" is given to a book which contains a record of the origin or beginning of all things.

Authorship and Date

There is no direct internal evidence that Moses wrote the book of Genesis, but tradition has preserved the idea of Mosaic authorship. The name of Moses has been closely bound to the authorship of the books of the Pentateuch, which are referred to as "The Five Books of Moses." The caption at the head of the first book in the OT is "The First Book of Moses, called Genesis." This pattern follows through to Deuteronomy, which is called the "Fifth Book of Moses."

There are sufficient statements in the other books of the Pentateuch to give Mosaic authorship to at least portions of Genesis as well as the other books in the Pentateuch (see Ex. 17:14; 24:4-7; 34:27; Nu. 33:2). Also, David referred to "the law of Moses" (1 K. 2:3) and in the synoptic period Luke used the same expression (Lu. 2:22). Jesus made frequent reference to the writings of Moses (Jn. 5:46-47; 7:19). Of particular interest is his reference to the threefold divisions of the Hebrew Bible, with these words: "All things must be fulfilled, which were written in the law of Moses, and in the prophets, and in the Psalms, concerning me" (Lu. 24:44; see also Lu. 16:29,31; cf. Jn. 5:46-47; Mt. 5:17). In this statement about "Moses" Jesus is making reference to the Pentateuch.

Bible Outline **4222a**

Creator **884-885**

Book of Genesis **4223**

Moses **2420-2421**

Prophecy Fulfilled **2892-2893**

One writer affirms that

Apostles
2080-2082

the apostles also used terminology which supports this contention (Ac. 26:22; 28:23). Christ referred to many items in the Genesis record as inspired Scriptures (Mt. 19:4-6; 24:38; Lu. 17:32; Jn. 7:22). It is clear that the apostles held to the Mosaic authorship of Genesis. The Jewish historian Josephus expressly stated the same view in about A.D. 90 (Against Apion 1.8). No ancient authority of value brings this view into question.[2]

A noted scholar concludes: "There is no valid reason to dispute the Mosaic authorship. The scriptures uphold it, and the style of the Pentateuch is in harmony with other records originating at an earlier date than the beginning of the Hebrew monarchy... Besides it is altogether possible that Moses used earlier documents and annals, such as 'The Ten Generations'...and compiled them into one account. Suffice it to say, whether compiled or originally composed, Moses was guided by the Spirit, as the Bible indicated,

Holy Spirit
Guides
1611

to write a redemptive or a religious history of 'first things.' "[3]

Objections to Mosaic Authorship Modern rejection of Mosaic authorship began in 1756, when Jean Astruc published a book entitled *Conjectures on the Original Memoirs which Moses Seems to Have Used in Composing the Book of Genesis.* He observed that in the book of Genesis the divine names YHWH (translated Jehovah in ARV and LORD in KJV, RSV and NIV)

Engish
Versions
4220

and Elohim (translated God in most English versions) were not used interchangeably and that one was more predominant in some sections than others.

In pursuing this problem a few decades later, the liberal theologians in Germany took the lead in constructing a documentary hypothesis by employing the "investigative technique" as is used for evaluating secular literature. They concluded that two separate and distinct deities were involved, not recognizing or considering the possibility that these designations or titles of deity related to the various functions of God.

According to their theory, the consonantal form of YHWH referred to the "Thunder God" of Mount Sinai; later this deity became the God of the Southern Kingdom (Judah). References to him in the Scriptures were grouped into a section specified as the "J" documents (J standing for Jehovah, the ARV rendering of YHWH). The divine name Elohim, translated "God" in almost all English versions, indicated the God of the Northern Kingdom (Israel). To this theory were added the "D" documents which related to the legal codes or the law. The parts of the Pentateuch dealing with priestly affairs were labeled the "P" documents. These theories were combined into what is now known as the JEDP hypothesis, subscribed to generally by liberal scholars but acknowledged as untenable by many within their own ranks. This theory leaves little, if any, place for Mosaic authorship or divine inspiration of the compilers and/or writers of the Scriptures.

Jehovah
1868-1872

"Word"
Inspired
417

"In the beginning God created the heaven and the earth."

One leading scholar gives an appraisal of this theory: "Scholars pursued this theory until they thought there had originally been five or six documents." Later many fragments of documents were pieced and fitted together, and then altered and added to by still later editors so that "according to some writers, some of the stories…in Genesis and other books were made of parts of stories from various documents and fragments. Moses was denied authorship of most of the Pentateuch. The theory was carried to such lengths of absurdity that it was far more difficult to believe than the simple, plain declaration of the Bible itself, that Moses wrote these things…They could see no other basis … for the use of different names for God in the OT than a literary significance which is no significance at all for the spiritual mind. There is, however, a functional significance in the use of these different names. It is much more 'rational' to believe that the great, infinite and eternal God has given us these different names to express different aspects of His being and the different relationships He sustains to His creatures."[4]

Divine
Ways
3796

Omni-
science
of Christ
3849

The Importance of Mosaic Authorship "The issue of Mosaic authorship of the Pentateuch is important to anyone who [considers] the NT as a truthful record of Jesus Christ's words and work. Faith in Christ and in the books of the OT canon stand or fall together. Christ and His apostles not only [consider] the Pentateuch as [having] Mosaic [authorship] but put their seal on it as Holy Scripture, as they did for the entire Jewish canon of their day (Ro. 1:2; 2 Ti. 3:16)."[5]

Thus, Mosaic authorship is important to the conservative, evangelical Christian because the entire system of doctrinal and Scriptural integrity rests on this question. To discount Moses as the author of the Pentateuch places a low estimation on the divine inspiration and the authority of the Scriptures.

God's Word
Sacred
427
God's Sure
Word
430
Analysis of
the Book
4223

Background, Purpose, and Content

The exact stages in which the Book of Beginnings developed are unknown. To outline this book is a difficult task because it is possible that the book of Genesis had its beginning with the family records referred to as the "Ten Generations." Moses probably used these family records as a basis for compiling the book of Genesis in its present form. The first part of Genesis was probably the preface and the Creation Hymn (Ge. 1:1-2:3)

The Ten Generations of Genesis	
1 The Generations of Heaven and Earth	2:4-4:26
2 The Generations of Adam	5:1-6:8
3 The Generations of Noah	6:9-9:29
4 The Generations of the Sons of Noah	10:1-11:9
5 The Generations of Shem	11:10-26
6 The Generations of Tereh	11:27-25:11
7 The Generations of Ishmael	25:12-18
8 The Generations of Isaac	25:19-35:29
9 The Generations of Essau	36:1-43
10 The Generations of Jacob	37:2-50:26

Importance of Genesis

The book of Genesis is a vast storehouse of knowledge, embracing many subjects. This book is, in a measure, the keystone of all redemptive doctrines. The very need of salvation rests upon the origin of sin as described in Genesis. Without the Genesis record there could not have been the other sixty-five books in the Bible. All of these books base their theology on what happened in Genesis. This book is the source book in which the message of the "cross" is prefigured through the lives and experiences of such men as Abel, Enoch, Noah, Melchizedek, and Moses. The wilderness journey, the tabernacle, and finally the entrance of the "Jacob tribes" into the "Promised Land" are object lessons of God's grace. The book of Genesis tells man where he came from and where he is going.

Some theologians have a tendency to divorce OT religion from any direct connection with the NT, placing it in the same category with other pre-Christian religions, such as that ascribed to Homer and the theology of Marcion. (For more information about Marcion, see the Introduction to the NT.) To this school of thought, the LORD of the OT is a dim and distant figure who has nothing to do with the redemptive process in the NT.

This point of view is closely related to that of the Gnostics, who considered the God of the OT to be an inferior god, a kind of "demiurge," who had created the evil world of matter, in contrast to the spiritual realm that Jesus had come to reveal. To this impersonal, transcendent god, love, mercy, and justice were completely foreign.[6]

However, the facts of revelation do not substantiate these conclusions. "The relationship of the New Testament to the Old is of such nature that they both stand or fall together. The NT assumes the existence of the OT law and prophecy as its positive presupposition ... We cannot have the redeeming God of the New Covenant without the creator and 'covenant God' preached in the Old; we cannot divorce the Redeemer from the OT predictions which He came to fulfill. The genesis of all the ideas of the NT relating to salvation lies in the OT."[7]

There is not a flower of truth blooming in the New Testament whose seed was not sown in the soil of the Old; and there was not a seed of truth planted in the OT which does not come to full fruitage in the NT. The very breath of the OT is the same breath that prayed, dying, on Calvary.

> The heavenly council met in extraordinary session in behalf of man's redemption long before the racial catastrophe [the Fall] took place. God the Father, with the Son and the Holy Spirit, constituting the Trinity, had the bridge of salvation built before man actually came to it. While the details of the plan of redemption were not known from the beginning, there was no uncertainty as to the [basic] facts...The Christ, promised [to man] in Eden, was the [eternal] Saviour of the world, making it possible that the first woman who yielded to the temptation of disobedience, might through faith in the promised Redeemer become a subject of His redemptive grace.[8]

A noted Bible scholar captured the significance of this truth in these words: "Before the first man sinned, God provided a way by which he might escape the death penalty and be made perfect again. That was through the atoning work of Christ who...was 'slain from the foundation of the world' " (Re. 13:8b).[9]

Doctrine
1029, 3558

Redemption
Through
Christ
2978-2979

River Chart
Page 4

Spiritual
Kingdom
2007-2011

Salvation
3116-3123

Prophecies
2890-2892

Spiritual
Kingdom
2007-2011

Salvation
Promised
3122

Immutability
2480

In Mt. 25:34 reference is made to the inheritance of "the kingdom prepared for you from the foundation of the world."With regard to the eternal relationship of Christ to salvation the Bible affirms that

God had appointed His Son to be the Mediator of salvation. The Son is the Lamb, without blemish before the foundation of the world was laid (1 Pe. 1:19-20). Christ is the Mediator of world redemption, for it was the good pleasure of the "...Father that in him [Christ] should all fulness dwell...to reconcile all things unto himself" (Col. 1:19-20). His death on the Cross was an offering of Himself to God (He. 9:14).[10]

From Genesis to Revelation, the Bible reveals one God, the Creator of the heavens and earth, and the Redeemer of mankind.

1:1 In the beginning God...

The Bible makes no effort to prove God, that he exists. It is a categorical assumption. "In the beginning God" is the eternal declaration echoing down through the halls of time. Who says there is no God? The Psalmist tells us that "the fool says in his heart, 'There is no God'" (Ps. 14:1, NIV).

The divine name in this verse is the Hebrew word *Elohim*, which appears over 2500 times in the OT. Its form is plural, but the meaning is uniformly singular. The plural form expresses "Majesty" or "Mightiness" — the One who brought order out of chaos. It is a generic rather than a specific personal name for the Deity. *Elohim* is the impersonal transcendent Creator-God, not subject to the historical process and above the world of phenomena. He is the nonpersonal Almighty Mind. There is a hint of his trinitarian nature when he says: "Let us make man in our image, after our likeness" (v. 26, NIV). Perhaps it would be correct to say that *Elohim* is the Great Almighty King, who stays in the background while he manifests and relates himself to man through the second and third persons of the Trinity. For commentary on other names of God in the Bible, see Ge. 15:1-2 (Adonai), Ge. 17:1 (El Shaddai) and Ex. 3:14, with chart (YHWH).

1:1 ...God created the heaven and the earth.

The book of Genesis is the frequent target of a certain type of "scientist." This book is not a scientific textbook, but at the same time it does contain scientific truth.

"Genesis is clear that God made the worlds and is the Lord of nature as well as of spirits; therefore where the Bible touches on science, it must be held to be correct. When fairly and accurately interpreted, the Bible in Ge. 1 and elsewhere declares that God created the worlds out of nothing. Matter is not eternal; with this view the current theories of science have no quarrel."[11]

1:5 ...And the evening and the morning were the first day.

There are at least two theories on the creation days: (1) the creation days are twenty-four-hour days, and (2) the creation days referred to in Genesis are long periods of time. It is true that God's redemptive plan does not "rise or fall" on whether the creation days were twenty-four-hour days or longer periods of time.

"The word 'day' has variable meanings. In this verse it is used as a term for Light. In 1:8,13 it seems to mean a day of 24 hours. In 1:14,16 it seems to mean a twelve-hour day. In 2:4 it implies the whole creation period. In such passages as 2 Ti. 1:12 it seems to refer to the era beyond the Lord's Second Coming, and in Ps. 90:4 and 2 Pe. 3:8 'one day is with the Lord as a thousand years, and a thousand years as one day.'"[12]

Creator
884-886

Fools
3853

Majesty,
God's
2234

Names
of God
3633

Jehovah
Titles
1868-1872

Truth of
God's Word
436

Creator
884-886

Day
920-926

The Organic Evolutionary Hypothesis vs. Divine Creation

By definition, "organic evolution" assumes that man ascended from the animal world. Some Biblical scholars have developed the theory of "theistic evolution" to explain the Genesis account of creation.
They see no conflict between divine creation and the evolutionary hypothesis. On the other hand, many traditional Biblical scholars do not accept this theory because it is contrary to the plain teachings of an authoritative and infallible Bible. It does not accommodate itself to the Biblical claim that "holy men of God spake as they were moved by the Holy Ghost" (2 Pe 1:21) and that "all scripture is given by inspiration of God" (2 Ti. 3:16). Certainly the Holy Spirit knew what the facts were, and he could have revealed the evolutionary process, if there had been one.

Creator
884-886

"Word" Inspired
417

The radical theory of organic evolution has a destructive effect upon the faith of men. In the early nineteenth century Charles Darwin was preparing for the Christian ministry. Darwin says, "Whilst on board the Beagle I was quite orthodox, and I remember being heartily laughed at by several of the officers (though themselves orthodox) for quoting the Bible as an unanswerable authority on some points of morality."[13] However, when evolution became his belief (1836-1839) the first casualty of his Christian commitment was belief in the Bible as the infallible Word of God. Soon thereafter he abandoned the Christian faith in which he had been reared. He wrote:

Faith-Unbelief
1201-1226

God's Sure Word
430

I had gradually come, by this time, to see that the Old Testament from its manifestly false history of the world…and from its attributes to God [of] the feelings of a revengeful tyrant, was not more to be trusted than the sacred books of the Hindoos, or the beliefs of any barbarian…I gradually came to disbelieve in Christianity as a divine revelation…Thus disbelief crept over me at a very slow rate, but was at last complete. The rate was so slow that I felt no distress, and have never since doubted even for a single second that my conclusion was correct.[14]

Evidently Darwin lost his faith because of an apparent conflict between plain Bible teachings and a dogmatic scientific approach to Biblical interpretation based upon the scientific investigative technique. R. Laird Harris concluded that "it is the feeling of many Biblical scholars that this conflict is due to misconception of the Bible's teaching and its relation to scientific theory…Much of the scientific— religious conflict can be avoided if extremes of scientific dogmatism on the naturalistic nature and animal origin of man are avoided."[15]

Ignorance of "Word"
432

Genesis states that God created things "after their kind." It seems reasonable to assume that "kind" as used in Genesis has to do with types which can interbreed. There has been change but there is a lack of evidence to support the evolutionist's claims that all living forms found today come from one common ancestor. Above all, man was created separately and in the "image of God" in a specific creative act and not through a process of evolution from a single-celled animal.

Creator
884-886

Image of God
4044

James D. Bales gives an interesting statement at this point:

It will be observed that the Bible does not say how God formed man's body from the dust of the earth, nor how long it took. However, it does not seem that [this] silence of the Scriptures...gives us any grounds, when we consider some other passages, for assuming that it was by an evolutionary process via the animal route...Although animal flesh was already in existence—and it, too, was formed of the ground (Ge. 2:19)—yet the passage of Ge. 2:7 does not say that man was formed from animal flesh but of the dust of the ground. Both animal life and dust existed when God created man. God made man from dust and not from living creatures.[16]

In addition to man, the Genesis account shows that God created animals and enabled them to bring forth "after their kind." "And God said, Let the earth bring forth the living creature after his kind, cattle, and creeping thing, and beast of the earth after his kind: and it was so. And God made the beast of the earth after his kind, and cattle after their kind, and every thing that creepeth upon the earth after his kind: and God saw that it was good" (Ge. 1:24-25). The law of reproduction in this passage reveals that the animals, who were created before man was created, were to reproduce after "their kind." However, if man came by evolution via the animal route, some animals would have had to produce not their own kind, but mankind.

In 1 Co. 15:39 Paul clearly tells the Corinthians that the flesh of animals is different from that of man: "All flesh is not the same flesh: but there is one kind of flesh of men, another flesh of beasts, another of fishes, and another of birds." If this is true, how can there be a biological relationship between the beasts and man, whom God made in his image?

| Animals |
| 150-189 |

| Man's Dominion |
| 2241 |

| Preeminence of Man |
| 2240 |

Thomas Henry Huxley, the famous zoologist and the first to be convinced of Darwin's analysis, stated unequivocally that evolution, if consistently accepted, makes it impossible to believe the Bible.

In summary, organic evolution is diametrically opposed to the Christian system of thought in at least seven important ways:

1. The theory of organic evolution excludes a transcendent God, thus leading to pantheism instead of theism.

2. The theory of organic evolution nullifies the idea of creation as clearly stated in the Biblical record.

3. The theory of organic evolution degrades man in that it denies the direct divine origin of man. Instead of recognizing man as having been created in God's image, the evolutionist believes that man evolved from a lower form.

4. The theory of organic evolution invalidates Biblical authority. Darwin, in his *Life and Letters,* stated that he did not believe there had ever been any revelation. Thus the Bible is reduced to a book conceived and produced by man without action on the part of God.

5. The theory of organic evolution denies the truth of Christ as to his incarnation and virgin birth and puts him in the same category with other men but somewhat higher up on the evolutionary scale. The Bible clearly teaches that Christ co-existed with God the Father from the beginning, but according to the theory of evolution, Christ is considered to be, if he is considered at all, the culmination of a process. This theory holds that his preex-

| Divine Omniscience |
| 3850 |

| Divine Image |
| 2239 |

| Methods of Revelation |
| 2495-2504 |

| Christ's Perfection |
| 2731 |

The Fertile Crescent (gray area) in relation to modern nations. The Garden of Eden was most likely located somewhere in the eastern end of the Fertile Crescent.

istence was limited to successive stages, from the lower to the higher, until he achieved some semblance of deity.

There is no place for Jesus Christ in the evolutionary program because Jesus

Jesus Christ
677-723

Christ, in the view of the evolutionist, is an exception in nature. This is supported by the fact that the so-called "upreach" of evolution ended with Jesus Christ. If Christ were a culminating figure in the ever upreaching scheme of evolution, why did not the human race continue from there to become 100 percent Christ-like charac-

Christ's Perfection
2731

ters? Humanity still has not evolved to the state of perfection demonstrated by the Savior. Man, who is still basically sinful, needs the divine intervention as expressed in the new birth. Evolution would deny the reality of miracles, including the new birth and the virgin birth. Apart from the virgin-born Son of God, the human race is basically the same now as it was before the birth of Christ. Evolution cannot accommodate the bodily resurrection of Christ nor his second coming. It

Resurrection
2407-2416

would seem that the plainly stated Biblical record is much more compat-ible with the facts than the theory of evolution.

6. The theory of organic evolution invalidates the Christian interpretation of sin and defines evil as a purely humanis-

Sin, Universality of
3340

tic force. Thus the logic of organic evolution destroys not only the doctrine of original sin but also the holiness of God, for it makes God the author of sin.

Holiness of God
1597

7. The theory of organic evolution is incompatible with ethics. If the principle of living is merely the "survival of the fittest," as among the beasts, the Christian teachings of love, service, and growth through self-sacrifice would have no effect in preventing selfish struggles against others.

Power of "Word"
421

It is obvious that the theory of organic evolution and the plain teachings of Genesis are incompatible. Furthermore, the evolutionary hypothesis would make Mosaic authorship irrelevant and there would be no basis for Scriptural authority.[17]

God's Sure Word
430

1:27 So God created man in his own image...

That Adam and Eve were created initially by God as two human beings is obvious in the Genesis account. However, in a day when study of the Bible is neglected and ignorance of the Bible is apparent, it is possible for the deceptive and subtle theories of liberalism to take up residence in one's mind.

To refresh one's memory it is well to cite the instances in the Bible where Adam is definitely presented as a historical person and not "a symbolic term for all mankind."

A. Genesis 1:27. Here it is stated that "God created man in his own image"; "male and female created he them." Jesus affirms the statement: "Haven't you read ... that at the beginning the Creator 'made them male and female'...?"(Mt. 19:4, NIV)

B. Genesis 2:19. "God formed every beast of the field, and every fowl of the air; and brought them unto Adam" to name.

C. Genesis 2:21-22. " ... the LORD God caused a deep sleep to fall upon Adam, and he slept: and he took one of his ribs, and closed up the flesh instead thereof; And the rib, which the LORD God had taken from man, made he a woman, and brought her unto the man."

D. Genesis 3:1ff. Here it is stated that Adam and Eve committed the sin of disobedience.

E. Genesis 4:1. "Adam knew Eve his wife; and she conceived, and bare Cain." Later Abel and other children were born.

F. Genesis 5:1-3. "This is the written account of Adam's line. When God created man, he made him in the likeness of God. He created them male and female and blessed them. And when they were created, he called them 'man.' When Adam had lived 130 years, he had a son in his own likeness, in his own image ..." (NIV)

G. Genesis 5:5. Here the Scripture states that Adam lived 930 years.

H. Deuteronomy 32:8. In this reference Moses clearly affirms the historicity of Adam. The nations of the earth are referred to as the "sons of Adam."

I. Joshua 3:16. In this passage a city is named after Adam.

J. First Chronicles 1:1. Here the name Adam is listed as the first in a chronology of the human race.

K. Job 31:33. Job clearly acknowledges Adam as a person and compares his own transgression to that of Adam.

L. Luke 3:38. Luke acknowledges Adam as a person and lists him as the first human being in his chronology of the human race.

M. Romans 5:12. Paul tells us that "by one man sin entered into the world, and death by sin; and so death passed upon all men, for that all have sinned."

N. Romans 5:14,18. Paul clearly acknowledges Adam to be a historical person: "Nevertheless, death reigned from the time of Adam to the time of Moses, even over those who did not sin by breaking a command, as did Adam, who was a pattern of the one to come ... Consequently, just as the result of one trespass was condemnation for all men, so also the result of one act of righteousness was justification that brings life for all men." (NIV)

Adam
34, 1240

Eve
1159

Creator
884-886

Pre-
eminence
of Man
2240

Disobedience
2620-2621

Divine Image
2239

Longevity
2190

Fall of Adam
1240

Sin Universal
3340

Death
Universal
2158

Death
Vanquished
1360

Death
Universal
2158

Enoch
1135

God's Voice
3301

Revelations,
Divine
2494

Sabbath
3098ff, 4317
Rest
3010
Poor
2799-2804
Bondservants
2138
Death
2158-2163
Moses
2420-2421
Command-
ments
444

O. First Corinthians 15:22. "For as in Adam all die, even so in Christ shall all be made alive."

P. First Corinthians 15:45. "And so it is written. The first man Adam was made a living soul; the last Adam was made a quickening spirit."

Q. First Timothy 2:13."For Adam was first formed, then Eve."

R. Jude 14. Jude affirms that Adam was a person: "And Enoch also, the seventh from Adam, prophesied of these [things]…"

The fact that Adam and Eve were actual, historical human beings is thus clearly affirmed in both the Old and New Testaments. It is also apparent that Jesus Christ recognized the historicity of Adam when he discussed the problem of divorce with the Pharisees (cf. Mt. 19:4ff with Ge. 1:26-28).

1:28 God…said to them… (NIV)

The first recorded instance when God spoke to human beings concerns his explaining the rules of the Garden to Adam and Eve. Exactly how a spirit could speak to flesh and blood is a mystery, but there are recorded instances when his Son and other beings heard God's voice. At the baptism of Jesus, John said that there " …came a voice from heaven, saying, Thou art my beloved Son, in whom I am well pleased" (Mk. 1:11). At the Transfiguration of Jesus the same basic pronouncement was made with this addition, "Listen to him!" (Mt. 17:5, NIV). On the Damascus road Scripture states that the resurrected Jesus spoke these words to Saul (Paul): "Saul, Saul, why do you persecute me?…I am Jesus, whom you are persecuting" (Ac. 9:4-5, NIV).

When we speak of God revealing himself and speaking, we use the theological word "theophany," a Greek compound word meaning "God appearing," or "the appearance of God to man." God seems to reveal himself in some quasi-mystical human form, sometimes as the Angel of the Lord, the pre-incarnate Christ. (See the essay on "Theophanies in the OT" on p. 72.)

2:3 And God blessed the seventh day, and sanctified it…

One of the greatest blessings which has come down to man is the idea of the Sabbath, a rest day, one in seven days.Various sociological experiments have been conducted regarding this practice, but no system has proved so beneficial as the one-day-in-seven formula.

In ancient times the poor, and especially the slaves, were required to work every day. Life expectancy was low. People were expended, literally worked to death, in mines, in building projects, and on farms.

When Moses proclaimed the Fourth Commandment, the introductory words, "Remember the Sabbath Day…" suggest that the Sabbath did not originate on Mount Sinai, but rather that the people should adhere to, preserve, and observe a practice forgotten or neglected. Actually the idea of one rest day a week is implied when God rested from his labor on the seventh day of creation (Ge. 2:2) and required his people to do likewise (Ex. 23:12; 16:23).

This great blessing, one rest day a week, has been transmitted to the Christian world. Even in officially atheistic countries, like Russia, and Moslem countries, such as Turkey, Sunday is the official rest day. There is something in the warp and woof of nature that demands recognition of this formula. Man's history has demonstrated his need for the recuperation of his physical, mental, and spiritual energies once every seven days.

See additional commentary on the Sabbath at De. 5:14.

Rest
Enjoined
3010

3:6 ...the woman...did eat, and gave also unto her husband with her; and he did eat.

As God is holy and eternally the same, his hatred for sin and his love for holiness have always been consistent. With him is "no variableness, neither shadow of turning" (Ja. 1:17). The psalmist had this in mind when he said, "Thou art the same, and thy years shall have no end" (Ps. 102:27). Malachi, as a spokesman for the Lord, emphasizes this conclusion, "For I am the LORD, I change not" (Mal. 3:6). Parallel to this plain teaching of Scripture is the fact that God does not have two redemptive plans, one for the people in the OT and one for those in the NT. It is not likely that God exposed the human race at any time to hopeless fate. Because of God's foreknowledge and love, a recovery plan would be imperative. When Adam and Eve sinned, they had a standby plan of salvation provided for them (Ro. 4:13; 9:6-8).

God Eternal
2481
Immutability
2480

Salvation
for All
3119
Adam
34
Eve
1159
Conviction
of Sin
1764

After their transgression, Adam and Eve, suddenly realizing that they were sinful and naked, made aprons from fig leaves for a covering. Afterward "did the LORD God make coats of skins, and clothed them" (Ge. 3:21). The account indicates that the price of this covering was the life of an animal. This seems to foreshadow the innocent dying for the sinner. Thus

The Shofar, or ram's horn, used to announce the Sabbath in ancient Israel.

the covering of their nakedness was a gracious token from…God, that the sin which had alienated them [Adam and Eve] from him…was henceforth to be in his sight as if it were not. It was done…to denote the covering of guilt from the eye of Heaven, an act which God alone could have done. But he did it…by a medium of death, by a sacrifice of the life of those creatures which men were not yet permitted to kill for purposes of food, and…with grace which laid open the prospect of recovered life and of blessing for the fallen. It is probable that Adam and Eve appropriated God's redemptive provision before they died.[18]

Guilt
1763
Sacrifices
3107-3111

3:9 And the LORD God called unto Adam, and said unto him, Where art thou?

Since the human race comes from common stock and is polluted with sin, it becomes clear that God's concern for man's salvation began with Adam and Eve. The first intimation of this appears when the first couple tried to hide themselves from their Creator and God's voice came booming through the garden, " Where art thou?" God was not seen but his voice was heard.

Salvation
3116-3128
God's Voice
3301

3:15 And I will put enmity between thee and the woman, and between thy seed and her seed; it shall bruise thy head, and thou shalt bruise his heel.

It is evident that this prophecy refers to Christ because he did truly bruise Satan's [the serpent's] head. Paul, in his letter to the Galatians, states that "when the fulness of the time was come, God sent forth his Son, made of a woman, made under the law, to redeem them that were under the law"(Ga. 4:4-5).

Christ
Prophesied
2890

Initially, when Christ hung on the cross, and finally at the resurrection, he bruised Satan's head, even as satanic forces, incarnate in man, bruised Christ's heel when the cruel spikes were driven through his quivering flesh. Finally, he will cast Satan into the lake of fire and the defeat of Satan will be complete. The writer of Hebrews tells the Jewish converts that, "as the children are partakers of flesh and blood, he [Christ] also himself likewise took part of the same; that through death he might destroy him that had the power of death, that is, the devil" (He. 2:14). Jesus was "declared to be the Son of God with power, according to the spirit of holiness, by the resurrection from the dead" (Ro. 1:4).

Satan's
Defeat
3149

Resurrection
2413-2414

In the Genesis reference, one recognizes the promise of him who was to be born of a woman and whose seed was to be at odds with the seed of Satan. The enmity that prevails between the righteous on the one hand and the evil forces on the other is continually manifesting itself. A war has been going on between the forces of righteousness and those of evil since this judgment of God was pronounced (2 Co. 10:4; 1 Ti. 1:18; 6:2; 2 Ti. 2:4).

Spiritual
Warfare
358

The Scripture (Ge. 3:15) is addressed not to Adam and Eve, but to Eve alone; the consequence of this purpose of God was that Jesus Christ was born of a virgin. This is what is implied in the promise. Jesus Christ died to redeem sinful man by the sacrifice of himself, and eventually to destroy him who had the power of death, that is, the devil. Although Satan will be defeated, Christ indicated that Satan is now the prince of this world and that he goes about seeking whom he may devour, or as an "angel of light" deceiving the very elect. Even though he is a potentially defeated foe, he is still active (1 Co. 2:6; 1 Pe. 5:8). In destroying Satan's power and lordship over mankind, God enabled man to turn the power of Satan unto God (Ac. 26:18), and Satan

Death
Vanquished
1360

bruised his heel. God so ordered it, because salvation could only be brought about by the death of Christ. By woman sin was introduced into the world, and by woman a Savior from sin was given (Ga. 1:4; 4:4).

3:20 Adam named his wife Eve, because she would become the mother of all the living. (NIV)

Adam's faith was expressed by the name he gave Eve.

From the first, Adam believed in the original good news of the coming seed of the woman (Ge. 3:15). This is suggested by the name Eve (Hebrew *Chavva*, "life") which he gave to his wife (*Isha*, fem. of *Ish*, "man") directly after the original promise, and immediately before the expulsion from Paradise (Ge. 3:20ff.). "Sunken in death he nevertheless gave his wife so proud a name" (Calvin), and thereby expressed his faith in the conquest of death by life. So it was an "act of faith that Adam named his wife Eve" and from that time the new name of his wife was for man the "reminder of the promise of God's grace."[19]

Adam called her "woman" in Ge. 2:23, for she was "taken out of man," and he called her "Eve" in Ge. 3:20, "because she was the mother of all living."

It has been said of the original good news: "On this, Adam trusted and thereby was saved from his fall. That Eve also in faith took her stand on the ground of the word of promise is shown by her statement in Ge. 4:1."[20]

4:4-5 …And the LORD had respect unto Abel and to his offering: but unto Cain and his offering he had not respect…

We do not know what details of God's redemption plan were revealed to this first family, but there is direction toward the sacrificial atonement in the acceptable blood sacrifice of Abel and the rejection of Cain's humanistic offering. In this episode the formula of "justification by faith" is dimly seen in the apocalyptic affirmation: " … the Lamb slain from the foundation of the world" (Re. 13:8). As time advanced, God progressively unfolded his redemptive pattern.

"Cain must have been in a position to have the same knowledge of sin and mercy as did Abel, but the offering which he brought was rejected. In what way did the two offerings differ? One offering, that of Abel, was of such a nature that it required the shedding of blood. The other was bloodless."[21] The blood sacrifice (Re. 13:8b) was sufficient ground for the faith of Abel. "It is quite evident that we have an intimation, at least, in the sacred records, that the sacrifice in its earliest history, was instituted by God Himself, either by example or immediate command … The shedding of the blood of the sacrifice, and the yielding up of its life, must repeat continuously, to stupid, fallen humanity of every generation, the message of man's guilt, of divine justice and God's mercy. The promise made in Eden should be

An altar with four "horns."

Parents' Sin
3341

Adam
34
Eve
1159

Grace,
Divine
1445-1449

Faith
1201-1206

Conception
306

Offerings,
Unacceptable
2635
Justification,
by Faith
1203, 1985
Knowledge
2020-2035
Offerings
Acceptable
2625
Blood of
Sacrifices
516

Evil
Generation
1401

Remission
of Sin
3127
Blood of
Christ
679
Abel
4

Cain
618

Sin
3558-3359

Redemption
2978-2979

fulfilled."[22] The loss of life is the penalty of sin, and its typical vicarious sur-render was necessary to remission (He. 9:22). "The blood of animals was used in all offerings for sin… (Le. 17:11). The 'blood of Jesus,' the 'blood of Christ,' the 'blood of Jesus Christ,' or the 'blood of the Lamb,' are figurative expressions for his atoning death (1 Co. 10:16)."[23]

Redemptive acceptance is most strongly reflected in Abel whose righteousness cannot be doubted (Mt. 23:35). On the other hand, Cain is presented as one who rejected God's requirement as evidenced by his act of murdering his brother (Ge. 4:5-15). Abel accepted God's plan "by faith" (He. 11:4). Cain rejected it by doubt. Abel's faith was evidenced by righteousness; Cain's sinful rebellion, by his crime. In brief, "by their fruits ye shall know them" (Mt. 7:20).

4:8 …Cain rose up against Abel his brother, and slew him.

The origin of human sin points back to Adam and Eve. How sin is transmitted from one generation to the next is not fully stated, but sin manifested itself when Cain killed his brother Abel. The remedy for sin is seen in the atoning blood of Christ which was foreshadowed, symbolically, in the animal sacrifice. Man can appropriate this redemptive provision by repentance, confession and an exercise of faith. Before the Advent, man expressed his faith symbolically, by offering an animal without spot or blemish on the altar for sin. Ceremonially and symbolically Christ's blood was prefigured in "the Lamb slain from the foundation of the world" (Re. 13:8). This can be called a standby sacrifice within the context of God's

Noah and his family building the mid-section of the ark.

foreknowledge that man would commit sin. When man sinned, this pre-creation sacrifice was automatically invoked. The blood is the central element in all redemptive considerations and is so expressed in all thirty-nine books of the Old Testament.

Blood
512-517

6:8 ...Noah found grace in the eyes of the LORD.

Noah was a faithful follower of the Lord, as this verse so clearly states. We are also told that he was a "just man and perfect in his generations, and Noah walked with God" (Ge. 6:9,22; 8:20; 9:1,9).

Noah
2597, 4289

7:24 The waters flooded the earth... (NIV)

Concerning the Flood, science and the Bible both agree that the earth was once covered with water. This agreement is apparently verified by the fact that fossils and sea shells are found at high elevations. Science says that water covered the earth millions of years ago and that cataclysmic upheavals created the mountains. The Bible states that the earth was covered with water in Noah's day.

Deluge
973
Ark
214-216

8:20 ...Noah built an altar unto the LORD...

Scripture points out that Noah took clean animals into the ark (Ge. 7:2ff.), evidently for sacrificial purposes, and after the flood,

Animals
150

> Noah built the Lord an altar and offered burnt offering...To him the hearts of the pious lift...To heaven...must their offering and prayers ascend, if they are to reach his throne ...So as to give this "upward" direction to the sacrifice,...there were erected...high places and altars from which [the prayers] should 'ascend' heavenwards in the fire.

Altars
120, 4316

The presence of God is indeed everywhere and is not restricted by the boundaries of an above or beneath (Ps. 139)...The clean animals offered, as well as the sacrifices from the beginning of the world, themselves point to the sacrifice on Golgotha, the Lamb, without blemish and without spot (1 Pe. 1:19-20) who is in truth the fountain of all preservation and salvation of the world.[24]

In his devotion to God, Noah observed the requirements given by God to the Adamic generation. Adam Clarke states that

the old world began with sacrifice, so also did the new...(Ge. 8:20). The proper mode of worshiping the divine Being is the invention or institution of God Himself; and sacrifice, in the act and design, is the essence of religion. Without sacrifice, actually offered or implied, there never was, there never can be any true religion. Even in the heavens, a lamb is represented before the throne of God as newly slain (Re. 5:6). The design of sacrifice is two-faced, the slaying and the burning of the victim point out: first, that the life of the sinner is forfeited to divine justice; secondly, that his soul deserves the fire of perdition.[25]

The Jews have a tradition that Noah built his altar on the same spot where Adam built his worship center and where Abel later offered his sacrifice. It is thought that this place was Mount Moriah in Jerusalem, presently called the Dome of the Rock, where Abraham offered Isaac.[26]

The Dome of the Rock, on Mount Moriah in Jerusalem. This is thought to be the area where Abraham went to offer Isaac (Ge. 22:1-4) and the spot where David purchased the threshing floor of Ornan the Jebusite (2 Chr. 3:1). It is also the site that King Solomon chose on which to build the Temple.

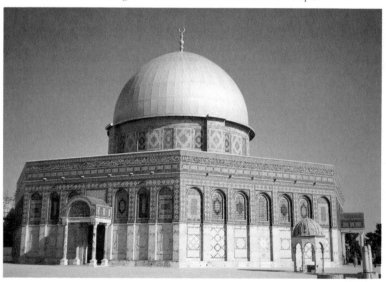

Lamb of God
3365

Sacrifices
3107-3111

Burnt-offerings
2626

Moriah
2439

The Altar

In the beginning, when worship centers were first set up, the altar was merely a site or location where man sought communication with his God. Worshipers in the patriarchal period built altars wherever they pitched their tents (Ge. 8:20; 12:7; 22:9; 35:1,7). Almost any kind of marker used in communication with deity became an altar. Frequently it was nothing more than a stone or several stones laid one on top of another, or it might have been a mound of earth. Sometimes an altar was made of metal (2 K. 16:14). The altar was in a measure a testimony or a witness to the heathen world that surrounded early Yahweh worshipers.

Altars
120

Worshiper
3952

Picture of Altar
4316

Immediately after Noah left the ark, he built a simple stone altar on which he offered sacrifices unto the Lord, who responded favorably and promised Noah many great blessings. Abraham built altars in several places as he went from Ur of the Chaldees to Haran and on into Canaan and Egypt (Ge.12:7; 13:18). Jacob made an altar out of the stones that he had used for pillows while he was camping in Bethel (Ge. 28:18-19; cf. Ge. 33:20; 35:7).

Abraham
4290

Jacob
4291

As time passed different forms of worship centers have been used: the tabernacle, the temple, the synagogue and the church. For a chart on this development of worship centers, see pp. 402-403.

Places for
Religious Worship
4316

9:20-21 Noah...proceeded to plant a vineyard. When he drank some of its wine, he became drunk... (NIV)

In the interest of exegetical integrity, the question of Noah's drunkenness must not be evaded. There are several approaches to the question; of these, two categories will be considered: (1) that he was guilty of sin and was restored, and (2) that he did it innocently.

1. It must be recognized that devout people have succumbed to temptation and have committed sin, but because of the mercy and grace of God, "if we confess our sins, he is faithful and just to forgive us our sins, and to cleanse us from all unrighteousness" (1 Jn. 1:9). Those who acknowledge this aspect of God's grace would be inclined to give Noah the benefit of the doubt. David also sinned and was forgiven (2 S. 11:3-4; cf. Ps. 32:1-5).

2. It is generally agreed that revelation of grace—its details—has been progressively revealed, e.g., man's understanding of grace is broadened through personal experience and the example of others (1 Co. 10:6).

Wine is not mentioned before the Noah incident (Ge. 9:20-21), nor is there a prohibition for the use of it prior to the time when "Noah began to be a husbandman"—a man of the ground, a farmer. This may have been the first time that wine [grape vine] was cultivated (see NIV text note, Ge. 9:20); and it is probable that the strength or intoxicating property of wine was never known before. The process of fermentation might have overtaken Noah without his being aware of the fact of its effects. A right-minded person would hesitate to deprive Noah of innocence for doing something (end in itself) like this without knowing the consequences.

In the interest of charity and candor it would seem that Noah should be given the benefit of the doubt, especially since Noah's name was still listed on the roster of faith when the book of Hebrews was written (He. 11:7).

11:9 Therefore is the name of it called Babel; because the LORD did there confound the language of all the earth...

According to the Genesis account, mankind migrated to the plain of Shinar, where people decided to build a city and a tower into heaven. The specifications called for substantial construction of fire-hardened brick and mortar (Ge. 11:1-4). For some reason the people's action displeased God, who proceeded to disrupt their plans by confounding their language and scattering them abroad upon the face of the earth (Ge. 11:5-9). Scholars generally assume this was the beginning of a multiplicity of languages. According to Biblical genealogies this event took place about 100 years after the flood and 325 years before the call of Abraham (about 2000 B.C., contemporary to Hammurabi).

Where was the tower of Babel located? Some scholars think it was within the immediate environs of ancient Babylon, citing a large pit located there out of which huge quantities of brick have been dug for building purposes. It is assumed that the pit once contained the foundation of a massive tower.

Other scholars, notably the English Orientalist Sir Henry Rawlinson, favor a location about ten miles southwest of Babylon, in the ancient city of Borsippa. There archaeologists have discovered a massive pile of brick rubble with a 50-foot tower rising out of the conal peak. The rubble base is about one-half mile in diameter. Enough of the original structure remains to show it was a solid mass of masonry sufficiently strong to support a large tower. It was obviously not a dwelling. The exposed tower and brick walls below were made out of fire-hardened brick and mortar. The archaeologists also found a cuneiform text inscribed on a clay cylinder in the ruins giving

Shinar
3272
Wicked
Confounded
3067
Dispersion
1022

Tower of
Babel
328
Babylon
4338

Bricks
545

A massive crumbling tower near Babylon. Some scholars associate this with the tower of Babel. The tower may have been built on ruins of a previous structure.

*Ur of Chaldees. A view of the archaeological excavations
in the area where Abraham lived.*

an account of a huge tower which was not finished at first, but later at the urging of the god Marduk it was completed.

Irrespective of the exact location of the tower of Babel, the ruins at Borsippa give us an idea of the structural nature of the original tower. The picture on the previous page shows how the tower appeared in 1966.

12:1-3 The LORD said unto Abram...
in thee shall all families of the earth be blessed.

This prophetic statement, as well as the one in Ge. 18:18, assured Abraham that he would be the progenitor of a nation which would be a spiritual blessing to the nations of the earth. In retrospect the Bible student can see that
this blessing has come to the world through Christ, who was a descendant of Abraham. It is said of Abraham that he saw the promises "afar off," and that he was "persuaded of them," and "embraced them" (He. 11:8-13). Paul tells the Galatians that Abraham was justified by faith, that the gospel was
preached to Abraham (Ga. 3:8), and that the believers in Christ are the spiritual children of Abraham.

The Messiah was to be of the promised seed of Isaac and Jacob (Ge. 17:19; Nu. 24:17). He would be a descendant of the tribe of Judah (Ge.
49:10), one of the twelve tribes. When Jesus was born in Bethlehem of Judea, the other tribal nations had vanished. It is most singular that the prophet was able to designate Judah, the only tribe with a political identity at the time of Jesus' birth. Certainly only divine inspiration could have foreseen this outcome (Ge. 49:10).

**12:2-3 ...I will make of thee a great nation...
and I will bless them that bless thee, and
curse him that curseth thee...**

A fascinating study can be made of the nation of Israel from a historical perspective. Many attempts have been made to destroy the Jews, yet they have survived. A timeline showing the threats to the Jewish nation is located on pp. 190-191.

Israel—
the Jews
1807-1829

**12:10 Now there was a famine in the land, and
Abram went down to Egypt to live there for a while
because the famine was severe.** (NIV)

It is interesting to note how important a role ancient Egypt played in the Genesis accounts. Its earliest contact with the Biblical account is in this story, when Abram and Sarai go there seeking relief from a famine. Again, it was a famine that prompted the sons of Israel (Jacob) to go to Egypt, seeking to buy food (Ge. 42:1-2).

Egypt
1100

Famine
21-23

Egypt, with the fertility of land around the Nile River, was the breadbasket of the ancient world. A great deal of wealth poured into this country from surrounding parts of the world, and splendid structures were created.

Perhaps the most famous of these structures are the pyramids, constructed in the Third to Sixth Dynasties (2500 B.C. and following). Abram and Sarai may have seen them, since they probably went to Egypt about 2000 B.C. See the essay on the following pages.

Memphis
4413

The Pyramids of Egypt

Pyramids numbering in the hundreds can be seen along the Nile River all the way from Cairo to Khartum. Most significant of these monuments are the three massive stone structures near Cairo, known as the "Pyramids of Giza." These huge structures are among the most massive in the world, and were built to house the remains of kings, queens and sometimes lesser officials. All three pyramids had adjacent funerary temples in which the morticians prepared the bodies for burial.

The Sphinx was erected at the head of the burial valley to guard the

The Sphinx in the Giza location. It is now over 4,000 years old.

tombs. It had the body of a lion with the likeness of a head, probably that of one of the kings. The Sphinx is sixty-six feet high from the base to the top of the head and 240 feet long. Between the paws is a small worship center with a tablet telling about Pharaoh's second son, not his first son, who by custom would have inherited the throne. Some scholars think that this plaque,

| Pharaoh |
| 2747-2748 |

placed there at a later date, implies that the first son died in the plague under Moses.[27]

Heroditus reports that 100,000 slaves and seasonal volunteers worked twenty years on one tomb alone. It is possible that the captive Hebrews built some of the later monuments in the area. The pyramids represent engineering feats which would be difficult to duplicate today. Manpower, along with primitive tools such as the lever, roller, rocker, and inclined plane, were the only known means for construction.

| Israel, Bondage of |
| 1820 |

Above: One of the pyramids in the Giza group. A small amount of the alabaster casting still remains on the crest.

Left: Khafre (Cheops) in the Giza group. A cross section is presented, showing the passageways leading to the Queen's chamber as well as the subterranean compartment where burial preparation was made.

Grand Gallery

Queen's Chamber

Spark Chamber

14:20 …And he gave him tithes of all…

The first direct reference to tithing in the Bible appears in this passage of Genesis, where Abram paid tithes to Melchizedek, "king of Salem [Jerusalem]…and…the priest of the most high God."

Obviously Melchizedek was high enough in the priestly hierarchy to make demands on Abram (Ge. 14:18-24). "Apparently from the approving manner in which this mysterious king-priest is mentioned here, the way in which Abram himself used his name for God (v. 22), and the place given him in Biblical typology (cf. Ps. 110:4 with He. 5:6-7), he had somehow risen above the pagan worship of his environment and was serving the True God by this significant name…God Most High…He proceeded to bless Abram in that name of God which he commonly used, and Abram gave him a tenth of all."[28] (For more on Melchizedek, see commentary on He. 6:20.)

It is thus a matter of record that the paying of tithes had its origin in the early part of Genesis. It is another phase of the animal sacrifices which the worshiper of the Lord was to make as an expression of his devotion to and faith in his Creator.

The word *tithe* comes from the Hebrew word *ma'aser* (Gr. *dekato*) and means giving a tenth part of the produce. Later, when the medium of exchange became money, a tenth part of the money was to be given to the cause of the Lord.

The Jews had the custom of tithing long before it became a means of support for the Levitical tribe under the Law of Moses. Giving the tithe carries with it the idea of commitment and dedication, as in the case where Jacob made a covenant with God and promised to pay his tithe to the LORD (Ge. 28:22). The tithe also implied "not the least and the last" but the "first and the best" for the LORD. Also, in it is the idea of paying rent to the LORD, the owner of all things. Someone has suggested that the "Divine Landlord" is most generous in that he permits the tither to keep 90 percent.

The idea of "free will" is at the heart of the tithe and is an expression of thankfulness as well as an acknowledgment of God's claim on one's possessions. However, by the time Jesus came, the institution of tithing had degenerated into an expression of self-righteousness (Lu. 18:11-12). Jesus rebuked the scribes and Pharisees who tithed their "mint and anise and cummin, and have omitted the weightier matters of the law, judgment, mercy, and faith" (Mt. 23:23).

Actually the tithe is a part of one's self because in giving the tithe a person gives a vital part of himself. In working to earn substance, one burns up vital energy. Tithing is also a way by which a person develops interests outside and beyond himself, thus avoiding selfishness. No one can maintain a spiritual outlook on life when "self" is the end. One should love one's self but not to the exclusion of loving his neighbor. Jesus said, "Love thy neighbor as thyself." A normal relationship with God includes a normal relationship with man.

Jesus expressed it this way, "Thou shalt love the Lord thy God with all thy heart, and with all thy soul, and with all thy mind…Thou shalt love thy neighbor as thyself" (Mt. 22:37-39). This standard of man-God relationship has been in force from the very beginning. Actually the quotation above was an OT standard which Jesus quoted from Deuteronomy 6:5 and Leviticus 19:18. The Ten Commandments support this idea because the first four commandments have a man-to-God relationship and the other six are man-to-man. It becomes clear that the practice of tithing in "the spirit of free will" helps the worshiper to develop a devotion to God and an interest in others.

15:1-2 …Fear not, Abram: I am thy shield, and thy exceeding great reward. And Abram said, Lord GOD…

When Abraham addressed God in this verse he used the word "Adonai" for the first time recorded in the Scriptures. Adonai is translated "Lord" in the English Bible, only the first letter being capitalized. It is used over 300 times in the OT, almost always in the plural and the possessive form.

> The name Adonai signifies ownership or mastership and indicated the truth that God is the owner of each member of the human family [sic], and that He consequently claims …obedience of all … The first occasion of its use, as with the name El-Shaddai, is with Abraham in Ge. 15:2…After the rescue of Lot, and Abram's military achievement (Ge. 15:1) the word of the Lord came unto Abram in a vision saying, 'Fear not, Abram; I am thy shield, and thy exceeding great reward.' Abram then makes his reply, addressing God as Adonai — Lord — an acknowledgment that YHWH is also Master. Certainly Abram understood what this relationship meant;…Lordship meant complete possession on the one hand and complete submission on the other…In addressing the Lord as Adonai he acknowledges God's complete possession and perfect right to all that he was and had.[29]

For other names of God in the Bible, see commentary on Ge. 1:1 (Elohim), Ge. 17:1 (El Shaddai) and Ex. 3:14, with chart (YHWH).

15:6 And he believed in the LORD; and he counted it to him for righteousness.

Abraham was a child of faith. Accordingly Abraham "believed God … By this heroic faith, was he justified… Abraham believed; he had faith in the Lord and the Lord reckoned it to him as [righteousness] … This is one of the mountain peaks of Scripture. It is higher than Sinai. It joins together the two Testaments. Already it reflects the light of Christ … Abraham, is now at peace, and [has] lived on in faith."[30]

The most significant event in Abraham's life was the revelation he received on a starry night when God concluded the covenant of faith with the patriarch (Ge. 15:5,18).That was the time when Abraham received the divine declaration of justification, and it is there that in the annals of salvation the very first plain and express mention is made of the justification by faith of a sinner (Ge. 15:6).

It is evident, however, that all responses to God require an act of faith, and it has been by faith in God's provision that people of all the ages have been justified. The reality of "justification" transcends its theological statement.

The question should be raised: When was faith reckoned to Abraham for righteousness? Was it before or after his circumcision (Ro. 4:10)? The answer is: Not less than thirteen years before he was circumcised. We know this because the covenant of circumcision was first introduced when Abraham was ninety-nine years old (Ge. 17:1-14); but the covenant of faith and justification took place even before the birth of Ishmael, and therefore before Abraham's eighty-sixth year (Ge. 17:1,11). Consequently Abraham had been justified already thirteen years before he was circumcised.

Abraham	**15, 4290**
Master	**693**
Divine Ownership	**3455-3460**
Abraham	**15, 4290**
Faith	**1201-1218**
Justification by Faith	**1203, 1985**
Circumcision	**765-767**
Ishmael	**1805**

It is significant that Paul builds his case for justification by faith upon the OT. In Romans he draws liberally upon the Hebrew Scriptures to prove that justification is through faith (Ro. 3:21ff.; 4:1ff.). Abraham's justification prior to circumcision is prophetically significant because through it Abraham was to become the father of all who would be justified through faith alone. By this fact it became evident that circumcision was not necessary for salvation but only a "seal of righteousness" by faith.

Abraham
15, 4290

To obtain salvation the Gentiles were not required to pass through the anteroom of the Jews—that is, through the law—but through the anteroom of that faith which Abraham already had before he was circumcised. Thus the Scriptures teach that salvation is without human merit, that redemption is of grace, a free gift entirely by faith, and that the gospel of the church age was foreshadowed in the covenant with Abraham. The "new covenant" is the continuation and glorious perfection of the covenant with Abraham (Ro. 4; Ga. 3:9,14).

Gentile
Believers
4038

Salvation
by Grace
1447

Abraham's faith in God's resurrection power was also manifested in his willingness to sacrifice his son, Isaac, upon whom so much depended, for he reckoned "that God was able to raise him up, even from the dead" (He. 11:19). The words of Abraham to his servants attested his confidence: "...and I and the lad will go yonder and worship, and come again to you" (Ge. 22:5). Thus Abraham's faith became the type of faith manifest in the NT resurrection.

Resurrection
Promises
2407

Isaac
1802

"The sacrifice which represented, in the fullest measure, Christ in His work of expiation and atonement was the particularly great offering of the Levitical system ...Whether from the herd of cattle, the flock of sheep or goats, or the clean fowl ... without blemish ... This represents Christ, the choice one of heaven, the unblemished one, whose life was sacrificed, and consumed, as it were, upon the altar of divine justice, in behalf of sinful men."[31] From the beginning, offering the sacrifice was a testimony to saving faith in God's promise.

Sacrifices
3107-3111

Lamb
of God
3365

In addition to Abraham, there were other men of faith. Isaac, Jacob, Joseph, and Moses also believed the promises (He. 11:20-24). Of these men it is said: "These all died in faith, not having received the promises, but having seen them afar off, and were persuaded of them, and embraced them, and confessed that they were strangers and pilgrims on the earth" (He. 11:13). Faith has always been the basic fundamental in a sinner's redemption. By faith and repentance a sinner can be reconciled to God.

Jacob
1837

Joseph
1917

Moses
2420-2421

God is the Creator of all and he has a standing offer of pardon to all men who turn from their evil ways and do that which is right (Eze. 33:11-14ff.). The song of redemption and of personal salvation is the eternal theme in the hymnbook (Psalms) of the OT church and in the books of the prophets. This shows that OT saints enjoyed a conscious realization of sins forgiven; "Let the God of my salvation be exalted" (Ps. 18:46); "For thou art the God of my salvation" (Ps. 25:5); "The LORD is my light and my salvation" (Ps. 27:1); "The salvation of the righteous is of the LORD" (Ps. 37:39). Obviously the psalmist makes salvation personal when he says: "The law of the LORD is perfect, converting the soul" (Ps. 19:7) and "Restore unto me the joy of thy salvation ... Then will I teach transgressors thy ways; and sinners shall be converted unto thee" (Ps. 51:12-13).Certainly the psalmist cannot be an

Creator
884-886

Songs of
Victory
2477

Spiritual Joy
1930

Conversion
834-836

evangel until he himself is forgiven and restored. The prophet Isaiah adds a note to the certainty of redemption: "God is my salvation" (Is. 12:2), and the prophet Micah joins in the refrain: "I will wait for the God of my salvation" (Mi. 7:7).

Faith was the key to salvation not only for OT penitents but for Paul and Silas as well. The writer of Hebrews states: "Without faith it is impossible to please him: for he that cometh to God must believe that he is, and that he is a rewarder of them that diligently seek him" (He. 11:6). The faith here expressed is faith in the atoning merits of the blood of "the Lamb" (1 Pe. 1:18-19; Re. 13:8b). If "Jesus Christ [is] the same yesterday, and to day and for ever" (He. 13:8), then his relationship to the redemption of man is the same always.

In speaking to the "people of Israel" about Jesus Christ, Peter says, "He is the stone you builders rejected, which has become the capstone. Salvation is found in no one else, for there is no other name under heaven given to men by which we must be saved" (Ac. 4:11-12, NIV). Here the truth is projected into every age. It is evident that salvation has never been available through any other name. Only by faith in God's Christ can anyone be saved, and people who will be gathering around the "Great White Throne" in heaven will be there because they exercised saving faith in him.

For more on this subject of salvation in the OT period, see the essay and chart on the following pages.

Salvation
of God
3116

Salvation
by Faith
1203, 1206

Blood of
Christ
679

Salvation
Possible
to All
3119

Name of
the Lord
2514-2517

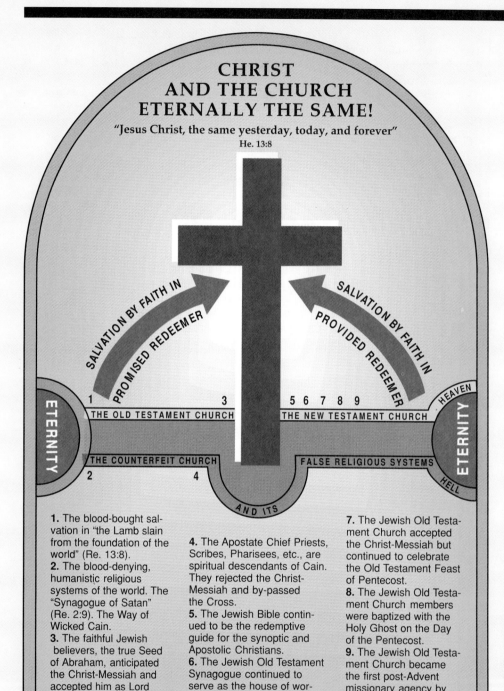

CHRIST
AND THE CHURCH
ETERNALLY THE SAME!

"Jesus Christ, the same yesterday, today, and forever"
He. 13:8

SALVATION BY FAITH IN PROMISED REDEEMER

SALVATION BY FAITH IN PROVIDED REDEEMER

ETERNITY

HEAVEN

ETERNITY

HELL

THE OLD TESTAMENT CHURCH

THE NEW TESTAMENT CHURCH

THE COUNTERFEIT CHURCH

FALSE RELIGIOUS SYSTEMS

AND ITS

1. The blood-bought salvation in "the Lamb slain from the foundation of the world" (Re. 13:8).
2. The blood-denying, humanistic religious systems of the world. The "Synagogue of Satan" (Re. 2:9). The Way of Wicked Cain.
3. The faithful Jewish believers, the true Seed of Abraham, anticipated the Christ-Messiah and accepted him as Lord and Saviour.

4. The Apostate Chief Priests, Scribes, Pharisees, etc., are spiritual descendants of Cain. They rejected the Christ-Messiah and by-passed the Cross.
5. The Jewish Bible continued to be the redemptive guide for the synoptic and Apostolic Christians.
6. The Jewish Old Testament Synagogue continued to serve as the house of worship for Synoptic and Apostolic believers in the Christ-Messiah.

7. The Jewish Old Testament Church accepted the Christ-Messiah but continued to celebrate the Old Testament Feast of Pentecost.
8. The Jewish Old Testament Church members were baptized with the Holy Ghost on the Day of the Pentecost.
9. The Jewish Old Testament Church became the first post-Advent missionary agency by the name of Christian.

The Mechanics of Salvation in the Old Testament Period

One of the Articles of Religion in many Protestant churches reads, in part: "The Old Testament is not contrary to the New; for both in the Old and New Testaments everlasting life is offered to mankind by Christ."

| Salvation through Christ |
| 3117 |

The problem of how Christ could save the people in the OT before the crucifixion is one which few writers have really faced. Some of the writings on this subject leave the impression that God has used a vacillating "trial and error" method — environment, influence, and example — but failed to save man until he finally conceived the idea of sending his Son. Some writers convey the idea that the sacrificing of animals, and/or obeying the Law, were sufficient to bring salvation. Still others have developed a complicated system of morality and ethics closely related to Greek philosophy and Liberation theology. These indefinite theories do not speak to the facts. God is absolute in all areas of his being, and it little behooves man

| Immutability |
| 2480 |

to place God in a labyrinth of uncertainty.

It is evident that the Scriptures present a simple plan of salvation from Genesis to Revelation; it is not necessary for man to superimpose his personal theories before he can have a rudimentary knowledge of salvation. There is a unity in the OT and NT in the basic Christian doctrines; and the NT doctrines amplify those in the OT.

| Good Doctrines |
| 1029 |

God is eternally the same, and he has saved men throughout the ages by an act of faith in his promise (Eze.

18:31-32). God is "no respecter of persons," and he looks upon the human race as a whole, without regard to national or racial distinctions. The only chosen people God has are those who have responded to his invitation and have accepted their election to salvation. "God so loved the world, that he gave ... " (Jn. 3:16).

| God's Impartiality |
| 1979-1980 |

| Chosen Ones |
| 2725 |

Although the early Genesis record includes little formal teaching about redemption, the book presents enough to show that a theology based on blood was common knowledge. The same pattern of redemption is discernible in the lives of such early Old Testament characters as Enoch, Noah, Abraham, and Melchizedek.

| Redemption |
| 2978-2979 |

Before going further in this study, certain basic assumptions should be considered, namely that:

1. Man's constitution and moral nature have not changed from those of fallen Adam (Ro. 5:12).
2. Man's need for salvation from sin has never changed (Ro. 3:23).

| Sin Universal |
| 3340 |

3. God's provision for man's salvation has been eternally the same.
4. By virtue of God's absolute nature, the plan of salvation could not be one thing for one generation and something else for another.
5. Jesus Christ, the Covenant Agent, is the same yesterday, today and forever (He. 13:8).
6. The act of faith has always been the means whereby man has been able to appropriate salvation (Hab. 2:4; Ro. 1:17; Ga. 3:11; He. 11:6).

| Faith |
| 1206 |

The educational process which God adopted for man is basically the same as that used in modern education. In his curriculum, God has slowly unfolded over a period of time the details of this provision. Even though the basic plan of salvation was revealed in the beginning, the Scripture spells out the details, "precept upon precept …line upon line; here a little, and there a little" (Is. 28:10). "First the blade, then the ear, after that the full corn in the ear" (Mk. 4:28; cf. Mt. 13:35).

> Learning Process
> 2028

At the appropriate time "God sent forth his Son, made of a woman, made under the law to redeem them that were under the law…" (Ga. 4:4-5). Here is a specific reference to God's clock, pointing to high noon—to an hour when the time was full. This noon hour was revealed in the Advent of God's Son. It is evident there was a period in history when the time was not full; the fullness of time was preceded by a period of preparation.

> Redemption
> 2978

> Fullness of Time
> 1343

The "dawn of redemption" compares favorably to the dawn of a new day. There is a moment when the sun becomes visible but before that time,

the light and life-giving properties of the sun have started to become effective. Sufficient light appears whereby man can find his way about. The benefits of the sun are effective long before it reaches its zenith or apex.

By analogy then, the dawn of God's revelation in his Son was prior to man's fall into sin. In other words, God's cure was provided for man before the need arose (Re. 13:8). However, there is a difference between the fundamental provision and man's full understanding of this provision.

In God's plan the fullness of this revelation was to be manifest in the incarnation, which was not practicable until an educational process could prepare the mind of man for the fuller revelation.

> Incarnation
> 720

The idea that salvation was provided for man from the beginning is suggested in Is. 53. Whatever the provision was, it had already been made in the mind of God as seen in the use of past tense: "he hath borne our griefs, and carried our sorrow… he was wounded for our transgressions, he was bruised for our iniquities: the chastisement of our peace was upon him; and with his stripes we are healed" (Is. 53:4-5). This same tense is also expressed in Jn. 3:16 at a time

> See Isaiah's Portrait of Christ
> 4301

when Christ was still actively engaged in his human ministry. The statement is clear: "For God so loved the world, that he gave his only begotten Son, that whosoever believeth in him should not perish, but have everlasting life" (Jn. 3:16).

These references, in addition to Re. 13:8, certainly indicate that the provision of salvation in Christ was made long before the actual crucifixion on Golgotha. This still leaves unanswered the question: How could God save a person before the crucifixion? This question can best be answered with an analogy from life.

> Golgotha
> 4353

Through the use of a note at a bank, a penniless man can enjoy all the financial benefits he would have if he already had the money. The maker of the note agrees to redeem it, to make full settlement at some future date, and on the basis of this promise the banker opens his vault and makes the funds available. By this analogy, God's redemptive promissory note was given to the human race. God, who "cannot lie," promised or pledged to redeem the note at some future date by the payment of his Son on the cross. The date of this note was "the fullness of time." God's note was sufficient legal tender for people to enter the kingdom of God. The only requirement was that

> God's Kingdom
> 2009

the people should repent of their sins and have faith in the Maker of the note. By faith, the saints of the OT were able to draw checks of salvation on the bank of heaven with full realization that the note would one day be fully redeemed. Ultimately this "faith" was justified when God redeemed his promissory note at the cross.

> Faith
> 1203,1985

The blood of animals did not atone for man's sin. The offering of these animals had been only a testimony, a symbolical expression of the faith the believer had in the blood of the atoning Savior who would die for humanity. How well these early believers understood the theology of Atonement is not known. However, the people of the OT found satisfaction in the same "redemptive fountain" at which the present generation finds satisfaction for their souls today. This was verified when Moses and Elijah joined hands with Jesus, Peter, James and John (Mt. 17:1-3). The Savior of the OT period is the same as that of the New (Is. 43:11-12).

> Atonement
> 304

16:1-21:21 Now Sarai, Abram's wife, had borne him no children. But she had an Egyptian maidservant named Hagar; so she said... "Perhaps I can build a family through her." (NIV)

Sarah
3145
Hagar
1474

The story of Sarai (Sarah) and Hagar is filled with lessons about impatience, jealousy, and mistreatment. It is also an instructive lesson in the mind of the apostle Paul as he writes to the church at Galatia about their faith in Christ. These are his words:

> ...it is written that Abraham had two sons, one by the slave woman and the other by the free woman. His son by the slave woman was born in the ordinary way; but his son by the free woman was born as the result of a promise. These things may be taken figuratively, for the women represent two covenants. One covenant is from Mount Sinai and bears children who are to be slaves: This is Hagar. Now Hagar stands for Mount Sinai in Arabia and corresponds to the present city of Jerusalem, because she is in slavery with her children. But the Jerusalem that is above is free, and she is our mother...Now you, brothers, like Isaac, are children of promise. At that time the son born in the ordinary way persecuted the son born by the power of the Spirit. It is the same now. But what does the Scripture say? "Get rid of the slave woman and her son, for the slave woman's son will never share in the inheritance with the free woman's son." Therefore, brothers, we are not children of the slave woman, but of the free woman (Ga. 4:22-31, NIV).

Spiritual
Bondage
2139

Reversion
to Judaism
4092
Judaizers
1958
Ceremonial
Law
Abolished
435
Faith
1203

Apparently the Galatians were too easily persuaded by the Jewish teachers who were insisting upon the observance of Mosaic law (Ga. 3:1-22). Some Judaizers had gone so far as to reinstate the Jewish festivals and ceremonies as essential to Christian worship (Ga. 4:8-11). Stating his argument in the form of a question, Paul shows the weakness of the position of the Galatians: "Does God give you his Spirit and work miracles among you because you observe the law, or because you believe what you heard?" (Ga. 3:5, NIV), i.e.,"or by the hearing of faith" (AV).

Paul's letter emphasizes once again the message that is found throughout the Bible: It is faith, not works, that makes man right with God (see commentary on Ge. 15:6 and essay following). The fact that he uses this example from early Genesis to make his point shows the thematic unity of the Word of God.

16:7 The angel of the LORD found Hagar... (NIV)

Angel of
the Lord
141
Hagar
1474

In this verse "the angel of the LORD" is to be distinguished from more general references to angels (see commentary on Re. 5:11). When this angel appeared to Hagar, she said to him, "Thou God seest me" (Ge. 16:13). Similarly when the angel of the Lord appeared to Abraham on Mount Moriah, he spoke to him out of heaven and the angel referred to himself as the Lord (Ge. 22:15-16). While Moses was at Mount Sinai "God called unto him out of the burning bush" (Ex. 3:4). Other instances are found in Ge. 32:30, Jos. 5:13-15 and Zec. 1:10-13.

Burning
Bush
556

One writer said:

> The angel of the Lord came in "human" form to Abraham, Hagar, Moses, Joshua, Gideon and Manoah. While any angel sent to execute the commands of God might be called the angel of the Lord (2 S. 24:16; 1 K. 19:5,7), yet mention is made of an angel under circumstances that justify one in always thinking of the same angel, who is distinguished from the Lord, and yet identified with Him (Ge. 16:10,13; 22:11-12,15-16; Ex. 3:2,4; Jos. 5:13-15; Zec. 1:10-13), who revealed the face of God (Ge. 32:30),

in whom was the Lord's name (Ge. 22:16), and whose presence was equivalent to the Lord's presence (Ex. 32:34; 33:14; Is. 63:9). The angel of the Lord thus appears as a manifestation of the LORD Himself, one with the Lord and yet different from Him.[32]

Further, Thomas Rees says, "The angel *(Malakh)* of God is a frequent mode of God's manifestation of Himself in human form, and for occasional purposes. In many passages it is assumed that God and His angel are the same being, and the names are used synonymously" (Ge. 16:7-13; Ex.3:2-7).[33]

Divine Appear-ances **206**

Thus the "angel of the LORD" is not a being lower than God, but is to be identified as God himself appearing to man in the unique form of an angel. As mentioned in the commentary on Ge. 1:28, the appearance of God to man is called a "theophany" in theological terms. The following essay gives more information on the subject.

Theophanies in the Old Testament

The compound divine name YHWH-Adonai, translated LORD, is the name used when OT people came face to face with the deity (see commentary on Ex. 3:14).

Divine Appearances
206

Such appearances by deity to man are called "theophanies" or "Christophanies." Both of these words are compound Greek words meaning "God appearing" or an "appearance of God" (or Christ). *Theos* is the Greek term for God, *Christos*, the Greek term for Christ, and *Messiah* is the Hebrew equivalent. It is reasonable to suppose that the idea of theophany was adopted by the Greek religions in which the priests showed the images of their gods to the people. At the festival of Delphi the statues of Apollo and other gods were prominent. Since the theophanies in the OT predate heathen religions, it is obvious that they borrowed the idea from Biblical revelation. Certainly no event in history would precede the appearance of God to Adam and Eve.

The noted scholar James A. Borland has written a scholarly book on this subject: *Christ in the Old Testament.* He states: "All Old Testament theophanies that involve the manifestations of God in human form were appearances of the Second Person of the Trinity, and as such, their purpose was not only to provide immediate revelation but also to prepare mankind for the incarnation of Christ."[34]

Trinity
3694

There are many different kinds of divine manifestations; this discussion is limited to a few of "those unsought, intermittent and temporary, visible and audible manifestations of God the Son in human form, by which God communicated something to certain conscious human beings on earth prior to the birth of Jesus Christ."[35] According to James Borland, the purposes of Christophanies (manifestations of the Second Person of the Trinity) suggest the following long-range implications:

Christ, Personal Appearance of
690

1. "God the Son anticipated his future incarnation, intimated its possibility, prefigured its human form and even prophesied its coming royalty."

Incarnation
720

2. "God was using a form of revelation suited to His purposes in the early history of His redemptive plan."

3. "God connected his work in the Old and New Testaments by appearing in human form in both."

4. "God was able to reveal aspects of his person in this way that no other form of revelation allowed."

5. "God may have sought to intimate Christ's Deity and the Trinity."[36]

Christ's
Divinity
709-718

In the light of such statements by Jesus as "all things must be fulfilled, which were written in the law of Moses, and in the prophets, and in the psalms, concerning me" (Luke 24:44), it is needful to show without equivocation that Christ is indeed a living reality in the OT. Matthew states that Jesus Christ was the son of David and the son of Abraham (Mt. 1:1). John declared that it is not the Elohim God who had been made manifest but the "only begotten Son, he hath declared him" (John 1:18).

The terms *Messiah* and *Logos* (Christ/Word) are definite in their expressions of

Messiah
695

God's revelation to man. Here the Lord carries on the office of Redeemer in behalf of God's overall plan during the OT period. However, the Advent of Christ did not finalize the plan of salvation. Without the death and resurrection there would have been no salvation. Without shedding of blood, there is no remission for sins. If Christ had not been resurrected from the dead, all humanity would still be dead in trespasses and sins.

At the Advent it is YHWH, the LORD, who finally appears in Jesus Christ, the God-Man. When Paul writes to Timothy, he speaks of eternal life as something "which was given us in

Lord
2514

Christ Jesus before the world began" (2 Ti. 1:9; Tit. 1:2). There are over 200 titles in the Bible for Christ. These reveal the fullness of his nature and the many-

Titles and Names
of Christ
3632

sided relationships he has with his people. When God made a special revelation of himself in the OT, he used the name YHWH-LORD, expressing his moral and spiritual attributes of love, holiness, and righteousness.

The historical display of the divine essence lies essentially in the idea of the LORD who enters into the phenomenon of space and time in order to manifest himself to mankind. From the beginning of time, when he spoke with Adam and Eve in the Garden of Eden, God has "at many times and in various ways" (He.1:1, NIV) made his presence known to mankind.

17:1 ...I am God Almighty... (NIV)

The Hebrew for "God Almighty" in this verse is El-Shaddai, a special name of God. El-Shaddai means "the God who is manifested in his mighty acts" or "God Almighty." In the Septuagint the Hebrew name *Shaddai* is translated a number of times as the Greek word *ikanos,* which can be translated "all sufficient." Rabbinical tradition points out that the word consists of two participles which, when combined, means sufficient or self-sufficient. Thus in this name, Shaddai or El-Shaddai, the idea is conveyed of the sufficiency of the Almighty One (Ph. 4:19; De. 2:7; 1 K. 19:6; 2 K. 4:6; 7:8).[37]

The name Almighty God speaks of the inexhaustible stores of his bounty, of the riches and fullness of his grace in self-sacrificing love pouring itself out for others. It reveals that every good and perfect gift comes from God, that he never wearies of bestowing his mercies and blessings upon his people (Ja. 1:17). But it must not be forgotten that his strength is made perfect in weakness and that his sufficiency makes it possible for believers to have "a well of water springing up into everlasting life" (Jn. 4:14), which they can share with a thirsty and needy humanity.

For other names of God in the Bible, see commentary on Ge. 1:1 (Elohim), Ge. 15:2 (Adonai) and Ex. 3:14, with chart (YHWH).

17:9-10 And God said unto Abraham...
Every man child among you shall be circumcised.

It is evident that blood symbolism is reflected in the OT rite of circumcision. This act was a covenant sign between Abraham and the Lord. "In order that Abraham might become 'the friend of God' he was commanded that he should be circumcised as a token of the covenant between him and God (Ge. 17:10-11). The blood exuding from the operation was a testimony of faith in God's blood atonement."[38]

Atoning
Blood of
Christ
679
Redemption
2978-2979
Sacrifice of
Christ
3366

The use of blood in the OT is "everywhere vested with cleansing, expiatory, and reverently symbolic qualities ... From the OT to the NT we see an exaltation of the conception of blood and ceremonies. In Abraham's covenant [circumcision] his own blood had to be shed ...There must always be a shedding of blood. 'Without shedding of blood there is no remission' (He. 9:22). The exaltation and dignifying of this idea finds its highest development then in the vicarious shedding of blood by Christ himself (1 Jn. 1:7)."[39]

For the OT church the rite of circumcision was the symbol of faith by which believers were distinguished from the heathen; the rite effected admission to the fellowship of the covenant people, securing for the individual his share in the promises and saving benefits provided by God from the beginning (Re. 13:8b).

It is evident that ethical demands are made on the adult who is spiritually circumcised, namely "born again"; he is obliged to obey God, whose covenant sign he bears in his body, and to walk blamelessly before him (Ge. 17:1). Thus circumcision is the symbol of heart purification after the new birth (Col. 2:11). The spiritual significance is brought out in the use of the

The vicinity of Bethel, where Jacob's dream took place.

phrase "uncircumcised of heart" to note a lack of receptivity to the things of God (Le. 26:41; Je. 9:25; Eze. 44:7); "while, on the other hand, the purification of the heart, by which it becomes receptive to the things of God and capable of executing God's will, is called circumcision of the heart" (Col. 2:11-13: cf. De. 10:16).[40]

From this evidence it is apparent that the physical operation (circumcision) is symbolic of the spiritual change wrought in the heart by the Holy Spirit, "circumcision of heart," or the "new birth" (see Ro. 2:25ff.). It can be noted that Abraham was "spiritually circumcised," or "born again," before he submitted to the physical operation of circumcision (Ro. 4:11).

Gradually baptism with water superseded circumcision. Reference to sprinkling of water and cleansing from filthiness is found in the OT (Nu. 8:7; Eze. 36:25). It is certain that John the Baptist found in such passages the ground for his practice of baptizing the Jewish believers who sought "to flee from the wrath to come" (Mt. 3:7; Jn. 1:25-28). The time period of the Gospels took place in the OT era. The NT Period did not come into being until after the death of Jesus Christ. The baptism of John was a connecting link between the OT and the NT churches because John ministered in the synoptic OT period — before Jesus died.

It has always been necessary for sinful man to accept the promised salvation proffered by the Lord. The cleansing so often referred to is in reality the circumcision of the heart (De. 30:6) rather than of the flesh. As God takes the initiative in making the covenant, it is apparent that human sin and depravity can be effectively eliminated only by the act of God himself renewing and transforming the heart of man (Ho. 14:4).[41]

New Man
2582

Moral
Filthiness
957

John's
Baptism
760

Spiritual
Circumcision
766
Renewed
Heart
1544

22:14 And Abraham called the name of that place Jehovah-jireh…

Jehovah
Titles
1868-1872

The NIV rendering of this verse begins, "So Abraham called that place 'The LORD will provide.' It is an interesting study to compare the Jehovah titles throughout the OT, because each shows a unique aspect of God's relationship with man. A chart at Ex. 3:14 in this book shows some of the most meaningful of these.

Substitute
3361
Rams
183

Jehovah-jireh means "LORD our provider" and is associated with the times of great crisis in the life of Abraham. In this setting he is commemorating the great deliverance of Isaac through the provision of a ram as a substitute sacrifice (Ge. 22:13). The ram as a substitute can typify Christ, who sacrificed himself on the cross as a substitute for sinful man.

28:12 …a ladder set up on the earth…and behold the angels of God ascending and descending on it.

Bethel
406, 4342

After Jacob experienced his dream about the ladder that ascended into heaven with the Lord standing at the upper end, he named the place Bethel, meaning "house of God."

37:17 …And Joseph went after his brethren, and found them in Dothan.

Joseph
1917

Dothan was a small town near Shechem on the caravan route (see also 2 K. 6:13). Joseph was cast into the pit here and sold to the Midianites by his brothers. The mound (or tel) of Dothan is today partially excavated, as shown in the picture below.

The tel of Dothan, where Joseph found his brothers.

JOSEPH		CHRIST	
Ge. 37:3	He was highly esteemed and set apart by his father	Mt. 3:17; Jn. 3:35	
Ge. 46:29	He was devoted to his father	Lu. 2:49; 10:22	Joseph, Son of Jacob **1917**
Ge. 37:4	He was hated and rejected by his brothers	Jn. 15:25	
Ge. 37:18	His brothers conspired against him	Mt. 26:3-4	Conspiracy Against Christ **2779**
Ge. 45:5	He forgave his brothers' sin	Lu. 23:34	
Ge. 37:24, 39:20; 41:41	He suffered great humiliation, but later was highly exalted	Ph. 2:6-11	Exaltation-Abasement **1164-1174**
Ge. 50:19-21	He returned good for evil	Lu. 22:51	
Ge. 50:19-21	He provided a way of salvation from death	Jn. 3:16-17	Deliverance **968-972**

Though the Bible nowhere states that Joseph was a type of Christ, it is an interesting study to compare the similarities in their lives. The chart above can provide a basis for such a study. See also the comparison of Joseph's life with that of Esther (p. 189) and Daniel (p. 249).

Joseph, Char. Study **4292**

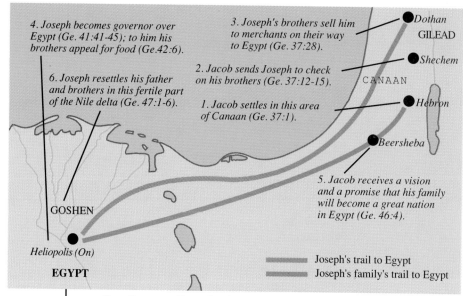

From Canaan to Egypt: Jacob's family resettles in a foreign land

49:1 Then Jacob called for his sons and said: "Gather around so I can tell you what will happen to you in days to come." (NIV)

The Blessing of Jacob (Israel) is one of several poetic blessings in the book of Genesis. This one is particularly fascinating for the student of the history of the nation of Israel, for it reveals a father's final thoughts about his sons and what they and their posterity will experience.

Dr. Charles W. Slemming, perhaps the greatest authority on Hebrew symbolism, has contributed insights about the tribes from a unique perspective. He has studied the symbolism of the breastplate that the High Priest of Israel wore when he represented the children of Israel to Jehovah (Ex. 28:29). Twelve precious and semi-precious stones were mounted on the face of the breastplate and each tribe had its own stone on which its name was engraved. For Israel this symbolized the watchful care of Jehovah, not only over Israel as a nation, but over Israel as individual tribes. For us this is suggestive of the personal interest God directs to each individual believer. Dr. Slemming writes:

> "A careful study will reveal the fact that these names were not written haphazardly but rather that the stones were purposely chosen for the engraving of the particular name. In each case a definite connection between the character of the person and the nature of the stone is to be seen."[42]

The following is a concise look at the twelve sons, the stones that symbolize their tribes, some of the events their families experienced, and some of their descendants. In addition, symbols for each of the tribes are pictured.

Israel's
Inheritance
1752

High
Priests
2064

Divine
Care
2911

The Children of Israel

Reuben

Genesis 29:32, born to Leah; 35:22, commits adultery with his father's concubine; 37:21-22, intercedes for Joseph's life; 49:4, Jacob calls him "turbulent as the waters" and states that he will not have preeminence.

Numbers 26:5-11, Reuben has four sons from whom descend four tribes; 1:20-21, Reubenites number 46,500 fighting men; 16:1-50, three descendants join a revolt against Moses and Aaron and are killed; Jos. 4:12, took part in all of Joshua's wars in Canaan; Jud. 5:15-16, vacillated in the battle against Sisera, perhaps fulfilling Jacob's prophecy.

1 Chronicles 5:1-10, genealogical records; Eze. 48:6-7, territorial description in Canaan; Re. 7:5, 12,000 descendants sealed.

Symbolic Stone: Emerald. Sea-Green in color, suggestive of the restless sea. Reuben was unstable as water.

Simeon

Genesis 29:33, born to Leah; 34:24-31, a part of the massacre of the Hivites to revenge their assault of his sister Dinah; 42:24, chosen to be held prisoner in Egypt as security for the return of his brothers; 49:5-7, his father predicts that his descendants will be scattered.

Joshua 19:1,9, descendants absorbed into the territory of Judah, a fulfillment of his father's prophecy. 1 Chr. 4:24-43, descendants listed; Re. 7:7, 12,000 Simeonites sealed.

Symbolic Stone: Sapphire, a rich azure color, the color of the sky on a clear day. The word "sapphire" comes from the Hebrew *sappeer*, signifying to "scratch or polish" and also "to cut off and divide." Simeon's descendants were scattered.

Levi

Genesis 29:34, born to Leah; 34:25-31, takes part along with Simeon in massacre of the Hivites; 46:11, has three sons from whom three tribes descend; 49:5-7, Jacob predicts that his descendants will be scattered.

Numbers 1:50, Levites are set apart for service to the sanctuary; Nu. 26:62, census showed 23,000 Levites; Nu. 1:47-53, duties spelled out; Jos. 14:4, "received no share of the land," fulfilling Jacob's prophecy; 1 Chr. 6:1-30, descendants listed.

Malachi 2:4-8, covenant discussed; He. 7:5-10, priesthood evaluated; Re. 7:7, 12,000 Levites sealed.

Well-known descendants: Moses, Aaron, Miriam, Samuel.

Since the tribe of Levi was set apart for service, it is not listed as a tribe by the time of the High Priest. Therefore there is no stone symbolizing this tribe.

Reuben

Simeon

Levi

Judah

Genesis 29:35, born to Leah; 38:1-10, two sons killed by divine judgment for their sins; 38:11-30, his treatment of Tamar and the birth of Pharez and Zarah; 37:26-28, saves Joseph's life; 49:3-10, Jacob gives Judah the blessing of the birthright.

Judah
1955-1956

1 Chronicles 2:3-6, genealogical records; Jud. 1:1-20, first tribe sent to take possession of its allotted territory; 2 S. 2:4, David anointed king over Judah; Re. 7:5, 12,000 descendants sealed.

Well-known descendants: Jesus Christ (fulfilling Jacob's prophecy), David, Solomon, Caleb, Othniel, Achan, Zerubbabel, Nehemiah.

Symbolic stone: Sardius (ruby). Since it is blood-red it is a strong symbol of the atonement that would come through the tribe's most important descendant, Jesus Christ.

Dan

Genesis 30:5-6, born to Bilhah; 46:23, has only one son;

Dan
909-911

49:16-17, Jacob mentions his future destiny as "one of the tribes of Israel."

Deuteronomy 33:22, Moses' blessing; Jos. 19:47, Danites take over the town of Laish and rename it Dan; Jud. 18:30; Danites guilty of idolatry; Re. 7:5-8, Dan is omitted from the list of the tribes that are sealed.

Well-known descendants: Oholiab and Samson.

Symbolic stone: Beryl, known for its hardness. The tribe of Dan seemed to be always fighting or taking over others.

Naphtali

Genesis 30:7-8, born to Bilhah; 46:24, four sons; 49:21, his

Naphtali
2520-2521

father refers to him as a "doe set free."

Numbers 1:42-43, fighting men number 53,400; Jos. 19:32-39, descendants settle in hill country of northern Palestine, perhaps showing their independent spirit (cf. Jacob's prophecy) since this was a somewhat isolated location; 1 K. 15:20, land overtaken by Syrians; Is. 9:1-7, comforting prophecy from Isaiah; Mt. 4:12-16, fulfillment of Isaiah's prophecy, because Christ's ministry was located in this territory; Re. 7:6, 12,000 of the tribe of Naphtali sealed.

Well-known descendant: Hiram, the skillful worker in metal (1 K. 7:13-14).

Symbolic stone: Jasper, of which there are several kinds, but this particular one was probably the transparent variety. The tribe of Naphtali reflected very clearly the glory of God, as Christ's ministry was located in their territory.

Gad

Genesis 30:10-11, born to Zilpah; 46:16, seven sons; 49:19, Jacob prophecies about future

Gad
1378

Judah

Dan

Naphtali

raids on Gad.

Deuteronomy 33:20-21, Moses blesses God for the enlargement of the tribe of Gad and praises the tribe's valor (cf. Jacob's prophecy); Nu. 1:24-25, fighting men numbered at 45,650; 1 Chr. 12:8, brave Gadites fight with David at Ziklag; Re. 7:5, 12,000 Gadites sealed.

Symbolic Stone: Diamond, a stone so hard it scratches all the other stones. The tribe of Gad had hard determination to get the first part of the Canaan inheritance for itself, ahead of everyone else (Nu. 32:1-36).

Asher

Genesis 30:12-13, born to Zilpah; 46:17, four sons; 49:20 his father refers to rich food and delicacies for the family of Asher.

Asher
269

Joshua 19:24-30, allotment of land for the tribe of Asher includes fertile farmlands near the Mediterranean coast (cf. Jacob's prophecy); De. 33:24, Moses' blessing; Jud. 1:31-32, failure to expel the Canaanite inhabitants of the land; Re. 7:6, 12,000 of the tribe of Asher sealed.

Symbolic stone: Onyx, a precious stone marked by parallel layers or bands of different shades of colors.

Issachar

Genesis 30:17-18, born to Leah; 46:13 four sons; 49:14-15,

Issachar
1830

Jacob describes a people that will submit to the oppression of foreign rule as long as they are permitted to stay in their pleasant land.

Numbers 1:28-29, fighting men number 54,400; 1 Chr. 7:5, fighting men increase to 87,000; 1 Chr. 12:32, political insight; Re. 7:7, 12,000 of the tribe of Issachar sealed.

Well-known descendants: Tola, a judge (Jud. 10:1) and King Baasha (1 K. 15:27).

Symbolic stone: Topaz, called so because it was found only after a diligent search. The meaning of the name Issachar is "reward."

Zebulun

Genesis 30:19-20, born to Leah; 46:14, three sons; 49:13,

Zebulun
3985-3986

Jacob predicts that Zebulun will "live by the seashore."

Numbers 1:30-31, fighting men number 57,400; Dt. 33:18-19, Moses' blessing refers to the affluence of the seas; Jos. 19:10-16, allotment of land for Naphtali was close to, though not bordering, the Mediterranean Sea (cf. Jacob's prophecy); Re. 7:8, 12,000 sealed from the tribe of Zebulun.

Symbolic stone: Carbuncle, derived from a Hebrew root used sometimes for "lightning" or "flashing." Jacob prophesied that Zebulun would "live by the seashore," perhaps calling up an image of a flashing light by the sea.

Gad

Asher

Issachar

Joseph (Ephraim and Manasseh)

Joseph
1917, 4292

Genesis 30:22-23, Joseph born to Rachel; 37:3, favorite son of his father; 46:20 sons Manasseh and Ephraim born in Egypt; 48:5, Jacob adopts Joseph's two sons as his own; 48:12-20, Jacob blesses the boys and places Ephraim ahead of Manasseh; 49:22-26, Jacob predicts the success of the two Joseph tribes.

Ephraim: 1 Chr. 7:20-22 Ephraim loses two sons to death; Nu. 1:33, fighting men number 40,500; Jud. 5:14, patriotically assist Deborah in battle; Jud. 8:1-3, quarrel with Gideon; Jos. 16:5-10, allotment of land for the Ephraimites; Is. 7:1-2, supremacy over the northern tribes; Re. 7:8, 12,000 sealed from the tribe of Joseph (Ephraim).

Ephraim
1144-1145

Well-known descendants: Joshua, Jeroboam.

Symbolic stone: Ligure, thought by some to resemble the jacinth or yellow jargoon. Its uncertainty of nature causes one to refrain from seeking any spiritual meaning.

Manasseh: Genesis 50:23, firstborn son is Makir, ancestor of the Gileadites (Jos. 17:1); Nu. 1:34-35, fighting men number 32,200; 26:34, number of fighting men increase to 52,700; Jos. 17:12-13, fail to expel the Canaanites from the

Manasseh
2244

land; 1 Chr. 12:19-21, give support to David at Ziklag; 1 Chr. 5:18-26, wage war with the Hagrites; 7:14-19, genealogical record; Re. 7:6, 12,000 sealed from the tribe of Manasseh.

Well-known descendant: Gideon.

Symbolic stone: Agate, which, when cut and polished, produces beautiful and precious variegated stones. Manasseh became a large tribe and experienced much success.

Benjamin

Benjamin
401

Genesis 35:16-20, born to Rachel; 43:1-17, especially beloved by his father; 43:29-34, affectionate relationship with Joseph; 49:27, Jacob describes him as "a ravenous wolf."

Joshua 18:11-28, the allotment of land for the Benjamites; Nu. 1:37, fighting men number 35,400; Jud. 3:15, strong deliverer for Israel from this tribe; Jud. 19-21, savagery of the tribe recorded (cf. Jacob's prophecy); 1 S. 10:20-24, first king of Israel from this tribe; 1 Chr. 7:6-12, 8:1-40, genealogy recorded; Ps. 68:27, Benjamin a leader; Re. 7:8, 12,000 sealed from the tribe of Benjamin.

Well-known descendants: King Saul, Mordecai (Est. 2:5), the apostle Paul.

Symbolic stone: Amethyst, a bluish-violet stone, which might apply to Benjamin because he and his tribe were hard and often headstrong in their warlike character.

Zebulun

Joseph (Ephraim & Manasseh)

Benjamin

Exodus

The Name

In the Hebrew Torah the book of Exodus, the second book in the Pentateuch, is called *We' elleh Shemoth,* meaning "these are the names." This expression, however, does not really describe the book. The English is a transliteration of the Greek work *exodus* and means "going out" or "departure." The title *Exodus* is used in the Greek OT (Septuagint).

Book of Exodus **4224**

Authorship and Date

The book of Exodus, as part of the Pentateuch, is attributed to Moses. He is the central human figure in the book. Internal evidence indicates that

Moses **2420-2421**

> the author must have been originally a resident of Egypt (not of Palestine), a contemporary eye witness of the Exodus and wilderness wanderings, and (must have) possessed a high degree of education, learning and literary skill. No one else conforms to these qualifications as closely as Moses, the son of Amram...The author was well-acquainted with Egyptian names, titles, words and customs. He correctly referred to the crop sequence for lower Egypt (Ex. 9:31-32)...He spoke only of the shittim tree or acacia, the one known desert hardwood tree in the Sinai peninsula, as the source of lumber for the tabernacle (Ex. 25:5, etc.)...the badger skins used as the outer cover for the tabernacle (Ex. 25:5; 26:14)...He knew about the reeds in the marshes of the Nile delta (Ex. 2:3) and that the desert sand begins abruptly at the edge of the cultivated fields (Ex. 2:12). He seems to have been an eye witness of the events...he listed for no apparent reason the exact number of springs (12) and of palm trees (70) at Elim (Ex. 15:27).[1]

Wilderness of Zin **3995**

Acacia Wood **24**

Nile **2591**

Finally, the proof of Mosaic authorship is strengthened by Jesus' reference to rising from the dead. He states "...as touching the dead, that they rise; have ye not read in the book of Moses, how in the bush God spake unto him, saying, I am the God of Abraham, and the God of Isaac, and the God of Jacob?" (Mk. 12:26; see also Lu. 20:37). The book of Exodus may have been written while Moses and the Israelites camped around Kadesh-Barnea.

Background, Purpose, and Content

The starting point for the Exodus is Rameses, as indicated in Ex. 12:37 and Nu. 33:5, and is associated with the eastern edge of the fertile delta area called Goshen (Ge. 47:6).

Rameses **2946**
Goshen **1439**

The book of Exodus is thoroughly redemptive in its content. It is the period when the Passover was instituted, foreshadowing Christ, "the Lamb of God." The outline theme of the book deals with liberation from enslavement, idolatry, and death. It continues to develop revelation concerning man's redemption, which is introduced in brief capsule form in Genesis.

Bond-servants **2138**

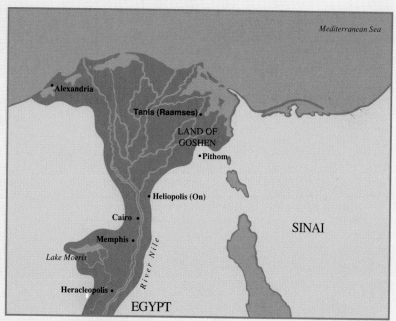

The land of Goshen in Egypt.

In the book of Exodus, YHWH, the LORD, the second person in the Trinity, declares himself to be "Israel's Covenant God." He delivers the Israelites and brings them out of the land of Egypt; he takes them to himself to be his people and to be their God; and he will bring them into the land promised to Abraham, Isaac, and Jacob (Ex. 6:6-8).[2]

False
Worship
3928-3952

As a background for Israel's monotheism there stands the polytheism of Egypt. There appears to have been a time in ancient Egypt when a monotheistic type of religion was practiced, but by the time of the historic period, a religion developed in which each native tribe adopted its own god represented by an animal. Among the animals in the Egyptian pantheon were the bull, cow, vulture, falcon, hawk, crocodile, goat, ape, frog, beetle, and serpent.

False Gods
3934-3941

Jacob
1837

Egypt
1100

The book of Exodus begins about 430 years after Jacob and his sons migrated to Egypt (Ex. 12:40-41). During this time the population of Egypt had increased appreciably. At the time of the exodus the Israelites numbered more then 600,000 men over 20 years of age, besides women and children (Nu. 1:45-46). According to the best scholarly estimate, that would place the total population at about 3,000,000. Some scholars object to this high figure but for 70 persons to reach this number in 430 years it would only be necessary to double the population about every 25 years.

The Highlights of the Book of Exodus

The outline in the TCRB Helps No. 4224 gives four main subtopics for the content of the book of Exodus:

Bondage
of Israel
1820, 2141,
2143

1. *The Period of Bondage.* The oppression of Israel began under the new pharaoh. The great increase in the Israelite population made this pharaoh feel insecure. To slow their increase the Israelites were subjected to oppression and abuse. The period ends with the marriage of Moses while he was in exile.

2. *The Period of Deliverance*. This topic includes the call of Moses at the burning bush, the twelve plagues, the deliverance under Moses from Pharaoh, and the institution of the Passover.

3. *The Period of Discipline*. In this division is an account of Israel's travel experiences from Egypt to Mount Sinai.

4. *The Period of Legislation and Organization*. During this period the Lord gave the Ten Commandments, the ordinances, and the plans for the tabernacle to Moses. YHWH, the LORD, gave the Israelites three religious institutions at Mount Sinai:

> a. The tabernacle for a formal worship center;
> b. The levitical priesthood, that was to supervise all religious activities;
> c. The Ten Commandments and the ordinances which ultimately were incorporated into the Jewish Bible.

Deliverance
968-972
Chastise-
ment
497
Command-
ments
444-445

Ordinances
2662

Ramesses II, commonly thought to be the pharaoh of the exodus.

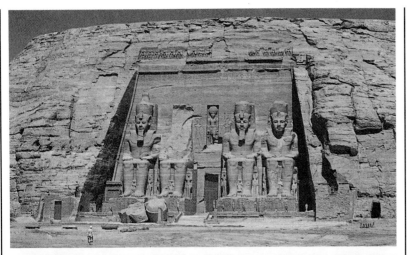

Top: Abu-Simbel—The colossal statues of Ramesses II and his temple as they appear reconstructed high above Lake Nassar.
Bottom: The Temple Ramesses II, built 100 yards downriver in honor of his wife and queen, Nefertari.

1:11 So they put slave masters over them to oppress them with forced labor, and they built Pithom and Rameses as store cities for Pharaoh. (NIV)

The oppressed children of Israel "sighed by reason of the bondage, and they cried, and their cry came up unto God by reason of the bondage" (Ex. 2:23). Who was the pharaoh who so oppressed the nation of God and whose "heart was hardened" many times throughout the book of Exodus?

Perhaps there is a clue from archaeology. A monument erected on the banks of the Nile River about 1250 B.C. depicts four sitting figures, each 67 feet high, and each a likeness of the Egyptian pharaoh Ramesses II. Scholars assume that he was the originator of the shrine, and certainly the egotism reflected in the many statues he had cut of his likeness is in keeping with the arrogant way the pharaoh treated the Hebrews in the story of the exodus.

Pharaoh
2748

Egypt
1100

How did the Egyptians form the massive rocks used in statues like that of Ramesses II? These pictures illustrate a technique used to split massive boulders into the shapes desired for statues and monuments.
Top: This from Aswan Quarries—a 137–foot obelisk abandoned by the stone cutters because of an accidental fault.
Bottom: A line cut showing the holes into which soaked wooden pegs were inserted. The wood then expanded, breaking the rocks in the desired place.

3:14-15 God said to Moses, "I AM WHO I AM ... Say to the Israelites, 'The LORD, the God of your fathers... has sent me to you.' This is my name forever, the name by which I am to be remembered from generation to generation. (NIV)

The consonantal divine name YHWH, translated LORD in the KJV and NIV, Jehovah in the ASV, and Yahweh in some modern English versions is the most significant name of God in the OT and appears over 6,000 times. In the post-exilic period, when a strong Messianic hope developed among the Jews, the name was not pronounced for fear of committing blasphemy; the penalty for doing so was stoning (Le. 24:16). In theological terminology Adonai was substituted for this most holy personal name of God.

The Jewish Masoretic scholars combined the consonantal form of YHWH with the vowels from Adonai to remind the synagogue readers that they were to pronounce only the term Adonai. From the combined form of the two terms for the Deity the name Jehovah developed. The imposition of the vowels of Adonai upon YHWH provided an approximate pronunciation of this word of four letters YHWH, namely Yahweh or Jehovah.

The meaning of this awesome name, YHWH, was shrouded in mystery and speculation. During the OT period the temple leaders gave credence to the idea that YHWH was the name of the Messiah and that the meaning and the pronunciation of the name would not be revealed until the advent of the Messiah. When Jesus applied this name to himself, therefore, it was a highly significant statement of identity (see commentary on Jn. 8:58).

Erich Sauer says

> Throughout the Old Testament the LORD-Messiah is regarded as 'the coming One'... Exactly the same verbal form Christos was used in the third century before Christ's birth in the Bible of the exiled Jews in Egypt, the Septuagint, the Greek translation of the OT prepared by the Jews. It is to be found in such passages as Ps. 2:2; Is. 2:10; Da. 9:25 ...In the old covenant the Gospel is coming into being (formative period)...the OT is the dawn of morning. The dawn belongs to the sun. Thus the OT belongs to Christ, and tells what Christ is. The NT tells who He is and in such a way that it becomes manifest that He alone knows who the Christ is; He is Jesus. So do the two Testaments correspond to the two chief names of the Redeemer; the Old to the name of His vocation, Christ; the New to His personal name, Jesus. But both are inspired by one Spirit and explain each other. Before He became man, Christ [was] is already the center of the history of salvation. His anticipatory presentation in the OT is at the same time a self-presentation, for the 'Spirit of Christ' was in the prophets (1 Pe. 1:11). The pre-Christian history of revelation is a 'history of Christ' before He came (Is. 25:9; 33:2).[3]

The Scribes, Pharisees, and other temple leaders never spoke the name Jesus. Since they could not utter the name of Jesus as Lord and Savior, they could not utter it at all.

At the time the Hebrew OT was translated into Greek, the combined name YHWH-Adonai was rendered Kurios. When the Greek NT was translated into English, the term was LORD. R. Alan Killen explains that "Adonai is an honorific title used both as an intensive plural of rank meaning 'Master,' 'Sovereign,' or 'Lord,' and as an appellative meaning 'My Lord.' Its alternate form occurs in Ps. 110:1 which reads: 'The LORD (Yahweh) said unto my Lord (Adonai).' Matthew 22:41-45 shows how Christ identified this title with himself. The Greek equivalent is Kyrios [*Kurios*] 'Lord,' representing both Yahweh and Adonai in the OT Septuagint. In the NT it is applied to Christ equally with the Father and the Spirit."[4]

The combined YHWH and Adonai is always rendered LORD (with

Jehovah
1867-1872

Blasphemy
473

Egypt
1100
Messiah
695

Redeemer
2977

Salvation
3116
Christ
Eternal
709
Christ,
Names
691-700

Wonderful
Name
2516

capital letters). A noted professor puts it thus: "The name Kurios (LORD) occurs very frequently. It seems to gather into itself the combined significance of Adonai, of which it is the equivalent, and Yahweh or Jehovah. The name is applied with equal clarity to God the Father and to Jesus Christ. Thus in the unfolding of the redemptive message of the New Testament, the richness of Old Testament nomenclature for the Deity is presupposed."[5]

God's special relationships to Israel are expressed in the many divine names/titles recorded in the OT. Some of the most meaningful are the titles which combine the name Jehovah or LORD with an attribute or act of God. Each of these has a special meaning in "God-to-man" and "man-to-God" relationships. The following chart lists the most familiar of the Jehovah/ LORD titles. For commentary on other names of God, see Ge. 1:1 (Elohim), Ge. 15:1-2 (Adonai) and Ge. 17:1 (El Shaddai) and the essay on "Theophanies in the OT," p. 72.

Names of God
1868-1872,
3633

Divine Name	Meaning of Name	Biblical Location	See Also Page
Jehovah-jireh	"the LORD our provider"	Ge. 22:13-14	76
Jehovah-rophe	"the LORD who heals you"	Ex. 15:22-26	100
Jehovah-nissi	"the LORD is my banner"	Ex. 17:15-16	100
Jehovah-m'kaddesh	"the LORD that sanctifies you"	Ex. 31:13	124
Jehovah-shalom	"the LORD is peace"	Jud. 6:24	158
Jehovah-rohi	"the LORD is my shepherd"	Ps. 23:1	204
Jehovah-tsidkenu	"the LORD our righteousness"	Je. 23:6	235
Jehovah-shammah	"the LORD is there"	Eze. 48:35	244

3:18 The elders of Israel will listen to you... (NIV)

The word "elder" in Hebrew means "one who is bearded," suggesting maturity and a high rank among the people. For more on the office of elder, see commentary on 1 Ti. 5:17.

Elders
2078-2079

12:1-2 The LORD said..."This month is to be for you the first month, the first month of your year." (NIV)

The Hebrew calendar that was used before the exile is described at length in the TCRB Helps No. 4451. It was based on the seasons and agricultural events of ancient Israel.

Months
2398

Actually the Pentateuch does not describe a calendar as such. Reference is made to the six-day work week plus the Sabbath. In Genesis a general reference is given to time keeping: "Let there be lights in the firmament of the heaven to divide the day from the night; and let them be for signs and for seasons, and for days, and years" (Ge. 1:14). The earliest division of the year was thus lunisolar: spring for sowing and fall for harvesting.

Sabbath
3098

Sabbatical Year
3104

For a study of the development of a reliable calendar, see the next essay.

The Calendar

The matter of a reliable calendar is now taken for granted, but it has not always been so. The Genesis record speaks of days, seasons and years, but presents no systematic menology. The pristine human race groped about in an effort to develop a meaningful, consistent time-keeping system. In early times small groups in an isolated community might point back to a leader's birth or to some significant event. Frequently a new event would supersede one that had been in use.

The earliest practical system developed out of the two seasons, winter and summer, and then increased to include spring and fall. From earliest times the time element, connected with the lunar, solar and stellar phenomena, was incorporated into a broader menology. The system was based on the movement of the earth in relation to the appearance of the sun, moon and other solar bodies.

The development of a calendar came about to satisfy the practical needs of the farmer, the hunter, and the religious. Agriculture required a system for determining the various periods of sowing, reaping and plowing. The hunter needed a time-keeping system to determine the movement of game and gestation. And the religious needed a menology to synchronize the fast and feast days along with the agricultural process.

A well-defined calendar for extensive use was not feasible until there was political unity and continuity over a large geographical area. There was a tendency to adopt local systems in the absence of one government controlling a large area. The Sumerians had one of the best documented calendars because of their strong central government. The names of the months and days were invoked for all commercial, business, legal and civil transactions. Their strong central government was especially noticeable in the time of Hammurabi — about 2000 B.C.

The Canaanites had no unified time-keeping method because they were divided into many warring groups including the Amorites, Arkites, Arvadites, Gerasites, Hamathites, Hittites, Hivites, Jebusites, Sinites and the Zemarites (Ge. 10:15-18).

The Egyptians had a time system based on the rise and fall of the Nile River. Nileometers still stand on the banks of the river. They divided the high and low levels into four seasons of three months each. The hieroglyphic sign for a month is the crescent.

When Hebrew national unity was strong, in the post-exilic period, a twelve month time-keeping system was adopted. This was especially useful for tax collection, conscription and the keeping of business records. Though there were still some fragmentary systems in local communities, all matters relating to the central government were required to use the unified twelve month system.

For religious practices, the unified system of reckoning time was necessary to keep a chronological record of the sabbatical year (every seven years), the Year of Jubilee (every fifty years), as well as the annual feasts of Dedication, Passover, Pentecost, Purim, Tabernacles and Trumpets. The management of the ecclesiastical calendar was the responsibility of the priests. The twelve month system they used and the interrelationships within it are shown in the chart in the TCRB Helps No. 4451.

At various times during the Old Testament period, the Hebrews used five different systems:

1. The Abib Calendar: Moses commanded the people to remember the month of Abib; it was Israel's Emancipation Day. All future events pointed back to this month (Ex. 13:3-4; 34:18; De. 16:1). The other time units followed the festivals outlined in the levitical law.

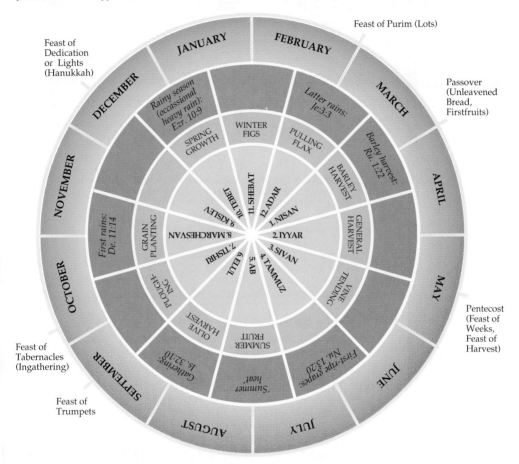

The Hebrew calendar. For more on the six annual feasts, see chart on pp. 126-127.

Feast of Purim (Lots)

Feast of Dedication or Lights (Hanukkah)

Passover (Unleavened Bread, Firstfruits)

JANUARY

FEBRUARY

MARCH

DECEMBER

NOVEMBER

OCTOBER

Rainy season (occasional heavy rain): Ezr. 10:9

Latter rains: Je:3:3

SPRING GROWTH

WINTER FIGS

PULLING FLAX

Barley harvest: Ru. 1:22

BARLEY HARVEST

First rains: De. 11:14

GRAIN PLANTING

11.SHEBAT

10.TEBET

9.KISLEV

8.MARCHESVAN

12.ADAR

1.NISAN

2.IYYAR

3.SIVAN

4.TAMMUZ

5.AB

7.TISHRI

6.ELUL

PLOUGH-ING

OLIVE HARVEST

Gathering: Is. 32:10

SUMMER FRUIT

'Summer heat'

First-ripe grapes: Nu. 13:20

GENERAL HARVEST

VINE TENDING

APRIL

MAY

JUNE

JULY

AUGUST

SEPTEMBER

Feast of Tabernacles (Ingathering)

Feast of Trumpets

Pentecost (Feast of Weeks, Feast of Harvest)

2. The Gezer Calendar: This practical system correlated the seasons with the lunar phases; it defined months by the crop being planted, tended, or harvested at the time.

3. The Phoenician Calendar: This ancient calendar had three months: Ziv, Ethanim and Bul (1 K. 6:1; 8:2; 6:38).

4. The Monarchy Calendar: This system came about through practical demands under the monarchy. It incorporated some of the Gezer elements. In this menology, Solomon's civil year seems to have started in the fall with the Feast of Trumpets (Le. 23:24 ff.). The dedication of the Temple (1 Ki. 8) was apparently deferred for eleven months (1 K. 6:38) in order to make it correspond to the New Year festivities (Rosh Hashana).

5. The Babylonian Calendar: This menology used the twelve month system and eventually became fixed in the entire Near East as the ancient world unified. Their year consisted of 364 days and was divided into four quarters. This was the system adopted by the Qumran community and probably also by Jesus and his disciples.[6]

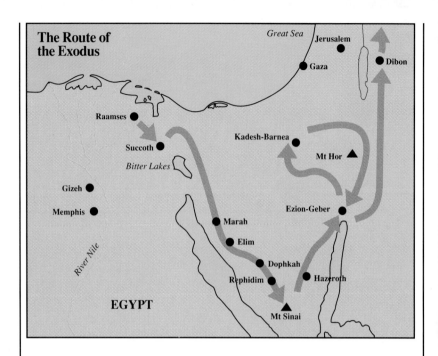

The Route of the Exodus

Great Sea · Jerusalem · Gaza · Dibon · Raamses · Kadesh-Barnea · Mt Hor · Succoth · *Bitter Lakes* · Gizeh · Ezion-Geber · Memphis · Marah · Elim · Dophkah · *River Nile* · Rephidim · Hazeroth · **EGYPT** · Mt Sinai

12:17 ...ye shall observe the feast of unleavened bread...

Feasts, Jewish
1256-1261
Passover
2686

The Passover, or the Feast of Unleavened Bread, was a day inaugurated in Egypt to commemorate the deliverance of the Israelites. This was the night when the death-angel smote the firstborn in the land of Egypt but passed over the houses of the Israelites where the blood had been sprinkled on the doorposts and the lintel. The festival began on the fifteenth day of Abib at evening with the sacrificial meal. A lamb was slain, roasted whole, and eaten with unleavened bread, accompanied by bitter herbs, to commemorate the Israelites' exit from Egypt in haste, not waiting for their bread to rise (Ex. 12:18; 1 Co. 5:8). The festival lasted for seven days. The first day was kept as a Sabbath and likewise the seventh. On the second day of the festival the priest waved a sheaf of barley before the Lord to consecrate the opening harvest.

Sabbath
3098

Lamb
3365

The Passover has a powerful Christian implication. The Passover lamb was a foreshadowing of Christ, the Lamb of God (1 Co. 5:7). Like the paschal lamb, he was without blemish (Ex. 12:5; 1 Pe. 1:18-19) and not a bone was broken (Ex. 12:46; Jn. 19:36). His blood was presented to the Lord (Ex. 12:13). As the Israelites ate the Passover with each other, so also Jesus ate this memorial meal with his disciples (Lu. 22:1-18).

Feast of Passover
1256

12:51 ...the Lord brought the Israelites out of Egypt... (NIV)

God's redemptive program of delivering the nation of Israel from the land of Egypt is a picture of his redemptive plan of rescuing mankind from the oppression of sin. Since the early formative years of the Christian church, Bible scholars have been able to see the plan of salvation prefigured in the exodus from Egypt (see 1 Co. 10:1-4). The following essay further discusses this great Biblical theme.

S alvation Symbolized in the Exodus

The OT abounds in rich doctrinal symbolism. In addition to the symbolism of the tabernacle, a most interesting redemptive pattern is found in the exodus experience of the Israelites. Grace Saxe points out that the Epistle to the Hebrews "explains the significance of the whole Jewish ritual" and that a study of the exodus through the barren wilderness presents God as protecting the Israelites from danger, supplying their needs, teaching them, training them, and eventually bringing them into the rich land of Canaan, their permanent home. So Christ is, at this time, gathering together a people for his name, taking them through a hostile world, protecting, teaching, training, and preparing them for their eternal home.[7]

The apostle Paul tells the Corinthians that "all our fathers were under the cloud, and all passed through the sea; and were all baptized unto Moses in the cloud and in the sea; and did all eat the same spiritual meat; and did all drink the same spiritual drink: for they drank of that spiritual Rock that followed them: and that Rock was Christ" (1 Co. 10:1-4). Paul concludes that "all these things happened unto them for ensamples: and they are written for our admonition" (1 Co. 10:11). The word *ensample* is translated from the Greek word *tupos* meaning literally "a figure, image, or pattern prefiguring a future person or thing."

A few of the places, persons, and events will be examined to show their symbolical meaning.

1. *Egypt.* This land of bondage symbolizes sin. The Hebrews who were

> Moses
> 2420-2421

> Rock
> 3096

> Egypt
> 1100

slaves in Egypt found their plight was almost hopeless. They could not deliver themselves but were dependent upon help from the outside such as God gave to them through his servant Moses.

> Bondage, Physical
> 1820, 2138

2. *Pharaoh* —a type of Satan. This Egyptian king ruled Egypt with an iron hand. Exodus 1:8-22 presents an account of Pharaoh's oppression of the Hebrews. He, a "prince of the world," held his slaves in bondage. "Israel sighed by reason of the bondage, and they cried, and their cry came up unto God…" (Ex. 2:23). Is this not a picture of distressed and burdened people who, when they cry out to God in sincerity, get a sympathetic response from God?

> Pharaoh
> 2747-2748

3. *The Children of Israel.* The Hebrew children typify the people, who, being dissatisfied with the unjust treatment and the tyranny of the king, long for deliverance. When people are ready to turn from sin to righteousness, there is a leader who is ready to take them from Egypt to Canaan. Even one sinner is important enough to be led to the promised land. The Lord not only delivers, but he gives continual guidance.

> Israel
> 1808

4. *Moses.* Moses, compared to Christ, the Great Deliverer (De. 18:15), leads the people out of the land of sin. Moses was given to the people at the proper time, even as Christ came forth when the "fulness of time was come." He, who was called the son of Pharaoh's daughter, chose "rather to suffer affliction with the people of God, than to enjoy the pleasures of sin for a season" (He. 11:24-25). As the son of

> Moses
> 2420-2421

Pharaoh's daughter, he was in line for the throne. Although he had all the social and economic advantages of Egypt at his command, he chose privation with his people. Jesus, too, "was rich," yet for our "sakes he became poor, that [we] through his poverty might be rich" (2 Co. 8:9; Ph. 2:5-8).

Moses, like Jesus, was rejected by his people. When Moses received his call to service, he said, "Behold, they will not believe me, nor hearken unto my voice: for they will say, The LORD hath not appeared unto thee" (Ex. 4:1). Jesus also "came unto his own, and his own received him not" (Jn. 1:11).

God gave credentials to Moses so that the people might know that he

was sent from God. Moses performed miracles, as did Christ, although of a different nature.

| Miracles |
| 2361, 2369 |

However, the miracles of Christ, like those of Moses, were intended to give credence to his divine commission.

From the narrative about the Hebrews' desire to sacrifice unto God comes the insight that man cannot build his altar of worship in "the land of sin." They could not sacrifice because the Egyptians wanted to keep the people in Egypt. Pharaoh wanted the people to offer their sacrifices within his borders. Moses was divinely compelled to go "three days' journey" from the land (Ex. 8:25-28).

It is also necessary for true believers to separate themselves from Egypt. "Friendship with the world is enmity with

| Separation |
| 290 |

God" (Ja. 4:4, RSV). It is impossible to serve the God of heaven and the god of the world at the same time. Man must serve either one or the other (Mt. 6:24).

5. *Pharaoh's Imitators.* Pharaoh called his magicians together and they duplicated some of the miracles of Moses. Satan also has a counterfeit religion

| Sinful |
| Imitation |
| 3916 |

which is so close to the genuine that many are deceived. Satan is willing for people to be religious. As long as he can keep people satisfied with a bloodless religion, he is happy. Imitating real religion is much more effective than promoting outright infidelity. Religion with some semblance of reality is always dangerous because there is enough truth in it to make it attractive.

| Religion |
| True-False |
| 2985-2991 |

God wants forthright Christians, not people who compromise. Moses stated the case plainly and to the point, "There shall not an hoof be left behind" (Ex. 10:26). God demands complete separation from the world, sin, and the devil.

Bricks without straw. The task of the Hebrew slaves was made more difficult when pharaoh ordered that no straw be given the people for making bricks. These are bricks with straw. (Ex. 5:7-13)

6. *The Passover.* The redemptive work of Christ is evident in the Passover (Ex. 12:1 ff.). The

Passover
1256, 2686

lamb was to be without spot or blemish, and its blood was to be sprinkled upon the door post and the lintel so that the death angel could see it. The applied blood was necessary to life: without the blood, death was certain. Paul states that "Christ our Passover is sacrificed for us" (1 Co. 5:7). The importance of Christ's blood is symbolized by the blood of the Passover lamb. The Lord informed the people that "the blood shall be to you for a token upon the houses where ye are:

Lamb of God
3365

and when I see the blood, I will pass over you" (Ex. 12:13). Many people of Egypt were good, moral, law-abiding citizens, but this was not enough. Only the blood availed.

With the assurance of safety, the Hebrews were able to feast upon their lamb with peace of mind. They enjoyed communion and fellowship such as only the redeemed can have. The feast is not for unbelievers, but for those who have been redeemed by the blood of the lamb.

7. *The Pillar of Cloud* (Ex. 13:21-22). The pillar of cloud speaks of the presence of God through his Holy Spirit. Dur-

Pillar of Cloud
2501

ing the day the pillar took the shape of a mushrooming cloud so that the Israelites might be guided as well as be protected from the hot desert sun. At night the pillar turned into a column of fire so that the people might have evidence of God's presence. It is of importance that the pillar was a light for the Hebrews but utter darkness for the Egyptians (Ex. 14:19-20). So it is

with Christians versus sinners. The believer receives light and revelation from God, but to the sinner this mystical

Light
2166-2175

presence is foolishness (1 Co. 2:11-14).

When the Hebrews began to move out of Egypt, Pharaoh and his army gave pursuit. So it is when a seeker starts to leave the bonds of Egypt. Satan always makes it difficult for the repentant soul to escape. He always attempts to keep the captive from crossing the "Red Sea."

8. *The Red Sea* (Ex. 14:9ff.). In preparation for their escape from Egypt the children of Israel had been delivered by the

Red Sea
2975

blood. At the Red Sea they were delivered from Egypt by the power of God. The Red Sea (symbolizing a separation from the forces of sin) opened a path for the Hebrews, but when they had crossed, the waves closed upon Pharaoh and his men. The Red Sea means death. The Red Sea experience might symbolize a type of water baptism marking the end of service to Satan and the beginning of service to God (1 Co. 10:1-4).

9. *The Redemption Song* (Ex. 15:1-21). When the Hebrews saw that Pharaoh and his army had been drowned in the sea, they sang a song of victory. A similar response occurs when a repen-

Songs of Victory
2477

tant sinner crosses the Red Sea and obtains salvation. Does he not find within him a compelling urge to sing the songs of Zion as an expression of praise and thanksgiving to God for saving him from his enemy, Satan? When he looks at Calvary and sees that his own sins are gone, he, too, enters into an understanding of the hymns that have been sung by the saints of other days. The Song of Moses is a type of Christian hymn.

10. *The Wilderness* (Ex. 17:1ff.). After the people had been redeemed the trials

Wilderness of Zin
3995

and hardships began to press in upon them. During these physical hardships, many began to think about the flesh pots and the garlic of Egypt. The human outlook for survival was dark. Wilderness testings came to them from every hand. This experience symbolizes the experiences many believers go through who do not hasten on to complete consecration. Neglecting prayer, Bible study, and personal service are some of the wilderness dangers that believers must avoid. Every Christian should become established by making his complete dedication to God, going on without delay to possess his Canaan land. This is the believer's reasonable service (Ro. 12:1-2).

11. *Canaan*. This was the ultimate goal of the Israelites, that God had promised to

Canaan
626-634

the Hebrew children; it was a land flowing with milk and honey, where the grapes of Eschol grew so large they touched the ground. This land was their reward for completing the conquest, not just going part way.

God also offers the "milk and honey" experience to all believers who consecrate themselves completely to him. They can live in the land where pomegranates and grapes abound. Paul gives the formula: "I beseech you therefore, brethren, by the mercies of God, that ye present your bodies a living sacrifice, holy, acceptable unto God, which is your reasonable service" (Ro. 12:1).

It is the will of God that all believers should be filled with the Holy Spirit and

Holy Spirit
1601-1614

this can come about only by obeying the divine injunction: "Wait for the promise of the Father" (Ac. 1:4).

When the members in the infant church in Jerusalem met the condition, "they were all filled with the Holy Ghost" (Ac. 2:4). This Canaan experience is a believer's privilege, his birthright, and his responsibility, but it is more than this—it is the believer's obligation. God has provided it, and he expects every believer to appropriate it.

A complete surrender to God with the resultant filling of the Holy Spirit

Sanctification
3140-3142

will save Christians, both old and young, from wasting many precious years in the wilderness. It was God's desire for the Hebrews to go immedi-

Surrendered Life
3508-3511

ately to possess the land, but because of their unbelief, they doomed themselves to aimless wanderings in the snake-infested desert. What folly! Why should any believer spend tortuous years in the wilderness when the murmuring brooks of Canaan and the grapes of Eschol beckon him on?

God intends for every believer to be radiant, happy, and victorious. Pentecost changed the early believers from a state of uncertainty to one of

Pentecost
2722

victory and joy. What God did for the early Christians he can do for any Christian.

15:26 ...I am the LORD that healeth thee.

Names of
God
**1868-1872,
3633**

In this verse one of the divine names is introduced (see chart at Ex. 3:14-15). Jehovah-rophe means "LORD that healeth thee," and here Christ (LORD) is presented as the Great Physician. The Gospels reveal that he is physician not only of the body but also of the soul (Lu. 7:21-22). In this Exodus reference, the LORD miraculously changed the bitter waters of Marah into sweet drinking water for the murmuring children of Israel. He also stated that if Israel would be obedient to him he would keep from them all the diseases that were inflicted on the Egyptians. The Divine Healer was concerned with not only their physical well-being, but also their spiritual health.

Spiritual
Healing
1543

After this experience at Marah with the Great Physician, the children of Israel came to Elim, a refreshing oasis, where there were "twelve wells of water, and threescore and ten palm trees" (v. 27).

17:15 And Moses built an altar, and called the name of it Jehovah-nissi.

Altars
120-123
Rod of
Moses
3092

Jehovah-nissi, another divine name that reflects the character of God, means "the LORD is my banner." Moses gave this name to the altar which he built to memorialize the defeat of the Amalekites at Rephidim. The Amalekites, descendants of Esau, were avowed enemies of Israel. The uplifted rod in Moses' hand became the symbol of the LORD's strong arm or banner. See chart at Ex. 3:14-15.

19:20 The LORD descended to the top of Mount Sinai and called Moses to the top of the mountain. So Moses went up... (NIV)

It is possible for a religious pilgrim to retrace the steps of Moses and the Hebrew children from Egypt to Canaan provided there are no international

Sinai Campground. When the Hebrews arrived at Mt. Sinai they pitched their tents on this plain, about one mile from where St. Catherine's monastery now stands. (Ex. 18:5).

The peak of Mt. Sinai. After several hours on the trail, the peak of the mountain still seems far away. It involves a climb of about five hours.

border restrictions. See map showing the traditional route of the exodus, p. 94. Twelve to fifteen hours of hard driving are involved in a journey from Cairo to Mount Sinai. The traveler crosses the same bleak, desolate desert wilderness the children of Israel traversed over 3,000 years ago. The sand, the desert insects, the rocks, the dreary ridges, and the rugged mountain peaks are still there. Much of the journey is through a dry river bed with marks of erosion on either bank.

20:1 And God spoke all these words... (NIV)

Moses was given a formal set of laws from God on Mount Sinai. It is interesting to note the similarity between some of the Codes of Hammurabi with the Mosaic Laws. Since it is assumed that Hammurabi was a contemporary of Abraham, it seems evident that the worship of YHWH (LORD) was known in Babylon and beyond Ur of the Chaldees when Abraham was called out to become the progenitor of the Christ-Messiah who would come more than a thousand years later. Thus a measure of divine revelation is evidenced long before these Mosaic laws were given.

One of the Ten Commandments given to Moses states: "Remember the Sabbath day, to keep it holy" (v. 8). The word "remember" indicates that the idea of the Sabbath did not originate here, but it had probably been neglected or forgotten, and the people were to revive a custom not practiced in Egypt. For more on the origin of the Sabbath, see commentary at Ge. 2:3.

Mount
Sinai
2444

Messianic
Hope
4186
Decalogue
949

The Mosaic Law: The Unity of the Legal Structure in Both Testaments

The essential substance of law in all civilized countries is reflective of the Mosaic code. No one has improved upon these laws because they are the perfect legal code given by God to Moses and in some form to earlier societies. There is danger in every age of civilization of abandoning or modifying the laws of God. Scripture teaches that the law is ordained by God (Ro. 13:1), that it is the duty of man to obey the law, and that it is the duty of duly appointed officials to administer punishment for breaking the law (1 Pe. 2:13-14).

Obedience
2614

As both the OT and NT are the infallible Word of God, it is obvious that the Advent of Christ did not repudiate, indeed could not repudiate, the moral and ethical laws of the OT (2 Ti. 3:16-17). Though the grace of God became more strongly emphasized, grace does not abolish the moral law. The authority by which Jesus taught came from the OT, and his message was the "Good News" that the Messiah "written in the law of Moses, and in the prophets, and in the psalms" had come (Lu. 24:44).

Grace
1445-1449

An area of vital importance in the Christocentric message of the Scriptures is God's attitude toward sin and its punishment. God, by the very nature of his holiness, cannot tolerate sin. Adam and Eve's disobedience in the Garden introduced sin into the world and separated man from God. OT history is replete with instances which show that sin leads to destruction. Because of this destructiveness of man's sin, God's law has been given for his good. The Commandments must become a "way of life" if man is to survive.

Sin Defined
3338

The prophet Amos vigorously denounced the sins of Israel (Northern Kingdom). Ignoring his warning resulted in complete destruction of the nation and enslavement to the Assyrians. The punishment was harsh, but it was commensurate with Israel's sins. Ezekiel gives a description, in dramatic and figurative language, of the frightful consequences when a nation forsakes God and turns to unrestrained sin (Eze. 20). The standard of punishment prescribed in the OT may seem severe, but who is to pass judgment on these laws? History clearly reveals what happens when a nation defies God and breaks the laws embodied in the Ten Commandments.

Sin Destructive
3350, 3352-3356

As to civil and social codes as well as moral ones, Jesus insisted that citizens must obey the law (Mt. 22:21; see also Ro. 13:1; Tit. 3:1; 1 Pe. 2:13-14). He certainly affirmed the validity of the Commandments when he said, "Thou shalt do no murder, Thou shalt not commit adultery..."(Mt. 19:18). Paul also recognized the binding claim on man to observe the Commandments: "Thou shalt not commit adultery, Thou shalt not kill, Thou shalt not steal, Thou shalt not bear false witness, Thou shalt not covet; and if there be any other commandment, it is briefly comprehended in this saying, namely, Thou shalt love thy neighbor as thyself" (Ro. 13:9; see also 1 Pe. 4:15; 1 Jn. 3:15).

Some people have a problem reconciling the OT law of "eye for eye, tooth for tooth" (Ex. 21:24) with the teaching of Jesus on turning the other cheek (Mt. 5:39) and forgiving the offending brother "seventy times seven" (Mt. 18:22). The "eye for eye" law, rightly interpreted, affirms the overall intent of the law, that the punishment must be commensurate with the crime. Divine law states that he who murders a man forfeits his right to live (Ge. 9:6).

Retaliation
2279-2281

In many instances a clear distinction should be made between the redemptive teachings in the OT and the "traditions of the elders" by which temple matters in the NT were decided. This structure of "traditionalism" had in it so many additions that the pharisaical legal code had little resemblance to the basic teachings of the OT. The Judaism of Jesus' day was a flagrant departure from the religion of the OT. Peter, Paul, and Jesus all denounced the nonbiblical interpretation the temple leaders superimposed upon the plain teachings in the OT (Mt. 15:3-6; Mk. 7:7-8; Col. 2:8; Tit. 1:14; 1 Pe. 1:18).

Legalism
2990

These references show the unity of the entire legal structure between the OT and NT, and that the plan of salvation, basically and substantially, is the same in both Testaments (see essay on "The Mechanics of Salvation in the OT Period," p. 67). God foreknew that man would sin and therefore he planned salvation before man was created (2 Ti. 1:9; Tit. 1:2). However, after the essence of God's redemptive plan was initially revealed, there was a progressive unfolding of revelation with succeeding generations gradually receiving additional light on the various phases. "When the fullness of the time was come," the final details of God's plan were manifested in Jesus Christ.

Revelations
2494-2498

Jesus came to reinstate the spirit of the law which, in his day, had been twisted into letter-of-the-law legalisms. Jesus pointed out that acts of murder, adultery, or other infractions are the result of mental assent before the thoughts are put into action (Ps. 37:8; Pr. 14:17; 16:32; 19:11). He explained that in the sight of God, the sin has already been committed when man conceives the act in his mind (Mt. 5:27-28). For a discussion of OT/NT unity regarding Jesus' forgiveness for "the woman taken in adultery," see commentary on Jn. 8:11.

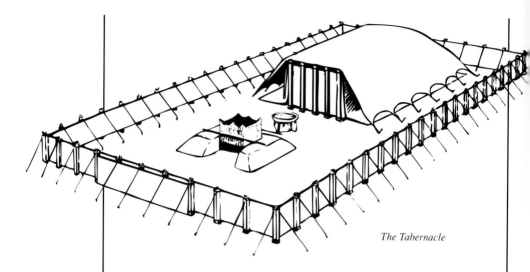

The Tabernacle

23:11 ...during the seventh year let the land lie unplowed and unused... (NIV)

Sabbatic
Year
3104

The sabbatical year (see also Ex. 21:2; Ne. 10:31) was the first year in a cycle of seven years within the Hebrew calendar, set aside as a year for resting. It provided rest for the soil, for man and for beast, and it allowed for the care of the poor. It was also the year when all debts were remitted or canceled and all slaves were set free. Apparently an Israelite could sell himself for a certain sum, to serve a fellow Israelite as a slave, but his servitude could last for no more than six years (Je. 34:14). In the seventh year all slaves were freed. During the sabbatical year the land was to remain uncultivated so that poor people and wild animals could live on it (Le. 25:4-7).

In the seventh year everyone could return to his own family estate. The only properties exempt from the law were houses which were not redeemed within one year (Le. 25:29- 31) and the houses of the Levites, the priestly tribe (Le. 25:32-34). In the book of Deuteronomy the sabbatical year is called the "year of release" or the "year of cancellation." All debts between Israelites were canceled with a warning against refusing to lend to a poor neighbor, in view of the nearness of the sabbatical year (De. 15:7-11). The law, in effect, was given for a special period of time but eventually it became obsolete by default. Later, when undue hardship developed from the letter-of-the-law interpretation, the Jews invented a system of credit which enabled the debtor to spread his obligation over a longer period of time.

A parallel ordinance was the Year of Jubilee (see commentary on Le. 25:10).

23:16 Celebrate the Feast of Harvest with the firstfruits of the crops you sow in your field. (NIV)

This is the first reference in the Bible to the Feast of Harvest or Pentecost, also called the Feast of Weeks. For more on Pentecost, see commentary on Ex. 34:22.

25:8-9 Then have them make a sanctuary for me, and I will dwell among them. Make this tabernacle and all its furnishings exactly like the pattern I will show you. (NIV)

The architectural wonders of man grace various nations of the earth. Greece boasts of its Acropolis and Parthenon; Italy, its leaning Tower of Pisa; and France, its Eiffel Tower. The United States has the Empire State Building, the Washington Monument, and countless other architectural works. Only the Jews, however, can boast of a structure planned, designed, and revealed by God. Over fifty times it is said [of the building of the tabernacle], "As the Lord commanded Moses, so did he."[8]

Since the Israelites would be spending forty years as nomadic travelers in the Sinai desert, they would need a portable center of worship. The tabernacle in the wilderness, God's dwelling place among his people (Ex. 25:8), was their movable sanctuary. For the development of other worship centers through history, see the chart at Ac. 2:47.

A Christological study of the tabernacle has been popular for Christians throughout the ages. In the Bible, many of the more than 212 references to the tabernacle specifically foreshadow Christ. At least 25 references to the tabernacle appear in the NT. In He. 9:11 the writer states that Christ became "an high priest of good things to come, by a greater and more perfect tabernacle, not made with hands." In God's wisdom he revealed the full plan of redemption progressively through the life and experiences of the Hebrews. Thumbnail sketches of the Anointed One begin in the third chapter of Genesis and continue to Malachi. The tabernacle in the wilderness is one of the great object lessons in the OT on Christ the Savior.

The construction details for the tabernacle are specific, and every detail has special spiritual significance. It is evident that God chose to accomplish the greatest number of ends by the fewest and simplest means possible. Building materials for the tabernacle such as acacia wood, hair, and skins were obtainable in its immediate vicinity. Gold, silver, brass, and linen were brought from Egypt (Ex. 25:3-7).

The kind of wood, the colors, the skins, the rings, the stones and embroidery, the lamps and the candlestick, even the priests' robes—all were to convey divine truth, not only for Moses and his people but for those of future generations. It is significant that God gave only two chapters in the Bible to the creation of the world and the fall of man, while he set apart no less than fifty chapters for the subject of the tabernacle. Many of the details in the tabernacle prefigure the Lord Jesus Christ, who became flesh and tabernacled (dwelt) among men.

The outside of the tabernacle was commonplace and unattractive. It was made of drab badgers' skins "but when we come inside, we find ourselves surrounded by shining gold: looking up to the curtained roof, we see the wings of the cherubim woven in blue and purple and scarlet and fine twined linen.... So it is with Christ himself. The natural man, beholding him, sees no beauty that he should desire him (Is. 53:2b) but to those who know the Lord Jesus Christ, his beauty satisfies their souls."[9]

Tabernacle
3528

Bethel
406, 4342

Priesthood of Christ
2863

Tabernacle
3528

Fulfillment
2892

Incarnation
720

Ark of the Covenant

The tabernacle contained two rooms designated as the Holy Place and the Holy of Holies. The table of shewbread (Ex. 25:23-30), the golden candlestick (Ex. 25:31-40), and the altar of incense were placed in the Holy Place. The Holy of Holies accommodated the ark of the covenant. The veil was made out of white, blue, purple, and scarlet colored materials, and separated the two rooms. Over the ark rested the Shekinah glory (Ex. 40:34-35). Inside the ark was placed Aaron's rod that budded, the tables of the Law, and a pot of manna—all objects of veneration for the Hebrews. The brazen laver stood in front of the Holy Place (Ex. 30:17- 21) and the brazen altar just inside the "eastern gate." The tabernacle was within, in a curtain-enclosed court, rectangular in form, 100 cubits long and 50 cubits wide with a wall 5 cubits high (Ex. 27:11-19).[10]

The arrangement of the fixtures is suggestive of the cross. The brazen altar, the brazen laver, the altar of incense, and the ark of the covenant form the upright of the cross. The golden candlestick on the left and the table of shewbread on the right form the crosspiece. Here is seen one of the many prophetic implications of Christian symbolism in the OT.

Moses was instructed to begin the construction of the tabernacle by making the ark of the covenant. The lid covering it was called the mercy seat. The two cherubim of gold on the cover were symbols of the presence and the approachability of the Lord (Ex. 25:10ff.). God began the redemptive plan from the focal point, while man appropriates it from the peripheral. God initiates the redemptive plan at the mercy seat while man appropriates the redemptive provision at the brazen altar. At the altar the sin problem is settled for time and eternity.

The steps in the tabernacle blueprint were sevenfold. "First, the seeker made a decision at the gate; second, he made provision for his acceptance at the brazen altar; third, he was ceremonially cleansed at the brazen laver; fourth, he made intercession at the altar of incense; fifth, he had communion and fellowship at the table of shewbread; sixth, he testified at the golden candlestick, and seventh, his faith turned into sight within the veil."[11]

For the significance of the encampment of the tribes around the tabernacle, and especially the location of the tribe of Judah, see commentary on Nu. 2:2-3.

Beyond the tribe of Judah was located the continually burning fire which consumed the bodies of the sin offerings and the refuse of the camp. Here the fire becomes representative of the eternal fires that will ultimately torment the souls of men who have not settled the problem of sin at the brazen altar (cf. De. 32:22; Ps. 55:15; 86:13).

25:10,17 And they shall make an ark...and...a mercy seat...

The ark of the covenant, or ark of the testimony, was the focal point of the tabernacle. It was the appointed meeting place between the Lord and the priests, who represented the people (Ex. 25:22). It is described at length here in chapter 25 and also in Ex. 37:1-9.

The ark of the covenant was the only piece of furniture in the inner sanctuary, except on the Day of Atonement when the altar of incense was taken inside for the day. The ark served also as the mercy seat. The acacia wood out of which the ark was made is suggestive of Christ's humanity, and the gold with which it was overlaid symbolized his deity. "The ark being placed in the Holy of Holies is a type of Christ in glory in the presence of God the Father."[12] The Shekinah glory, typifying God's presence, hung over the ark of the covenant (Ex. 40:35).

The ark contained three objects:

1. The two tables of the law (Ex. 19; 20:1-17; 31:18; Mt. 22:36-40). These tables were a testimony to the law of God as given to Moses and recorded in the Pentateuch (Ex. 20:1-17). The law of God contained three areas, namely the moral law, the civil law, and the ceremonial law. "The law, which man could not keep, was deposited within the ark of the covenant and beneath the mercy seat."[13]

2. The golden pot of manna (Ex. 16:11-31; Nu. 11:1-9). The manna supplied the physical needs of the people on their pilgrimage even as Christ supplies the Christian's spiritual needs as he goes on his journey to the "promised land." The manna came down from heaven as Christ himself came down from above. As Christ came in a supernatural manner, so the manna fell in a miraculous way. As the manna came in the night time, so the Lord came in the world's night of sin, when man was steeped in formalism and the "traditions of men" rather than in true repentence and faith (Mt. 15:1-9).

3. Aaron's rod that budded (Nu. 16-17). Aaron's rod "budded...and bloomed...and yielded almonds" (Nu. 17:8). The budding of this rod confirmed a God-chosen priesthood.

The room in which the ark was located was a perfect cube. Once each year, on the Day of Atonement, the high priest carried the names of the people on his breast and shoulders and made peace with God for their sins. First, the high priest sacrificed a bullock for himself and his fellow priests. The censer with live coals was placed inside the Holy of Holies so that the smoke might cover the mercy seat. The priest then sprinkled blood from the bullock upon the mercy seat and the floor.

After the high priest made an atonement for himself and his house (Le. 16:6), he presented two goats "before the Lord at the door of the tabernacle of the congregation. And Aaron...cast lots upon the two goats; one lot for the

| Judah |
| **1955-1956** |
| Fire |
| **1284** |

| Religious |
| Testimony |
| **3599-3605** |

| Ark of the |
| Covenant |
| **216** |
| Christ's |
| Divinity – |
| Humanity |
| **701-722** |

| Tablets of |
| Stone |
| **3543** |

| Manna |
| **2248** |
| Christ, |
| Bread of |
| Life |
| **1308** |

| Traditions |
| **3652** |
| Rod |
| **3092-3093** |

| Ark |
| **216** |

| Holy of |
| Holies |
| **1599** |

| Goats |
| **169** |

Lord, and the other lot for the scapegoat…And Aaron shall lay both his hands upon the head of the live goat, and confess over him all the iniquities of the children of Israel, and all their transgressions in all their sins, putting them upon the head of the goat, and shall send him away by the hand of a fit man into the wilderness: and the goat shall bear upon him all their iniquities unto a land not inhabited: and he shall let go the goat in the wilderness" (Le. 16:7-8, 21-22).

The blood of the goat killed for a sin offering was taken within the veil and sprinkled upon and before the mercy seat "because of the uncleanness of the children of Israel, and because of their transgressions in all their sins…" (Le. 16:16).

Table with "bread of the Presence"

The time the high priest spent behind the veil was always an occasion of anxiety and suspense. As long as the high priest moved about behind the veil, the golden bells gave forth a tinkling sound and the people knew that all was well. Silence in the inner sanctum indicated that the priest had completed his ministration before the Lord, and he was standing before the mercy seat waiting for the Lord to indicate his pleasure by a movement of the Shekinah or pillar of cloud.

Tradition has it that a scarlet cord was tied around the high priest's leg so that he could be dragged out if he suffered death inside. It meant certain death for the high priest if he went into the presence of the Lord without being ceremonially clean and fit to officiate for the people. Only holy, set-aside people could come into the presence of the Lord God (Ex.19:22; cf. 2 S. 6: 7-8).

There was a season of rejoicing among the worshipers when the short period of silence was broken by the tinkling bells. The sounding of the bells meant that all was well and that sin had been expiated for that year. For more on the Day of Atonement, see commentary on Le. 16:16.

25:30 And thou shalt set upon the table shewbread before me alway.

The table of shewbread got its name from the bread placed upon it. "Shewbread" in Hebrew is "bread of faces," faces signifying presence. The bread stood in the divine presence always before the face of the Lord. Here it is suggested that all the supplies for the children of Israel, both material and spiritual, come from the Lord. Believers, too, have the assurance that Jesus will supply all their needs (Ph. 4:19).[14]

The table stood on the right side upon entering the outer room, just opposite the candlestick. The bread is suggestive of Christ, the spiritual food. The table on which the loaves were placed each Sabbath was made of acacia wood, which grew in the desert where there was little else. This is perhaps emblematic of the lonely adverse conditions under which the Son of God was born and reared. The gold with which the table was overlaid speaks of his divinity.

Twelve fresh loaves were placed on the table each Sabbath by the officiating priests. The loaves were arranged in two rows, each loaf sprinkled with a small amount of frankincense as a memorial to the Lord. The week-old loaves were eaten by the priest (Ex. 25:30; Le. 24:5-9; 1 S. 21:6; Mt. 12:4). The bread is a type of the word of God, that is Christ the Written Word, who is also seen as Christ the Living Word (Jn. 6:35,41).

The fine beaten flour out of which the loaves were made can symbolize the mill of suffering through which Christ passed. "As bread must be crushed in the mill stones and kneaded in the baker's hand, and baked in the fierce heat of the oven, so...the heavenly bread has been prepared under the crushing pressure and in the consuming flame of suffering. As the bread passed through the hot oven, even so Christ passed through the fire of Calvary and came out the Bread of Life to satisfy those who trust him."[15]

The shewbread was eaten by the priests representatively for the twelve tribes of Israel. As there was a loaf for each tribe, so there is a satisfying loaf for every believer, who becomes a priest in the faith and is privileged to eat of the bread which is Christ. In Christ adequate provision has been made for the whole church. Truly, it is a miracle that as bread satisfies the physical, so Christ, the bread from heaven, satisfies every repentant soul.

The loaves of bread served a twofold purpose. First, they were offered to God as an oblation, and second, they were eaten by the priests. "When we offer ourselves in complete dedication, God responds by giving us a satisfying portion of his heavenly manna, and makes us a blessing to others. Peace that passes human understanding comes over us as we make our consecration complete. Every day requires new strength, and grace, and one must have 'daily bread.' The whole of the true believer's life is a Sabbath in the sense that he has entered into rest, rest from sin and self in Christ, and in the enjoyment of his peace he can sing: 'I shall not want. He maketh me to lie down in green pastures. He leadeth me by the waters of rest.' "[16]

25:31 And thou shalt make a candlestick of pure gold...

The candlestick of gold has a base and a perpendicular shaft with six branches, three coming out of one side and three out of the other (Ex. 25:31-39). The candlestick and its associated vessels were to be made exactly as directed on the mount (Ex. 25:40).

Light is a very important provision in the creation, and light was created first in the natural world. Physical light dispels darkness, and spiritual light dispels spiritual darkness. Light is essential to existence. "It is that which clothes everything with beauty and color. It is that which gives glory to the rainbow and the ruby. It is that which makes the diamond anything but a bit of charcoal. It is that which makes the human face so full of

Candlestick of pure gold

Gold	**1431-1432**
"Word" as Food	**416**
Christ the "Word"	**700**
Christ's Sufferings	**3489**
Fire	**1284**
Bread	**536-539**
Offerings	**2625-2636**
Rest	**3010-3017**
Candlestick	**637**
Light	**2165-2180**
Rainbow	**2943**

loveliness; and it is that which gives us everything that is beautiful in our human relationships and in all the wonder of the natural world."[17] Many of the figures used in the Bible in relation to God are figures of light. The pillar of fire and the burning bush are reminders of the words of Jesus Christ when he said, "I am the light of the world" (Jn. 8:12).

The golden candlestick was the first object that the priest saw as he entered the tabernacle. God wants the pure light of his divine illumination to shine forth in his church, so that his light may shine through believers.

The light on top of the candlestick is a reminder that Christ is the light of the world. The flame was fed with oil which symbolizes the Holy Spirit who makes manifest the light of Christ. In a sense the base symbolizes Christ and the branches suggest the Christian's relationship to Christ. In the Sermon on the Mount Jesus said, "Ye are the light of the world" (Mt. 5:14). As the flame was fed by the oil, so the Christian's light must be fed by Christ through the Holy Spirit.

The only light in the tabernacle was the candlestick which illuminated the room and the objects in it. The candlestick symbolizes the light of Christ which Christian believers radiate into the world. The lights on the candlestick show the purpose of the church—to radiate the light that comes from above.

There is one more important fact: The candlestick had to be filled with oil each day. The officiating priest had to trim the wick and keep it clean. This may be a symbol of the Christian's need to attend to his spiritual condition each day by prayer, the study of God's Word, and service so as to keep his light burning brightly at all times.

26:33 ...The curtain will separate the Holy Place from the Most Holy Place. (NIV)

The central part of the tabernacle complex was the tabernacle itself, composed of two rooms. The outer room, the Holy Place, was twice as large as the inner room, or the Holy of Holies.

The Holy of Holies was the secret place of the Most High where all repentant sinners were represented through the high priest. A view of the inside was obstructed by the veil. Now the veil has been rent in twain and all believers are priests in the faith and may go personally to the mercy seat. When the sinner meets the condition of repentance for sin at the foot of the cross, the veil for him becomes "rent in twain" and it is then that he can rejoice over the invitation: "Having therefore, brethren, boldness to enter into the holiest by the blood of Jesus, by a new and living way, which he hath consecrated for us, through the veil, that is to say, his flesh; and having a high priest over the house of God; let us draw near with a true heart in full assurance of faith, having our hearts sprinkled from an evil conscience, and our bodies washed with pure water" (He. 10:19-22).

The inner veil, or curtain, separating the two sanctuaries was truly lovely and is a beautiful reminder of Christ. It hung upon four pillars and on it were embroidered golden cherubim (Ex. 26:31) which indicated that this was the dwelling place of deity. The white in the curtain symbolized Christ's purity; the blue his flawless character, the purple his royal nature, and the scarlet his sacrifice for sin. The Epistle to the Hebrews states that the veil was a type of the flesh of Christ (He. 10:20). The human frame that Christ took

Pillar of Fire
2501

Christ the
Light
2168

Light
2166-2171

Testimonies
3598

Oil
2638

Holy Place
1600
Holy of
Holies
1599
Priesthood
of Believers
2864

Priesthood
of Christ
2863

Cherubim
672-673

upon himself was a veil which hid the inner glory of the divine life. Once during his life on the earth that glory burst through the veil, on the Mount of Transfiguration.[18]

"Let us proceed now with bowed heads and reverent hearts into those sacred precincts, reserved for priests unto God, pausing…first to examine ourselves. Are we really entitled to such a close relationship with God? Have we come by the way of the cross of Calvary, typified in the brazen altar? Have we been washed at the laver? If so, there is but one thing still needed, and that is to step, by faith, within the door. We cannot behold God's glory until we come into his presence."[19]

Self –
Examination
3197

27:1 And thou shalt make an altar…

The brazen altar was where a penitent dealt with the problem of sin before he could go into the redemptive court (Ex. 27:1-8; 38:1-9). "The only way the sinning Israelite could be right with God, and safe from the penalty due his sins, was through the sacrifice offered on the brazen altar [symbol of the cross of Christ], and the mediation of the high priest who took the blood of the sacrifice into the Holy of Holies on the great Day of Atonement."[20]

Brazen
Altar
122

To punish the Israelites in the wilderness for their rebellious conduct, God sent "fiery serpents" into their midst; many were bitten and died (Nu. 21:6). For their relief, Moses lifted up a brazen serpent on a pole with a crosspiece, to keep the serpent from sliding down (Nu. 21:9). When, in obedience and faith, the people looked upon the serpent, they were healed, and by looking unto Jesus (He. 12:2) a sinner may receive spiritual healing. Christ gave the analogy that "as Moses lifted up the serpent in the wilderness, even so must the Son of Man be lifted up: That whosoever believeth in him should not perish, but have eternal life" (Jn. 3:14-15). Here it is seen that the serpent on the pole symbolized Christ on the cross. As the serpent symbolized sin (and sin's origin) so Christ, having taken our sins upon himself, symbolized the sins of the world. Christ promised, "If I be lifted up from the earth, [I] will draw all men unto me" (Jn. 12:32).

Brazen
Serpent
535

Cross of
Christ
892

The brazen altar stood directly in the entrance, and no one could gain admittance to the court without presenting a sin offering without spot or blemish (Ex. 12:5; Nu. 19:2; De. 15:21). Does this not suggest the requirement for salvation— that of repenting for sin and confessing Christ before one can come unto a saving experience?

Unblemished
3717

The Hebrews presented a choice animal as a sin offering whereas post-Advent penitents plead the atoning merits of the Lamb, slain for all mankind. The pattern of animal sacrifice dates back to Abel (Ge. 4:4) and then to the days of the flood when Noah stepped out of the ark and offered sacrifices to God (Ge. 8:18-20).

Sacrifices
3107-3111

Abel
4

Noah
2597

Brazen Altar

This practice was continued by the Jewish church until the Lamb of God was offered on the cross.

Charles Slemming puts it well when he says, "Even so we must ourselves visit the 'altar' and see our 'sacrifice' dying for us ere we can step into any blessing of a Christian walk or know anything of the fellowship of a living Christ...As a Holy God he has irrevocable claims which must be fully realized before he can show forth mercy: sin must be punished, either in person or substitute. The lamb, goat, and bullock were Israel's substitute, and God accepted them at the altar. These great claims of God have since been met to the full in Christ at Calvary when he became the Offering, the Altar, and the Priest."[21]

27:9,16 ...thou shalt make the court of the tabernacle...there shall be hangings for the court of fine twined linen...and for the gate of the court shall be a hanging...of blue, and purple, and scarlet...

The linen fence served as the line of demarcation between the world of sin on the outside and the redemptive court on the inside. Entrance could be made into it only by way of the gate (Ex. 27:9-21). Efforts to gain admittance over the fence would result in death, for touching the fence was fatal. "It was made of fine twined linen, and might speak typically of the righteous

requirements of the law, as linen symbolizes righteousness. There is no chance of getting into God's presence by law keeping."[22]

The eastern gate was the only way into the court of God's favor. Jesus said on one occasion, "He that entereth not by the door into the sheepfold, but climbeth up some other way, the same is a thief and a robber" (Jn. 10:1). Climbing over the fence could be representative of man's attempt to gain salvation through humanistic efforts. Some have considered plans to avoid Christ and his cross, but none of these have met God's standard. The fence around the tabernacle with its one gate is

suggestive of Christ as the only door to salvation. Jesus said, "I am the door: by me if any man enter in, he shall be saved" (Jn. 10:9). In another place he said, "No one comes to the Father, except through me" (Jn. 14:6, NIV).

High Priest

Over the one and only entrance to the court there was a curtain "of blue, and purple, and scarlet, and fine twined linen" (Ex. 27:16), which symbolized the character of Christ. Each of the four colors suggest figurative significance. The blue speaks of Christ's heavenly character, the purple tells of his kingly or royal nature, and the scarlet symbolizes his atonement, while the white speaks of Christ as the Spotless One who dwelt among men. The curtain before the gate marked the place where men could step from the world of sin into the world of true righteousness. No one guarded this gate. It was always ready to admit those who would repent and be saved. "Whosoever will may come" was and will always be the divine invitation.

The linen fence and the gate are also the subject of Ex. 38:9-20.

28:1 ...they may serve me as priests. (NIV)

Before the establishment of the levitical priesthood at Mount Sinai, individuals like Cain and Abel and patriarchs such as Noah, Abraham, Isaac, Jacob, and Job performed the essential office of priest for the family and tribe. The religious head, who was divinely ordained as mediator between God and the people, had the responsibility of ritual and administration. When the Hebrew nation was organized at Mount Sinai, a religious order of an unusual nature came into being. Here the Jewish religion became institutionalized with a priesthood, a worship center, and a religious code, including the Ten Commandments and sundry ordinances.

> Priesthood
> **2863-2864**
> Patriarchs
> **2696**
> Sinai
> **2444**
> Command-
> ments
> **444**

The priests were ordained to care for the religious needs of the people. Aaron and his sons were appointed to that office and Aaron was ordained high priest. The tribe of Levi, of whom Aaron was a descendent, was designated as the priestly tribe. It was hereditary and restricted to the one family (Ex. 28:1). All the sons of Aaron were priests unless banned by legal disabilities (Le. 21:16ff.). The high priestly family had special duties which included (1) officiating at the altar, (2) teaching the law to the people in the tabernacle services, and (3) using the Urim and Thummin, objects placed under the breast plate, for the purpose of determining God's will in doubtful matters concerning the nation (Ex. 28:30; Nu. 27:21; De. 33:8; Ezr. 2:63; 1 S. 14:36-42).

> Priests
> **2058**
> Altars
> **120-123**
> Urim and
> Thummin
> **2497**

The priests were subject to very strict laws pertaining to their personal lives (Le. 10:6ff.); they also had to wear special priestly garments (see next entry).

28:2 Make sacred garments for your brother Aaron, to give him dignity and honor. (NIV)

Moses was commanded to make holy garments for Aaron, and these served as object lessons in God's plan of redemption. Every part and appointment of the high priest's garments were designed to symbolically convey spiritual truth.

> Garments
> of Priests
> **1050**

The Ephod and the Robe (Ex. 28:6ff.)

The ephod was an upper garment worn by the high priest during his official ministrations. It contained the same brilliant colors as those found in the veil. Heretofore the white, blue, purple, and scarlet were manifest only in the hangings of the tabernacle and court, but now the colors are brought into a more personal relationship. The high priest wore these brilliant colors upon his own body, which is suggestive of the personal relationship all believers have to Christ. The ephod was suspended by two shoulder straps, one over each shoulder. On each shoulder strap was an onyx stone encased in a setting of gold and engraved, each with the names of six tribes of Israel (Ex. 28:9; 39:6-7).

> Ephod
> **1143**

The robe was distinct from the ephod itself and was fringed at the bottom with bells of gold alternating with pomegranates of blue, purple, and scarlet (Ex. 28:31-35; 39:22-26). "The small golden bells were attached to the lower part of the official blue robe of the high priest in order to send forth a sound that might be heard when he went into the holy place before the Lord."[23]

The Girdle (Ex. 28:8)

Girdle
1420-1421

The girdle was functional as well as emblematic of service. Truly, service characterizes the life of Christ. "He went about doing good" (Ac. 10:38). The lame were healed, the palsied were made whole, the blind were given their sight, and the demon-possessed were restored to sanity. Even now his good work continues "seeing he ever liveth to make intercession for [us]" (He. 7:25). Christ is "a minister of the sanctuary, and of the true tabernacle, which the Lord pitched, and not man" (He. 8:2).

The Onyx Stones (Ex. 28:9,14)

Onyx
2856

The onyx stones were mounted on the shoulder pieces and on each stone were engraved the names of six tribes of Israel "according to their birth" (Ex. 28:10). The stones were to be in plain view of everyone and gave continual testimony to the watchful care of the priest over his people. They were kept constantly before the Lord. The high priest was divinely instructed to "put the two stones upon the shoulders of the ephod for stones of memorial unto the children of Israel" (Ex. 28:12).

Intercession
1785

This concern of the high priest for his people is suggestive of Christ the high priest's continual care. "He ever liveth to make intercession" for his own (He. 7:25). The name of each child of God is engraved in the Lamb's book of life and it is comforting to know that he cares for us (1 Pe. 5:7).

The Breastplate (Ex. 28:15-29)

Breastplate
540-541

The breastplate, made out "of gold, of blue, and of purple, and of scarlet, and of fine twined linen" (Ex. 28:15) was square. Twelve precious and semiprecious stones were mounted on it. Moses was commanded to "set in it settings of stones, even four rows of stones" (Ex. 28:17).

Precious
Stones
2843-2860

Each tribe had its own stone on which its name was engraved. No two were alike. There was a sardius (ruby), a topaz, a carbuncle, an emerald, a sapphire, a diamond, a ligure, an agate, an amethyst, a beryl, an onyx, and a jasper (Ex. 28:17ff). For a description of each stone relative to the character of the person or tribe it represents, see pp. 79-82.

Divine Care
2911

The breastplate was suspended on the high priest's chest by two chains of gold. By divine instruction Aaron was to "bear the names of the children of Israel in the breastplate...for a memorial before the Lord continually" (Ex. 28:29). The breastplate had a function somewhat related to the onyx stones on the shoulders of the high priest, but assigned a single stone to each tribe. For Israel this symbolized the watchful care of the Lord, not only over Israel as a nation but over individual tribes. For the believers this is suggestive of the personal interest God directs to each individual.

The Urim and the Thummin (Ex. 28:30)

Urim and
Thummin
2497

The Hebrew meaning of these words is "lights" and "perfections." These objects were placed underneath the breastplate next to the high priest's heart. With Urim and Thummin the high priest learned the will of God in doubtful cases. Through these devices the perfect will of God was ascertained for the nation. This is suggestive of Christ, the High Priest who reveals the Father's will. "What satisfaction it is to know that the One who...pleads man's cause with the Father has unlimited power, fathomless love, and unsearchable wisdom. What a settled peace should be ours in the consciousness of this!"[24]

The Mitre and the Plate of Gold (Ex. 28:36-38)

The Lord instructed Moses to "make a plate of pure gold, and grave upon it, like the engravings of a signet, HOLINESS TO THE LORD" (Ex. 28:36). This plate was to be suspended upon Aaron's forehead. The head of the high priest was "crowned with the symbol of holiness and righteousness, an important factor for those who hold the responsibility of leadership and particularly those who lead in religious affairs. This was decidedly true of the Lord Jesus Christ the great High Priest. His was holiness in the...fullest sense of the word."[25] As believers in Christ what could be a more fitting heart attitude than holiness to the Lord?

The Linen Coat and Breeches (Ex. 28:39-43)

The high priest and his sons wore the linen coat and breeches. "The linen typifies righteousness, and...God clothes each believer with the righteousness [Re. 19:8] that is in Christ...Is there anything about us to indicate to others that we are sons of God? Do we have in our lives a well-balanced fruitage and testimony represented by the alternate arrangement of the pomegranates and bells?...Are we consecrated to His service, holy unto the Lord? These are some of the questions all believers might ask themselves."[26]

29:33 They are to eat these offerings by which atonement was made... (NIV)

This verse contains the initial instruction regarding the Day of Atonement. For more on the importance of this concept in both Testaments, see commentary on Le. 16:16; Ro. 3:25.

30:1 And thou shalt make an altar to burn incense...

The receptacle holding the incense is one of the three main objects in the Holy Place. It is described at length here in chapter 30 and also in chapter 37:25-29. It was made of acacia wood overlaid with gold and stood in the center of the Holy Place just outside the veil which concealed the Holy of Holies. Each morning while the priests dressed the lamps, smoke from the altar of incense ascended toward heaven. Once each year, on the Day of Atonement, the high priest took the censer into the Holy of Holies where incense was burned in connection with his ministration at the mercy seat.

The smoke was typical of the intercession of the appointed high priest as well as of the prayers of the saints. This principle applies to the psalmist's request that his prayer might be set forth before the Lord as incense (Ps. 141:2), and also to the worshipers praying outside the temple while Zacharias offered incense within its walls (Lu. 1:10). In the Apocalypse an angel was seen burning incense on the golden altar in connection with the prayers of the saints (Re. 8:3-5).

Great things happened at the hour of prayer when incense was being offered. "And it came to pass at the time of the...evening sacrifice, that Elijah the prophet came near, and said, Lord God of Abraham, Isaac, and of Israel, let it be known this day that thou art God in Israel...Then the fire of the Lord fell" (1 K. 18:36-38).

Mitre
2387

High Priests
2064

Linen
2185

Fruitfulness
1336-1339

Atonement
304-305

Incense
1747

Censers
652
Intercessory Prayer
1785
Zacharias
3979-3980

Fire
1282-1285

The smoke from the burning incense filled the sanctuary, making it fragrant with perfume, and it helped the priest to realize that he was standing on holy ground (Ex. 30:34-38). The formula for this incense was used exclusively for its intended purpose. Using it for other purposes involved serious consequences.[27]

The ascending smoke is suggestive of various spiritual truths. The central message for us is its symbolization of prayer and communion with God. "There is something in the sense of smell which is perhaps finer than any other of the senses. The perfume which this sense appropriates is almost like the breath of nature, expressing the finer sensibilities of the soul of the natural world. And the fragrance became an expression of the sweet breath of prayer and it is the chosen emblem of the heart's homage to our heavenly Father.[28] The perpetually burning fire in the censer is a reminder of our Lord's continual intercession at the right hand of God the Father Almighty (He. 7:25).

Incense Altar

30:18 Thou shalt also make a laver of brass…

Between the brazen altar and the tabernacle stood the brazen laver (Ex. 30:18-21). The laver was located beyond the altar; this altar spoke of atonement and expiation for sins. For the priests the laver was a basin for symbolically cleansing themselves in preparation for service and worship.

The brazen laver was made from the looking glasses of the women (Ex. 38:8). This is significant. Their willingness to give them symbolized the complete consecration God requires. Life is a treasure, the prized possession that God asks of his servants.

As the priest approached the laver, he could see his reflection in its shiny surface. Seeing himself reminded him of his sinful nature and his need for cleansing. "And the Lord spake unto Moses, saying, Thou shalt also make a laver of brass, and his foot also of brass, to wash withal…and thou shalt put water therein. For Aaron and his sons shall wash their hands and their feet thereat. When they go into the tabernacle of the congregation, they shall wash with water, that they die not; or when they come near to the altar to minister, to burn offering made by fire unto the Lord" (Ex. 30:17-20). This washing symbolized the priest's ceremonial cleansing and fitness for ministering before God on behalf of Israel.

The brazen altar was for the people. The brazen laver was for the priest who presented himself before the Lord within the Holiest Place. The priest rendered for the people a service they could not perform for themselves. Since the veil has been rent in twain, every believer in this dispensation may become a priest to offer spiritual sacrifices. Peter declared that, "Ye also…are…an holy priesthood, to offer up spiritual sacrifices, acceptable to God by Jesus Christ" (1 Pe. 2:5).

James stated that those who would draw near to God must cleanse their hands (Ja. 4:8), typified by washing at the brazen laver. Preparation for worship and service demands a clean heart. No state of grace permits active and willful sin. Holiness unto the Lord is the minimum that is acceptable unto God (1 Jn. 3:6).

Spiritual Cleansing 962

The author Iris McCord points out that "if we would serve him [Christ], then we must be vessels purged, sanctified and thus made meet 'for the master's use, and prepared unto every good work' (2 Ti. 2:21). Or if we would worship him in song, prayer, praise, Bible study, or in any way whatever, we must go into his presence by way of the laver. A holy life is the Christian standard; but 'if any man sin, we have an advocate with the Father, Jesus Christ the righteous: and he is the propitiation for our sins: and not for ours only, but also for the sins of the whole world' (1 Jn. 2:1-2)."[29]

Holiness Enjoined 1598

31:12-13 The LORD said to Moses, "Say to the Israelites, 'You must observe my Sabbaths...so you may know that I am the LORD, who makes you holy.' " (NIV)

The detailed instructions for building the tabernacle and making the priestly garments are concluded with this reminder about the importance of the Sabbath. For more on the Sabbath, see commentary on Ge. 2:3 and De. 5:14.

Sabbath 3098

32:4 ...an idol cast in the shape of a calf... "These are your gods, O Israel." (NIV)

According to Ex. 12:38 (NIV), "many other people" joined the Israelites in their exodus from Egypt. Some of them may have been Egyptians who were members of the Apis cult. Apis was an Egyptian god in the line of the fertility cults, worshiped mainly around Memphis. He had a dual nature: the creator and the guardian over the dead. Perhaps, from the mixed multitude that left Egypt, someone provided this mold for casting the golden calf at Mount Sinai.

Idol Making 3932

34:22 ...thou shalt observe the Feast of Weeks...

The book of Exodus contains the first reference in the OT to Pentecost, or Feast of Weeks (Ex. 23:16ff). It was the second of the annual feasts at which every male was required to appear before the Lord at the tabernacle, and the first of the two agricultural festivals (Ex. 34:22-23; 2 Chr. 8:12-13). The Feast of Weeks was so called because it came seven weeks after the harvest consecration and featured offering a sheaf of the first ripe barley. The sheaf was waved on the morrow after the Sabbath, or for seven complete weeks plus the morrow which would make the fiftieth day—Pentecost. On the Sabbath, the forty-ninth day, no work was permitted; so the physical effort to wave the grain before the Lord was postponed until the morrow or the first day of the week. No one could eat new grain until he had waved the sheaf before the Lord or until after the priest had blessed it for the Lord.

Feast of Pentecost 1257, 2722

Sabbath 3098

Pentecost was set aside as a special Sabbath in which no ordinary work should be done. All activity was limited to the needs of the Holy Convocation.

According to tradition, the day of Pentecost commemorated the giving of the Law on Mount Sinai, fifty days after the Passover. According to Christian tradition, Pentecost came fifty days after the resurrection of Jesus. The correlation is indeed impressive.

See chart on "Six Annual Hebrew Feasts," pp. 126-127.

Convocation 837
Day of the Pentecost 2722

35:4 Moses said to the whole Israelite community, "This is what the Lord has commanded..." (NIV)

Chapters 35-39 in Exodus are nearly parallel to chapters 25-28, emphasizing the intricate details that were given for building the tabernacle and making the priestly garments. See the commentary on the earlier chapters for the typological significance of these verses.

Cloud
780
Special
Manifes-
tation
2501
Divine
Presence
1271

40:38 So the cloud of the Lord was over the tabernacle by day, and fire was in the cloud by night, in the sight of all of the house of Israel during all their travels. (NIV)

The Lord provided not only a tabernacle where he would dwell, he also made his presence visible to "all of the house of Israel during all their travels." This assurance of God's presence is a comforting theme throughout Scripture. Years before, he had promised the patriarch Jacob, "...I am with thee, and will keep thee in all places whither thou goest..." (Ge. 28:15). And years later the Lord Christ promised his followers, "...I am with you alway, even unto the end of the world" (Mt. 28:20).

Leviticus

The Name

The book of Leviticus deals largely with the levitical priesthood and the national festivals and ordinances which developed during the first month of the second year after the Israelites left Egypt. The word *leviticus* comes into the English version from the Greek OT (LXX) where the term is rendered *levitikon*. The Hebrew title, *Wayyiqra*, is actually the first word in the book of Leviticus (Hebrew) meaning "and he called." The term is descriptive of the content in the book.

Book of
Leviticus
4225

Levites
2114

Authorship and Date

The book of Leviticus is placed third in the Pentateuch, the Five Books of Moses. The question of authorship is related to the continuing narrative from Genesis to Deuteronomy. In the book of Leviticus, as well as in Exodus, Numbers, and Deuteronomy, Moses is the central character. The name Moses is mentioned in all but two of the 27 chapters of this book (chs. 2-3) — over 80 times in all. The caption at the head of the book of Leviticus, "The Third Book of Moses called Leviticus," was placed there by scribes at a very early date to preserve author identification.

Moses
2420-2421

The liberal view ignores these considerations and classifies Leviticus as "the priestly code." This code is known as "P" within the "JEPD" documentary formula (see commentary at the Introduction to Genesis, p. 37). According to this approach the book was compiled by priests in Jerusalem between 500 and 450 B.C. Robert H. Pfeiffer presents this view: "The priestly code is a fifth century Midrash or historical commentary on the embryonic Pentateuch (JED), including a series of narratives often illustrating legal precedents and a codification of ritual laws based on earlier codes."[1] The JED formula has very little place for Moses or the historical setting the book of Leviticus describes.

Dating the book about 600 years after the events it described was based on a wish to view the history of the OT religion and literature in terms of the liberal philosophies of the age. For example, Julius Wellhausen laid down the principle that the sense of sin in Israelite sacrifice was a decidedly late development.[2] Robert O. Coleman addresses himself to this consideration: "The fact that there would have had to be regulations before there could have been orderly worship by the priests and people demands a central controlling force and fixed time. We can best understand this as the role of Moses at the establishment of tabernacle worship...there is no need to believe that this

Sin's Origin
3339

Tabernacle
3528

fixing of rites in worship of Jehovah was a gradual one of evolution or that the record of Leviticus is a late invention of Ezra's day."[3]

Inspiration
1774, 4173

The conservative position is that the writers of the Bible books were inspired by the Holy Spirit, and the events they set forth are factual and relevant to the period in which the described events took place. Even though Leviticus does not state that Moses wrote the book, the many instances of the use of the words, "The Lord spoke to Moses" (Le. 4:1; 5:14; 6:1, 8, 19, 24; 7:22,28) and the relationship Moses had in the establishment of the grand national festivals of the Jews such as the Passover, Pentecost, and the Feast of Tabernacles lead conservative Christians to accept the traditional view that Moses wrote the book of Leviticus. He most likely wrote it sometime before arriving on the plains of Moab, because the historical review Moses gives there verifies the existence of Leviticus in some form. A well-organized plan of worship was already in use, based on the levitical ordinances and national feast days.

Finally, one can see that the general subject matter of Leviticus is so intertwined with the content of other books in the Pentateuch that to deny Moses' authorship of one book would affect the entire Pentateuchal structure. Leviticus is very definitely Mosaic in its subject matter, style, scope and terminology.

Background, Purpose, and Content

The general theme of Leviticus is holiness, both as a description of the nature of God and as a way of life for his subjects. God's divine injunction to the people was "Sanctify yourselves therefore, and be ye holy: for I am the Lord your God" (Le. 20:7).

In the OT the people were commanded to bring their sacrifices to the Tabernacle, but in the NT the Hebrew Christians were told that "it is not possible that the blood of bulls and goats should take away sins" (He. 10:4). What then, was the worth of the blood sacrifices? It is believed that the value was symbolic. The true spiritual worshiper of the Lord brought his blood sacrifice as an expression of his love and devotion to God. It is obvious that the bringing of a sacrifice was not adequate (see 1 S. 15:20-22; Ps. 51:15-16), but that it merely symbolized the worshiper's obedience and devotion to God. Holiness of heart is carried through into the NT and expressed forcibly in Peter's sermon: "But as he which hath called you is holy, so be ye holy in all manner of conversation; Because it is written, Be ye holy; for I am holy" (1 Pe. 1:15-16). (The latter part of that verse is a quotation from Le. 11:44.)

The entire book of Leviticus is designed to deter Israel from the polytheistic culture of Egypt and to establish a unified monotheistic concept of divine worship. The TCRB No. 4225 divides the book of Leviticus into four main sections to show how God endeavored to hold Israel's attention to the claims of the living God:

1. The first division outlines "The Way of Access to God." The chief principle the Lord wanted Israel to learn was that they should approach God only at the altar designated. To this end the tabernacle with its altar was built. The offertorial ceremonies were developed to help romanticize the worship of the Lord and to help Israel keep its undivided attention upon God. This provided a dramatic expression through which the worshipers could manifest their faith in God. To help the Israelites express their inner motivation, God

Hebrew
Festivals
1276

Jewish
Feasts
1256-1261

Worship of
God
3921

Holiness
1596-1598

Sacrifices
Insufficient
3108

Idolatry
3928-3947

Altars
120

gave them a priesthood and a high priest to lead them.

2. The second division tells of "Special Enactments Governing Israel." The Lord provides very specific instructions about personal habits, customs, and morals to teach the nation of Israel a purity of life. The purity of the priests was especially emphasized.

3. The third division describes the "Six Annual Solemnities, or Feasts" that Israel should observe. Each feast had a different purpose, but collectively they reminded the nation of their history with God and provided a way to keep their relationship right with him through atonement for sins. See chart on pp. 126-127.

4. The fourth division provides "General Enactments and Instructions." It includes the guidelines for the sabbatical year and for the year of Jubilee.

Priests
2058-2064
Purity
1759

Hebrew
Times,
Seasons
and
Festivals
4317

1:4 He is to lay his hand on the head of the burnt offering, and it will be accepted on his behalf to make atonement for him. (NIV)

The burnt offering was the first ritualist ceremony described in the book of Leviticus (Le. 1:2-9). It was designed to help Israel express undivided devotion to God by a complete dedication of themselves. As the animal "without spot or blemish" was offered to God on the altar by fire, the worshiper's own dedication would result in "self" being purified and directed by God. No one can give a more complete offering than himself. Paul states this principle well in Ro. 12:1-2.

2:1 And when any will offer a meat offering unto the LORD...

The second ceremony specified (Le. 2:1-16, 6:8-14) was the meat or meal offering (or grain offering, NIV). It was designed to develop appreciation and thankfulness. Spiritual grace is a measure of a free gift from God; it is unmerited. Thus the recipient of a gift was to show his appreciation. God did not demand expensive sacrifices from poor people, but he expected each one to give freely according to his means.

Even a pigeon or a small wafer was acceptable to the Lord as long as it was from a "broken spirit...and a contrite heart" (Ps. 51:17). So, when a worshiper made an offering, no matter how small, that person was giving a part of himself because some energy had to be expended to earn the cost of a small offering. Jesus summarized this principle in his reference to the "widow's mite" (Mk. 12:42-44).

3:3 From the fellowship offering he is to bring a sacrifice made to the LORD by fire... (NIV)

The peace offering (fellowship offering, NIV) was the third ceremony (Le. 3:1-17; cf. 7:11-18) that the Israelites were to observe. It was designed as a fellowship experience with God. One part of the offering was consumed by fire on the altar; the other part was reserved for a meal with close friends and loved ones. The human association symbolized their joyful fellowship with the Lord.

4:3 ...let him bring for his sin...a young bullock without blemish unto the LORD for a sin offering.

The fourth ceremony, the sin offering, was a means of expressing to the Lord guilt for sin (Le. 4). All sins, whether intentional or unintentional, had to be atoned for by the prescribed blood sacrifice and confession.

4:15 And the elders of the congregation shall lay their hands upon the head of the bullock before the LORD...

The elders were to represent the people in making atonement before the Lord. During this period the title was one of high authority, both in religious and political matters. Elders are first mentioned in the Bible in Ge. 50:7 and last mentioned in Re. 19:4. For a study of the office and how it changed over the years, see commentary on 1 Ti. 5:17.

5:15 If a soul commit a trespass, and sin through ignorance, in the holy things of the LORD; then he shall bring...a trespass offering.

The fifth and last ritual in this series was the trespass offering (guilt offering, NIV), designed for the intentional offender. This person had committed an offense against God and man, and both had to be satisfied. It required not only a sacrifice for sin but also restitution with compensation to the person offended. The idea of atonement was involved in both the sin and the trespass offering.

Trespass-offerings **2634**

Atonement **304**

8:10 Then Moses took the anointing oil and anointed the tabernacle and everything in it, and so consecrated them. (NIV)

For a study of the Christological significance of the tabernacle and "everything in it," see commentary on Ex. 25:8-9 and the verses immediately following.

Tabernacle **3528**

8:12 And he [Moses] poured of the anointing oil upon Aaron's head, and anointed him, to sanctify him.

This chapter of Leviticus tells of the ordination of Aaron and his sons to the priesthood. Their ordination was for life and they were subject to very strict laws. Even their clothing was detailed and symbolic. For the Christological significance of their garments, see commentary on Ex. 28.

Ordination **1490**
Priests **2058-2060**

16:16 And he shall make an atonement for the holy place, because of the uncleanness of the children of Israel...

The initial instruction by Jehovah to Moses for the Day of Atonement is given in Ex. 29:33. Further directions are given in Ex. 30:10, where it is stated that Aaron the high priest is to make an atonement upon the horns of the altar once a year with the blood of the sin offering which is used for the purpose of atonement for sin. This ritual is further amplified in Le. 23:26-32. According to Le. 25:9, the year of Jubilee begins with the Day of Atonement.[4]

Atonement **304-305**
High Priest **2064**

In the NT the Day of Atonement is referred to as "the fast" (Ac. 27:9), and is the supreme act of national atonement for sin. Fasting was commanded from the ninth until the evening of the tenth day in the seventh month, Tishri (Le. 23:27). The ritual was divided into two parts: one for the priesthood and one for the people.

Fasting **3212-3214**

On the Day of Atonement the high priest arose and laid aside his high priestly garments, after which he underwent a ceremonial cleansing with water at the laver. Following this ritual, he dressed himself in a holy white linen garment and presented a young bullock for a sin offering for himself and his house, after which he slew the sin offering and entered the Holy of Holies with an incense burner. The cloud of incense coming from the brazier filled the room and covered the ark. Next the high priest sprinkled the blood of the sin offering upon the mercy seat and seven times before the mercy seat, for the symbolic cleansing of the Inner Sanctum or the Holy of Holies. After making atonement, he returned to the court of the sanctuary.

Priest's Garments **1050**

The high priest then presented two goats to the Lord at the door of the tabernacle as a sin offering for the people. He cast lots over them, one marked for the Lord and the other for Azazel, the scapegoat. The goat on which the lot fell was slain and the priest repeated the sprinkling of the blood as before (Le. 16:17).

The scapegoat is a symbol of Jesus, who bore the sins of mankind.

High Priest 2064

In the second stage of the ceremony the high priest laid his hand on the scapegoat's head and ceremonially transferred the sins of the people to the goat through a ritualistic prayer. The goat was then led into the wilderness to perish among the wild beasts, never to return again. Thus Jesus, the crucified Christ, is identified as the sinner's "scapegoat," the innocent one taking the sins of the guilty. Some authorities suggest that the goat was led to a cliff and tossed over. His expiatory death was symbolic of ridding the people, the priests, and the sanctuary from all impurity. In later Judaism the Day of Atonement has been observed as a day of penitence and prayer.[5]

Scapegoat 3160

For more information on the Day of Atonement, the "Good Friday of the OT," see commentary at Ro. 3:25.

17:11 For the life of a creature is in the blood, and...it is the blood that makes atonement for one's life.

Sacrifices 3107

Blood of Sacrifices 516

From the time of Cain and Abel there is revelation about the importance of the blood sacrifice. Cain's offering was rejected; Abel's required shedding of blood and it was accepted. For more on the importance of the blood sacrifice, see commentary on Ge. 4:4-5.

20:8 And ye shall keep my statutes, and do them: I am the LORD which sanctify you.

Sanctification 3140-3141

Consecration 3508-3509

Calling 622

This verse reveals a special name of God. LORD-m'kaddesh expresses spiritual completeness, "I am Jehovah that sanctifies you" (Ex. 31:13). Frequently referred to in the book of Leviticus, the name indicates the importance of sanctification. A well-known Bible professor makes this comment: "Leviticus is the book of life, or the walk and worship of a people already redeemed. Therefore, sanctification is its most appropriate theme. It could not appropriately be presented until redemption was fully accomplished. It...sets forth that holy way in which a people already redeemed should walk worthy of their calling (Ep. 4:1) and the spiritual worship which the LORD demands of them. Thus in connection with their moral and spiritual purity, this title of God is repeated six times in the two chapters following its first appearance."[6] It is the indwelling LORD sanctifier that enables people to live a holy life (Ex. 28:36; Le. 19:2; 20:8; 22:32; 1 Co. 1:30; Ep. 4:24; 2 Ti. 1:9; He. 3:1; 12:14).

20:10 If a man commits adultery with another man's wife...both the adulterer and the adulteress must be put to death. (NIV)

When Jesus showed mercy to the woman taken in the very act of adultery (Jn 8:3ff), the religious leaders were confounded. The leaders' one-sided attitude toward the law was self-evident because they did not also bring the man who was involved; the law clearly stated that the man as well as the woman taken in adultery were both guilty. In fact, even the ones who brought the woman were themselves guilty of sin, because when Jesus asked the person without sin to cast the first stone, they all slowly slunk away. In the absence of any further accusations, Jesus refused to condemn the woman and commanded her to "go and sin no more" (Jn. 8:11).

Law is intended to be fair and just; it would have been unfair for the woman to have been punished alone. For the question of OT/NT unity concerning this incident, see commentary on Jn. 8:11.

Adultery
1662

Guilt
1763

23:3 There are six days when you may work, but the seventh day is a Sabbath of rest... (NIV)

The importance of the Sabbath is a vital part of the message of the Pentateuch. For its origin and development, see commentary of Ge. 2:3; De. 5:14; Ac. 1:12.

Sabbath
3098-3102

23:4 These are the LORD'S appointed feasts, the sacred assemblies you are to proclaim at their appointed times. (NIV)

The description of the feasts given to Moses is recorded also in Numbers, chs. 28-29. This parallel passage provides very detailed instructions about the offerings to be made at each feast. See the chart on the next pages.

Jewish
Feasts
1256-1264

Six Annual Hebrew Feasts

Name of Feast	To Commemorate
Passover (Unleavened Bread, Firstfruits)	Deliverance of Israelites from Egypt. When the Death-angel smote the first-born of Egypt he "passed over" the houses of Israel.
Pentecost (Feast of Weeks, Feast of Harvest)	Giving of the Law on Mount Sinai (50 days after Passover). NT Pentecost came 50 days after Christ's resurrection.
Feast of Trumpets	New civil year
Feast of Tabernacles (Ingathering)	Thanksgiving for harvest. (They lived in booths as a reminder of their fore-fathers' nomadic life in the wilderness.)
Feast of Dedication or Lights (Hanukkah)	Purification of the temple and restoration of the altar in the temple by Judas Maccabaeus in 165 B.C.
Feast of Purim (Lots)	Deliverance of Jews of Persia from slaughter by Haman (see book of Esther).

Hebrew Date	Approximate Modern Date	Biblical Reference	See TCRB	See Page
Began 15th day of Abib (Nisan)	March-April	Ex. 12:13,17	Chain 1256; also 4451	94; also 93
6th day of Sivan	June	Ex. 34:22-23	Chain 1257; also 4451	117; also 93
1st day of Ethanim (Tishri)	October	Le. 23:24	Chain 1258; also 4451	128; also 93
15th-22nd of Ethanim (Tishri)	October	Le. 23:34	Chain 1259; also 4451	128; also 93
25th day of Kislev	December	Jn. 10:22	Chain 1260; also 4451	392 also 93
14th and 15th day of Adar	March	Est. 9:20-22	Chain 1261; also 4451	192 also 93

23:24 ...a memorial of blowing of trumpets...

The Feast of Trumpets, inaugurated by Moses (Le. 23:24ff.), ushered in the new civil year. It was celebrated at the first New Moon of Tishri, the first civil month and the seventh sabbatical month in the religious year. People were summoned to the holy convocation by the sound of trumpets. Special offerings were presented and no common work was done on this day. (See chart on "Six Annual Hebrew Feasts," previous page.)

23:34 ...the feast of tabernacles...unto the LORD.

The Feast of Tabernacles, occurring five days after the Day of Atonement, was also known as the Feast of Ingathering (Sukkoth). It came when the moon was full in the seventh month, Tishri (September or October) and lasted

Man with Shofar.

seven days. On the eighth day it culminated in a "holy convocation" (Le. 23:34-36).

    This autumn festival (De. 16:13-17) was important as the beginning of the new civil year. It came at the end of harvest after all the fruits and grain were gathered in. This crowning event of the year was a great homecoming time of family reunions and celebration when families lived in booths made from tree branches. There was thanksgiving to the Lord for a good harvest and also paying of respect to their nomadic forefathers who had lived in tents in the wilderness. This autumn feast resembled New England Thanksgiving festivities and is also reminiscent of the old-fashioned camp meetings. In the fall when crops were harvested, our forefathers gathered in the woods for religious services and family reunions. They, too, erected temporary dwelling places—brush arbors and tents.[7]

Convocation
837

Thanksgiving
1457

24:5 ...bake twelve loaves of bread...set them... on the table of pure gold before the LORD. (NIV)

Shewbread
3269, 3530

For the Christological significance of the table of shewbread, see commentary on Ex. 25:30.

25:10 Consecrate the fiftieth year and proclaim liberty throughout the land...it shall be a jubilee for you...(NIV)

Year of
Jubilee
1953

The year of Jubilee was ushered in by a trumpet blast on the tenth day of the seventh month (Tishri) on the Day of Atonement (Le. 25:9). The Israelites were to keep the day holy and proclaim liberty throughout the land (Le. 25:10). This year is mentioned in only three chapters, Le. 25 and 27 and Nu. 36. Most of the ordinances were parallel to those in the sabbatical year (see Le. 25:1-7; commentary on Ex. 23:10): e.g., the land was to rest, it was to revert to its original owners, and slaves were to be freed.

Sabbatic
Year
3104

The whole idea behind the sabbatical year and the year of Jubilee was to give relief to labor, both human and animal, and to avoid enslavement, either financial or physical. These rest days were safeguards against usury and profiteering. The pattern is similar to developing countries where a few landed men own the land and the common people are reduced to serfdom or tenant farmers. In some areas the tenant farmers are always so deeply in debt to the landlords that they are never free from obligation.

Under the Law of Jubilee the landed man was the steward, not the owner. Under the theocratic order, God owned the land and "the cattle on a thousand hills." The value of the land was based on the number of years remaining before the Jubilee year. It appears that the forty-ninth and fiftieth years were both free years. Perhaps the forty-ninth year under this circumstance was purely a calendar event.

The Mishna takes the view that the year of Jubilee was abolished after the exile. Josephus, the historian, does not mention the year of Jubilee or its abolishment, although he makes reference to the sabbatical year. [8]

26:41 ...if then their uncircumcised hearts be humbled...

Circumcision
765-767

Throughout Scripture the term "uncircumcised hearts" denotes a lack of receptivity to the things of God. The physical operation of circumcision is a symbol of the spiritual change that comes about in the human heart when it is "born from above." For more on the spiritual significance of circumcision, see commentary on Ge. 17:10.

Numbers

The Name

The title of this book in the Hebrew canon is *Bemidgar,* a term found in the first verse which means "in the wilderness." In the Greek OT the term is rendered *Arithmoi,* from which the English word arithmetic is derived. In the Latin Vulgate the word is translated "number." Although the book of Numbers suggests a census, the actual numbering of the tribes occurs only in chapters 1, 2, 3, and 26.

Book of
Numbers
4226

Authorship and Date

The book of Numbers is the fourth book of the Pentateuch, and Mosaic authorship of this book is assumed with Mosaic authorship of the Pentateuch. The name "Moses" appears 245 times in the book of Numbers, and many of these references have the words, "the Lord spoke to" or "Moses spoke."

Moses
2420-2421

Certainly Moses was eminently qualified to write this book because he was present and a participant in the drama which unfolded in the Sinai desert.

One writer points out that certain passages in Numbers have the "appearance of having been written by Moses...those which bear evidence of having been intended for a people not settled in cities but dwelling in tents and camps, e.g., Nu. 1-4, describing the arrangements for the census and the formation of the camp; the high priestly benediction is given in Nu. 6:24-26; orders for marching and halting the host are given in Nu. 10:35-36; the direction for the sounding of the silver trumpets in Nu. 10:1-9; the legislation which obviously presupposes the wilderness as the place for its observances (Nu. 19:3, 7, 9, 14)...It is not too much to say that the preponderance of evidence lies on the side of the substantial Mosaicity of the book of Numbers."[1]

Wilderness
of Zin
3995
Tents
3596

Trumpets
2466-2467

Background, Purpose, and Content

The twelve tribes of Israel have behind them the Passover (Ex. 12:22), the crossing of the Red Sea (Ex. 14:22), the experience of the bitter waters at Marah (Ex. 15:23-25), the

The silver trumpet was used to call together the Israelite community.

sweet water wells at Elim (Ex. 15:27), the giving of the Law (Ex. 20:1-21), the tabernacle (Ex. 25:1-9), and the priesthood (Ex. 28:1-5) at Mount Sinai; their next main encampment was at Kadesh-Barnea (Nu. 13:26; 32:8).

A brief analysis of the book shows that the tribes received organization and legislative instruction and that they prepared to break camp at Sinai and resume their journey toward the promised land. Every tribe was identified by the name of one of the twelve sons of Jacob. The two sons of Joseph, Ephraim and Manasseh, were designated as half-tribes (Nu. 1-2). After the tribes were numbered and organized, they were assigned with respect to the service which they were to render in maintaining and moving the tabernacle (Nu. 3). Each male from 20 to 50 years was to serve in some official capacity. Strict rules for camp sanitation were given (Nu. 5). Rules for commemorating the Passover were defined (Nu. 9).

It becomes evident that all the members in the tribe were not true Jehovah worshipers. There was in their midst a "mixed multitude." Judgment was pronounced upon those who murmured and doubted God's promises (Nu. 11). The marriage of Moses to a Cushite wife resulted in sedition by Aaron and his sister, Miriam (Nu. 12). Twelve men, one from each tribe, were sent into Canaan to spy out the land (Nu. 13). The pessimism produced by the

A diagram of the tribes of Israel in camp.

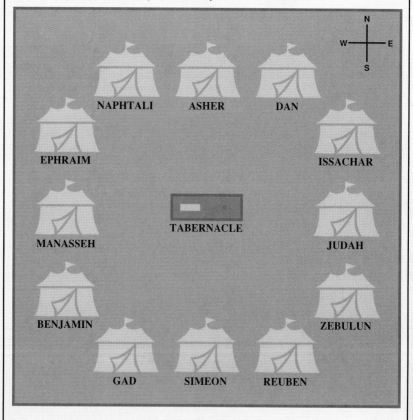

majority spy report caused rebellion in the camp. God decreed that all Israelites twenty years and older were to perish in the wilderness (Nu. 14). God established worship guidelines (Nu. 15). The earth swallowed Korah, Dathan, and Abiram for their part in the insurrection against Moses (Nu. 16). The authentic priesthood was to be determined by the budding rod (Nu. 17). The priests were to be supported by tithes and offerings (Nu. 18); the red heifer ordinance outlined the ritual of purification for sin (Nu. 19). Miriam died and Moses was informed he would not be permitted to enter the promised land (Nu. 20).

> Moses' Rod 3092

Many of the people, bitten by serpents, were healed by looking up to the brazen serpent, a type of Christ (Nu. 21; cf. Jn. 3:14). The Israelites faced Balak and the prophet Balaam (Nu. 22) and had a running encounter with Balaam, the false prophet, until they arrived at the plains of Moab (Nu. 22-25). The second census was taken; Joshua, Caleb, and Moses were the only adults who had survived from the first count (Nu. 26). The inheritance laws were revised, and Joshua was appointed as Moses' successor (Nu. 27). The laws relating to burnt offerings, the Sabbath, and the Passover were restated (Nu. 28). Additional instructions were given regarding the feast days (Nu. 29-30), and Israel's victory over the Midianites followed (Nu. 31).

> Serpents 3238
>
> Joshua 1922, 4293

Reuben, Gad, and Manasseh settled for a tract of land on the east side of Jordan (Nu. 32). Israelite history was reviewed (Nu. 33), and a formula for dividing the land was worked out (Nu. 34). Forty-eight cities were assigned to the Levites, including four cities of refuge (Nu. 35); inheritance laws were given (Nu. 36). The period of the exodus covered between 38 and 39 years.

> Cities of Refuge 771

2:2-3 The Israelites are to camp around the Tent of Meeting some distance from it, each man under his standard with the banners of his family. On the east, toward the sunrise, the divisions of the camp of Judah are to encamp... (NIV)

Moses and Aaron camped near the entrance of the Tent of Meeting (the tabernacle) while the tribe of Judah was positioned just beyond the eastern gate. The other tribes were located in their appointed places around the outer edge of the linen fence (see Nu. 2-3).

The prophetic implication found in the position of the camp of Judah is very significant. Its location to the east is not accidental but intentional (Nu. 2:3). From early times in Hebrew history the people looked for a great leader. Ancient Biblical records gave sketches about the Holy One that was to come. Moses was inspired to prophesy that the Messiah would come out of the tribe of Judah (Ge. 49:10). The location of the camp of Judah suggests the idea that as the sun rising in the east ushers in the dawn of a new day, so the tribe of Judah located eastward would usher in the "Son of Righteousness" with healing for the nations. See the diagram on p. 132.

3:6,8 Bring the tribe of Levi...they are to take care of all the furnishings of the Tent of Meeting, fulfilling the obligations of the Israelites by doing the work of the tabernacle. (NIV)

The Levites were responsible for the maintenance of the tabernacle (here called the Tent of Meeting) and the court, and pitched their tents around its walls. For a study of the tabernacle and its Christological significance, see commentary on Ex. 25:8-9ff.

9:2 Have the Israelites celebrate the Passover at the appointed time. (NIV)

The first Passover was celebrated in Egypt, and the second was here at Sinai. See commentary on Ex. 12:17.

9:17 Whenever the cloud lifted from above the Tent, the Israelites set out; wherever the cloud settled, the Israelites encamped. (NIV)

The Lord's presence in the cloud to guide his people was also mentioned in Ex. 40:38 (see commentary there). The pillar of cloud and the fire was one of the special ways God manifested himself to people in OT times. Another special manifestation of divine power and glory was the Shekinah, the supernatural light or cloud which appeared on the mercy seat of the tabernacle.

11:7 The manna was like coriander seed and looked like resin. (NIV)

Manna was the Lord's provision for his people during their journey in the wilderness. In order to remind future generations of his faithfulness in providing food for their journey, a sample was kept in the ark of the covenant. This "golden pot of manna" is described in Ex. 16:11-31. For a parallel

---

Tabernacle
3528

Judah
1956

Christ our
Righteous-
ness
686

Levites
2114

Passover
2686, 1256

Pillar of
Cloud and
Fire
2501
Shekinah
2502

Manna
2248
Ark of the
Covenant
216

between manna, which met the Israelites' needs, and Christ, who meets our needs, see the commentary on Ex. 25: 10,17 (regarding the contents of the ark).

11:16-17 The Lord said to Moses: "Bring me seventy of Israel's elders…they will help you carry the burden of the people…"(NIV)

At this time elders were recognized as the highest authoritative body over the people. For more on the development of elders throughout the Scriptures, see commentary on 1 Ti. 5:17.

Elders
2078-2079

Bread of Life
1308

11:25 Then the Lord…put the Spirit on the seventy elders… (NIV)

It is evident from this verse that the work of the Spirit of God is not limited to the New Testament, though there are certain variances in how it was manifested in different historical times. A study of the work and nature of the Holy Spirit's work shows that his coming upon persons in the OT was limited to specially selected leaders such as the elders in this verse. The Spirit gave Moses and the seventy elders the gift of divine wisdom that they would need to guide the people.

In both Testaments, it is through the Spirit that divine revelation penetrates the heart and mind of man. For more on the subject, see commentary on De. 6:4; Jn. 16:13.

Holy Spirit
**1601-1614,
1774**

Divine Revelations
2494-2498

11:31 Now a wind went out from the Lord and drove quail in from the sea… (NIV)

At a certain season of the year, quail fly across the eastern Mediterranean from Europe. After they cross they are so exhausted, they land in the coastal area. Natives stretch their nets near the coast to capture them for market.

God may have used this natural phenomenon in a miraculous way to provide quail for the Israelites when they complained against him. The strong wind referred to in the verse above could have sent the quail beyond their customary landing place so that they were available in the wilderness.

This miracle brings to mind Jesus' feeding of the 5,000 (Jn. 6:5-13) and the feeding of the 4,000 (Mt. 15:29-39). Throughout Scripture God is the Master of natural phenomena.

Quails
464

Multitude Fed
2448

15:32, 35 …a man was found gathering wood on the Sabbath day…the Lord said to Moses, "The man must die…" (NIV)

The importance of keeping the Sabbath is once again evident. The Lord had told the Israelites, "You must observe my Sabbaths" (Ex. 31:12-13, NIV) and "Whoever does any work on the Sabbath day must be put to death" (Ex. 31:15, NIV). The man in the verse above willfully disobeyed the divine command.

For more on the Sabbath, see commentary on Ge. 2:3; De. 5:14; and Ac. 1:12.

Sabbath
3098-3102

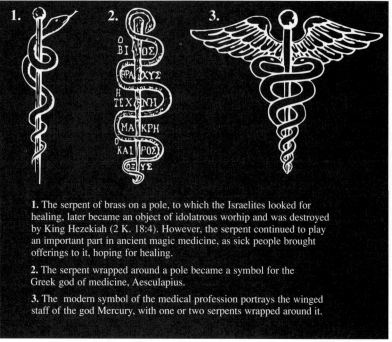

1. The serpent of brass on a pole, to which the Israelites looked for healing, later became an object of idolatrous worhip and was destroyed by King Hezekiah (2 K. 18:4). However, the serpent continued to play an important part in ancient magic medicine, as sick people brought offerings to it, hoping for healing.

2. The serpent wrapped around a pole became a symbol for the Greek god of medicine, Aesculapius.

3. The modern symbol of the medical profession portrays the winged staff of the god Mercury, with one or two serpents wrapped around it.

The Brazen Serpent as a Symbol.

Brazen Serpent 535

21:9 And Moses made a serpent of brass, and put it upon a pole, and it came to pass, that if a serpent had bitten any man, when he beheld the serpent of brass, he lived.

Regeneration 2154

Son of Man 722

Jesus gave this incident typological significance when he instructed Nicodemus about the concept of the new birth. Nicodemus, a Pharisee and a member of the Jewish ruling council, would have been very familiar with the historical event. Jesus, applying it to himself, said, "And as Moses lifted up the serpent in the wilderness, even so must the Son of man be lifted up" (Jn. 3:14).

Satan 3148-3155

Christ 710, 4136

The serpent as a symbol of Satan had been introduced in Ge. 3:15, when God told the serpent regarding Eve, "I will put enmity between you and the woman, and between your offspring and hers; he will crush your head, and you will strike his heel"(NIV). Throughout the Testaments and throughout the ages Satan has been trying to "bite" mankind, but by looking to Christ man can be saved from otherwise certain death. Ultimately it is Christ who has supremacy, and he will crush the serpent's head forever.

22:41 And it came to pass on the morrow, that Balak took Balaam, and brought him up into the high places of Baal...

Baal 3936

The word "baal" comes from a root word meaning "master." Reference to this deity in the Bible appears first in this verse and then occurs about 40 other times. The greatest religious conflicts the Israelites had were with the

Baal gods. At one time Israel's destiny hinged on Elijah's contest with the Baal prophets on Mount Carmel (1 K. 18:19-40).

The first time Baalism appeals to the Israelites in the Biblical record is here in Numbers. Balak of Moab, terrified by reports of how Israel has defeated the powerful Amorite kings, sent for Balaam, a soothsayer who he hoped would curse Israel and insure their defeat. Instead Balaam seduced Israel to worship the Canaanite god Baal. When Israel "joined in worshiping the Baal of Peor ... the LORD'S anger burned against them" (Nu. 25:3, NIV) and in the plague that followed 24,000 Israelites died (Nu. 25:9).

Baal is often identified with the place in which he is worshiped by using "Baal" as a prefix. For example, there is Baal-gad (Jos. 11:17), Baal-hazor (2 S. 13:23) and Baal-zephon (Nu. 33:7). Baal-zebub (probably Baal-zebul originally) is the name used for Baal worship in Ekron (2 K. 1), and this may be the source of Jesus' mention of Beelzebub, the prince of demons (Mt. 10:25). The name came to be used of Satan, the epitome of all evil gods.

For more on the nature of Baal and the city built in his honor, see the following essay.

Temple of Jupiter at Baalbeck. Only six of the original 19 Corinthian columns have survived the earthquakes.

Baalbeck

Baalbeck is a city which rises out of the mists of time. No records exist which remotely suggest its origin or date. It is often linked with the arrival of the Baal religion from Mesopotamia. The city represents the primitive nature religion its name suggests.

Baal
3936

The city of Baalbeck was a bastion of the god Baal and built in his honor. Baal was identified with the storm god Hadad. He was the god of fertility and his nature was most deceptive and treacherous because it condoned the sexual act as a religious rite. Young girls were expected to serve as temple prostitutes for a predetermined time.

Baalbeck, Lebanon, occupies a central place in the Beqaa valley, 55 miles northeast of Beirut at the base of the ante-Lebanon mountains. Archaeologists have also unearthed a Baal religious center at Ras Shamra on the Syrian coast, not far from Baalbeck.

The Roman emperor Augustus built the city whose ruins we see today. The city contains the most gigantic complex of Roman temples ever built. It was built in a broad valley, at an elevation of 65 feet above the surrounding terrain and can be seen for many miles. It is one of the architectural wonders of the world. Visitors stand in amazement as they contemplate what the Romans did in the interest of their religion.

All the stones in this complex were fitted together so tightly that a knife-blade cannot be inserted between them. No mortar was used in its construction. Some of the stones in the Jupiter temple are 64 feet long, 15 feet

The pre-fabricated steps leading to the Temple of Jupiter cut out of stones 64 feet long and 8 feet square.

Baalbeck Quarry. A 1200 ton cut stone abondoned in the quarry. Stones similar in size are visible in the temple complex.

high and 12 feet wide and weigh over 1,000 tons. One stone abandoned in the quarry is said to weigh 1,200 tons.

The temple of Jupiter, dedicated to the storm god Hadad, was one of the most spectacular temples ever built. It was surrounded by a peristyle of 19 Corinthian columns 62 feet high and more than 7 feet in diameter at the base. Only six of these columns still stand (see picture). Mosaic steps (see picture) lead to the temple of Jupiter. The steps were prefabricated in single sections from stones 64 feet long and 8 feet square. Some restoration work has been done.

The Romans rebuilt the city as a bulwark against the ever-expanding Christian religion, but history shows Baalbeck crumbling in ruins while the Cross continues to march on from victory to victory. When the Roman emperor, Constantine the Great, was converted to Christianity, he decreed Christianity to be the lawful religion of the Roman Empire. Shortly thereafter he had a Christian church built in the middle of the Baalbeck complex.

Deuteronomy

The Name

The name, Deuteronomy, is derived from the Septuagint (Greek OT) and means "the second law."

The title Deuteronomy in the English is an Anglicized form of the Greek compound word *Deuteronomion*, which means "second law" (*deutros* means second; *nomos* means law). This Greek term is an interpretative paraphrase of the Hebrew *Aleh (Hadebarim)*, which means, "These be the words" (De. 1:1). In some of the Hebrew Commentaries the rabbis call this book *Misneh Torah*, which means "the repetition of the law." Others call it *Sepher Tukhhuth*, which means "the book of reproofs." This book is rightly referred to as the "second law" because it contains the levitical laws and ordinances in a more concise and systematic form that previously given.[1]

Authorship and Date

The book of Deuteronomy is the fifth book in the Pentateuch and is linked to Mosaic authorship. This view was held by both Jewish and Christian scholars until liberal scholars developed the Documentary Hypothesis, known as the JEDP theory (see Introduction to Genesis, p. 37). Jesus and the NT writers alluded to the book of Deuteronomy over 100 times, usually indicating that the reference came from Moses (Mt. 19:8; Mk. 12:19; Ro. 10:19). The name of Moses is frequently mentioned, and he is the central figure in Deuteronomy.

Background, Purpose, and Content

The book of Deuteronomy covers a period of five weeks. It begins on the first day in the eleventh month of the fortieth year after the Israelites left Egypt and ends one lunar month later. The book consists mainly of the three great addresses of Moses to the new generation that had grown up since the law was given at Mount Sinai. The rebellious generation, twenty years old and upward (Nu. 14:29), had died; of the adults only Joshua, Caleb, and Moses were still living.

In his first great address (De. 1-4) Moses reviewed the events of the wilderness and reminded the people of God's faithful protective care from Sinai to the plains of Moab.

Book of Deuter-
onomy
4227
Book of
the Law
525

Moses
2420-2421

The
Decalogue
949

Sinai
2444

Wilderness
of Zin
3995

In his second address (De. 5-20) Moses gave a commentary on the Ten Commandments, which had been given at Mount Sinai (Ex. 20). In this discussion he emphasized that the love of God is the practical formula for obeying the Commandments (De. 6:5; 10:12; cf. Mt. 23:36-40; Le. 19:18).

Circumcision
765-767
Jewish
Feasts
1256-1261
Covenants
877-881

Moses also pointed out that the idea behind the initiatory rite of circumcision is spiritual circumcision of the heart (De. 10:16; see also 30:6; Je. 4:4; Ro. 2:29; Col. 2:11). (For additional information on circumcision see commentary on Ge. 17:10.) In this address Moses explained the importance of such feast days as the Passover, Pentecost, and Tabernacles, reminding the people that the covenant God had made with Abraham, Isaac, and Jacob was equally binding for the new generation. Many of this generation were old enough to remember that obedience resulted in rewards and that the penalty of disobedience was punishment (De. 6:1-9; 7:12-26).

Cities of
Refuge
771

To insure justice, six levitical cities of refuge were set aside where the law violator could be protected until legal machinery could be set up for a just trial (Nu. 35:6ff.).

Parental
Duties
1629-1631
Spiritual
Adultery
1814

The parents were cautioned to provide religious training for their children. The priests were urged to read the Law to the people once every seven years. In this address Moses warned the people against the temptation of spiritual adultery or idolatry.

In his third address (De. 27-31) Moses directed his attention to the future, thereby expressing his faith in God's providential plan for the people after they crossed the Jordan River. The leaders were instructed to call a judicial council after arrival in Canaan for the purpose of ratifying and renewing commitment to the covenant given the patriarchs.

Moses blessed each of the twelve tribal leaders (De. 33). Moses was permitted to view the promised land from "Pisgah's lofty height," the highest

Mount
Nebo
2440,
2572, 4417

point in the Mount Nebo range, but was not permitted to enter because of his disobedience in the desert (Nu. 20:7-13).

Deuteronomy 34 contains an account of the death of Moses: some critics object to Mosaic authorship of Deuteronomy because of this death account. Since the literary content and continuity in Deuteronomy 34 is such

Joshua
1922,
4307c,
4293

that it could easily fit at the head of Joshua's chronicle, some scholars suggest that Joshua wrote the postscript for Deuteronomy. It is possible that Joshua was present when Moses died.

5:14 ...the seventh is a Sabbath...
you shall not do any work... (NIV)

The Sabbath was to be observed by all: the servants, the beasts of burden, the members of the Hebrew household, their guests, and the visitors within their gates—all were commanded to stop work and rest on this day (De. 5:14-15). Verse 15 implies that the captives in Egypt did not have the benefit of the Sabbath rest.

The priests were to set the table in the Holy Place on the Sabbath. The rite of circumcision was to be performed on the Sabbath if it was the eighth day after the child's birth (Le. 12:3; Jn. 7:22). A "Holy Convocation" or the assembly of the community for religious purposes was within the bounds of Sabbath activity. However, the church fathers of the second and third centuries were very much opposed to the legal aspects of the Sabbath. The rift between the Jews who rejected the Messiah and those who accepted him became so great that everything Jewish was looked upon with hostility.

Following the reforms under Nehemiah and Ezra, the Jewish leaders developed an elaborate code of regulations and restrictions. The rabbis worked out a table of thirty-nine main divisions of labor forbidden on the Sabbath Day. In their zeal for the law, the rabbis increased the commandments of the written law to include 613 precepts. "Of these, 365 are negative—things a Jew must not do—the number corresponding to the number of days in the solar year. The remaining 248 are positive—things a Jew must do—the number corresponding, according to the Rabbinic view, to the 248 bones in the human body."[2] It is evident that under this interpretation the Sabbath would become burdensome.

For more on the Sabbath, see commentary on Ge. 2:3; Ac. 1:12.

6:4 Hear, O Israel: The LORD our God is one LORD.

This verse emphasizes the fact that even though God is trinitarian in nature, he is still one God. He is God the Father (Elohim) and God the Son (YHWH) and God the Holy Spirit (Ruach). The Father, Son and Holy Spirit are distinct from each other and are able to send and be sent by one another (Jn. 13:20), but their unity constitutes the one Godhead.

A study of the trinity in the OT affords insight into the nature of the triune God. The Scriptures teach that God is the Creator and the Keeper of the Universe, the Father of the Lord Jesus Christ, and that he does not change (Mal. 3:6; He. 1:12; 13:8; Ja. 1:7). The idea of the trinity is first suggested in a passage from Genesis, "Let us make man in our image" (Ge. 1:26). The reason for the delay in the full revelation of the trinity may have been to avoid conflict with the polytheistic culture of OT times. To establish firmly the concept of monotheism, one God, the idea of the trinity was not developed until Jesus the Messiah came, and then the disclosure was gradual.

Reference to the Spirit, or the Spirit of God, or the Holy Spirit, is found in many books of the Bible. The word for Spirit in the Hebrew Bible is *rauch,* meaning "the breath of God." In the NT the Greek word for Spirit is the verb *pneuman,* meaning "breathe" and has the same basic meaning as that of the Hebrew *rauch.* The Spirit of God "moved upon the face of the waters" (Ge. 1:2) in the precreation period and at the command of Elohim (God) order was brought out of chaos (see Ps. 36:6).

Sabbath	3098-3102
Holy Place	1600
Nehemiah	2577
Ezra	1199
Law	435-441, 4055
Trinity	3694
Creator	884-886, 680
Immutability	2480
Holy Spirit	1601-1614
Holy Spirit as Creator	886

Holy Spirit	
1603-1604	

The Spirit of God worked in the OT period but was divinely limited to the leaders. Even though the ministry of the Holy Spirit was restrained in the OT, his work did pre-

Day of	
Pentecost	
2722	
Book of	
Joel	
4251	

pare the way for the full demonstration of the Holy Spirit on the day of Pentecost. The prophet Joel had a vision of this event (2:28-29). The Spirit of the Lord came upon Othniel (Jud. 3:9-11), upon Gideon (Jud. 6:34) and upon Jeph-

Just as God provides physical food, he also gives man spiritual bread–his Word.

thah (Jud. 11:29). For more on the Holy Spirit see essay on "The Work of the Holy Spirit in the Old and New Testaments," p. 394.

Bread	
536-537,	
1308	

8:3 ...man does not live on bread alone but on every word that comes from the mouth of the LORD. (NIV)

Jesus himself emphasizes the unity of the Biblical message by quoting these words in response to the devil's temptation (Mt. 4:4; Lu. 4:4). He also gives authority to the Old Testament Scriptures by quoting them as the resource for judging right from wrong.

Feeding	
the Flock	
2090	

Both this verse and the words Jesus spoke refer to the feeding of the people of God supernaturally. Moses told the nation of Israel that God "humbled you, causing you to hunger and then feeding you with manna, which neither you nor your fathers had known..." God provided something for his people that they did not have the capability of providing for them-

Word of	
God	
416	

selves. So, too, he provides spiritual food—his Word—as a gift to his people that will give them life. It is something man could not do for himself.

Moses warns, "When you have eaten and are satisfied...be careful that you do not forget the LORD" (De. 8:10-11, NIV). Man must remember that God is the source of all food, both physical and spiritual.

Food,	
Physical-	
Spiritual	
1296-1309	

15:9 Be careful not to harbor this wicked thought: "The seventh year, the year for canceling debts, is near," so that you do not show ill will toward your needy brother and give him nothing... (NIV)

Concern and provision for the poor is an important theme throughout the Scriptures. This verse refers to the sabbatical year, a year given to protect

Sabbatic	
Year	
3104	

the poor and also to allow the land to rest (see commentary on Ex. 23:11). God tells his people that they must give generously and with pure motives; "then because of this the LORD your God will bless you in all your work and in everything you put your hand to" (De. 15:10, NIV). See TCRB section beginning 2115 for an enlightening study on liberality and the blessing it brings.

16:1 ...celebrate the Passover of the LORD your God...

This important festival is especially significant because of its fore-shadowing of Christ. For the Christological implications of it, see commentary on Ex. 12:17 and also the discussion of it in the essay, "Salvation Symbolized in the Exodus," p. 95.

Passover
2686, 1256

16:10 And thou shalt keep the feast of weeks unto the LORD thy God...

The Feast of Weeks, or Day of Pentecost, commemorated the giving of the Law on Mount Sinai, fifty days after the Passover. Instructions for observing this special Sabbath are found here as well as in Le. 23:15-22 and Nu. 28:26-31. It is also the subject of Ex. 34:22ff and further commentary is given there. The descriptions of many of these celebrations are repeated throughout the Pentateuch.

Feast of Weeks
1257

16:13 Celebrate the Feast of Tabernacles for seven days after you have gathered the produce of your threshing floor and your winepress. (NIV)

This joyful celebration of the harvest is somewhat like a Thanksgiving Day celebration. For an explanation of the Feast of Tabernacles, see commentary on Le. 23:34.

Feast of Tabernacles
1259

18:15 The LORD thy God will raise up unto thee a Prophet from the midst of thee, of thy brethren, like unto me; unto him ye shall hearken.

This verse is quoted in the New Testament by both the apostle Peter (Ac. 3:22) and Stephen (Ac. 7:37). Both affirm its Messianic meaning. Jesus himself may have been referring to this verse when he told the self-righteous Jews, "...Your accuser is Moses, on whom your hopes are set. If you believed Moses, you would believe me, for he wrote about me" (Jn. 5:45-46, NIV).

Prophecies, Messianic
2890-2891, 4306b

24:1 If a man marries a woman who becomes displeasing to him...and he writes her a certificate of divorce... (NIV)

The question of divorce was the subject of a dialogue between the Pharisees and Jesus (Mt. 19:7-8; Mk. 10:3-5). In the discussion, both referred to this verse from the law of Moses, using it as an authoritative basis for doctrine. This not only affirms Mosaic authorship of Deuteronomy, it also indicates the value that was placed upon its teachings.

Divorce
1666
Marriage
1620-1623

25:5 ...the wife of the dead shall not marry...a stranger: her husband's brother shall...take her to him to wife...

The Sadducees of Jesus' day questioned him about the levirate law, which is based on this verse (Mk. 12:18-23). Jesus, in response, said, "have you not read in the book of Moses..." (Mk. 12:26, NIV) and quoted from the Pentateuch, the only five books the Sadducees considered authoritative.

Directly following this incident, a teacher of the law came and asked Jesus which, of all the commandments, was most important. Jesus quoted

Widows
3829-3830

Book of the Law
525

De. 6:4, "Hear, O Israel: the LORD our God, the LORD is one" (NIV), and then he gave the Great Commandment—that man is to love the Lord with all his heart, his soul, his mind and his strength and he is to love his neighbor as himself. (Mt. 22:37-39; Mk. 12:30-31).

It would be difficult to overstate the value that Jesus placed on the writings of Moses, the Pentateuch. These writings were foundational to his message and purpose.

28:58 ...this glorious and awesome name—the LORD your God... (NIV)

The divine name YHWH, translated LORD in both the KJV and NIV, is the most significant name of God in the OT. For more on its meaning, see commentary on Ex. 3:14-15.

Mount Nebo –where Moses viewed the promised land.

30:6 And the LORD thy God will circumcise thine heart…to love the LORD thy God with all thine heart, and with all thy soul, that thou mayest live.

Circumcision, instituted in Genesis, became a symbol of heart purification throughout the Scriptures. For more on the symbolic significance of circumcision, see commentary on Ge. 17:10.

Circumcision
765-767

32:21 …I will make them envious by those who are not a people; I will make them angry by a nation that has no understanding. (NIV)

The fact that this verse was written by Moses is affirmed by Paul in Ro. 10:19. He uses the writings of both Moses and Isaiah to make his point that the Gentiles (the "nation that has no understanding") understood God's message better than the Jews of his time. He was exhorting the nation of Israel

Gentiles
2383-2384

to put her faith in God, a message that Moses preached throughout the book of Deuteronomy.

34:1 Then Moses climbed Mount Nebo...There the LORD showed him the whole land... (NIV)

Mount Nebo is opposite the point where the Hebrews crossed the Jordan River. The mount is the point from which Moses viewed the promised land and the place where he died.

The elevation of this spot is 4,000 feet above the Dead Sea and from this vantage point one can gain a magnificent view of the area of Palestine immediately west of the Jordan. On a clear day it is possible to see clearly the towers on the Mount of Olives at Jerusalem.

Archaeologists have excavated an ancient Christian church on top of the mount.

Joshua

The Name

The book of Joshua is named for one of the faithful spies who, with Caleb, brought back a true report from Canaan. Joshua is the first book of the second group of Hebrew writings known as "The Former Prophets." Other writings in this series include Judges, 1 and 2 Samuel, and 1 and 2 Kings.

The name Joshua underwent a progressive change in spelling. When Joshua was listed with the other eleven spies, he was called "Oshea the son of Nun" (Nu. 13:8). Before the spies departed on their mission, Moses called Oshea "Jehoshua" (Nu. 13:16). (The addition of "Jeh" indicates a more responsible relationship to Jehovah.) When the spies returned, Jehoshua became "Joshua" (Nu. 14:6). He was so called from that time on.

In the NT the name Joshua is Grecized and appears as Jesus (Ac. 7:45; He. 4:8). Why this change of spelling came to be is uncertain, but it is known that Hebrew custom was to change the name of a person at a time of crisis or in changed relationships. For example, Abram was changed to Abraham; Jacob to Israel; and Saul to Paul. It is possible that Joshua's name was changed to reflect the continuing revelation of the Messianic hope. As a leader, Joshua is a type of Christ, and the name Jesus (Greek, *Iesous*) is the equivalent of the Hebrew Joshua (*Yehoshua*) meaning Yahweh, or "salvation." (For more on the significance of names in the Bible, see commentary on Mt. 1:21.) Joshua's character is reflected in his consecration (Nu. 14:6-8); he is notable for his spiritual mindedness (Jos. 3:5; 8:30), his godly reverence (Jos. 5:14), his courage (Jos. 10:25), and his obedience (Jos. 11:15).

Joshua was an Ephramite (Nu. 13:8) who settled in Timnath-serah (Jos. 19:50) and was buried in the hill country of Ephraim.[1] Because of his loyalty to Moses and his spiritual integrity the Lord appointed Joshua to succeed Moses (De. 31:22-23) and to lead the children of Israel into Canaan. Joshua was eminently qualified for this office, having served as personal minister to Moses (Ex. 24:13; 32:17). He was in attendance when the Lord communicated with Moses (Ex. 33:11); he learned about the power of the Holy Spirit from Moses (Nu. 11:27-29). His experience as a spy familiarized him with the Canaanites' territory in Palestine.[2]

Authorship and Date

According to tradition, the book of Joshua was written by the man whose valiant achievements it relates. Both Jewish and Christian scholars have held to this view. Joshua certainly is the central human figure throughout the entire book. His name appears at least once in every chapter except the

Book of
Joshua
4228
Caleb
621

Joshua
1922, 4293

Names
Changed
2518

Names of
Christ
3632

Journeys of
Joshua
4307c
Moses
2420

sixteenth. However, with the advent of the documentary hypothesis theory, this book suffered literary altercation along with the books of the Pentateuch. (For a discussion of this liberal theory see the Introduction to Genesis, pp. 37-38).

The most likely answer to authorship is found in the "Deuteronomist Theory" which supposes that Joshua preserved a record of events, written and/or oral, which was later compiled and edited to form the book as it appears in the Bible. There may have been an editor after the time of Joshua because the book contains a record of Joshua's death and burial (Jos. 24:29-31).[3]

Background, Purpose, and Content

The book of Joshua continues the historical narrative begun in the Pentateuch, and it is sometimes called the last book in the Hexateuch. (The Hexateuch consists of the five books of the Pentateuch plus Joshua, which form a six-book literary unit having historical continuity.) Some believe that the Hexateuch preceded the Pentateuch as a literary unit and that the book of Joshua was removed about 400 B.C. on religious and theological grounds, namely to emphasize the importance of the Torah—the Pentateuch—as the Five Books of Moses.[4] As to subject matter, Joshua is more closely related to the Pentateuch than the books of the Former Prophets of which it is a part.

The book of Joshua records the crossing of Jordan, the people's encounter with the fortress city of Jericho, and the establishment of the twelve tribes in their homeland (a privilege Jacob's descendents did not have for four hundred years). All of the tribes received their land allotment except the priestly tribe of Levi, who controlled only the six cities of refuge.

Joshua was faithful in carrying out the instructions of Moses. The covenant made by God with the fathers was reaffirmed (Jos. 24:14-33). Joshua proved himself to be a strong leader (Jos. 1:2-9). The words in Joshua's farewell address challenged the tribes as well as the countless followers of the Lord in later generations: "Now therefore fear the LORD, and serve him in sincerity and in truth...as for me and my house, we will serve the LORD" (Jos. 24:14-15).

Important information about the early topographic details of Palestine have been preserved in this book. Archaeological evidence in many parts of Palestine confirms the accuracy of the book of Joshua. (See the archaeological section in TCRB Helps: No. 4326, Ai; No. 4378, Gerizim; No. 4387, Hazor; No. 4390, Jericho; No. 4402, Lachish; No. 4432, Shechem; No. 4433, Shiloh.)

Genesis 4223

Joshua 4293

Jordan 1915-1916
Jericho 1878

Covenants 877-881

Serve God 3894
Land of Canaan 626-634

**1:1 Now after the death of Moses the servant
of the LORD it came to pass, that the LORD spake
unto Joshua the son of Nun, Moses' minister...**

Joshua was well-prepared for the Lord's call to lead the Hebrew nation into the land of Canaan. He had been a faithful servant to Moses (Ex. 24:13; 32:17) and had personally witnessed God's mighty hand in Moses' life. He was also known for his military skill (see Ex. 17:9).

The Lord had told Moses who his successor would be so that there would be a smooth transition of leadership (see Nu. 27:12-23). Perhaps most significant was the Lord's description of Joshua as "a man in whom is the spirit" (Nu. 27:18). For more on the Holy Spirit in both the Old and New Testaments, see p. 394.

Journeys
of Joshua
4307c

Moses
4307

Holy Spirit
1601-1614

Jericho ruins. A massive corner bastion and watchtower.

2:1 Then Joshua son of Nun secretly sent two spies…"Go, look over the land," he said, "especially Jericho…" (NIV)

Jericho was an important city of this time, located about 5 miles north of the Dead Sea and about 17 miles northeast of Jerusalem. It is the oldest city in Palestine and archaeologists believe it to be the oldest city in the world, dating back to at least 7000 B.C. Since it was strongly fortified its conquest was essential to the Israelites' settling of the area.

The story of its destruction by divine command is well-known. Except for Rahab all living inhabitants were slain and Joshua decreed that if anyone ever fortified the city he would lose his elder son when the foundations were laid and the younger one when the gates were set up (see Jos. 5:13-6:26). Accordingly when Hiel of Bethel fortified the city during the reign of Ahab he suffered the curse Joshua pronounced (1 K. 16:34).

The city is rich in Biblical history. It was at Jericho that Jesus restored sight to Bartimaeus (Mk. 10:46-52) and brought salvation to Zacchaeus (Lu. 19:1-10).

Jericho
1878, 4390

Rahab
2942

2:1 ...So they went and entered the house of a prostitute named Rahab and stayed there. (NIV)

Though the word for "prostitute" could possibly mean innkeeper (see NIV text note), Rahab is mentioned elsewhere in the Bible as a "prostitute" (see He. 11:31; Ja. 2:25). In vv. 8-11 she makes a remarkable confession of faith in the God of Israel, which the writer of the book of Hebrews emphasizes in the famous He. 11 "roll call" of the faithful. The fact that she not only believed in God, but was willing to place her own life in jeopardy for the cause of the Hebrew spies prompted James to include her in his treatise on faith and works (Ja. 2).

Rahab's family was spared as a result of her faith and was incorporated into the Hebrew nation (see Jos. 6:22-25). It was no doubt this Rahab who became the wife of Salmon and the mother of Boaz, an ancestor of Christ (see Mt. 1:5). Rahab is a powerful testimony to the changing power of God, whose grace is extended to people of all nations and walks of life.

Prostitutes
3881-3882

Spies
3429

Boaz
520

These dwellings atop the walls at Ankara, Turkey, may typify the house on the wall where Rahab lived in Jericho.

Hazor. Cultic objects and statue from "C" temple.

11:10-11 And Joshua…took Hazor, and…smote all the souls that were therein with the edge of the sword, utterly destroying them: there was not any left to breathe: and he burnt Hazor with fire.

Hazor
4387

Idolatry
3928-3933

Hazor was the capital city of the northern Canaanite kingdom and its conquest was perhaps Joshua's greatest victory. The destruction of the entire city was in obedience to the divine command regarding the conquest of the cities of Canaan (see De. 7:2, 16). Israel was to have no relationship with the people of Canaan and their idolatry.

The city of Hazor was rebuilt later and included in the territory allotted to Naphtali (Jos. 19:32-36).Today there are extensive archaeological excavations of the city by Israel's Department of Antiquities.

Joshua
1922, 4293

13:1, 6 When Joshua was old and well advanced in years, the LORD said to him…"Be sure to allocate this land to Israel for an inheritance, as I have instructed you." (NIV)

Obedi-
ence–
Disobedi-
ence
2614-2621

The next chapters of Joshua record the land still to be subdued by the nation of Israel and the assignments of specific areas for certain tribes. Joshua was between 90 and 100 years old at this time and still so much remained to be done. In ch. 23 Joshua gives his farewell message to the nation, with much the same focus as the address by Moses in the book of Deuteronomy. He reviews the goodness of the Lord and his faithfulness to all his promises, then exhorts the Israelites to be obedient to the law of Moses. He warns them that disobedience would bring ruin while obedience would bring blessing. Joshua's death is recorded in Jos. 24:29-31.

22:19 …come over to the LORD'S land, where the LORD'S tabernacle stands… (NIV)

Tabernacle
3528

The tabernacle was the central place of worship for the Israelites during this period of their history. It had been designed, planned and revealed by God. Ex. 25:9 is where God's instruction to Moses regarding the tabernacle begins. For more on the tabernacle as a step in the development of worship centers, see chart on pp. 402-403.

Judges

The Name

The title of the book of Judges was derived from the special rulers, the judges, appointed by God to assume governmental control after the death of Joshua (Jud. 2:16). Judges is the eighth book in the OT and the second in a group called "The Former Prophets."

The name Judges comes from the Hebrew *shaphatim* (pl.) and refers to men who ruled and directed the affairs of state in Israel from the death of Joshua until the crowning of Saul as king. The term *shaphatim* (pl.) is unlike the term *shaphat* (sing.), meaning "one who judges controversies in court."

Book of
Judges
4229

Judges of
Israel
1821-1822

Authorship and Date

The authorship of the book of Judges is unknown. Some scholars suggest that each judge maintained a diary or executive log and that eventually some redactor (editor) compiled the book into the form as it appears in the Bible. "Some ascribe it to Phinehas, to Samuel, to Hezekiah, and some to Ezra. But it is evident that it is the work...of a person who lived posterior to the time of the judges...and most probably of Samuel."[1] Others have suggested that the final compilation of the book may have come after the Josiah reform.[2]

Charles R. Wilson writes that "the dates for the period ot the Judges may be set between 1250 and 1050 B.C. This includes the history of Israel from the death of Joshua to the rise of the monarchy under Saul. Joshua's death may be dated in 1417 B.C., as seen from comparing the following references: Ex. 17:8ff.; 16:35; Jos. 24:29; 1 K. 6:1. This would make the period of the Judges roughly 367 years."[3]

Samuel
**4295,
4307d**

Joshua
1922

Background, Purpose, and Content

No leader had been provided to succeed Joshua, so when he died the nation of Israel was without a central government or an executive head. The nation soon degenerated and began to serve the gods of the heathen nations. Law and order became a personal matter and soon ceased to exist. "Every man did that which was right in his own eyes" (Jud. 17:6). Repeatedly God intervened and provided a judge to deliver the people from their life of bondage.

Israel –
the Jews
1807-1829

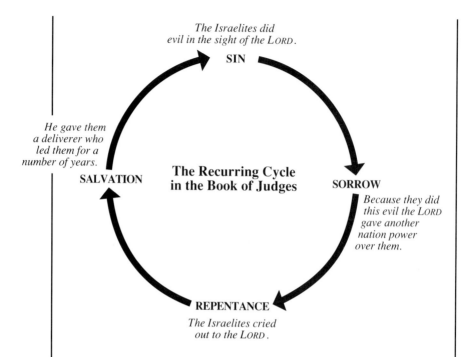

The Recurring Cycle
in the Book of Judges

*The Israelites did
evil in the sight of the LORD.*

SIN

*He gave them
a deliverer who
led them for a
number of years.*

SALVATION

SORROW

*Because they did
this evil the LORD
gave another
nation power
over them.*

REPENTANCE

*The Israelites cried
out to the LORD.*

Apostasy **1235-1236**	The pattern of Israel's apostasy was consistent. When the "children of Israel did evil in the sight of the LORD, and forgat the LORD their God, and served Baalim and the groves...the anger of the LORD was hot against Israel." The LORD turned them over to a heathen rule for a season (Jud. 3:7-8,12; 4:1; 6:1).
Deliver- ance **968-971**	The pattern of deliverance was also consistent. When the people repented and cried unto the Lord, the Lord raised up a deliverer for the children of Israel, to conquer the enemy and to deliver the people from bondage (Jud. 3:9,15; 4:3; 6:7). At times of victory some of the leaders composed and sang a ballad of triumph (Jud. 5:1ff.; see also Ex. 15:1ff.).
The Decalogue **949**	The general teaching of Judges is consistent with the law as revealed to Moses by God. The book of Judges constantly manifests the discipline which the Lord had imposed upon his people. In the national development of Israel, the cycle of sin, sorrow, repentance, and salvation occurred repeatedly.
Samuel **4295**	The instability in the national and religious affairs of Israel continued until the days of Samuel. This last judge, and the first prophet, led the way for Israel's spiritual and national renewal.

2:11 And the children of Israel did evil in the sight of the LORD, and served Baalim.

In the Hebrew *Baalim* is the plural of *Baal*, the god that was worshiped by the nations surrounding Israel. There were various Baals and the OT often differentiates between them. Also, "Baal" was a prefix that was sometimes used to identify the name of the place where he was worshiped (such as Baal-gad, Jos. 11:17). For more on the worship of Baal and the city of Baalbeck, which was built in his honor, see commentary on Nu. 22:41.

Baal
3936-3937

2:16 ...the LORD raised up judges, which delivered them...

The office of judge was not hereditary nor were the judges elected by the people. They were special rulers chosen by God and were always selected by him in a supernatural way. Adam Clarke says:

Judges of
Israel
1821-1822

> They [the judges] had no power to make or change the laws; they were only to execute them under the direction of the Most High God; therefore God was king in Israel: the government was a theocracy; and the judges were his deputies. The office, however, was not continual, as there appear intervals in which there was no judge in Israel. And, as they [the judges] were extraordinary persons they were only raised up on extraordinary occasions to be instruments in the hands of God [in] delivering their nation from the oppression and tyranny of the neighboring powers.[4]

Guidance
1465-1471

Deliverance
968

Major Judges		Minor Judges	
Othniel	(3:7-11)	Shamgar	(3:31)
Ehud	(3:12-30)	Tola	(10:1-2)
Deborah	(chs. 4-5)	Jair	(10:3-5)
Gideon	(chs. 6-8)	Ibzan	(12:8-10)
Jephthah	(10:6 -12:7)	Elon	(12:11-12)
Samson	(chs. 13-16)	Abdon	(12:13-15)

3:9-10 But when they cried out to the Lord, he raised up for them a deliverer...The Spirit of the Lord came upon him, so that he became Israel's judge...(NIV)

Holy Spirit
1601-1614

The interrelationship of the "Lord" and the "Spirit of the Lord" in these verses shows that while they are distinct from each other, they are able to send and be sent by one another (see Jn.13:20). This affirms the concept of the triune God, which is found throughout Scripture. For more on the Trinity, especially in the OT, see commentary on De. 6:4.

Trinity
3694

6:23 And the Lord said unto him, Peace be unto thee; fear not: thou shalt not die.

Peace
3012-3017

Lord-shalom, "The Lord is peace," was the title Gideon gave to the altar he built at Ophra, in response to the word spoken to him by the Lord, "Peace be unto thee." The land of Canaan had long been possessed by the Hebrews. Joshua was dead and the people had entered into their Canaan rest (see Hebrews, chapter 4).

For more on the names of God see chart on p. 90.

6:32 ...that day they called Gideon "Jerub-Baal"...(NIV)

Gideon
1414,
4307d
Names
Changed
2518

In Bible times great value was placed upon the meaning of a person's name. When a character had developed, a new name was sometimes given as being expressive of it, as when Jacob received the name Israel, meaning "he strove with God," (Ge. 32:28) and Simon became Cephas, meaning "rock" (Jn. 1:42). For the apostle Paul's name change, see commentary on Ac. 7:58.

8:16 And he took the elders of the city...

In the Bible the word "elder" is used in various ways. There are elders in government, elders who are Jewish religious leaders, and elders in the Christian church. In general it has to do with seniority and authority.

Elders
2078-2079

For more on the title of "elder" in the Bible, see commentary on 1 Ti. 5:17.

11:29 Then the Spirit of the Lord came upon Jephthah...

The Holy Spirit in the Old Testament is the same member of the Trinity that is written of in the New Testament, but the nature of his work is somewhat different. During the period of the judges, the Spirit came upon specially selected leaders who were called to do a specific task. For more on the subject, see "The Work of the Holy Spirit in the Old and New Testaments," p. 394.

Holy Spirit
1601-1614

Ruth

The Name

The name Ruth is not a translation but a transliteration of a Moabite name into Hebrew characters. This is one of the few instances where the meaning of a name in Hebrew is unknown. No Hebrew stem can be positively identified. The fact that Ruth was not a Jew may account for a lack of etymological identification. The book was obviously so named because Ruth is the central character. In the Hebrew canon Ruth is one of the Five Scrolls (*Megilloth*) and is listed in the category of the Writings (Heb., *kethubim;* Gr., *hagiographa*).

Ruth
3097a

Moabites
2392

Authorship and Date

According to Jewish tradition, Samuel wrote the book of Ruth, but certain internal information raises the question of whether Samuel was the sole author. It is, however, quite possible that Samuel helped to preserve information on the events in Ruth. The reference to (King) David (1000-960 B.C.) in Ru. 4:17-22 makes it unlikely that Ruth in its present form was written in Samuel's lifetime. The opening words in the book suggest a backward look: "It came to pass in the days when the judges ruled" seems to indicate that the period of the judges was a comparatively distant event (Ru. 1:1). Miller and Miller say, "It is believed to have been written in the post-exilic period (c. 400 B.C..); the chief reasons for assigning it to this period are (1) the language it employs; (2) the obsolete customs it depicts which must be explained to its readers (Ru. 4:7); and (3) its implied protest against Nehemiah's and Ezra's censure of the mixed marriages so popular after the exile (Ru. 1:4; Ne. 13:1-3,23-27; Ezr. 10)."[1]

Book of
Ruth
4230
David
919, 4307f

Marriage
with the
Heathen
Forbidden
2255

Background, Purpose, and Content

The book of Ruth is one of the shortest books in the OT, but few books surpass it for historical background. It is a natural sequel to the book of Judges. Adam Clarke suggests that it might have originally been an appendix to the book of Judges.[2]

The description of King David's ancestry makes the book of Ruth a connecting link with later historical books. The friendly relationship expressed in the book of Ruth by the Moabites toward this Jewish family is again manifested when David placed his mother and father in the care of the king of Moab (1 S. 22:3-4; cf. Mt 1:5).

Book of
Judges
4229

Moab
2391

A typical threshing scene. The camel was used to pull the threshing sled for separating the grain from the straw.

Racial Prejudice 4083

One of the motives for this book probably was to combat racial prejudice. This story shows that "God is no respecter of persons" (Ac. 10:34) and that all nationalities are welcome into the kingdom when they repent and have faith in Jehovah. (For more on this subject, see commentary on Ac. 10:34-35.) Ruth is an example of one who separated herself from her people, the Moabites, and became loyal to the nation and religion of Israel. In this book the Moabitess, Ruth, became a link in the Messianic line.

Concerning the book of Ruth, Arthur E. Caudell wrote, "It enshrines so much of what is basic in human relationships and in true Israelite religion. It is a story of a loyal, disinterested relationship which secured its just reward...

Boaz 520

Love of God 2206

The upright, considerate, and industrious Boaz was a model Israelite. It demonstrated an overruling Providence and the all-embracing love of God, illustrating the fact made explicit in Ac. 10:34-35. It is a story of ordinary people [who]...appeal to the heart. It speaks a word of hope to the hopeless, the desolate, and the bereaved."[3]

Perhaps the spirit of the book is expressed in Boaz's statement to Ruth: "It hath fully been shewed me, all that thou hast done unto thy mother in law since the death of thine husband and how thou hast left thy father and thy mother, and the land of thy nativity, and art come unto a people which thou knewest not heretofore" (Ru. 2:11-12). The book of Ruth also communicates the providential care by the Lord Jehovah for two widows, Ruth and Naomi, in desperate circumstances, and the ancient customs of courtship and marriage.

Widows 3873

The ethical values of the book must not be overlooked. Here a good example is presented of "steadfast filial piety." The loyal commitment of Ruth to Naomi and her God brought to Ruth prosperity, happiness, a good husband, and the honor she received as an ancestress of the House of David.

1 and 2
Samuel

The Name

The name Samuel comes from the Hebrew *Shemuel*. The two books of Samuel originally formed a single book called by that name; 1 and 2 Kings were also one book. It is evident that both the Samuel and Kings books are a continuation of the book of Judges because they contain an account of the last judge and the election of Saul, as well as the chronicles of the kings of Israel and Judah.

Herbert W. Wolf explains that when the OT was translated into Greek (Septuagint, early third century B.C.) the books of Samuel were divided into two books, called the "Books of Kingdoms." "In similar fashion Kings became 'Kingdoms III and IV'...Jerome affixed the title 'Books of the Kings'...His modification of 'Kingdoms' to 'Kings' was intended to reproduce the Hebrew title for the present 1 and 2 Kings...Eventually the Latin Vulgate reverted to the name 'Samuel' for the first two books."[1]

The Rabbinic Bamberg Bible, published in 1516, divided the Samuel book into Parts 1 and 2. When the Bible was translated into English, Jerome's modified arrangement of 1 and 2 Samuel and 1 and 2 Kings was adopted.

Authorship and Date

It is impossible to ascribe the authorship of the Samuel books to any one person. The name Samuel was probably given to these books because of the prominent place that the prophet has in the first twenty-five chapters; his death is recorded in chapter 25. Elmer B. Smick remarks that

> There are indications in Scriptures that the prophets Samuel, Nathan, and Gad were the authors. 1 S. 10:25 says that Samuel wrote a book and laid it up before the Lord, while 1 Chr. 29:29 states that the acts of David were 'written in the book of Samuel, the seer, and in the book of Nathan the prophet, and in the book of Gad the seer' (cf. 2 Chr. 9:29 are the acts of Solomon). It is not likely that Samuel could have been responsible for more than the early part of 1 Samuel since his death is recorded in Ch. 25. 2 S. 5:5 speaks of the complete reign of David in the past tense, so someone who outlived David wrote the section.[2]

Reference is also made to the book of Jasher (2 S. 1:18), which is now in print but its origin is questioned. The books of Nathan and Gad are no longer in existence; therefore, verifying their content is impossible. However, since the books are referred to in Scripture, one may assume that they contained reliable information. It is possible that the final edition of the Samuel books, under the leading of the Holy Spirit, drew some information from these

Book of
1 Samuel
4231
Book of
2 Samuel
4232
Book of
1 Kings
4233

Book of
2 Kings
4234

Samuel
3138, 4295
Nathan
2523

David
919, 4307f

"Word"
Inspired
417

sources as well as from the royal records such as those David preserved (1 Chr. 27:24). It is evident that much of the material in 1 Samuel is contemporary with the prophet Samuel. These noncanonical sources are very important and have much historical value.

Background, Purpose, and Content

Old Testament History
4222b
Bible
414-445

The books of Samuel had a twofold purpose: first, to narrate the historical events preceding the prophet Samuel's time and, second, to teach the moral and spiritual lessons portrayed in God's revelation. Charles R. Wilson comments,

> The authenticity and completeness of the history of Israel recorded in the books of Samuel give great emphasis to the significance of history in the Bible. It was through the outworking of the historical process that God revealed His acts. The compiler of Samuel was aware of that and perceived that what had happened in the course of Israel's history was vital to his contemporaries for their instruction and admonition concerning God's activity in their time.[3]

Apostasy
1235-1236

The books of Samuel record the reformation work begun by the prophet following the confusion and apostasy recorded in the book of Judges. This revival began when, during Samuel's tenure as judge, Israel was delivered from the Philistines at Mizpah (1 S. 7:3-14).

Though it was not God's choice, the people insisted on having a king. With Samuel's guidance, Saul was selected as Israel's first king (1 S. 11:15).

Saul
3158,
4307e
Estrangement
1272-1273

Even though Saul began his reign under favorable circumstances, he soon showed contempt for his obligations. Saul was commanded to totally destroy the war booty taken from the Amalekites, but he disobeyed God and chose to save the best oxen and sheep (1 S. 15:9). After his loss of fellowship with God, Saul was troubled by an evil spirit (1 S. 16:14-16). When Saul's condition continued to deteriorate, his servants urged him to "seek out a man, who is a cunning player on an harp" (1 S. 16:16). Samuel chose David, the son of Jesse,

David
4296, 4307f

to be Saul's comforter. David's superior qualities aroused Saul's jealousy. As a result, Saul determined to murder David (1 S. 19:1). After the danger to his life became great, David left the court and became a wanderer (1 S. 18-20); he even aided the Philistines in their warfare against Israel (1 S. 29-30).[4]

Witchcraft
2231

Eventually Saul sought the counsel of the witch at Endor (1 S. 28:7ff.), who brought Samuel back from the dead, but instead of friendly reunion Samuel rebuked Saul (1 S. 28:15). Finally Saul's loss of fellowship and

Suicide
1699

communion with God led to his suicide (1 S. 31:4). David was anointed king by the men of Judah.

*An archaeological dig at Gath. Many scholars believe this Gath
is the one to which the ark of covenant was brought in 1 S. 5:8.*

1 S. 3:20 And all Israel from Dan even to Beersheba knew that Samuel was established to be a prophet of the LORD.

Samuel
4295, 4307d

The books of Samuel deal at length with Samuel's life; a biographical sketch of the prophet follows. Scripture records that Samuel, whose name means the "name of God," was the last of the judges (1 S. 7:15; Ac. 13:20) and the earliest Hebrew prophet after Moses (2 Chr. 35:18; Je. 15:1). Samuel's father was Elkanah, a Levite, who with his family lived in the hill country of Ephraim (Jos. 21:5; 1 Chr. 6:66). Hannah, Samuel's mother, was barren, but after special prayer she gave birth to Samuel, whom she dedicated to the Lord. While he was yet a child, Samuel ministered in the tabernacle at Shiloh, living in a chamber in or near the tabernacle. The Lord revealed himself to Samuel in his early boyhood (1 S. 3:4ff.).

Judges of
Israel
1821-1823

Samuel was unlike some of the prophets who succumbed to the temptation of rendering pleasing prophecies during times of stress (Je. 14:13-14; 27:1,10,14; see also Am. 7:10-17). He and the other prophets (Jeremiah, Ezekiel, Daniel, Amos) shunned this temptation; they obediently proclaimed the whole counsel of God.

Prophets
2065-2066

1 S. 8:5 "...appoint a king to lead us, such as all the other nations have." (NIV)

Israel was to settle in the land of Canaan as a people of God, the Great King. However, they allowed the surrounding nations to influence them to desire a human king. The main theme of the books of Samuel relates to this human king—how he was selected and how he was to rule in relation to God's kingship. The account of Saul, who showed his unwillingness to submit to God's leadership, and the story of David, the king faithful to the Lord, provide contrasting examples.

Saul
3158, 4307e

David
919, 4307f

1 S. 13:14 But now thy kingdom shall not continue: the LORD hath sought him a man after his own heart...

David
4296

The importance of King David, both to the people of his day and to all of mankind, can hardly be overestimated. He was the founder of the Hebrew monarchy. His spiritual influence through his writings is known by all of Christendom. He is sometimes called a type or picture of the Messiah because of his character and the nature of his leadership of the people of Israel.

Jesse
1889

However, there could be no greater commendation than the Lord's own description, "a man after my own heart." The apostle Paul quotes this Scripture in his sermon at Pisidian Antioch: "After removing Saul, he made David their king. He testified concerning him: 'I have found David son of Jesse a man after my own heart; he will do everything I want him to do' " (Ac. 13:22, NIV).

1 S. 15:22 "...To obey is better than sacrifice, and to heed is better than the fat of rams." (NIV)

Sacrifices
3107-3111

The meaning of sacrifice is consistent throughout the Bible, though the practice was different in the OT. Symbolically it was to show God's mercy and to provide man a way to seek redemption and salvation. It was always meant to involve a consecration to God and a willingness to listen to and obey him.

Love
2200-2209

The ultimate end of all the sacrificial ritual in the OT was to communicate love. Jesus made this clear when he was questioned about the commandments and told a scribe, "Thou shalt love the Lord thy God with all thy heart, and with all thy soul, and with all thy mind, and with all thy strength...Thou shalt love thy neighbor as thyself." When the scribe replied that this "...is more than all whole burnt offerings and sacrifices," Jesus replied, "thou art not far from the kingdom of God" (Mk. 12:30-34).

Obedience
2614-2619

Further, Jesus commanded "If ye love me, keep my commandments" (Jn. 14:15), emphasizing the correlation between love and obedience. These NT teachings shed light on the meaning of OT sacrificial rituals, but the essence of sacrifice—the attitude of the heart—is the same from Genesis to Revelation.

2 S. 7:2 ...the king said unto Nathan the prophet, See now, I dwell in an house of cedar, but the ark of God dwelleth within curtains.

Ark of the
Covenant
216

The ark of the covenant was also the subject of chs. 4-6 of 1 Samuel, when it was captured by the Philistines, who then suffered many disasters and returned it to Israel. David placed it in a temporary tabernacle (2 S. 6:17; 7:1-2), where it remained until it was placed in the Holy of Holies in Solomon's temple (1 K. 8:1-9). For the progression from tabernacle to temple as the place where Israel worshiped God, see chart on the "Development of Worship Centers," pp. 402-403.

2 S. 7:12,16 When your days are over... I will raise up your offspring to succeed you... your house and your kingdom will endure forever... (NIV)

Solomon
3414,
4307g

Though the immediate reference is to Solomon, who will succeed David and build the Temple, ultimately this promise is fulfilled in the incarnation of Jesus Christ, David's greater Son.

1 and 2 Kings

The Name

The word for king comes from the Hebrew *melakhim*. The other meanings or titles of the book of Kings have been many. The earliest title, consisting of the first three words in 1 Kings, "Now king David" (1 K. 1:1), is similar in origin to the title for the book of Genesis, which came from the first word, *bereshith,* which translates "in the beginning" (Ge. 1:1).

In early times the Samuel and Kings books were 1 and 2 Kings (the Samuel Books) and 3 and 4 Kings (the Kings Books). These divisions were justified on the basis that all of these writings were one continuous religious-political unit. The books of Kings cover a period of about 400 years.

In the original Hebrew there were only consonant forms (without vowels). After A.D. 600 the vowel points were added and with this addition the scrolls doubled in size. Dividing the scrolls into two parts may have been functional, i.e., to facilitate their use.

Book of 1 Kings **4233**
Book of 2 Kings **4234**

Authorship and Date

The author of the Kings books is unknown. Some scholars suggest that Ezra was the compiler or editor. As a priest, Ezra was a zealous servant of the Lord, a reformer opposing the corruption which had filtered in. He was also approved and accepted by the Jews.[1] Others suggest that a prophet in Babylon wrote the book during or after the exile, in about 550 B.C. The "synchronism between the northern and southern kingdoms throughout the Kings books favors the idea that these records were kept by the prophets."[2] The material for the compilation of these books may have come from public and private records similar to the Samuel books.

Ezra **1199**

Some scholars suggest that Isaiah and Jeremiah may have participated in the compiling and editing of these books because of the similarity of several chapters in both prophetic writings to some in 1 and 2 Kings. Compare 2 K. 18:19-20 with Is. 36, 37, 38, and 39; and 2 K. 24:18 and 25:1 with Je. 52:1. An alternate view is that the prophets perhaps used some material from the Kings books.[3] The uniformity of the style and the connection of the events suggest a single author or editor. That this person had access to ancient documents is suggested by his own words, "the rest of the acts...are they not written in the book of the chronicles of the kings of Judah?" (1 K. 11:41; 14:19,29; 15:7,23,31; 16:5,14,20,27).

Isaiah **1803**
Prophecy **2889-2894**

Cyprus

Mediterranean
Sea

**THE KINGDOM OF
DAVID AND SOLOMON**

Kingdom of Saul

Area conquered by David

Area under Solomon's economic control

Extent of Solomon's kingdom

Aleppo

Y A M H A D

Euphrates R.

Tiphsah

H A M A T H

Hamath

Qatna

Arvad

Kadesh (on the Orontes)

Tadmor

S Y R I A N

D E S E R T

Byblos

Lebweh

Sadad

Qaryatein

Berothai

Sidon

Damascus

Mt. Hermon

Tyre

Dan

A R A M

Kedesh

Hazor

Accho

Sea of Galilee
(Sea of Chinnereth)

Dor

Megiddo

Ashtaroth

Taanach

Beth-
shan

Edrei

Salecah

Ramoth-gilead

Shechem

Mahanaim?

A M M O N

Joppa

PHILISTIA

Gezer

Gibeah

Rabbath-ammon

Ashdod

Jerusalem
(Jebus)

Medeba

Gaza

Gath

Beth-shemesh

Ziklag

Hebron

Lachish

Dead
Sea

Raphia

Beersheba

Kir-hareseth (Kir-moab)

M O A B

A M A L E K

Tamar

Bozrah

Kadesh-
barnea

E D O M

Petra

Ezion-geber

S I N A I

Gulf of
Aqaba

Oronies R.

Leontes R.

Litani R.

Jordan R.

W. el Arish

Background, Purpose and Content

The first book of Kings begins with the close of David's reign. His son Solomon took the kingdom into its golden age during which time the temple was built. At Solomon's death the territory was divided into the Southern Kingdom (Judah) and the Northern Kingdom (Israel). The writer of these books usually gave the length of each king's reign and the name of the queen of the kingdom of Judah. As to the spiritual history, the writer stated each king's relationship to God. The whole viewpoint is Deuteronomic, with emphasis on loyalty and obedience to Jehovah.

The books of the Kings show that the rulers of Israel did not hesitate to violate the Davidic covenant (2 S. 7:8-16) nor the covenant God made with Israel at Sinai (De. 29:1-22).

The Kings books started with a stable kingdom and ended with a total collapse and deportation of the people, the net result of rebellion and idolatry.

The chart on page 1602 in TCRB Helps shows the moral heights and depths in the lives of the kings of Judah. It pictures the causes of the downfall of the kingdom which eventually led to the Babylonian captivity.

David
4307f
Solomon
4307g
Kings of
Judah
1824

Rebellion
3231-3232

Captivity of
Israel
1825-1827

1 K. 3:11-13 So God said to him [Solomon], "...I will do what you have asked. I will give you a wise and discerning heart, so that there will never have been anyone like you, nor will there ever be. Moreover, I will give you what you have not asked for—both riches and honor—so that in your lifetime you will have no equal among kings." (NIV)

Wisdom
3838-3851

The kingdom of Solomon was proverbial for its splendor, its vastness and its power. People came from all over the world to glimpse the magnificence of Solomon's wealth and political power as well as to hear his wisdom (1 K. 4:34; 10:1-13).

Solomon
3414, 4297
Wisdom
3538-3851

Jesus spoke of "Solomon in all his splendor" (Mt. 6:29, NIV), and later referred to himself as "one greater than Solomon" (Mt. 12:42, NIV). Only Jesus, the Son of God, could say this, because God had told Solomon that never in the course of human history would there be anyone so wise and discerning.

Solomon
4307g

Solomon was born to David and Bathsheba at Jerusalem and was named "Solomon" from the Hebrew word *shalom,* meaning peace and welfare. God had long before revealed to David that his son's kingdom would be one of peace and quietness in contrast to David's own militant reign (2 S. 7:5ff.). Solomon began his reign about the time he was 20 years old and reigned 40 years. During that time he fortified several cities, but otherwise devoted himself to the development of his own kingdom and the arts. Solomon showed great astuteness in government and administration, surrounding himself with

skilled officials. He brought great wealth to the kingdom and developed commerce and trade, building store cities such as Palmyra.

Riches
2805-2811

Solomon's construction of a magnificent temple to God fulfilled the dream of his father David. Solomon also followed his father's interest in literary pursuits. He wrote and collected many proverbs, some of which constitute the OT book of Proverbs, and he is credited with the writing of at least two Psalms (Ps. 72, 127).

Solomon's Temple
3577

Solomon's greatest downfall was his establishment of a harem which included about 1,000 women. Many of his marriages were to women from other countries who were idolatrous in their religion, and Solomon allowed himself to be persuaded by them to build pagan altars (1 K. 11:1-8). One result of this apostasy was the division of Solomon's great kingdom, which led eventually to the exile of the nation of Israel from their homeland.

Idolatry
3928-3951

1 K. 6:1 ...he began to build the house of the LORD.

The temple of Solomon was one of the most beautiful and expensive buildings ever constructed. The tabernacle had been drab, covered with animal skins, whereas the temple was glorious and golden. The tabernacle had been moved from place to place as the patriarchal tribes traveled from Mount Sinai to Canaan, while the temple was a permanent structure for use after the children of Israel had settled on their assigned land allotments in Canaan.

Tabernacle
3528

Solomon's Quarry. The entrance to the quarry where Solomon dug stone with which to build the temple.

For more on the development of worship centers over the course of history, see the chart on pp. 402-403.

The temple contained over 1,000,000 talents of silver and 100,000 talents of gold. To these Solomon added 3,000 talents of gold and 700 talents of silver from his own private fortune. The princes contributed additional gold and silver. In modern times the value of the gold and silver would be equivalent to billions of dollars.

Fine Lebanese cedar wood was imported from Tyre. Large work crews, transported to the mountains of Lebanon, cut and shaped the cedar wood. One hundred and fifty thousand Canaanites were drafted to hew stone. The temple was erected on Mount Moriah, where Abraham, many years before, had expected to offer Isaac and where Araunah, the Jebusite, had had his threshing floor (2 S. 24:16; 2 Chr. 3:1). The general plans for the temple were like those for the tabernacle, but the dimensions were doubled and the ornaments were richer. The stones were cut to size in the quarry beneath the city. All the timber was shaped and finished before it arrived at the temple site. It was probably the first prefabricated building in the world; certainly it was the largest and most beautiful. The interior was overlaid with gold.

The Holy Place, within the temple, which contained the golden candlestick, was symbolic of God, the Light; the table of shew bread symbolized spiritual bread; the altar of incense suggested man communing with God through prayer. A veil separated the Holy of Holies or the Inner Sanctum from the Holy Place. Behind the veil was the ark of the covenant with its two cherubims ten cubits high. Once each year, on the Day of Atonement (Yom Kippur), the high priest entered here and officiated for the people. Before the priests could minister inside either sanctuary, they were required to undergo a ceremonial cleansing at the brazen laver located outside the entrance to the Holy Place. The laver, made out of brass, contained water for the ablution ritual. Scripture records show that the brazen laver was made of the "looking-glasses of the women" (Ex. 38:8). Giving up their mirrors symbolized the women's complete dedication.

A place in the temple complex was provided for the Gentiles who desired to receive religious instruction which would lead to conversion to Judaism. Such converts were called proselytes. The temple served the worship needs of the people until it was destroyed by Nebuchadnezzar in 586 B.C.

1 K. 9:15 Here is the account of the forced labor King Solomon conscripted to build...Megiddo... (NIV)

Megiddo's strategic location, which provides a view of the Valley of Jezreel, gave the city prominence from the pre-Canaanite period. King Solomon fortified this valuable city and stabled some of his chariot horses there; archaeological excavations have revealed that there were well-constructed stables built for about 450 horses.

1 K. 17:2 Then the word of the LORD came to Elijah... (NIV)

Throughout the accounts of the kings of Israel, the prophets Elijah and Elisha serve as official representatives of the Lord, Israel's spiritual King. Nothing is known of Elijah's parentage, though he was at some point given a name which means, "The LORD is my God." He is one of the most unique and dramatic figures in Bible history. Because of his ruggedness in appear-

---

Gold
1431-1432
Silver
3315-3319

Canaanites
635

Solomon's
Royal
Buildings
4316

Holy of
Holies
1599

Priests
2058-2064

Gentiles
2383-2384

Megiddo
2283, 4411

Elijah
1112-1113

ance and dress, and because of the nature of his messages, he is sometimes seen as a prototype of John the Baptist (2 K. 1:8; Mt. 3:4).

When a chariot of fire carried Elijah to heaven (2 K. 2:1-11), the prophet Elisha succeeded him. As a model spiritual leader, he was a man of great energy (1 K. 19:19), he was a surrendered servant of God (1 K. 19:20-21), he desired spiritual equipment for his task (2 K. 2:9), he spoke with authority (2 K. 3:16-17), he put his entire personality into the work (2 K. 4:34-35), he was a man of integrity (2 K. 5:16), he lived in a spirit of victory (2 K. 6:15-16), he exhibited spiritual vision (2 K. 6:17), he died a victorious death (2 K. 13:14-19), and he had a wonderful posthumous influence (2 K. 13:20-21).

Elijah
2366, 4298

2 K. 19:35 That night the angel of the LORD went out and put to death a hundred and eighty-five thousand men in the Assyrian camp... (NIV)

Throughout Scripture angels are commissioned to carry out God's decrees of judgment: death, pestilence, and military defeats (Ge. 19:15-26; Jud. 5:23; Ac. 12:23). These messengers are spirit beings who usually appear in quasi-anthropomorphic form (Ac. 1:10; He. 1:14; 13:2) and are usually visible only to those whom they address (Nu. 22:22; 1 Chr. 21:16).

Angels
143-149

When the angel is called "the angel of the LORD" reference could be to the very Son of God, who was higher than the angels but, when he took on a human body, condescended to become a being "a little lower than the angels" (Ps. 8:5-6; Hc. 2:7-8). This appearance of deity to man is called a "theophany," or if it is Christ appearing, a "Christophany." For more on the subject, see the essay "Theophanies in the Old Testament," p. 72.

Son of God
707

2 K. 22:19 Because your heart was responsive and you humbled yourself before the LORD when you heard what I have spoken... I have heard you, declares the LORD. (NIV)

In both the Old Testament and the New Testament repentant people consistently experience divine forgiveness and restoration to God's favor. For a study of how the plan of salvation relates to both Testaments, see the essay "The Nature of the New Birth: Is It Unique to the NT?" pp. 384-386.

Forgiveness
1314-1316

2 K. 23:21 ...Keep the passover unto the LORD your God, as it is written in the book of this covenant.

Josiah's instruction to keep the Passover celebration is a major step in covenant renewal. The Passover inaugurated the deliverance of the Israelites from Egypt, when the death-angel killed the firstborn in homes where blood had not been sprinkled on the doorposts. For the Christian implications of this important celebration, see commentary on Ex. 12:17.

Feast of the Passover
1256

2 K. 25:19 ...the principal scribe of the host, which mustered the people of the land...

The word "scribe" has various meaning and implications throughout Scripture. In some cases scribes were a political party or a religious sect, but scribes could also refer to a professional group of royal officials, such as state record keepers.

Most likely that is the case in this verse. For more on the subject of scribes, see commentary on Ezr. 7:6.

Scribes
3165

The Divided Kingdom

Kings of Israel	Jeroboam	Evil	22 years	933-911
	Nadab	Evil	2 years	911-910
	Baasha	Evil	24 years	910-887
	Elah	Evil	2 years	887-886
	Zimri	Evil	7 days	886
	Omri	Evil	12 years	886-875
	Ahab	Evil	22 years	875-854
	Ahaziah	Evil	2 years	855-854
	Joram	Evil	12 years	854-843
	Jehu	Evil	28 years	843-816
	Jehoahaz	Evil	17 years	820-804
	Joash	Evil	16 years	806-790
	Jeroboam II	Evil	41 years	790-749
	Zechariah	Evil	6 months	748
	Shallum	Evil	1 month	748
	Menaham	Evil	10 years	748-738
	Pekahiah	Evil	2 years	738-736
	Pekah	Evil	20 years	750-730
	Hoshea	Evil	9 years	730-721

Kings of Judah	Rehoboam	Evil	17 years	933-916
	Abijah	Evil	3 years	915-913
	Asa	Evil	41 years	912-872
	Jehoshaphat	Good	25 years	874-850
	Jehoram	Evil	8 years	850-843
	Ahaziah	Evil	1 year	843
	Athaliah (Queen)	Evil	6 years	843-837
	Joash	Evil	40 years	843-803
	Amaziah	Good	29 years	803-775
	Uzziah	Good	52 years	787-735
	Jotham	Good	16 years	749-734
	Ahaz	Evil	16 years	741-726
	Hezekiah	Good	29 years	726-697
	Manasseh	Evil	55 years	697-642
	Amon	Evil	2 years	641-640
	Josiah	Good	31 years	639-608
	Jehoahaz	Evil	3 months	608
	Jehoiakim	Evil	11 years	608-597
	Jehoiachin	Evil	3 months	597
	Zedekiah	Evil	11 years	597-586

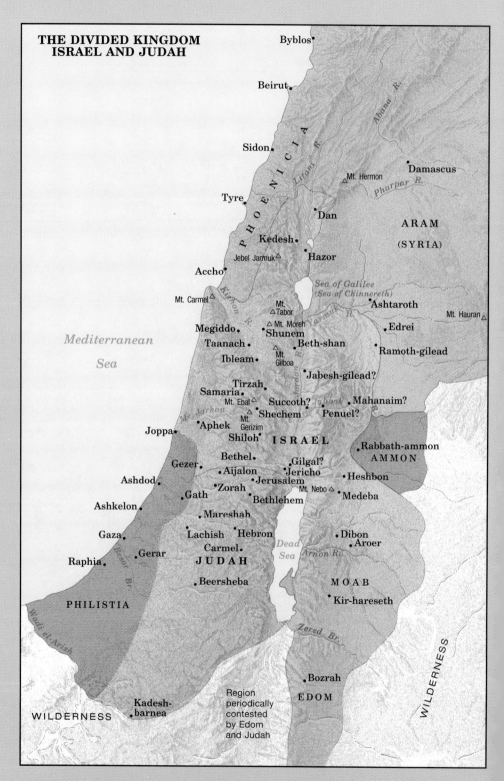

THE DIVIDED KINGDOM
ISRAEL AND JUDAH

Byblos

Beirut

PHOENICIA

Sidon

Mt. Hermon   Damascus

Tyre

Dan

ARAM
(SYRIA)

Kedesh

Jebel Jarmuk   Hazor

Accho

Sea of Galilee
(Sea of Chinnereth)

Mt. Carmel

Mt.
Tabor   Ashtaroth

Mt. Hauran

Megiddo   Mt. Moreh
Shunem   Edrei

Mediterranean   Taanach   Beth-shan   Ramoth-gilead

Sea   Ibleam   Mt.
Gilboa

Jabesh-gilead?

Tirzah

Samaria   Succoth?   Mahanaim?
Mt. Ebal
Shechem   Penuel?
Mt.
Gerizim

Joppa   Aphek

Shiloh   I S R A E L

Bethel   Rabbath-ammon
Gilgal?   AMMON
Gezer   Aijalon   Jericho
Jerusalem   Heshbon
Ashdod   Zorah
Mt. Nebo
Gath   Bethlehem   Medeba

Ashkelon

Mareshah

Gaza   Lachish   Hebron   Dibon
Carmel   Dead   Aroer
Raphia   Gerar   Sea
JUDAH

M O A B
Beersheba

PHILISTIA   Kir-hareseth

WILDERNESS

Zered Br.

WILDERNESS

Bozrah
Region
periodically   E D O M
Kadesh-   contested
WILDERNESS   barnea   by Edom
and Judah

1 and 2 Chronicles

The Name

The Chronicles, once a single continuous scroll, written in chronological order, are so named because of their historical accounts of the reigns of the kings of Judah and Israel. There is no structural reason for dividing the books into two parts; the beginning narrative in book two is a continuation of the kingly line which ends book one. In the Hebrew canon the Chronicles books are listed under the category of the Writings (Heb., *kethubim;* Gr., *hagiographa*).

These books have had several names. One of the great commentators writes:

> In Hebrew they are denominated…*dibrey haiyamim;* literally, "The Words of the Days," i.e., the Journals, particularly of the kings of Israel and Judah…The Septuagint (Greek OT) has…"of the things that were left omitted" which seems to suggest that these books were a supplement either to Samuel and the books of Kings, or to the whole Bible…In our English Bible these words are termed "Chronicles from the Greek…A History of Times, Kingdoms, States, Religion, etc. with an Account of the most memorable Persons and Transactions of those Times and Nations."[1]

In the Greek OT the word *paralipomena* is used for Chronicles and means "of the things that were left or omitted."

Authorship and Date

The authorship of the Chronicles books is unknown. Some think that they are the work of different authors. There is internal support for this view in a number of references. The Jews took great care to record their civil, military, and religious transactions, and to make sure that the men who did the recording were indeed "holy men of God" who wrote "as they were moved by the Holy Spirit" (2 Pe. 1:21). The reign of David was recorded by Samuel, Nathan, and Gad (1 Chr. 29:29); the acts of Solomon were written by Nathan, Ahijah, and Iddo (2 Chr. 9:29). Some of the acts of Jehoshaphat were written by "Jehu the son of Hanani" (2 Chr. 20:34); Isaiah recorded the royal records of Uzziah (2 Chr. 26:22), and those of Hezekiah (2 Chr. 32:32). Other references to authors are found in 2 Chr. 28:9 and 33:19. Frequently the prophets were closely associated with the kings and had scribal responsibility. However, one commentator concludes that "the uniformity of the style, the connection of the facts, together with the recapitulation and reflections which are often made, prove that they are the work of one…person."[2] Both Jews and Christians have long had the opinion that Ezra was the man who

Book of 1 Chronicles **4235**
Book of 2 Chronicles **4236**
Kings of Israel **1823**
Divine Inspiration **1774-1776**
Prophets **2065-2070**
Ezra **1199**

Central Avenue in Tadmor. The street is almost a mile long and has 750 columns, each 55 feet high.

finally organized, edited, and compiled the Chronicles as they appear in the Bible. Some suggest he was assisted by Haggai, Zechariah, and Malachi.

Second Chronicles concludes with the reference to Cyrus, the Persian king who conquered the Babylonians and set the Jewish captives free (2 Chr. 36:23). Ezra, Haggai, Zechariah, and Malachi were prominent and active at the time when Cyrus published his emancipation decree included in the book of Ezra, which follows 2 Chronicles. Some of the terms in these postexilic writings which do not appear in prior writings may have been acquired in exile: e.g., "golden cups" in 1 Chr. 28:17 and in Ezr. 1:10, 8:27 and "a drachma" or drams in 1 Chr. 29:7; Ezr. 2:69; Ne. 7:70; "rafts" or floats, 2 Chr. 2:16 and 1 K. 5:9. Calmet considers these words as strong evidence that these books were the work of Ezra, which he penned after the captivity.[3]

Ezra returned to Jerusalem in about 457 B.C., and Nehemiah assumed the position of governor in about 444 B.C. (The temple had been rebuilt in 520-515 B.C.) Then followed a period of extreme Jewish laxity in matters of Mosaic law and indifference to religious obligations. Ezra may have written the Chronicles at this time of low spirituality, possibly during the time he went from Babylon to Jerusalem and after the walls were rebuilt, between 450 and 397 B.C. However, debate continues among scholars, and all specific dates are at best only suppositions.

Haggai
1475
Malachi
4261
Persia
2744

Captivity of
Israel
1825-1827
Nehemiah
2577
Neglect
1085

Background, Purpose, and Content

Ezra felt a pressing need for a religious revival. To stimulate and challenge the people, he may have been prompted to write a historical homily to remind his readers of their rich heritage and the providential oversight which the Lord Jehovah had provided for them throughout the generations. This may explain why the Chronicles books are historical sketches and not complete history. They may have been written specifically to promote revival.

Revivals
312-315

The Chronicles books are neither solely a record of events occurring at that time, nor are they a supplement to previous books. The writer relates in them many things which had already occurred, but he also omits some important events in the history of Israel. However, he includes little that is not recorded in other books. Genealogy predominates until the tenth chapter in 1 Chronicles, which begins abruptly with the unsuccessful battle of Saul and his ensuing death. The writer gives many details in the life of David, but he omits reference to David's adultery with Bathsheba and the consequences. Nothing is recorded about the incest of Amnon and his sister Tamar nor of the rebellion of Absalom.

David
919, 4307f

Absalom
16

The purpose of the books was to give the people a partial genealogy from Adam to about 500 B.C. (1 Chr. 1-9) and to establish family descent (cf. Ezr. 2:59); to review the Kingdom of David (1 Chr. 10-29), and to enumerate the principles of the ideal theocratic state.[4] Second Chronicles 1-9 portrays the glory of Solomon with emphasis on worship in the temple. Second Chronicles 10-36 gives a history of the Southern Kingdom with its "religious reforms and the military victories of Judah's more pious kings."[5]

Sovereignty
of God
3415-3421

Left: The remaining seven columns of the Temple of Bel (known also as Baal).

Below: The Triumphal Arch and the main gate to Tadmor.

2 Chr. 8:4 [Solomon]...built up
Tadmor in the desert... (NIV)

Tadmor
3544, 4439

Palmyra, known as Tadmor in the Bible, was one of the most impressive cities between the Mediterranean Sea and the Euphrates River. Even today Palmyra impresses the traveler as the most spectacular ruins of the ancient world (see picture on p. 176). The city is located on the edge of the Syrian desert, about 200 miles northeast of Damascus. It is referred to, even today, as the "City of Palm Trees," because of its mineral springs, fertile soil, walled-in gardens and date palm groves. It was the only significant supply center for the trade caravans traveling from India to Egypt via the coastal highway.

Solomon
3414,
4307g

Tadmor is referred to in Assyrian texts dating to the 19th century B.C. and the Mari Tablets (1100 B.C.). It is probable that Solomon added considerably to the already existing city. Classical writers tell about the great wealth of the caravans passing through. During the reign of Augustus, the first Roman emperor (27 B.C.-A.D.14), a temple was built to the Babylonian sun-god Marduk (Bel). Of its 390 original towering columns, only seven still stand. References to this god are found in Is 46:1 and Je. 51:44.

Several very powerful Roman emperors succeeded Augustus and today Palmyra's massive and mammoth ruins point their towering columns toward the sky. The modern village stands in the shadow of the ruins of great empires of the past.

2 Chr. 32:30 This same Hezekiah also stopped
the upper watercourse of Gihon, and brought it
straight down to the west side of the city of David.
And Hezekiah prospered in all his works.

Jerusalem
1881-1885

Near Eastern cities, even when walled, were very vulnerable when their water supply was threatened. Jerusalem, built on a high elevation, gathered some rain water in cisterns but was still dependent on water from outside the walled city. In David's day one of the sources of water was the Gihon Spring outside the city in the Kidron Valley. The threatened invasion by the Assyrian king Sennacherib prompted King Hezekiah of Judah to take protective measures. He put a group of stone cutters to work cutting a tunnel through solid rock from the Gihon Spring to the Pool of Siloam (see 2 K. 20:20). He then extended the city wall to embrace the end of the tunnel. In 1880 a boy discovered the Siloam inscriptions in the tunnel which told how the stone cutters, working from each end, met in the center only four feet apart; each side could hear the voices of the men on the opposite side. Other water sources around Jerusalem were blocked to deprive the invading force of needed water (2 Chr. 32:30). When Sennacherib, King of Assyria, had captured most of the area in Palestine he sent an ultimatum to Hezekiah. Sennacherib bragged that he had conquered forty-six walled cities and had taken 200,000 captives.

Hezekiah
1585

Isaiah
1803

When Hezekiah saw Sennacherib's 185,000 troops camped on Mt. Scopus, he summoned Isaiah the prophet and together they put on sackcloth and went to the temple to pray all night (2 Chr. 32:1-22). The next morning 185,000 soldiers had been overcome by the angel of the LORD (see commentary on 2 K. 19:35). Sennacherib made a hasty retreat to Nineveh where his two sons assassinated him (Is. 36-37).

Ezra

The Name

The book of Ezra derives its title from the man who is thought to have been the compiler and author. In Hebrew the name is *Ezra* and appears fourteen times in the book. In the Hebrew canon the historical book of Ezra is listed in the category of the Writings (Heb. *kethubim;* Gr., *hagiographa*).

Authorship and Date

There is evidence to support the conclusion that the books of Ezra and Nehemiah were originally one book. Furthermore, the style, continuity, connective links, and approach suggest that these two books, forming a large, single scroll, also included the Chronicles books. It is significant that the last two verses of 2 Chronicles are almost identical to the first two verses in Ezra.[1] Charles R. Wilson points out that "Ezra and Nehemiah have affinities with I and II Chronicles. The most satisfactory explanation is that these writings are the work of one compiler...Two sections in Ezra are in Aramaic (4:7-6:18; 7:12-26)...If these sections represent the Aramaic language of Babylon that was prevalent during that part of the period of the restoration included in the Old Testament narrative, these writings may be dated between 430 and 397 B.C."[2] The Aramaic content would indicate that the author was familiar with the language of Babylonia, the country in which the Jews were enslaved. "Ezra was a very holy man; so also was he a very learned man, and especially skilled in the knowledge of the Holy Scriptures; and therefore he is said to have been a very ready scribe in the law of God, for which he was so eminent that Artaxerxes takes [sic] particular notice of it [sic] in his commission."[3]

Certainly Ezra was well qualified to write the books of Ezra and Nehemiah as well as the Chronicles books. One may assume the date of the books to be somewhere between 430 and 397 B.C. However, among the scholars the debate on the issue has not been resolved.

Background, Purpose, and Content

In 2 Chronicles and 2 Kings we are given an account of the disaster which befell both the northern kingdom (Israel) and the southern kingdom (Judah) because of their backslidings and rebellions. Israel was carried into captivity by the Assyrians, never to regain its political identity. Judah, a less

Book of
Ezra
4237
Ezra
1199

Book of
Nehemiah
4238

Babylon
329, 4338

Scribes
3165

Backsliding
993

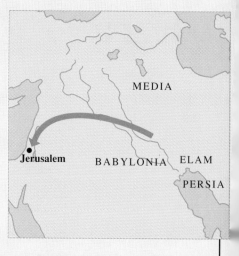

idolatrous country, was taken into Babylonian captivity for seventy years. When Cyrus, the Persian king, conquered Babylonia, the Jews were emancipated and were permitted to return to Jerusalem. It is evident that God's providential hand was at work to provide a deliverer for the Jews in Cyrus. It seems apparent that Cyrus had been greatly influenced by the Jewish religion, so much so that he provided economic and military support for their cause. "Some suggest that Daniel showed Cyrus the prophecies that were thus fulfilled by his conquest (Je. 25:11-12; 29:10) and also the prophecies of Isaiah, who 200 years before, had called Cyrus by name, stating that under him the Jews would return and rebuild Jerusalem (Is. 44:26-28; 45:1,13). No wonder Cyrus had high regard for the Jew's God."[4]

The books of Ezra and Nehemiah tell how Judah was restored—how the workers rebuilt the Jerusalem altar, temple, and walls during the reigns of the Persian kings Cyrus, Darius and Artaxerxes (Ezr. 6:14). A scholar of note observes:

> In the beginning of the year 458, before the Christian era, Ezra obtained of King Artaxerxes and his seven counsellors a very ample commission for his return to Jerusalem, with all of his nation, the Jews, that were willing to accompany him…giving him full authority there to restore and settle the state, and reform the Church of the Jews, and to regulate and govern both according to their laws.[5]

There is no way to measure the extent of the influence the dispersion of the Jews had in the spreading of the Jewish faith. For more on the subject the essay on pp. 285-286.

Captivity of Israel 1825-1827

Cyrus 907

Isaiah 1803

Restoration of Israel 3026

Dispersion of the Jews 1023

3:8 ...Zerubbabel...began the work, appointing Levites twenty years of age and older to supervise the building of the house of the LORD. (NIV)

There were three temples built on the same site in Jerusalem at different times in Biblical history. King Solomon constructed the first one in the fourth year of his reign (2 S. 7; 1 K. 6:1-38; 2 Chr. 3:1-14). When the Babylonians catpured the city in 587 B.C. Solomon's temple was plundered and burned.

Temples
3577-3581

The second temple was built by the Jews who returned from Babylonian exile. The plan of Solomon's temple was followed, though the scale was far less grand. Because of the personal interest Zerubbabel had in building it, and because of his position (he was a Persian governor under Darius), the second temple is often called "Zerubbabel's Temple." Zerubbabel was an ancestor of Jesus Christ (Mt. 1:12-13; Lu. 3:27).

Zerubbabel
3991

The third temple was built over and around the existing second temple by King Herod around 20 B.C. It was destroyed in A.D.70 during the seige of Jerusalem by the Romans.

Herod's Temple
4319

7:6 ...Ezra...was a ready scribe in the law of Moses...

The word "scribe" has a very broad application. From ancient Babylonian and Egyptian times the scribe held a place of prominence. In the Hebrew nation the scribes were neither a religious sect nor a political party but a professional group. "Lawyer," "scribe," and "teacher" are synonymous terms.[6]

Scribes
3165

In a day when education was not generally available to the common people, the scribe served as a public stenographer, secretary, and legal advisor for the people who needed personal, social, and legal services. In the days of walled cities the scribe usually kept a desk near the outside of the gate where he could make his services available to the people. It can be presumed that Boaz transacted business in the presence of a scribe (Ru. 4:1ff.). There are also instances where the scribe was called upon to read and write letters for the illiterate. Scribes can still be seen near the gates of some walled cities.

Gates
1391, 1393

The scribes were the learned men of that day, well versed in social decorum and legal matters. As a royal official or a secretary with cabinet status, such scribes might serve as state record keepers (2 Chr. 26:11; 2 K. 25:19; 2 S. 8:17; 1 K. 4:3).

In the Biblical context the scribe would be thoroughly trained in all aspects

Book of
the Law
525

Tablets of
Stone
3543

Teachers of
the Word
2092

Pharisees
3171
Sadducees
3172

of legal matters dealing with the legal codes of Moses and Biblical laws in general. The Talmud laid down strict rules for handling Biblical manuscripts. The scribes were meticulous in their efforts to make an exact copy of the Biblical text being copied, carefully giving attention to each "jot" and "tittle." Every word was checked and double checked. "It was customary for them to count the words and even the letters in each scroll, noting the middle word and letter, to guard against both omissions and additions of any kind."[7]

Never has the world known more painstaking copyists than the Jewish Sopherim, or scribes. Ezra was both a priest and a scribe who contributed greatly by compiling the holy oracles and who studied and taught the law to Israel (Ezr. 7:6,11). After the exile, when the writing prophets had completed their work, scribal activity in the area of Biblical manuscripts increased greatly. By the second century B.C. the scribes were recognized as members of an honored profession. They were the religious scholars and theologians with the responsibility to maintain the purity of the Scriptures. During the time of Christ the scribes were active in politics and exerted a powerful influence. Because they were the teachers of the Law and because of their ability to make judicial decisions based on scriptural exegesis, they occupied important positions in the Sanhedrin. However, by that time the scribes and the Pharisees had perverted the meaning of Scripture into pure legalism disregarding the spiritual intent. The scribes together with the Pharisees and Sadducees opposed Jesus when he tried to bring the religious community back to the spirit of the Law. The problem is clearly stated by Jesus in Mt. 23:13-35.

For more on the religious leaders of Jesus' day see commentary on Jn. 8:44; Re. 2:9.

Nehemiah

The Name

Nehemyah is the Hebrew word for Nehemiah, which appears seven times in the book. The book of Nehemiah is so named because Nehemiah is its principal figure. Unlike Ezra the priest, Nehemiah was a layman—a zealous builder who became the civil governor with authority from the Persian king to rebuild the walls of Jerusalem.[1] In the Hebrew canon the historical book of Nehemiah is listed under the category of the Writings (Heb., *kethubim;* Gr., *hagiographa*).

Nehemiah
2577

Book of
Nehemiah
4238

Authorship and Date

For discussion of authorship and date see commentary on Ezra. The author is thought to be Ezra and the date of writing 430-397 B.C.

Background, Purpose, and Content

In about 444 B.C. Hanani visited his brother in the palace at Shushan. Hanani brought sad tidings about the reconstruction program in Jerusalem. Through enemy intrigue the rebuilding program had stopped (Ne. 4:7-13). Nehemiah was the king's cupbearer who tasted the food and wine as a precaution against the king's being poisoned.

Shushan
3281, 4434

"Nehemiah was a man of prayer, patriotism, action, courage and perseverance. His first impulse always was to pray (Ne. 1:4; 2:4; 4:9; 6:9-14). He spent 4 months in prayer before he made his request to the king (Ne. 1:1; 2:1)."[2] With a heavy heart Nehemiah communicated his concern for Jerusalem to the king (2:1-3). Sympathetic to the request of Nehemiah, the king sent Nehemiah to Jerusalem with letters of identification and recommendation bearing the king's seal. To insure the execution of the king's intent, "captains of the army and horsemen" were sent to accompany Nehemiah (2:4-9). Upon arrival in Jerusalem, Nehemiah made a secret inspection of the walls and found breaches in them, and many of the gates destroyed. In spite of the hostility from his enemies, the Moabites, Ammorites, Ashdodites, Arabians, and Samaritans, Nehemiah began the rebuilding of the walls. Notwithstanding the opposition, they were finished in 52 days. Jerusalem was again a city enclosed with walls 142 years after its destruction in 581 B.C.[3]

Prayer
2816-2841

Gates
1393

The next phase in the reconstruction period was spiritual: Ezra and his helpers called a special convocation and read God's law to the people. This

Restoration
3025-3026

The city walls, Jerusalem.

Repentance
2706-2712

effort resulted in a great wave of repentance and in turn a great revival and a new commitment to keep God's law (Ne. 9-10). The wall was dedicated and temple service was reorganized (Ne. 9-12).

Marriage
with the
Heathen
Forbidden
2255

After numbering the priests and Levites, Nehemiah condemned the practice of marriage between Jews and heathen wives. He reminded the people of the sin of Solomon and the evil effects these heathen women had upon Solomon and the nation (Ne. 13:26-31).

Nehemiah supervised the rebuilding of the wall, but his most important contribution was spiritual in nature. He made the people realize the intimate relationship they had with God and that his message was a practical implementation of the exhortation of the pre-exilic prophets such as Jeremiah, Ezekiel, Habakkuk, and Zephaniah. In addition, the people began to realize

Stewardship
3451-3460

the faithful stewardship of Nehemiah. As a layman, he had come to Jerusalem to deal with an almost impossible task, as well as with vigorous opposition.

Religious
Reforms
316-320

"With the help of the Lord, he revived a desolate Jewish Community and sought to make it well-pleasing to God through reforms. He toiled diligently and sacrificed personal popularity in order to gain the divine approval 'Well done.' His deep desire was expressed in his prayer: 'Remember me, O my God, for good' (Ne. 13:31)."[4]

Esther

The Name

The name "Esther," from the Hebrew *'ester,* comes from the Jewish girl Esther, who became queen of Persia. In the Hebrew canon, the book of Esther is one of the five scrolls *(Megilloth)* and is listed in the category of the Writings (Heb., *kethubim;* Gr., *hagiographa*).

Authorship and Date

The authorship of the book of Esther is unknown. The terminology in Est. 9:29-32; 10:3 seems to eliminate Mordecai as a contender for authorship. Mordecai is the subject being discussed by the writer, whoever he may be. The writer is obviously a Jew who is familiar with the palace and with Persian customs. He quotes the legal documents written by Mordecai. The Hebrew style of writing closely resembles that in the books of Ezra and Nehemiah, and the Chronicles books. This similarity of style suggests that Ezra may have been the author.[1]

It is estimated that Esther became queen of Persia in 478 B.C. and that she saved the Jews from destruction in 473 B.C. "Esther appears about 40 years after the temple was rebuilt and about 30 years before the wall of Jerusalem was rebuilt."[2]

From this historical background one may conclude that a likely date for the book of Esther is in the mid-fifth century B.C.[3]

Background, Purpose, and Content

The purpose of the book of Esther is to relate the origin of the Feast of Purim.

The liberal view is that this book is a historical novel and that "the story has not been confirmed by any Persian records nor is it referred to by any New Testament writers."[4]

Although the name of God is not mentioned in this book, the author communicates the spiritual element of God's overruling providence. Mordecai's stand against the evil Haman is typical of the three Hebrew children's resistance to the edict of the king and the evil Chaldeans (Da. 3:8-12). The courageous action of Mordecai to expose Haman's plan for revenge because of his refusal to bow down to Haman is a reminder of God's intervention for his people.

"The outstanding religious motive is divine providence. The Jews learned under God's affliction what they would not learn under His forbearance...No Jew could have penned this without the intention of presenting the providence of God in the sparing of His people."[5] If Haman's plot had succeeded there would have been no Jewish race from which Christ the Messiah came.

Another evidence of Jewish influence is the appointing of a fast by Esther (Est. 4:16; 9:31; Ps. 69:10; Is. 58:3; Je. 14:12; Joel 1:14; 2:12). The Feast of Purim is so ingrained into the history and customs of the Jews that the historicity of Esther cannot be doubted.

4:14 ...who knows but that you have come to royal position for such a time as this? (NIV)

The story of Esther in many ways parallels the story of Joseph, who also became prominent in the court of a foreign king and delivered his people from disaster. This verse may be compared to Joseph's statement to his brothers, "...God sent me ahead of you to preserve for you a remnant on earth and to save your lives by a great deliverance" (Ge. 45:7, NIV).

Joseph
1917, 4292

7:4 For I and my people have been sold for destruction and slaughter and annihilation... (NIV)

The history of the Jewish nation is full of turbulence, oppression, and threats to their very existence. From the time of the Pharaoh in Egypt who "knew not Joseph" (Ex. 1:8), the Jewish nation has been misunderstood, mistreated, and blamed for all manner of problems. The miraculous survival of this nation attests to the sovereignty and power of God. Though his name is not mentioned in the book of Esther there can be no doubt of divine superintendence of the events that protected the nation through whom the Savior would come.

Israel—The Jews
1807-1829

Divine Preservation
2913

When the nation of Israel was divided and then sent into exile, the Jews became a minority group in a foreign land. Throughout history they have remained a minority group and, while there have been times when they have experienced peace with the nation in which they have lived, there have been many times that either natural phenomena or external foes have almost destroyed the Jewish race. On the following pages a timeline shows some of the most difficult times in the history of the nation.

In 1947 the United Nations voted to establish both an Arab and a Jewish state in Palestine. On May 14, 1948, the Jews declared their independence and a viable government was established in the land of Palestine, the area to which Abraham was called so many years before.

Canaan
632-634

Prophecy of the future state of Israel is difficult. This is an area in which many prophetic interpretations have developed; only time will reveal the details. There are two aspects of Jewish history which are most unusual: the preservation of the nation and its language. These developments give reason to expect the continued fulfillment of prophecy concerning the Jews.

1. Politically, the nation came to an end with the destruction of Jerusalem under Titus in A.D. 70. The resurrection of Israel, as a nation, in 1947 is unique. There is no instance in history where a nation has revived as a political entity after its dissolution. The passing of 2000 years definitely put Israel into the same category with other "dead" nations.

Restoration of Israel
3026

2. Hebrew, as a national language among dispersed Jews, was considered to be dead by about 250 B.C., except in the immediate area of Jerusalem among those of the temple hierarchy. The scattered Jews had adopted the universal Greek language and/or the local dialects of the area in which they lived; they were out of touch with their "mother tongue." Today Hebrew is the unified language among the Jews who have assembled in Israel from over 70 language areas.

Hebrew Language
1553

What God has in mind for the Jews and Israel remains to be seen, but it is clear in the Scriptures that a Jew, if he is to be saved, must accept Jesus Christ the Messiah as his personal Savior.

Jesus the Only Saviour
4188

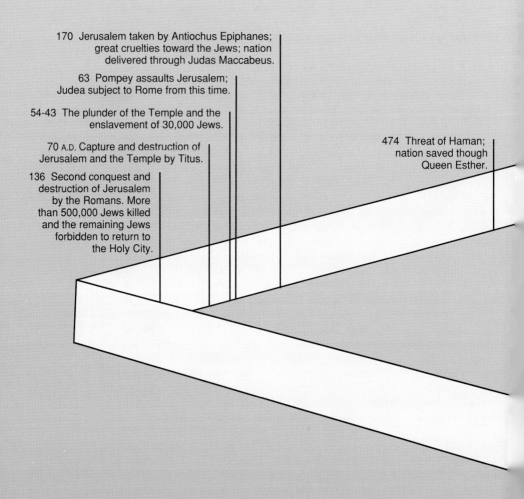

170 Jerusalem taken by Antiochus Epiphanes;
        great cruelties toward the Jews; nation
            delivered through Judas Maccabeus.

63 Pompey assaults Jerusalem;
Judea subject to Rome from this time.

54-43 The plunder of the Temple and the
            enslavement of 30,000 Jews.

70 A.D. Capture and destruction of
Jerusalem and the Temple by Titus.

136 Second conquest and
destruction of Jerusalem
by the Romans. More
than 500,000 Jews killed
and the remaining Jews
forbidden to return to
the Holy City.

474 Threat of Haman;
nation saved though
Queen Esther.

**Difficult Times in the
History of the Jewish Nation**

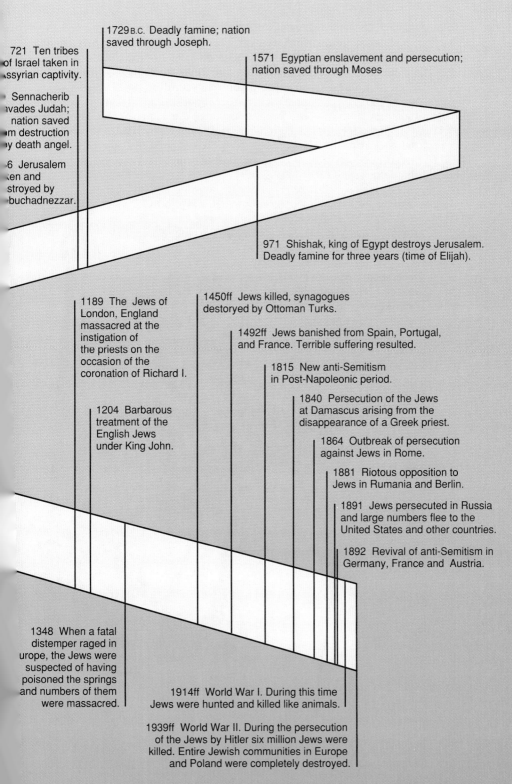

1729 B.C. Deadly famine; nation saved through Joseph.

721 Ten tribes of Israel taken in Assyrian captivity.

Sennacherib invades Judah; nation saved from destruction by death angel.

6 Jerusalem ken and stroyed by buchadnezzar.

1571 Egyptian enslavement and persecution; nation saved through Moses

971 Shishak, king of Egypt destroys Jerusalem. Deadly famine for three years (time of Elijah).

1189 The Jews of London, England massacred at the instigation of the priests on the occasion of the coronation of Richard I.

1450ff Jews killed, synagogues destoryed by Ottoman Turks.

1492ff Jews banished from Spain, Portugal, and France. Terrible suffering resulted.

1204 Barbarous treatment of the English Jews under King John.

1815 New anti-Semitism in Post-Napoleonic period.

1840 Persecution of the Jews at Damascus arising from the disappearance of a Greek priest.

1864 Outbreak of persecution against Jews in Rome.

1881 Riotous opposition to Jews in Rumania and Berlin.

1891 Jews persecuted in Russia and large numbers flee to the United States and other countries.

1892 Revival of anti-Semitism in Germany, France and Austria.

1348 When a fatal distemper raged in Europe, the Jews were suspected of having poisoned the springs and numbers of them were massacred.

1914ff World War I. During this time Jews were hunted and killed like animals.

1939ff World War II. During the persecution of the Jews by Hitler six million Jews were killed. Entire Jewish communities in Europe and Poland were completely destroyed.

9:28 These days should be remembered and observed in every generation by every family, and in every province and in every city. And these days of Purim should never cease to be celebrated by the Jews, nor should the memory of them die out among their descendants. (NIV)

Feast of
Purim
1261
Deliverance
968-971

The Feast of Purim is held on the fourteenth and fifteenth of the twelfth month, Adar or March. Mordecai instituted it to commemorate the deliverance of the Jews of Persia from national slaughter by Haman as recorded in the book of Esther. The celebration is also referred to as the Feast of Lots because Haman had cast lots to ascertain on which day he would carry out the murderous decree.

This festival is celebrated with "feasting and joy, and of sending portions [of food] one to another, and gifts to the poor" (Est. 9:20-22). Its popularity with the Jews is attested to by Josephus (Ant. XI.6.13). Services in the synagogue on Purim include the reading of the book of Esther.

Other annual Hebrew feasts commemorate the deliverance of the nation of Israel from oppressors. The Feast of the Passover celebrates the deliverance of the Israelites from Egypt. The Feast of Hanukkah is a reminder of the revolt against the Syrians led by Judas Maccabeus. For more on annual Hebrew feasts see the chart on pp. 126-127.

Jewish
Feasts
1256-1261

Drawing from a carving of a Persian spearman.

Job

The Name

The name Job comes from the Hebrew *'iyobh,* meaning "object of enmity" or "he who turns." The book of Job derives its name from its central character Job, whose name appears 55 times in the book. Because of its antiquity the etymology of the name defies literary analysis. Some scholars note that an early form of Job in ancient literature is *Ayyab* meaning "where is father" or "no father." The translation suggests that Job may have been an orphan or perhaps an illegitimate child.[1] In the Hebrew canon the poetical book of Job is listed in the category of the Writings (Heb., *kethubim;* Gr., *hagiographa*).

Authorship and Date

The book of Job has been the center of literary debate from earliest times. Scholars have presented various theories: some say Job is a fictional character; others say the book of Job is about a real person, while some deny that Job existed. However, the evidence is strong that the work is historical and factual.

It is impossible to determine an author or a date for the book of Job because of its antiquity, but the identity of such a character as Job is established in the Old Testament and in nonbiblical sources. The book is first noted in Hebrew literature in the Old Testament. The name of Job is mentioned in extra-Biblical literature such as the tell-el-Amarna tablets from Egypt, in the clay tablets found at Mari on the Middle Euphrates, and in the Ugaritic texts from Ras Shamra on the Mediterranean coast of Syria. These places are widely separated, but they were all stopping places for the Hebrew people. Job's name appears in Ezekiel with the names of two other righteous men—Noah and Daniel (Eze. 14:14,20). A Job is also mentioned in the genealogical table of the tribe entering Egypt with Jacob, where Job is catalogued with the sons of Issachar (Ge. 46:13). His historicity is confirmed by James who commends Job's perseverance (Ja. 5:11).

Jewish tradition says that Job was a descendent of Abraham, Isaac, and Jacob. The fact that the book of Job has a place in the OT canon further

---

Book of
Job
4240
Job
1899
Fatherless
3829-3830

Law
Perfect
436

Noah
2597
Daniel
914
Issachar
1830

A view of the Sinai mountains, where God appeared to Moses. Job states that "...God comes in awesome majesty." (Jb. 37:22, NIV)

confirms that Job has a place in history. Because of the divine inspiration accorded canonized books, the integrity and authenticity of Job is further confirmed.

Deserts
978-979

The writer of Job was obviously well acquainted with the desert east of the Jordan River as well as with the cultural background of Egypt. A well-known scholar says of Job: "There are several indications that he [Job] lived in the patriarchal age: the longevity of Job (he apparently lived two centuries), the flourishing of true religion, supported by special divine revelation outside the community of Abraham's covenant, and certain early, social and ethnic features such as the still nomadic status of the Chaldeans and the patriarchal form of worship and sacrifice."[2]

Patriarchs
2696

With respect to authorship a noted writer states that "the case for a Hebrew author rests largely on references to civil and moral prescriptions (Jb. 22:6; 24:9; cf. Ex. 22:26; 25:2; cf. De. 19:14), familiarity with a few OT writings and mention of the name of the God of Israel. Yahweh is in the prologue and epilogue and in the superscriptions of God's speeches and Job's answers."[3]

Israel
1807-1829

Authorship of the book of Job has always been debated. Learned men have suggested the names of Elihu, Job's friend, Solomon, Isaiah, Ezra, and others, but the evidence available points to Moses as the possible author. According to Hebrew tradition, the book of Job was compiled/edited/written

Moses
2420

by Moses in Midian exile. It is thought that Moses had direct contact with Job, or with those who knew Job intimately and who possessed authoritative information, oral or written, on the material in the book of Job.[4]

Adam Clarke gives the consensus of the great scholars in his day with reference to authorship. The conclusions still remain valid:

That Moses was the author of Job has been the opinion of most learned men…the writer of this poem must, in his style, have been equally master of the simple and the sublime: that he must have been minutely and elaborately acquainted with astronomy, natural history and the general science of his age; that he must have been a Hebrew by birth and…that he must have flourished and composed the work before the exodus…every one of these features is consummated in Moses and in Moses alone…Instructed in the learning of Egypt, it appears…that he composed it during some part of his forty years residence with the hospitable Jethro, in that district of Idumea which was named Midian…In addition to these external proofs of identity…a little attention will disclose to us an internal proof of peculiar force, in the close and striking similarity of diction and idiom which exists between the book of Job and those pieces of poetry which Moses is usually admitted to have composed…the order of creation, as detailed in the first chapter of Genesis is precisely similar to that described in Job XXXVIII:1-20, the general arrangement that occupied the first day;—the formation of the clouds, which employed the second;—the separation of the sea, which took up a part of the third;—and the establishment of the luminaries in the skies which characterized the fourth…the combined simplicity and sublimity of Ge. 1:3 "and God said, Be light! and light was," has been felt and praised by the critics of every age…and has by all of them been regarded as a characteristic feature of the Mosaic style.[5]

Background, Purpose, and Content

The Bible states that Job lived in the land of Uz (border between Palestine and Arabia) and that he was a very wealthy and influential sheik or desert rancher. Scripture relates that he was "perfect and upright, and one that feared God, and eschewed evil" (Jb. 1:1). Disasters struck in quick succession. "His vast herds of camels were stolen, and their attending servants killed, by a band of Chaldean robbers. At the same time, his herds of oxen were stolen and their attending servants killed by a band of Sabean robbers...About the same time his 7,000 sheep and their attending servants were killed by a thunderstorm, and...his family of ten children were all killed by a cyclone...A little later Job himself was smitten with the most hideous and painful disease known to the ancient world."[6] This evidence supports the assumption that Job was a historical figure and that the message in the book has a legitimate claim to a place in historical literature.

The book of Job is the first in a group of four books known in the OT canon as wisdom literature and is in dialogue form with a narrative prologue and an epilogue in prose. Its poetical form employs parallelisms, rhythmic expressions, and synonymous or antithetical couplets. The other wisdom books are Psalms, Proverbs, Ecclesiastes, and Song of Solomon; they are all classified as poetical books. Outstanding literary men have paid high tribute to the book of Job as being the greatest of all literary compositions. Victor Hugo said, "The book of Job is the greatest masterpiece of the human mind." Thomas Carlyle referred to Job as "one of the greatest things ever written." Philip Schaff said, "It rises like a pyramid in the history of literature."[7]

The book of Job presents both philosophical and theological problems. It deals with the age-old question: "Why do the righteous suffer?" "Is God unjust because the righteous Job is punished so severely—nigh unto death?"

Midian	2339
Moses	4307a
Egypt	1100
Genesis	4223
Day	920
Uz	3742
Uprightness	3737
Blessings—Afflictions	480-499
Wisdom–Folly	3838-3855
Suffering	3474-3495

A misinterpretation of the Mosaic law assumed that a good man would always be rewarded without experiencing punishment but the wicked man would always be punished with no material rewards. The true Biblical view, however, is that "it rains on the just and the unjust" (Mt. 5:45). The righteous man can suffer from the elements as much as the wicked man. A hailstorm can wipe out the crop of a good man as well as that of a bad man. The facts are that disease will strike in all families regardless of their moral state.

Further insight results from the account of the conversation between God and Satan. (The name "Satan" is used in both the OT and NT while "Devil" is used only in the NT. However, the two terms can be used interchangeably.) The book of Job illustrates Satan's attack on man (Job 1:6-9,12; 2:1-7). He is no mythical figure but personal and real with power to inflict harm upon human beings. Peter gives a dramatic description of Satan in these words: "your adversary the devil, as a roaring lion, walketh about, seeking whom he may devour" (1 Pe. 5:8). Satan's purpose and design is to do evil continually. He is the enemy of the soul of man, opposing goodness of every kind. He is the chief opponent of God and man and is determined to undo the work of God and persuade men to sin (Lu. 22:3). One writer says,

> When permission is granted him [Satan] to carry out his evil plots, it is only that he may become an instrument in furthering the divine plan. In Job's case, the vain efforts of Satan to induce the patriarch to sin resulted in disciplining his character and maturing his faith in God. In the fully revealed doctrine of Satan, which is seen in the NT, he is the god of this world who has access to the hearts of men, deceives them, and receives their willing or unwilling obedience (Lu. 22:3; Ac. 5:3; 26:18; 2 Co. 4:4, 2 Th. 2:9; Re. 12:9).[8]

An overview of the book indicates that the story revolves around Job and three dogmatists, Eliphaz, Bildad, and Zophar, who assume that Job's difficulty was attributable to secret sins. It is the contention of Eliphaz that no innocent man will be chastised through affliction and that God destroys only the wicked. The speeches of Bildad and Zophar support this thesis (Jb. 8:3-7; 18:5-21; 22:3-11). Job insisted that he was not a wicked man (Jb. 10:7), that God is no respecter of persons and that he sends affliction on the righteous as well as upon the wicked (Jb. 9:22); in moments of despair and intense pain Job regretted his birth (Jb. 10:18-22). Zophar countered with the assertion that Job's punishment should be more severe (Jb. 11:6) where-upon Job became sarcastic and challenged the assumptions of his comforters (Jb. 12:13).

As the dialogue proceeded each became more caustic than the other (Jb. 13:3-4). Job rebuked his friends for being unmerciful and insisted on his innocence (Jb. 16:17). Bildad reproved Job for his presumption and impa-tience (Jb. 18). In his agony Job expressed his faith in the resurrection (Jb. 19). Zophar and Eliphaz continued their attack on Job (Jb. 20,22). Job agreed that in the end the wicked suffer (Jb. 21) but insisted upon his own innocence (23-24). Bildad made his last speech (Jb. 25). Job concluded his rebuttal and grew more confident of his innocence (Jb. 26-31).

In Jb. 32 the whole dramatic scene changed. The three comforters ceased to reprove Job; Elihu, a fourth member of the team, entered the controversy and rebuked the original three comforters for their inability to subdue Job. Elihu took the position that suffering is intended by God to be corrective rather than punitive.

God, in a whirlwind, spoke against ignorance, impatience, helplessness, and the infinitesimal smallness of man as compared to God and asked question after question, which "awed" Job into silence and drove him to his knees (Jb. 38-41). In the last chapter, the Lord reprimanded the three comforters for the wrong they had done to Job. God commanded them to give a special burnt offering of seven bullocks and seven rams and informed them that Job would pray for them (Jb. 42:8).

Job's fortunes changed when he "prayed for his friends" (Jb. 42:10). Perhaps this indicates that Job should have prayed for his friends in the beginning instead of arguing with them. The concluding verses give an account of the great prosperity Job enjoyed after his deliverance. The Scripture states that "the LORD gave Job twice as much as he had before" (Jb. 42:10b).

Whirlwind
2330-2331

Submission
3233-3234

Prayer
2816-2841

Prosperity
2900

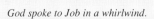
God spoke to Job in a whirlwind.

Parallels Between Early Genesis and the Book of Job

(References from NIV unless specified)

The Creation of the Heavens	And God said, "Let there be an expanse…" God called the expanse "sky…" (Ge. 1:6-8)	He alone stretches out the heavens… (Jb. 9:8)
The Creation of Animals	And God said, "Let the land produce living creatures…" (Ge. 1:24)	In his hand is the life of every creature… (Jb. 12:10)
The Creation of Man	The LORD God…breathed into his nostrils the breath of life, and the man became a living being. (Ge. 2:7)	In his hand is the breath of all mankind. (Jb. 12:10)
Man Made from Dust	The LORD God formed the man from the dust of the ground… (Ge. 2:7)	Remember that you molded me like clay. Will you now turn me to dust again? (Jb. 10:9)
The Sin of Adam	And the LORD God called unto Adam…Where art thou? And he said, …I was afraid…and I hid myself. (Ge. 3:9-10, KJV)	If I covered my transgressions as Adam, by hiding mine iniquity… (Jb. 31:33, KJV)
The Great Flood	God saw how corrupt the earth had become…so God said to Noah…"I am going to bring floodwaters on the earth to destroy all life under the heavens…" (Ge. 6:12-17)	Will you keep to the old path that evil men have trod? They were carried off before their time, their foundations washed away by a flood. (Jb. 22:15-16)
The Promise of No More Universal Floods	"Never again will all life be cut off by the waters of a flood…" (Ge. 9:11)	"Who shut up the sea behind doors…when I said, 'This far you may come and no farther; here is where your proud waves halt.'" (Jb. 38:8-11)
The Dispersion of Nations	…the LORD scattered them over the face of the whole earth… (Ge. 11:9)	…he enlarges nations, and disperses them. (Jb. 12:23)

Psalms

The Name

The Hebrew title is *Sepher Tehillim,* meaning "book of praises." In the Greek OT (LXX) it is rendered "Psalmoi" and in the English Bible it is translated "Psalms"; the title means "Songs set to Music." In the Hebrew canon the poetical book of Psalms is listed in the category of the Writings (Heb., *kethubim;* Gr., *hagiographa*).

Book of Psalms **4241** Songs **2475-2477**

Authorship and Date

Tradition says that David was the principal author of the Psalms; seventy-three are ascribed to him. Asaph, a Levite skilled in playing the cymbal and a leader in David's choir, was the author of thirteen (50, 72-83); eleven are ascribed to Korah, probably a family of musicians (42, 44-49, 84, 85, 87, 88). Solomon is credited with two (22, 127), Moses with one (90), Ethan with one (89), and forty-nine are anonymous.

Asaph **267**

The Targum has assigned two psalms of the anonymous group to Adam (92, 139), one to Melchizedek (110), and one to Abraham (89). New Testament writers assumed that at least some of the psalms were written by David (Lu. 20:42; Ac. 1:16). The Hebrew prepositions, "of," "to," and "for" make identification difficult. A psalm may have been dedicated "to David" or it may have been a psalm "for David"; on the other hand, it may have been a psalm "of David."

Solomon **3414**

Melchi- zedek **2284**

No doubt David was the author of some of the anonymous psalms or those which have uncertain authorship. It seems quite probable that David was the author of over one-half of these psalms, making him the major contributor.

Background, Purpose, and Content

The book of Psalms is the first in the category of writings called the poetical books. The language in some of the psalms is figurative, and Hebrew poetry and hyperbole are used to express ideas (Ps. 58:10). The primary interpretation of the psalms is usually found within their historical context, but because of their nature the psalms are applicable to any age. As one reads the psalms, he becomes aware that they are speaking to him. They are devotional in nature and are designed to satisfy the need of the human heart.

"Word" Endures **415** "Word" in Heart **418**

The book of Psalms has five sub-divisions: Book One, chs. 1-41; Book Two, chs. 42-72; Book Three, chs. 73-89; Book Four, chs. 90-106, and Book Five, chs. 107-150. Each book closes with a doxology (Ps. 41:13; 72:18-19; 89:52; 106:48; 150:6). From ancient times the fivefold division has been indicated in both the Hebrew and Greek (LXX) and is thought to be comparable to the fivefold division of the Pentateuch.

The headings of the psalms give the key to their musical rendition with the title being determined by the superscription; e.g., "To the chief Musician upon Gittith" (Ps. 8, 81, 84). "To the chief Musician on Neginoth" indicated that the psalm was to be sung with stringed instruments (Ps. 4, 6, 54, 55, 67, 76). "To the chief Musician upon Nehiloth" signified that wind instruments were to be used (Ps. 5), and "A song upon Alamoth" designated a musical composition to be sung by some young women (Ps. 46). The refrain of the choral response is included in the second part of each verse in Psalm 136. Such other words as "Maschil" (Ps. 32) and "Michtam" (Ps. 16; 56-60) furnish further musical direction. Some psalms were to be sung antiphonally,

Praise to God
1451-1452

Musical Instruments
2454-2469

A view of Jerusalem. "Glorious things are spoken of thee, O city of God." (Ps. 87:3)

or responsively (Ps. 15, 24). The familiar words "Hallelujah" and "Amen" were congregational responses.

There are eight main categories of psalms:

Singing
2472-2473

1. The Psalms of Praise
2. The Psalms of Degrees (120-134)
3. The Nature Psalms (19, 29, 50, 65, 104)
4. The Historic or National Psalms (14, 44, 46, 53, 66, 68, 74, 76, 79, 80, 83, 85, 87, 108, 122, 124-126, 129)
5. The Social Psalms (8, 78, 104, 139, 146)
6. The Imprecatory Psalms (52, 58, 59, 69, 109, 137)
7. The Penitential Psalms (6, 32, 51, 102, 130, 143)
8. The Messianic or Royal Psalms

The Importance of the Psalms

Historical
Bridge
4219a
Songs
2476-2477

The book of Psalms provides us with a bridge over which saints pass from the OT church period into the New (see commentary on p. 315). This book was the hymn book of the church during the Old Covenant period and served almost exclusively as the basic hymnbook of the NT church for over fifteen hundred years. The Psalms provide a union of spirit in the church through the ages. Believers find here a vehicle of expression for the soul as it endeavors to praise God for salvation. Every redemptive emotion finds an avenue of expression in the Psalm book and the Christian finds that he has a common emotional experience with his brethren of the OT. Believers can meditate upon this book and feel the same heartfelt inspiration that they receive from reading the Gospels.

Good
Doctrine
1029

Truly, the Psalms have been an exceedingly important instrument for the expression and spread of doctrine and devotion, both in the OT and the NT church periods. Expressions of praise and thanksgiving to God for the joy of salvation are found on every page, with a grand culmination in a "hallelujah chorus."

Christ
Jesus
677-700

For the Christological significance of the book, see the essay, "Christ in the Psalms," pp. 209-210.

8:3-4 When I consider thy heavens…what is man, that thou art mindful of him? and the son of man, that thou visitest him?

Psalm 8 can be categorized as a "Social Psalm" (along with Ps. 78, 104, 139 and 146). Although the purpose of the book of Psalms is not to be a sociological study, the book does contain many insights into the origin and activities of the human race. Man is a special creation of God (100:3). Adam was to rule over God's creation (8:5-6).

In Psalm 8 the poet looks up to the heavens and sees the glory of God and observes the fingers of God at work. The observer looks down to the fields and sees the result of the works of God in the animal world. The sheep and the oxen and the beasts of the field are all God's creation and subjects for praise by the psalmist.

Man, as an individual, received new life from God (Ps. 139:13); the eternal destiny of man has been recorded in the Bible (Ps. 139:16). Man has a physical body and yet he is a spiritual being made in the image of God (Ps. 8:5; 103:14) and has an immortal soul (Ps. 31:5). The security of the redeemed soul is described in Psalm 4:8.[1]

Divine Image **2239**

Glory of God **1426**

The Redeemed **2976**

9:11 Sing praises to the LORD…

Since early times, people have engaged in music by which the soul expresses its emotion and may reach to God in prayer. The mood in the psalms ranges from the deepest sorrow and grief to the highest expression of joy (1 Pe. 1:8).

The Bible is replete with songs of praise and thanksgiving to Jehovah. Both Judaism and Christianity engage in singing. Finally, in heaven the redeemed will continue to sing God's praises (Re. 5:9-14).

Music and ritual played a prominent part in the festive occasions of Israel. Upon the completion of Solomon's temple and the placing of the ark of the covenant in the Holy of Holies, the chronicler described the event: "…the priests that were present were sanctified [set aside and cleansed for holy service]…The Levites which [sic] were the singers…being arrayed in white linen, having cymbals and psalteries and harps, stood at the east end of the altar, and with them an hundred and twenty priests sounding with trumpets. It came even to pass, as the trumpeters and singers were as one, to make one sound to be heard in praising and thanking the LORD…" (2 Chr. 5:11-13). The 150 psalms contain expressions of joy and praise. Moses and Miriam composed and sang a psalm of thanksgiving on the banks of the Red Sea after being delivered from the host of Pharaoh (Ex. 15), a song which may be typical of those sung on their journey to the promised land (Nu. 21:17). The victory of Deborah and Barak over

Joy– Sorrow **1926-1952**

Singing **2472-2473**

Solomon's Temple **3577**

Praise God **1451-1452**

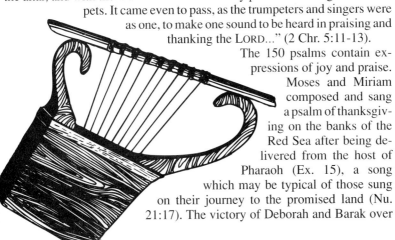

David's harp.

Sisera resulted in a song of praise (Jud. 5:1ff.); Hezekiah's singers put the words of David to music (2 Chr. 29:28-30). When the inaugural convocation was held for King Solomon, the Scripture states that "four thousand praised the LORD with the instruments which [David] made...to praise therewith" (1 Chr. 23:5).

The use of psalms as hymnody was carried over into the NT church (Mk. 14:26; 1 Co. 14:26). Paul and Silas even sang in prison (Ac. 16:25).

Jesus was familiar with the Psalms and used them frequently. He and the disciples sang at the Last Supper (Mt. 26:30) and on the cross Jesus used phrases of the Psalms in his dying agony (Ps. 22:1; 31:5; cf. Mt. 27:46; Lu. 23:46); thus he affirmed the Christological content of the Psalms (Lu. 24:44).[2] (See the essay, "Christ in the Psalms," pp. 209-210.)

19:1 The heavens declare the glory of God; and the firmament sheweth his handiwork.

The psalmist was able to see God reflected in the creation all around him—the things the Creator made for man to enjoy. In Psalm 19 the sweet singer of Israel sees God's redemptive revelation portrayed in the heavens. He sees in the sky a revelatory language which can be understood by persons around the world. He points out that there is no language in the world in which this revelation of the sky would not be understood. He calls the heavens the "tabernacle for the sun." All is governed by "the law of the LORD" and leads to "converting the soul." The fear of the Lord is to be the natural consequence of this revelation. He concludes with a benediction which many Christians have known from their youth: "Let the words of my mouth, and the meditation of my heart, be acceptable in thy sight, O LORD, my strength, and my redeemer (v. 14)."

23:1 The LORD is my shepherd...

God's special relationships to his people are expressed in the many divine names and titles recorded in the OT. The LORD (Jehovah) is the predominant divine name used in the book of Psalms. An instructive study can be made of the combination of the name Jehovah or LORD with a characteristic of God (see chart at Ex. 3:14).

LORD-rohi means "The LORD is my shepherd" and this example in Ps. 23 is the most outstanding one in Scripture. This title probably has brought more comfort to people's hearts than any other. It is in the name of the LORD-

The shepherd boy.

rohi that this relationship finds its highest and tenderest expression, for the LORD is the Shepherd of his people. No other name of the LORD has the tender intimate touch of this one name.

Names of God **3633**

Some scholars recognize seven titles of the LORD, in principle, in the twenty-third Psalm. These titles are outlined in the chart below.

Jehovah Names **1868-1872**

LORD-jireh	"LORD our provider"	v. 5
LORD-rophe	"LORD our healer"	v. 5
LORD-m'kaddesh	"LORD our sanctifier"	v. 6
LORD-shalom	"LORD our peace"	v. 6
LORD-tsidkenu	"LORD our righteousness"	v. 3
LORD-rohi	"LORD our shepherd"	v. 1
LORD-shamma	"the LORD is there"	v. 4

29:2 Give unto the LORD the glory due unto his name; worship the LORD in the beauty of holiness.

In Psalm 29 the psalmist describes in poetical ecstasy the glory and beauty of the environment around him. He is awed and inspired by the waters and thunder, the cedars of Lebanon, the flames of fire, the wilderness, and the flood. In all of this natural phenomenon the psalmist sees God in the beauty of his holiness.

Beauties of Nature **380**

44:1 We have heard with our ears, O God; our fathers have told us what you did in their days, in days long ago. (NIV)

Psalm 44 is an example of a historic, or national psalm. The God of Israel is preeminent in both the national and religious affairs of Israel. It is through the nation of Israel that Christ the Messiah appeared on earth. In the historical psalms the writer reviews God's providence in the lives of Abraham, Isaac, and Jacob. Jerusalem, the holy city of Zion, is mentioned many times.

God's Holiness **1597**

Preeminence of Christ **716** Divine Providence **2905-2913** Exodus **4224**

Some of the psalms in this group deal with the events in the lives of the kings of Israel (Ps. 18, 21, 22, 89, 101, 110, 144). However, some psalms, reflecting critical national situations, have a tone of woe and despair (Ps. 44, 74, 79, 80, 137).[3]

Psalm 80:8 deals with the exodus from Egypt; Psalms 78 and 105 speak of the ten plagues; the crossing of the Red Sea is mentioned in Psalm 66, 74, 78; God leading Israel through the wilderness is the subject of Psalm 78; the promised land comes into focus in Psalm 105. The psalmist acknowledges that when Israel disobeyed God, they suffered the consequences, as at Shiloh (Ps. 78:10,37,60). Every aspect of life is touched in these psalms, including the times of peace and prosperity as well as times of war, stress, famine, and disaster.[4]

Obedience– Disobedience **2614-2621**

51:3 For I acknowledge my transgressions: and my sin is ever before me.

Sin **3338-3359**

Even though the psalmist David succumbed to the temptation of the flesh, he was sensitive to sin and its serious consequences. A noted scholar offers this definition of sin and its implications:

Deliverance Sought **971**

> "Transgression" denotes an overt act of stubborn revolt and wilful defiance of a known law. "Iniquity" is an unnatural, distorted state due to the presence of a life-sapping, deadening, evil force which eventually will destroy all ethical qualities, leaving one in a state of helplessness. "Sin" indicates missing the mark, falling short of the goal...these companion words are used in the appeal for pardon. "Blot out" means to erase or expunge, as words from a manuscript or data from a careful record, the misdeeds of the past. "Purge" and "wash" are strong terms used to describe the completeness of the purification needed. "Cleanse me" is a familiar phrase carried over from the ritual of the priests in the purification of lepers, and here given a wider application. The power of God alone could bring such deliverance.[5]

The Penitential Psalms (6, 32, 51, 102, 130, 143) give expressions of regret or remorse for committed sin. The instances in the Psalms of human wrong-doing, repentance, and forgiveness are many. Man's iniquity is presented as original and Adamic which is transmitted from generation to generation (Ps. 51:3; 58:3).[6]

David **4296, 4307f**

Sin's Penalty **3352-3356**

The outstanding example of sin committed and forgiven by God is that of David's adultery with Bathsheba, the wife of Uriah the Hittite, a soldier in Israel's army (2 S. 12ff). After David committed this sin, the prophet Nathan called upon the king and related that a wealthy citizen in his realm had taken from a poor man his only pet lamb and had served it to his guests. David was angered and pronounced the penalty of death upon the guilty offender (2 S. 12:5). By the words, "Thou art the man," David was made to realize that he was the sinner, that he had taken the wife of another man (2 S. 12:6-11) and committed adultery (2 S. 12:9-10). Nathan told David that for this sin the Lord would exact punishment upon him and the sword would never depart from his house (2 S. 12:9-11).

Confession of Sin **816-818**

Restoration **3025**

Psalm 51 records David's confession of his sin and his plea for the mercy of God. In vv. 1-4 David admits his transgression, acknowledges his sinful nature and asks God to cleanse him thoroughly. In v. 10 he pleads for a "clean heart" and "a right spirit." Psalm 32 is an expression of the "blessedness" David experienced after his sins were forgiven and he was restored to God's favor. David is quite outspoken in his testimony. In v. 1 he says, "Blessed is he whose transgression is forgiven, whose sin is covered." In v. 2 he indicates his justified state in these words, "Blessed is the man unto whom the LORD imputeth not iniquity, and in whose spirit there is no guile." This declaration reflects the joy explicitly stated in the NT (1 Pe. 1:8).

104:1 Bless the LORD, O my soul. O LORD my God, thou art very great; thou art clothed with honour and majesty.

Glory of God **1426**

The majesty and glory of God the Creator is the theme in Psalms 50, 65, and 104. Because the glories of the Lord cannot easily be described or expressed in ordinary speech, the psalmist uses much figurative language.

109:8 May his days be few; may another take his place of leadership. (NIV)

David's enemy no doubt held an official position and was probably seeking to bring about David's death. In the New Testament Peter quoted this verse in reference to Judas (Ac. 1:20).

Psalm 109 can be classified as an "Imprecatory Psalm." Others in the category include Ps. 52, 58, 59, 69, 137. The Imprecatory Psalms are the most difficult to interpret because in them man invokes the wrath of God upon his enemies. Perhaps these statements acknowledge the evil which rises up in man's heart at times. These prayers do not reflect the pronouncement of God's attitude but are prayers by men for vengeance upon evildoers. Some feel this is in direct contradiction to the teachings of Jesus that one should love his enemies. One writer explains these psalms thus:

> In the Old Testament God's purpose was to maintain a nation and to pave the way for the Coming of Christ. He was working with human nature as it was, and did not necessarily endorse everything that even His most devoted servants did or said. Some of these Psalms are Battle Hymns, expressing intense patriotism...life and death struggles with powerful enemies to help the nation to survive. With the Coming of Christ, God's Revelation of the meaning of human life, and its standards of conduct were completed; and God shifted the direct emphasis of His work from the maintenance of a nation to the transformation of individuals into the kind of persons He wants us to be.[7]

Christians frequently pray for the defeat of the enemy in wartime, as if the enemy were a spiritual one, the personification of Satan and his forces of darkness. In a measure, the imprecations against the enemy are actually directed against the principle of evil and not so much against the person. When righteous people are persecuted or oppressed, there is justification for the righteous to make an appeal to God for deliverance and victory.

God has an abhorrence of sin, the cause of all trouble in the world. Liberals have criticized the OT for the national destruction commanded by God on nations, as found in the OT, but an evil society can finally forfeit its right to survive, as man can forfeit his right to live in a decent, law-abiding society when he commits murder (Ge. 9:6). It is acknowledged that there is a difference between righteous indignation and defensive action for one's own personal interest. The Imprecatory Psalms seem to have been expressed in terms of concern for causes of righteousness and not for personal vindication. J. Barton Payne points out that: "three things must be observed positively: that the Psalms and other Biblical imprecations are not hasty, emotional expressions, but carefully written literature; they are prayers and songs...written in good conscience; and that they are not, in the last resort, human products, but are rather inspired works of the Holy Spirit."[8]

111:1 Praise ye the LORD. I will praise the LORD with my whole heart, in the assembly of the upright, and in the congregation.

The Hebrew word *hallelujah* is a compound word meaning "praise Jehovah" or "praise the LORD" (*hallel* means "praise" and *JAH* means "Jehovah"). The Greek form is *alleluia*. Because of alphabetical differences between Hebrew and Greek, these words are usually transliterated in the various languages.

Impre-
cations
1744
Enemies
3395
Good for
Evil
1437

Evil Activity
31-32
Prayer
2816-2841

Social Life
3393-3410

Written with
a Purpose
424

Praise God
1451-1452

The expression "hallelujah" in any country would be understood by the religious community to mean "praise the Lord," and its use is indeed universal. The psalms beginning with "hallelujah" or with "praise the Lord" include Psalms 106, 111-113, 117, 135, 146-150; those ending in praise are Psalms 104-106, 113, 115-117, 135, 146-150. The *hallel* psalms were sung at family devotions during the Feasts of the Tabernacles, Pentecost, and Dedication.

Jewish
Feasts
1256-1261

119:1 Blessed are they whose ways are blameless, who walk according to the law of the LORD. (NIV)

Psalm 119 is sometimes called an acrostic or alphabetic psalm because there are in it twenty-two divisions, each with eight verses; each section begins with one of the twenty-two Hebrew consonants; i.e., vv. 1-8 use the Hebrew character *aleph*. Each of the eight verses in this section begins with an *aleph*. Verses 9-16 employ the second consonant in the Hebrew alphabet—*beth*—and each of the eight verses in this section begins with a *beth*. This formula continues throughout the psalm to vv. 169-176 (the twenty-second section) which have *tau* as their superscription, and each of the eight verses begins with a *tau*. Almost all of the 176 verses in the psalm make reference to the Word of God in some form: "testimonies," "thy word," "percepts," "statutes," "law," "judgments," and "commandments" are a few of the terms used.

Word of
God
414-445

120:1 In my distress I cried unto the LORD, and he heard me.

This psalm begins a section of psalms (Ps. 120-134) that have a degree of thematic unity. They are called the "Psalms of Degrees" and are said to be postexilic. Probably they were used as a source of inspiration in the days of Nehemiah by the laborers while they were rebuilding the walls of Jerusalem. The laborers kept a sword in one hand and a trowel in the other (Ne. 4:17-18). The title, "A Song of Ascents," may well signify "Songs of going up, upon the walls," because the songs were short and could easily be sung from memory by the workmen and the guards.[9]

Jews'
Return
1827
Jerusalem
1881-1885

Christ in the Psalms

In addition to praise and thanksgiving there is also present in the Psalms a prophetic spirit which recognizes the reality of Christ. Jesus certainly affirms the fact that the Psalms have Christological

content when he says: "all things must be fulfilled, which were written in the law of Moses, and in the prophets, and in the Psalms, concerning me" (Lu. 24:44). In many of the Psalms one discovers elements of religious life and experience that are thoroughly Christian (Ps. 146-150). While Jesus hung on the cross his mind turned to Ps. 22:1; 31:5; 69:21. In this book a composite picture of the suffering Savior is clearly revealed. In it we read that he was patterned after the order of Melchizedek (Ps. 110:4); that he would be betrayed by a friend (Ps. 41:9); that another person would be elected to Judas' office (Ps. 109:7-8); that false witnesses would accuse him (Ps. 27:12); that he would be hated without a cause (Ps.69:4); that his hands and feet would be pierced (Ps. 22:6-8); that he would be given gall and vinegar (Ps. 69:21); that his prophetic words would be repeated in mockery (Ps. 22:8); that he would pray for his enemies (Ps. 109:4); that soldiers would cast lots for his garments (Ps. 22:18); that not a bone would be broken in his body when he was crucified (Ps. 34:20); that he would be resurrected from the dead (Ps. 16:10); that he would ascend to heaven after his resurrection (Ps. 68:18). Many of these statements can be applied to Jesus without misconstruing their meaning.

C. S. Lewis says, "In a certain sense Our Lord's interpretation of the Psalms was common ground between Himself and His opponents. The question...how David can call Christ 'my Lord' (Mk. 12:25-37), would lose its point unless it were addressed to those who took it for granted that the 'my Lord' referred to in Psalm 110 was the Messiah, the regal and anointed deliverer...The 'scriptures' all had a 'spiritual' or second sense. Even a gentile 'God-fearer' like the Ethiopian eunuch (Ac. 8:27-38) knew that the sacred books of Israel could not be understood without a guide, trained in the Judaic tradition, who could open the hidden meanings. Probably all instructed Jews in the first century saw references to the Messiah in most of those passages where Our Lord saw them; what was controversial was His identification of the Messianic King...with Himself."[10]

Wonderful, indeed, is the bond which unifies worshipers in the OT period with that of the New. This bond is exemplified by "Christ and the Eleven singing the second half of the Hallel (Ps. 113-118) after the transition from the passover to the Lord's Supper; of the disciples at Jerusalem 'praising God' (Ac. 2:47); of James urging his readers, when cheerful,to 'sing praises' (Ja. 5:13); and of Paul similarly emphasizing the place of 'psalms and hymns and spiritual songs'...the NT inferentially suggests that the Church will do wisely, nevertheless, to retain a large place in its liturgy for the Psalter, as a precious inspired gift of God, for the use of the NT Church."[11]

In Paul's address to the church at Corinth he observed,"when ye come together, every one of you hath a psalm..." (l Co. 14:26), and in his letter to the Ephesian and Colossian believers, a similar reference is made (Ep. 5:19; Col. 3:16).

Before the period of the Reformation, church services were usually opened with the reading or singing of a psalm. The Hebrew practice of singing psalms continued in the post-Advent church (see Ps. 62:4; 111:1; 132:16; Je. 33:11; Ezr. 3:11, and so on).

After the Reformation the Psalter was re-emphasized "so that Christ's people might once again drink freely of this fountain of salvation...The Psalter gave joy, courage, and strength in days of trial and danger."[12] In addition to their use in singing, many churches made a wise use of the Psalter in responsive reading. It is thought that the Psalter has contributed more to Biblical unity than any other portion of the Bible, and its importance as devotional literature is seen in the fact that most editions of the New Testament include the Book of the Psalms at the end. One divine says that along with the NT, the aged Christian desires a copy of the Psalms. He passes easily from the Gospel to the Psalter and back again without the sense of shifting from one spiritual level to another. Religious experience was enjoyed and was portrayed by the ancient psalmist so well that no Christian book in the apostolic period was composed to displace the Psalms.[13]

A noted scholar sums up the Messianic content of the Psalms in these words:

> No one can read the Psalms without being aware that the individual verses have a deeper, further significance beyond the simple meaning of the words. The Messiah is not mentioned by name, but his figure is foreshadowed, as later generations of Jews came to realize. And the New Testament writers are quick to apply these verses to Jesus as the prophesied Messiah.

Other psalms depict human suffering in terms which seem farfetched in relation to ordinary experience, but which proved an extraordinarily accurate description of the actual sufferings of Christ. Under God's inspiration, the psalmists chose words and pictures which were to take on a significance they can hardly [sic] have dreamed of. Psalm 22, the psalm Jesus quoted as he hung on the cross (v. 1; Mt. 27:46), is the most amazing example. Compare v. 16 with Jn. 20:25; v. 18 with Mk. 15:24. (See also Ps. 69:20 and Mt. 27:34,48.)[14]

Sufferings of Christ
3489-3495

Proverbs

The Name

The book of Proverbs derives its name from the first two words in the first chapter: "The Proverbs." The word "proverbs" is derived from the Hebrew word *mashal,* meaning "a comparison of one thing to another."

In the Hebrew canon the poetical book of Proverbs is listed in the category of the Writings (Heb. *kethubim;* Gr. *hagiographa*).

Book of
Proverbs
4242

Authorship and Date

Internal evidence links "Solomon the Son of David, king of Israel" with the authorship of Proverbs (1:1). Tradition credits Solomon with writing most of the book of Proverbs; however, it is apparent that some other authors participated in the compilation of this book. Among those mentioned in the book are "the men of Hezekiah," who copied out and compiled some proverbs which apparently were written by Solomon (Pr. 25:1). The name Agur appears as a caption at the head of chapter 30. Lemuel is credited with chapter 31.

A careful study of the Proverbs indicates that these wise sayings were collected over the years and that Solomon was one of the wise men who collected, compiled, added to, and edited these sayings of wisdom. That there is repetition would indicate that several men shared in the compilation, all possibly drawing materials from the same general source. Presumably these sayings were preserved in oral and written form by many different people and ultimately recorded by a Spirit-filled editor, as they now appear.

It is thought that the proverbs were finally compiled by Solomon in about 950 B.C. The proverbs copied by Hezekiah's men and those written by Agur and Lemuel were probably added in about 700 B.C.

Solomon
3414,
4307g

Hezekiah
1585

Solomon
4297

"Spirit"
Filled
1125
Proverbs
2904

Background, Purpose, and Content

The book of Proverbs contains aphoristic literature, duplicated in other parts of Scripture but only on a fragmentary basis (Psalms, Ecclesiastes, Job). The entire book is made up of short epigrams (wise sayings) which are concise and easy to memorize. It is possible that in Israel maxims constituted a large part of the early childhood training. Parents probably

Wise
Thoughts
2356

"...he who refreshes others will himself be refreshed." Pr. 11:25 (NIV)

instilled them in their children, and the proverbs may have formed the basis for the earliest educational curriculum. Likewise the proverbs were recited by men and women in all strata of life—from the learned and rich to the poor and ignorant. They were repeated while men worked in the fields, in shops and on the roads, as well as in the schools.

Parental Duties 1629-1633

The proverbs are definitely influenced by Deuteronomic social and religious ideals. They were a personification of law and order. OT wisdom grew out of experience and action in life, but the "fear of the Lord" was the first step in gaining wisdom. One writer speaks of the book of Proverbs as "a Manual of Sanctified Common Sense." He says,

True Wisdom 3840

> The main object that the writers of our book had in view was to teach men how to live happy and contented lives as long as they were on earth: for this reason they deal very largely with the relationship between man and man, between parents and children, husband and wife, friend and foe, rich and poor, high and low; they teach what is right behaviour in every phase and occupation of life; how to accept adverse fortune, and the fitting attitude of him who enjoys wealth; to practice self-control in all things, to cultivate consideration for others, and so on, in a word, how to live to the best advantage, to do right, because it brings its own reward, to avoid wrong doing because it entails disadvantages...It is pointed out that wisdom and godliness are really the same thing and that the origin and essence of the highest form of wisdom is the fear of the Lord.[1]

Spiritual Relation- ships 740

The Wise Man vs. the Prophet and Priest

The wise men shared in the religious educational process with the priests and prophets. The priests interpreted God and his law of sacrifice to the people, while the prophets (the *Nebhiim*) were the divinely inspired foretellers of the consequence of a certain course of action. The wise men endeavored to enlarge on the teachings of the priests and the prophets. They condensed the essence of truth into short and pithy sayings, so they could be grasped and understood by the common people. One writer puts it thus:

Wise Men 3847

> The wise men attempted to present a composite picture of the ideal man. It is not a sentimental, apologetic saint they portray, but a man of red blood and practical ability. He is a devoted husband, a true friend, a wise counselor and a charitable neighbor. He is industrious, honorable and righteous. His insight into life is simple, yet profound. Above all he is sane, normal, and motivated by a sound faith in God and a desire to evidence his loyalty to God by living in accord with the divine precepts. He is happy and content.[2]

Man 2237-2243

Wisdom was dispensed wherever people met, because schools or institutions as known today had not yet developed. Through memorization, truth was communicated, not only by "wise men" but also by the father and mother to the children and by the children to each other. The ideal mother and wife is presented as a virtuous woman, industrious, ever desiring to provide for the well-being of her family. She is respected and admired and is a leader in the community for the causes which will strengthen and bless society.

Contentment 829 Truthfulness 3701

A large body of axiomatic truth floated in the minds of the people. These wise sayings influenced and became a part of the cultural pattern. Men of wisdom collected these wise sayings and compiled them into written form as they appear in the wisdom books of the Bible.

Spiritual Conversation 3299

The Wise Man vs. the Philosopher

Hebrew wisdom had in it a striking difference from the speculative Greek philosophy of the Western world. The wise men dealt with divine revelation; the philosophers, with human reason. The Jews had their "wise men"; the Greeks had their "philosophers." The "wise men" dealt with everyday practical truths; the philosophers dealt with abstract theories. The "wise men" were concerned with ethics and morality, based on divine revelation, whereas some of the "philosophers" based the test of validity upon whether certain courses of action were reasonable and pleasurable.

W. T. Purkiser sums up the difference between the "wise men" and the "philosophers" thus: "While reason was the method of Greek Philosophy and argumentation its form, intuition or insight was the method of Hebrew wisdom and the epigrammatic proverb its form. The Jewish wise man had no argument to sustain, no chain of reason to follow. He presents his truth with the simple assurance of one who has seen."[3]

Ecclesiastes

The Name

A precise name for the book of Ecclesiastes does not appear in the Bible text. The name is derived from the second word in the first chapter of both the Hebrew and Greek Old Testament. In the Hebrew Bible the word is *qoheleth*, meaning a presiding officer or one who speaks to an assembly, a school or a religious body such as a synagogue.

The word in the Greek OT is *ekklesiastes,* meaning a member of or a presiding officer of an *ekklesia* (a religious body) or a preacher. A scholar of note phrases the meaning thus: "The English title Ecclesiastes is taken from the Greek translation of the Hebrew word *Qoheleth* and means 'one who gathers an ekklesia,' *ekklesia* being the Greek word for 'church' or 'assembly.' From this, Luther interpreted it as meaning 'the preacher,' a title which found its way into our English version."[1] Luther translates the word *qoheleth* as *prediger,* (German), which in English means "preacher."

In the Hebrew canon the book of Ecclesiastes is one of the Five Scrolls *(Megilloth)* and is listed in the category of the Writings (Heb., *kethubim;* Gr., *hagiographa).*

Authorship and Date

Positive identification of the author of the book of Ecclesiastes is not given in the Bible text; however Jewish tradition has always assumed that Solomon was the author.

The introduction refers to "the Preacher" (Heb., *qoheleth*), the son of David, king of Jerusalem (Pr. 1:1). Ecclesiastes 1:12 states that "I the Preacher was king over Israel in Jerusalem."

Solomon, with all of his royal glory and wealth, was eminently qualified to describe the experimentation and the conclusion portrayed in this book. He probably wrote the manuscript in his declining years when he could look in retrospect upon his life with its varied experiences of wealth, power, royal prestige, and every conceivable sensuous pleasure. Solomon died in 931 B.C., after a reign of forty years.

Background, Purpose, and Content

The general purpose of Ecclesiastes may be to communicate the unhappy consequences of a life given to unrestrained self-indulgence. The key to this pessimistic conclusion is found in these words: "Vanity of vanities, saith the Preacher, vanity of vanities; all is vanity" (Ec. 1:2).

Book of
Ecclesiastes
4243

Work of
Ministers
2087-2092

Solomon
3414,
4307g

Solomon
4297

Earthly
Riches
2805-2811

Deceptive
Treasures
2810
Emptiness
or Vanity
1120-1122

Despondency in the Bible

Much of the book of Ecclesiastes is given to a pessimistic outlook on life: "Everything is meaningless" (1:2, NIV). Finally, though, the author does wisely conclude: "Fear God and keep his commandments, for this is the whole duty of man" (12:13, NIV). It is helpful to remember that the Bible records moments of despondency, even in the lives of godly people. Hope and optimism return, however, when one remembers that to honor and worship God and do what he commands is the whole purpose of life.

Moses And if thou deal thus with me, kill me, I pray thee, out of hand, if I have found favour in thy sight; and let me not see my wretchedness. (Nu. 11:15)

Joshua And Joshua said, Alas, O Lord GOD, wherefore hast thou at all brought this people over Jordan, to deliver us into the hand of the Amorites, to destroy us? would to God we had been content, and dwelt on the other side Jordan! (Jos. 7:7)

Elijah But he himself went a day's journey into the wilderness, and came and sat down under a juniper tree: and he requested for himself that he might die; and said, It is enough; now, O LORD, take away my life; for I am not better than my fathers. (1K. 19:4)

Job My soul is weary of life; I will leave my complaint upon myself; I will speak in the bitterness of my soul. (Jb. 10:1)

David O my God, my soul is cast down within me: therefore will I remember thee from the land of Jordan, and of the Hermonites, from the hill Mizar. (Ps. 42:6)

Jeremiah Woe is me, my mother, that thou hast borne me a man of strife and a man of contention to the whole earth! I have neither lent on usury, nor men have lent to me on usury; yet every one of them doth curse me. (Je. 15:10)

The Disciples And he said unto them, What manner of communications are these that ye have one to another, as ye walk, and are sad? (Lu. 24:17)

Solomon's conclusion seems to deal with periods when God had little or no place in his life.

Solomon presents some of the great beauties of life, but the predominant tone of this book is desperation, futility, and melancholy. He had grown up under a father (David) who faced difficulties, hardships, and struggle but was forever proclaiming "Rejoice" and "Praise the Lord." David had brought Israel to the brink of the "golden age" with its wealth, power, and glory. Solomon was "born with a silver spoon in his mouth," as it were, and he never confronted the realities of life. Though he gave his heart "to seek and search out by wisdom concerning all things that are done under heaven" (Ec. 1:13), all he found was gloom: "I have seen all the works that are done under the sun; and, behold, all is vanity, and vexation of spirit" (Ec.1:14). He adopts a defeatist attitude toward life; though he claims to have had great "wisdom and knowledge," he knows only the "vexation of spirit" (Ec. 1:17); to him wisdom and knowledge "increaseth sorrow" (Ec. 1:18).

Solomon set out to buy happiness with his great wealth. He wrote, "Whatsoever mine eyes desired I kept not from them, I withheld not my heart from any joy" (Ec. 2:10). He gave himself to "enjoy pleasure," to "laughter" and "mirth" and the "wine cup." He planted great "vineyards," "gardens," "orchards," and "trees," and made "pools of water," with which to irrigate them. In his lifetime Solomon acquired many "servants," "maidens," wives, and concubines (1 K. 11:3) as well as great cattle ranches. He accumulated much gold (1 K. 10:14-17). He was entertained by great musicians with many instruments, but in spite of what he had, he was not satisfied.

He expresses his stark pessimism in these words, "Then I looked on all the works that my hands had wrought...and behold all was vanity and vexation of spirit, and there was no profit under the sun" (Ec. 2:1-11). The term "under the sun" is interpreted to mean that he sought and enjoyed all these things by his own efforts and not as blessings from God.

The attitude of Solomon is typical of a man in any age who has the "golden platter" placed in his lap. He soon discovered that without struggle and hardship the fruit of fame and fortune is futile and empty. His riches were his sufficiency; he seemed to think he had no need for God. He was in a position to taste the fruits of luxury and pleasure in every area of life, but found them bitter and meaningless. The unceasing refrain in the entire book is the word "vanity," which occurs 37 times.

The king of Israel saw earthly life at its best; he could gratify every sensuous desire. He made it his business to taste every earthly pleasure, but he found it all to be vanity and vexation of spirit. Even though the name of God is mentioned twenty times in the book, the main thrust is that he sought satisfaction and meaning in life through his own efforts (Ec. 1:2-2:23). To Solomon, God seemed to be abstract, impersonal and transcendent, so far away that Solomon was not conscious of God's availability.

Solomon found life disappointing (Ec. 4:1-16). The worldly attainments proved to be futile and inadequate (Ec. 6:1-7). Yet, shrouded in philosophical speculation, there are some suggestions of hope. He gives words of wisdom for living in a world where all is vanity (Ec. 7:1-12:8). He does not totally ignore the Deuteronomic Law—"obey the earthly king and

Hopeless-
ness
1694

Despair
1697-1699

Riches
Perilous
2806

Disap-
pointing
2811
Sin
Unprofit-
able
2873

Conceit
1728

Vanity
1120
Sexual
Impurity
664-666

Disappoint-
ment
1190

Keep the
Law
437

fear the heavenly king" (Ec. 8:1-17). He makes honorable mention of death (Ec. 9:1-12). The writer admits that wisdom is better than folly (Ec. 9:13-10:20); that hard work and benevolence in a troubled world may bring satisfaction (Ec. 11:1-8). He exhorts youth to "Remember now thy Creator" (Ec. 12:1-2). Apparently the writer, now in his old age, comes to the conclusion that his own humanistic approach is vain, that others should not follow his example, and that the way to start life is with God. Solomon himself appears to be so much confused in his "humanistic prison that he cannot break out." He seems to maintain his pessimistic view of life— "vanity of vanities, saith the preacher; all is vanity" (Ec. 12:8). Finally in the last two verses a burst of light comes forth. He concludes that to "Fear God, and keep his commandments" is the best way to live (Ec. 12:13).

A legitimate question may be asked: Why was such a book included in the canonized Scripture? No absolute answer is available, but succeeding generations can and should profit from Solomon's experience. "God gave Solomon wisdom and unparalleled opportunity to observe and to explore every avenue of earthly life. And, after much research and experimentation, Solomon concluded that, on the whole, humanity found an unutterable yearning for something beyond himself [sic]. Thus the book, in a way, is humanity's cry for a Saviour. With the coming of Christ, the cry was answered. The vanity of life disappeared. No longer vanity, but joy, peace, gladness prevailed...In Christ humanity found the Desire of the ages: Life, Abundant, Joyous, Glorious Life."[2]

(margin notes:)

Wisdom-Folly
3838-3855

Fear God
3034

Crying to God
1071

The Song of Solomon

The Name

The Song of Solomon is frequently called "The Song of Songs" or "Canticles." The book derives its name from the first verse in the book: "The Song of songs, which is Solomon's" (Song 1:1). In the Hebrew Bible this title appears as *Sir hassirim;* in the Septuagint as *Asma;* and in the Latin Vulgate as *Canticum* or *Canticorum.* In the Hebrew Canon the Song of Solomon is one of the Five Scrolls and is listed in the category of the Writing (Heb., *kethubim;* Gr., *hagiographa*).

Song of
Solomon
4244

Authorship and Date

Traditionally, the Song of Solomon has been attributed to Solomon because of the reference to Solomon in the first verse and other parts of the book (Song 1:1; 3:7,9,11; 8:11-12). This opinion is consistent with the view that the Bible is the authoritative Word of God. A likely date for this book is about 950 B.C., the middle of Solomon's reign, which ended in 931 at his death.

Solomon
3414,
4307g
Bible, Word
of God
414-445

The first verse is vague, according to the Hebrew idiom. It could mean that Solomon was the author or that the song was about Solomon. This uncertainty is acknowledged, but the probability is that Solomon was the writer.

Background, Purpose, and Content

The Song of Solomon has been a difficult book for the religious community to deal with because of its general eroticism. The language is passionate and sensuous; the description of man and woman relationships are in intimate terms. It is made more difficult because there is not a religious sentence in it nor is the name of God ever used.

Chastity-
Impurity
663-667

However, it is a book in the canon, and this is the basis for accepting it as a part of the inspired Word of God. Therefore readers must seek a wholesome, positive interpretation of this Song. The Jewish church has always cherished the Song and used it as a part of the ritual on the eighth day of the Passover, in memory of the exodus when God, the Bridegroom, espoused Israel as his bride. In the third century A.D., Origin introduced this book to the Christian church as representing the blissful relationship between Christ, the Bridegroom, and his bride, the church. It is obvious that the study of the Song of Solomon demands a pure, sanctified attitude, especially in an age of sexual permissiveness and perversion.

Passover
1256, 2686
Christ
Bridegroom
736
Bride
737

En Gedi, an oasis where water falls from the desert cliffs above.
David hid in a nearby cave when Saul sought to kill him (1 S. 24:1).
Solomon mentions the "vineyards of En Gedi" in Song 1:14.

There are at least five major approaches to, or interpretations of, the Song of Solomon.

1. *The Cultic View.* Some persons assume that this book presents a liturgy of Baalism, the Canaanite fertility cult, prevalent in Palestine when the tribes arrived. This cult had as its purpose the stimulation of nature. The priest and priestess performed a sexual ritual in the temple. This observance was supposed to have a magical influence upon the fertility of the land and the productivity of the herds.

False Worship 3928-3952

2. *The Lyrical View.* According to this interpretation, the book contains a series of love songs, in which the sensuous beauty of the bride is discussed and dramatized.

3. *The Literal View.* There are several versions of the literal view. The most popular one is the "conjugal love version," which portrays the beauty and sacredness of sexual love within holy matrimony, a husband-wife relationship sanctified by God. The sacredness of marriage is further enhanced by the participation of Jesus in the marriage at Cana of Galilee (Jn. 2:1ff.). One writer justifies this love poem in these words:

Conjugal Love 1623 Marriage 1620-1621

> Even if Canticles is merely a collection of songs describing the bliss of true lovers in wedlock, it is not thereby rendered unworthy of a place in the Bible…If Canticles should be rejected because of its sensuous imagery in describing the joys of passionate lovers, portions of Proverbs would also have to be excised (Pr. 5:15-20). Perhaps most persons need to enlarge their conception of the Bible as a repository for all things that minister to the welfare of men. The entire range of man's legitimate joys finds sympathetic and appreciative description in the Bible. Two lovers in Paradise need not fear to rise and meet their Creator should He visit them in the cool of the day.[1]

Creator 884 Biblical Manuscripts 4220

4. *The Dramatic View.* This view is sometimes referred to as the "Shepherd Hypothesis," a view popular a few decades ago. It was assumed that the "Song of Solomon" is one of the few survivors of ancient Hebrew art. This theory is strengthened by the "stage directions" found in the Codex Sinaiticus. In this Biblical manuscript various verses are assigned to "different speakers such as 'the bride to maidens,' 'the maidens to the bride' and 'the bridegroom to the bride.' Clearly some sort of drama is here presupposed."[2]

A further analysis suggests a:

> drama in fine arts, thirteen scenes. There are three main characters and three choruses-court ladies-citizens of Jerusalem. The play opens with the Shulamite girl yearning for her absent lover. Solomon tries to woo her but is unsuccessful. She replies that "there is a true love that cannot be excited artificially." The simple country maiden has no adequate conception of palace life and conduct. She answers Solomon in language borrowed from the shepherd life familiar to her. She draws imagery from the pastoral and horticultural mountain life.

Conjugal Love 1623

> In the second act the Shulamite describes a date she had with her shepherd lover in the mountains. She tells about a dream she had since coming to the palace and how she searched the streets of Jerusalem for her lover until she found him.

> In the third act Solomon enters dressed in all his splendor in an effort to overwhelm the maid, but in her inner subconsciousness she hears only the passionate pleas of her absent lover; this is followed by another dream about her lover.

> In the fourth act the social set in Jerusalem express their surprise at her rejection of the king. Solomon then renews his efforts to win the maiden, telling her how he first saw her in a nut orchard, but she maintains her loyalty to her shepherd lover and in the last act she is permitted to return home to be reunited with her lover. Some ancient sages point out that through this experience, Solomon is converted to higher ideals because of the loyalty the maid demonstrated for her lover under the most severe enticements; she demonstrated to Solomon that pure love is more powerful than sensual love.[3]

Pre-eminence of Love 2209, 4182

5. *The Allegorical View.* Perhaps the most popular and abiding interpretation of the Song of Solomon is the allegorical view, which presupposes that the Song portrays the love relationship between Jehovah and Israel. Jehovah is the Bridegroom and Israel, the bride. It is probably this view that made the canonization of this love poem possible. The allegorical view is supported in the oldest Jewish sources such as the Targum, Talmud, and Midrash.

It is a matter of record that marriage is the symbol in the OT illustrating the relationship between Jehovah and Israel. The Jews expressed this belief in their use of this poem during the Passover Feast. When Israel turned its face from God and worshiped the gods of Canaan, they were called adulterers; this was spiritual adultery. The terms "whoredom" and "whoredoms" are frequently used in citing Israel's spiritual infidelity (Je. 3:9; Eze. 16:17,33; Ho. 1:2; 4:10).

Isaiah makes clear the idea embraced by the allegorical position: "As the bridegroom rejoiceth over the bride, so shall thy God rejoice over thee" (Is. 62:5). Other prophets affirm this position (Ho. 2:18-23; Je. 3:1-10; Eze. 16,23). The application of Jehovah, the bridegroom, and Israel, the bride, was transferred to Christ and his church. Jesus made frequent reference to the bridegroom and bride imagery and did not hesitate to identify himself as the bridegroom, who would one day complete the age and take unto himself his bride, the church.

Christian scholars readily adopted and developed the Jewish allegorical interpretation, for the figure of wedlock is used in the NT by both Paul and John to represent the ultimate and vital union of Christ and his church (2 Co. 11:2; Ep. 5:22-23; Re. 21:2-9). One writer has contributed this explanation:

> The pure spontaneous, mutual love of a great king and a humble maid was seen to exemplify the mutual affection between Jehovah and His people. And the story was told, not merely because it was beautiful, but chiefly because it was typical of this great religious truth. The Song of Songs is thus analogous to Messianic Psalms, which are based on the personal experiences official position of David and Solomon, and exhibit truths regarding the great king. The comparison of the mutual love between the church and its divine head to that of the bride and bridegroom frequently occurs in the NT (Ep. 5:25-33; Re. 19:7; 21:9, etc.).[4]

Isaiah

The Name

The name Isaiah is derived from the Hebrew *yeshayahu,* meaning "Jehovah saves," or "Jehovah is salvation." The Greek form *Esaias* is used in the English NT, KJV. In the Latin Vulgate the rendering is the same as the Greek—*Esaias*. The title of the book originated from the reference in the first verse, "Isaiah the son of Amoz," as explained under "Authorship and Date." The name Isaiah also appears a number of times in various sections of the book, as well as in other parts of the OT.

Isaiah is the first of the Major Prophets in the English Bible and the first of the Latter Prophets in the Hebrew canon.

Authorship and Date

The authorship of Isaiah (758-698 B.C.) was not questioned by scholars in Judaism and traditional Christianity until the development of Biblical criticism in the eighteenth century. One supposition of this approach was that the prophets always spoke only in immediate historical situations, that there was no miraculous intervention by God, and that the prophets could not foretell the future. On the basis of this assumption, the book of Isaiah, the book of Daniel, and other sections of the OT which contain reference to miracles and prophetic statements of future events have been reassigned to dates later than the historical events these writings describe.

As most of the content in chapters 1-39 was considered to be unified and within the period of Isaiah's ministry, most critics have been willing to grant authorship of these chapters to the prophet. However, chapters 40-66 contain some references to events not in his lifetime; consequently these chapters were assigned to writers living in a later period, after the predicted events had become history. An imaginary second Isaiah (Deutero-Isaiah), supposedly living after the Babylonian captivity (536 B.C.), was credited with writing the chapters in question. Because of differences in historical background, a third Isaiah (Trito-Isaiah), was created. Since then, other Isaiahs have been suggested to deal with the so-called textual problems. At the present time the book of Isaiah is "in large part distributed among various writers from Cyrus to Simon (538-164 B.C.)."[1] The process of this arbitrary

Book of Isaiah **4245**

Isaiah **1803**

Prophets **2065-2066**

Miracles **2360-2374**

Prophecy **2889-2894**

Captivity of Israel **1825-1827**

division of the book of Isaiah by such extreme critics as J. Wellhausen, B. Stade, A. Kuenen, F. Ruckert and others is well presented by Robert H. Pfeiffer.[2]

Messianic
Prophecies
2890,
4306b

The Messianic prophecies were either ignored or disposed of by the use of a "gloss"—an imaginary explanation or false interpretation used to dispose of a difficult problem. This approach brought into question the whole idea of Scriptural integrity. According to this approach, certain passages relating to "universal peace" (Is.11:1-9), "universal judgment upon the whole earth" (Is. 14:26), and the Apocalyptic chapters (Is. 24-27) transcended Isaiah's range of thought; so these passages were lifted out of their chronological context and reassigned to a later date, when, it was supposed, these concepts had developed.

Universal
Judgment
4123

Another argument used in favor of multiple authorship, but not developed in this study guide, is style; i.e., internal and linguistic evidence in matters of diction and tone. Some critics have favored the assigning of two or more Isaiahs in the authorship of the book because of the variations in content and style that they have noticed in certain passages. However, a study of various authors' works sometimes shows a difference in style within the individual author's writing. The author's style may vary with content and emotion. Such variation within Isaiah's long ministry could support the view of single authorship of the book of Isaiah.

Isaiah
1803

Both Jewish and Christian tradition accepted Isaiah as the author of the entire book bearing his name. Isaiah is the recognized author in both the Talmud and in the writings of the early church fathers. Not only is the author of the book identified in the first verse, his name is mentioned sixteen times in the body of the book with such notations as, "then said the LORD unto Isaiah" (Is. 7:3); "Isaiah said unto them" (Is. 37:6); and "then came the word of the LORD to Isaiah" (Is. 38:4). Jesus referred to Isaiah at least four times as the author (Mt. 13:14-15; 15:7; Mk. 7:6-7; and Lu. 4:17; cf. Is. 6:9-10; 29:13; 61:1-2). Philip identified Christ with the passage of Isaiah that the Ethiopian eunuch was reading (Ac. 8:28-29; cf. Is. 53:6-8). Paul affirmed that Isaiah is the author of the book of Isaiah (Ac. 28:25-27; Ro. 9:27,29; 10:16; 15:12).

Philip
2753
Paul
2697

The evidence for a single author and the traditional view that the prophet Isaiah wrote the book of Isaiah is overwhelming. Isaiah's prophecies follow a general chronological order from chapter one to sixty-six. In Isaiah 6:1 the writer refers to the death of King Uzziah (740 B.C.); in Isaiah 20:1 to the Tartan's arrival in Ashdod (711 B.C.); in Isaiah 36:1 he makes reference to the fourteenth year of Hezekiah's reign when Sennacherib came to attack Jerusalem (701 B.C.). Chapters 40-61 were written soon after 701 B.C.[3]

Uzziah
3744
Hezekiah
1585

In addition to the book of Isaiah, Isaiah wrote two other books: *The Life of Uzziah* (2 Chr. 26:22) and *The Book of the Kings of Judah and Israel* (2 Chr. 32:32). The best information available is that Isaiah's prophetic life extended from 758 to 698 B.C.[4]

Palaces
2669

Background, Purpose, and Content

Isaiah was the "stately gentleman," equally at home in the palace (Is. 7:3) or in the temple (Is. 8:2). He served the court of Jerusalem for about sixty

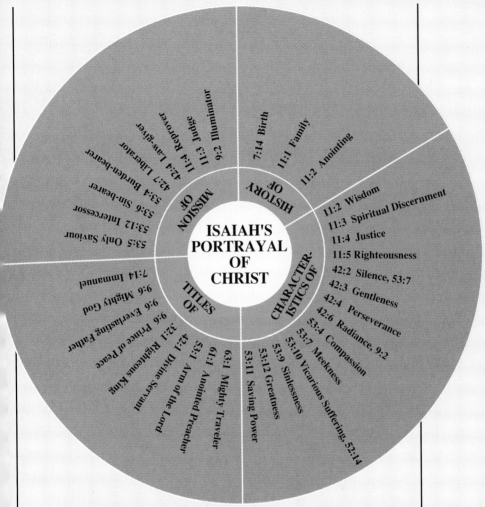

Isaiah's Messianic Prophecies. This prophet looked down the centuries and saw the coming Messiah. He has given us the most perfect picture of the history, mission, titles, and characteristics of Christ of any of the great Hebrew prophets.

years under the reign of four kings: Uzziah, Jotham, Ahaz, and Hezekiah. When Sennacherib, the conqueror of Assyria, demanded Jerusalem's surrender, King Hezekiah "prayed before the Lord." God sent an answer to King Hezekiah through the words of the prophet Isaiah. During the night God answered by sending the death angel to destroy the 185,000 Assyrian troops (2 K. 19:15,20,35). Sennacherib hastily retreated to his capitol, Nineveh, where his two sons assassinated him (2 K. 19:36-37).

Nineveh
2593, 4418

As a prophet, Isaiah ranks above the other seers. He is the prince of all the prophets; his writings excel in their scope and in prophetic insight; he is a man of God. Isaiah's major theme is "salvation by faith" (Is. 43:10-11). He is the St. Paul of the OT, and the book by his name is often referred to as

Seers
2069

Christ
Jesus
677-700

Galilee
1384

Anointed
One
677
Christ's
Death
3367

Remnant
of Israel
1828

Dead Sea
Scrolls
4362

Divine
Grace
1445-1449
Universal
Judgment
4123

the fifth Gospel because of its Messianic content. When all of Isaiah's prophetic statements are assembled into a composite collection, a perfect portrayal of Christ emerges, showing Jesus in his various sufferings and death. The fifty-third chapter alone contains sufficient Christological information to keep a Bible student occupied for a lifetime.

Handel drew much of his imagery for his great oratorio, the *Messiah,* from Isaiah. So fully does Isaiah describe the person and office of the coming Messiah that from the time of Jerome he has been known as the evangelist of the Old Testament.[5] Through his "prophetic telescope" Isaiah views the Messiah as the heir to the throne of David (Is. 9:7) and his virgin birth is clearly predicted (Is. 7:14; cf. Mt. 1:18).

The mention of the Messiah's ministry in Galilee (Is. 9:1) is an unusual prediction, because the Messiah was expected to set up his kingdom in Jerusalem, in the very heart of Judaism. Isaiah's prediction proved to be true; Jesus did grow up in the lowly village of Nazareth (Jn. 1:46), in the very heart of Galilee—far removed from the temple hierarchy. It was here that he selected his disciples and conducted much of his earthly ministry. He was expected to redeem Israel, yet Isaiah accurately predicted that he would be rejected by the Jews (Is. 53:3; cf. Jn. 1:11), that he would be anointed by the Holy Spirit (Is. 11:2), and that he would be cruelly abused. All this the prophet Isaiah clearly foretold (Is. 53:4-7). The prediction of his crucifixion between two sinners (Is. 53:12) and other prophecies give a perfec preview of Christ's suffering and death.[6]

Some of the ideas presented throughout the book are peculiar to Isaiah. He refers to Jehovah as "the Holy One of Israel" twenty-five times. This phrase appears only six times in other parts of the OT. The "highway" is an expression peculiar to Isaiah (Is. 35:8; 40:3; 49:11; 62:10) and is found throughout the book; also note such terms as "remnant" and the position occupied by "Zion." "Pangs of a woman in travail," the "wrath of Jehovah hath spoken it," and "streams of water" are expressions used at intervals from chapter 1 to chapter 66 and appear nowhere else in the OT. These phrases are indicative of the probable single authorship of the book of Isaiah.

The discovery of the Isaiah scroll at Qumran was no doubt the greatest Biblical discovery of this century. Albright places the date of the scroll in the second century B.C. Another well-known scholar expresses the same opinion in these words: "This makes it [the Isaiah scroll] the oldest known complete Hebrew manuscript of any Biblical book, and it agrees in almost every respect with our traditional Hebrew texts, as used in the translation of the King James Version of our Bible."[7]

Another scholar evaluates this view:

To deny to Isaiah of the 8th century [B.C.] all catholicity of grace, all universalism of salvation or judgment, every highly developed Messianic ideal, every rich note of promise and comfort, all sublime faith in the sacrosanct character of Zion, as some do, is unwarrantably to create a new Isaiah of greatly reduced proportions, a mere preacher of righteousness, a statesman of not very optimistic view, and the exponent of cold ethical religion without the warmth and glow of the messages which are actually ascribed to the prophet of the 8th century.[8]

6:3 ...Holy, holy, holy, is the LORD of hosts: the whole earth is full of his glory.

This verse is the basis for our hymn, "Holy, Holy, Holy." Our hymnody contains many other selections whose inspiration came from the book of Isaiah. "O Zion Haste" was inspired by Is. 12:6; "Heralds of Christ" came into being out of Is. 40:3-5; Toplady's "Rock of Ages" owes its origin to Is. 32:2; "Savior, Like a Shepherd Lead Us" was born out of Is. 44:28, and "All Hail the Power of Jesus' Name" came from Is. 28:16. Many other great Christian classics in the realm of music find their inspiration in the book of Isaiah. Foster's solo, "Fear not, I am with Thee" has Is. 43:5 for its foundation; Simper's anthem, "Sing, O Heaven," comes from Is. 44:23; and Harker's solo, "How Beautiful upon the Mountains," finds expression in Is. 52:7. The solo by Roberts, "Seek ye the Lord," is keyed to Is. 55:6, and Handel's *Messiah*, one of the greatest of all musical compositions, draws over one-third of its texts from the book of Isaiah.

Isaiah is influential in our Christian hymnody because he was dedicated to the Christ of the Bible.

7:14 ...Behold a virgin shall conceive, and bear a son, and shall call his name Immanuel.

The fact that this son was to be called *Immanuel,* meaning "God with us," is a clear indication that a "sign" would accompany the manifestation of the Redeemer, clearly set forth in prophecy. This divine name could not have been given to an ordinary human being; it could have been given only to the God-man Jesus Christ, who truly was born as the prophets had foretold.

World history does not reveal another human being of whom it could be said, "God with us." This reference "can refer only to Christ because Christ is God. Thus Christ is the Only One who can be rightfully called Immanuel, 'God with us.' This is indeed an appropriate name for His coming to earth. He is God...manifest in the flesh (1 Ti. 3:16). He (Christ) 'was made flesh, and dwelt among us' (Jn. 1:14). Christ is the Immanuel, a name which carries with it the true meaning of the Incarnation, namely God with us in human flesh."[9]

Isaiah is specific; the prophecy clearly stated that the Messiah to come was to be a son, born of a virgin. No one in history, other than Christ, can be found who has this identification. It is to be acknowledged that the Isaiah 7:14 passage is couched in a historical reference pertaining to the prophet's own time. Critics of the "Messiah interpretation" at this point ask: "How can the coming of Christ seven centuries later be made to establish the time for the forsaking of the land of Israel and Syria? What relevance does this text have to King Ahaz?"

Some prophetic and especially Messianic texts in the Old Testament are found in settings quite foreign to their nature; they appear as a kind of prophetic parenthesis (Ps. 34:20; 41:9; 69:21; 110:4). Frequently these prophetic texts have the same relationship to the context as does a precious stone in the native ore in which it is imbedded. This idea is further illustrated in such Messianic prophecies as Ps. 22:16,18; 34:20; 41:9; 69:21 and Zec. 9:9; 11:12-13.

Holiness
of God
1597
God,
a Rock
3178
Christ as
Shepherd
3264-3267

Christ
Jesus
677-723

Immanuel
1741

Christ's
Divinity–
Humanity
701-723

Incarnation
720
Virgin Birth
4217

Messianic
Prophecies
2890-2892

From a literary point of view the Scriptures cannot be made to conform to the "scientific investigative techniques" which are so commonly applied to secular literature. The Scriptures are uniquely "God breathed" and are designed to convey redemptive revelation inherent in the Christ Messiah. "Holy men of God spake as they were moved by the Holy Ghost" (2 Pe. 1:21); the ways of God are foolishness to the natural or sinful man (see 1 Co. 2:10-14). Certainly Matthew understood the passage in Isaiah 7:14 to mean the virgin-born Christ (Mt. 1:23).

J. Gresham Machen says,

> It is certainly clear that something more than the Israelitish people is meant by the figure of the "Servant of Jehovah" in the latter part of Isaiah: and it is certainly clear that something more is meant by "Immanuel" in our passage than the child of the prophet or of Ahaz or of any ordinary young woman of that time. A really sympathetic and intelligent reader can hardly...doubt but that in the "Immanuel" of the seventh and eighth chapters of Isaiah, in the "child" of the ninth chapter, whose name shall be called "Wonderful, Counsellor, mighty God, everlasting Father, Prince of Peace," and in the "branch" of the eleventh chapter, one mighty divine personage is meant. The common minimizing interpretations may seem plausible in detail; but they disappear before the majestic sweep of the passages when they are taken as a whole.[10]

Divine Inspiration 1774-1776

Christ as Servant 3901

Christ's Name 2516-2517

"I stand continually upon the watchtower..." Is. 21:8. Isaiah's imagery is drawn from the watchtower on which the vineyard owner posted a guard, protecting his property from predatory animals and thieves.

During the first century most of those who embraced the Christian faith were Jews—Jews in the strict spiritual sense—who anticipated the Messiah and accepted him when he came. To what extent they understood all the intricate details of Jesus' birth is a matter of conjecture, but the fact remains that they recognized him as the Messiah.

Adam Clarke observes that:

> According to the original promise there was to be a seed, a human being, who should destroy sin; but this seed or human being, must come from the woman alone; and no woman alone could produce such a human being without being a virgin. Hence, a virgin shall bear a son, is the very spirit and meaning of the original text, independent of the illustration given by the prophet; and the fact recorded by the evangelist, is proof of the whole. But such a reading of prophecy will not be induced, in those who have abandoned it, by any considerations that we can now bring forth; indeed, it will come only when there is a mighty revulsion from the shallowness of present religious life, and when men are again ready to listen to the voice of the living God.

It may perhaps at first sight seem strange that if Isaiah 7:14 is really a prophecy of the virgin birth of the Messiah, the later Jews should have so completely failed to interpret it in that way. But a parallel in the Old Testament which seems to the Christian heart to

Christians
725
Israel—
The Jews
1807-1829

Sin-Bearer
3362

Virgin Birth
4217

be a prophecy of the redeeming work of Christ…is that matchless fifty-third chapter of Isaiah. We read it today, often in preference to New Testament passages, as setting forth the atonement which our Lord made for the sins of others upon the cross. Never, says the simple Christian, was there a prophecy more gloriously plain.[11]

It is evident that the Isaiah 7:14 passage relates to Jesus Christ because reference is made to the divine name *Immanuel,* or "God with us." (The name which appears as *Immanuel* in the OT shows up as *Emmanuel* in the King James Version NT because of alphabetical peculiarities between Hebrew and Greek.) Emmanuel is indeed "God with us" to comfort, enlighten, protect and to give inner resources that sustain faith in the hour of persecution and death. Believers throughout the ages have testified to saving faith in Jesus Christ, and many have died in defense of that faith.

In conclusion, if the reference to the virgin in Is. 7:14 were a single, isolated reference, its relevance to the virgin birth of Christ might be questioned. But since this book is so saturated with descriptive prophecies concerning the life, death and redemptive work of our Savior, it is not unreasonable to assume that this passage is indeed in the Messianic compendium and must be coupled with *Immanuel,* "God with us."

Jeremiah

The Name

The name Jeremiah, derived from the Hebrew, *Yirmeyahu,* and abbreviated *Yirmeyah,* means "Jehovah founds or establishes." In the Greek OT (LXX) the word appears as *Iermais* and in the later Vulgate as *Jeremias.*

The name of the book of Jeremiah is taken from the first verse: "The words of Jeremiah the son of Hilkiah" (1:1). There are other places in the book where the name Jeremiah appears. Jeremiah is the second of the Major Prophets in the English Bible and the second of the Latter Prophets in the Hebrew canon.

Book of
Jeremiah
4246

Authorship and Date

According to both Jewish and Christian tradition, Jeremiah is the author of the book bearing his name. The basis for this assumption is strengthened by the prominence of Jeremiah's name in 34 of the 52 chapters, for a total of 132 times. Other parts of the OT mention Jeremiah's name 15 times. It is quoted once in the NT as "Jeremias" (Mt. 16:14).

Jeremiah
1877

Jeremiah was a native of Anathoth, a small community about six miles northeast of Jerusalem. This village was located in the area belonging to the tribe of Benjamin and was appointed by Jehovah for use by the priests, the descendants of Aaron (Jos. 21:13-18).

Priests
2058-2064

Jeremiah received his call to the prophetic office, possibly at the age of 20 (Je.1:6), in the thirteenth year of King Josiah's reign (Je. 1:2), about 626 B.C. He was active in Jerusalem until its fall in 586 B.C.[1]

Josiah
1923

Background, Purpose, and Content

A student of Jeremiah soon discovers that the structure and contents of the book are not arranged chronologically. Apparently Jeremiah circulated individual scrolls, each one illustrating some aspect of his total message. Later the scrolls were compiled into a single book. The names of the five kings under whom Jeremiah served are listed on the next page.

Kings of
Judah
1824

Josiah, 639-608 B.C.	Je. 1:2
Shallum (Jehoahaz), 608 B.C.	Je. 22:11
(as **Shallum** in 1 Chr. 3:15)	
(as **Jehoahaz** in 2 K. 23:30)	
Jehoiakim, 608-597 B.C.	Je. 1:3
Jehoiachin, 597 B.C.	Je. 22:24
Zedekiah, 597-536 B.C.	Je. 1:3; 32:1-5

It is evident from this list that there is a difference between the order of the chapters and the dates. One writer describes this chronological irregularity:

> It will be seen that the book is not arranged in chronological order. Some late messages come early in the book, and some early messages come late in the book. The messages were delivered orally and perhaps repeatedly, for years, possibly, before Jeremiah began to write them. The writing of such a book was a long and laborious task. Writing parchment, made of sheep skin was scarce and expensive. It was made into a long roll, and wound around a stick. This may account, in part, for the lack of order in Jeremiah's book. After writing an incident or discourse, some other entrances delivered previously would be suggested, and he would write them down, in some cases, without dating them, thus filling up the parchment as he unrolled it.[2]

God called Jeremiah to the prophetic office especially to warn the people of Judah to repent and turn to God. Because of their idolatry, the Northern Kingdom had fallen to the Assyrians. Next, Judah was about to be attacked by Nebuchadnezzar, the Babylonian conqueror. Most of Judah had been conquered; only the capital of Jerusalem remained, and it was surrounded by hostile forces. One commentator describes the moral and spiritual state of Judah in these words:

> Altars to Baal were erected, and Asherim were built. Molech, the Ammonite deity, was acknowledged by the sacrificing of children in the Hinnom valley near Jerusalem. Worship of stars and planets was instituted. Official approval was given to astrology, divination, and occultism. The Temple itself was desecrated with graven images of Asherah, the wife of Baal. God was openly defiled at altars in the court of the Temple where the host of heaven was worshiped (cf. Je.19:13). Innocent blood was shed...[3]

A brief analysis of the book shows that Jeremiah and his fellow prophets, Habakkuk and Zephaniah, made desperate attempts to warn Judah to repent and "flee from the wrath to come" but the religious and political leaders persisted in moral and spiritual degradation. Jeremiah likened Judah

to an unfaithful wife who has forsaken her husband and has become a prostitute. Not only was sexual promiscuity and adultery common among the people (Je. 5:7-8), but also the nation was given to spiritual adultery, so called

because of their unfaithfulness to Jehovah and their worshiping of pagan gods. The people scoffed at the prophet's warning (Je. 5:12); the leaders did not hesitate to oppress and rob the people (Je. 5:26-28); the government was corrupt (Je. 5:30-31); the leaders listened to the false prophets (Je. 5:31), but

they ignored the men of God.

Jeremiah, a man of sorrows, found a people totally abandoned to everything vile; they were a "wicked and adulterous" generation.[4] Even Pashur the priest cast his lot with the evil forces. When Jeremiah's severe warnings persisted, he was put in prison and in stocks (Je. 20:2). Finally when Jeremiah advised the Jewish leaders to surrender and take their punishment, he was accused of treason (Je. 37-38). The advice of the false prophets was contrary to that which Jeremiah gave the people. Jeremiah predicted that Jerusalem would be destroyed and that Judah would be taken into captivity for 70 years (Je. 25). Jeremiah, again placed on trial and accused of treason by the priests and the false prophets, barely escaped execution (Je. 25-26).

Jerusalem
1881-1885

After preaching for twenty-three years, Jeremiah wrote his prophecies in a book so that his warnings could be read to all the people, but King Zedekiah burned the book and again imprisoned the prophet (Je. 38:6). Soon thereafter Nebuchadnezzar destroyed Jerusalem (Je. 39) and appointed Gedaliah governor to rule over the remaining citizens; however, in three months Gedaliah was assassinated by the rebellious element who then fled to Egypt, forcibly taking Jeremiah with them (Je. 40-43). In Egypt, Jeremiah continued his warning (Je. 44) and foretold the destruction of Egypt. When Nebuchadnezzar had completed the destruction of Judea, he attacked and conquered Egypt, according to the prophet's prediction (Je. 43:8-13). After the conquest of Egypt, Jeremiah predicted the fall of Babylon (Je. 50:37-43).

Zedekiah
3988

Warnings
1794-1795

Jeremiah 50 and 51 were copied in a separate book and sent to Babylon. The book was to be read to government officials. Then in solemn ceremony the chapters were sunk in the Euphrates river with these words: "Thus shall Babylon sink, and shall not rise from the evil that I will bring upon her...thus far are the words of Jeremiah (Je. 51:64)."[5] To this day the empty ruins remain.

Babylon
329, 4338

1:5 "Before I formed you in the womb I knew you, before you were born I set you apart; I appointed you as a prophet to the nations." (NIV)

Prophets
2065

Moses
2420

Warnings
1794-1799
Persecution
3480-3484

Divination
2226

The prophets were usually laymen divinely called to deliver a special message from God to the people. Prophets were inspired foretellers or forthtellers, who declared and interpreted divine revelation. Moses stands out as the chief prophet and father of the prophetic movement.

The OT does not explain how divine revelation was disclosed to the prophets; but when it was revealed, they became burdened to deliver the message even in the face of opposition. Usually a prophet's message was a serious warning from God against the sinful practices of the people (Ho. 9:17). As a result, many prophets suffered bodily harm and persecution for their efforts (Je. 37:15). The prophets of the Lord were men of integrity and absolute honesty. Their message was consistent with the moral nature of the God they represented and their message was reinforced with "thus saith the Lord." The revelation given them was not human but divine in origin (2 Pe. 1:20-21). The prophet Micah claimed that he was filled with the Spirit of the Lord to make known to the nation of Israel its sin (Mi. 3:8). As a counter-action to the continuous duplicity of the Canaanite soothsayers and diviners, God promised to send Israel men who would declare the whole counsel of God (De. 18:15-22). As the priests took the needs of the people before God, the prophet took special messages from God to the people (Am. 3:7ff.; cf. Ex. 4:16; 7:1).[6]

Behold, as the clay is in the potter's hand, so are ye in my hand, O house of Israel. (Je. 18:6)

Many of the prophets came from among the people; they were men with a sincere concern for the community who felt that they were commissioned by God to warn their contemporaries of the judgment to come and to give guidance concerning moral issues.

History has no parallel to the courageous witness the prophets of Israel gave the people, such as was demonstrated by Amos in 750 B.C. Under God, the prophets created Israel's spiritual greatness. They were "holy men of God."

The prophets of Israel emphasized the holiness of God, fearlessly criticized the immorality of their day, and tried to point their people to a nobler way of life. In the courts of Israel the prophets boldly rebuked the rulers, as Nathan did David (2 S. 12), and Jeremiah, the princes of Judah (Je. 26). They did not hesitate to castigate the selfish rich (Am. 4:1; 6:4-6).

The prophets were extremely patriotic and scornful of all who would invade their lands. Their written messages declare the ultimate triumph of good and the certain downfall of evil, but they had pity for the penitent and a charitable concern for the wayward (Is. 1:18). They kept believing that a righteous remnant would survive (Is. 10:20-22; 37:32; Eze. 6:8). Some of their pronouncements were bright with hope of a Messianic age.[7]

In the Hebrew canon the former prophetic books comprise Joshua, Judges, 1 and 2 Samuel, and 1 and 2 Kings and contain information on the period from the occupation of Canaan (thirteenth century B.C.) to the fall of Jerusalem in 587 B.C. The major prophetic books in the OT are Isaiah, Jeremiah, and Ezekiel. The writings of the minor prophets include Hosea, Joel, Amos, Obadiah, Jonah, Micah, Nahum, Habakkuk, Zephaniah, Haggai, Zechariah, and Malachi. These prophetic books are called major and minor because of the length of their writings.

There were also women in the prophetic office. Among them were Miriam, the sister of Moses and Aaron (Ex. 15:20-21), Deborah (Jud. 4:4), and Huldah (2 K. 22:12-20).

23:6 In his days Judah shall be saved, and Israel shall dwell safely: and this is his name whereby he shall be called, THE LORD OUR RIGHTEOUSNESS.

LORD-tsidkenu translates as "the LORD, our righteousness" and appears in Jeremiah's prophetic statement of a "righteous Branch" and a "King who is to come." The prophecy was given when Judah was about to fall—to be taken into captivity. The nation had sinned so greatly that judgment was inevitable, but in that day of darkness Jeremiah gave a word of encouragement to the people. Even though punishment was to come upon them, it was to be inflicted by the LORD, who loved them. Their immediate present was dark and hopeless; nevertheless, as the LORD is righteous, in the end righteousness will prevail.

This designation appears hundreds of times in the Scriptures and is used in the sense of rendering justice and making right. The LORD himself is perfect righteousness or the perfectly Righteous One. He then, is a *tsadik*,

Guidance
1465-1471

Holiness
of God
1597

Avarice
2131-2132

Canaan
626-634

Miriam
2375
Deborah
948

Jehovah-
Tsidkenu
1872
God's
Judgment
1966-1974

Justice—
Injustice
1975-1986

a righteous One, wrote the psalmist (Ps. 129:4). As an *El-tsadik,* a righteous God, there is none to compare with him, declared Isaiah (Is. 45:21). He is the Rock whose work is perfect, all of whose ways are just; *tsadik* is righteous and "right is he" (De. 32:4). His "righteousness is an everlasting righteousness," and his testimonies are righteous forever (Ps. 119:142,144). Righteousness and justice are the very foundations of his throne (Eze. 43:1-7). Therefore in all his dealings he is righteous.

For other Jehovah titles in the Bible, see chart at Ex. 3:14.

Lamentations

The Name

The original title of Lamentations was taken from the first word in the book. In the Hebrew canon it is called *Ekkah* (1:1), meaning "How" or "Alas!" A modern expression might be "how come" this disaster. In the Greek OT (LXX) the word is rendered *threno.* In Latin it is *thren,* meaning "lamentations." This book has a collective name which tradition has applied to the five elegies in the Hebrew canon lamenting the fate of destroyed Jerusalem. In the Hebrew canon the book of Lamentations is one of the five scrolls *(Megilloth)* and is listed in the category of the Writings (Heb., *kethubim;* Gr., *hagiographa*).

Authorship and Date

Many scholars believe that Jeremiah wrote the book of Lamentations. The style and phraseology of the entire book appear similar to the writings in the book of Jeremiah.

Jeremiah certainly was qualified to write the dramatic description of horror and destruction. Only an eyewitness could do this.

Background, Purpose, and Content

Jeremiah lived in Jerusalem for about forty-five years under most trying conditions. He had suffered persecution in an effort to save the city from destruction and her people from captivity. Tradition says that Jeremiah took a position on the western slope of the Mount of Olives and mourned as he watched the city of Jerusalem being burned to the ground.

The composition of this poem is very technical. Chapters 1, 2, 4 and 5 each have twenty-two verses. They are called acrostic or alphabetic because each of the twenty-two Hebrew consonants is used as the initial letter for one of the twenty-two verses. For instance, in chapters 1, 2, 4 and 5 the first verse begins with the *aleph,* verse two with the *beth,* the third verse with a *gimel,* verse four with *daleth,* and so on to the end of each chapter.[1]

Chapter 3 has sixty-six verses or three sets of twenty-two verses. In this chapter the first three verses begin with *aleph,* the second three with a *beth,* the third three with a *gimel,* and so on to the end of the chapter. The

Lamenta-tions	**1945-1946**
Lamenta-tions of Jeremiah	**4247**
Jeremiah	**1877**
Jerusalem	**1881-1885**
Jerusalem	**4391**

order of *ain* and *pe* in chapters 2 and 4 is reversed. This arrangement is comparable to Psalm 119 which is an alphabetic poem with twenty-two eight-verse sections.

Joy
Departed
1812

Sin's
Misery
788

Prayer
2816-2841

One scholar describes the sadness of the book of Lamentations in these words:

> One would think…that every letter was written with a tear; every word the sound of a breaking heart: that the author was compacted of sorrow; disciplined to grief from his infancy; one who never breathed but in sighs, nor spoke but in a groan…

> All the expressions and images of sorrow are here exhibited in various combinations…Misery has no expression that the author of Lamentations has not employed…Take him through his life to his death, and learn from him what true patriotism means. The man who watched, prayed and lived for the welfare of his country; who chose to share her adversities, her sorrows, her wants, her afflictions, and disgrace, when he might have been a companion of princes, and have sat at the table of kings; who only ceased to live for his country when he ceased to breathe;—that was a patriot, in comparison with whom almost all others are obscured, diminished and brought low, or totally annihilated.[2]

Jerusalem, as seen from the Mount of Olives. Jeremiah prophesied and witnessed the city's destruction.

Ezekiel

The Name

The name Ezekiel is derived from the Hebrew *Yehezkel* meaning "God strengthens." In the Greek OT (LXX) it appears as *Iezehiel* and in the Latin Vulgate as *Ezechiel*.

The name of the book is taken from Ezekiel 1:3, "The word of the LORD came expressly unto Ezekiel." The book of Ezekiel is the third of the Major Prophets and the third of the Latter Prophets in the Hebrew canon.

Authorship and Date

Ezekiel 1:3 records that the prophet was the son of a certain Buzi and that he was also a priest as well as a prophet. This identification would presuppose that Ezekiel was a man of letters, well-versed in the rabbinical law of his day. Some writers see special levitical elements in Ezekiel 40-46, and high-priestly characteristics in his portrayal of the Messiah (Eze. 45:22).[1]

Background, Purpose, and Content

Ezekiel was taken into Babylonian captivity with King Jehoiachin during Nebuchadnezzar's second attack upon Jerusalem in 597 B.C., eleven years before the city was totally destroyed. His place of residence in Babylon was in the vicinity of the Chebar River, "the great ship canal branching off from the Euphrates north of Babylon and running through Nippur to the Tigris."[2]

When Ezekiel arrived in Babylon, Daniel had already attained great fame. Daniel was the prophetic statesman in the palace, and Ezekiel was minister to the captives in the slave areas. Ezekiel was of aristocratic rank, a member of the priestly tribe, accustomed to association with the upper echelon of society. In Babylon he was suddenly thrust into the society of the poor, a new experience for him. Before he assumed parish responsibility among the common people, he lived in their midst to work and eat as they did for a time. This experience put him in a better position to understand the problems of the people so that he could say, "I sat where they sat" (Eze. 3:15). In spite of all his pleading, the people were still rebellious and

Ezekiel	**1197**
Book of Ezekiel	**4248**
Prophets	**2065-2066**
Captivity	**1825-1829**
Jehoiachin	**1859**
Nebuchadnezzar	**2573-2574**
Daniel	**914, 4300**
Poor	**2799-2804**
Rebellion	**3231-3232**

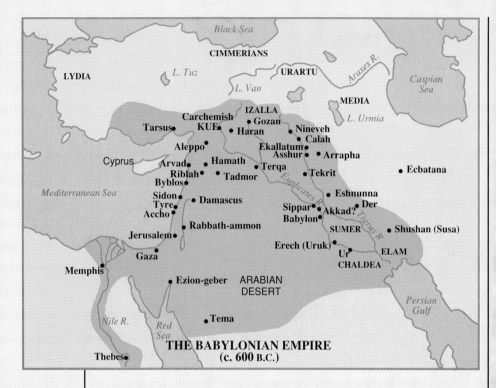

THE BABYLONIAN EMPIRE
(c. 600 B.C.)

Prophetic
Visions
2495

refused to turn to the Lord (Eze 2:1-5). Ezekiel's revelation from God came in the form of a scroll (Eze. 2:9-10) which the prophet was commanded to eat (Eze. 3:3).

The people who had gone into exile with Daniel (606 B.C.) were hopeful that Ezekiel's arrival (579 B.C.) would signal a return to Jerusalem, but their hopes were dashed when Ezekiel told them that the city of Jerusalem would soon be destroyed by fire and that more captives would be arriving. Ezekiel made it clear that the people would be homeless for many years and would stay in exile until they repented and accepted God (Eze. 4-7).

Repentance
2706-2710
Restoration
3025-3026

Ezekiel had many visions of the final destruction of Jerusalem (Eze. 8-9), but he prophesied that there would be an eventual restoration after the exiles were humbled, and ceased their idolatry (Eze. 10-12).

The prophecy in chapter 12 describes accurately the fate which would befall king Zedekiah five years later. Zedekiah was forced to see his sons put to death. Then his captors put out his eyes and led him as a slave to Babylon to join the other captives. Zedekiah, no doubt, was the victim of the advice given him by the false prophets (Eze. 13-14).

False
Prophets
2100
Idolatry
3928-3933

Ezekiel had a vision of a burning vine tree which symbolized the burning of Jerusalem (Eze. 15). Through the symbol of a bride, the prophet gave a vivid description of Judah's idolatry (Eze. 16). The parable of the two eagles symbolized the destruction of Jerusalem under Zedekiah (Eze. 17), the result of the national and personal sins of Judah. In the parable of the lion cubs, the prophet lamented for the princess of Israel (Eze. 19). The elders' continual rebellion against God (Eze. 20) eventually resulted in their destruc-

Destruction
990-991

tion (Eze. 21-23). A cauldron symbolized the siege of Jerusalem and the dispersion of the people (Eze. 24). Nations other than Israel were also subject to divine punishment. The prophet directed his prophetic attention against Ammon, Moab, Edom, and Philistia (Eze. 25), later against Tyre and Sidon (Eze. 25-28).

Dispersion
1023

Ezekiel's prophecy of judgment upon Tyre is unusual. The prophet predicted that Nebuchadnezzar, king of Babylon, would set his engines of war against the walls of Tyre, that with axes he would break down the walls, and that the conqueror would put stones, timber, and the dust of Tyre into the sea (Eze. 26:7-12). When Nebuchadnezzar's army approached Tyre, the leading citizens and the government moved to an island a mile or so off the coast. It took the Babylonian conquerors thirteen years to destroy the city on the shore (585-573 B.C.). Years later, when Alexander the Great conquered the city in 332 B.C., the island city had become a formidable fortress.

Tyre
3716, 4445

War
3766-3773

Alexander was a land soldier without ships, so to attack the city on the island he built a causeway with the stone and timbers from the old city. The need for fill-in material became so great that he literally scraped the dirt from the surface down to the bare rock to complete the project.[3] Bible scholars see in this episode the minute fulfillment of Ezekiel's prophecy that the "stones," the "timber" and "dirt" would be put into the water (Eze. 26:12). For centuries the site of the former city was a bare rock, just as Alexander the Great had left it. It was a place where the fishermen spread their nets to dry. Thus the prophecy of Ezekiel was fulfilled in detail (Eze. 26:4-5,14).[4] For more of the city of Tyre, see the essay on pp. 347-350.

Warriors
3779

Ezekiel next pronounced judgment and desolation upon Egypt (Eze. 29-30) and Assyria (Eze. 31). Shortly thereafter Ezekiel lamented when his prophecy against Egypt was fulfilled (see Eze. 29-30; 32).

Egypt
1100

When news of the fall of Jerusalem reached Babylon, Ezekiel received a new call to prophesy (Eze. 33). He pronounced judgment upon the shepherds of Israel who fed themselves but did not "feed the sheep" (Eze. 34). Edom was the next nation to fall because of the help the people gave Nebuchadnezzar when their Jewish cousins were being slaughtered by the Babylonians. (See the book of Obadiah for further pronouncements of doom upon Edom.)

Feeding the Flock
2090

Ruins of the Hippodrome at Tyre from Ezekiel's time.

In the "vision of dry bones" Ezekiel saw the resurrection of Israel, the return of the Jews to Judah (Eze. 37) and the destruction of the enemies of Israel (Eze. 38-39). Ezekiel's concluding prophecies deal with the rebuilt temple and the restoration of offerings and sacrifices (Eze. 40-48).

Offerings
2625-2636
Jews' Return
1827

27:9 Veteran craftsmen of Gebal... (NIV)

The Biblical city of Gebal, referred to here and in Ps. 83:7, is a very ancient city, now known as Byblos. It is located about thirty miles north of Sidon on the coast of Lebanon at the base of the Lebanon mountains. Its harbor, along with that of Beirut, Tyre and Sidon, helped to make this area one of the great commercial centers in the Mediterranean world. It is the oldest known Phoenician city, with a tradition going back to 5000 B.C.

Byblos had diplomatic contact with Egypt as early as 1400-1360 B.C. The Tel Amarna tablets contain the first known alphabetic writing including a Ugaritic system with 31 signs as well as a more cursive script with 22 characters.

Archaeological activity in this area began with Ernest Renan in 1860. In 1924 the French started the most thorough excavation at Byblos under the direction of Pierre Montet and Maurice Dunard. They found artifacts dating

The remains of the harbor facilities at Byblos (Gebal).

from the second millenium to the Roman Period. Later the Lebanon Department of Antiquities continued the excavations.

From very early times Byblos was a center for the Baal nature culture. The Baal gods, along with their female counterpart, Ishtarte, were worshiped exclusively. Worship was associated with the seasons. The gods were said to die in the fall when plant life dried up and were resurrected in the spring when nature came back to life. The fall festivities were accompanied by mourning and funeral rites along with self-torture and mutilation. Sacramental sex indulgence characterized the spring resurrection festivities. Both male and female prostitutes served in these activities.

Byblos has become a household word because of its paper business. Egypt shipped the papyrus reed to Byblos, who in turn processed the reed paper and then shipped the finished product abroad. The Greeks named the

Baal
3936

False
Worship
3928-3951

Paper
2676

paper "Byblos." Thus, Byblos became synonymous with papyrus paper and from this came the word "book," from which developed "The Book" or the Bible.

48:35 ...the name of the city from that day shall be, The LORD is there.

By his various titles the Lord revealed himself in the power and majesty and glory of his person in meeting all human needs. His name Elohim revealed him as the Creator of the universe. His name LORD revealed his special relationship to man. The title for Jehovah in this verse is perhaps the most fitting one with which to climax the OT. LORD-shammah conveys the meaning "The LORD is there" (Eze. 48:35; see also Eze. 43:1-7).

Justification
by Faith
1203
Future
Rest
1366

The name LORD-shammah reveals the promise to complete the pledge to bring man to his final rest and glory, for "man's end is to glorify God and to enjoy Him forever. For, as Paul states, 'Whom he called, them he also justified: and whom he justified, them he also glorified' (Ro. 8:30), a past tense, but the language of eternity."[5]

The reference by Ezekiel (48:35) appears at the very end of his message. Even though Israel's temple was destroyed and the people were separated from Jerusalem, they were assured of the Lord's presence with them.

For other Jehovah titles in the Bible, see chart at Ex. 3:14.

Daniel

The Name

The name "Daniel" is derived from the Hebrew *Daniyel* and means "God is my judge." In the Greek OT (LXX) this name is rendered *Daniel* corresponding to the form used in English. The book is so called because Daniel is the principal character. His name is mentioned 75 times in the book, appearing in all but chapters 3 and 11.

The book of Daniel is usually referred to as a prophetic book. It follows Ezekiel as the fifth book of the Major Prophets, but in the Hebrew canon it is placed in the third division, the Writings (Heb. *kethubim,* Gr., *hagiographa*). This book was not put with the other prophets, although Daniel was called a prophet (Mt. 24:15) and was marvelously gifted with the spirit of prophecy. Nevertheless he did not have the prophetic vocation but was an official statesman and spent his life in the business of the state. He does not use the common prophetic declaration, "thus saith the Lord," nor does he exhort his contemporaries as it was the function of prophets to do.[1]

Authorship and Date

The Bible refers to three Daniels: (1) a son of David and Abigail (1 Chr. 3:1); (2) a priest in the days of Nehemiah (Ezr. 8:2; Ne. 10:6) and (3) the celebrated Jewish prophet in the Babylonian Court.

Daniel was taken, as a youth, into Babylon with the other captives in the first deportation during the reign of Jehoiakim (606 B.C.). In Babylon he and his companions were selected to be trained and to serve as liaison officers between the captives and the Babylonian government. Daniel stands out as a man of intelligence, integrity, and dedication to Jehovah. People in all ages have been inspired by his loyalty to God (Da. 1:8-17).

The book of Daniel, like the book of Isaiah, has been attacked by certain critics. However, both Christian and synagogue scholars have been committed to the assumption that the book was written by Daniel. Around him the account centers. The words in Daniel 12:4 indicate that Daniel wrote a book and was instructed to seal or conclude it (see also Da. 7:1).

Daniel
914, 4300

Book of
Daniel
4249

Prophetic
Visions
2496

Babylon
**329-331,
4338**

Piety
2986

Wall decoration from the palace of Babylon.

The book of Daniel deals with the prophet's relationship to government officials and people in the Babylonian-Persian area. The book also contains prophetic statements concerning the development of future nations and predictions relating to the coming of the Messiah and the founding of his kingdom.

Messianic Prophecies 2890

The authorship of Daniel remained unquestioned until, in the third century, Malchus Porphyry (or Porphyrius) attacked the historical integrity of Christianity and the book of Daniel (A.D. 233-304). He vented his antagonism against the Christian religion in his fifteen books entitled *Against the Christians.*[2] In the twelfth book the critical thrust was against the apocalyptic sections in the book of Daniel, and the foretelling of future events.

Philosophy 2759

Porphyry, a scholar, was educated in the heathen philosophy of Athens and Rome. "With Platinus, he believed in good and evil demons and respected Greek mythology with its philosophical tenets. He relied upon enchantment as a means of acquiring power over demons and the souls of the dead, believing that all matter was polluted."[3]

Evil Spirits 3156

The translation of the Latin Vulgate version of Jerome assists the student to a better understanding of Porphyry's opposition to revealed truth. Jerome interprets Porphyry's view thus:

he went through the various kings in order, stated the actual number of years involved and announced beforehand the clearest signs of events to come, and because Porphyry saw that all these things had been fulfilled and could not deny that they had taken place, he overcame this evidence of historical accuracy by taking refuge in this evasion, contending that whatever is foretold concerning the antichrist at the end of the world was actually fulfilled in the reign of Antiochus Epiphanes (175-164) because of certain similarities to things which took place at his time. But this very attack testifies to Daniel's accuracy. For so striking was the reliability of what the prophet foretold, that he could not appear to unbelievers as a predictor of the future, but rather a narrator of things already past...Porphyry makes his objection to us concerning the book of Daniel, that it is clearly a forgery, not to be considered as belonging to the Hebrew Scriptures but an invention composed in Greek...[4]

Antichrist
196

Of course, Porphyry was mistaken in assuming that the book of Daniel had its origin in Greek and not in Hebrew; he initiated the destructive criticism of the Bible which followed. The references in the Bible that fore-tell the future and give an account of the miracles which occurred have been the focal point of attack by some critics. They assumed that the prophets could not foretell the future; those who disbelieved placed the prophetic section at a date subsequent to the actual event.

Bible
414-445
Miracles
2360-2374

When modern theological rationalism developed in the seventeenth and eighteenth centuries, the critics adopted Porphyry's approach to Daniel. Instead of leaving the book of Daniel in its historical context (606-535 B.C.), they placed it in the period of Antiochus Epiphanes or during the Macca-bean Revolt (175-164 B.C.), even though Antiochus is not mentioned in the book. They assumed that the people needed encouragement in those trou-blesome times. Consequently a clever scribe was invented who used the figure of Daniel to write a kind of fictional historical novel to stimulate loyalty to God and to maintain enthusiasm for the national cause against the Seleucid ruler, Antiochus Epiphanes. Thus historicity of the events de-scribed in the book of Daniel became totally irrelevant. These critical scholars have classified a respectable book in the OT canon with a group of spurious books akin to the pseudepigrapha. So it has been with all scholars such as Emil K. Kraeling in *Encyclopedia of Religious Knowledge,* p. 216; Robert R. Pfeiffer in *Introduction to the Old Testament,* p. 420; and others.

God's
Word
Sacred
427

In recent years archaeological and other kinds of new discoveries have strengthened the traditional, conservative view. Clyde J. Hurst con-cludes that

despite prevalent critical opinion against the 6th century dating of the book [Daniel] a gradual trend is discernible toward earlier dating. The discovery of Belshazzar's (q.v.) name on Babylonian clay tablets, and the probable identification by Whitcomb of Darius the Mede (q.v.) with Gubaru (Gr: Gobryas) have gone far to validate the 6th cent. historical accuracy of the book. Alleged linguistic and exegetical problems have been more than adequately answered by conservative scholars...Qumran fragments of the book of Daniel (150 B.C.) are also weighing heavily in pushing back the date of the authorship of the book toward the conservative date.[5]

Darius
915

The many references in the book of Daniel to the immediate Babylo-nian and Persian background indicate that the writer was present to make these cultural observations. The internal evidence is supplemented by the external.

Babylon
329-331

It is evident that Jesus considered Daniel to be a historical person and the author of his book and that what Daniel had said about the "abomina-tion of desolation" was important (Mt. 24:15; Mk. 13:14; cf. Da. 9:27).[6] William Smith writes: "The book represents, in many respects, a startling

Christ
Jesus
677-700

and exceptional character, yet it is far more difficult to explain its composition in the Maccabean period than to connect the peculiarities which it exhibits with the exigencies of the Return."[7]

Jews'
Return
1827

Favor–
Disfavor
1250-1255

Dreams
1037-1039

Meshach
2305

Background, Purpose, and Content

A brief analysis of the book of Daniel shows that Daniel was the young prophet who won court favor in Babylon because of his intellectual, physical, and moral excellence. Even though he was challenged several times for his faith, he apparently retained his official relationship as well as his spiritual and moral integrity for about seventy years.

Through his dream-image Daniel prophetically identified the four on-coming world powers: Babylonia, Persia, Greece, and Rome. Between the time of Daniel and the coming of Christ each prediction was minutely fulfilled (Da. 2). After Daniel and his three friends had been in Babylon twenty years, Shadrach, Meshach, and Abednego defended their spiritual integrity. For this allegiance they were thrown into the fiery furnace; through divine intervention the three emerged from the furnace unsinged (Da. 3). Daniel showed his courage when he told the king that his dream meant that the king would temporarily lose his sanity, join the animals in the field, and eat grass (Da. 4). Following this experience the king made a profession of faith in Daniel's God (Da. 4:37).

Divine
Hand
1484-1486
Euphrates
1157

After Daniel had been in Babylon seven years, Belshazzar put on a "royal feast." During that time a mysterious hand begin to write on the wall. That same night Cyrus, the Persian king, took the city, marching his troops into the city over the dry river bed. Historians state that Cyrus's engineers diverted the course of the Euphrates River around the city. No additional historical record has been found so far which mentions Darius the Mede or any other ruler between Nabonidus, Belshazzar, and Cyrus, nor have the various identifications of Darius satisfied all scholars. This does not mean that Darius did not exist (Da. 5:31). Some scholars suggest that Darius was a sub-king under Cyrus.

Prayer
2816-2841

Because of Daniel's popularity in the court, his political enemies determined to attack him through his religion (Da. 6:5). When he violated a decree which forbade praying to anyone other than the king, Daniel was cast into the lion's den, but God protected him just as he had preserved the life of his friends who were cast into the fiery furnace (Da. 6). Chapter 7 records Daniel's vision of four beasts coming out of the sea—a lion, a bear, a leopard, and a nameless beast with iron teeth and ten horns. The four beasts are usually interpreted to represent four world empires—Babylon, Persia, Greece, and Rome. The ten horns are thought to represent the ten kingdoms into which the Roman Empire was divided.

End of the
World
1126
Last
Judgment
1351-1353

In this vision Daniel seems to have been carried into the "end time" or the final judgment (Da 7:9-10,13-14). The eighth chapter is a continuation of chapter 7. In the ninth chapter Daniel has a vision of "The Seventy Weeks." J. W. Purkiser presents a commonly held interpretation among evangelicals:

The angel...reveals to Daniel that the seventy years in reality stand for seventy weeks (of years) or a period of seventy times seven years. Of these seventy weeks, sixty-nine ("seven weeks, and threescore and two weeks") represent the time "from the going forth of the commandment to restore and build Jerusalem" to the coming of the Messiah

DANIEL		JOSEPH
Da. 1:3-7	Carried captive in youth	Ge. 37:28
Da. 1:4	Model young man	Ge. 39:2-6
Da. 1:4-5	Employed in the king's court	Ge. 41:40
Da. 2:13; 6:16	Unjustly persecuted	Ge. 39:20
Da. 6:28	Hardships led to honor	Ge. 41:14
Da. 1:17	Interpreted dreams	Ge. 40:16; 41:15
Da. 1:17-21; 2:48	Exalted to rulership	Ge. 41:40, 44
Da. 1:8	Lived a pure life in a corrupt court	Ge. 39:7-13
Da. 12:13	Died in a foreign land	Ge. 50:26

A comparison of the lives of Daniel and Joseph

(9:25). The remaining week seems to refer to the reign of the Antichrist and to be delayed until the time of the end (9:27). The command referred to is commonly thought to be the commission given to Ezra by Artaxerxes, king of Persia, in 458 or 457 B.C. (Ezr. 7:11-28). If the latter date is used, we note that the time from Ezra's commission until the beginning of Christ's ministry in A.D. 26 was exactly 483 years (sixty-nine times seven years)—a remarkable fulfillment of prophecy)![8]

Daniel's last vision took place two years after the Jews returned to their homeland (434 B.C.). God showed Daniel some of the hidden conflicts which were going on in the unseen world. Michael and his angels were at war with Satan and his angels (Da. 10). Chapter 11 represents a continuation of the four great empires from the time of Daniel to Christ. These revelations seem to be progressive, culminating in the "end of time." There is to be a time of trouble such as had never occurred before. In Chapter 12 Daniel brought a glorious message on the resurrection: "and many of them that sleep in the dust of the earth shall awake, some to everlasting life, and some to shame and everlasting contempt" (12:2).

Finally, Daniel was commanded to seal the book, presumably the one he had written and which is to be opened at "the time of the end" (Da. 12:4).

The Future
1344-1375

Spiritual
Conflict
358-360
Angels
143-149

End of the
World
1126

The City of Babylon

The Babylon to which Daniel and his friends were carried was one of the mighty cities of antiquity and was located in the general area where civilization had its beginning, in the Garden of Eden. The tower of Babel was built in or near the immediate environs

Babylon
329-331

Towers
3651

of the city (see commentary and picture at Ge. 11:9).

Babylon was the capital city of the Babylonian Empire and reached the peak of its glory under King Nebuchadnezzar in the sixth century. Nebuchadnezzar enlarged and repaired the old palace, making it the most splendid capital of that time. In Daniel 4:30 he boasts, "...Is not this

Nebuchadnezzar
2573-2574

great Babylon, that I have built for the house of the kingdom by the might of my power, and for the honour of my majesty?"

It is thought that the famous Hanging Gardens, one of the Seven Wonders of the Ancient World, were built near the palace for the benefit of Nebuchadnezzar's wife, who missed the hills of her homeland (in the region of Media).

> Media
> **2268**

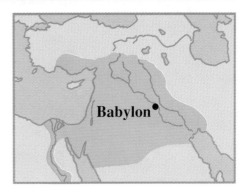

Historians agree that the city of Babylon was square—about 15 miles to each side—and that the walls were 300 feet high and 80 feet thick with 250 water towers.[9]

This seemingly impregnable city was destroyed just as the Biblical prophets foretold. Jeremiah declared, "...Babylon shall become heaps, a dwelling place for dragons, an astonishment, and an hissing, without an inhabitant" (Je. 51:37). Today all that is left of the once glorious city is ruins.

> Desolation
> **987**

A view of thr ruins at Babylon.

An artist's impression of Processsion Street, Babylon, which began slightly north of the famous Ishtar Gate.

Hosea

The Name

The Hebrew name for Hosea is *Hoshea,* probably meaning "Help, God," or "God is help." It comes from a Hebrew verb from which *salvation* is derived. In the Greek OT the name is rendered *Osee.* The title for the book of Hosea comes from the book itself where the name appears once in the first verse and twice in the second verse.

The book of Hosea is listed in the English Bible as the first of the Minor Prophets, probably because Hosea's book is the longest of those of the minor prophets. In the Hebrew canon it is listed as that of the fourth Latter Prophet.

Authorship and Date

Authorship has been ascribed to Hosea in both Jewish and Christian tradition. Verse 2 states: "The beginning of the word of the LORD by Hosea." Verse 1 identifies Hosea as the son of Beeri, and states that the Word of the Lord came to him in the days of Uzziah (787-735), Jotham (749-734), Ahaz (741-726), and Hezekiah (726-697), kings of Judah, and in the days of Jeroboam (790-749). It is evident that Hosea had a long life span; his ministry lasted for about fifty-seven years (782-725). Hosea was one of the eighth-century prophets and "was a younger contemporary of Amos, an older contemporary of Jonah and Micah."[1]

Background, Purpose, and Content

The book of Hosea has presented problems concerning moral principles to both Jewish and Christian scholars. According to the levitical law, no priest or prophet was to marry an adulterous woman (Le. 21:7). Yet the text of Hosea clearly states: "The LORD said to Hosea, Go, take unto thee a wife of whoredoms and children of whoredoms" (Ho. 1:2). Verse 3 records that Hosea "went and took Gomer the daughter of Diblaim; which conceived, and bare him a son" (Ho. 1:3). The remaining part of ch. 1 and ch. 2 deal with the children conceived in this union, and the meaning of the names given them, as well as the judgment God proposed for Israel. It is apparent that Gomer continued to practice her prostitution while she was married to Hosea, for the writer stated the offspring are the children of whoredoms and "their mother hath played the harlot: she that conceived

Prominent
Bible
Characters
4300a
Book of
Hosea
4250

Hosea
1704

Prophets
2065-2066

Adultery
1662

them hath done shamefully: for she said, I will go after my lovers" (Ho. 2:5). Gomer left her husband's home to associate herself with a lover who could better satisfy her fondness for luxury.

Despite Gomer's infidelity, Hosea continued to love his wife. The Lord commanded Hosea to bring his wife back. When the lover refused to release Gomer without monetary compensation, Hosea redeemed her for fifteen pieces of silver and some barley (Ho. 3:1-2). The rest of Hosea deals with the various aspects of judgment which are to befall Israel. Students of the Bible have an interest in the interpretation of this story. For what purpose was it considered to be the infallible, inspired Word of God? Of the many theories, there are four leading ones:

1. *Allegorical*. According to this view, the story is purely allegorical (having hidden meaning), designed to communicate a truth, but it has no actual authority. However, if the events did not occur, it would be difficult to know what is truth and what is fiction. The book of Hosea does not support the assumption that the account is merely an allegory. The story is told clearly and simply: What God said and did and what Hosea said and did.

2. *Literal*. The literal interpretation presupposes that Hosea loved Gomer and thought that he could reform her.

Casual thinking would lead one to wonder how God could command Hosea to violate the very commandments he had instituted at Sinai. To better comprehend God's direction to Hosea, one needs to recognize something of the extent of the apostasy and immorality which prevailed in Israel. Jehovah, the true and living God, had been forsaken; in his place the people worshiped the Baals— the nature gods and goddesses. The pagan temple ritual involved sexual immorality in which the people participated, the outstanding example being the Baal priests and the temple harlots or prostitutes. The belief was that to influence the productive forces of nature, the priest and priestess must engage in sexual orgies. Male prostitution and homosexuality were included in the ritual. Thus, the people were completely under the control of the Baal gods.

About forty years before Hosea, Jezebel, a dedicated champion of the Baal religion, married

The god Baal — artist's interpretation of a bronze figure from Ras Shamra.

Israel, where Hosea was the resident prophet.

Ahab, the king of Israel. As the queen, she brought hundreds of Baal priests and prophets into the royal court and started a systematic persecution and murder of God's prophets. She threatened the great Hebrew prophet Elijah, who escaped death at her hands only because of God's providence. One scholar describes Jezebel's reign:

> She was a devoted worshipper of Baal, and intolerant of other faiths. To please her, Ahab reared a temple, and an altar to Baal in Samaria, and set up an Asherah (1 K. 16:32-33)...She slew all the prophets of Jehovah on whom she could lay hands (1 K. 18:4-13). When she planned the death of Elijah (1K. 19:1-2), and afterward effected the judicial murder of Naboth, she similarly ignored the king's authority, though he condoned the deed (1 K. 21:16-22).[2]

The moral and religious degradation which existed in Israel resulted in disregard for social and ethical values. Corruption had affected every segment of society. In fact, this total disregard for righteousness finally resulted in a disaster for the nation such as could be compared only to the Canaanite nations who perished under Joshua. Israel embraced the very system which had brought total judgment upon the heathen nations (see Jos.1-2).

The Baal religion was one of the most depraved religions in the world (see commentary on Nu. 22:21). Even young girls were expected to give themselves to the temple hierarchy for sexual purposes before marriage. Their service was usually for a month or more.

One reason God commanded Hosea to marry a prostitute may be that most, if not all, marriageable young women had served their time in the temple as religious prostitutes. Halley writes: "The idolatrous worship of the land was so universally accomplished with immoral practices (Ho. 4:1-14) that it was hard for a woman to be chaste, and 'whoredom,' in its literal sense, was probably true of most of the women of the time. For Hosea, possibly, it was that kind of woman, or none at all."[3]

Although the story of Hosea and Gomer is repulsive to the pure mind, history shows that God can use the evil experiences of men for his glory. Some parables drawn from this story show that as Hosea continued to love Gomer, despite her infidelity, so Jehovah continued to love his bride, the children of Israel, even though they had turned their faces from him and

Ahab
102

Persecution
3480, 3484

Places
Devoted to
Idolatry
3948-3951

Degradation
967
Righteousness—
Unrighteousness
3077-3085

Chastity–
Impurity
663-667

Spiritual
Adultery
1814

Bride
737

Discern-
ment–
Dullness
1007-1014

Compassion
of God
3517

Adultery
1662

Conjugal
Love
1623

Old Age
2191-2195

committed spiritual adultery. One writer summarizes the matter thus:

> Whatever the difficulties of determining the correct interpretation may be, the basic message of the prophet is clear, Israel is the wife of Yahweh (Ho. 2:19-20; cf. 2:2). She has entered into this holy relationship by way of a covenant (Ho. 6:7; 8:1). However, like Gomer, the nation is guilty of spiritual infidelity, having been corrupted by Baal worship (Ho. 2:8,13,17; 4:13;11:2).

> More fundamental than their idolatry is the people's lack of personal knowledge of their God (Ho. 4:1, 6; 5:4; 6:6; 13:4). They have rejected a close, warm contact with His loving heart (Ho. 4:6); in return they must press on to know Yahweh (Ho. 6:1-3). Coordinate to their infidelity and the spurning of His love is the absence of covenant loyalty and devotion…on their part (Ho. 4:2; 6:4, 6)…A revival of its observance is essential (Ho.10:12; 12:6).

> Even though Israel has fallen to this despicable level, Yahweh still loves her with yearning compassion (Ho. 11:8-9; 14:4). If she will but repent (Ho.10:12; 12:6; 14:1), He will have mercy and restore her…Just like Luke writes of the prodigal son, so Hosea tells of the prodigal wife.[4]

3. *The Conditional Literal View.* This view accepts the textual statements but with interpretive qualifications. It is more charitable toward Gomer, because even though the text states that Hosea "took a wife of whoredoms," this view allows for the possibility that it was her family that was involved in harlotry, but that she was pure when she married Hosea. However, after her marriage Gomer drifted into prostitution, and Hosea continued to love her and to hope that she would return to him.

4. *The Literal View with Historial Adjustments.* This view assumes that Hosea wrote the book in retrospect, after he was an old man and`had ministered about fifty years. Having learned some things at a later date, Hosea pushed back the narrative and spoke them as though he had known them from the first. He had married Gomer thinking she was free of her family's whoredoms. The erotic style of the text encourages this viewpoint.

Joel

The Name

Names, Meaning 4300a

In Hebrew, the name Joel is *Yoel* and means "Jehovah is God." In the Greek OT (LXX) this name is rendered *Ioel*. Nothing is known about this prophet other than that he was the son of Pethuel (Joel 1:1). This particular Joel is not mentioned in the OT other than in the book bearing his name.

Book of Joel 4251

In the English Bible the book of Joel is listed under the Minor Prophets in second place; in the Hebrew canon it is the fifth under Latter Prophets.

Authorship and Date

Both Jewish and Christian traditions attribute authorship of the book of Joel to the prophet whose name it bears. The first verse states: "The word of the LORD that came to Joel."

Famine 21-23

Joel gives a description of destruction by famine and insect hordes (Joel 1:4), but this reference does not contain a statement as to the date of its writing or its author. Natural disasters happened frequently in Judea, e.g., the famine mentioned in the book of Ruth and the one in Genesis which occurred in the days of the patriarch Jacob (Ge. 41:54 ff.). The book contains passages similar to those in Jeremiah (46:10), Isaiah (2:12), Ezekiel (7:19), and Amos (5:16, 20), especially with reference to an apocalyptic event. Joel is considered to be an eighth-century prophet. McRae suggests that Joel began his ministry in 837 B.C. and ended it in 800 B.C.[1]

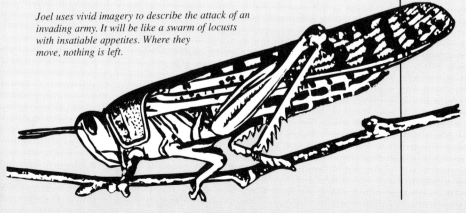

Joel uses vivid imagery to describe the attack of an invading army. It will be like a swarm of locusts with insatiable appetites. Where they move, nothing is left.

The name Joel is quite common in the OT but in each instance the reference is to a Joel other than the prophet; e.g., a Levite in the family of Kohath, the father of Heman, the singer (1 Chr. 6:33); the older son of Samuel (1 S. 8:2); a Gershomite Levite who helped carry the Ark (1 Chr. 15:7, 11-12); a chief of the tribe of Issachar (1 Chr. 7:3); a brother of Nathan and a soldier under David (1 Chr. 11:38); a son of Pedaiah and ruler in the tribal domain of Manasseh (1 Chr. 27:20); a chief Gadite in Basham (1 Chr. 5:12-17); a Reubenite (1 Chr. 5:4, 8-9); a Kohathite Levite during Hezekiah's reign (2 Chr. 29:12); one of the Simeonite princes (1 Chr. 4:35-43); a son of Nebo (Ezr. 10:43); and a Benjamite in Jerusalem under Nehemiah (Ne. 11:9).[2]

Background, Purpose, and Content

There is almost no narrative in the book, except a short passage in 2:18. The first part of the book is an account of the invasion and destruction caused by the palmerworm, the locusts, the cankerworm, and the caterpillar. Each successive invader ate what the other had left. These insects grew rapidly from larva to winged adult (Joel 1:4) and at every stage their appetite increased so that when they had finished no green thing remained.

In warning the nation Joel used the insect swarms as a symbol of enemy hordes of the north that would sweep across the land leaving it scorched and desolate. He affirmed that no one need fear God's judgment if he would repent and turn his face to God (Joel 2:11-13). Joel pled with the whole nation to repent and assured them that God was merciful (Joel 2:12-18). Upon their repentance, God promised to rid the land of the insects and to restore it to a bountiful supply.[3]

The second part of the book is apocalyptic; Joel describes prophetically a distant day when the LORD, their God, "will pour out [his] spirit upon all flesh," without regard to social distinction (Joel 2:28-31). In this day "Whosoever shall call on the name of the LORD shall be delivered (saved)" (Joel 2:32). On the Day of Pentecost Peter quoted this passage as a prophetic statement which was being fulfilled in the Upper Room (Ac. 2:16-21). For more on the pouring out of God's spirit, see commentary on De. 6:4 and the essay "The Work of the Holy Spirit in the Old and New Testaments," p. 394. For more on God's call to all people, see commentary on Ac. 10:34-35.

Joel prophesied that a day of retribution would come for those who had inflicted evil upon God's "chosen people" (Joel 3:2-8) and that the final destiny of people and nations would be determined on the Judgment Day. After an earthquake and fire God would abolish all evil and make his home in the City of Zion (Joel 3:16-18).

In his prophetic vision Joel saw a day when God's people would dwell forever in a heavenly Jerusalem (Joel 3:20).[4]

Prophets
2065-2066

Agriculture–
Horticulture
57-100

Destruction
990-991

Last
Judgment
1351-1353

Holy Spirit
1601-1614
Retribution
3049-3050

New
Jerusalem
1886

Amos

The Name

In Hebrew the name Amos is *amos* and means "burden" or "burden bearer." In the Greek OT (LXX) the name appears as *Amos*. The prophet Amos appears seven times in the book bearing his name, but he is never mentioned in the rest of the OT. Another unknown Amos is mentioned in the NT (Lu. 3:25).

The book of Amos appears in the English Bible as the third Minor Prophet; in the Hebrew canon it is the sixth Latter Prophet.

Amos
132, 4300a

Authorship and Date

Both Jewish and Christian tradition attribute authorship of the book of Amos to the Amos referred to in the book. The first four words of the book read, "The words of Amos." Other references to him appear in Amos 7:8, 10-12,14.

Amos 1:1 states that Amos prophesied in the days of Uzziah (787-725 B.C.) king of Judah, and in the days of Jeroboam (II) the son of Joash (806-790 B.C.) king of Israel. Verse 1 also states that this is what he saw concerning Israel "two years before the earthquake." The reference to the earthquake cannot be linked positively with a known historical event. One writer interested in antiquity concluded that the earthquake "was coincident with the imposition of Uzziah's leprosy (2 Chr. 26:16-21), according to which, Amos's prophecy was about 751 B.C."[1] The best estimate is that Amos discharged his prophetic office between 750 and 760 B.C.

Book of Amos
4252

Uzziah
3744

Earth-quakes
1091

Background, Purpose, and Content

Amos was not a professional prophet, and his prophetic experience seems to have been limited to one time. He said that he was not a prophet nor the son of a prophet but only a "herdman, and a gatherer of sycomore fruit" (Am. 7:14). The sycamore tree in Palestine grows to a great height—40 to 50 feet—and is not related to the sycamore tree of the Western world. This tree bore a pithy quality of fig, edible for both man and beast.

Amos was a layman in the small community of Tekoa in Judah, about ten miles south of Jerusalem. God called him with a message for Israel, the Northern Kingdom, approximately 200 years after the founding of the Kingdom. Israel was in the midst of great national prosperity but in a state of extreme apostasy. Calf worship had become the religion of Israel, now

Herdsman
1573

Tekoah
3565
False Worship
3928-3951

...let justice roll on like a river,
righteousness like a never-failing
stream! (Am 5:24, NIV)

260   *Amos*

further corrupted with Baal-worship which brought with it many of the abominable practices of Canaanite idolatry. Elijah and Elisha had pleaded with the nation to repent but to no avail.

When Amos arrived at Bethel, the center of religious apostasy in the Northern Kingdom, he employed a psychological approach. Instead of stating his prophecy against Israel at once, he pronounced judgment on Israel's neighbors in Damascus (Am. 1:3), Gaza (1:6), Tyrus (1:9), Edom (1:11), Ammon (1:13), Moab (2:1), and Judah (2:4). The denunciation Amos directed toward Judah must have created a favorable receptivity in the minds of the leaders. However, when Amos began his condemnation of the social and religious sins of Israel (Am. 2:6), the leaders soon directed their hostility against Amos.

The evils in their religious practices were paralleled by their social sins. Drunkenness and adultery were common practices (Am. 2:7-8); the righteous were scorned, chastened, mocked, and sold as slaves for a few pieces of silver; the poor were sold for the price of a pair of shoes (Am. 2:6-7). Apparently the rich religious-political leaders lived in luxury while the poor struggled to survive (Am. 3:15).

Amos denounced the sins of Israel. In reproving the Israelites he addressed them as the cows or "kine of Bashan" (Am. 4:1). They were like fatted animals awaiting the slaughter, for one of their sins had been the oppression of the poor.

Amos pleaded with the leaders of Israel to repent and turn to God (Am. 5:4-9). Apparently they were willing to offer sacrifices to God but without repentance. Amos looked with contempt on their offerings as sheer mockery. The LORD said, "I hate, I despise your feast days...Though ye offer me burnt offerings and your meat offerings, I will not accept them; neither will I regard the peace offerings of your fat beasts" (Am. 5:21-22). Even their songs were an abomination to God (Am. 5:23).

Finally the nation reached the point where God would pronounce his judgment. Punishment in the form of Assyrian captivity was to be their lot (Am. 6:7-14). Soon they were led away "with hooks."[2] The religious and political leaders were equally involved in the degenerate practices of the nation. When Amos declared that the impending judgment could not be avoided, "Amaziah the priest of Bethel sent to Jeroboam king of Israel,

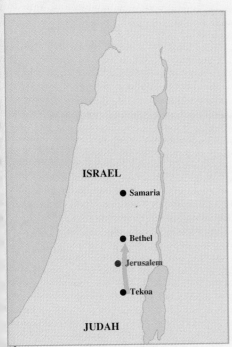

Amos, the "guest prophet," traveled from his native Tekoa, in Judah, to deliver God's message to Israel.

ISRAEL
● Samaria
● Bethel
● Jerusalem
● Tekoa
JUDAH

Baal
3936

Bethel
406, 4342

Hyprocrisy
2994-2995

Adultery
1662

Oppression
2005-2006

Pentence-Impenitence
2706-2718

God's Judgments
1966-1974

saying, Amos hath conspired against thee in the midst of the house of Israel: the land is not able to bear all his words. For thus Amos saith, Jeroboam shall die by the sword, and Israel shall surely be led away captive out of their own land" (Am. 7:10-11).

Destruction
990-991

Grass-
hoppers
80

Imminence
1743

"Word" as
Food
416

Amaziah commanded Amos to leave the country and return to "the land of Judah, and there eat bread, and prophesy there: but prophesy not again any more at Bethel: for it is the king's chapel, and it is the king's court" (Am. 7:12-13). The homily of Amos on the grasshoppers foreshadowed the destruction of Israel. Amos interceded for the people and God extended the grace period (Am. 7:1-3). The message on fire also symbolized destruction (Am. 7:4-6). Once again Amos interceded for the people, and God relented. In the message on the plumb line the city was measured for destruction (Am. 7:7-9). By that time the grace period had ended and the fate of Israel was sealed. The message of summer fruit (Am. 8:1) symbolized that the kingdom was ripe for destruction. Additional details of the destruction follow in the succeeding passage (Am. 9:1-8). Amos described what it would be like when there is a famine of hearing the Word of God (Am. 9:8-12).[3]

Obadiah

The Name

In Hebrew the name Obadiah is *Obadyah* and means "Serving the LORD," or "A Servant of the LORD." It is a compound name from *Obed,* "servant," and *Yah,* an abbreviated form of YHWH, pronounced *Adonay* by the Jews. In the Greek OT the word is *Obidou.*

The name Obadiah is used nineteen times in different OT passages, but only one reference, in the book by this name, pertains to the prophet. The other Obadiahs are: a steward or prime minister under Ahab (1 K. 18:3-16), a descendant of David (1 Chr. 3:21), a leader in the tribe of Issachar (1 Chr. 7:3), a descendant of Saul (1 Chr 8:38), a Levite (1 Chr. 9:16), a Gadite (1 Chr. 12:9), a Zebulunite (1 Chr. 27:19), a teacher of the law (2 Chr. 17:7), a supervisor under Josiah (2 Chr. 34:12), a leader from Babylon under Ezra (Ezr. 8:9), a scribe under Nehemiah (Ne. 10:5), and a gate keeper in Jerusalem (Ne. 12:25).[1]

The book of Obadiah appears in the English Bible as the fourth Minor Prophet; in the Hebrew canon it is the seventh in the list of the Latter Prophets.

Authorship and Date

The only link of identification for the writer of this book is found in the first verse: "The vision of Obadiah. Thus saith the Lord GOD concerning Edom." There is no consensus as to which Obadiah wrote this book, but because the narrative deals with the Edomites when Jerusalem was being burned by the Babylonians, the most likely Obadiah is the one living during the reign of Zedekiah, who ruled from 587-586 B.C. (see 2 Chr. 36:11-21; Ps. 137:7).

One commentator calls attention to the parallel passages in Jeremiah and Obadiah. He says, "The first nine verses of this shortest of all Old Testament books closely parallels parts of Jeremiah 49, though the sequence of the material is different (cf. Obad. 1-4 with Je. 49:14-16; Obad. 5-6 with Je. 49:4,10; Obad. 8-9 with Je. 49:7,22). The question is: which prophet is dependent upon the other? The most likely answer is that both writers used an earlier well-known prophecy. Doubtless the present arrangement in this book is the work of Obadiah."[2]

Both Jewish and Christian traditions credit Obadiah, the prophet, with authorship, between 586 and 583 B.C.

Meaning of the Name
4300a

Book of Obadiah
4253

Prophets
2065-2066

Prophetic Visions
2496

Babylon
329-331

Jeremiah
4246

Above: Inside the entrance passage at Petra.

Left: Petra. Entrance to the fortress is a narrow
passage three miles long.

Background, Purpose, and Content

Edomites
1098

Israel-
The Jews
1807-1829

Petra
4424
Egypt
1100

Babylon
329, 4338

Stubble
3470

Obadiah's prophecy is directed against Edom, a country south of the Dead Sea. The Edomites were the descendants of Esau and were cousins of the Jews whose progenitor was Esau's brother, Jacob. Their capital was Petra, a fortress city situated in a bowl-shaped depression surrounded by high sandstone mountains. The only approach to Petra was, and is, through the Seq, a crack in the mountain range caused by an earthquake, through which the Wadi Musa flows, entering on the east side and exiting toward the west, emptying into the Aravah, a valley connecting the Gulf of Akaba and the southern end of the Dead Sea.

Petra was an almost impregnable cliff city which was easy to defend and difficult to attack. Through the years the Edomites prospered by raiding caravans enroute from Mesopotamia to Egypt, and then retreating into their fortress city.

The descendants of Esau (Edomites) and the descendants of Jacob (Jews) were always bitter enemies and jealous of each other (Ge. 25:23; 27:41). The Edomites refused passage to Moses and the twelve tribes while they were enroute to Canaan (Nu. 20:14-21). The Edomites were always ready to aid an enemy attacking the Jews. When the Israelite tribes were fighting the Canaanites, the Edomites aided and abetted the enemy. Again they assisted the Babylonian army when Jerusalem was under siege (Obad. 11-14). Obadiah pronounced judgment upon the Edomites for this treachery; they would have to suffer the same fate as the ones defeated (Obad. 15).

Within four years after the fall of Jerusalem, the same Babylonians, whom the Edomites aided, attacked this mountain stronghold, conquered it and carried most of the inhabitants to Babylonia as slaves.

A note of hope for the restoration of the Jewish nation is prophesied in the closing verses (Obad. 17-18) but the "house of Esau" was to be reduced to ruin (Obad. 15). This has been literally fulfilled. Jerusalem continues to be a thriving city while the capital city of the Edomites, Petra, is only a mass of vacant ruins.

Vari-colored sandstone formations at Petra.

Jonah

The Name

The Hebrew name of Jonah is *Yonah,* meaning "dove"; in the Greek OT (LXX) it is *Ionas*. In the English OT it is rendered *Jonah* and in the NT (KJV) *Jonas*. The name appears eighteen times in the book of Jonah, beginning in verse one: "Now the word of the LORD came unto Jonah the son of Amittai…" The same Jonah is referred to in 2 K. 14:25 where it is said that his home community was Gath-hepher, now known as Galilee. In the KJV Jonah's name is used ten times in the NT under the name of *Jonas* (Mt.12:39-41; 16:4; Lu. 11:29-30,32; Jn. 21:15).

The book of Jonah appears in the English Bible as the fifth Minor Prophet; in the Hebrew canon it is the eighth in the list of the Latter Prophets.

Authorship and Date

Determining the authorship of a work is sometimes related to its historical verification. The conservative view takes into consideration the historical-internal evidence and has concluded that the book is historical. The liberal view tends to interpret Jonah as fictional. This view is probably best represented by Robert H. Pfeiffer: "The story of Jonah is neither an account of actual happenings, nor an allegory of the destiny of Israel, or the Messiah (cf. Mt. 12:40); it is fiction—a short story with a moral—like the book of Ruth…or legendary character like Daniel."[1]

Some liberal views would take issue with Pfeiffer and insist that the book is an allegory which assumes that Jonah was identified with Israel and that the mission of Israel was to declare God's truth to the world. According to this view the fish is Babylon who swallowed the Israelites and took them into exile. The fish expelling Jonah on the beach represented the Jews returning from exile. Jonah's negative attitude to Nineveh's repentance represents the Jews after returning from exile.[2]

However, the book of Kings makes reference to Jonah as a historical person and identifies him as a son of Amittai (2 K. 14:25). Halley points out:

Jesus unmistakably regarded [the Jonah story] as a historical fact (Mt. 12:38-41). It takes considerable straining to make anything else out of the language. He called it a "sign" of the resurrection. He put the repentance of the Ninevites, his resurrection and the Judgment Day in the same category. He surely was talking of Reality when he spoke of his resurrection and the Judgment day. Thus Jesus accepted the Jonah story. For us that settles it. We believe that it actually occurred, just as recorded; and that Jonah

Jonah
1909

Galilee
1384

God's
Sure Word
430

Book of 2
Kings
4234

Christ
Jesus
677-700

Nineveh. The ancient walls of Nineveh stretch as far as the eye can see. Ancient Nineveh is said to have been 30 miles long and 10 miles wide.

Inspiration
of the Bible
417

himself, under the direction of God's Spirit, wrote the book…and that the book, under the direction of God's Spirit, was placed among the Sacred Writings in the Temple as a part of God's unfolding revelation of Himself.[3]

By accepting the historicity of the book, which is clearly asserted in both the OT and NT, it seems that Jonah must have written the book during the reign of Jeroboam II (782-753). Traditionally he has been considered an eighth century prophet."[4]

Jeroboam
1880

Background, Purpose, and Content

Nineveh
2593, 4418

Nineveh was the capital of Assyria, a world empire for about 300 years (900-607 B.C.). The Assyrian capital was a center of vice, corruption and heathen immorality. These vices are not specifically described in the book but the city was widely known as a center of fertility cult worship and of cruelty to its war victims.[5] The book makes reference to the wickedness of Nineveh (Jona. 1:2), and the fact that God sent Jonah to Nineveh on an evangelistic mission suggests spiritual need.

Wicked
3065-3085

Jonah was obsessed with the idea that the Jews were God's chosen people without any consideration to moral or spiritual obligation, and that they were not to associate with the heathen gentile world. Peter, too, had this problem until his experience on the housetop at Joppa where his ministry to Cornelius had its inception (see commentary on Ac. 10:34-35).

Joppa
1914, 4393
Tarshish
3550

Jonah tried to escape his prophetic duty by taking a ship to Tarshish (probably in southern Spain). However, at sea, God intervened and had Jonah thrown overboard. After a large fish swallowed Jonah, and disgorged him on the beach, he went in haste to Nineveh. For those who have problems with the fish, it can be pointed out that there are several instances where a large fish swallowed a man; thus the claim that a large fish could not have swallowed Jonah is not well taken. The account states that God prepared a great fish for the task (Jona. 1:17). The Hebrew word here used is *da'g*, meaning fish, not whale. Two other words in the Hebrew OT are translated whale: *tanniym* in Jb. 7:12 and *tan* in Eze. 32:2, but in all three instances the intended meaning is a large fish, or sea monster. In the NT the translators rendered the Greek word *ketos* to read "whale" but it can mean either a great fish or a whale. The word "whale" is frequently used as a descriptive adjective.

The book of Jonah is part of the inspired, infallible Word of God and has a place in the Hebrew canon, certifying its validity. This should be enough reason for authenticity to those with a high regard for Scriptural integrity.

When Jonah arrived in Nineveh he found it to be a very large city. The main part, including the palace and temple area, was enclosed with a high wall. The residential section extended for miles up and down the Tigris River and for many miles eastward. One archaeologist gives this description of the ruins:

> The city walls, clearly visible in outline, are eight miles long and enclosed two important mounds. One is called Nebi Yonus, and according to local legend, is the tomb of the prophet Jonah [mound covers 40 acres]. It is covered by a modern village with cemetery and mosque; consequently only very superficial excavation has been possible. The northern and larger mound, Kuyunjik, is one of the largest in Mesopotamia; it is estimated that over 14 million tons of earth would have to be moved to excavate it completely. The main buildings thus far discovered are three royal palaces and two temples.[6]

The modern visitor to Nineveh finds a limited number of archaeological test pits whose findings testify to the splendor and glory of this ancient city (see pp. 276-277). Unfortunately, most of the important archaeological finds have been removed to museums in London, Paris, and Berlin. Currently the Department of Antiquities in Iraq is restoring some of the walls and city gates. The massive ruins as seen today indicate the tremendous size of ancient Nineveh. The size of the city is also suggested in the text: "And Jonah began to enter into the city a day's journey" (Jona. 3:4).

When Jonah arrived in Nineveh, the people took his prophecy of impending judgment quite seriously. "The people of Nineveh believed God, and proclaimed a fast, and put on sackcloth, from the greatest of them even to the least of them" (Jona. 3:5). Even the king joined the repentant people (Jona. 3:6). The putting on of sackcloth and sitting in the ash pit symbolized

Omnipotence of God
3809

Whales
3821

Nineveh
2593, 4418

Meso-potamia
2306

Imminence
1743
Fasts Proclaimed
2710

Some of the walls of Nineveh which are being rebuilt. The main gate is at the right.

a spirit of repentance and humility. God saw that "they turned from their evil way" (Jona. 3:10) and withheld his judgment.

This is the first example of Jewish evangelism reaching out to the Gentiles. It is evident that "God is no respecter of persons: but in every nation he that feareth him, and worketh righteousness, is accepted with him" (Ac. 10:34-35). When Jonah saw the Ninevites repent and turn their faces to the living God, the prophet was displeased. He still carried in his heart a prejudice against Gentiles. He cared little whether or not more than 620,000 persons might be destroyed. Jonah expressed his desire to die rather than see salvation come to this great city (Jona. 4:1-3). Livingston describes Jonah's experience with the gourd vine and the hot east wind in these words:

> In order to teach the prophet a lesson, God prepares a fast growing plant to shade him from the sun, but the next night He allows a worm to destroy it. Then he sets a hot east wind blowing. As a result Jonah is faint in spirit and wishes for death. The story closes with a declaration that whereas Jonah is concerned for gourds, God is concerned for the salvation of sinful men.[7]

This book teaches that God is concerned for the salvation of souls, irrespective of nation, race, or creed. He is "not willing that any should perish" (2 Pe. 3:9). The evasion of responsibility, as with Jonah, is still man's weakness; God is powerful and can change the designs and will of man.

God's judgment is always tempered with mercy; the most unlikely mission fields are the most fruitful, and finally God is anxious to extend his mercy and grace to all who repent and seek his face.[8]

Impartiality
1979-1980

Salvation
3116-3128

Salvation of God
3116

Power of God
3808

God's Grace
1445

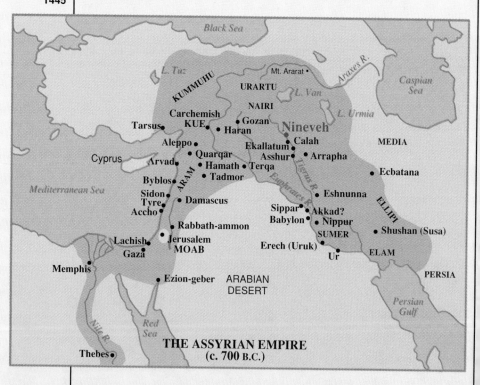

THE ASSYRIAN EMPIRE
(c. 700 B.C.)

Micah

The Name

The Hebrew name for Micah is *Mikkan* meaning "Who is like Jehovah?" The translation indicates Micah's character and concept of righteousness and holiness. The Greek rendering of Micah (LXX) is *Michaias*. There
are thirty instances in the OT where the name Micah appears, besides the
single reference in the first chapter of the book (1:1). Some of the leading
persons by this name are: an Ephramite who stole 1,000 pieces of silver (Jud.
17), a descendant of Reuben (1 Chr. 5:5), a son of Meribbaal (1 Chr. 8:34),
a Levite during the reign of David (1 Chr. 23:20), a son of Zichri (1 Chr.
9:15), and the father of one of Josiah's messengers (2 Chr. 34:20).

Meaning
of Name
4300a

The book of Micah is the sixth of the Minor Prophets in the English
Bible and ninth of the Latter Prophets in the Hebrew canon.

Book of
Micah
4255

Authorship and Date

Micah's name in the book establishes the author's identity: "The word
of the LORD that came to Micah" (1:1). Jewish and Christian tradition has
credited Micah with writing this book although certain critics question its
authenticity, especially on the basis of its prophetic content—foretelling
future events. Micah lived in the days of Jotham, 749-734 B.C., Ahaz, 741-
726 B.C., and Hezekiah, 726-697 B.C., all kings of Judah. Of the three, only
Ahaz was a wicked king. Micah was a native of Moresheath, about 25 miles
southwest of Jerusalem along a military highway over which the Assyrians
marched in 734 and 711 and again in 701 B.C.

Micah
2333

Kings of
Judah
1824

It is difficult to ascertain the origin of certain passages in some of the
prophetical books. The passage in Micah 3:12 (740-700 B.C.) is almost
identical with that in Je. 26:18 (627-586 B.C.). Similar phraseology exists
between Micah 4:1-3 and Isaiah 2:2-4 (758-698 B.C.). The three prophets
may have used a "floating oracle" or a common source for their information,
probably composed by an earlier prophet of hope.[1]

Isaiah
4245

Micah, one of the eighth-century prophets, probably wrote the major
portion of the book sometime before the fall of the Northern Kingdom (721
B.C.) since he predicts its downfall. As there were sacred oracles in circulation by that time, it is possible that through the leading of the Holy Spirit,
some interborrowing of information took place. The writers at that time did
not have the documentation ethic that is prevalent today.

Divine
Inspiration
1774

Background, Purpose, and Content

Isaiah
1803

Micah was a contemporary of Amos and Hosea, who prophesied in the Northern Kindgom, and of Isaiah, the prophet-statesman in Jerusalem. Micah, the country preacher, directed his prophecies to both Judah and Israel as did Isaiah, the prophet of the palace.

Poor
2799-2804

The idolatrous curse of the north was beginning to become a problem in Judah. Micah denounced rulers, priests, and false prophets. He condemned the exploitation of the poor and dishonesty in business as well as the apostasy which was developing in the Southern Kingdom.[2]

Sin
3338-3359

In the book of Micah, which contains only seven chapters, the prophet first denounced the transgressions and sins of Israel. He predicted that Samaria would become a "heap of the field" (Mi. 1:6). In 722 B.C. the Assyrians literally made a "heap" or a pile of rubbish out of Samaria (the palace area is nothing more than that at the present time). In chapters 2 and 3 Micah challenged certain social and moral abuses in the land (Mi. 2:1-3; 3:1-3). Claude Ries describes these abuses thus:

Samaria
3134, 4430

Riches
Perilous
2806

> The sins he (Micah) excoriated were those which bore upon the plain people whom he knew as farmers, agriculturists and small land owners. These were made the victims of the rapacity of the wealthy...the social sins of cruelty and inhumanity bulk large in his writings.

"They will beat their swords into plowshares and their spears into pruning hooks..."
(Mi. 4:3, NIV)

The rulers, the wealthy, the conniving priests and prophets in the capital cities, feeling secure within strong fortifications, made the most of their power to oppress the poor. The peasants had no protection from either the Assyrians or from the "grafters" of their own nation.[3]

The religious and political rulers lived within the walled cities whereas the peasants had their homes and fields on the outside of the walls.

In chapter 4 Micah had a vision of a "warless, prosperous, God-fearing world with Zion at its head." Isaiah also had a glimpse of this glorious society (2:2-4).[4] Henry H. Halley makes this observation:

Suddenly in the midst of this rhapsody of the future, the prophet reverts to his own troublesome times and the doom of Jerusalem, which he had just mentioned (3:12), announcing that the people would be carried away captive to Babylon (4:10). It is an amazing prophecy. At the time, Assyria was sweeping everything before it. This was 100 years before the rise of the Babylonian empire. Yet, Jerusalem survived the Assyrian onslaught (2 K. 19:35-37) and lived on until Assyria was overthrown by Babylon, at whose hands Jerusalem fell, 606 B.C.; and its people were carried away to Babylon.[5]

In the fifth chapter Micah prophesied the coming of the Messiah (Mi. 5:2). The specific nature of Micah's prophecy was apparent—the Messiah was to come in Bethlehem. The prophet specified the political sub-division,

Ephraim
1144-1147

Hypocrisy
2994

Punishments
2553-2565

Ephratah, originally "the tribal domain of Ephraim," in order not to confuse it with the Bethlehem located within the territory of Zebulun (Jos. 19:15), about seven miles northwest of Nazareth in Galilee.

In chapter 6 Micah reviewed the sins of ingratitude to God, religious pretense, dishonesty, idolatry—each of which was to receive its due punishment. Micah watched the breakdown of his country. The corruption which had begun at the government level permeated the whole nation, and human relationships crumbled. Friendship and families had deteriorated; the human aspect was bleak and discouraging.

But with God there was always hope. In his mercy, love and compassion, it was still possible for forgiveness and restoration to take place, if the people would repent and turn their face to God.

Nahum

The Name

The name "Nahum" in the Hebrew canon means "consolation" or "consoler," and expresses the purpose of the book—to comfort the oppressed and afflicted people of Judah. The name "Nahum" does not occur in any other OT book and it is used only once in the book by that name (1:1): "The burden of Nineveh. The book of the vision of Nahum the Elkoshite." In the genealogical table by Luke the name "Naum" appears (Lu. 3:25), but it has no relationship to Nahum the prophet.[1]

The book of Nahum is the seventh in the list of books by the Minor Prophets and the tenth of the Latter Prophets in the Hebrew canon.

Authorship and Date

Both Jewish and Christian tradition ascribe the authorship of this book to the prophet Nahum. Nothing is known about the author's ancestry or background, but he was one of the men whom God chose to write a book which became a part of the Hebrew Bible. The date for the writing of Nahum could be within the bounds of about fifty years. The tone of the message suggests that it was written shortly before Nineveh fell in 612 B.C. A most probable date is between 614 and 612 B.C., "after the Medes and Babylonians began to close in on Nineveh."[2]

Background, Purpose, and Content

Nineveh was the great and mighty capital of Assyria. It was founded by Nimrod, shortly after the flood (Ge. 10:11-12) and was a rival of Babylon from the beginning. Nineveh was located in the northern part of the country on the Tigris River and Babylon in the southern part on the Euphrates River. For a description of Nineveh, see the commentary on the book of Jonah.

About 150 years after Jonah had witnessed a great spiritual revival and a turning of the Ninevites to the worship of Jehovah, they reverted to their heathen worship. Nahum declared that God was jealous and would take vengeance upon the Ninevites. The days of the nation that had destroyed the Northern Kingdom and threatened Jerusalem were numbered. The fall of Nineveh would bring rejoicing throughout the Tigris-Euphrates area. The 300 years of terror and destruction were about to come to an end for the once proud and mighty Assyria of which Nineveh was the home and capital of the militant kings.

Meaning of Name 4300a

Book of Nahum 4256

Nineveh 4418

Nimrod 2542

Worship, True and False 3921-3952

Assyria 299

Above: According to Muslim tradition, Jonah died and was buried in Nineveh. This Muslim shrine is called the Mosque of Jonah.

Left: A view of the new wall of Nineveh as it extends eastward.

The prophet gives a vivid description of the battle which was to take place on the streets of Nineveh (Na. 2:3-4); when the gates opened, the palace was to "be dissolved" by the flooding Tigris River (Na. 2:6). (The effects of this flood damage are still visible in old Nineveh.) The destruction of the "bloody city" was at hand (Na. 3:1-3). No power on earth would now be able to save Nineveh; it had gone to the "point of no return." The defenses of the city would be destroyed (Na. 3:12-18) and there would be great rejoicing by the people in the neighboring countries. The prophet gives a vivid description of the battle scenes in the streets; the flaming chariots shall rage and "justle one against another" and they "shall run like the lightnings" (Na. 2:4).

Henry H. Halley describes the total destruction of the once great city:

Its destruction was so complete that even its site was forgotten. When Xenophon and his 10,000 soldiers passed by 200 years later he thought the mounds were the ruins of some Parthian city. When Alexander the Great fought the famous battle of Arbela, 331 B.C., near the site of Nineveh, he did not know there had ever been a city there.

So completely had all traces of the glory of the Assyrian Empire disappeared that many scholars had come to think that the references to it in the Bible and other ancient histories were mythical; that in reality such a city and such an empire never existed. In 1820 an Englishman, Claude James Rich, spent 4 months sketching the mounds across the Tigris from Mosul, which he suspected were the ruins of Nineveh. In 1845 Layard definitely identified the site; and he and his successors uncovered the ruins of the magnificent palaces of the Assyrian kings, whose names have now become household words, and hundreds of thousands of inscriptions in which we read the history of Assyria as the Assyrians themselves wrote it, and which to a remarkable degree supplement and confirm the Bible.[3]

Imminence
1743

Desolation
987

Destruction
990-991

Bible
414-445

Habakkuk

The Name

The Hebrew name for Habakkuk is *habhakkuk,* and means "embrace" or "ardent embrace"—"to cling." He clung to God. The Greek OT (LXX) renders this name *Hambakoum.* The only instances where the name Habakkuk appears in the entire Bible are the two times it is included in the book (1:1; 3:1).

Habakkuk
1472

The book of Habakkuk is the eighth in the Minor Prophets; it is the eleventh in the Latter Prophets in the Hebrew canon.

Book of
Habakkuk
4257

Authorship and Date

Little reliable information is available as to the identity of the prophet Habakkuk other than that he had a burden for his nation and that he prayed to God for it. Most scholars are willing to credit Habakkuk with writing the entire book. However, some of the more critical writers are hesitant to ascribe chapter 3 to this prophet even though it mentions the prophet's name (Hab. 3:1). They argue that this chapter must have been written by a later compiler because the views are more typical of another age, that this chapter was designed to be used in the temple worship, and that the theology expressed in it reflects a period after the exile. To support their contention they point out that the third chapter was not found in the Habakkuk manuscript at Qumran on the Dead Sea.

Patriotism
2528

Dead Sea
Scrolls
4362

The book may have been written at some time during the early part of the seventh century B.C., during the time of Josiah (639-608) and Jehoiakim (608-597).[1]

Background, Purpose, and Content

The dialogue between Habakkuk and God seems to have taken place in the midst of the Babylonians' military campaigns around Jerusalem. Most of the country had been greatly damaged. Many of the citizens, including Daniel and the three Hebrew children, had been carried into Babylon in 606 B.C.

Babylon
329-330

The prophet was bewildered by the savage attack of the enemy and engaged God in a debate, similar to a conversation. Habakkuk was unable to understand how God could permit a nation more wicked than his own to savagely attack the covenant people. From God's answer the prophet concluded that in the end a nation that sins but repents will be restored by God, whereas the heathen nation, temporarily prosperous and victorious, will be

Restoration
3025-3026
Instruments
of Judgment
2566

ultimately destroyed. The great heathen political and religious capitals of the ancient world are still a "heap of ruins" (e.g., Babylon, Nineveh, Ur, and Ephesus), while Jerusalem is a thriving city. History seems to bear out the idea that God sometimes used wicked nations to chasten his people.

From his insight into God's judgment and justice, the prophet saw that the essence of a satisfying relationship with God was faith. He formulated the statement: "The just shall live by his faith" (Hab. 2:4), and this assertion has become the base upon which the doctrine of justification by faith is developed in the NT. Paul quotes the verse twice (Ro. 1:17 and Ga. 3:11).[2] It is also repeated by the writer to the Hebrews (10:38).

Habakkuk may have been a chorister in the Levitical choir. Musical references occur in the first and last verses of the third chapter. The first verse includes a reference to *shigionoth,* which is a musical term meaning a "dithrambic ode," a lively, enthusiastic musical sequence. The last verse mentions singers and stringed instruments. The Hebrew designation for the use of stringed instruments is *neginoth* and is found frequently in the superscription of the Psalms (Ps. 4,6,55,67,76).

Wall decoration of a guard in the palace at Babylon.

Zephaniah

The Name

The Hebrew name for Zephaniah is *Sephanyah*, meaning "bids" or "Jehovah has bidden." In the Scriptures the name appears a total of ten times but only once in the book of Zephaniah. At least four other men bear this name: a Babylonian captive executed by Nebuchadnezzar (2 K. 25:18; Je. 52:24), a Levite, descendant of Kohath (1 Chr. 6:36), a priest in the reign of Zedekiah (Je. 21:1; 37:3), and the father of Josiah, who returned from Babylon (Zec. 6:10,14). The single reference to Zephaniah in his book appears in the first verse.

The book of Zephaniah is the ninth in the list of Minor Prophets and the twelfth of the Latter Prophets in the Hebrew canon.

Authorship and Date

Jewish and Christian tradition credit Zephaniah with the authorship of the book bearing his name. In the first verse the writer states, "The word of the LORD which came unto Zephaniah..."

Some of the liberal critics give credit to Zephaniah for having written the first chapter but do not accept his authorship of chapters 2 and 3 because of the prophetic elements in these sections. This position is not acceptable to conservatives because it holds that there is no validity in prophecy, i.e., foretelling of future events.

Since Zephaniah affirmed (in Zep. 1:1) that he had entered the prophetic office during the reign of Josiah, king of Judah (639-608 B.C.), he was probably a leader in the reform during Josiah's reign. MacRae suggests that the prophet ministered from 640-610 B.C.[1] He may have written his prophecy about two years before the first attack on Jerusalem by the Babylonians, or about 608 B.C.

Background, Purpose, and Content

Little is known about Zephaniah other than that he was a fourth-generation descendant of King Hezekiah, and thus a prince of royal lineage.[2] Zephaniah received his call to the prophetic office while he was quite young and was one of the first prophets in seventy years, after Isaiah and Micah. It is apparent that Nineveh had not yet fallen to Babylon (Zep. 2:13).

The book of Zephaniah divides itself "into two parts, of unequal length. Chapters 1:2-3:8 contain denunciation and threats; chapter 3:9-20 contains

Book of
Zephaniah
4258

Prophets
2065-2066

Prophecy
2889-2894

Josiah
1923

Hezekiah
1585

a promise of salvation and glor-
ification."[3] One scholar describes
the seriousness of the national
situation at the time Zephaniah
(also Jeremiah) accepted his call
to the prophetic office: "Zephaniah's sensitive, moral and religious spirit was overwhelmed by
the impending doom that awaited
the disobedient: in such a spiritual atmosphere disaster was sure.
The Day of Wrath (Zep. 1:14-
18)—borrowed from Amos (5:18-
20) and Isaiah—here for the first
time became apocalyptic...the
Day of the LORD became not only
the Day of Wrath, but the Last

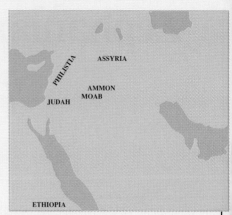

*Zephaniah prophesied that the wrath
of God would come upon these areas.*

Day...Zephaniah envisaged an attitude of life in which there remained
nothing but judgment of an Outraged God."[4]

The basis of Zephaniah's prophecy is the impending universal judgment which God is about to unleash. The extent of the coming destruction
can be compared to that of the flood under Noah (Zep. 1:2-4; Ge. 6:5-7). The
surrounding nations would not escape the wrath of God. Judgment would
come upon Philistia (Zep. 2:4-7), Moab and Ammon (2:8-11), Ethiopia
(2:12) and Assyria (2:13-15), but punishment of these nations would be no
consolation for Jerusalem. Religious and political leaders had become so
corrupt that the nation could not escape retribution (2:1-4).

The prophet does offer hope for a remnant who will ultimately enjoy
exaltation "as a redeemed daughter of Zion."[5] Some critical scholars question the integrity of 2:1-3, 4-15, which refers to the "meek of the earth" and
"seek meekness." The claim is that the concept of "meekness," as mentioned
here, did not develop until the post-exilic period. "There can be no question
that the words occur more frequently in post exilic psalms and proverbs than
in pre-exilic writings, but it cannot be proved, or even shown to be probable,
that the words might not have been used in Zephaniah's day (cf. Ex. 10:3;
Nu. 12:3; Is. 2:9ff.; Mi. 6:8)."[6]

In chapter 3 the prophet again denounced the "filthy and polluted" city
(Zep. 3:1-5). Nevertheless, the prophet again opened the door of hope for a
surviving remnant (3:12-13).

In Zephaniah 3:9 the prophet speaks of a "pure language," "a prediction of a complete and perfect revelation of God to man (obviously meaning
the Gospel of Christ) as a result of which converts from among the nations
would be brought to God, joyful with glad songs of redemption, all the earth
resounding with the praise of God's people."[7] It is also possible that the
fulfillment of this prophecy came to pass when Greek became the universal
language.

Haggai

The Name

In Hebrew the word for Haggai is *haggay,* meaning "festival." The name may suggest he was born on a festival day or it may refer to the anticipation of the return from captivity. In the Greek OT (LXX) this name is rendered *Haggaios*. The prophet is mentioned ten times in the entire Bible—two times in the book of Ezra (Ezr. 5:1; 6:14), and eight times in the book bearing his name (Hag. 1:1,3,12-13; 2:1,13-14,20). No other man by this name appears in the Bible.

The book of Haggai is the tenth in the list of Minor Prophets and the thirteenth of the Latter Prophets in the Hebrew canon.

Authorship and Date

The book of Haggai is short and concise. The unity and continuity are such that tradition has always given the prophet credit for writing it. His name, being frequently mentioned in the book and referred to by one of his associates, Ezra, makes authorship quite certain. R. K. Harrison comments that "there is no element in the prophecy as it now stands that points to diversity of authorship. Indeed, the weight of internal and external evidence supports the contention that the prophet Haggai was himself the author of the work attributed to him, and that he furnished a narrative of contemporary events involving himself in an objective manner"[1]

Haggai was a contemporary of Zechariah, and this fact, with the internal evidence, makes it possible to date the book as having been written in 520 B.C.

Background, Purpose, and Content

The prophet Haggai, as well as Zechariah and Malachi, was a post exilic prophet, so called because he prophesied after the Babylonian exile. Soon after the emancipation proclamation was given by Cyrus, the Jews began to return to Jerusalem. Haggai and Zerubbabel were two of the leaders returning with the first contingent. The reference in Hag. 2:3 is usually interpreted to mean that Haggai had seen Solomon's temple and that he had been among the persons, including Daniel, who were deported in 606 B.C. If this is correct, Haggai was an old man—about 85 years of age—when he prophesied.

The idea of returning to their homeland, at that time devastated and occupied by their enemy, was not a popular prospect for the Jews who had

Haggai	**1475**
Festivals	**1276**
Book of Haggai	**4259**
Prophets	**2066**
Zechariah	**3987, 4260**
Jews' Return	**1827**
Solomon's Temple	**3577**

become established in Babylon. Many were profitably engaged and had no desire to return. However, a group of about 42,000 people (Ezr. 2:64), including priests and religious leaders, who had nothing to lose, and those with an adventurous spirit, responded (Ezr. 1:5).

Zerubbabel
3991

Zerubbabel (Sheshbazzar) was commissioned to be governor over the new Jerusalem community (Ezr. 1:8; 5:14). Later, when the returnees saw the

Zeal
1073

rubble and the ruins of the old city, the initial wave of spiritual zeal and enthusiasm abated. When Haggai and his workers began

Opposers
1567-1568

to rebuild the altar and the temple, the Samaritans and the neighbors who had established "squatters rights" during the Jews' absence opposed the work and, in fact, stopped it temporarily by legal action (Ezr. 4:1-6; 5:1-5; 6:1-13).

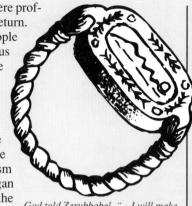

God told Zerubbabel, "...I will make you like my signet ring, for I have chosen you..." (Hag. 2:23, NIV). The signet was a symbol of royal authority, implying that Zerubbabel was given highest honor.

The book of Haggai contains four main prophecies which were delivered over a four-month period:

1. After the exiles had been engaged in their building project for a short time, their attention was diverted to building their own "ceiled" houses, while the temple remained roofless. Haggai told the people that a lack of dew from heaven and their short crops had been due to God's displeasure at their

Religious Indifference
1083

indifference and religious apathy (Hag. 1:6, 10). After Haggai exhorted them to resume work on the temple, they complied (Hag. 1:12-15).

2. In less than a month the work slackened. The people were discouraged because of the humble appearance of the new building as compared

Encourage-ment
1019

with the old. Haggai assured them that when completed, the glory of the new temple would be greater than that of the old. Work once more resumed (Hag. 2:1-9).

3. The third prophecy is a sequel to the first. Haggai drew an analogy: as the unclean pollutes the clean, so the work of the laborers done grudgingly and without zeal had polluted their undertaking, and God had withheld his

Blessings-Afflictions
480-499

blessings of plenty (Hag. 2:10-19).

4. The fourth prophecy is a sequel to the second. The prophet uttered words of encouragement, telling the people that God was about to shake the

Civil Strife
2532

nations of the earth (cause revolutions and turmoil among them) with a prophetic intimation regarding the final overthrow of the heathen nations in the Day of Judgment (Hag. 2:20-22).

One scholar succinctly wrote: "The prophecy of Haggai (2:20-23)

Future
1344-1375

looks to the future. Furthermore, there is significance in the use of the singular 'throne.' (Hag. 2:22)...One may see here, along with many able expositors, a reference to the ultimate overthrow of this world system, dominated by Satan, when the rightful King, the Lord Jesus Christ, returns to take the reign of government."[2]

Messianic Hope
4186

Haggai concluded his final message with a note of hope. Although Zerubbabel, the governor, did not fulfill the expectation of the vision (Hag. 2:21-23), nevertheless the prophet was faithful in proclaiming Messianic hope for future generations.

Unanticipated Blessings of the Exile and Dispersion of the Jews

Following the downfall of Judah in 586 B.C., the conquering hordes of Babylon took the inhabitants into captivity in Babylon. To all outward appearances, the nation's political and religious existence had been dealt a mortal blow. But the result was that the captive years for Judah became actually a period of spiritual growth. One is reminded of Joseph's statement to his brothers: "You intended to harm me, but God intended it for good to accomplish what is now being done, the saving of many lives" (Ge. 50:20, NIV). The following points show some of the ways in which many lives were affected for the good as a result of the exile and subsequent dispersion of the Jews (known also as the Diaspora).

1. *The development of the synagogue.* The Jewish people had become dependent upon the temple and its hierarchy for their spirituality. Following its destruction and the separation of the Jews from Jerusalem by hundreds of miles, they could no longer practice the levitical sacrifices. A substitute place of worship became a necessity and out of this need the synagogue developed, giving the Jews worship centers within easy reach of all members in the community (see chart on "The Development of Worship Centers," pp. 402-403). It was indeed a very practical solution to the problem. As slaves, the Jews were limited in their movement; they could not go to a central worship center. They were scattered throughout Babylon and needed local worship centers. Many of these small centers were in the homes. The synagogue was basically a layman's institution, an example of laymen preserving the faith in troubled times.

> Synagogues
> 3521-3523

By the time the Jews came back from Babylon to Jerusalem, the synagogue had become an established part of their religious life. Synagogues were built in every community, large or small, so that worship could be carried on without going to the temple in Jerusalem. The synagogue also provided an easy transition for the Jews when the temple was destroyed under Titus in A.D. 70. It was a developing link between the animal sacrifices and the believer's living sacrifice (Ro. 2:1-2).

An additional advantage was that the synagogues abroad provided easily accessible preaching places for the early missionaries. Since the Christ-Messiah movement was Jewish, it was logical for the missionaries to make their local contacts in the synagogues. Frequently Paul and the early evangels "reasoned in the synagogue every sabbath, and persuaded the Jews..." (Ac. 18:4) and "straightway he preached Christ in the synagogues, that he is the Son of God" (Ac. 9:20).

2. *The holy records were organized.* Under Ezra the holy records were codified and organized into what later became the Old Testament.

3. *The Jews lost interest in Baal worship.* There was no longer a question as to who the God of Abraham, Isaac, and Jacob was. For them Yahweh was the living God, the creator of the universe.

> Baal
> 3936

4. *God's miraculous power was displayed in their midst.* During the seventy years of captivity, God revealed his supernatural power in the lives of Daniel and the three Hebrew children. God demonstrated that he could preserve faith even in the lion's jaw and in the heat of the fiery furnace (Da. 3:27).

Finally God showed his mighty power by sending a friendly nation to conquer Babylon and set the captives free. When Babylon was conquered by Persia, King Cyrus immediately decreed that the Jews were free and that they could return to Judea.

5. *Witness to the true God reached the far outreaches of the heathen world.* Following the Jews' return to Palestine, many of them scattered all over the Tigris-Euphrates river area including Persia. They took with them their faith, their synagogue service, and their holy oracles.

Actually the dispersion of the Jews ("dispersion" comes from the Hebrew

Dispersion
of the Jews
1023

word *golah* and means "forced exile") began when the Assyrians took the Israelites into captivity in 721 B.C. Then in 586 B.C. the natives of Judea were taken into Babylon, and with the fall of Jerusalem in A.D. 70 Titus took many Jews to Rome as slaves. Some Jews went voluntarily into other lands for economic opportunities. Egypt had one of the largest Jewish communities in the Near East. Over 1,000,000 Jews lived in Egypt in the days of Christ. In fact, by the time of Christ more Jews lived outside of Palestine than lived in Judea.

6. *The Septuagint was translated.* The Septuagint (Greek OT) was another result of the dispersion of the Jews. Since the Greek language became universal, the availability of the Jewish

Greeks
1464

Scriptures in Greek greatly facilitated Bible religion. The Diaspora also produced the Targums, the Aramaic translation of portions of the OT, which communicated the Scriptural message of the Lord to the Babylonian area.

There is no way to measure the witness the Jews gave for the Lord in the many areas in which they were scattered. Clearly the hand of God was in work in this seemingly very difficult period of time.

Zechariah

The Name

The Hebrew name for Zechariah is *Zekharayah,* which means "Jehovah has remembered." It is mentioned at least twenty-nine times in the OT. The Greek OT (LXX) renders this name *Zacharias.*

Names,
Meaning
4300a

Ezra makes two references to the prophet Zechariah (Ezr. 5:1; 6:14), and the name is included four times in this book (Zec. 1:1,7; 7:1,8). Each instance is a definite identification, e.g., "the word of the LORD unto Zechariah" (1:1) or similar words.

Zechariah
3987

The book of Zechariah is the eleventh in the list of Minor Prophets and the fourteenth of the Latter Prophets in the OT canon.[1]

Book of
Zechariah
4260

Authorship and Date

Jewish and Christian traditions have always considered the prophet Zechariah to be the author of the book of Zechariah, written about 521 B.C. Some liberal critics who hold the view that prophets could not foretell the future have questioned the last six chapters because they contain Messianic prophecies and other references which foretell the future (Zec. 14:1-3).

Prophets
2065
Messianic
2890

Background, Purpose, and Content

Zechariah was first a priest by birth and then a prophet by special call, as were Jeremiah and Ezekiel. Zechariah ("Jehovah has remembered") was the son of Berechiah ("Jehovah blesses") and the grandson of Iddo ("timely," or "the appointed time") as shown in Zec. 1:1,7; Ne. 12:4,16. The meaning of these names along with the words "jealous" and "jealously" and such terms as "in that day" and "the day of the Lord" suggest the key to the meaning of the book.

Jealousy
1850-1851

However, the book of Zechariah is still difficult to understand. George L. Robinson observes: "Few books of the OT are as difficult of interpretation as the book of Zechariah; no other book is as Messianic...The scope of Zechariah's vision, and the profundity of his thought are almost without parallel...his book is the most Messianic, the most truly apocalyptic and eschatological, of all the writings of the OT."[2]

Messianic
2890,
4306b

The prophet Zechariah was a "contemporary of Zerubbabel, the governor, Joshua, the high priest, and Haggai the prophet (Zec. 3:1; 4:6; 6:11; Ezr. 5:1-2), and united with Haggai in exhorting the leaders of the Jewish colony to resume work on the house of God."[3] The prophet Haggai had been

Zerubbabel
3991

preaching two months and the temple work had started when Zechariah began his prophetic work. Zechariah's formal ministry lasted about three years.

Zechariah sensed an apathy in the people's devotion and a tendency to revert to the ways of their disobedient forefathers. The prophet's concern resulted in a message which had a twofold purpose: to exhort the people to repentance and to encourage them with visions of a glorious future (Zec. 1:1-6).[4]

The book of Zechariah has two major divisions—apocalyptic (chs. 1-8); and prophetic (chs. 9-14). During one night God granted the prophet eight visions, which inspired the people to finish rebuilding the temple:

The first vision, of the myrtle trees and the horses, meant that the whole world was at rest under the hand of the Persian Empire (Zec. 1:7-17). Certainly the Jews were greatly favored in the freedom granted them and the financial assistance given them by the Persian king.

The second vision, of the horns and the carpenters, represented the nations who had destroyed Judah and Israel and through the image of the four carpenters the prophet foretold the overthrow of Israel's enemies (Zec. 1:18-21).

The third vision, of the measuring line (Zec. 2), was a forecast that Jerusalem would prosper and grow until it would overflow its walls, and the nations of the world would come to seek counsel in Jerusalem.

The fourth vision, of Joshua, the high priest, gave a pre-vision of the atonement of Christ (Zec. 3). The filthy clothing of the high priest represented the sins of the people, and the removing of these garments symbolized that the people's sins were forgiven (Zec. 3:4-7). A foreshadowing of Christ the Messiah is seen in the Branch to which the prophet makes reference (Zec. 3:8-10).[5]

The fifth vision, in the fourth chapter, has a "double reference." The first one is for the immediate time while Zechariah was building the house, while the second is for a later, more glorious House, to be built by a descendant of Zerubbabel. He is called "The Branch," the candlestick representing God's House, and the light-bearer to the world. The two olive trees seem to represent Joshua and Zerubbabel.

Zechariah was a prophet to the Jews who returned to Jerusalem after 70 years of captivity in Babylon.

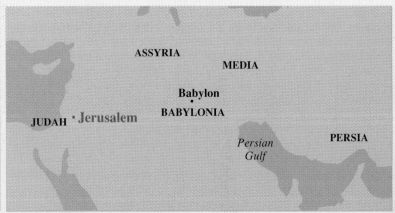

ASSYRIA

MEDIA

Babylon

JUDAH • Jerusalem   BABYLONIA

Persian Gulf   PERSIA

Margin notes:

Haggai
1475

"Fear-Nots"
1020

Persia
2744

Enemies
1128-1129

Atonement
304-305
Sin
Forgiven
3345

Christ,
a Branch
691

The Life of Christ in the Prophecy of Zechariah

	Zechariah	Other Biblical References
Given a Messianic title (Branch)	3:8; 6:12	Is. 4:2; 11:1; Je. 23:5; 33:15
Referred to as the Shepherd	13:7	Is. 40:11; Mt. 26:31; Mk. 14:27; Jn. 10:11; He. 13:20
His Priesthood	6:13	He. 2:17; 4:14
Builder of the Temple	6:12-13	Jn. 2:19; 1 Co. 3:16; Ep. 2:20, 22
Triumphal Entry	9:9	Is. 62:11; Mt. 21:1-11; Jn. 12:12-14
Sold for 30 Pieces of Silver	11:12	Mt. 26:15; 27:3-10
Money to be Returned for a Potter's Field	11:13	Mt. 27:3-10
His Side Pierced	12:10	Jn. 19:34
His Death	13:7	Jn. 10:11; Ro. 5:6
Apostles scattered after his death	13:7	Mt. 26:56; Mk. 14:49-50 Mt. 26:31; Ac. 8:1
Establishment of Peace	9:10	Is. 9:6; Lu. 2:14; Jn. 14:27; 16:33; Ep. 2:14
His Kingship	6:13; 9:9; 14:9, 16	Is. 9:7; Je. 23:5; Da. 7:14; Jn. 1:49; 18:37; 1 Co. 15:25
His Universal Reign	9:10, 14	Is. 9:7; Je. 23:5; Da. 7:14; Re. 19:6
Coming in Glory	14:4, 9	Jn. 17:5; Ac. 1:11-12; Re. 5:12

The sixth and seventh visions, picturing a "flying roll" or scroll and an ephah represent a curse against stealing and swearing (Zec. 5:1-4; 5:5-11). In the end the Lord will separate sin and the sinner from the kingdom (Zec. 5:1-11).[6]

The eighth and final vision, of the four chariots (Zec. 6:1-8), is similar to the first, showing a completion of God's work (Zec. 6:4-15).

In chapters seven and eight the prophet recalls that the people fasted in the fourth, fifth, seventh, and tenth months and mourned for the temple. The people asked whether they should continue their fasts as before and

Ephah
1141
Profanity
475
Fasting
3212-3214

Penitence- Impenitence 2706-2718	Zechariah reminded them that previously their fasts had the ingredient of penitence for their former sins, but now the fast had become a mere outward rite without spiritual significance. Then the prophet changed the scenes and gave a picture of the age when fasts would become joyful (Zec. 7:5-7; 8:19-23).

Zechariah reminded them that previously their fasts had the ingredient of penitence for their former sins, but now the fast had become a mere outward rite without spiritual significance. Then the prophet changed the scenes and gave a picture of the age when fasts would become joyful (Zec. 7:5-7; 8:19-23).

Seekers
3192

The people were discouraged because their number was small and they were despised, existing only by permission of the Persian king. The prophet tried to convince the people that the day would come when the enemy nations would be broken and God's people would again prosper and rejoice (Zec. 8:3-5). All the nations would one day come to the Jews to learn about their God (Zec. 8:22-23; see also 1:17; 2:4, 11; 14:8,16).

Spiritual
Kingdom
2007-2013

The judgment God's prophet pronounced on the neighboring nations was fulfilled. Chapters 9-14 contain references discussing the Greek wars which came 200 years after Zechariah. Chapter 9 seems to point to Judah's struggle with Greece which took place when Alexander the Great invaded Palestine in 332 B.C.[7], and suggests the final triumph of God's kingdom.

Part two of Zechariah's work contains Messianic prophecies; it is quite evident that the prophet was speaking of the coming Messiah and the establishment of Christianity. The following references reflect the nature of Zechariah's Messianic insight: He predicted that Christ would enter Jerusalem triumphantly on a colt (Zec. 9:9), that he would be sold for thirty pieces of silver (Zec. 11:12), that the enemy would pierce the Savior while he was on the cross (Zec. 12:10), that his blood would open up a "fountain" in the House of David "for sin and for uncleanness" (Zec. 13:1), that his wounds would be inflicted in the house of his friends (Zec. 13:6) (cf. "He came unto his own, and his own received him not," Jn. 1:11). In a glorious foreview Zechariah parts the curtain and shows the Savior in his triumphant arrival on the Mount of Olives (Zec. 14:4).

Messianic
Prophecy
4306b

God's
Grace
1445

The prophet has something to say about the Jews returning to their homeland: He will gather them "out of the land of Egypt" and "out of Assyria…into the land of Gilead and Lebanon" (Zec. 10:10). A severe warning is directed against "the nations that come against Jerusalem" (Zec. 12:9). In that final day the prophet envisions that Jehovah "will pour upon the house of David, and upon the inhabitants of Jerusalem, the spirit of grace and supplications: and they shall look upon me whom they have pierced, and they shall mourn for him, as one mourneth for his only son, and shall be in bitterness for him" (Zec. 12:10).

J. Kenneth Griner says,

Repentance
2706-2712

> Some have spoken of the Gospel of Isaiah. We could also speak of the Gospel of Zechariah. It begins with a call to repentance (Zec. 1:4) even as Christ's own ministry does (Mt. 4:17); and it is inlaid all through with references to the Messiah…Zechariah has more to say about Christ than all of the other Minor Prophets…Nowhere else in the Old Testament is there such a concentrated and rich revelation of Messianic prophecies.[8]

Incarnation
720

Thus the prophet Zechariah projects one of the most dramatic foreviews of both the first and the second coming of Christ. Few OT writers, with the exception of Isaiah and the Psalmist, give such a comprehensive picture of the things that deal with the Messiah, the coming King and Redeemer.

Malachi

The Name

The Hebrew name for Malachi, which appears only once in the entire Bible (Mal. 1:1) is *mal' akhi* and means "messenger," in a ministrative sense, as a "minister of religion." Some scholars suggest this form may be an abbreviation of *Malachiah,* a Hebrew personal name meaning "the messenger of Jehovah."[1] In the English Bible the word "messenger" appears twice in the book of Malachi (2:7; 3:1) and is rendered from the Hebrew *Mel'ak* meaning "to dispatch," as a deputy, a special messenger or courier, and sometimes "the Angel of the Lord."

The book of Malachi is listed in the English Bible as the twelfth work of the Minor Prophets; in the Hebrew canon it is the fifteenth of the Latter Prophets.

Meaning
of Name
4300a
God's
Messengers
2074

Book of
Malachi
4261

Authorship and Date

Tradition has ascribed authorship of this book to the prophet Malachi, mainly because of the reference to his name in verse one: "The burden of the word of the LORD to Israel by Malachi." Some scholars question the prophet's authorship because the word "Malachi" is not generally a proper noun. The meaning of the word "messenger" may imply the prophet's actual name or a pseudonym for Ezra.[2]

No other book in the OT is written anonymously, and evidence is lacking to support this deviation for Malachi. The conservative view is that the book has unity and continuity of subject matter sufficient for one to ascribe authorship to the prophet Malachi. As the prophet was a contemporary of Ezra and Nehemiah, one can assume that the book was written about 450 B.C.

Ezra
1199

Background, Purpose, and Content

There is scant information about the prophet Malachi. The single reference to this prophecy (1:1) gives no information concerning his ancestors nor the date when he prophesied. It is generally assumed that he ministered about 100 years after Haggai and Zechariah, and that he continued the reform movement which they had started.

The Jews who returned to Jerusalem under the leadership of Haggai and Zechariah had rebuilt the temple; Nehemiah completed the walls thirteen years later. By this time the Babylonian experience had cured the Jews of

Haggai
1475

Second
Temple
3578

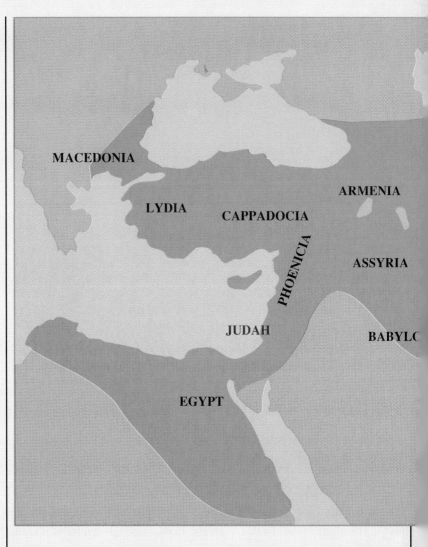

MACEDONIA

LYDIA

CAPPADOCIA

ARMENIA

PHOENICIA

ASSYRIA

JUDAH

BABYLO

EGYPT

a desire to worship the Baals. However the people had become at "ease in Zion." The people had fallen into an attitude of indifference, largely because leadership had become corrupt and self-centered. The priests were using blemished animals for sacrifice (1:8), and their neglect of duties connected with the temple caused people's interest in worship to diminish. Religion became a form without spiritual meaning.

According to the Law, the Jews were to marry only within their own group, but instead these Jews were intermarrying with the people who worshiped "strange gods" (Mal. 2:11). Older men were discarding the wives of their youth for young foreigners (Mal. 2:15).[3] God was receiving more favorable worship from the Gentiles than from the Jews (Mal. 1:11). The priests had been ordained to lead the people in truth and righteousness, but instead they were causing others to stumble in the path of righteousness

Indifference
1083-1084

Divorce
1666

Corrupt
Priests
2102

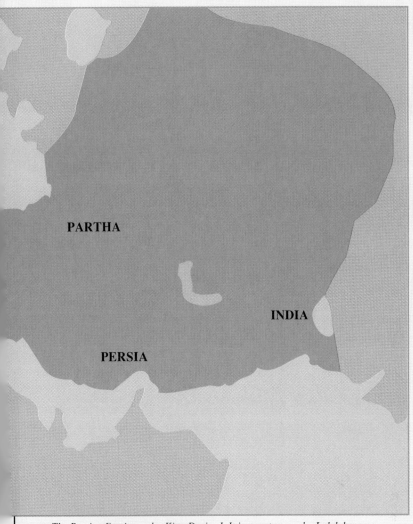

The Persian Empire under King Darius I. It is easy to see why Judah became discouraged: Though God had promised to exalt his kingdom in the sight of the nations (see Ps. 68), their land remained a miniscule province in a vast empire. Malachi rebukes their doubt and reassures his readers that the "great and dreadful day of the LORD" is coming (Mal 4:5).

(Mal. 2:8). The prophet does not spare the religious leaders from the severest condemnation and rebuke (Mal. 2:1-4).

Many scholars agree that Malachi was speaking of "the Forerunner," or John the Baptist, in his reference to the messenger (Mal. 3:1). This is in keeping with the Hebrew word used for messenger—*Mal'ak*. Some apply this name to the coming Messiah himself. The Messiah was to come with terrible judgment, but also to refine and purify his people, including the priests (Mal. 3:2-6). The Messianic reference (3:1-7) is a kind of parenthesis between the prophet's condemnation of Judah's immorality (2:11-17) and

John the
Baptist
1903-1906

the people's robbing God by withholding their tithes and offerings (3:8-10). The tithe was a kind of income tax which the people were expected to pay for the upkeep of the temple and the support of the priests. However the people had refused to pay their religious obligations (Mal. 3:8-9); therefore, the prophet urged his audience to put God's promise of bounty and plenty to the test by paying their tithes (3:10). The people refused the challenge to bring the tithes (3:13-15).

The prophet shifted back into an apocalyptic declaration in chapter four. Four times the prophet looked forward to "the Day of the Lord" (1:11; 3:1-6, 16-18; 4:1-6). The reference to "the Day" (3:2, 17; 4:1, 3, 5) seems to mean the Christian era. In the closing prediction, Elijah is to usher in a new day. Four hundred years later the "second Elijah," John the Baptist, appeared (Mt. 3:1-12; 11:14).

"Thus closes the Old Testament. Four hundred years elapsed. Then came the Messiah, whom the Hebrew nation had been born to bring forth. As through the centuries, the Jews had rejected the prophets of God, so when the Messiah arrived, they rejected him. Since which time Jews have been homeless wanderers over the earth, the tragedy and miracle of the ages."[4]

Margin notes:
Tithes
2123

Impenitence
2714

Messianic
Stars
4221
Wanderers
1273

INTERTESTAMENTAL PERIOD

The Intertestamental Period
How Events in the "Silent Years" Provide a Link Between the Testaments

Galatians 4:4 states that when the "fulness of time was come, God sent forth his Son." God did not send the Messiah until the world was fully ready; not even the minutest detail was neglected. The four-hundred-year period between the Testaments is sometimes referred to as the "Silent Period," because no canonized book was written during this time. However, this was a time of great importance for Christianity. It was during this time that propitious events converged for the coming of the Messiah and for the foundation of the Christian church. There never was a period in time before or after the Messianic event when the political, social and religious conditions were so favorable. This was a time when three nations were used of God to lay the foundation for the Christian era. Persia, Greece, and Rome all had a part in setting the Messianic stage.

The Persian Period (430-332 B.C.)

Following the Jews' return to Palestine, many of them scattered all over the Tigris-Euphrates river area including Persia, taking with them their faith, their synagogue service, and their holy oracles. They gave witness to the true and living God in the far outreaches of the heathen world.

Through the conquest of Babylon by Cyrus, God provided a sympathetic deliverer for the Jews in exile. During Belshazzar's feast in the great banquet hall in Babylon, detached fingers of a man's hand wrote a frightening message on the wall. It read: "MENE, MENE, TEKEL, UPHARSIN," which meant: "God

| Fullness of Time |
| 1343 |

hath numbered thy kingdom and finished it...Thou art weighed in the balances, and art found wanting... Thy kingdom is divided, and given to the Medes and Persians" (Da. 5:5,25-28). During the night the great king of Babylon was slain. Persian engineers had diverted the bed of the Euphrates River around the city. The next morning, under the direction of Cyrus, the Persians marched their army over the drained riverbed and captured the city. Both Darius and Cyrus, Persian kings, are mentioned as rulers of Babylon.[1]

| Persia |
| 2744 |

When Babylon was conquered, Cyrus immediately decreed that the Jews were free and that they could return to Judea. It seems clear that the hand of God was at work to provide a new political power that would be friendly to the Jews. By the Edict of Cyrus (Ezr. 1:2-4) the prophecy of Jeremiah was fulfilled to the letter (Je. 25:12-13). However, many of the Jews were well established in business and in the political life of Babylon and Persia and had no interest in going back to Jerusalem. On the other hand, priests and the religious party wished to reestablish temple worship. The older people and the poor had nothing to lose but a great deal to gain by returning to Jerusalem; so they joined the religious group for the trek back to the land of their forefathers.[2]

In addition to providing financial help for the venture, Cyrus returned to the Jews the sacred gold and silver vessels which Nebuchadnezzar had taken from the temple. An offering was received from "the chief of the fathers of Judah and Benjamin" (Ezr. 1:5-6; see also 6:1-5). Not only did the people and the priests take an offering among themselves, but also Darius and the counselors offered

| The Second Temple |
| 3578 |

expense money for tribute, bullocks, lambs, and rams for their sacrifices, as well as silver and gold for the reconstruction of Jerusalem (Ezr. 6:8-9; 7:15-16).

The question has been raised: Why did Cyrus befriend the Jews? Some have suggested that Daniel showed Cyrus some of the prophecies which had been fulfilled by Babylon's conquest (Je. 25:11-12; 29:10). The prophecy by Isaiah concerning the "dry river" must have attracted the king's attention (Is. 44:26-28). It seems that Cyrus was a willing and ready agent whom God could use to carry out his divine purpose. Cyrus freely acknowledged the hand of the Lord in these words: "The Lord God of heaven hath given me all the kingdoms of the earth; and he hath charged me to build him an house at Jerusalem, which is in Judah" (Ezr. 1:2).

Under the friendly dominion of Persia and with little or no political or military responsibility, Jerusalem once again became the center of Jewish

> **Jerusalem**
> **1881**

national life. However, when the Persians extended their military power into Greek territory, they suffered a crushing defeat at Salamis in 479 B.C. The decisive battle was at Issus when Alexander defeated Xerxes; this ended Persian influence in Europe. When Greece finally gained control of Palestine from the Persians, the Jews continued to enjoy favor and freedom.

The Greek Period (331-167 B.C.)

The origin of the Greek state is uncertain. A scholarly guess is that it began in about the twelfth century B.C., about the time the Hebrews arrived in Canaan under Joshua, or perhaps in the period of the Judges. The Trojan war occurred in 1193-1184 B.C. The Homeric age was parallel to

the time of David and Solomon's reign (1043-933 B.C.). Reliable history makes reference to the first Olympiad in 776 B.C. The Hellenistic states were formed in the period between 776 and 500 B.C. Then came the Persian wars, culminating with the battles of Thermopylae and Salamis in 480 B.C. In 336 B.C. Alexander the Great, at the age of 20, assumed command of the Greek army and swiftly conquered Egypt, Syria, Babylon, Persia, and the lands beyond. After reaching the Indus Valley (326 B.C.) he is said to have wept for more worlds to conquer.

Throughout the conquered area Alexander established Hellenism— the dissemination of Greek ideas, learning, dress, customs, festivals, and athletic

> **Greeks**
> **1464**

contests. The Greek language—one of the most expressive of all languages— became the *lingua franca*, the common language of the realm. This provided a lingual vehicle by which God could communicate his redemptive message without translators.

The Egyptian city of Alexandria was founded in honor of the great conqueror and became an example of Hellenistic culture and learning. At the invitation of Alexander thousands of Jews moved to Alexandria, where they were introduced to Greek culture and the Greek language. Many of the Jews developed a Hellenistic form of Judaism.

By the time of the advent of Christ, however, Greek philosophy had run its course: it combined pious platitudes and great ideas, but it did not have the power to fulfill itself. People were ready and willing for something more satisfying and this they experienced in the Gospel.

> **Characteristics of**
> **True Christianity**
> **4139**

When Alexander died in Babylon at the age of 33, his empire was divided among his several generals. Most prominent were the two whose dynasties would have lasting importance for the Near East area. Seleucus gained control of Syria and Ptolemy took control of Egypt. Palestine went first to Syria and then to Egypt, where it remained until 198 B.C. Under the kings of Egypt, called the "Ptolemies," the Jews enjoyed peace and tranquillity. They built many synagogues in Alexandria, and through their economic and political participation the city became a great center for Judaism.

Antiochus III (the Great) (223-187 B.C.) reconquered Palestine in 198 B.C., and it reverted to the kings of Syria, called the "Seleucids." When Antiochus IV (175-164 B.C.) ascended the throne, he assumed the name of Antiochus Epiphanes (the manifest [god]). Bitterly opposed to the Jews, he made a determined effort to strengthen Hellenism. At the same time he took steps to exterminate the Jews and their religion. The final break came in 167 B.C. shortly after Antiochus was forced to withdraw from Egypt on Roman orders. Treating Jerusalem as an enemy city, he loosed his army upon it; the result was widespread death, looting, and destruction.[3] This utter lack of feeling and respect for the Jews made the ensuing rebellion of 166 B.C. inevitable (1 Macc.).

The Maccabean (Independence) Period (167-63 B.C.)

In 198 B.C. Palestine passed back to Syrian control under the Seleucids. Later, in 175-164 B.C., a violent outrage developed against the Jews under Antiochus Epiphanes III. Being hard pressed for funds to carry on his feud with the Ptolemies, Antiochus increased the tax levy against the Jews and offered the position of high priest to the highest bidder. He removed the rightful high priest, Onias, from office

```
Jews Persecuted
1829
```

and installed a man named Jason, who agreed to assist Antiochus in his effort to Hellenize the Jewish nation. Jason built a gymnasium in Jerusalem and forced some of the Jewish males to submit to surgery to disguise their circumcision and then to participate in the sports in the nude (1 Macc. 1:14-15). Many of the Jews were horrified. To challenge this blasphemous practice, an opposition party, called Hasidim (Pious ones) was organized. The Hasidim fought bravely against efforts to impose Greek customs upon them because to them these practices were very immoral. In desperation, Antiochus finally decided to destroy the religion of the Jews by forbidding the practice of Judaism in all of its forms and by erecting in the Jewish temple an altar to Zeus and offering upon it the flesh of a sow. Heathen altars were set up all over the country. The Jews were commanded to worship at them and to eat food forbidden by the Torah, but the Hasidim refused to obey.

```
Temple
Polluted
960
```

Finally the Jews revolted under the leadership of a priest named Matthias and his five sons. Foremost among the sons was Judas. Matthias summoned all the faithful Jews to join him in a war of resistance against Antiochus. Immediate support came from the Hasidim. Matthias died shortly thereafter and his leadership was quickly assumed by Judas, whose nickname was Maccabeus—"the Hammer."

In December 164 B.C., three years after the temple was desecrated, Judas defeated the forces Antiochus had despatched from Syria to Jerusalem and declared a state of independence. Judas immediately fortified and garrisoned the city. He gave his attention to cleaning up the temple and rededi-

```
Temple
Cleansed
318
```

cating it to God. This event, which comes near Christmas, has been celebrated ever since as the feast of Hanukkah. The Independence period lasted about a hundred years (167-63 B.C.).

The Roman Period
(63B.C. – A.D. 638)

The eighth century B.C. saw the founding of Rome, and the fifth century, the organization of a republican form of government. Two centuries of war with the North African rival city of Carthage ended in victory for Rome (146 B.C.). The great Roman general and statesman, Pompey, conquered Jerusalem in 63 B.C., making it a part of the greater Roman Empire.

Thus, by the time of the advent, Rome had unified the Mediterranean world into one great empire. Roman roads with guard stations crisscrossed the empire, thereby providing safe travel. This later provided the way for Christian missionaries to travel freely without visas. Roman philosophy too had been tested and found inadequate to satisfy the demands of life. The entire Roman world was ready for a new and better way. The Gospel way was practical and pragmatic: it gave new meaning to life.

Throughout the period between the Testaments and the era of the New Testament, Rome played a part in the setting of the Gospel. Following is a brief recounting of the history of the empire during this time.

In 40 B.C., Herod became ruler of both Judea and Samaria, with the title of king. However, disturbances in Jerusalem made it impossible for him to ascend the throne until 37 B.C., after which he ruled until 4 B.C., the time of Jesus' birth. During Herod's rule, Peraea in Trans-Jordan, Galilee, and the territory north and east of the sea of Galilee were added to his kingdom. Because of his political skill, Herod proved to be one of the most successful of Rome's puppet rulers. He came to be known as Herod the Great. Under him a degree of law and order was restored in troubled Palestine. He set the country as a buffer state between Rome's territories and the hostile Arab tribes, who constantly threatened Rome's lines of communication.

Herod gave support to the imperial cult and built many temples honoring Augustus Caesar. He also built gymnasiums, theaters, and stadiums to encourage the Hellenistic way of life.[4] However, to maintain a semblance of peace in his territory, Herod was forced to show some favor to the Jews. To gain their cooperation, he lowered their taxes and rebuilt the temple with great splendor. But behind the facade of friendship he filled the land with secret officials and took ruthless vengeance on any Jew who created visible dissension. He even had his favorite wife, his brother-in-law, and his two sons murdered because he was suspicious of their loyalty. When it was reported that a new king was born in his realm, he sent his soldiers out to slaughter all the male children in Bethlehem up to two years old.

In his will Herod designated his sons as his successors. The Jews, in their anxiety not to have a continuation of the Herodian dynasty to rule them, sent a petition to Rome requesting a nullification of this will. With encouragement from the Hasidim, the Jews began to riot in protest. In addition to the Hasidim there were the extremely fanatical zealots who helped to keep the spirit of the rebellion at the boiling point. To counteract this, the Roman governor in Syria was sent to put down the uprising, and shortly thereafter

Intertestamental Period

The fortress at Masada, which had come into the possession of Jewish loyalists, was attacked by the Romans prior to the destruction of the temple in A.D. 70. After the Romans built and ascended this ramp they found that the defenders had committed mass suicide rather than submit to Roman rule. It is not mentioned in the Bible.

Herod the Great's North End Palace at Masada. Herod had many fortresses in which to seek refuge from his enemies. Masada, at the Dead Sea, was the most formidable.

Augustus Caesar approved Herod's will, dividing the kingdom among his three sons.

Judea was turned over to Archelaus (4 B.C.-A.D. 6); Herod Antipas was to rule over Galilee and Peraea; and Iturea was given to Philip. During the troublesome period between A.D. 6 and 66, Rome sent at least 14 procurators to Judea. The increased tension and Jewish rejection of Hellenism made the rulers' task progressively more difficult. Many of the procurators were low-grade politicians who sought only their selfish interests. To these men, graft and immorality of every kind were an accepted way of life. They had difficulty in comprehending the Jews' religious faith and devotion to God. Pontius Pilate (A.D. 26-36), before whom Jesus appeared, is a good example of how the procurators failed to under-

Pontius
Pilate
2763

stand the Jewish mind and heart.

Pilate's acts of poor judgment, such as bringing the military insignia, with its image of Caesar, into the holy city of Jerusalem and commanding his soldiers to attack a group of defenseless Samaritans, forced Rome to remove Pilate from office.

In A.D. 66 the situation became so critical that a revolt broke out in Jerusalem. The misrule of Florus, the

Excavations from inside Herod's fortress palace.

last of the procurators, brought things to a climax. When the revolt raged beyond local control, Nero dispatched his star general, Vespasian, to crush the revolt with military force. Vespasian had been in command only a short time when he was proclaimed Emperor of Rome to succeed Nero. The general returned to Rome to assume the seat of government and placed military command in the hands of his son, Titus, who marched on Jerusalem and completely destroyed all resistance in Jerusalem by A.D. 70. The temple and city were completely leveled. A pall of smoke hung

> Temple
> Destroyed
> 3581

heavily over the ruins of what was once the proud city of Jerusalem. This brought an end to temple worship and its sacrificial system. The synagogue became the sole place of worship. Rome continued to have political influence and power in Palestine until the Mohammedan Arabs gained control of Jerusalem (A.D. 638).

How Sacred Documents Provide a Link Between the Testaments

The last few centuries before the coming of Christ are shrouded in a peculiarly silent darkness as far as written revelation is concerned. The Old Testament, the Septuagint, the Dead Sea Scrolls, and the noncanonical apocrypha and the pseudepigrapha, give insight and information on the events during that period. They also provide links between the Old Testament period and the advent of the Messiah.

> Advent
> Awaited
> 1348

The Canon of the Old Testament

In A.D. 90 the great Jewish scholars met in Jamnia to place the final seal of canonization upon the Jewish Holy books. However, long before that time the Old Testament books were generally accepted as the authoritative Word of God. The New Testament gives conclusive evidence that there existed an OT canon to which one could turn for an authoritative reference (see references listed in the Introduction to the Old Testament: How it Became the Official Canon). Thus it is clear that when the Messiah came a closed canon of Scriptures was in use all over the empire.

The Septuagint (LXX)

The Septuagint (LXX) came into being when the Hebrew language had been almost forgotten, especially among the dispersed Jews in the Roman Empire. Hebrew language began to decline during the Babylonian captivity (606-536 B.C.), and was practically dead in the Roman Empire outside Jerusalem and its environs. The Aramaic Targums developed as oral paraphrases to Scripture reading in the postexilic synagogue. Aramaic words are especially noticeable in the exilic books of Daniel and Ezekiel.

The Greek language became the vernacular in most of the eastern Mediterranean world after the conquest of Alexander the Great (334-323 B.C.), with the exception of priestly circles. By 250 B.C. the Jews were left without a Bible they could read. A Jewish Bible for Greek-speaking Jews in the educational and cultural library in the city of Alexandria, Egypt, was not available. The need for a Jewish Bible in the commonly spoken Greek

> Ignorance of
> "Word"
> 432

language of the day became so great that a special appeal was made to the King of Egypt to authorize a translation of the Hebrew Bible into Greek.

Knowledge of just how the Septuagint (LXX) came into being is not clear. According to a little-known scholar in Alexandria, Aristeas, the Jews brought pressure upon the king, pointing out that his great library was incomplete without a Jewish Bible in the common language. Following this request, Ptolemy Philadelphus III is said to have ordered seventy-two Jewish scholars shut up in a monastery to undertake the translation separately, each without comparing notes with his neighbor. When the work was finished, each man's translation was in total agreement, word for word. Thus, the translation was called the New Greek Septuagint (LXX), after Aristeas' romantic story of the seventy-two scholars. The truth probably is that some Hebrew-Greek scholars in Alexandria began translating the Torah in about 250 B.C., and eventually completed the entire OT.

In the Greek-speaking world of that day, the Septuagint became a powerful force in spreading Bible knowledge in a heathen world. Later it became a ready vehicle for the spread of the Messiah-Christian religion.

The Apocrypha

The word *apocrypha* means *hidden* or *secret* and is the name given to fourteen books of a religious nature which contain information on events between 400 B.C. and the Advent of Christ. Even though they contain information on matters of religion, these books are considered to be noncanonical, especially by most Protestants. At the Council of Trent in 1546 the Roman Catholic Church adopted all but three of the Apocryphal books as canonical. I and II Esdras and the Prayer of Manesseh were omitted. They are called Deutrocanonical and not apocryphal in the Douai Version—the official Roman Catholic Bible.

The apocryphal books were written in Greek between the first and the third centuries B.C. and were never a part of the Hebrew canon, which concluded with Malachi about 400 B.C. However, the Apocrypha was included in Wycliffe's translation. Likewise, Luther recognized these works as having literary value but placed them between the OT and the NT with this notation: "These books are not held equal to the sacred scriptures and yet are useful and good for reading." As far as content is concerned these writings do not contain anything new in the area of redemptive revelation. All the necessary redemptive information is contained in the sixty-six books of the Protestant Canon.

The apocryphal books bear the following titles:

1 Esdras. The purpose of this book was to present Cyrus and Darius to the Jews as being benevolent persons. It contains the debate of the three soldiers who concluded that the truth is the greatest thing, and parts from Ezra, 2 Chronicles, and Nehemiah with legends about Zerubbabel.

2 Esdras. In this book Ezra is said to have had visions of a new world government and the coming of a new age.

Tobit. A romantic novel about a young Israeli captive in Nineveh who was led by an angel to wed a "virgin widow."

Judith. This book is a supposedly historical account of a rich, beautiful Jewish widow who, in the days of the Babylonian invasion, went to the tent of a Babylonian general and cut off his head to save the city.

The Rest of Esther. These are fragments of accounts gathered by Jerome to show the hand of God in the OT Book of Esther.

Wisdom of Solomon. A mixture of Hebrew thought and Greek philosophy was written by an Alexandrian Jew who claimed to be Solomon.

Ecclesiasticus. A book of proverbs and wise sayings by Jesus, the son of Sirach, gave rules of conduct for civil, religious, and domestic life.

Baruch. A book of paraphrases from Jeremiah, Daniel, and other prophets. It appears to have been written in Babylon by Baruch, the scribe of Jeremiah.

Song of the Three Holy Children. This song is an addition to the book of Daniel, giving the prayers of the three Hebrew children while they were in the fiery furnace. It also contains their triumphal praise for deliverance.

History of Susanna. As another addition to Daniel, this narrative tells about the wife of a wealthy Jew in Babylon who was cleared of a charge of adultery by the wisdom of Daniel.

Bel and the Dragon. Intended as an addition to the book of Daniel, this writing includes Daniel's proof that the idols of Bel and the Dragon are not gods.

Prayer of Manasseh. The volume contains the supposed prayer of Manasseh when he was a captive in Babylon, referred to in 2 Chr. 33:12-13.

1 Maccabees. The Maccabees is recognized as a historic book of great value, containing an account of the heroic struggle by the Jews for independence (175-135 B.C.).

2 Maccabees. This book is also an account of the Maccabean struggle (175-166 B.C.), supplementing 1 Maccabees. It is said to be an abridgment of a work written by Jason of Cyrene, of whom nothing is known. In general these were written by unknown authors and were added to the Septuagint which was composed about the same time. Several reasons exist for rejecting the Apocrypha as part of the Bible canon:

1. The books were not in the Hebrew OT and were written after the Hebrew canon was closed.

2. Josephus rejected them as a whole.

3. They were never recognized by the Jews as Hebrew Scripture.

4. They were never quoted by Jesus or by anyone else in the New Testament.

5. They were never recognized by the early church as having canonical authority nor as having been divinely inspired.

6. When the Bible was translated into Latin (Catholic Bible) in the second century, its OT was translated from the Greek OT (Septuagint) and not the Hebrew. When the Protestants rejected the Apocrypha, the Catholic Church affirmed it as Scripture at the Council of Trent in A.D. 1546, in an effort to stop the Protestant movement. The Apocryphal books are still in the Douay [Douai] version.

7. A final reason for rejecting these books as canonical is that the quality of the writings is inferior to the canonical Scripture. The dignity and integrity of the writers of the canonical books is lacking. Identification of authorship is almost impossible in the Apocryphal books.

The Pseudepigrapha

These books were written by Jewish authors between 200 B.C. and A.D. 100. The word *pseudo* means "false" or "hidden." Even though the works deal with religious subjects, they are far below the quality of the canonized Bible books. Some of the books include the following:

Palestinian Books Written in Hebrew in 200-100 B.C. The Testaments of the Twelve Patriarchs contain legends, moral codes, and apocalyptic expectations which the twelve patriarchs are said to have passed down to their descendants.

(a) The Psalms of Solomon, written about 40 B.C.

(b) The legendary lives of the prophets, dating A.D.1-100.

Palestinian Books Written in Aramaic, about 200-1 B.C.

(a) The Book of Jubilees, a legendary account of Genesis and Exodus through ch. 12.

(b) The Testament of Job (legends).

(c) The Book of Enoch (apocalyptic). This is quoted in Jude 14-15.

It is acknowledged that even these books contain some truth. Where passages are singled out under the leading of the Holy Spirit they are true, as in the aforementioned quotation from Jude.

Books and Legends Written A.D. 1-100

(a) Legends with Christian additions

(b) The Martyrdom of Isaiah

(c) The Additions of Jeremiah

(d) The Life of Adam and Eve

(e) The Assumption of Moses

(f) The Apocalypse of Abraham

Alexandrian Books Written in Greek 200 B.C.-A.D. 100

(a) Written about 200-75 B.C. Letter of Aristeas giving a legendary account of the translation of the Pentateuch into Greek in about 250 B.C.

(b) 3 Maccabees written in 75-1 B.C. Gives an account of the miraculous deliverance of the Egyptian Jews from a death sentence.

(c) 4 Maccabees is a philosophical and historical demonstration of the stoic statement, "Devout reason is master of the passions." Written in A.D. 1-100.[5]

These writings are anonymous. Appended names of canonical authors were used to give dignity to the heretical writings.

The Dead Sea Scrolls

The discovery of the Dead Sea Scrolls is one of the most significant archae-

Dead Sea
Scrolls
4362

ological finds of the twentieth century. These scrolls constitute some of the earliest OT manuscripts known to man, dating back to within several hundred years of the autographs. In addition, there are extrabiblical books which give heretofore unknown information about the pre-Christian Jews and the "pre-Advent church." The particular scrolls to which this study makes reference are definitely of the B.C. period and have in them vivid glimpses of the period not covered in the Bible.

A scholar of note relates that "in the Qumran texts and Damascus Document we now have considerable quantity of literature cherished and produced by a dissident group of Jews during the time when the Temple was standing, just after the composition of the latest books of the Old Testament..."[6]

The Dead Sea Scrolls and the religious movement which they represent help Bible students to comprehend and to reconstruct the spiritual situation of pre- and post-Advent Christianity. By enriching one's knowledge of Judaism in the period in which Christianity arose, the Dead Sea Scrolls supply material for a better understanding of the NT and of early Christianity.

Many volumes have been written on the Dead Sea Scrolls, with varying shades of interpretation. An objective look at the scrolls reveals startling similarities between the pre-Messianic dwellers at the scroll community (Qumran) and the early Christian church. Though there are a great many differences in the interpretation of the scrolls, most scholars are agreed that there is a close affinity between the scrolls and the gospel records.

Many scholars of the Dead Sea Scrolls are in agreement that it should not be surprising to find similarity in language and thought between the early church and the Qumran community. Jesus was baptized by John the Baptist in the Jordan River during the time when the community of covenanters was flourishing not many miles away. It is further agreed that there are many points at which John's ideas resemble those expressed in the Dead Sea Scrolls. Like the covenanters, he was devoted to preparing the way of the Lord in the wilderness. He insisted that without previous spiritual cleansing, bathing in water could not signify the removal of guilt. There is also a striking similarity in that the "conception of a Messianic baptism by the Holy Spirit is present also in the scrolls. The statement in the *Manual of Discipline* that at the end of this age God will cleanse men by sprinkling upon them the spirit of truth recalls John's proclamation that the Messiah will baptize His people with the Holy Ghost" (Mt. 3:11; Jn. 1:33; Ac. 2:16-21).[7]

John's Baptism 760

Since the similarities which exist between the Gospels and the Qumran texts are striking, one can conclude that there may have been association of the two. This conclusion is justified because the dwellers at Qumran were representative of the pre-Christian (Messianic) religion as revealed in the OT. An objective examination of the scrolls may dictate the conclusion by Burrows that "Christians should have no reluctance to recognize anticipations of Christianity in the Dead Sea Scrolls. The Gospel was given as the fulfillment of what was already revealed. God who spoke in many and various ways to the fathers by the prophets, spoke more clearly and fully in His Son."[8]

From the scribal tables and benches, as well as from the scrolls and the thousands of scroll fragments found, comes the evidence that the Qumran community was a literary center. Many of these scrolls and fragments are Biblical in nature. One of the most important scrolls in this group is the Scroll of Isaiah which portrays most graphically the vicarious sufferings of the Messiah to whom these holy people were dedicated. The prophet Isaiah states, "Surely he hath borne our griefs, and carried our sorrows...He was wounded for our transgressions, he was bruised for our iniquities...with his stripes we are healed...He was oppressed, and he was afflicted" (Is. 53:4-7).

Isaiah's Portrait of Christ 4301

Many of the Messianic passages are in the past tense. This particular tense is also used in John 3:16, which clearly states that salvation had been provided before Christ actually died on the cross. There is a sense in which Jesus Christ had already been crucified and had already been resurrected—that is, in the mind of God—long before the incarnation. The redemptive promise by God was as good as its ultimate fulfillment. And by faith, pre-Advent humanity could be saved. In addition, the nonbiblical scrolls found in the Qumran area abound in matters relevant to the doctrine of redemption.

In the Dead Sea Scrolls are the authentic forms and idioms reflected in the Gospel of John and other NT writings. It is possible that the ritualistic ideas expressed in the scrolls helped to formulate a blueprint of the religious organization which later developed in the post-Advent church. This is evidenced by the Dead Sea scriptures in which NT parallels are numerous.

The affinities between the thought and language of the Dead Sea Scrolls and that of the NT may best be gauged by a representative list of examples. By permission from the publisher a few excerpts given below show how the Dead Sea Scrolls provided a long-needed document portraying the forerunner of Christianity. In these scrolls one of the many bridges is provided over which religious entry can be made from the OT Church to the New. Gaster's work cites the following parallels:

1. The members of the community styled themselves "the elect" or "the elect of God." Compare Titus 1:1.

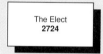

The Elect
2724

2. The truth of God, as revealed in His law, is constantly called the light. Compare John 1:7-9 and 8:12.

3. The "enlightened" members of the community described themselves as "Sons of Light." Compare John 12:36.

4. In the *Book of Hymns*, the faithful frequently declare that they stand in the eternal congregation of God, and hold direct converse with Him, and share the "lot of the holy beings." Compare Eph. 2:19.

5. A basic tenet is the doctrine of the "remnant," the belief that their community constitutes the true "relic" of Israel, faithful to the Covenant. See Ro. 11:3-5.

6. The spiritual leader of the community is called "teacher" or "right teacher." In Jn. 3:2 Jesus is hailed as the teacher sent by God...So too in Jn. 7:14.

7. In the *Manual of Discipline* is the statement that "if the community abide by the prescribed rules it will be a veritable 'Temple of God, a true holy of holies.'" Compare 1 Co. 3:16-17.

8. In the *Manual of Discipline* there is a long passage describing the Two Ways, viz., of good and evil, light and darkness, which God sets before everyman. See Mt. 7:13ff.

Light-
Darkness
2165-2180

9. The *Manual of Discipline* quotes the famous words of Isaiah in Is. 40:3. In John 1:23, the Baptist quotes exactly the same passage in exactly the same context.[9]

A leading scholar summarizes the linkage between the OT and the NT thus:

> These scrolls provide a link between the Old and New Testament periods...unlike the pattern of life prevailing in the Judaism of the Temple. This community observed poverty, chastity, and obedience as rigid disciplines and practiced daily baptisms. Admission to membership was highly selective. They flourished when the Christian movement was taking root...It is possible that the import of this group and others like them was much stronger on Judaism (and thus on Christianity) than we had imagined before finding the scrolls.[10]

How a Small Jewish Sect Provides a Link Between the Testaments

The discovery of the Dead Sea Scrolls provides enlightenment on a small religious sect of Jews known as the Qumran community. According to the testimony given in the scrolls, the people residing in the covenant community believed that they constituted the "Israel of God" (Ga. 6:16), the spiritual seed of Abraham (Ro. 9:6; 11:5) or the remnant which preserved "the faith which was once delivered unto the saints" (Jude 3). They believed that God always had his faithful witnesses and that they were, in fact, the successors to previous "remnant" groups professing the true Messianic faith. The term "remnant" had

Remnant of
Israel
1828

a very peculiar significance to these people because in their thinking they were the small segment of people that would welcome the Messiah.

They thought of themselves as the spiritual descendants of Moses. They were looking for a new covenant but also for the reaffirmation of the Old, which had been given in Eden and was periodically reaffirmed, not alone at Mount Sinai, but to all believers in all ages.

They considered themselves the "elect" or "chosen people," not because of their lineal descent from the patriarchs, but rather because they had responded to and had met the condition of God's redemptive plan. They had gained membership in the "household of God" by virtue of their professed faith in God's promised Messiah. These people were not attempting to change the legal code they already had. It was their aim to assert the law and "to deliver it from the realm of darkness in which it had become engulfed....and perverted by 'false expositors.'"[11]

| Chosen Ones |
| 2725 |

These spiritual children of Abraham endeavored to exemplify and promulgate the spiritual intent of the Scriptures. In their writings they made reference to a teacher, but not *just* a teacher—a godly, righteous teacher who would come. This teacher was probably typified by the true prophets, but all of these types pointed forward to the One who would fulfill all righteousness, even the Messiah (De. 33:9-10; see also Ac. 3:17-23). The true and righteous teachers, in contrast to the false prophets, taught the people that as Moses was raised up a prophet and teacher, to lead the church through the wilderness, so God would soon raise the Great Prophet and Teacher, the Messiah, to lead the church through the wilderness of the world. The Messiah would proclaim that which the people in the pre-Advent period had appropriated by faith and expressed. The book of Deuteronomy asserts this view: "The Lord thy God will raise up unto thee a Prophet from the midst of thee, of thy brethren, like unto me; unto him ye shall hearken..." (De. 18:15ff.; see also Ac. 3:17-23). Special significance is seen in the fact that some of the fragments found in the caves indicated passionate Messianic expectation.

The doctrine of the new birth was understood at least in principle by these faithful believers and was considered definitely a part of divine revelation. The Qumran dwellers taught that man could see and receive the deep spiritual things of God only through an inner enlightenment. In their *Book of Hymns*, reference to the "shining faces" identifies the people with the special enlightenment. They believed that this enlightenment accrued membership for them, not only in a consecrated earthly brotherhood, but also in an eternal fellowship with God. This is certainly consistent with the teachings of the OT (Jb. 19:25-27; Da. 12:2-3; Ps. 16:10-11; 17:15; 23:6).

| New Birth |
| 2154 |

Within this group the supreme authority in all theological matters was assumed by the priests ("right teachers"). The administrative functions were handled by a group of officials whose counterpart today would be stewards, deacons, elders, or presbyters. A noted scholar of the scrolls points out that "these Presbyters were known as 'the men of special holiness' and they had to undergo a year's probation before appointment" (Ac. 6:1ff.).[12] The Qumran sect held an annual conference for the discharge of community affairs which was provided for by the *Manual of Discipline*, similar to the regulative discipline which church denominations have today.

Scholars differ regarding the identity of this Qumran community. Evidence is strong to support the conclusion that these dwellers at Qumran were in fact the Judaistic sect known as the Essenes, a small group that was active in the Jewish community during the last two

| Jewish Sects |
| 3171-3173 |

Above: Three of the most important of the Dead Sea Scrolls: Isaiah, Habakkuk and the Manual of Discipline.

Below: The interior of a cave where some of the Dead Sea Scrolls were found.

The receding shore of the Dead Sea reveals ancient tree stumps preserved by salt and chemicals in the water.

centuries B.C. The presence of the Essenes in the Dead Sea area is attested to by Philo, the Jewish philosopher, Flavius Josephus and Pliny the Elder, both historians of the first century A.D.; and by the Damascus Document. Père de Vaux, one of the pioneer scholars in a study of the Dead Sea Scrolls, says that the Essenes must have lived at Khirbet Qumran, except for a few years, from about 100 B.C. or a little before, to A.D. 66-70.[13]

Another reason to believe that the Essenes were the sect who produced the Dead Sea Scrolls and who perceived that they were the "remnant" of true believers, the "Israel of God," was their separation from the hierarchy of the organized church of the day. Supervision and direction of formal temple worship had been taken over by the apostate ecclesiastical leaders within Judaism to such an extent that true worshipers found it difficult to carry on their form of worship within the religious system of the temple. When Jesus arrived at the temple, he referred to it as a "den of thieves" instead of a house of worship. The pre-Advent apostasy within the established ecclesiastical temple hierarchy was so great after Christ began his public ministry that it was considered a serious religious offense to acknowledge Jesus of Nazareth as

the Messiah. Offenders were removed from synagogue membership without question (Jn. 9:22; Ac. 7:51-52).

Distinction must be made between the apostate religious leaders and those pious ones, the Essenes and other "like groups" who refused to compromise on the moral, ethical, and social standards clearly taught in the OT. These OT principles were frequently quoted by Jesus (Mt. 22:36-40; cf. De. 6:5; Le. 19:18) and the NT writers.

Ancient historians state that the Essenes had their origin in the period of religious protest about the same time the Pharisees and Sadducees became active (see commentary on Jn. 8:44). It is difficult to find a favorable reference to the Pharisees and Sadducees in the entire NT. The Pharisees assumed a strict letter-of-the-law, legalistic position; the Sadducees accepted only the Pentateuch as being authoritative and had no share in the Messianic hopes of which the Prophets spoke at length. They believed in neither angels nor spirits and had no hope of immortality (Ac. 23:8). On the other hand, "nothing could be farther removed from the Essene spirit and doctrines as recorded in the apocalypses. The Messianic hopes bulk largely: angels are prominent; their hierarchies are described and their names given. The doctrine of immortality is implied, and the places of reward and punishment are described."[14]

The Essenes were caught in the legalistic cross fire of the religious parties. This Covenant community might be compared to the Waldensian brotherhood of the twelfth and thirteenth centuries. From a religious viewpoint the comparison is indeed suggestive of the common reaction both groups had against the doctrinal

| Pharisaism |
| 2750 |

degeneration of the established hierarchy.[15]

It is not known exactly when the Essenes separated themselves from the temple and its activities and withdrew into communal settlements where they could have freedom of worship. Many of the faithful believers who anticipated the imminent coming of the Messiah withdrew to the Judean wilderness where they worshiped more in accordance with Judaism in the days of the prophets. It is significant that it was in the wilderness area, in the proximity of the Qumran community, rather than in the temple, that John the Baptist and Jesus inaugurated their public ministries. The prebaptism ministry of both Jesus and John the Baptist took place in Essene territory.

It is a matter of historical record that the believers in Christ were separated from traditional Judaism as represented by the Pharisees and Sadducees. True Israel (the church) was closely linked with those who looked for the Messiah and who accepted him when he came. The NT church is indeed an extension or continuation of the OT church. This precious faith has been preserved by mystical groups such as the Essenes and the Therapeutae (Jewish monks and other like groups to which Philo makes reference in his treatise "De Vita Contemplativa"). One noted scholar observes that "the Essenes and the Therapeutae were given over to a study of the laws and sacred oracles of God enunciated by the holy prophets, and hymns, and psalms and all kinds of other things by reason of which knowledge and piety are increased and brought to perfection."[16] It is evident these intertestamental groups help one to make closer contact with

> Church
> Precious
> **729**

that spiritual Judaism out of which Christ the Messiah came. From this, one can see that the temple hierarchy rejected Jesus but at the same time other Jews accepted him and became the vanguard for the Christian church.

At times in history the Christian faith has not been evident, but there have always been minority groups through whom the faith has been nurtured and preserved. Thus God is not dependent upon "ecclesiastical cloth" for the preservation of the faith (Ac. 13:27ff.). In periods of spiritual darkness God has preserved the faith within the hearts of humble people. Is it possible that Simeon and Anna, living at the beginning of Jesus' earthly life, were acquainted with the Essenes and at the end of his life, Joseph of Arimathea also? It seems reasonable to suppose that these believers were Essene in spirit, but perhaps bearing another name. J. E. H. Thompson points out, for example, that the "term 'Methodist' was derived from a purely temporary characteristic of the society that gathered around Wesley. As the name Essene is not found in the NT it is possibly a nickname, as the term 'Quakers' was, applied to the Society of Friends."[17]

> Faithful
> Servants
> **603**

Many of the rites and concepts of worship among the Essenes are similar to those in the NT, particularly in the Gospel of John and the Pauline Epistles. Both the Essenes and the Christians were inspired and influenced by the Messiah: The Essenes looked forward to the promises of the OT prophets; for the Christians those promises had become a reality. The essence of redemption in the OT is the same as that in the NT. The Essenes and the Christians both developed their ritual from the sources which inspired Abel, Enoch, Joseph, Daniel, and the

> Redemption
> Through Christ
> **2979**

other spiritual giants in the OT. Frank M. Cross, of the American School of Oriental Research, says:

> The New Testament and Essene writers...draw on common sources of language, common theological themes and concepts and share common religious institutions...For God chooses to give meaning to human history, not to suspend it. This means he uses its continuities, its language, its events, its institutions in speaking to men and in building His church...No Christian need stand in dread of these tests.[18]

One of the scholars who took an initial lead in the translation and interpretation of the Dead Sea Scrolls points out that instead of looking for the Jewish substrata of Christian doctrines in Pharisaic and Talmudic quarters, as had hitherto been done, henceforth the same search must be conducted from the direction of Essenism as revealed by the new documents. The gospel does not emerge out of Pharisaic Judaism. On the contrary, in the gospel accounts, Jesus was the target of the Pharisees' hostility. They spared him neither the strongest criticism nor the bitterest invective (see Jn. 8:33ff.).

From the Scriptures it is evident that the revelation of Christ was gradually unfolded over the centuries so it was natural and normal that the basic ritual would undergo slow changes in order to fit itself to the changing culture, economy, and functional needs of the people. These changes in the ritual facilitated the passing of "spiritual Judaism" into the Christian era and into the Gentileworld.

Père de Vaux states:

> The most startling disclosure of the Essene documents so far published is that the sect possessed, years before Christ, a terminology and practice that have always been considered uniquely Christian. The Essenes practiced baptism and shared a liturgical repast of bread and wine presided over by a priest. They believed in redemption and the immortality of the soul.[19]

John the Baptist's use of baptism has led scholars to believe that he was either an Essene, or strongly influenced by the sect. The noted historian Will Durant tells us that the asceticism and piety of John the Baptist and that of the Essenes had a very close affinity and that the name "the Baptist" may be a Greek equivalent of "Essene" (bather). This would draw John the Baptist closer to the Essene camp.[20] Bathing the body and washing the raiment had ceremonial significance among both the Israelites and the Essenes (Le. 8:6; 14:8; 15:5; 17:15; Nu. 19:7-8. See also Josephus, *Antiquities*, XIII, 5).

Another significant fact is that Essenism disappeared with the advent of Christianity. Could it not be that Christianity became a continuation of this "Mosaic ideal" nurtured by the Essenes? Is it not possible that the terminologies and the practices of the Essenes, such as baptism, carried over into the institution known as the Christian church? It is evident from the data presented that the literature at Qumran provided a very logical transitional link between OT Judaism and NT Christianity.

A renowned Bible scholar says, "If we are to understand the Palestine in which our Lord's ministry was carried on, we must comprehend the place occupied by the Essenes." He continues with this very surprising statement: "The Essenes are brought forward as the very flower and perfection of Mosaism...They use a threefold criterion—love of God, love of virtue and love of man...No one can fail to be struck with the resemblance all this has, in the first place, to the teaching of the Sermon on the Mount and to the practice of the early church."[21]

A perspective of the ruins at Qumran.

Why the Essenes are not mentioned in Scripture is only conjecture. In the first place, they were a minority group, perhaps less that 4,000. Their protest against the temple hierarchy, both political and religious, culminated in a radical withdrawal from normal social and religious associations in Jerusalem. Such religious extremists were not popular and probably not thought to be worthy of public attention. Their separation and withdrawal soon resulted in complete oblivion. A parallel to this would be the absence of any reference in Egyptian records to the Hebrew residency or to the exodus.

Regardless of what the final judgment about the Essene community might be, it is obvious that, although there were differences, there are sufficient similarities between the teachings of these people and the later teachings in the Gospels, especially those of John, to form a bridge of communication between the Old and the New Covenants.

Other Links Between the Testaments
The Hymnody of the Church

The Psalms bring the Old and NT church together, as pointed out in the introduction to the book of Psalms, p. 202. In the same way the Christian hymns evolving after the Reformation attest

> Hymns
> 2476-2477

their OT ancestry. The frequent references to OT places, persons, and things in Christian hymns suggest a common theology, doctrine, and background. "I will sing my great Jehovah's praise" and "When I see the blood I will pass over you" or "Just inside the Eastern Gate" are just a few of the terms and phrases compatible to the OT church. (See the commentary on Is. 6:3 for references from the book of Isaiah in Christian hymns.)

Most of our Protestant hymnals contain many references to the OT subjects including the saints. For example, one of the poets related Jesus to a common heaven with the prophets of the OT: "Jesus my all, to heaven has gone...the way the holy prophets went." In another hymn we read: "Hail to the brightness of Zion's glad morning, long by the prophets of Israel foretold." Another poet refers to the common loyalty of the OT prophets and the apostles to Christ, the Word: "For our Prophets and Apostles, Loyal to the living Word; For all heroes of the Spirit, Give we thanks to Thee, O Lord." In another hymn we read about the affinity between the two Testaments:

Join, O Man, the deathless voices,
    Child of God, lift up thy head!
Patriarchs from the distant ages,
    Saints all longing for their heaven,
Prophets, psalmists, seers and sages,
    All await the glory given.

The NT poets not only emphasize the theological unity between the Testaments but also make reference to "The God of Abraham...who was, and is, and is to be...the same one Eternal God." Another poet shows that "poet, prophet and saint received his word from this one Eternal God." In another hymn OT and NT saints have a common cause: "Finding , following, keeping, struggling, Is He sure to bless? Saints, apostles, prophets, martyrs, Answer, Yes." In some hymns OT saints and their relationship to the Savior are projected into NT thought patterns: "Hail to the Lord's anointed, Great David's greater Son!"[22]

| Eternal God |
| 2481 |

The Liturgy of the Church

In the liturgy of the church one again finds compatibility with the religion of the OT. In our responsive readings frequent reference is made to the Psalms and other OT texts. On Palm Sunday we read responsively selections from Psalms 40 and 45, and on Good Friday we read from Psalm 22. Ascension Day calls for readings from Psalm 21. Selections from the Psalms and/or other OT books appear in almost every responsive selection, and this is as it should be since the entire OT abounds in references to Christ. It is Christ, and only Christ, who makes the OT alive and pulsating with redemptive life; take Christ out of the OT and we have remaining only a lifeless religious shell.

The Word Ekklesia (Church)

A single word can be a most powerful link between periods of time. The Greek word *ekklesia* is such a term, forming an undeniable bridge between the church in the OT period and the church in the NT period.

| Foundation of Church |
| 3177 |

This word *ekklesia* comes to us from the classical Greek, meaning an assembly such as a political group or gathering. The ecclesiastical writers appropriated this term to designate a religious community comprising members on earth or saints in heaven or both. Strictly speaking, it is used when reference is made to the "called out ones" or the "believers in the Lord's Christ-Messiah." This term is never used to designate a church building, nor is there reference in the NT to such a structure.

In the third century before Christ the Greek language became dominant in the Mediterranean world, and in the middle of this century the Hebrew Bible was translated into Greek because Hebrew was an almost forgotten language among the dispersed Jews. When Paul and the early missionaries began their journeys to announce the glad tidings that Jesus of Nazareth was indeed the Messiah, they went to the synagogues in which the Greek OT was used. It can be demonstrated that most of the OT quotations in the NT use the terminology of the Septuagint (Greek OT) rather than the Massoretic text (Hebrew OT). It can be said that even the Greek language provided a religious inter-Testament bridge. The *ekklesia* in the NT takes its name and primary idea from the *qahal* of the OT. The *qahal* of the OT is a continuing idea in the NT and becomes the *ekklesia* (church).

Although the term "church" is understood by many to mean an institution brought into existence on the day when the Holy Spirit baptized a certain group in the Upper Room, let us ask ourselves: Were these Holy Ghost-baptized people saints or sinners? Does the Holy Spirit baptize sinners? Obviously not. Those in the Upper Room already bore the mark of the cross and had the blood applied before they assembled there.

> Accessions
> **733**

Let us consider the facts. The English word *church* appears many times in the Authorized (King James) Version of the NT. To be specific, it appears three times in the Gospels and about seventy-eight times in the entire NT. However, the fact that *church* in the English language is used in reference to both a building and the body of Christ, has caused no end of confusion—perhaps more than has been caused by any other key term of the NT.

It can then be asked which Greek word has been translated "church." The answer is *ekklesia*, which means the "called out ones." The term defies trans-

> Christian
> Calling
> **622**

slation, and should be transliterated in all versions and tongues. The ekklesia is the institution in which saints of all ages find their repose. This term is equally at home in the Greek OT and the Greek NT.

Fenton Hort, once Professor of Divinity at Cambridge and co-compiler with Brooke Foss Westcott, of the Greek text, makes this observation: "The English term 'church,' now the most familiar representative of 'Ekklesia' to most of us, carries with it associations derived from the institutions and doctrines of later times, and thus cannot, at present, without mental effort, be made to convey the full and exact force which originally belonged to Ekklesia."[23]

Scholars are generally agreed that the Greek word *ekklesia* could also be translated "congregation," and was thus rendered in most English versions throughout Henry VIII's reign.

> Congregation
> **820-821**

The Geneva revisers translated *ekklesia* to read "church," and it was the accepted rendering in the authorized version of 1611. The general conclusion among scholars is that the only neutral word to denote the church is the transliteration of *ekklesia*, pointing back to the beginning of Christianity. It is impossible to fully understand the actual ekklesia of postapostolic times without first gaining some clear impressions of the ekklesia of the apostles from which it came. In the lifetime of our Lord such language was peculiarly likely to be misunderstood by the outer world of Jews, and therefore it is not surprising if it formed no part of his ordinary public teaching.

As a final consideration, let it be noted that the passage in Matthew 18:17 uses the term *ekklesia* in a sense of something already in existence.

Here the Lord is speaking not of the future but the present, instructing his disciples how to deal with an offending brother. In a functional sense the ekklesia was already in existence during the lifetime of our Lord, as it was in the wilderness with the Hebrews on their way to Canaan (Ac. 7:38).

In the major passage of Matthew 16:16-18, Jesus addresses Peter in Caesarea Philippi, and evokes from him the confession, "Thou are the Christ, the Son of the living God." In turn the Lord says to Peter: "I say also unto thee, That thou art Peter [*Petros*] and upon this rock [*petra*, Peter's confession] I will build my church [*ekklesia*] and the gates of hell shall not prevail against it." Here there is no question of a partial or narrowly located ekklesia. The congregation of God in the OT is what the disciples must have come to understand to be the meaning of the church which was, for the present, mysterious. If one may venture for a moment to substitute the name "Israel" and read the words as "on this rock I will build my Israel," one may have at least an approximation of the probable sense. The ekklesia of ancient Israel was the "ekklesia of God," and since Jesus was confessed

Church Divinely Instituted
731

to be God's Messiah, our Lord could, without risk of grave misunderstanding, claim the ekklesia as his own. The ekklesia (the called out ones) of the apostles has antecedents in facts and words recorded by the Evangels and historically in the institutions and teachings of the OT.

The Exhaustive Concordance of the Bible by James Strong defines the word *ekklesia* thus: "a calling out...a popular meeting, especially a religious congregation (Jewish Synagogue, or Christian community of members on earth or saints in heaven, or both): assembly, church." The precise meaning of the term in the OT is a common one. The Greek OT (Septuagint) renders the OT term *qahal* as "ekklesia." Two important words are used in the Hebrew OT for the gathering of the people of Israel or their representative heads: *edhah*, translated "congregation"; and *qahal*, rendered "assembly" in the Revised Version. "Synagogue" is the usual, almost the universal, Septuagint rendering of *edhah*; "synagogue" is also the usual translation of *qahal* in the earlier

Synagogues
3521-3523

books of the Pentateuch. It is well to remember that the use of these terms in a Biblical sense has to do with a group of people who are followers of God.

Fenton Hort says, "In the NT period the term 'Ekklesia' already has a history of its own, and was associated with the whole history of Israel....Its antecedents, as...used by our Lord and His Apostles, are of two kinds, derived from the past and present respectively. The most important meaning came from its ancient, or religious use. This is the sense in which it was used in the Jewish Scriptures. This was combined with the sense in which it was still current in the everyday life of the Jews..."[24]

The actual word *ekklesia*, as many know, is confined in the Gospels to two passages in Matthew (which was written to the Jews) where Peter's name is used in connection with building the Messiah's ekklesia. Thus the way was paved for the use of this term by the apostles in that it was founded on an impressive saying of Christ the Lord. What he declared that he would build was in one sense old, and in another new. It had a true continuity with the ekklesia of the Old Covenant; the building of it would be a rebuilding, as suggested in Acts 15:16, where James quotes Amos 9:11, "In that day will I raise up the tabernacle of David that is fallen, and close up the breaches thereof; and I will raise up his ruins, and I will build it as in the days of old." Hence, this single word, ekklesia, forms another bridge between the OT and the NT.

The Sacraments of the Church

Many other bridges provide free and easy passage between the Testaments. The Christian sacraments of baptism and the Lord's Supper (referred to by some as "sacraments" or "ordinances") are important links which have their meaning and origin in the Old Testament.

> Sacraments of Church
> **756-757, 761**

Basically the need for the sacraments or ordinances existed from the time salvation was first presented to man. Many believe that the plan and the promise (Ge. 3:15) were presented to Adam and Eve. Abel, their son, certainly gives evidence that he had been taught the way of salvation and the acceptable sacrifice. The stages of the religious ritual are revealed in the Bible. Since salvation could not be fragmented, one may assume that salvation was complete from the time God presented the plan to man, and essentially it has not changed.

Two sacraments were practiced in the OT—circumcision and the Passover; the one was initiatory, the other commemorative. Before these sacraments were introduced, there may have been other rites which God had established to fulfill this purpose. Before the Advent, all the rituals and ceremonies referred to the time when circumcision and the Passover were inaugurated. However, they also looked toward the Messiah's coming.

Salvation in the OT as well as in the NT required faith: a forward look of faith in the promised Messiah and a backward look of faith in the provided Savior

> Faith in Christ
> **1206**

satisfied the redemptive requirement. Some of the rituals, customs, and modes that were exceedingly useful and appropriate before Christ's Advent, were inappropriate and useless afterward. The Bible record reveals changing forms and modes of the ritual. The OT forms of circumcision, the Passover, the Day of Pentecost, the Sabbath, all take on new significance after the advent of Christ.

Substantially Christ was and is the center of all salvation relevance in both the OT and the NT. In the OT he is referred to as the coming King and Savior; in the NT he is presented within the context of history. He had come; this was the Good News. In the OT, Christ stands in the prophetic tradition, illustrated by the animal sacrifices, symbolizing faith in him who was spoken of by Moses and the prophets. In the NT Christ is the fulfillment of all that the prophets foretold (Ro. 1:1-5). When Jesus said, "I am the way, the truth, and the life: no man cometh unto the Father, but by me," he made a statement which is timeless. It was a statement of eternal truth. There never was a time when this statement was not true. He always stands in the same relationship to sinners and saved men (He. 13:8),

> Salvation Only Through Christ
> **3117**

but in the one case the literal consummation of his great atoning acts was in the prophetic future, and in the other, in the historical past. In the NT, the OT sacraments continue, but the mode changes from circumcision to baptism and from the Passover to the Lord's Supper. Each one will be considered separately:

Circumcision-Baptism

The word "circumcision" comes from the Hebrew word *mula* and from the Greek word *peritome*. Both have the basic meaning of "cutting around."

> Circumcision
> **765**

The natures of the "natural man" and the "redeemed man" are such that in society it is necessary for the redeemed man to have a mark of identification and a symbolic witness. Circumcision was the mark chosen by God to identify believers in the days of Abraham (Ge. 17:1-13). It was understood to be a mark of separation from the practices of the sinful world in which the believers lived. History affirms that circumcision was an early Semitic institution and the idea was borrowed by some other religions. It is assumed that the worship of Elohim-YHWH (God the Lord) was the first religious system and that the other religious systems are corrupted "spinoffs" from this pure religion.

The ritual always commemorated the historical event but it also looked forward to the reality which it symbolized. Circumcision was definitely a vital part of God's plan as it was unfolded in the time of Abraham from Genesis to Malachi. The validity of the event was dependent upon the prophetic event to which it looked forward. The coming of the Messiah, a future event of grace, was always an integral part of OT religion. The person who submitted to circumcision thereby sealed a promise to God and the qahal, or the OT church, to carry out and observe all the things implied in OT church "membership." The believing Jew was under this obligation, and the rite was the seal which bound him to be true to the faith.

Now if the sacrament of circumcision was necessary, why did it not continue after Christ? The sacrament of initiation did continue uninterruptedly, but in a different form. Nothing changed but the form in which the sacrament was administered, and this was done for most obvious and necessary reasons. The particular form in which the sacrament was administered before the coming of Christ had peculiar significance and appropriateness to the blood-letting in the animal sacrifices. The significance of all this was the forward look, to the cross, which foreshadowed "the Lamb of God" who died once for all. Since the animal sacrifices looked forward to the redemptive event, they no longer had relevance. It was now necessary to change, to introduce a sacramental mode which would be historical. The "Lamb of God" on the cross took the place of the "slain animal," and water baptism as an historical attestation was adopted as the mode of the initiatory rite.

Of course sacramental modes do not change suddenly. There is a gradual, preparatory phase so the people can become adjusted to the change. As an example, the use of the metric system is being introduced gradually, and both the mile and the kilometer are on sign posts and speedometers. Since circumcision was the sacramental mode before the Advent, it had no real relevance after the Advent because what it had pointed to was fulfilled in Christ. Paul repeatedly explains this in his epistles to the Galatians and to the Romans. "Behold, I Paul say unto you, that if ye be circumcised, Christ shall profit you nothing. For I testify again to every man that is circumcised, that he is a debtor to do the whole law" (Ga. 5:2-3). Circumcision of the flesh now becomes "spiritual circumcision" of the heart of which baptism is the symbol (Ro. 2:28-29; De. 10:16; Je. 4:4; 9:25-26).

Spiritual
Circumcision
766

Even in the OT, physical circumcision was intended to be the outward sign of inward grace, the circumcised heart (Eze. 44:7), and in the NT, it is the new birth. It is well to bear in mind that the introduction of water baptism as an initiatory rite developed gradually in a time when both circumcision and water baptism were used concurrently. Ritualistic washing with water was well known in the OT (Ex. 29:4; 30:20; 40:12; Le. 15; 16:26-28). John the Baptist used water in his initiatory rite, and it is significant that both John and Jesus ministered during the OT period. The NT period did not start until after the death of Christ on the cross.

Sacrament of Baptism 756-760

The Passover-Lord's Supper

In considering the relationship between the Passover and the Lord's Supper, again one observes how an OT rite gradually changed to fit the religious need of the New Covenant. Sometimes it is difficult to focus on the point at which the actual change becomes evident.

Passover 2686

The Gospel record contains several accounts of Jesus going to Jerusalem to celebrate the OT Passover. The earliest instance occurred when Joseph and Mary took the boy Jesus to Jerusalem (Lu. 2:41ff.). John the Beloved gives an account of the three separate Passover feasts attended by our Lord during his formal earthly ministry (Jn. 2:13,23; 6:4; 11:55; 12:1; 18:28,39). The Synoptic writers make it clear that Jesus was crucified on the first day of the Passover (Mt. 26:17; Mk. 14:16; Lu. 22:15). John gives a vivid description of Jesus' last Passover with his disciples (Jn. 13:1ff.).

John associates Jesus with the "Passover Lamb" in his reference: "Behold the Lamb of God, which taketh away the sin of the world" (Jn. 1:29). In Paul's letter to the Corinthians he stated that "Christ our passover is sacrificed for us" (1 Co. 5:7). In John's account of Jesus' last Passover with his disciples, Jesus states that he is the "bread of life"; this fits well into the Paschal context (Jn. 6:31-35; cf. Mt. 26:26-29). The early church recalled the analogy between the Jewish Passover and the death of Christ (Mt. 26:17ff.; Mk. 14:12ff.; Lu. 22:7ff.). Like a Paschal lamb, he was without blemish (Ex. 12:5; cf. 1 Pe. 1:18-19); not a bone was broken (Ex. 12:46; cf. Jn. 19:36). In 1 Corinthians 5:7-8 reference is made to the unleavened bread of sincerity and truth within the context of "Christ our passover who is sacrificed for us." Jeremiah's reference to the New Covenant of the future led the NT Church to interpret the death of Jesus as a prophetic fulfillment (Je. 31:31). For more on the Christological significance of the Passover, see the essay "Salvation Symbolized in the Exodus," p. 95.

It becomes progressively clear that the annual celebration of the OT Passover was adopted as the vehicle in which the NT celebrated the death of Christ but under a new name, the Lord's Supper. It is still a sacrament but has been changed to the NT context. Note

Sacrament of the Lord's Supper 761

that in both instances the central point is the "shed blood." In the OT the blood was sprinkled on the visible door post, in the NT the blood is mystically applied to "the door post of the heart." In each celebration the idea of freedom from enslavement is present—the Israelites from Egyptian bondage, the church from the bondage of sin.

The OT Passover has no significance for the Christian who wishes to commemorate the Savior's sacrifice. It commemorates the deliverance from the bondage of Egypt. Of necessity there had to be some changes in it, or the rite would become meaningless. These obvious changes were that, first, the Passover had looked forward to the shedding of Christ's blood, and now that has been accomplished. Something must be substituted for the Paschal lamb, which prefigured Christ. Second, the Passover had looked forward to the great deliverance by Christ, so long anticipated by every act of worship. The acts of worship must now be continued by the NT church and in remembrance of him (Lu. 22:19; 1 Co. 11:24-25).

The OT Passover is now behind; it is history. Christian believers cannot commemorate the Paschal lamb because the "Lamb of God" has died on the cross, has arisen from the grave, and

> Christ the
> Lamb of God
> 3365

is now at the right hand of God the Father (Mk. 16:19; He. 1:3). Like that of baptism the name of the sacrament became changed at the time of Christ. He, "the Lamb of God, which taketh away the sin of the world" (Jn. 1:29) has taken the place of the Paschal lamb of Egypt.

The liturgical section of most denominational hymnals includes a responsive reading on, "Christ Our Passover." The response quoted below is from the United Methodist Hymnal (1966):

Christ Our Passover

Christ, our paschal lamb, has been sacrificed. Let us, therefore, celebrate the festival,

not with the old leaven, the leaven of malice and evil, but with the unleavened bread of sincerity and truth.

For we know that Christ being raised from the dead will never die again; death no longer has dominion over him.

The death he died he died to sin, once for all, but the life he lives he lives to God.

So you also must consider yourselves dead to sin and alive to God in Christ Jesus.

Christ has been raised from the dead, the first fruits of those who have fallen asleep.

For as by a man came death, by a man has come also the resurrection of the dead.

For as in Adam all die, so also in Christ shall all be made alive.

1 Co. 5:7b-8; Ro. 6:9-11; 1 Co. 15:20-22

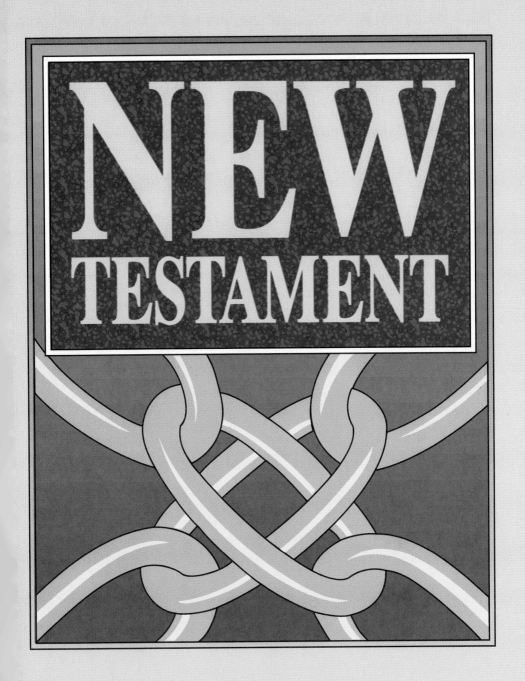

NEW TESTAMENT

The New Testament

The New Testament books as they are today are twenty-seven in number. Jesus himself established the authority of the New Testament by relating it to the Old Testament. He had previously attested to the authenticity of the Old Testament Scriptures as being "the Word of God," referring to Moses, the Prophets, the Psalms, and words and incidents of the OT books. Jesus further verified the message of the NT when he based his own authority on the Scriptures. On the road to Emmaus "...he expounded...in all the scriptures the things concerning himself" (Lu. 24:27).

> **The Word of God**
> **414–445**

The historical books (the four Gospels and Acts) relate almost everything known about what Jesus said and did. Also, the book of Acts contains a record of the spreading of the gospel to other parts of the Roman world after Jesus was crucified. The Epistles deal mainly with doctrinal instruction, exhortation to Christian conduct, and rules of church polity. The book of Revelation, the last book in the New Testament canon, deals with the struggle between good and evil and the ultimate triumph of Christ at his Second Coming. It is also called the Apocalypse, meaning to "uncover" or to "reveal secret meanings."

> **Words of Christ**
> **3885–3887**

The general assumption is that all of the New Testament books were written during the first century. The Gospels and the Epistles are usually dated between A.D. 50 and 90; the Gospel of John, John's Epistles, and Revelation are dated about A.D. 90.

> **N.T. History**
> **4222b**

How It Was Written

From the beginning, Christian churches accepted the Old Testament as the Word of God. In fact, this is the only Bible the early Christians had. How, then, did the New Testament come into being?

The recording of the gospel events and teachings was delayed for some time for several reasons. The disciples of Jesus saw no need of a written record as long as Jesus was with them. Initially their understanding had been that the "kingdom of God" on earth was soon to be realized.

> **God's Kingdom**
> **2009**

Also, because they considered Christ's ministry to be exclusively Palestinian, they saw no need for a written account of his life. Since the Christian movement was strictly a Jewish phenomenon at that time, there was aversion to writing religious books other than the OT, which was regarded as being sufficient.

Other reasons for the hesitancy to write included the fact that the OT was the source from which Jesus, the apostles, and the early missionaries quoted, to affirm their message. Jesus frequently cited the OT passages for his authority. In addition, eyewitnesses attested what Jesus said and did. Finally, as the leaders in the Christian movement were, in the main, poor, and writing materials were very expensive, it was not feasible for the disciples to engage in literary activity. They placed much emphasis upon the "inner life of the spirit" rather than upon the "written letter of the word."

As some of the apostles died, however, and it became evident that Jesus was not coming back as soon as believers had anticipated, an urgency developed to record the gospel events. The four Gospels became the means of communicating the birth, life, teach-

ings, death, and res-
urrection of the Lord.
Gospel means "good
news"; the good

Gospel
1440–1442

news was that "he of whom Moses and
the prophets spoke" had arrived. Thus
the gospel records are especially important; they are the "divine package"
in which all of the dependable information about Jesus and his life has
been preserved.

As the Christian movement spread,
the apostles and other inspired men
wrote letters of instruction to the
several congregations relative to
doctrine, ethical and moral conduct,
and the rules for ordaining church
officers. Some of the letters were
written to meet certain local needs as
well as to clarify misunderstandings.
However, these writings contained
broad principles of truth which made
them relevant to the problems and
needs of people in every age. This fact
is sometimes referred to as the "double
reference" formula.

As copies of letters were received by
a congregation, they were recognized
as documents with a broad application,
relevant to other Christian groups.
Interested congregations sent their
scribes to copy the letters, which were
soon circulated among other Christian
groups. The traditional church believed
that as the Holy Spirit
inspired men to write
these letters, so also
he superintended the

Inspiration of the Bible
417

preservation of these books and finally
guided the minds of men in the formation of the canon.

How It Became the Official Canon

In Biblical use, the word "canon"
means a measuring
rod or standard by
which genuinely
inspired Bible books

Word, Standard of
Truth
426

were separated from the many spurious religious writings, which contained

Biblical truth mixed with heathen philosophy and superstition. Thus the
canonized books came to mean the
"written rule of faith" verified by
apostolic sanction.

One of the most important problems the early church officials faced
was that of distinguishing between
these genuine apostolic writings and
the apocryphal or spurious books
which were written by men with
heretical tendencies. For example, the
Gospel of Peter was a book supporting
the Docetic heresy that Christ only
seemed to have a human body. The
Epistle to the Laodiceans was a mixture of the Epistle to the Philippians
and heathen myths and philosophies.
The apocryphal epistles approximating
Paul's letters were 3 Corinthians and
the Epistle to the Laodiceans. The
apocryphal Apocalypse of Peter was
the only rival to the book of Revelation
by St. John. By assuming the name of
those in whose spirit they professed to
write, the apocalyptic approach provided heathen philosophers a vehicle
in which to shroud their ancient superstitions. The inferior quality of these
writings and the lack
of true apostolic back-
ground were quite
marked. These NT

Apostles
2080 – 2082

apocryphal books were never compiled in a form comparable to the OT
apocryphal books. Only the heretical
sects placed them on a par with the canonical books.

Another cause of concern for the
early church fathers was that Marcion,
an influential church leader in Rome
with an inclination toward Gnosticism,
introduced a short "canon" of books to
the church. He accepted only the
Gospel of Luke and ten of the Epistles
of Paul (excluding the pastorals). He
eliminated the first two chapters of
Luke because they described the miraculous stories of Jesus' birth. Marcion's compilation of New Testament

materials created a serious problem in the church. Scholars are agreed that the challenge by Marcion was one of the factors which caused Christian leaders to compile a canon consistent with apostolic authority.

The church leaders felt a moral obligation to separate the spurious from the authentic books. This brought up the question of what measuring device should be used to determine the true apostolic writings from the spurious.

God's Sure Word
430

The first consideration was whether the book had been written by an apostle or someone close to the apostolic times. It is probable that this measure was applied to all of the twenty-seven New Testament books. There was no problem with Matthew and John. Since Mark was a close associate of Peter and Luke of Paul, it was decided that they would meet the apostolic standard. James Iverach asserts that "The place of the Gospels in church tradition is secure. Eusebius [264-340] places the four Gospels among the books that were never controverted in the church…It is acknowledged that by the end of the second century these four Gospels… [were] ascribed to authors whose names they bear, [and] were in universal circulation and undisputed use throughout the church."[1]

Another question was whether the contents of the book were of unquestionable, high spiritual character. The apocryphal and pseudepigraphal books fell far short of this standard.

Other considerations were whether the book had received universal approval throughout the church and whether the book had the aura of divine inspiration. This decision was difficult to determine at times, although the contrasting inferior tone of the spurious books was usually apparent. It is true, however, that during the canonization process some of the New Testament books were in question for short periods of time.

God's Word Inspired
417

In the third century, Origen classified the New Testament books into two categories: acknowledged and disputed. He placed James, 2 Peter, 2 and 3 John and Jude in the questionable category. In A.D. 326 Eusebius wrote that Hebrews and Revelation were also in dispute, the former in the West and the latter in the East. However, in the course of the canonization period the Holy Spirit permitted the process of time to be a factor in the leaders' sifting the genuine books from the false.

The writings of Justin Martyr (A.D. 150) and Clement of Alexander (A.D. 165-220) contained affirmation of the books as they are now in the New Testament canon. "In 367 Athanasius issued a list of twenty-seven books which tally with the twenty-seven books which are accepted by the synods of Hippo Regius (A.D. 393) and Carthage (A.D. 397-419). There was much opposition to including any of the apocryphal books." At no time were they ever included in the Protestant canon.[2]

Apocrypha
4219b

The official canonization of the New Testament books took place at the Council of Carthage (A.D. 397),

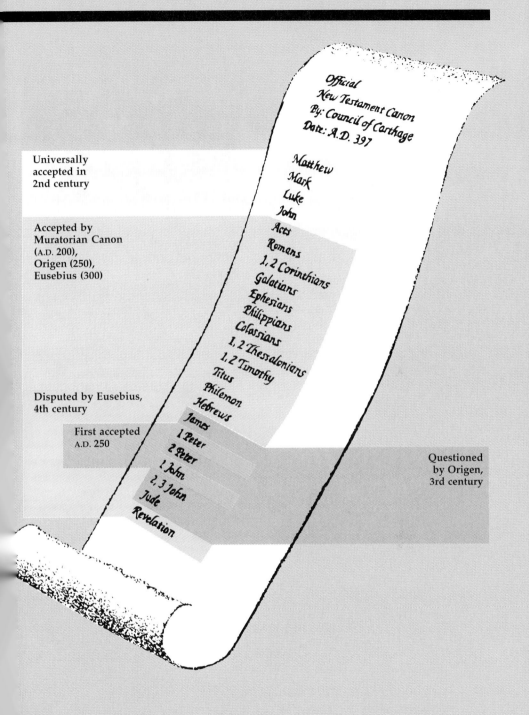

Universally
accepted in
2nd century

Accepted by
Muratorian Canon
(A.D. 200),
Origen (250),
Eusebius (300)

Disputed by Eusebius,
4th century

First accepted
A.D. 250

Questioned
by Origen,
3rd century

Official
New Testament Canon
By: Council of Carthage
Date: A.D. 397

Matthew
Mark
Luke
John
Acts
Romans
1, 2 Corinthians
Galatians
Ephesians
Philippians
Colossians
1, 2 Thessalonians
1, 2 Timothy
Titus
Philemon
Hebrews
James
1 Peter
2 Peter
1 John
2, 3 John
Jude
Revelation

when the Council merely affirmed what the consensus of the church had been for many years.

How It Was Preserved

Most of the early manuscripts were written on papyrus sheets, made from the papyrus reed growing along the Nile River in Egypt. This is the term from which the word "paper" comes. A small amount of the reed still grows in the Lake Huleh area near the Sea of Galilee. To process it, the papyrus reed was peeled, the pith inside was sliced and rolled into thin strips, laid crisscross in sheets, and then pressed between two heavy flat surfaces. After a few days these sheets became writing material, which was in use in the Old Kingdom of Egypt as early as 2700 B.C. Some of this ancient papyrus has been preserved in the sands and tombs of Upper Egypt. The Edwin Smith surgical documents of 5,000 years ago were written on Egyptian papyri.[3]

> Origin and Growth of the English Bible
> 4220

Most of the papyrus manuscripts have been discovered since 1890 and of these the most important are the Chester Beatty papyri found in Egypt. Mr. Beatty, an English scholar, had the good fortune to discover NT papyrus sheets in Egypt in 1930-31. They came from what was originally a three-volume codex (page form) manuscript consisting of thirty-two sheets from the Gospels and the book of Acts, eighty-six leaves from a codex of Paul's epistles, and ten leaves of an original thirty from the book of Revelation. These manuscripts were especially valuable

> Manuscripts
> 4220

Papyrus growing in Cairo, Egypt.

because they date back to the third century and provide an early form of the NT.

Writing instruments in early times were brushes, pointed quills, and slender sticks of papyri. The papyrus pens were ideal because the pithy interior could absorb ink through capillary action. This is perhaps the forerunner of the modern fountain pen, or felt-tipped pens. The writing fluid was an ink made of charcoal, gum and water.

The early manuscripts were copied by hand and sewn together to form rolls up to 30 feet long. Unrolling the manuscripts frequently caused much wear, and eventually they became fragile and broke up into small pieces. Some museums have large quantities of these fragments and at times it is difficult to find two pieces which fit together.

> Scribes
> 3165

Because the ancient manuscripts were carried to many areas in the world by ship, caravan, and on foot, and because Christianity was an outlawed movement in some parts of the world for the first three centuries after Christ, readers had little opportunity to bring manuscripts out into the open for comparison. However, with the advent of Constantine (A.D. 313) and his Edict of Toleration, it was no longer necessary to keep NT manuscripts concealed.

Soon thereafter, in making comparisons, scholars discovered variant readings. Many of these variants were unintentional or accidental, in areas of sight, of writing, and of judgment. Sometimes errors were caused by the confusion of letters or pairs of letters that looked very much alike. Sometimes an abbreviation might be mistaken for a full word, or a similar word. An error might be caused by

> Scripture
> Wrested
> **4099**

faulty hearing when a group of scribes copied manuscripts by dictation. Sometimes intentional changes were made by the scribe to correct what he thought was a mistake in the manuscript. However, "there is virtually no evidence of a scribe's intentionally weakening the theology or purposely introducing heresy into his manuscripts."[4] Generally speaking, the scribes were professional men and took great pride in their accuracy and in the fact that they were men with a holy mission. Complications arose from the natural limitations of transmission.

Even more complicated are the texts themselves. There were no chapter and verse divisions in the manuscripts, but in 1228 Stephen Langston worked out a chapter division for the entire Bible. In 1551 Robert Stephens divided the NT into verses. About A.D. 700 the Masorites had begun to work out a verse division for the OT.

Another type of error resulted from the absence of word separation; ancient manuscripts neither separated

Above: Copy of Sinaiticus manuscript on display in St. Catharine's Monastery. This is the earliest complete NT manuscript still available.

Below: St. Catharine's Monastery at the base of Mount Sinai. Codex Sinaiticus was discovered here in the nineteenth century.

words nor used punctuation. Thus Jn. 1:3 would read: "ALLTHINGSWERE MADEBYHIMANDWITHOUTHIM WASNOTANYTHINGMADETHATWAS MADE." It is self-evident that errors could develop within this kind of composition.

When scholars speak of verifying a Biblical subject by the original Greek or Hebrew text, they do not mean to imply that they will actually read an original autograph. Unfortunately no autographs have been preserved; only copies of copies of originals remain. Almost all of the ancient copies which have survived are hand copied and are on deposit in school libraries, in museums, and in a few private collections. Photographic reproductions provide a base for scholarly studies.

> Dea Sea Scrolls
> (picture)
> 4362

Bible readers are very much indebted to the scholars of the ages who sifted, compiled, edited, and, through a system of synthesis, have produced from the "raw materials" remarkably accurate Biblical documents.

How It Relates
To The Old Testament

As foretold in the OT, the NT is a historical verification of God's plan for man (Mt. 21:42; Mk 14:49; Lu. 24:32). Eventually a fully canonized set of writings describing the events in the lifetime of Jesus the Savior was made and was acknowledged to have equal authority with the OT.

James clearly states that by revelation the prophets spoke in the name of Christ (Ja. 5:10). Luke writes that the law and the prophets were until the

> Voice of Prophets
> 4088

coming of John the Baptist (Lu.. 16:16). In speaking of Jesus Christ, Philip said, "We have found him, of whom Moses in the law, and the prophets, did write" (Jn. 1:45). Certainly the Lord in the OT is identical with Jesus

Christ in the NT.[5] Peter states positively that "all the prophets witness" to Christ, that "through his name" all believers "receive remission of sins" (Ac. 10:43). Paul, in his message to Agrippa, bases salvation on belief in the Messiah of whom the prophets testified (Ac. 26:27).

The writer of Matthew's Gospel definitely relates the kingdom to him "that was spoken of by the prophet Esaias" (Mt. 3:3); that is, to him who was in existence before and during the lifetime of Esaias, although he did not take upon himself the form of man and become manifest or physically visible until the "fulness of the time was come" (Ga. 4:4). Christ is the principal theme in the Scriptures, and it is he whom God "promised afore by his prophets" (Ro. 1:2).

> Christ Prophesied
> 2890

The Spirit of Christ, which was in the prophets, testified of the sufferings of Christ and the glory that should follow (1 Pe. 1:10-11). It is obvious that the men of God in ancient times thought of Christ as the one through whom salvation was provided (cf. Ps. 51:12 and Ac. 4:12; Is. 7:14 and Mt. 1:18; Zec. 9:9 and Jn. 12:13-14).

When Philip talked to the Ethiopian he opened the "Scriptures" at a passage spoken by the prophet Isaiah (Is. 53:7-8), and "preached unto him Jesus" (Ac. 8:32-35). As soon as Paul was able to do so after his conversion, he also "preached Christ in the synagogues, that he is the Son of God" (Ac. 9:20). Even the children of Israel had Christ preached to them (Ac. 10:36). Throughout the Bible, Christ is the eternal focal point; he is the Redeemer and the dispenser of salvation in every age. He is always one with the Father, whether he is called LORD God in the OT or Jesus in the NT.[6]

Jesus established his divinity to preach, to overcome temptation, to expose false leaders and to teach

Christian concepts, particularly those of the Sermon on the Mount, by quoting and referring to the OT Scriptures. These Scriptures offer positive proof that Christ has always been eternal and co-creator with the Father. Paul testified that the incarnation of the Lord fulfilled his historical portion of the redemptive plan: "When the fullness of the time was come, God sent forth his Son, made of a woman, made under the law, to redeem them that were under the law, that we might receive the adoption of sons" (Ga. 4:4-5).

> Incarnation
> 720

When the Lord walked with the disciples on the Emmaus road, He said, "O fools, and slow of heart to believe all that the prophets have spoken: Ought not Christ to have suffered these things, and to enter into his glory?" (Lu. 24:25-26). Luke adds these words, "And beginning at Moses and all the prophets, he expounded unto them in all the scriptures the things concerning himself" (Lu. 24:27). When the Lord came to Nazareth, he read a passage from the book of Isaiah: "The Spirit of the Lord is upon me, because he hath anointed me to preach the gospel to the poor; he hath sent me to heal the brokenhearted...to preach the acceptable year of the Lord" (Is. 61:1; cf. Lu. 4:18-19). He concluded with these words: "This day is this scripture fulfilled in your ears" (Lu. 4:21).

While the disciples were locked in their hideaway chamber, the resurrected Jesus appeared in their midst and said unto them, "These are the words which I spake unto you, while I was yet with you, that all things must be fulfilled, which were written in the law of Moses, and in the prophets, and in the psalms concerning me" (Lu. 24:44).

During the temptation in the wilderness, Jesus made exclusive reference to the Scriptures (OT) in his conflict with Satan (De. 6:16; cf. Mt. 4:1-11). Furthermore all the great truths spoken by the Lord were based on OT theology; he went about "teaching...and preaching the gospel of the kingdom" (Mt. 4:23), as revealed in the OT (Ps. 22:28; Ps. 103:19; Da. 4:3).

> Scriptures
> 3166

To illustrate these parallels between the OT and the NT, the book of Matthew is an appropriate source, particularly the Sermon on the Mount. Almost every idea presented in Matthew can be traced to the OT; a similar result would be obtained using other NT books. There are many references for each idea in Matthew, but only a few will be presented here.

The Sermon on the Mount was a presentation of "old gospel wine" in new theological wineskins (cf. Mt. 5:3 with Ps. 51:17; Pr. 16:19; cf. Mt. 5:4 with Is. 61:2-3; cf. Mt. 5:5 with Ps 37:11; cf. Mt. 5:6 with Is. 65:13; cf. Mt. 5:7 with Ps. 41:1; cf. Mt. 5:8 with Ps. 15:2). The terminology used in this sermon was appropriate for the worldwide or universal gospel mission to which divine revelation was directed. The Master gathered the ideas and concepts of the Kingdom as they had been preached in the OT by men of faith (Jude 3) into a homily especially suited to the need at hand. By so doing, Jesus Christ linked the NT Church to the OT. His statement, "Ye are the light of the world" (Mt. 5:14), is another way of saying "The path of the just is as the shining light, that shineth more and more unto the perfect day" (Pr. 4:18). The command to turn the "right cheek" (Mt. 5:39) is clearly the spirit of the statement in Isaiah (50:6).

> Sermon on the Mount
> 3237

When Jesus made reference to entering the closet, he no doubt restated a principle of private devotion known to Elisha when "he went in…and shut the door…and prayed unto the LORD" (2 K. 4:33). The entire Sermon on the Mount, including the Lord's Prayer, is a restatement of divine concepts well-known in the OT (cf. Mt. 6:9 with De. 32:6; Is. 6:3; cf. Mt. 6:10 with Ps. 103:20; cf. Mt. 6:11 with Pr. 30:8).

> **Prayerfulness**
> **1003**

Fasting as taught by our Lord (Mt. 6:16) was a common practice among OT saints (Ps. 35:13; 69:10; Is. 58:3; Je. 14:12; Zec. 7:5). The warning against laying up treasures on earth is obviously drawn from the Proverbs (23:4; 28:20). Seeking first the "kingdom of God" (Mt. 6:33) is a divine principle illustrated in the inauguration of Solomon as king (1 K. 3:11ff.). "False prophets" in Mt. 7:15 were a problem in Moses' day (De. 13:3). The healing power manifested by Jesus (Mt. 8:14ff.) is the same that healed people in the OT. It is certain that the healing ministry of Christ was already in operation long before the incarnation. Use of the past tense supports this thought in Isaiah 53:4-5, "He hath borne our griefs…he was wounded…he was bruised…with his stripes [already provisionally existing] we are healed" and people were healed in OT times (Nu. 21:9; 2 K. 5:14).

> **Fasting**
> **3212–3214**

All of the redemptive provisions (healing for the body and soul) were contained in the provision made in the crucified Savior who was projected in the foreknowing mind of God. Rebuking the winds and the sea (Mt. 8:26) was a prerogative Christ the Lord had during

> **Salvation**
> **3116–3128**

the OT period (Jb. 38:8-11; Ps. 65:7). The concept that mercy was more desirable than sacrifices (Mt. 9:13) was an accepted truth in the OT (1 S. 15:22; Ps. 51:16-17; Is. 1:11; Ho. 6:6). The principle of God providing words for an hour of need (Mt. 10:19) was well-known to Moses and Jeremiah (Ex. 4:12; Je. 1:7). The idea that a person receiving a prophet would receive a prophet's reward (Mt. 10:41) is illustrated in the relationship between the widow and Elijah (1 K. 17:10ff.) and between the woman and Elisha (2 K. 4:8).

John the Baptist was comparable to Elijah in the OT (Mt. 11:12-14). Christ shows from the book of Malachi that John was another Elijah (Mal. 4:4-6); John the Baptist was to the NT church what Elijah was to the OT church. Jesus Christ came to emphasize the spirit of the law which had been lost by Pharisee/Sadducee Judaism. These leaders of the counterfeit church had substituted the "doctrines and commandments of men" for the spiritual interpretation of divine revelation (cf. Is. 29:13 with Mt. 15:9 and Tit. 1:14). The "apostate vipers" in the temple had perverted the faith of Abraham, Moses, and Elijah to such an extent that formal worship was mere shallow mockery. With few exceptions, Jesus Christ was making reference to "commandments and doctrines of men" when he said, "Ye have heard" or similar expressions. Of their legalistic application and interpretation he said, "from the beginning it was not so," but rather, "it is the spirit that quickeneth…the words that I speak unto you, they are spirit, and they are life" (Jn. 6:63).

> **John the Baptist**
> **1903–1906**

> **Traditions of Men**
> **3652**

For more on the counterfeit church, see commentary on Re. 2:9.

Matthew

The Name

The Greek name for Matthew is *Matthios*, meaning "Gift of God" or "of Jehovah." This name appears five times in the NT and in each instance the citation relates to the apostle Matthew (Mt. 9:9; 10:3; Mk. 3:18; Lu. 6:15; Ac. 1:13). In the second reference, the qualifying words indicate the apostle's former occupation; he was Matthew the publican (10:3). Some NT references name this same man "Levi" (see Mk. 2:14; Lu. 5:27). However, no satisfactory explanation for this variation is available.

Robert McL. Wilson indicates that both names are Hebrew, and he raises the question: "Could it be that he [Matthew] was the son of a man named Levi, 'Matthew ben Levi,' and that he was a Levite? Perhaps, as in Peter's case, Jesus gave him the name Matthew as a Christian-Jewish name, because it means 'a gift of Yahweh'...Only God could change a tax collector named Levi into a Christian apostle named Matthew."[1]

Authorship and Date

The authorship of the book of Matthew is important to contemporary Christians because it comes from the pen of an eyewitness of the gospel events. To assign its message, especially the prophetic aspects of it, to a writer other than an eyewitness seems to violate the integrity of the Scriptures. Those of liberal persuasion usually take the position that the writer of Matthew was dependent upon Mark for his sources. If Matthew was an eyewitness of what Jesus said and did, it does not seem reasonable that he needed to consult anyone else in order to write a first-hand account of the Gospel.

It is true that the Gospel does not name Matthew as the author; little is known about him. However, the ancient church attributed authorship of this book to Matthew. The caption, "The Gospel according to Saint Matthew," is not a part of the original manuscripts, but it has appeared as the title of Matthew (as have the captions in the other NT books) since the beginning of the second century A.D. and is confirmed by such other writers as Justin Martyr (A.D. 100-165) and Irenaeus (A.D. 125-202). These

Gospel of Matthew
4262

Matthew
2265

New Name
2585

God's Sure Word
430

Gospel
1440-1442

ancient writers say that Matthew wrote his Gospel originally in Hebrew and Aramaic. Presumably the writer had "field notes" and later, in about A.D. 60, he incorporated the abbreviated Hebrew version into a more complete Greek edition. Many Greek copies of Matthew have survived but no Hebrew or Aramaic versions are in existence today.[2] The testimony of these ancients, who lived so close to the synoptic period, would seem to be trustworthy, and certainly no other person would have been more qualified to write this book than Matthew himself.

Dating the book of Matthew is closely related to the question of authorship. Wilson points out that "the traditional view of the time and place of writing has been that Matthew was the first evangelist to write a Gospel and that he wrote in Palestine, possibly in Jerusalem itself, shortly after the events of Mt. 27:58 and 28:15 in about A.D. 60…A different place now seems more plausible…Antioch in Syria about A.D. 60 is both the probable and plausible time and place of writing of the first Gospel."[3] This place was the headquarters and pivotal point for the early Christian Church and would have provided a favorable environment for writing such a book.

Some assume that the book was written after A.D.70—the date of the destruction of Jerusalem—because of the prophetic statements Jesus made in this regard (Lu. 19:43-44; 21:24). The parable of the kingdom of heaven (Mt. 22:7) provides another base for assuming late authorship, but such an interpretation of this text ignores the fact that foretelling future events is an integral part of Scripture. Christians of the conservative view would not deny this power to Jesus.[4]

Background, Purpose, and Content
It was no accident that the book of Matthew was placed first in the NT canon. As the Holy Spirit inspired the writers and revealed to them what they should write, so the Holy Spirit could have guided the compilers in their selection and placement of the holy books. The book of Matthew was rightly placed at the beginning of the NT canon because it correlates the OT prophecies with their fulfillment in the NT. It contains more fulfilled prophecies pertaining to the Messiah than any of the other three Gospel records. At least 60 references and 40 quotations, such as "that it might be fulfilled" and "thus it was written by the prophet," appear — more than in either Mark or Luke.

The Jewish community seems to have been foremost in the mind of the writer Matthew. His message is the good news that the Jewish Messiah came in the person of Jesus Christ. The first verse clearly states that Jesus Christ is a kinsman of the Jews, "the son of David, the son of Abraham," and was intended to attract the attention of the Jews. Because Abraham was the founder of the Hebrew nation and the Jews called him their Father (Mt. 3:9; Jn. 8:33,39), they would be attracted to Jesus by this kinship. The rest of the apostles, who were Jews, and the many other people who were attracted to the Savior, came to realize that Jesus of Nazareth was he "of whom Moses in the law, and the prophets, did write" (Jn. 1:45). Another indication that the book of Matthew had the Jews in mind is the genealogy (mentioned also in Lu. 3:23-38). Matthew's genealogy goes back only to Abraham, which was of special interest to the Jews, since they claimed Abraham as the founder of their nation.

PALESTINE IN THE TIME OF OUR SAVIOUR

— Extent of the kingdom of Herod the Great

▣ Herodian fortress city

○ Decapolis city

• Other city

Mediterranean Sea

ABILENE

•Sidon

Abila

ITUREA

○Damascus

SYRIA

△ Mt. Hermon

Pharpar R.

Leontes R.

•Caesarea-Philippi

PHOENICIA

TRACHONITIS

•Raphana

Tyre.•

J. Jarmuk △ •Hazor

L. Hula

GALILEE

GAULANITIS

TETRARCHY

OF PHILIP

Ptolemais • (Accho)

Chorazin.•

•Bethsaida

Gennesaret• •Capernaum •Gergesa

Mt. Carmel △

Magdala• Sea of Galilee (Chinnereth)

BATANEA

Cana•

Nazareth•

Tiberias•

△ Mt. Tabor

•Hippos

Dor.•

•Nain

○Gadara •Abila

AURANITIS

Caesarea (Strato's Tower).•

•Megiddo

Scythopolis○ (Beth-shan)

•Pella

Dothan.•

•Dion?

SAMARIA

DECAPOLIS

Sebaste• (Samaria)

Salim?•

Amathus▣

•Gerasa

△ Mt. Ebal

Jabbok

Mt. Gerizim △ •Sychar

Me Jarkon

•Antipatris (Aphek)

Joppa•

Alexandrium▣

PEREA

(SEMI-INDEPENDENT MUNICIPALITY)

Lydda• Bethel•

•Ephraim

•Philadelphia (Rabbath-ammon)

Jamnia•

•Berea?

Cyprus▣ Jericho

•Esbus (Heshbon)

Azotus (Ashdod)•

•Emmaus △Mt. Olivet

Kedron?• Jerusalem•

•Bethany

Bethabara?

•Medeba

Bethlehem•

•Hyrcania

JUDEA

•Herodium

Ashkelon.•

•Hebron

▣Machaerus

Gaza.•

•Adora

Engedi• *Dead Sea*

Arnon R.

•Raphia

Besor Br.

IDUMEA

Masada▣ •Arad

Beersheba.•

▣Malatha

N A B A T E A

Zered Br.

Bozrah•

Punon•

Jordan

Kishon R.

Me Jarmuk R.

In the early days of the human family God chose one family line—that of Abraham—through which his Son was to enter the human family. The Hebrew nation was founded and nurtured by God to prepare them for this great mission of providing the human agency for the coming Messiah. The genealogy in Matthew is somewhat abbreviated but adequate to present the line of descent.

The genealogy in Luke differs from that of Matthew, who, in presenting the descending line, uses the word "begat." Luke presents the ascending line using the term "was the son of." From David, there are separate lines touching in Shealtiel and Zerubbabel. "The commonly accepted view is that Matthew gives Joseph's line, showing Jesus to be the legal heir to the promises given Abraham and David: and that Luke gives Mary's line, showing Jesus' blood descent ('Seed of David, according to the flesh,' Ro. 1:3). Mary's genealogy, in accord with Jewish usage, was in her husband's name. Joseph was the 'son of Heli,' (Lu. 3:23), that is, 'son-in-law' of Heli. Heli was Mary's father. Jacob was Joseph's father…Carefully guarded through long centuries of special vicissitudes, they contain a family line through which a promise was transmitted…a fact unexampled in history."[5]

Another clue to Matthew's Jewish appeal is seen in his reference to geography. One writer notes that it "is seen, incidentally, that he presupposes the reader will know the geography of Palestine and its customs, manners and ceremonies…[For] instance, in the matter of washing the hands before eating bread, Matthew takes for granted that the readers are acquainted with that custom (Mt. 15:1-2); but Mark feels that he should explain to his readers that this was the tradition among the Jews (Mk. 7:3)…He wanted the Jews to see that Jesus was the long promised Messiah."[6]

Further evidence that this Gospel was written for the Jews is suggested in the presentation of the conflict between the true concept of the Messiah and the false. The Jewish religious leaders were jealous and so absorbed with using their office for their own selfish interests that they showed hostility toward Jesus when he warned and rebuked them, which brought to the surface their false righteousness. He distinguished between the true OT teachings and the "tradition of the elders," indicating the deplorable state of the Jewish church in such statements as "O generation of vipers" (Mt. 12:34) and "ye hypocrites" (Mt. 15:7), as well as "blind leaders of the blind" (Mt. 15:14; see also Mt. 23).

The increasing resentment by the temple hierarchy is expressed in such accusations against Jesus as "this man blasphemeth" (Mt. 9:3), and "Why eateth your Master with publicans and sinners?" (Mt. 9:11), and "He is guilty of death" (Mt. 26:66).

There are many other Jewish distinctions in Matthew's Gospel including the term "kingdom of heaven" rather than the "kingdom of God" to avoid uttering the name of God for fear of blasphemy (Mt. 13:31; cf. Lu. 13:18-19) and the parable of the "wheat and the tares"(the field of the world, Mt. 13:38).

However, there is also a tone of universality in Matthew's account. He presents the first Gentile pilgrims—the Magi—to the Savior (2:1-2), and mentions the faith of the Roman centurion (8:5-10). He foretells of the future inflow into Jerusalem to hear the Christ-Jehovah gospel; he cites the statement by Jesus: "many shall come from east and the west, and shall sit down with Abraham, and Isaac, and Jacob, in the kingdom of heaven" (8:11).[7]

Religious leaders expressed strong reaction when Jesus prophetically stated that "the kingdom of God shall be taken from you, and given to a nation bringing forth the fruits thereof" (Mt. 21:43) and when he presented the Great Commission, commanding them to make disciples in all nations (Mt. 28:19-20).

The Synoptic Problem

Under the inspiration of the Holy Spirit, Matthew, Mark, and Luke formulated written records which have been passed down to the present. They are called the synoptic Gospels because, viewed together, they are parallel to each other, and their content is similar.

A critical examination of these records shows that the synoptic Gospels have many similarities as well as differences. Clark H. Pinnock notes some of these peculiarities: "Some 606 verses out of Mark's total 661 appear, although somewhat abridged, in Matthew, and 380 reappear in Luke. Only 31 verses in Mark have no parallel in either Matthew or Luke. In addition, there are some 250 verses common to Matthew and Luke that have no parallel in Mark."[8]

In the TCRB Helps No. 4308a, a chart shows "The Harmony of the Gospels," giving a comparative analysis of the specific content of the four Gospels. At first glance the "Synoptic Problem" becomes apparent: Why are the Gospels so similar and yet so different?

First, each Gospel writer had his own personality, as well as social and economic background. Second, each Gospel was written to a different group of people and with varied motives. The Gospel according to Matthew was written by a Jew to the Jewish community, as a piece of evangelistic literature. The Gospel written by Mark was to the Romans, the people of action. Their ability as engineers and builders is attested by their great engineering projects still standing. The Gospel recorded by Luke was directed to the intelligentsia of that day, the Greeks. The literary quality of this book gives ample testimony that its author was a man of "letters."

Scholars are still unable to give definite answers concerning the synoptic problem. Serious discussions have continued and larger issues have been raised, but no adequate solutions have been found. Three major theories have evolved out of these debates:

1. The Oral Tradition. This theory assumes that each Gospel writer obtained his materials independently, not from written records, but from oral narratives of the sayings and activities of Jesus, which, through repetition, had assumed a relatively fixed form.

2. The Mutual Use Theory. Many variations of this theory exist. The basic assumption is that a single source, one of the Gospels, was used by the other writers. In this approach each of the Gospels has been put first, each second, and each third, and each in turn has been regarded as the source of the others.

Some studies conclude that 90 percent of the content in Mark was incorporated in the other two Gospels and that in the order of events Matthew and Luke have mainly followed Mark. Thus some feel that the book of Mark contains the central core of Gospel information and that Matthew and Luke were probably largely dependent upon Mark for their

Jerusalem
1681-1885
Kingdom
2007-2013

Matthew
4262
Mark
4263
Luke
4264

Harmony of
the Gospels
4308a
Christ as
Portrayed in
the Synoptics
4302
Jews
1807-1829
Romans
772
Greeks
1464

Christ's
Words
3885

Mark
4263

Matthew
4262

Christ in the Synoptic Gospels

Matthew

Jesus, the Kingly Messiah

Called "The King," eight times; Called "The Son of David" nine times. Examples: ch. 2:2, "Where is he that is born king..."; ch. 21:5, "Behold thy king cometh"; ch. 25:34, "Then shall the king say..."

Recurrent word: "fulfilled," indicating that the Messianic prophecies were fulfilled in him.

material. However, if Matthew was an eyewitness of what Jesus said and did, it does not seem reasonable that he needed to consult a man who was not an apostle nor a witness of Jesus' ministry.

3. The Source Theory. Those who hold to the source theory assume that there was a common depository of some kind (oral or written) from which all three synoptic writers drew their information; however, there is no consensus on this theory among scholars. The source in this theory is believed to be very similar to, if not identical with, the Gospel of Mark. Consideration is also given to the idea that there was a second source in addition to Mark, now generally called "Q" after the German word *quelle*, meaning a "spring" or "source." Some scholars raise the question as to why "Q" has not survived. To this there is no answer available.

It has been suggested that the "Q" document comprised the "in-class

Mark	Luke
Jesus, the Wonder–Worker and Tireless Servant of God and Man	**Jesus, the Friend of Sinners and Outcasts**
Demonstrated his divinity and compassion by his mighty works of mercy and help, ch. 6:2. Called "teacher" (or variant) 39 times.	Came to seek and save the lost, ch. 19:10. See stories of the Good Samaritan (10:30-37); The Lost Sheep 4-7); The Prodigal Son (15:11-32); The Pharisee and the Publican (18: 10-14); Zacchaeus (19: 2-10); The Penitent Thief (23:39-43).
Recurrent word: "straightaway" indicating immediate action.	Recurrent word: "Son of Man," indicating Jesus' humanity and concern for mankind.

notes" which Matthew recorded and that later Matthew as well as Mark and Luke used these notes in compiling their Gospel records. In these early days the writers freely borrowed from each other without benefit of footnotes because, in the first place, Gospel information was in the "public domain," and, second, in this early day there was no concept of plagiarizing or copyright. It is evident that the materials of which the Gospels were composed existed before they were put in final form. At least thirty years elapsed from the time Jesus ascended to heaven until the Gospels, in their present form, were written. Of the three synoptic writers, only Matthew was an apostle and the sole eyewitness. Mark and Luke obviously had access to Gospel materials of some kind. Mark was in close contact with Peter, and Luke was a frequent companion of Paul, who is considered to be an apostle because of his personal encounter with the resurrected Lord on the Damascus Road.[9]

Names of Apostles
2081
Apostleship of Paul
202

"Word"
Inspired
417

Luke
4264

Acts
4266

God's Sure
Word
430

Irrespective of human instrumentality it must be acknowledged that the compilation of the Gospel record was superintended and directed by the Holy Spirit. The promise is that "He shall teach you all things, and bring all things to your remembrance" (Jn. 14:26). It is logical to assume that materials of an oral or written nature would be valid Gospel material as long as the Holy Spirit sanctioned the selection.

Luke established authority in this area: Note Lu. 1:1-4. Luke, a physician, was a man of literary ability. Under the leadership of the Holy Spirit, Luke made extensive research in his preparation for writing the books of Luke and Acts.

From these observations comes the conclusion that God used three men of unquestioned integrity and piety to make a record of the events surrounding the birth, life, death and resurrection of Jesus Christ. The fact that these Gospel documents have stood the test of time for almost two thousand years, gives credibility to the belief that in them mankind has trustworthy redemptive information from the eternal, living God.

1:21 ...thou shalt call his name JESUS...

In Bible times people placed great value on the name of a child. They frequently gave it symbolic or character meaning. Hebrew is especially relevant in this connection. Modern names are intended merely as identification, but most Bible names, in addition to identifying the person, are also descriptive and often prophetic. Frequently religious significance resided in the name parents gave their child. Sometimes the name suggested the service the child should render to the Deity. Perhaps the name commemorated the favor of God in the gracious gift of the child; for example, Nathaniel, "gift of God"; Adonijah, "the Lord is God"; Samuel, "heard of God." The name Jacob meant "the supplanter," Sarah, "a princess," Shallum, "recompense," Nabal "foolish or churlish," and Esau, "hairy." Martha signified "lady or mistress." Some names were given prophetically, as that of Jesus, because he was to be the Savior (Mt. 1:21). When character had developed, a new name was sometimes given as being expressive of it, as Israel, "He strove with God," and Cephas, "Rock."

The name Jesus (Greek, *Iesous*) is the equivalent of the Hebrew Joshua *(Yehoshua)* meaning Yahweh, or "salvation." This is the personal name of the Lord in the Gospels and in Acts. In the Epistles, Jesus, with a few exceptions, takes on a compound form, Jesus Christ, or Christ the Lord. In the first case the human name, Jesus, is linked with Christ, the divine name.

Divine direction concerning a name is illustrated by the name specified when the angel appeared to Mary and declared, "Thou shalt call his name Jesus, for he shall save his people from their sins" (Mt. 1:21). This was indeed he of whom Moses and the prophets spoke.

1:22 All this took place to fulfill what the Lord had said through the prophet... (NIV)

There was a general expectation among the people of the Messiah, but the prophetic vision had become corrupted by legalistic interpretations so that the dominant concept of a Messiah was that he would be an earthly king who would overthrow the Roman rule and establish Israel as the people in power.

The appearance of the angel to the Virgin Mary with the message that she would conceive by the Holy Ghost and give birth to the Savior was not generally known, although Isaiah had made this prophecy over 500 years earlier (Is. 7:14). Unaware of this information, Judaism at large was not prepared to accept the "meek and lowly Jesus" who preached a non-violent message. He taught about a kingdom of love and peace and a humble people who would repent and believe in order to enter his new order. The religious establishment, on the other hand, believed that the Messiah would come marching into Jerusalem with "pomp and circumstance" wearing an earthly crown and thus they were not prepared to accept the babe born in a stable at Bethlehem.

For a description of prophets, see commentary on Je. 1:5.

Children Named
1653

Name
2513

Names Changed
2518
Christ's Name
2516-2517

Angels Appear
144
Christ, Savior
3360

Prophecies Relating to Christ
2890-2892, 4306b

Prophets
2065-2074

Isaiah's Messianic Prophecies
4301

These nomads crossing the Sinai Desert remind one of the wise men coming to worship the baby Jesus.

Immanuel
1741

1:23 "The virgin will be with child and will give birth to a son, and they will call him Immanuel" — which means, "God with us." (NIV)

Matthew, writing to the Jews, takes many Messianic quotations from the OT. For more on the name "God with us," see commentary on Is. 7:14.

Herod the
Great
1578
Payment of
Taxes
2529-2530
Decapolis
950

2:1 ...in the days of Herod the king...

The Gospel story had its setting in Palestine, a small province on the eastern edge of the Roman Empire. Herod the Great was its puppet ruler with the responsibility of taxing the people and skimming off the productivity of the land to help support the extravagant lifestyle of the central government in Rome. Revenue collection cities, including the Decapolis on the Transjordan, were designated in strategic locations.

Rome
4428
Infanticide
2452

The skimming off process was so severe that little remained for the people to live on. Discontent and despair obsessed the working class so that revolutionary groups including the Zealots organized secretly to overthrow the Roman yoke.

When Herod the Great heard about the "New King" from the wise men, he became jealous and decided to protect his crown by killing all the male children under two years of age. This action was for him routine, since he had already executed one wife and three sons in a jealous rage. The life of Jesus was spared when an angel warned Joseph in a dream to flee into Egypt.

Wise Men
3847
Esther
1152, 4239

2:1 ...there came wise men from the east...

The wise men of the East, having read the Holy Oracles left behind by the Jews in the days when Esther was the Persian queen, learned about the Savior who was to be born in Bethlehem (Mi. 5:2). They were so forceably impressed and inspired that they made the long journey to take gifts to the Bethlehem babe.

3:7 But when he saw many of the Pharisees and Sadducees come to his baptism, he said unto them, O generation of vipers…

Before Jesus began his public ministry, John the Baptist had already confronted the hypocritical Pharisees and Sadducees. For more on the religious leaders of Jesus' day, see commentary on Jn. 8:44; Re. 2:9.

3:11 I baptize you with water for repentance… (NIV)

Paul interprets John's baptism as having a relationship to belief in Jesus Christ who had not yet arrived on the scene. Paul said, "John verily baptized with the baptism of repentance, saying unto the people, that they should believe on him…that is, on Christ Jesus" (Ac. 19:4). This raises the question: At what point in history, before Jesus came, could people be saved through faith in Jesus Christ? If they could be saved a few months before he came by exercising faith in him who was to come (foretold by the prophets), it seems logical that they could be saved by faith one year, ten years, yes one hundred years from the time "the Lamb [was] slain from the foundation of the world" (Re. 13:8; see also 2 Ti. 3:15; Tit. 1:2).

Pharisees
3171

Sadducees
3172

John's Baptism
760

Foreordained Plan of Salvation
4154

Lamb of God
3365

Air view of the Herodian Fortress Palace, built by Herod the Great to enclose and protect his person, a place of refuge. It became his tomb. Inside were terraced gardens, baths and a marble throne room.

When John the Baptist said, "Repent ye: for the kingdom of heaven is at hand" (Mt. 3:2), he made a statement that was applicable to every age. The Kingdom and the King have always been at hand; the Fountain of David has always been open with the invitation that "whosoever will may come." In this connection Jesus made it clear that there was no other way into the Kingdom: "I am the way, the truth, and the life: no man cometh unto the Father, but by me" (Jn. 14:6). This is a statement of fact not subject to any tense of time. The Great "I AM" is speaking.

"I Am"s of
Christ
4166

4:25 And there followed him great multitudes of people...from Decapolis...

Decapolis
950
Multitudes
2786-2787

Mark's Gospel also refers to the Decapolis as an area where Jesus taught and people responded (Mk. 5:20; 7:31). The Decapolis was actually a group of ten Greek cities and one of them, Jerash (Biblical Gerasa), is particularly interesting because history tells us that it became a strong Christian community and that it sent a bishop of the church to the Council of Chalcedon in A.D. 451. This Christian presence is affirmed by archaeological evidence.

Roman
Citizens
772

The city was located in a fertile valley where many roads converged and was designated by the Romans as a customs and tax collection center. These ruins are the best preserved of any Roman/Greek city.

5:3 ...theirs is the kingdom of heaven.

Kingdom of
Heaven
2013

The expression "kingdom of heaven" is found in Matthew's Gospel, while the other synoptic Gospels use the words "kingdom of God." For more on the subject see commentary on Mk. 1:15.

5:17 Do not think that I have come to abolish the Law or the Prophets; I have not come to abolish them but to fulfill them. (NIV)

Keep the
Law
437
Law Perfect
436
Isaiah's
Messianic
Prophecies
4301
The Law
435-445, 949,
4055

When the Savior came, one of his first declarations was that he had not come to destroy the Law which God had provided in the past, but that he would fulfill or establish "the Law." NT teachings clarify his meaning as to his ability to accomplish this expectation in three principal areas: his relationship to the Law and his authority regarding it, his function as a perfect sacrifice, and his fulfillment of the Messianic prophecy.

Christ, the Lord, as envisioned by the prophet Isaiah, had the power to make the ritualistic Law effective: "He will save us" (Is. 33:22). The Scriptures provide further proof that Christ was indeed the source of the Law (Is. 51:4). The visible evidence of the Covenant (Tables of the Law) made by God was to be placed within the Ark (De. 10:2). Hence, Christ, author of the Law, and Son of God, could fulfill the Law of the Old Covenant and usher in the "New Covenant" (Je. 31:31-33; cf. He. 9:1-28).

New
Covenant
881
Christ's
Sacrifice
3366

When the incarnate Christ (God the Son in human flesh) came, he presented a new understanding of the Law. His purpose was to establish the Law (Ro. 3:31), which included the Decalogue that God had given Moses, but he did eliminate the levitical ritual and the animal sacrifices, which were to serve only in the pre-Advent period; these he fulfilled in his own death on the cross.

Jerash. The original 56 columns of the Oval Forum still stand.

The inner heart relationship now became more important and religion more personal. The Law, once written on stone tablets, was written within men's hearts (Je. 31:33; 2 Co. 3:3). Christ did not repudiate the Law, for its use in past generations had been directed by God (Le. 18:3-4). In fact it was in reference to the Old Covenant that Christ could explicate and establish the meaning of the New. The old Law, observed by use of ritual, was a means, not an end. The Law was to guide God's people, until the time when all the Law would be fulfilled; when the Prophet, who is Christ, "the end of the law for righteousness" would appear (Ro. 10:4). Law in the Heart **438**

Paul said, "I had not known sin but by the law" (Ro. 7:7). So the Law was put in charge to lead us to Christ that we might be justified by faith. Now that faith has come, we are no longer under the supervision of the Law (Gal. 3:24-25). Purpose of Law **4055**

Christ also fulfilled the Law because he was the perfect priest, the sacrifice, and the promised Redeemer. Thus Christ transcended the ritualist law of the OT in providing a better way to man's salvation. He was the sinless priest—the High Priest, who did not need "to offer up sacrifice... for his own sins" (He. 7:27) as the levitical priests were required to do daily (He. 7:16; 10:10,12). There was no permanence in the sacrifices offered by the regular priests (He. 7:23); these offerings had to be repeated. Nor could "the blood of bulls and of goats...take away sins" (He. 10:3-4). OT prophets had acknowledged this fact (1 S. 15:22; Je. 6:20; Ps. 40:16; 51:16). In the NT John declared that Jesus is "the Lamb of God, which taketh away the sin of the world" (Jn. 1:29). Priesthood of Christ **2863**

Sacrifices **3107-3111**

Lamb of God **3365**

The blood of Christ as the perfect offering was "as of a lamb without blemish and without spot" (1 Pe. 1:19). "Through the offering of the body of Jesus," believers are "sanctified...once for all" (He. 10:10,14). Finally, Atoning Blood of Christ **679** the coming of Jesus Christ fulfilled all the Messianic prophecies which the faithful Jews had waited for (De. 18:15,18; Zec. 9:9; Da. 9:25; Jn. 1:45).

Christ, Man's
Substitute
3361
Retaliation
Forbidden
2279
Good for Evil
1436-1437

5:39 ...whosoever shall smite thee on thy right cheek, turn to him the other also.

Some people have a problem reconciling the OT law of "eye for eye, tooth for tooth" (Ex. 21:24) with this verse. See the essay "The Mosaic Law: The Unity of the Legal Structure in Both Testaments," pp. 102-103.

9:9 ...Jesus...saw a man named Matthew sitting at the tax collector's booth... (NIV)

Publican
2926

Matthew was a publican who collected Roman taxes. The office was usually sold at auction to the highest bidder. Because of the finances involved, usually only men of great wealth were able to obtain such a position.

Zacchaeus
3977

The very nature of such transactions made the office of tax collector conducive to extortion and abuse, and the man an object of scorn. Frequently the tax collector farmed out portions, or all, of his territory, and this necessitated extra revenue to pay these "middle men." If Zacchaeus is an example of tax abuse, the financial hardship of the common people must have been severe (Lu. 19:8).

11:21 Woe unto thee, Chorazin! Woe unto thee, Bethsaida! for if the mighty works, which were done in you, had been done in Tyre and Sidon, they would have repented long ago in sackcloth and ashes.

Chorazin
4357
Capernaum
641
Bethsaida
411, 4345
Tyre
3716, 4445
Sidon
3282, 4435

Jesus severely rebuked Chorazin, Capernaum and the sister city Bethsaida—all Jewish towns—for rejecting the Gospel message. He said that if the mighty works which had been done in their cities had been done in the Gentile cities of Tyre and Sidon, the non-Jews would have repented in sackcloth and ashes. Reference to these cities would have been especially meaningful to Jesus' audience, because they had long histories relating to the people of God. For a more extensive look at each one, see the following essay.

Three Special Cities in Jesus' Ministry

Chorazin

Chorazin is an ancient city dating back to the Stone Age and is located in

Chorazin
4357

south Galilee about three miles from Capernaum. This area was once volcanic and is still covered with basalt rock. Most of the buildings are made out of this basalt stone.

Excavations in Chorazin are extensive; outstanding is a fourth century synagogue. Many of the other buildings are richly decorated with sculptured

Synagogues
3521-3523

animals as well as with grape-gathering and pressing scenes.

Archaeologists have uncovered a stone seat near the synagogue with an Aramaic inscription. Some scholars suggest that it is an example of "Moses' seat" referred to by Jesus (Mt. 23:2)—probably a seat of special honor.

Tyre

Tyre was an ancient Phoenician port city on the Mediterranean coast about fifty miles south of Beirut and a few miles south

Tyre
3716, 4445

of Sidon. Tyre and Sidon are usually mentioned together in the Gospel references (Mt. 11:21; 15:21; Mk. 3:8; Lu. 6:17). Joshua makes reference to it as "the strong city of Tyre" (Jos. 19:29). Isaiah refers to Tyre as the "city of antiquity" (Is. 23:7-8). Heroditus dates its founding in 2750 B.C. (Heroditus, II, 14). The seamen of Tyre were known to sail to places never before seen by man. Hiram, the king of Tyre, was a friend to David and Solomon and provided cedar for building the Great Temple in Jerusalem (1 K. 5:1-6; 7:13-46).

Solomon's Temple
3577

The Assyrian kings Tiglath-Pileser and Shalmanezer as well as the Babylonian king Nebuchadnezzar besieged Tyre

Chorazin. The archaelogical excavations at Chorazin showing a synagogue at the top.

for many years. Finally the citizens moved to an off-shore island and abandoned the coastal site. When Alexander the Great arrived at the old site, he had no ships with which to attack the island city. His engineers built a causeway to the island, using stones, rubble and the topsoil from the old ruins for filler. The king literally scraped all of the soil, down to bedrock, thus fulfilling to the letter Ezekiel's prophecy (Eze. 26:1-6). In the carnage 10,000 people were killed and 30,000 taken captive as slaves. In a few years the island city revived and became prosperous as a commercial and maritime center.

The Gospels tell us that Jesus visited the coasts of Tyre and Sidon (Mt. 15:21-31) and that the people in the region came to Lake Galilee to hear Jesus preach (Mk. 3:8; Lu. 6:17).

Popularity of Christ
2786-2788

When Tyre was captured by the Muslims the Christians were forbidden to build new churches or to hold any kind of religious services. On June 27, 1124, the crusaders subdued the city; Muslims recaptured it in 1291 and it

28 miles south of Beirut. It became a famous commercial and maritime city on the coastal highway going south to Egypt and north to Asia, with 40,000 inhabitants. Because of its proximity to the well traveled thoroughfare, it suffered much abuse by the armies of many nations as they marched to and from war.

During the Amarna period in Egypt (1400-1360 B.C.) Sidon asserted itself by throwing off the Egyptian yoke and then subjugating its neighbor, Tyre, which had been closely linked with Sidon over the years.

When Assyria began its conquest in Palestine, Sidon was put under constant

Assyria
299-300

pressure for tribute. When Sidon rebelled, Esarhaddon, the Assyrian king, son of Sennacherib (681-668 B.C.), obliterated the city and killed or captured most of its citizens. Alexander the Great rebuilt the city (332 B.C.).

Under Roman rule the people were given the right to self-government. Under this set-up the city prospered and became well-known as a commer-

Left: Tyre. These remains unearthed by archaeologists were once completely covered with coastal sand.

Bottom: A Sarcopagus. It was the custom to sculpture a likeness of the deceased on the lid. Here a man and wife are pictured.

has been in their hands ever since.

Today the island city of Tyre is connected to the mainland by a wide sandy neck, built up against the old causeway by tidal sand. Archaeological excavations have uncovered much of the ancient city of Tyre.

Sidon

Sidon is one of the oldest Phoenician cities, founded by Sidon, the son of

Sidon
3282, 4435

Canaan, in about 2750 B.C. (Ge. 10:15). It is located on the Lebanon coast about

Sidon. An aerial view of the ancient and modern city. The Crusader Castle can be seen in the upper left.

cial center; its fine harbor enhanced its maritime outreach.

In 150 B.C. the noted Zeno was born in Sidon. He established an Epicurean school in Athens where Cicero audited his lectures.

Sidon gained the attention of Bible writers in both the Old and New Testaments (Ge. 10:19; Jos. 13:6; 1 K. 16:31). Matthew tells us that Jesus went on a preaching mission as far north as Tyre and Sidon (Mt. 15:21). Great multitudes from Judea and Jerusalem came to hear Jesus (Lu.

6:17). When Paul, the prisoner, was on his way to Rome, he was granted permission to stop and visit with his friends in Sidon (Ac. 27:3).

The Crusaders captured the city (A.D. 1111) and held it until the Muslim conquest (A.D. 1187). Their Crusader Castle still stands as a landmark in Sidon off the Mediterranean coast. It is connected to the mainland by a heavy stone causeway, built out of stones from the ruins; granite pillars were built into the walls for reinforcement.

Paul's Missionary Journeys
2382

12:2 ...Behold, thy disciples do that which is not lawful to do upon the sabbath day.

The Jewish leaders had developed an elaborate code of regulations and restrictions for the Sabbath. For more on the subject, see commentary on De. 5:14. For the origin of the Sabbath, see commentary on Ge. 2:3.

Sabbath
3098-3102

13:55 Isn't this the carpenter's son? (NIV)

We can surmise that the boyhood of Jesus was like that of most other Jewish lads. His father was a carpenter making plows, yokes and other farming tools. It is probable that Jesus learned to work with his hands in the carpenter shop.

Carpenters
234

Scripture does indicate, however, that Jesus was unusually wise in spiritual matters as a child (Lu. 2:40-48), that he was an obedient son (Lu. 2:51) and that he grew intellectually, physically and socially in a manner worth noting (Lu. 2:52).

Christ's
Humanity
721

16:18 ...thou art Peter, and upon this rock I will build my church...

The work "rock" is frequently used to symbolize Deity. This sheds some light on the question of who the "rock" was in Christ's dialogue with Peter here at Caesarea Philippi. In the wilderness it is said that the "spiritual Rock which followed them was Christ" (1 Co. 10:1-4). For other Divine Rock passages see: Dt. 32:4, 15-18; 2 S. 22:32; 23:3; Ps. 18:2,31; 92:15.

Peter
2746
God, a Rock
3178
Rock of
Offense
698

16:18 ...I will build my church...

There have always been religious congregations from the earliest times. There is a sense in which Adam and Eve were a congregation when they had a conversation with God among the trees of the Garden (Ge. 3:8-21). In this regard there is unity between the teachings in the OT and the NT, which rests upon the assumption that there has always been a body of

Congregation
820-821

A primitive carpenter's shop in Nazareth.

believers in all ages who were essentially Christian in belief, to the extent of the revelation they had.[10] The Scriptures clearly show that an assembly of people or a church worshiping the Living God is of early origin; it may have been in operation by the time of Abel (Ge. 4:4).

In the Hebrew OT, the assembly of believers was called the *qahal* of God and in the Greek OT (Septuagint) this term was translated *ekklesia*. Though it was not a religious term, it has had its own pre-Christian history. In the Septuagint it was used to describe the "body of believers" in the OT times, denoting the "Congregation" or the "Community of Israel" (Job 30:28; Ps. 149:1). The term "OT church" is the functional equivalent of all

other terms used in the NT to designate believers. So it would seem that any objection to recognizing the OT church would be more semantic than real.

A noted church historian observes that, "If we are to understand the

nature of the church, we must begin with the OT. According to Ac. 7:38 there was already a church in the wilderness when God redeemed His people out of Egypt. Terms such as 'new Israel' and 'Israel of God' would be pointless

except against the background of a nation which had been so conceived as the people of God. If Christians were the 'true circumcision' (Ph. 3:3; cf. Eze. 44:7) and the 'real sons of Abraham' (Ro. 4:12), this OT background

is presupposed. A people of a New Covenant presupposed an Old Covenant."[11] The Chosen of God enjoyed this blessed relationship because individuals had conformed their lives to God's will and design. They were

the "children of the most High" (Ps. 82:6), "the congregation of the righteous" (Ps. 1:5), the constituency of the OT church. Thus the "basic

conception" of an organized congregation or church goes back to the OT. The "true remnant" about which the prophets had spoken had found fulfillment in the Christian community. The words of the Savior following

Peter's affirmation, "Thou art the Christ, the Son of the living God" (Mt. 16:16), "Upon this rock I [Christ] will build my church" (Mt. 16:18) suggests the continuity of the church from the OT to the NT.

The church in the OT can be compared to the foundation and basement of a new church building. Occasionally churches first appear as roofed-over basements, where all the functions of the church and worship are carried on. Later the superstructure rises, but the basic function in the roofed-over basement, as compared with the completed building, is essentially the same. Christ built his message and teachings upon the foundation of the patriarchs and prophets. In Matthew 16:18 Christ presents himself as

the (future) builder of the church and as he became the "corner stone" so he was and also is the foundation. No foundation, other than Christ, can support

the redemptive structure (1 Co. 3:11). He, who was the foundation of the plan of redemption from the beginning, has been ingrained in the work of salvation, and this redemptive work is the same, regardless of time. Christ

is the Lord of eternity, the "Alpha and the Omega." In speaking of the church, the Lord used the thought patterns of his day to fit the current need.

By adopting the term "church," Christ did not imply the abandonment of the purpose of the synagogue and the temple. He was merely reshaping

terminology to fit the day when the Gentiles would enter the fellowship of believers, the church.

When the word "church" comes to the mind of the average person, it evokes a variety of responses. Some people think in terms of a church building in which people worship God, while others think of denominational groups, but these ideas would have been strange to the early church. "Amid the ruins of war-torn cities many modern Christians are discovering anew that the Church is not made of stone or brick. The living stones of the true Temple of God are those who worship Him in spirit and in truth."[12] The church is, by definition, the "people of God" and the idea of more than one denomination was not present in early Christianity. In Jesus Christ all believers in God are one and belong to the same mystical body called the church. In the true church all human discrimination is abolished (Gal. 3:28; Col. 3:11). The unity of the Christian faith is indicated in "One Lord, one faith, one baptism, one God and Father of all" (Ep. 4:5-6) which unifies all believers and makes them a part of the glorious church.

"One can hardly say...that Jesus founded the Christian Church. For centuries there had been a people who looked upon themselves as set apart for God. When Christians applied the term *ekklesia* to themselves they redefined the *qahal* of God, in terms of the new acts and revelation of God in Jesus Christ for their redemption. It was not to be identified with Israel after the flesh, but with individuals from every tribe, nation, people and tongue" (Re. 7:9).[13]

A noted German scholar puts it this way: "Before the foundation of the world, God conceived the counsel of salvation for the church...from eternity, that amazing structure that...was determined by the Redeemer. Therefore, 'from before the ages,' the Christ mystery was...hidden in God for the Gentiles who would be fellow-heirs and fellow-members of the body of Jesus Christ our Lord" (Ep. 3:6).[14]

According to the conception of historic Christianity, the *ekklesia*, or the church, is made up of people who have committed their lives by faith to God through Jesus Christ and who witness to the work of the Savior among the communities of mankind. "It is the whole spiritual commonwealth of God's children, the company of all faithful people. It is represented by the organized or visible church in any or all ages."[15]

The term *ekklesia* is never used to mean a building or house of assembly but to designate a body whose unity does not depend on its meeting together in one place. It is not merely an assemblage of individuals but of members in their several places united to the one head, Christ, and forming one organic living whole (1 Co. 12). It is referred to as the Bride of Christ (Ep. 5:25-32), the household of God (Ep. 2:19), and the temple of the Holy Ghost, made up of living stones (Ep. 2:22; 1 Co. 3:16; 1 Pe. 2:5).[16]

17:3 Just then there appeared before [Peter, James and John] Moses and Elijah, talking with Jesus. (NIV)

The fact that Moses and Elijah were talking with Jesus just as surely as Peter, James and John were able to talk with him affirms that the Savior of the OT is the same as that of the New. For more on the subject, see the essay "The Mechanics of Salvation in the OT Period," pp. 66-69.

The Church
726-761

God's People
2723-2725

Unity of Believers
3724-3727

The Redeemed
2976

The Saved
1358
Redeemer
2977
Conversion of the Gentiles
2383

Body of Christ
726

Church as Bride
737
Names of the Church
3635
Moses
2420-2421
Elijah
1112, 4298

Whitewashed tombs in Samaria.

18:4 ...whoever humbles himself like this child is the greatest in the kingdom of heaven. (NIV)

Jesus' central message was the "kingdom of God" and the repentance necessary to enter it. But this is not strictly a NT concept. For its OT background, see commentary on Mk. 1:15.

Spiritual
Kingdom
2007-2013

21:12 Jesus...overturned the tables of the money changers... (NIV)

During Passion Week, when the sufferings of Christ began, Jesus drew the battle line when he drove the sellers of animals and the money changers from the temple.

Avarice
2131
Greed
2133
Christ's Zeal
1075-1076
Sacrilege
3038-3040

Temple hierarchy robbed the worshipers by charging unreasonable rates for exchanging money. This affected many pilgrims from other countries who were required to change their money into the Temple currency. The sellers of sacrificial animals also charged inflated prices to such an extent that Jesus drove the money changers and the animal merchants out of the Temple with the charge that they had made the House of God into a den of thieves (v. 13).

22:38 This is the first and greatest commandment. (NIV)

Command-
ments
444

Pre-
eminence
of Love
2209, 4182

When a lawyer asked Jesus what the most important commandment was, he restated the OT formula given by Moses in De. 6:5: Thou shalt love the LORD thy God with all thine heart, and with all thy soul, and with all thy might," and, "thou shalt love thy neighbor as thyself." These two commandments are the key to a happy relationship with God and man. This love fulfills all the demands of law. Jesus said, "on these two commandments hang [depend] all the law and the prophets" (v. 40). The message is simple: the commandment of love satisfies and fulfills all the other commandments of God.

23:27 Woe to you, teachers of the law and Pharisees, you hypocrites! You are like whitewashed tombs. (NIV)

Tombs above ground were whitewashed to make them conspicuous. Touching anything dead, even a tomb, resulted in the person being defiled (Nu. 19:11). For more on the Pharisees of Jesus' day, see commentary on Mk. 8:11; Jn. 8:44.

26:18 ...I will keep the passover at thy house with my disciples.

The Passover was set apart to commemorate God's great deliverance of the Israelites from Egypt. It was the night the firstborn throughout Egypt were killed, but the death angel "passed over" the houses of the Israelites which had been sprinkled with blood on the doorposts. For more on the important relationship of the OT Passover with Christ's memorial meal with his disciples, see commentary on Ex. 12:17.

Hypocrisy
2994-2995

Pharisees
3171

Passover
1256

Apostles
2080-2082

Lord's Supper
761

The City of Jerusalem

From the book of Genesis to the book of Revelation the reader's attention is drawn to the city of Jerusalem. The 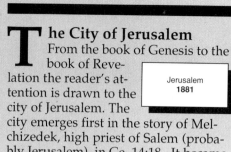 city emerges first in the story of Melchizedek, high priest of Salem (probably Jerusalem), in Ge. 14:18. It became the most important city of the Hebrews, when David made it the capital of his kingdom.

Jerusalem was the scene of the latter days of our Lord's life on this earth. His concern and love for the city were shown when he cried, "O Jerusalem, Jerusalem, you who kill the prophets and stone those sent to you, how often I have longed to gather your children together, as a hen gathers her chicks under her wings, but you were not willing. Look, your house is left to you desolate...not one stone here [at the temple] will be left on another; every one will be thrown down"(Mt. 23:37-38; 24:2, NIV). His prophecy was fulfilled in A.D. 70, when the Romans, under Titus, took Jerusalem, the Temple and nearly all the city and broke down all the walls. In 1968 archaeologists uncovered large numbers of the stones that were thrown down.

Jerusalem
1881

Love for Jerusalem
2528

Right: A beautified area around the east wall of Jerusalem.

Below: The Damascus Gate in Jerusalem.

Matthew

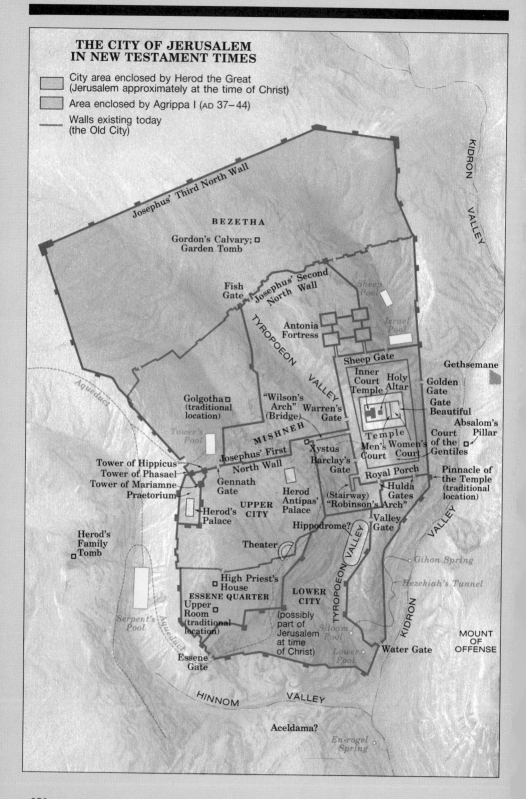

THE CITY OF JERUSALEM
IN NEW TESTAMENT TIMES

City area enclosed by Herod the Great
(Jerusalem approximately at the time of Christ)

Area enclosed by Agrippa I (AD 37–44)

Walls existing today
(the Old City)

KIDRON VALLEY

Josephus' Third North Wall

BEZETHA

Gordon's Calvary;
Garden Tomb

Fish Gate

Josephus' Second North Wall

Sheep Pool

TYROPOEON VALLEY

Antonia Fortress

Israel Pool

Sheep Gate

Gethsemane

Aqueduct

Golgotha
(traditional location)

"Wilson's Arch" (Bridge)

Warren's Gate

Inner Court Temple

Holy Altar

Golden Gate

Gate Beautiful

Tower's Pool

MISHNEH

Josephus' First North Wall

Xystus
Barclay's Gate

Temple

Men's Court

Women's Court

Court of the Gentiles

Absalom's Pillar

Tower of Hippicus
Tower of Phasael
Tower of Mariamne
Praetorium

Gennath Gate

Herod Antipas' Palace

Royal Porch

Hulda Gates

Pinnacle of the Temple
(traditional location)

UPPER CITY

(Stairway)
"Robinson's Arch"

Valley Gate

VALLEY

Herod's Family Tomb

Herod's Palace

Hippodrome?

Theater

Gihon Spring

Hezekiah's Tunnel

KIDRON

High Priest's House

ESSENE QUARTER

Upper Room
(traditional location)

LOWER CITY

(possibly part of Jerusalem at time of Christ)

TYROPOEON VALLEY

Siloam Pool

Water Gate

MOUNT OF OFFENSE

Serpent's Pool

Aqueduct

Lower Pool

Essene Gate

HINNOM VALLEY

Aceldama?

En-rogel Spring

Mark

The Name

The Gospel of Mark was written by John Mark. His first name, John, was his Jewish given name, translated from the Greek *Ioannes*. Mark (Gr, *Markos*) was his Roman (Latin) surname, meaning "a large hammer." He was called John among the Jews but Mark in the Gentile world (Ac. 12:12,25; 15:37).

John Mark's name appears five times in the New Testament (Ac. 12:12, 25; 15:37, 39; 2 Ti. 4:11). The first three references include the names John and Mark. Twice he is called John (Ac. 13:5, 13). In three other places he is referred to as "Marcus" (Col. 4:10; Phm. 24; and 1 Pe. 5:13).[1]

Authorship and Date

From the beginning, early church tradition credited John Mark with authorship of the Gospel of Mark. The caption at the head of the book, "The Gospel according to Mark," was not a part of the original manuscript but was placed there by the fathers to preserve the identification of the author. This fact is attested by such early Christian writers as Papias (A.D. 70-155), a pupil of John the Beloved and Bishop of Hierapolis; John Martyr (A.D. 100-167), a philosopher and defender of Christians; and Eusebius (A.D. 264-340), the father of church history. In general, there is agreement among modern scholars that John Mark was the author of the book bearing his name,[2] and by many conservative scholars that the book was written before the destruction of Jerusalem in A.D. 70, probably about A.D. 60.

Background, Purpose, and Content

In the book of Acts John Mark's name is mentioned first in Ac. 12:12, when Peter was released from prison, and went to the house of Mary, "the mother of John, whose surname was Mark; where many were gathered together praying." John Mark appears next in Perga where, for reasons unknown, he left the company of Barnabas and Paul and returned to Jerusalem (Ac. 13:13).

When Barnabas and Paul were making preparation for their second missionary journey, Barnabas was "determined to take with them John, whose surname was Mark" (Ac. 15:37), but Paul objected. After disagreement between the two men, Barnabas took John Mark on a tour independent of Paul of which nothing more is said. "Paul chose Silas" to accompany him on the second journey. Apparently John Mark later developed into a strong missionary witness. When Paul was in prison at Rome, he asked Timothy to bring Mark "for he is profitable to me for the ministry" (2 Ti. 4:11).

Most scholars are agreed that John Mark was a close associate of Peter and "that he…inquired of the Elders and the followers of the Elders [concerning Jesus' ministry]…Having become the interpreter, he wrote down accurately all that he remembered, not, however, in order, the words and deeds of Christ…Mark made no mistake in thus writing down some of the things as he remembered them. For one object was in his thoughts— to omit nothing that he had heard, and to make no false statements."[3] But some ancients believe that Peter, "through modesty, would not put his name to the work, but dictated the whole account, and Mark wrote it down…"[4] The book of Mark indicates, however, that the writer follows closely and substantially the well authenticated Gospel tradition, even though he was probably not an eye witness."[5]

The short, concise statements of fact show that Mark had remarkable organizational ability and literary skill to portray action. He gives dynamic movement to the events recorded in his Gospel with such words as "straight-way" (19 times) and "immediately" (17 times). The considerable amount of data which Mark includes in his book is illustrated in the first chapter. Mark made the declaration that Jesus is the "Son of God" (v. 1); that John is the messenger of God (v. 2) as well as "the voice of one crying in the wilderness" (v. 3), the baptizer (vv. 4-8), a rugged character (v. 6), and the forerunner of Jesus (v. 7). This introduction is followed by an account of the baptism of Jesus (v. 9), at which time the heavens were opened (v. 10) and God affirmed that Jesus is the Son (v. 11). In the next verse is a reference to Jesus being driven by the Spirit [sent him out—NIV] into the wilderness for 40 days (v. 12). He is "tempted of Satan" (v. 13). Following this experience, John was put in prison (v. 14). Jesus began to assemble his disciples by calling Simon and Andrew (vv. 16-18) and then added James and John (vv. 19-20). In Capernaum Jesus entered the synagogue (vv. 21-22) where he healed a man with an unclean spirit (vv. 23-27). Forthwith, Jesus went into a house and healed Simon's mother-in-law (vv. 29-31). When his fame went abroad, many others were healed (vv. 32-34). The following morning Jesus went out "into a solitary place" to pray (v. 35).

In the same chapter Mark verified that Jesus is the one anticipated by the prophets (vv. 2-3), that it would be he who baptized men with the Holy Spirit (v. 8) and that he was a receiver of visions (vv. 9-11). He is the One to whom angels ministered (v. 13), and who preached the Gospel of the kingdom (v. 15). Jesus also called men to become evangelists (vv. 16-20); he was a teacher with authority (v. 22) and the One who cast out demons (v. 25). He was a man of prayer, one who had compassion for the sick (vv. 30-34), and one with missionary interest (v. 39). This "action-filled" writing reflects the *dunamis* (power) of God. (The Greek Lexicon defines *dunamis:* to have inherent power, power residing in a thing by virtue of its nature, or which a person or thing exerts and puts forth, power…beyond our power.)

Silas
3288

Rome
3095, 4428

Peter
2746

Gospel
1440

Christ's
Divinity
701-718
Baptism
756-760

Holy Spirit
1604-1614
Temptation
3584-3595
Apostles
2080-2082
Christ Heals
1539
Private
Devotions of
Christ
2834
Prophesies
Relating to
Christ
2890-2892
Prayer
2816-2841
Power
3803-3816

A Roman aqueduct in Caesarea. The Romans (to whom Mark wrote) were famous for their engineering ability.

The book of Mark contains approximately 90 percent of all the material (in condensed form) contained in the books of Matthew and Luke. This phenomenal amount of information in Mark has created a problem for some scholars who have concluded that Mark wrote the first Gospel and that Matthew and Luke borrowed liberally from Mark for their writings. Another speculation is that there may have been a central source of information which all the gospel writers utilized, known as the "Q" document (Q" is the symbol for the German word, *quelle,* meaning source or spring). However, no such book or manuscript is in existence.[6] For more on the "Synoptic Problem," see the Introduction to Matthew.

The assumption that the gospel writers copied from each other is not necessarily true. In the days of Jesus the educative process involved a great deal of memorization. Thus the gospel events were communicated orally among the people. The sayings and activities of Jesus were the subject of conversation in the marketplace and at the synagogues. Possibly some of the people may have carried fragments of written materials—one person perhaps made notes as he heard the various stories about Jesus. Of course, the Holy Spirit superintended and regulated the written gospel records.

Most of the book of Mark seems to have been written for Gentile readers, probably those in Rome. The writer explains a number of Jewish customs and frequently employs Latin terms without translating them; but he does interpret a number of Aramaic terms (cf. Mk. 3:17; 5:41; 7:11,34; 15:34),[7] and discusses details of life in Palestine which would have been unfamiliar to the Gentiles (Mk. 7:3ff.; 12:42; 14:12, 15-22, 42).

Internal evidence shows the author to be a Christian Jew who was intimately acquainted with the Jewish life and who had a knowledge of the Scriptures. His knowledge of the general geography of Palestine, and especially Jerusalem, gives further support to this supposition.

Harmony of the Gospels
4308a

Christ as Portrayed in the Synoptic Gospels
4302

"Word" Inspired
417
Gentile Believers
4038

Jerusalem
4391

Unlike the book of Matthew, with its frequent OT citations, the book of Mark makes its appeal to Gentiles by its disapproval of Jewish dietary laws (Mk. 7:2-7) and strict sabbath observation (Mk. 2:28).

It is clear that there was a great need for a Gospel account with such terms as "straightway" and "immediately." The Romans were builders—the engineers of the world. Their method of construction was so thorough that many viaducts, bridges, and buildings of Roman origin are still in use.

The Romans were not interested in philosophizing. They were people of action; they built for permanency—they were more interested in what Jesus did, and less in what he said. Therefore Mark emphasized the actions of Jesus.

Mark called his writings the "gospel," using the terms six times in his book (1:1,14,15; 13:10; 14:9; 16:15). He selected the word from the Greek OT (LXX), used especially in the book of Isaiah—the Hebrew word *basar* meaning "good tidings," which is translated in the English as "gospel."

Mark did not propose to write a biography in the usually accepted sense, but a treatise with a religious-historical background. It is evident that originally, when Mark uses the word gospel he means the faith, not the book.

The book of Mark has a practical appeal to the modern church. J. Newton Davies puts it in these words:

> Just as the first readers in Rome, of this vivid portrayal of the Son of man, were encouraged to face cruel tortures and punishments of unheard-of severity, and above all to maintain their missionary zeal in the face of colossal obstacles and continuous disappointments, so the Christian Church today, in reading afresh the story of the life of Jesus as written by Mark, will be greatly strengthened and encouraged in its task of presenting the claims of Christ to an age bewildered by many conflicting emotions, torn by faction, burdened by many sorrows, weighed down by the spirit of material-ism, and yet in its heart of hearts yearning for one who will be its guide and shepherd through the perplexing mazes of its day. The road to the future, it has been well said, is the road back to the NT. We cannot more effectively begin to walk that road than by reading and rereading this striking presentation of the Lord of life by John Mark.[8]

The entire structure of the book is suggestive of a universal gospel.

Traditions
3652
Roman
Citizens
772

Christ Jesus
677-723
Gospel
1440-1442

Faith
1201-1213

Enabling
Grace
4030
Weakness –
Power
3797-3816

Universal
Gospel
1442

1:11 And there came a voice from heaven…

From the very beginning the Bible records instances when God speaks to man (Ge. 1:28, "God…said to them"). These times when human beings hear the voice of God audibly are called "theophanies," indicating a revelation of God to man. For more on this subject, see commentary on Ge. 2:18 and the essay "Theophanies in the OT," pp. 72-73.

Divine Revelations **2494-2496**

1:15 …The kingdom of God is near… (NIV)

"The Gospels clearly indicate that the central message of Jesus did not semantically deal with the church but was concerned with the 'kingdom of God' and the repentance which was necessary if men should enter in by the gracious mercy of God (Mk. 1:14-15). Jesus announced the nearness of the kingdom of God, a message which gave tremendous urgency to His ethical demands. A crisis was at hand; men must stand ready to pay the price to enter God's kingdom (Lu. 14:25-33). The term 'kingdom' was common in the old covenant and was understood to mean 'children of Zion' (Ps. 149:2), 'congregation of the saints' (Ps. 89:5), or 'those who had faith in the Lord.' "[9]

God's Kingdom **2009** Mercy **2297**

Congregation **820-821** Kingdom, Spiritual **2007-2013**

The expressions "kingdom of heaven" and the "kingdom of God" are identical.[10] "Kingdom of heaven" is found only in Matthew (32 times) and was originally intended for Jews; the other Gospels, written for Gentile readers, used the expression "kingdom of God" (for example, Luke 33 times; Mt. 13:31,33, cf. Lu. 13:18-21; Mt. 19:14, cf. Lu. 18:16-17).

John the Baptist and Jesus were not the first who spoke of the kingdom of heaven. Indeed "they adopted the language of the OT and of Judaism around them, filling the same expression with new meaning as in Lu. 15:21: 'Father, I have sinned against heaven, [i.e., God], and in thy sight'; Mt. 21:25: 'the baptism of John, whence was it? from heaven, [i.e., God], or of men'; Mt. 26:64: 'ye [shall] see the Son of man sitting on the right hand power [i.e., of God].' Therefore, with the Lord the prevailing description of the kingdom of God is the kingdom of heaven."[11]

Heavenly Kingdom **2008**

Kingdom of Heaven **2013**

Lake Galilee. Fishermen with their morning catch.

The Jesus Boat.

1:16-17 ....Jesus...saw Simon and his brother Andrew casting a net into the lake, for they were fishermen. "Come, follow me," Jesus said, "and I will make you fishers of men." (NIV)

About a year after beginning his public ministry, Jesus chose twelve disciples. The Temple authorities assumed that the Messiah would have chosen his disciples from among the Temple hierarchy, but to their consternation he made his selection from a wide spectrum of lowly country folk near Lake Galilee. Some were fishermen, one was a zealot and one was a despised tax collector. This worked against any interest the Temple leaders could have had in his movement.

1:21 ...on the sabbath day he entered into the synagogue, and taught.

Jesus was accustomed to worshiping in the synagogue on the Sabbath (Lu. 4:16). For more on the synagogue as a worship center, see chart and commentary on Ac. 2:47.

2:27 ...The sabbath was made for man, and not man for the sabbath.

The subject of the Sabbath was very important to the Pharisees of Jesus' day, because they had developed a very legalistic interpretation of how the day should be observed. For more on the subject of the Sabbath, see commentary on Ge. 2:3; De. 5:14 and Ac. 1:12.

3:9 Because of the crowd he told his disciples to have a small boat ready for him... (NIV)

Boats were commonly used in Biblical days for fishing, for cargo and human transport. The book of 2 Samuel speaks of David and his household crossing the Jordan River on a ferry (2 S. 19:18). John speaks of boats in Jn. 6:22-23. Mark and John both speak of "little ships" (Mk. 3:9; 4:36; Jn.

21:8). Apparently the words "ship" and "boat" were used interchangeably. Jesus and his disciples most likely used the smaller boats or ships which could be rowed with oars.

Ships
3273

In January, 1986, the Sea of Galilee was at its lowest level in many years. As a result, two Jewish brothers discovered the remains of an ancient boat, partially submerged in the mud near the edge of the shore. The Department of Antiquities excavated the boat and determined it dated back to the first century A.D. The boat was 8.20 meters long and 2.35 meters wide. Their estimate was that it would have accommodated 14 to 16 people.

Sea of
Galilee
1385

Because of its similarity to the boats used by Jesus and his disciples, the boat is referred to locally as "the Jesus Boat." After the boat was repaired it was immersed in a vat of water and is on display in a special museum on the property of Kibbutz Ginosar, near the northwest shore of the Sea of Galilee.

5:20 So the man went away and began to tell in the Decapolis how much Jesus had done for him. (NIV)

Decapolis
950

The Decapolis was Gentile territory, in contrast to many of the healings done in Jewish towns. It was a group of cities where Jesus taught. See commentary on Mt. 4:25.

Gentiles
2383-2384

6:30 And the apostles gathered themselves together...

Apostles
2080-2082

Mark uses the word "apostle" only once for the twelve. For more on the meaning of the word, see commentary on Ac. 1:26.

7:24 And from thence he arose, and went into the borders of Tyre and Sidon...

Tyre
3716, 4445

For more on the Gentile cities of Tyre and Sidon and how they relate to Jesus' ministry, see essay on pp. 347-350.

Sidon
3282

8:11 The Pharisees came and began to question Jesus...

Pharisees
3171

The Pharisees were laymen (not priests) dedicated to preserving the Mosaic Law. Their origin is not known but there is evidence that they were in existence in the time of Ezra when heathenism threatened Judaism. Their presence is more clearly pronounced during the Maccabean Revolt when heathen philosophies were creeping into Jewish religious life.

Heathen
1546

> The Pharisees...[were] esteemed most skillful in the exact application of their laws...but were not apt to be severe in punishments favoring "stripes and bonds" but not death.[12]

Sanctimony
2991

The Pharisees were the strict legalists. They stood for the rigid observance of the letter of the law, including the traditions. There were some sincere men among the Pharisees, but in the main they were known for their self-righteous attitudes. Their aim was sometimes commendable, but by stressing the letter of the law and neglecting the spirit they became victims of extremism. Because the Pharisees were concerned about preserving the law, they neglected that which the law intended to protect, the rights of the individual. The nature of their legalistic confusion is reflected in the Gospels, especially in the twenty-third chapter of Matthew where the Pharisees and scribes came in direct conflict with Jesus, who taught and emphasized the spirit of the law.

Legalism
2990

Self-
Righteous-
ness
3219-3220
Formalism
2992-2993

A more moderate spirit among the Pharisees prevailed in Gamaliel, a doctor of the law, who advised moderation when the apostles were brought before the council for teaching in the name of Jesus (Ac. 5:34-39). Some Pharisees accepted Jesus as the Messiah. Among them was Saul of Tarsus (Ac. 23:6ff).

For more on the religious leaders of Jesus' day, see commentary on Jn. 8:44; Re. 2:9.

10:25 It is easier for a camel to go through the eye of a needle than for a rich man to enter the kingdom of God. (NIV)

Central in the Master's teaching was that his kingdom was not of this world and that the treasure of this world was not legal tender in the kingdom he represented. He warned his disciples not to lay up great treasure in this world for it was subject to deterioration by "moth" and "rust" and to loss by thieves and robbers. This message was not well received by the rich who were opposed to giving their material treasure to the cause of charity.

Jesus did not bar the rich from his kingdom but pointed out that their possessive attitude toward their riches would make it very difficult for a rich person to enter heaven. In the verse above, the "eye of a needle" is usually interpreted to mean the small door in the large city gate reserved for late-comers. In order to get in, the traveler had to unload his cargo, then walk the camel through on his knees. The implication is obvious.

12:18 Then the Sadducees, who say there is no resurrection, came to him with a question. (NIV)

In their origin the Sadducees seem to have been contemporaries of the Pharisees. They are mentioned by the historian Josephus.[13] Unlike the Pharisees, the Sadducees reacted against Jewish legalism, but they favored the philosophical speculation inherent in Hellenism. They took no part in the Maccabean revolt. Although they were religious officials, at heart they were very irreligious. They were wealthy, worldly, and prominent in the Sanhedrin. They placed high value on the Law of Moses but relegated the prophetic writings to a place of lesser importance. They rejected the belief in angels, demons, evil spirits, and Jesus' resurrection. They were the extreme liberal philosophers of their day. Both the Pharisees and the Sadducees acknowledged the supremacy of the Torah, but the Sadducees held only to the written law and did not accept the traditions of the elders. Both the Sadducees and the Pharisees opposed Jesus (see Mt. 23; see also commentary on Mk. 8:11). For more on the religious leaders of Jesus' day, see commentary on Jn. 8:44; Re. 2:9.

Margin references:

Gamaliel
1388
Pharisees
3171
Sadducees
3172

Kingdom, Spiritual
2007-2013
Riches Perilous
2806

Avarice
2131

Christ the Door
4028

Sadducees
3172
Resurrection, Doubts Concerning
2408

Worldliness
3914-3917
Sanhedrin
862

Book of the Law
525

Garden of Gethsemane. Olive trees and perennial flowers grace this beautiful garden. The Golden Gate is visible in the distance.

12:33 To love him with all your heart...is more important than all burnt offerings and sacrifices. (NIV)

This wise comment followed Jesus' affirmation of the "Great Commandment" (see commentary on Mt. 22:37). The sacrificial system of the OT was intended to communicate love and to point out the mercy of God to fallen man. Its message was not, therefore, different in spirit from the heart of the NT message; its way of communciating it was simply different. For more on the sacrifices of the OT and the NT, see commentary on Ro. 12:1.

14:12 And the first day of unleavened bread, when they killed the passover...

During the Passover Feast a lamb was killed, roasted whole, and eaten with unleavened bread. Historically, it marked the exodus; symbolically it foreshadowed Christ's sacrificial death. For more on the subject, see commentary on Ex. 12:17.

**14:32 They went to a place called
Gethsemane, and Jesus said to his disciples,
"Sit here while I pray."**(NIV)

Gethsemane was a garden on the lower slopes of the Mount of Olives. Just before his death, Jesus chose this beautiful garden, one of his favorite places, to pray in agony, because he knew what he would face. The next day he would carry his cross to "The Place of the Skull," where he would be crucified.

The trunk of an olive tree in the Garden of Gethsemane.
This tree is possibly over 2,000 years old.

Luke

The Name

The name Luke comes from the Greek *Loukas* and appears three times in the New Testament—twice as Luke (2 Ti. 4:11; Col. 4:14) and once as Lucas (Phm. 24). He is not considered to be the Lucius who is cited twice in the NT (Ac. 13:1; Ro. 16:21). Luke is not mentioned in the Gospel by his name nor is he mentioned in the book of Acts, even as John does not mention himself in his Gospel.

Authorship and Date

Authorship of Luke cannot be separated from that of the book of Acts because these books are two parts of one whole. Luke was not making a boastful statement when he said that he had a "perfect understanding of all things" (Lu. 1:3) in the gospel accounts, nor in his second record when he stated that he had written "of all that Jesus began both to do and teach, until the day in which he was taken up…" (Ac. 1:1-2).[1] Rather, the indication is that Luke conducted thorough research before he began to write his book. Only such excellence could challenge the Greek mind. In the book of Acts, Luke gives a continuing account of what Jesus did through his commissioned evangels after his resurrection.

Although Luke's name does not appear in his books, the internal evidence provided by the use of the personal pronouns in certain parts of the book of Acts, along with Paul's reference to Luke's name serve to support the supposition that Luke is the author.

After Paul received his Macedonian vision, the writer of these books apparently joined Paul and Silas; this is indicated by the pronouns "we" and "us," which begin in the text at this point. They continue to appear until the party arrived at Philippi (Ac. 16:10-12), where Luke apparently stayed to practice medicine and to oversee the church, while Paul and Silas continued on their journey to Thessalonica. The first person plural pronouns are suspended at this point but begin again when Paul returned to Philippi and started his journey back to Jerusalem. The recurrence of the pronouns indicates that the writer had rejoined the missionary party (Ac. 20:5-21:17). Later, when Paul was delivered into the hands of Julius the centurion to be taken to Rome, the pronoun "we" again is used, indicating that the writer had again joined Paul (Ac. 27:1-28:16). These references in Luke and Acts show that Luke was the writer of the book.

Luke	**2216**
Gospel of Luke	**4264**
Acts of the Apostles	**4266**
Greeks	**1464**
Macedonia	**2222**
Philippi	**2756, 4425**
Thessa-lonica	**3610, 4442**

From the Epistles written during Paul's first imprisonment in Rome it is evident that nine people were with Paul: Tychicus, Epaphroditus, Onesimus, Aristarchus, Marcus, Jesus who is called Justus, Epaphras, Luke, and Demas (Ep. 6:21; Ph. 2:25; Col. 4:7-14; Phm. 10,23-24).

"Since the writer of Acts went with Paul to Rome, Epaphras and Epaphroditus are ruled out because they arrived later (Ph. 4:18; Col. 4:12). Aristarchus (Ac. 19:29), Mark (Ac. 12:25), Timothy (Ac. 16:1), and Tychicus (Ac. 20:4) are eliminated because they are all mentioned in the third person in Acts."[2]

It is doubtful if the runaway slave Onesimus, coming to Paul later, could have written the book. Demas is an unlikely author since he deserted Paul (2 Ti. 4:10). Only Luke and Justus remain, and since tradition does not mention Justus in this connection, it is obvious that Luke must be the author of both the Gospel of Luke and the book of Acts.

These books are addressed to Theophilus. The cultural and educational quality of the writings and the writer's interest in sickness and in healing are additional reasons why these books were written by a man of letters as well as one with a medical knowledge (Lu. 4:27; 8:29,43,49). It is thought that the book of Luke was written about A.D. 60.

Background, Purpose, and Content

Of Luke's background, little is known other than that he was a physician (Col. 4:14), and that he was a companion of Paul during a part of his missionary journeys. Scholars differ as to his religious background. Some think he was a Jew converted directly to Christianity, while others suggest he was a Gentile (Greek) and that he became a proselyte to Judaism, sometime later accepting Jesus of Nazareth as the Messiah in the same way that the apostles and other Jews had done.[3]

Apparently many people had written on what Jesus said and did, but Luke felt that there was still a need for another presentation of the gospel. The first four verses in Luke are filled with basic background information.

In the first verse Luke's scholarly background is clearly evident. He could not have made this statement without having read what the "many...had set forth." The subject matter of these writers is identified with the Christian faith—"those things which are most surely believed among us." There is no hesitation on the part of Luke to make this declaration; what he is saying is factual and not theoretical. It must be remembered that Christian profession entailed great risks. Men were severely persecuted and even put to death for making such declarations. Luke went further to describe the character of these writings. They were documents prepared "from the beginning...[by] eye witnesses, and ministers of the Word." They had in them the evidence of apostolic authority.

Apparently some gospel records had already been written, but there still was a need to satisfy Greek civilization representing culture, philosophy, reason, beauty, and education. The writer's appeal would have to be made by a brilliant scholar in excellent Greek form. Luke had the qualifications and attempted to satisfy this need.

He wrote a sympathetic, concise, and orderly account of the gospel which some call the most beautiful story ever written.[4] He presented Jesus in all of his beauty and perfection as the universal Savior, who is not for the Jews alone, but for all mankind. Luke directed his message to Theophilus. The salutation, "most excellent," suggests that he was writing to a high Roman official, perhaps in the Greek community, who had embraced Christianity. The name Theophilus is a compound word meaning "Lover of God." It is apparent that Theophilus already had some Christian instruction and that Luke was writing a more concise, orderly treatise, especially with the Gentiles in mind (Lu. l:1-4).

A Greek audience is further indicated by the detailed account Luke gave of the birth of both John the Baptist and Jesus. The writer deals at length with the priest Zacharias and his wife Elisabeth, the parents of John the Baptist. Luke goes into even greater detail in connection with the events surrounding the nativity story. Luke, the physician, trained in biology, went into detail to present the virgin birth as factual. Luke showed an interest in women, e.g., Anna, the prophetess; Mary the Mother; and Mary Magdalene.

The genealogy presented by Luke is evidence of his intellectual excellence. Matthew traces the Messianic line only to Abraham (Mt. 1:2). To the Greeks this limited view of world history would not be satisfactory. They would desire a more complete account. Luke satisfied this demand by tracing the genealogy back to Adam and God (Lu. 3:38).

It is true that Matthew presented some universal aspects of the gospel, but Luke went into greater depth. He refers to Jesus as being the light of the Gentiles (Lu. 2:32) and he quoted Isaiah (cf. Is. 52:l0): "All flesh shall see the salvation of God" (Lu. 3:6). Luke wrote of Elias being sent to befriend a widow (a Gentile) in Sarepta of Sidon during the drought, though his mission did not include the widows of Israel (Lu. 4:25-26), and of the healing of Naaman, the Syrian, without the cleansing of the lepers in Israel (Lu. 4:27).

Luke centered attention upon social outcasts, the poor and repentant sinners. One outstanding illustration is the immoral woman, who, in repentance, poured expensive ointment on Jesus' feet (Lu. 7:37-38). Luke mentioned that Jesus rebuked James and John for wanting to call down fire from heaven to consume a Samaritan village (Lu. 9:51-56). The story of the Good Samaritan is cited only by Luke (Lu. l0:25-37) as is the story of the Prodigal Son (Lu. 15:11- 32). Only Luke preserved the narrative of ten lepers (Lu. l7:11-l9). When the self-righteous Pharisee prayed by the side of the contrite publican, Luke reports that Jesus justified the latter rather than the former (Lu. l8:9-l4). The account of the repentant Zacchaeus would not be known if it had not been written by Luke (Lu. l9:l-l0), nor would the story of the penitent thief on the cross (Lu. 23:39-43).

Many other examples in Luke's account show that Christ was interested in the whole human race, not just the Jews. This universal acceptance made the Gentiles and all others, including the poor and the outcast, eligible for kingdom membership.

Universal Opportunity
4189

Gentiles
2383-2384

John the Baptist
1903-1906

Zacharias
3980

Virgin Birth
4217

Genealogies of Christ
1400

Universal Gospel
1442

Salvation
3119

Elias (Elijah)
1112

Naaman
2505

Samaritans
3135-3136

Lepers
2110

Pharisees
3171

Publicans
2926

Gospel Universal
1442

Promises to Poor
2885

2:7 ...there was no room for them in the inn.

Bethlehem
408, 4344

When the Holy Family traveled from Nazareth to Bethlehem they probably spent a few nights on the road and had to stay in an inn. However, when they reached Bethlehem all of the inns were full; so they had to spend the night in the stable.

Garden of
Eden
1096

Hospitality
3398-3399

Overnight accommodations are as old as the human race. Travel actually began when Adam and Eve were driven out of the Garden of Eden. For thousands of years people traveled by cart, wagon, camel, donkey, horse or on foot. Overnight accommodations included stalls and frequently food for the animals as well as sleeping quarters for the people. These shelters were called a *khan*, or *caravanasary*. Usually they were a quadrangular court with a well in the center and with rooms and stalls around the open courtyard for man and animals. The living quarters, usually above the stalls, had no furniture. The traveler brought his own bed roll and did his cooking on an open fire in the court. Entrance to the inn was through a door in one of the four sides of the court. Thus the inn provided shelter from the elements and protection from thieves and robbers, a constant problem to the wayfarer. Joseph's brothers stayed in an inn like this (Ge. 42:27; 43:21).

2:8 And there were in the same country shepherds abiding in the field, keeping watch over their flock by night.

Shepherds
3268

Angels
Appear
144

The angels of the Lord appeared to the lowly shepherds and told them about the birth of a heavenly King in a Bethlehem stable. After they paid their respects to the new King they spread around the word of his coming.

2:39 ...they returned...to their own city Nazareth.

Nazareth
2571, 4416

Galilee
1384

The town of Nazareth was located in an isolated spot, in the hills of Galilee, well removed from the main caravan route between Damascus and Egypt. In fact, by the time that it became known that Jesus lived there, Nazareth had already acquired a political stigma; skeptics later asked, "Can any good thing come out of Nazareth?"

A perspective of the city of Nazareth, from the east.
The hometown of the Holy Family

2:52 And Jesus grew in wisdom and stature, and in favor with God and men. (NIV)

Little information is available on the early years of Jesus. The Gospel records tell us that Jesus was circumcised when he was eight days old and shortly thereafter he was presented in the temple (Lu. 2:21-22). When he was 12 years old he was taken to the temple. His parents were unable to find him afterward and returned to the temple, where he was debating with the learned doctors of the law. When they questioned their son, he said, "Wist ye not that I must be about my Father's business?" (Lu 2:49). Even then they did not fully comprehend his mission.

See also commentary on Mt. 13:55.

4:16 ...as his custom was, he went into the synagogue on the sabbath day...

There are fifty references to the synagogue in the NT, but the term occurs only once in the OT (Ps. 74:8). It seems there was no need for a synagogue during the time the Jews were able to worship in the temple. But when the Babylonians took the Jews into captivity they totally destroyed the temple which was not rebuilt until after Cyrus liberated the Jews. During the 70 years in captivity, when the Jews were deprived of using the temple, expediency led to the development of a functional worship center for their use during this period. The steps in the development of the synagogue are not known but it is known that the Jews brought it from Babylon.

It has been estimated that the Jews had over 1000 synagogues in the Mediterranean world by A.D. 70. After the destruction of the temple under Titus (A.D. 70) the synagogue and Jewish worship spread even more. In the synagogue can be recognized the transitional step from the temple to the modern church. Animal sacrifices ended with the destruction of the temple, and this meant that worship took on a new meaning in the Christian-Messiah movement (1 S. 15:22; Ps. 51:16,17; Ho. 6:6).

Since it was not used for sacrifices, the synagogue was used for exposition of the Law, and in time, prayers and preaching were added to the services. The synagogue became an all-purpose worship center, a place for prayer and Bible study as well as fellowship. It ranged in size from the small home unit to special structures where large numbers could gather. The house synagogue which could accommodate a family and a few friends may be compared to the "house churches" in the Christian era (Phm. 2).

Only ten heads of families or households were needed to organize a synagogue. Frequently synagogues were built by one man, as was the case of the centurion in Capernaum (Lu. 7:5). Later these synagogues provided preaching places for the traveling missionaries.

The church described in the Synoptic Gospels found the synagogue adequate, and within the framework of this institution the NT church developed. It seems evident from the NT that Jesus gave his disciples no formal prescription for the organization of the church. In the first days after Pentecost (commemoration of the Law at Sinai) believers had no thought of separating themselves from the religious life of Israel and the OT church, and

Tree of
Jesus' Life
4308
Christ's
Wisdom
3838
Christ's
Words
3885
Youthful
Piety
3966

Synagogues
3521-3523

Temples
3577-3581
3040, 4319

Babylon
329-331,
4338

Temple
Destroyed
3581

Sacrifices
3107-3108

Church
727

Missionaries
2381

Day of
Pentecost
2722

A Caravansary (inn). The remains of an inn at Acre, similar to the one still standing near Bethlehem.

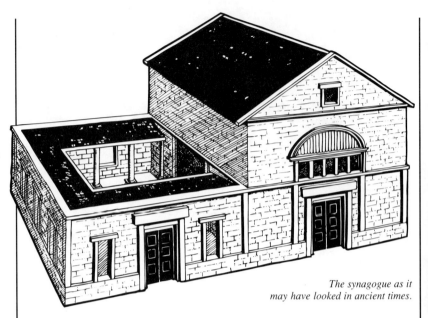

The synagogue as it may have looked in ancient times.

did not realize the need of any distinct organization of their own. The temple worship was still adhered to (Ac. 2:46; 3:1), though it was supplemented by apostolic teaching by prayer and fellowship, and by the breaking of bread (Ac. 2:42-46). For many years the NT church continued to use the physical agencies and edifices of the OT church. The synagogue was the place where the believers in Christ, the Messiah, assembled; the OT was their Bible.

The apostles maintained this close bond between the Jewish synagogue and the Christian church until resistance to the truth by the rejecting Jews led Christians to leave the term synagogue to them exclusively.[5] When the complete break came between the believers in Christ and those who rejected him, the Christians began to develop an institution which was more nearly suitable to the need of the combined Jewish-Gentile membership.

Organization was gradual, suggested by the needs as they arose. The oldest Christian meetings and meeting places were modeled on the pattern of the synagogue. Many years after the apostolic period "Christian Churches were built resembling synagogues, with the holy table placed where the chest containing the law had been; the desk and pulpit were the chief furniture in both. Common to both church and synagogue were the discipline (Mt. 18:17), excommunication (1 Co. 5:3-5), and the collection of alms (1 Co. 16:2)."[6]

The church today also has much in common with the synagogue. The similarity of the Christian church building to the synagogue gives credence to the affinity and common historical background of the two. In addition, each has a distinguishing mark: for the synagogue it is the Star of David, for the church it is the cross. Church services are quite similar to those in the synagogue: the congregation sang the Psalms, had responsive readings from the Scriptures, prayed, taught lessons from the Scriptures and their leaders preached sermons. Their hymn book, the Psalms, became the hymn book the church had for the first 1500 years of its history.

For more on the development of worship centers, see chart at Ac. 2:47.

4:24 "...no prophet is accepted in his hometown." (NIV)

Jesus referred to himself here as a prophet. For more on the meaning of "prophet" to the Jewish people, see commentary on Je. 1:5.

6:13 ...he called his disciples to him and chose twelve of them, whom he also designated apostles. (NIV)

Luke is the only Gospel writer who refers almost exclusively to the disciples as "apostles." For more on the terms "disciple" and "apostle," see commentary on Ac. 1:26.

11:32 The men of Nineveh...
repented at the preaching of Jonah... (NIV)

For more on the story of Jonah preaching to the city of Nineveh, see the book of Jonah and commentary there.

11:39 ...Now do ye Pharisees make clean the outside of the cup and the platter; but your inward part is full of ravening and wickedness.

The Pharisees of Jesus' day were the strict legalists, who concentrated on the letter of the law but neglected the spirit of the law. For more on this group of religious leaders, see commentary on Mk. 8:11; Jn. 8:44.

13:14 And the ruler of the synagogue answered with indignation, because that Jesus had healed on the sabbath day ..

A common target of the religious leaders against Jesus was his conduct on the Sabbath day. For more on the development of the Sabbath, see commentary on Ge. 2:3; De. 5:14; Ac. 1:12.

17:21 ...the kingdom of God is within you.

Luke uses the expression "kingdom of God" 33 times in his Gospel. Clearly it was central to the teaching of Jesus. For more on this expression and also its relationship to the "kingdom of heaven" phrase, see commentary on Mk. 1:15.

18:12 ...I give tithes of all that I possess.

The paying of tithes had its origin in the early part of Genesis. For more on the significance of this practice, see commentary on Ge. 14:20.

19:8 But Zacchaeus...said to the Lord, "...Here and now I give half of my possessions to the poor, and if I have cheated anybody out of anything, I will pay back four times the amount." (NIV)

The office of tax collector was so often open to extortion and cheating that the men who held them were treated with utmost scorn. If Zacchaeus is an example of tax abuse, the financial hardship of the common people must have been very severe. See commentary on Mt. 9:9.

20:27 Then came to him certain of the Sadducees, which deny that there is any resurrection; and they asked him...

The Sadducees were the extreme liberal philosophers of their day. Along with their denial of the resurrection, they also rejected belief in angels, demons, and evil spirits. For more on this group of religious leaders, see commentary on Mk. 12:18; Jn. 8:44.

24:31 And their eyes were opened, and they knew him; and he vanished out of their sight.

The appearances of God in Christ are clearly portrayed in the Gospel records as are the post resurrection appearances. On the Emmaus road the resurrected Jesus mysteriously appeared to two disciples as a man with whom they had normal conversation, but at the moment they recognized him, he disappeared from their sight. Many more examples of such divine manifestations are given throughout the Scriptures (see essay on "Theophanies in the OT," p. 72).

John

The Name

The Gospel of John derives its name from the apostle John (Gr., *Johanan*) which means "Jehovah has been gracious." The author does not mention his own name but refers to himself as the one "whom Jesus loved." Study affirms that John "was recognized as the one closest to Jesus. Five times he is spoken of as the disciple 'whom Jesus loved' (Jn. 13:23; 19:26; 20:2; 21:7,20). He must have been a man of rare qualities of character to thus attract the companionship of Jesus."[1]

Peter, James and John, who formed the inner circle of disciples, were frequently grouped together in a triumvirate (Mt. 17:1; 26:37; Mk. 5:37; 13:3; 14:33; Lu. 9:28). Of the three, John most nearly fits the "beloved" description. For some reason, John seems to be the disciple most devoted to the Lord; it was he who sat next to the Savior (Jn. 13:23).

Jesus called John a " 'Son of Thunder' (Mk. 3:17), which seems to imply that he had a...violent temper, but he brought this under control. The incident of forbidding the stranger to use the name of Christ in casting out demons (Mk. 9:38) and the desire to call down fire on the Samaritans (Lu. 9:54) are...(phases of) his nature."[2] Even though sometimes John was intolerant and vindictive, he was the disciple who would later say, "He that loveth his brother..." (1 Jn. 2:10). In spite of John's nature, he had an unquestioned devotion and love for his Master. Jesus must have recognized these qualities in John for "when Jesus was on the cross He committed Mary to the care of the 'beloved disciple.' His own brethren were not believers at this time."[3] John's desire was not for his own self-interest but to extol the Christ and his work.

Perhaps his change to a loving nature explains why he is referred to as "John the Beloved." Certainly love is an important subject in the Gospel of John and in his First Epistle.

Authorship and Date

From early Christian times John the apostle was credited with having written the Gospel of John. Early second-century writers, including Irenaeus (A.D. 125-202), Bishop of Lyons and author of *Against the Heresies;* Tertullian (A.D. 160-220), a Roman theologian and author; the theologian Saint Hippolytus (A.D. 160-223); and Origen (A.D. 185-254), a Greek philosopher and writer, ascribe authorship of the Gospel to John. Internal evidence supports John as being the author. John, who was a Jew, frequently quoted from the OT. His writings show that he was well acquainted with Jewish

Gospel of John
4265
John
1902

Peter
2746
James
1842

Samaritans
3135-3136
Brotherly Love
2200-2202
Mary
2259

Beloved Desciple
392
Love
2200-2209, 730, 4182-4183, 4124
Apostles
2080-2082

John
1902

Jewish
Feasts
1256-1261
Messianic
Prophecies
2890

Ephesus
1142, 4373
Elder
754, 2079

Christ's
Divinity
701-718

"Word"
Inspired
417
Divine
Inspiration
1774-1776

Mary
2259

The Seven
Churches
of Asia
762

John
1902

Zebedee
3984

Salome
3113
Cleopas
777

feasts (Jn. 7:2ff.), customs (Jn. 8:3ff.), and the Messianic prophecies (Jn. 1:41). John, upon hearing Jesus' call, readily accepted and became a follower (Mt. 4:21; Mk. 1:20).

Until the development of Form Criticism in the eighteenth and nine-teenth centuries, authorship of the books of the Bible was seldom ques-tioned. Since that time unresolved problems have developed in the Biblical field. A number of the books of the Bible have come under attack, especially the Pentateuch and the Gospels. In the case of the Fourth Gospel, some critics have relied upon an obscure statement by Papias, as quoted from Eusebius, and concluded that the author is a little-known presbyter in Ephesus by the name of John and not John the Apostle—since *presbyter* means "elder" and John the Beloved referred to himself as the "elder" (2 Jn. 1:1; 3 Jn. 1:1).[4]

This double reference to John is hardly a basis upon which to assume that the author of John's Gospel was an obscure presbyter in Ephesus (Ac. 19:4). Henry H. Halley says, "The same class of critics who deny the Virgin Birth of Jesus, His Deity, and His Bodily Resurrection…have inferred that the author was not John the Apostle but another John of Ephesus. This [con-clusion] would undermine the value of the book as a testimony to the Deity of Jesus."[5] George H. Turner says that "when both internal and external evidence is weighed, there seems no compelling reason to deny to John, the son of Zebedee, the honor of being its author."[6]

It is not known where John received his inspiration to write the Gospel of John; the only reference made to a revelation from God is the Apocalypse (Re. 1:9). The traditional place for his inspiration is on the Isle of Patmos where John had been banished in the reign of Domitian in about A.D. 95. Scholars are not in agreement as to whether John received his revelation at Patmos for all of his books (John, Revelation, 1,2,3 John); neither are they certain that he wrote any of them on the Isle. Some scholars think that he wrote all of his books at Ephesus, which has a strong traditional link with the Virgin Mary, who is supposed to have lived here with John in later years. The traditional house of the Virgin Mary is located on a hill at Panaja Kapoulu, a suburb of ancient Ephesus, and it is believed that she is buried there. In John's generation a strong church flourished in Ephesus. The congregation is listed as one of the Seven Churches of Asia Minor (Re. 2:1ff.).

It is generally assumed that the book was written about A.D. 90, about 30 years after the writing of the synoptic Gospels.

Background, Purpose, and Content

Biographical information about the apostle John is limited. He is men-tioned three times by Matthew, ten times by Mark, and seven times by Luke. John's family was apparently wealthy enough to have servants (Mk. 1:19-20). From Mt. 4:21 one learns that Zebedee was his father and apparently Salome was his mother (comparing Mt. 27:56 with Mk. 15:40 indicates that she was the wife of Zebedee). "It is further the opinion of many modern critics that Salome was the sister of Mary, the mother of Jesus, to whom reference is made in Jn. 19:25. The words admit, however, of another explanation, according to which they refer to the 'Mary, the wife of Cleophas' immedi-ately afterward mentioned. We can hardly regard the point settled, though the weight of modern criticism is decidedly in favor of the former view."[7]

The Gospel of John is selective in its choice of subject matter. Ninety percent of its content is different from the synoptic Gospels. John acknowledges that Jesus said and did many other things not included in his book (Jn. 21:25). John included many striking miracles (signs) which could inspire a belief that Jesus Christ was indeed God's Son. John clearly states that "these are written, that ye might believe that Jesus is the Christ, the Son of God; and that believing ye might have life through his name" (Jn. 20:31).

Differing from the writers of the synoptic Gospels, John recorded miracles, better designated as signs, of Jesus which were manifestations of his power and character. Jesus had:

1. Power over nature—changing water into wine (Jn. 2:1-11).
2. Power over disease—healing the nobleman's son (Jn. 4:46-54).
3. Power over the body—healing the lame and blind man (Jn. 5:1-9; 9:1-41).
4. Power over death—the raising of Lazarus and speaking of his own resurrection (Jn. 2:19; 10:18; 11:1-46).

Only the feeding of the 5,000 is common to all the gospel records.

John provides further evidence that the reader might believe that Jesus is the Christ; he spiritualizes water (Jn. 4:10; 7:38), light (8:12; 12:35), and bread (6:35,48) and gives special significance to such terms as world (3:16; 8:23), life (10:15; 14:6), know (3:11; 13:17), love (14:15,23; 15:12), truth (8:32; 16:13), and resurrection (5:29; 11:25).

At the time John wrote the Gospel (about A.D. 90) he was the only living apostle. The period of the synoptic Gospels was now past; 30 years had elapsed since the first three Gospel records had been written. The church, then about 50 years old, had been established in much of the Roman world.

Various heathen philosophies were pressing in upon the Christians. Among the views was that of the Gnostics, which was becoming a serious threat to the Church. Those who held the view of the Gnostics repudiated the OT and made Jesus merely a creature created by God, and his death only apparent. Concerning this philosophy Conrad Henry Muehlman writes that "The Gnostic god was a philosophical abstraction with mystical trimmings and redemption a divine Comedy. In Gnosticism the same god could not be both creator and judge and redeemer. If Gnosticism had triumphed, Christianity would have become just another Graeco-Roman mystery religion."[8] Another writer termed Christian Gnosticism the "acute Hellenization of Christianity."[9]

Greek philosophy, coupled with other aspects of Hellenism, had made deep inroads among the Jews of the Diaspora and had become the dominant way of life among the Jews. Greek had become the language of the Jews, and with the Greek language had come Greek influence. John challenged the encroaching Gnosticism and Hellenization of the Jews. The purpose of 1 John, and one purpose of the Gospel of John, was to combat error in the Christian church—especially, in 1 John, the heresy of Gnosticism.

To break through the philosophical facade of the Hellenized community, John interpreted Christianity by identifying Christ with the well-known and understood term *logos,* a word that was "as old as the Greek language. It was first introduced by Heraclitus of Ephesus, in the 5th century B.C. into a circle of philosophical ideas as a principle of cosmic interpretation."[10]

According to Heraclitus,

Philosophic wisdom…apprehends that the total process of cosmic being is subjected to the regulative control of an agency to which…the logos technique accounted for the orderliness of nature. He further postulated that change, if not chaos, must conform to fixed patterns; and that…therefore, order, law, measure and predictability, were formulations of cosmic transformations going on according to logos, thus the permanence of all things preserved, because all things observe their own measure.[11]

The Greek concept of the logos did not contain the idea of a transcendent God but only an imminent law or reason or a creativity responsible for the things as seen. There was resident in the Greek understanding a recognition that the world was a unity and "that basic to all human institutions is a spiritual, all-pervasive principle with which man must deal, i.e., the *logos*."[12] There is a sense in which the Greek concept of the logos is in accord with the fourth Gospel but there is a difference.

At this point John removed the term logos from the realm of principle and gave it Life and Personality and made of it a Person. In the English Bible (Jn. 1:1ff.) this term, meaning the "Living Word" or Christ, is used 22 times in the Gospel of John.

In identifying the logos as Christ, John did for the Hellenized Jews what Paul did for the Athenians when he identified their "unknown god" as Jesus Christ (Ac. 17:22-31). John says in substance that the "logos and God are two appellations of one single divine reality."[13]

Thus John breathes life and Christological meaning into a term that had heretofore been a philosophical abstraction.

Nature's
Lessons
4075

Creator
884

Spirit of
Man
2242

Christ the
"Word"
700

Names of
Christ
3632

1:29 …John seeth Jesus coming unto him, and saith, Behold the Lamb of God, which taketh away the sin of the world.

Lamb of God
3365

Jesus was mentioned only three times before John presented him at the Jordan River: at his birth (Lu. 2:1-7); at his presentation in the temple (Lu. 2:22-24); at his visit to the temple when he was twelve (Lu. 2:41-50).

When John saw Jesus he immediately identified the purpose of Jesus' life on earth — to offer himself as a sacrifice for the sins of mankind. Only through divine revelation could John have made this statement, that otherwise had no logical basis. Jesus was "the Lamb slain from the foundation of the world" (Re. 13:8).

Christ's Sacrifice
3366

The innocent lamb was sacrificed for the guilt of others.

3:3 …Except a man be born again, he cannot see the kingdom of God.

New Birth
2154
New Man
2582

The concept of the new birth is often linked to this verse. But is it unique to the New Testament? In the instances where the new birth comes into focus it is well to remember that the NT era did not begin until after Christ's crucifixion and thus the examples given in the Synoptic period took place in the OT era. The essay following takes up this subject in depth. See also the essay, "The Mechanics of Salvation in the OT Period," pp. 67-69. For the term "kingdom of God," see commentary on Mk. 1:15.

Spiritual Kingdom
2007-2013

Jacob's Well, where Christ spoke to the Samaritan woman (Jn. 4:6). The well is deep and the water cool and refreshing.

The Nature of the New Birth: Is it Unique to the NT?

An important question revolves around the problem of personal salvation in the OT. Is one to say that the just man not only walked in the faith of a future fulfillment of the promise and a future redemption, but also rejoiced in the present possession of salvation, and had the assurance that his sins were forgiven?

From the evidence gathered in the OT comes the conclusion that people enjoyed salvation before Christ's incarnation. It is assumed that the disciples and others were saved men before the crucifixion. Both the OT and NT teach and illustrate that all individuals experience divine forgiveness who have repented of their sins and who have turned to God in saving faith (Eze. 43:27; Ac. 10:34-36). David, as an individual, testified to personal forgiveness and salvation when he said, "Blessed is he whose transgression is forgiven, whose sin is covered" (Ps. 32:1). On another occasion the psalmist said: "There is forgiveness with thee" (Ps. 130:4; cf. Is. 55:7).

> Universal Call
> 1791

Many other instances are given in the OT of individuals repenting and being restored to God's favor (2 K. 22:19). "The sin of Israel is recognized as the sin of the individual, which can be removed only by individual repentance and cleansing. This is best seen from the stirring appeals of the prophets of the exile...This cannot be understood otherwise than as a turning of the individual to the Lord."[14]

There was no merit in the animal sacrifice brought by the individual worshiper, for "it is not possible that the blood of bulls and of goats should take away sins" (He. 10:4). It was only as the sacrifice symbolized and testified to faith in the blood of God's "Lamb" that sins were remitted. The "interposition of divine grace" is represented under the figure of a ceremonial washing and sprinkling from all iniquity and sin (Is. 1:18). Proselytes embracing Judaism had to repent and submit to the same ritual before they could be fully received into the covenant of Israel.

> Justification by Faith
> 1203,1985

In the teachings of our Lord, the concept of the "new birth" or regeneration is resident in the OT; the teaching is clear at this point and is graphically asserted by Jesus Christ in his conversation with Nicodemus (Jn. 3:1-21), "a man of the Pharisees... a ruler of the Jews." He was well versed in the Talmud and the Midrash as well as other great rabbinical teachings. Above all, he was a student of the Scriptures; and yet, despite this fact, Nicodemus was apparently ignorant of the OT teachings on "the new birth." He is a type of the church member who has not been regenerated, that is, "born again." Jesus takes this occasion to chide Nicodemus for his ignorance. "Art thou a master of Israel, and knowest not these things?" (Jn. 3:10). Adam Clarke paraphrases this verse thus: "Hast thou taken upon thee to guide the blind into the way of truth; and yet knowest not that truth thyself? Dost thou command proselytes to be baptized with water as an emblem of a new birth; and art thou unacquainted with the cause, necessity, nature, and effects of that new birth?"[15] Here Jesus Christ is speaking about a divine necessity existing before the crucifixion was actually carried out. Nicodemus could not become a member in the "kingdom" until he had experienced salvation, namely, the "new birth." The incarna-

> Regeneration
> 2154

tion did not in any way change the conditions by which believers entered the "congregation of the righteous" (Ps. 1:5; see also Eze. 11:19-20).

New Birth
2154

Professor Sauer says,

The whole pre-Christian revelation of salvation divides into two chief sections: the covenant of promise and the covenant of law—the sinner is to be redeemed, and to this end renewal and new-birth are needful. But this new-birth has man's conversion as a presupposition, and conversion is twofold: a turning from and a turning to, a "No" to ourselves and a "Yes" to God, or as the NT puts it, repentance and faith. Only here is revealed…the true meaning of the OT histories: throughout centuries God spoke the word "faith" into the history of salvation, this is the meaning of the covenant with Abraham. Through two thousand years it was an education in faith. Throughout centuries God spoke the word "repent" into the history of salvation; this is the meaning of the law of Moses. Through one thousand, five hundred years it was an education in repentance. "Repent" and "believe" the gospel (Mk. 1:15) says Christ…This is the NT purpose of the OT.[16]

Repentance
2706-2710

People were lost in "trespasses and sins" from the day the first sin was committed. They all, without exception, needed to be saved—to be "born again." Jesus Christ came to "seek and to save that which was lost" (Lu. 19:10), but he had always been seeking to save the lost (Ga. 4:4-5). Christ came in the person of Jesus to reveal God the Father more clearly, and to die on the cross. The principle of "new birth" is reflected in the story of the prodigal son; he is declared to have been "dead" and to be "alive again" (Lu. 15:24).[17]

The teaching on the "new birth" in the NT reiterates a truth that is, was, and always will be, effective; it is timeless. Moreover, every sermon and doctrine in the NT is initiated by the Spirit of God. Inspiration for the two Testaments came from a common source (2 Ti . 3:16; 1 Pe. 1:10-11). Paul distinctly reaffirms the basic OT concept that a new life is in store for those who have been spiritually dead; that at conversion a spiritual resurrection takes place. This regeneration causes a complete revolution in man. He has thereby passed from under the law of sin and death and has come under 'the law of the Spirit of life in Christ Jesus' (Ro. 8:2). The change is so radical that it is possible now to speak of a 'new creation,' of a 'new man,' that 'after God is created in righteousness and true holiness' (Ep. 4:24) and of 'the new man which is renewed in knowledge after the image of Him that created him' (Col. 3:10) and the image to which the sinner in the NT is renewed is the image of the OT God.[18]

New Creature
2582

To Paul, regeneration was a personal knowledge of God's Christ whereby the sinner acquired the imprint of the divine nature. Peter affirms, through OT phraseology, that by the "new birth," believers become "a chosen generation, a royal priesthood, an holy nation, a peculiar people" (1 Pe. 2:9). Behind the race, the priesthood, the holy nation, stand the redeemed ones—the born-again believers who constitute the church in every age. According to popular interpretation, the "new birth" is associated with the post-crucifixion period, but it must be pointed out that people were redeemed, that is, people were "born again" before Jesus Christ was crucified. Jesus' encounter with Nicodemus took place during the OT period. A never-changing God cannot have a double standard, one for the OT and another for the NT. Some examples are given of people who were con-

God, Immutability
2480

verted before the crucifixion.

1. In his high-priestly prayer Jesus Christ recognized the redeemed nature of his followers when he said, "I have given unto them the words which thou gavest me; and they have received them, and have known surely that I came out from thee, and they have believed that thou didst send me. I pray for them: I pray not for the world, but for them which thou hast given me; for they are thine" (Jn. 17:8-9). The Redeemer follows this testimony by saying: "Those that thou gavest me I have kept, and none of them is lost, but the son of perdition" (Jn. 17:12), and here the apostasy of Judas is verified. Eleven of the original twelve were still faithful; one had, by transgression, fallen from the faith (Ac. 1:25).

2. There can be no doubt but that Zaccheus was converted, i.e., born again, the day Christ visited him. The Scriptures clearly provide the evidence: "Jesus said unto him, This day is salvation come to this house" (Lu. 19:9). Following the Master's visit, Zaccheus brought forth works meet for repentance. The fruits of his life gave witness that he had experienced a "new birth;" he had come to a place in his life where old things had passed

Salvation
3116-3123

away and all things had become new (Lu. 19:1ff.).

3. To those already considered can be added the "many [that] believed in his name" (Jn. 2:23), "the Samaritans of that city [who] believed" (Jn. 4:39), "the man [that] believed the word that Jesus had spoken" (Jn. 4:50), "many of the people [that] believed on him" (Jn. 7:31), and the "many [that] believed on him there" (Jn. 10:42), as well as Peter, the profane fisherman, whose shadow later healed others (Mt. 26:74; Ac. 5:15-16).

The Master is explicit and insistent upon sinners being genuinely converted. "Verily I say unto you, Except ye be converted, and become as little children, ye shall not enter into the kingdom of heaven" (Mt. 18:3). Conversion has always been a prerequisite for membership in the living church.

Conversion
834-836

The statement, "He that hath the Son hath life; and he that hath not the Son of God hath not life" (1 Jn. 5:12), applies to all time. "Ye must be born again" (Jn. 3:7) is the irrevocable formula whereby sinful man is translated from death to eternal life. This divine truth, the "new birth," has been forever in effect for both the Jew and Gentile alike (Ro. 15:8-12).

See the essay, "The Mechanics of Salvation in the OT Period," pp. 67-69.

4:9 …For Jews do not associate with Samaritans. (NIV)

Jews believed that the Samaritans were "unclean," a race that was to be avoided and despised. However, nowhere in the Bible, in either of the Testaments, is there room for racial exaltation and discrimination. God has no favorites (Ac. 10:34-36), but wants everyone to be saved (1 Ti. 2:4). For more on the subject of Jew and Gentile in both the OT and NT, see commentary on Ac. 10:34-35.

Impartiality of God
1979-1980
Universal Call
1791

8:11 "Neither do I condemn you," Jesus declared…(NIV)

Some Christians have raised questions of OT/NT unity concerning the incident of the "woman taken in adultery" (Jn. 8:3). After the men had made their accusation and Jesus had written in the sand, no one remained to press charges against her. Jesus said, "Neither do I condemn thee: go, and sin no more" (Jn. 8:11). God's mercy and grace can always be extended to the penitent sinner, even when he must be punished. Salvation sometimes comes to men before they are sent to, or while they are in, prison. Even those who have been given the death penalty can receive forgiveness from God and salvation before they die. This is the beauty of grace; regardless of how sinful a person has been, by repentance and faith he can receive instant pardon from God. On this point the OT is clear: those who repent are promised escape from God's judgment (2 Chr. 7:14; Is. 55:7; Eze. 18:21). The entire book of Judges gives examples of Israel being forgiven after the people repented.

Adultery
1662
Forsake Sin
3346
Promises to the Penitent
2707
Sin Forgiven
3345
Forgiveness, Human
1315-1316

When Jesus spoke about men forgiving one another, he was referring to man-to-man interrelationships. God forgives anyone who repents; man is to do likewise, even to the extent of forgiving "seventy times seven" (Mt. 18:21-22; see also Mk. 11:25; Lu. 17:4; Ep. 4:32; Col. 3:13; Jona. 3:5-10).

Important in the case of the woman taken in adultery is the question of motive on the part of the men who brought the woman to Jesus. The legal issue (their bringing only the woman) suggests that their paramount concern may not have been what the woman had done; their motive was evidently to trick Jesus into an answer that would conflict with the law of Moses. If they accomplished this, they could accuse Jesus of blasphemy which was punishable by death (Le. 24:16). In any case they certainly had no legal authority to take the woman to Jesus for a crime which was punishable by death, because Jesus was not a civil judge nor did he claim to be. He always insisted that citizens should give to Caesar (civil law) that which was Caesar's (Mt. 22:21; see also Jn. 18:36). If the men truly had had concern for the law, they would have taken both the man and the woman to a duly appointed magistrate.

Mosaic Law
949
Blasphemy
473
Citizen's Duties
2525

The conclusion of the events surrounding this woman illustrates divine mercy and forgiveness, but the outcome did not waive the punishment which theocratic law (government by God) demanded for this particular offense. Under the circumstances the charges were so clearly one-sided that legal action was impracticable. Law is intended to be inherently fair and just; the woman could not be punished alone (Le. 20:10). Under modern law, the case would have been dismissed on legal technical grounds arising from the absence of the other offender. However, irrespective of legal technicalities, when one violates moral law, there are consequences within the human conscience. Certainly the woman experienced psychological and sociological sufferings. The same can be assumed for the man who probably was living in constant fear that he too might be taken into custody at any time.

Punishment of Sin
3047-3048
Misery of Sinners
788

8:12 ...I am the light of the world: he that followeth me shall not walk in darkness, but shall have the light of life.

The theme of light and darkness is constant throughout the Scriptures. From "Let there be light," the first event of creation in Ge. 1, to "there shall be no night there," the description of the city of God in Re. 22, the Bible speaks of light, both physical and spiritual. Light is essential to existence, and many of the figures used in the Bible in relation to God are figures of light. For more on the subject, see commentary on Ex. 25:31, where the golden candlestick placed in the tabernacle is shown to symbolize Christ, the light of the world.

8:44 You [religious leaders] belong to your father, the devil...(NIV)

In Jesus' day religious affairs were no longer controlled by true Jehovah worshipers; the priests, scribes, Pharisees, and other officials possessed the key to the temple precincts, but they were impostors and counterfeits.

God has never been dependent upon any visible ecclesiastical organization for preserving the faith, and this was certainly the case in the NT era. Interesting information comes, at this point, from the Dead Sea Scrolls. *The Manual of Discipline* was revered by the Sect of the Covenant at Qumran, an intensely separatistic sect; they rigidly avoided the "Sons of Darkness," contact with whom meant defilement and impurity. In *The Manual of Discipline* the expression "to be separated from all unrighteous men" (or "men of error") appears repeatedly (1 QS V:1,a,10; VIII:13, etc.).[19]

It is quite probable that these faithful believers, referred to at times as the "children of the prophets" (Ac. 3:25), withdrew from the formal temple precincts to escape the evil threats of the corrupt leaders whom they opposed and to establish themselves in wilderness caves and dens so that the "faith which was once delivered unto the saints" (Jude 3) could be preserved and that a way might be prepared for the coming of the Christ-Messiah (see commentary on pp. 308-315). Millar Burrows adds this sidelight: "The moral ideals of the covenant members at Qumran are much like those of similar monastic groups in other religions, but quite unlike those of orthodox Judaism at many points. They are the ideals of a group that has withdrawn from the world into a separate life or rigid discipline and purity, going into the desert to prepare the way of the Lord by the study of the Law."[20]

Asceticism and mysticism, represented by purely Jewish sects, were active in the century before the incarnation.[21]

Christ the Light
2168
Light
2165-2175

Candlestick
637

Corrupt Priests
2102
Unfaithful Ministers
2098

Separation
288-290
False Prophets
2100
God's People
2723

Messianic Hope
4186

Purity
1759
Deserts
978-979

Qumran Caves

Little is known about the earthly life of our Lord from age twelve until he assumed his public ministry, and nothing specific is said about the Lord's contact with the Essenes, but it is evident that his ministry and teaching were closely related to this pious "holiness group". It is certainly clear that he divorced himself completely from the Pharisee/Sadducee system of legalistic Judaism.

In certain historical periods "the faith which was once delivered unto the saints" (Jude 3) was severely resisted, but God has never been without a witness. At times "the faith" has made tactical retreats and has made its abode with small groups and sects, but it has always revived and flowered into revival movements in some localities. In the political world, the democratic ideal has at times been lost as far as the visible outline was concerned, but it continued to "glow" in the hearts and minds of the common people, later to manifest itself again, perhaps under a new name. So it has been with the "faith" throughout history.

The entire ecclesiastical hierarchy of Pharisee/Sadducee Judaism of the Savior's day stood condemned before God. Professing themselves to be the servants of God, they were instead administrators of murder. Instead of accepting the Lord, in the person of Jesus, they rejected him, the "chief cornerstone" (Ac. 4:10-12). Instead of serving the church, these "false prophets" served the "synagogue of Satan" (Re. 2:9). A further inquiry might be made relative to the identity of these apostles of evil. Did Christ call them by name? Jesus identified these "false prophets" and called them the "children of the devil" (Jn. 8:44-47; see also Mt. 23). The Gospels indicate that these servants of Satan were none other than the scribes, the Pharisees, the Sadducees, the chief priests, the elders, and the rulers who were in charge of the religious program in the temple.

Their interest in religion was limited mainly to use as a cloak behind which to hide their evil designs. Sin, to them, became a lucrative business. The poor were oppressed and driven into slavery; dishonest trading and bribery were common; public and private virtue were almost forgotten; the courts of justice were notorious; immoralities were practiced without shame or compunction. The appetites of the greedy temple authorities were such that they made the house of God "a den of thieves" (Mt. 21:13, see also Mt. 23). However, a few of these leaders did accept Christ (Jn. 3:1; Ac. 26:5; 15:5).

Through faith the "congregation of the saints" (Ps. 89:5), the church, stood up under persecution and abuse by these "children of the devil" (1 Jn. 3:10), i.e., the counterfeit church (see chart on p. 66; see also commentary on Re. 2:9). The faithful believers were subjected to disgrace and indignity as indicated in Hebrews (11:37-40). Jesus provided evaluation of the religious leaders as follows:

1. In addressing the scribes and Pharisees in Jerusalem, Christ called to mind the fact that Isaiah had pronounced condemnation upon the religious leaders of his day. The Lord then applied this condemnation to their descendants: "This people draweth nigh unto me with their mouth, and honoureth me with their lips; but their heart is far from me. But in vain they do worship me, teaching for doctrines the commandments of men" (Mt. 15:8-9). Isaiah had referred to this group as an "abominable branch" (Is.

Tree of Jesus' Life	**4308**
Faith	**1201-1213**
Testimony	**3599-3605**
Pharisees	**3171**
Sadducees	**3172**
Christ Rejected	**2965**
Cornerstone	**692**
False Profession	**2989**
Children of the Devil	**3063**
Avarice	**2131-2132**
Temple Despoiled	**3040**
Congregation	**820-821**
Martyrdom	**3487-3488**
Isaiah	**1803**
Traditions of Men	**3652**

14:19); "rebellious children" (Is. 30:1; see also 30:9). Teaching traditions of men instead of divine truth has always been characteristic of false prophets.

False
Prophets
2100
Spiritual
Blindness
500

2. Jesus advised the people to ignore the temple authorities because they did not discern spiritual issues. Said Jesus: "Let them alone: they be blind leaders of the blind. And if the blind lead the blind, both shall fall into the ditch" (Mt. 15:14). Certainly no blind man wants another blind man to lead him across the street, nor does one sinner care to have another sinner attempt to lead him into the way of salvation.

Hypocrites
2995

3. On another occasion the Pharisees and the Sadducees came to tempt Jesus with their trick questions, whereupon Jesus called them "hypocrites" (Mt. 16:1-3).

Take Heed
1799
Pharisaism
2750

4. The people were warned against the leaders: "Take heed and beware of the leaven of the Pharisees and of the Sadducees" (Mt. 16:6). By leaven, Christ meant the "traditions of the elders" as opposed to the doctrines of God. As leaven has a tendency to permeate the dough, so these false teachings endangered the entire religious body.

Christ's
Authority
710
Divinity
Challenged
4149

5. Evidence of corruption and perversion within the ranks of the priests and elders was seen in the manner in which they challenged the authority of Christ (Mt. 21:23). The fact that they did not recognize the Savior as the Son of God showed their ignorance of the Father (Jn. 8:19).

Christ
Defamed
4137
Stumbling
Blocks
1565
Sanctimony
2991
Fools
3853

6. The demon-possessed nature of these leaders is further shown in the efforts of the chief priests and Pharisees to lay hand on the Savior in order to harm him, even to kill him.

7. To further evaluate the status of the temple authorities the following facts should be considered: Jesus called the scribes and Pharisees "stumbling blocks" to the kingdom of heaven; they refused to go in, and they prevented others from so doing (Mt. 23:13). They devoured widows' houses (literally robbed the widow of her home and living) and then hid behind long sanctimonious prayers in public places (Mt. 23:14). This same group took great pains to convert the heathen to their way of life which made each of them "twofold more the child of hell" (Mt. 23:15). These false teachers were referred to as fools who pervert God's Word by their false teachings regarding the temple and the altar (Mt. 23:16-18).

Self-
righteous-
ness
3219-3220
Innocent
Blood
513
Serpents
3238-3239

The Pharisees, intoxicated with their own self-righteousness, boasted: "If we had been in the days of our fathers , we would not have been partakers with them in the blood of the prophets" (Mt. 23:30). But Jesus countered their claim: "Wherefore ye be witnesses unto yourselves, that ye are the children of them which killed the prophets" (Mt. 23:31). By their deeds and attitudes they witnessed to their true nature. Jesus then called them "serpents" and "vipers," the key symbol of sin, and asked the question: "How can ye escape the damnation of hell?" (Mt. 23:33). He next described prophetically the persecution and murder to which they would give themselves in their conflict with God's righteous forces (Mt. 23:34ff.). Our Lord gave the scribes and Pharisees a preview of their future wickedness: "...Behold, I send unto you prophets, and wise men, and scribes: and some of them ye shall kill and crucify; and some of them shall ye scourge in your synagogues, and persecute them from city to city: that upon you may come all the righteous blood shed upon the earth, from the blood of righteous Abel unto the blood of Zacharias son of Barachias, whom ye slew between the temple and the altar" (Mt. 23:34-35).

Future
State of the
Wicked
1368-1370
Murder
2450

But this is only part of the evidence of their wrong doing; "Now the chief priests, and elders, and all the council, sought false witness against Jesus, to put him to death" (Mt. 26:59). This same crowd violated their own law by holding our Savior's trial at night. The chief priests and elders used methods of bribery and political intrigue and "persuaded the multitude" that they should ask for the release of Barabbas rather than Jesus (Mt. 27:20).

Finally the chief priests, scribes, and elders mocked him as he died on the cross (Mt. 27:42), revealing an attitude totally unlike the spirit of the Beatitudes, as given by the Master: "Blessed are the merciful" (Mt. 5:7). The temple authorities, by their rejection of Christ, evidenced the fact that they did not know the Father and that the love of God was not in their hearts (Jn. 8:19ff.). The leaders made much of their faith in Moses, but Jesus told them that they stood condemned by Moses (Jn. 5:45-46). If they had been true spiritual descendants of Moses, they would have accepted Christ as the Messiah. He said to them: "For had ye believed Moses, ye would have believed me: for he wrote of me" (Jn. 5:46).

So perverted and blind to spiritual truth were the temple rulers that they rebuked some of their own number for believing in Christ. Said they, "Are ye also deceived?" (Jn. 7:47). When the officers came back empty-handed from their mission to take Christ, the authorities asked: "Have any of the rulers or of the Pharisees believed on him?" (Jn. 7:48). This is a familiar oriental custom, making a strong affirmative statement in the form of a question. The obvious inference is that few if any of the temple rulers or the Pharisees had openly professed belief in Christ. By their denial of him as the Christ-Messiah they gave testimony that their hearts were not right. Jesus told these "Satanic apostles" that they would die in their sins (Jn. 8:24). The leaders of the temple said much about Abraham being their father, but Jesus challenged them: "...If ye were Abraham's children, ye would do the works of Abraham. But now ye seek to kill me, a man that hath told you the truth, which I have heard of God: this did not Abraham" (Jn. 8:39-40). It is true, they were physical descend-ants of Abraham but they were not his spiritual descendants (see Ro. 2:28-29). Instead of being children of God they were children of the devil (Jn. 8:44; 1 Jn. 3:10).

The leaders continued to boast that they had "one Father, even God" (Jn. 8:41), but the Master said to them: "...If God were your Father, ye would love me: for I proceeded forth and came from God; neither came I of myself, but he sent me. Why do ye not understand my speech? even because ye cannot hear my word" (Jn. 8:42-43; Mt. 11:27).

In a final address Jesus made the indictment in these words; "Ye are of your father the devil, and the lusts of your father ye will do. He was a murderer from the beginning, and abode not in the truth, because there is no truth in him" (Jn. 8:44). Jesus then asked the question of them: "Which of you convinceth me of sin? And if I say the truth, why do ye not believe me?" (Jn. 8:46). Jesus then gave the answer: "He that is of God heareth God's words: ye therefore hear them not, because ye are not of God" (Jn. 8:47).

William Morehead states that "When Pharisaism, with its rigid legal-ism, with its intolerable burdens, became dominant, all liberty of worship and spontaneous service largely disappeared. The religious life of Israel stiffened into a dreadful monotony."[22]

False Witness **3856-3857**
Barabbas **339**
Christ Mocked **3493**
Christ Rejected **2965**
Ignorance of God **2038**
Christ Unknown **2039**
Contempt **827**
Pharisees **3171**

Denial of Christ **815**
Jewish Pride **1725**
Abraham **15, 4290**
Children of God **742**
Christ Divine **701**
Satan's Work **3151**

Children of the Devil **3063**
Unbelief **1221**

Pharisaism **2750**

Israel
1809-1811
Spiritual
Quickening
315
Abraham,
Father of
the Faithful
15
Ignorance
Concerning
Christ
2039
False
Teachers
2101
Corrupt
Priests
2102
Deceivers
3707
Moses
2420-2421

This certainly is a serious indictment of those who were clad in ecclesiastical garb; it has been noted that Jesus did not identify the natural descendants of Abraham (see Ro. 2:28-29) as the "Israel of God" (Ga. 6:16). The Jews became members in the "household of faith" (Ga. 6:10) only when they accepted Christ as their Lord; only then did they become "quickened" by the Spirit (Ep. 2:5; see Jn. 5:21) and have a spiritual relationship with Abraham (Ga. 3:7). In reference to the "enemy of all righteousness" (Ac. 13:10) Paul attested the union of Elymas, the sorcerer, and the devil.

The Pharisees expressed ignorance and unbelief of the work and mission of Christ. Without accepting Jesus they could not have known the Father (Mt. 11:27; see also Ac. 3:14-15,17). It is evident that the scribes, Pharisees, Sadducees, and other false ecclesiastical leaders are types and examples of which each generation has its counterpart (see De. 13:1-3; Je. 14:14; Mt. 7:15; 24:4-5,11,24; Mk. 13:5; Lu. 21:8; 2 Pe. 2:1-3). Abel is referred to as a righteous prophet who was slain by Cain (Lu. 11:50-51), a type of all succeeding "enemies of the cross" (Ph. 3:18).

For more on the Pharisees, see commentary on Mk. 8:11. For more on the Sadducees, see commentary on Mk. 12:18. For more on the counterfeit church, see commentary on Re. 2:9.

8:58 "...before Abraham was born, I am!" (NIV)

On the occasion of God's commissioning Moses to deliver the "children of Israel" from Egypt, Moses asked God how he should respond to the Hebrews when they asked the name of the God who had sent him. God told Moses to answer: "I AM hath sent me unto you" (Ex. 3:14).

"I AM"s of
Christ
4166

Fulfillment
of
Prophecy
2892

Appear-
ances of
God
206

Jesus, in addressing the Jews, related himself to and identified himself as "I am." Here Jesus was clearly saying that he was the One who appeared to Moses on the backside of Mount Horeb (Ex. 3:1-2; Jn. 8:58; see also Re. 1:18). This interpretation is strengthened by the reaction it drew from the Temple leaders. They were ready to stone Jesus for claiming that he was the "I am," or God (Jn. 8:58-59).

"In the Gospels and throughout the NT, Jesus appears as the goal of OT revelation and the point to which all providential development tended. Paul said, [He came] in 'the fulness of time' (Ga. 4:4). It has often been shown in history how politically, intellectually, and morally everything in the Graeco-Roman world was ready for such a universal religion as Jesus brought into it."[23]

See also the commentary on Ex. 3:14-15 and the essay "Theophanies in the Old Testament," pp. 72-73.

10:22 Then came the Feast of Dedication at Jerusalem...(NIV)

The Feast of Dedication began on the New Moon on the twenty-fifth day of Chislev, the ninth sacred month, which came in late November and/or early December, and continued for eight days. In the ceremony the people carried torches or candles which they put in homes and places of worship; hence the title, Feast of Lights. It commemorated the purification of the temple and the restoration of the altar in the temple by Judas Maccabaeus in 165 B.C. The historical source is described in one of the Apocryphal books, Maccabees 4:52-59. Josephus, the historian, makes mention of this feast

(Ant. XII. 7.7). This Feast of Lights was similar to the Feast of Tabernacles, celebrated by the carrying of boughs, palms, and branches and the singing of the Psalms. The use of lights during the Hanukkah celebration has always been a significant ritual in the homes, synagogues, and streets of Palestine. The feast is observed near the time when Christians are celebrating Christmas with lights on the tree.[24]

Feast of Tabernacles **1259**

11:43 ...he cried with a loud voice, Lazarus, come forth.

Raising Lazarus shook the very foundations of the temple hierarchy. Many people were converted to faith in Jesus as the Messiah; many of them called him their King. Both the religious and political implications created conditions which made the Sanhedrin decide to put Jesus to death.

Resurrections **2409** Sanhedrin **862**

16:13 ...when he, the Spirit of truth, comes, he will guide you into all truth... (NIV)

How does the Holy Spirit of the New Testament relate to the Spirit of the Old Testament? Is their nature and function the same? The following essay addresses these questions.

Spirit of Truth **1613** Holy Spirit, O.T. Ref. to **1604**

Lazarus' Tomb. The traditional tomb in Bethany where Jesus called Lazarus back to life.

The Work of the Holy Spirit in the Old and New Testaments

It can be assumed that God the Creator, Yahweh the Lord, and Ruach the Spirit of God are the "Three in One" in the OT. The Spirit of God in the OT is the Holy Spirit in the New; he reveals divine truth in both Testaments. Peter definitely attributes the inspiration of the OT to the Holy Spirit (2 Pe. 1:21).

Trinity
3694

A study of the work and nature of the Holy Spirit's work shows that his coming upon persons in the OT was limited to specially selected leaders such as prophets, priests, priestesses, and kings (Jud. 6:34; 1 S. 10:10), and "it is in the prophetic period that He becomes the organ of the communication of God's thoughts to men."[25]

Holy Spirit
1601-1614

It is only through the Spirit that divine revelation penetrates the heart and mind of man. The Spirit is represented as proceeding from the Lord and imparted by him, to a person, to be bestowed upon others (Nu. 11:17,25). A person can also lose the Spirit as Saul did (1 S. 16:14). In Isaiah the Israelites "rebelled, and vexed his Holy Spirit" (Is. 63:10). It is evident that as the Holy Spirit progressively revealed himself, the latter forms of his revelation are more distinct, appearing in a more personal way after the founding of the theocracy.

Holy Spirit
Inspires Prophets
1774

Dr. Gustave Oehler says that the Holy Spirit unfolds himself in proportion as the outward theophany disappears (see essay on "Theophanies in the Old Testament," pp. 72-73) and that it is the same with the course of revelation in the NT, especially since "Christophanies continued for some time after the ascension of our Lord [and] then disappeared and made room for the revelation of the Lord in the inwardness of the Spirit."[26] In the OT the Spirit's work in the divine kingdom is rather that of endowing the organs of the theocracy (government under God) with the gifts required for their calling, and these gifts of office in the OT are similar to the gifts of grace in the NT (1 Co. 14:12ff.).

Divine Gifts
485-486

The Spirit of God bestowed upon Moses and the seventy elders the gift of divine wisdom in guiding the people (Nu. 11:17ff.); which was given also to Joshua (De. 34:9), the judges (Jud. 6:34), and the kings (1 K. 3:12). Obviously this work is parallel to the work of the Spirit as promised by Jesus Christ. "When he, the Spirit of truth, is come, he will guide you into all truth...and he will shew you things to come" (Jn. 16:13). It would appear from this evidence that the full revelation of the Trinity and the Holy Spirit in particular in the New Testament is foreshadowed by the restrained work of the Spirit through the OT prophets, priests, and kings.

Spirit of Truth
1613

> The NT Church of the future...is founded upon the outpouring of the spirit upon all [saved] flesh (Jn. 12:28ff.)... The direct personal communication with God which is effected by the Spirit, and which afforded the prophets an insight into the divine counsels, is to become the possession of all members of the Church (Nu. 11:29). The impartation of the Holy Spirit, besides communicating a vital knowledge of God, purifies the heart and creates a readiness to fulfill the Divine Will (Eze. 36:25-27)... thus the end of the OT educational work is attained; the holy people of God are also a...holy church.[27]

Holy Spirit, Filling
Saints
1125

See also commentary on De. 6:4.

Acts

The Name

The book of Acts has had a variety of names: " 'The Acts or Transactions of the Apostles' is the title in the Greek BEZAE… 'The Acts of the Holy Apostles' is the title in the Codex Alexandrinus and several others…By some it has been…[called] a 'Fifth Gospel'…and the 'Gospel of the Holy Spirit,' [as well] as 'The Book, the Demonstration of the Holy Spirit.' "[1]

Other ancient manuscripts give the title as "Acts," "The Acts," "Acts of the Apostles," and "Acts of the Holy Apostles."[2] The title "The Acts of the Apostles" is used in the Authorized Version (1611) and the Revised Version (1881) as well as the Revised Standard Version (1946).

The patristic fathers probably assigned the caption, "The Acts of the Apostles," to the book of Acts to preserve an account of the work of the risen Savior and its continuance through the apostles by the power of the Holy Spirit. However, the account makes reference to the activities of only a few apostles by name. In a sense, the book is a "Fifth Gospel" because it is a continuation of the narrative begun in the Gospel of Luke.

Authorship and Date

Evidence for authorship of Luke and Acts has been presented in the introduction to the Gospel of Luke. Literary style, the chronological order of the writing, and the internal and external evidence make it impossible to separate authorship of the two books from that of a single writer. This leads to the conclusion that Luke is the author of both books.

Presumably the book of Acts was completed by Luke at some time near the end of Paul's two-year imprisonment in Rome. It is apparent that Luke's principal sources of information were his immediate personal contact with Paul and the notes he had accumulated while traveling with Paul. The date of composition for the book of Acts is uncertain but A.D. 80 seems to have the most probability. The book could not have been written earlier than Paul's final imprisonment because the narrative is continuous to that time, nor could it have been written later because the writings deal specifically with Paul's imprisonment in Rome.[3]

A study of the book of Acts should include comment upon the viewpoint of those critics who differ from the traditional view of establishing authorship of a book upon internal and external evidence. Some critics subject a book to question if it contains miracles, the supernatural power of Jesus, and the ability of prophets to foretell the future. The book of Acts has

Manuscripts
4220

Acts of the Apostles
4266

Apostles
2080-2082

Gospel of Luke
4264

Luke
2216

Tree of Paul's Life
4309
Paul's Missionary Journeys
2382

False Teachers
2101

been no exception to this procedure. "With [their reasoning]...instead of inferring the truth of the narrative from the overwhelming evidence that it is the narrative of eye-witnesses, and a contemporary, they conclude it is not the authoritative narrative because it contains...statements about the miracles which they are...[unwilling] to admit as true."[4]

Among the references not acceptable to those who use this form of interpretation are "the account(s) of the Ascension of our Lord and the Day of Pentecost...as well as the miracles of Peter, and John...and the other supernatural events throughout the book."[5]

Form Criticism is a device that the critics have created by which natural historical events can be shifted from their setting to a later date more compatible with the presupposed "scientific investigative technique."[6] This kind of exegesis is coupled with "rationalistic" assertions of "alleged contradictions," "inadequate accounts," and "omissions of facts," but these assertions are never clearly defined.[7]

Another device used by these critics for nullifying the traditional view is the creation of sources which a supposed "redactor" is said to have used, including (1) a biography of Peter, (2) a rhetorical work of the death of Stephen, (3) a biography of Barnabas and the memoirs of Silas.[8] None of these so-called sources have Biblical, historical, or literary certainty. In conclusion it is asserted that the book of Acts "is not historically reliable."[9] Most of this destructive criticism was developed by German critics of the eighteenth and nineteenth century of which the Tubingen school is representative.

Background, Purpose, and Content

Though the title reads "The Acts of the Apostles," the book deals only in a limited way with the activity of all the apostles. Of the apostles, the book

mentions "the eleven" (1:26), who witnessed Christ's ascension to heaven (Ac. 1) and the election of Matthias to replace Judas (Ac. 1), which was followed by the outpouring of the Holy Spirit (Ac. 2). Peter is the prominent figure in the first 12 chapters of Acts,[10] and Paul in the later chapters. References to the events occurring after Pentecost include Peter's imprisonment (Ac. 4), the tragic death of Ananias and Sapphira (Ac. 5), the healing of Aeneas, the raising of Dorcas from the dead (Ac. 9), and the conversion of Cornelius in Caesarea (Ac. 10), the election of Philip to supervise the social affairs (Ac. 6), Philip's planting of the church in Samaria (Ac. 8), and the baptizing of the Ethiopian eunuch (Ac. 8). John is mentioned as being with Peter at the healing of the man at the temple gate and being in prison with Peter (Ac. 3). In chapters 13-28 most of the references deal with those before, during, and after Paul's conversion on the Damascus Road.

The book of Acts is the key, not only to the continuing activity of the apostles but also to the Pauline Epistles. Information about Paul's Galatian ministry is contained in Ac. 16 and 18, his Philippian ministry in Ac. 16, his Thessalonian witness in Ac. 16 and 17, his labors at Corinth in Ac. 18 and 20, his work in Ephesus in Ac. 18 and 19, and his ministry among the Romans in Ac. 28. "No one could read Acts without realizing that Paul was a genuine apostle of Christ, independently commissioned by Him and providing by the 'signs of the apostles' which accompanied his ministry, the truth of his claim that he came in no way behind 'the very chiefest apostles' (2 Co. 12:11)."[11]

The Book of Acts as a Supplement to the Gospels

If the Gospel records were the only source of information available on the post-resurrection Christian movement, knowledge of the developing Jewish-Gentile church would be very limited. The prophetic statements in the OT regarding the outpouring of the Holy Spirit (Joel 2:28-29; cf. Ac. 2:16-17) and the replacement of Judas (Ps. l09:7-8; cf. Ac. 1:15-17) would not be understood.

In writing the book of Acts, Luke continued that which he had so ably begun in his Gospel narrative. The entire content in his Gospel makes the book of Acts imperative.

Joseph Exell says of Luke: "It is obvious that the first preaching of the Gospel [by Luke] in Jerusalem was necessary, both to connect his second work with the first, and also because...the Mission of the Gentiles sprang from the Mother Church in Jerusalem. The existence and establishment of the Jewish Church was the root from which the Gentile Church grew and the Gentile Church had a common interest with the Jewish Church in these great events."[12]

Holy Spirit
1601-1614, 3803
Day of Pentecost
2722
Judas
1959
Gentiles
2383-2384

Gentile Believers
4038

1:12 ...a sabbath day's journey.

The law of "a Sabbath day's journey" was invented by the rabbis to protect the Sabbath and to keep the people in close proximity to the center of worship on the Sabbath. Only a casual reference is made to this rabbinical ordinance here in Ac. 1:12, which states that the distance between the Mount of Olives and Jerusalem was a "Sabbath day's journey." Where this law began is uncertain, but no doubt a need developed in history to define the limits of labor on the Sabbath. Walking, as well as working, consumed human energy, so the rabbis determined that the permissible distance for travel on the Sabbath should be 2,000 cubits (two-thirds of a mile). In the Jerusalem Targum is the statement, "Let no man walk from the place beyond 2,000 cubits on the Sabbath Day." This is an arbitrary demand and has no basis in the levitical code. However, keeping the Sabbath day holy is clearly stated in the rabbinical ordinance, which possibly had its origin in the Mosaic period, when the Israelites were not to leave camp to gather manna on the Sabbath.[13]

At the beginning of the NT period the true meaning of the Sabbath had become obscured and shrouded in oppressive ordinances. Jesus sought to clarify the real meaning of the Sabbath by showing the original purpose of the institution: "The sabbath was made for man, and not man for the sabbath" (Mk. 2:27). The early Christians were loyal Jews. They worshiped daily in the temple at Jerusalem (Ac. 2:46); later they attended the synagogue and heard sermons.

For more on the Sabbath, see commentary on Ge. 2:3; De. 5:14.

1:26 ...the lot fell upon Matthias; and he was numbered with the eleven apostles.

The word *apostle* signifies "one sent forth" as a messenger or ambassador. The definition for *disciple* is a "pupil" or "scholar." It is a broad term used to indicate those with Christian faith. The twelve Jesus chose to be his followers were called disciples. Such a designation is seen in Mt. 10:1, but in the next verse the same twelve are referred to as apostles. They are Peter, Andrew, James, John, Philip, Bartholomew, Thomas, Matthew, James, Thaddeus, Simon the Canaanite, and Judas. Sometimes this group is referred to as "the twelve." In Mt. 10:1-2 the terms *disciple* and *apostle* are interchangeable. Frequently, in broad usage, the term apostle or disciple seems to include all believers in Christ, but in Ac. 1:21-22 a narrow definition would include only those who had been with Jesus from the time of his baptism. This definition of apostle is borne out by Ac. 1:21-26 where Matthias replaces Judas. The "lot" fell upon Matthias and he was numbered with the eleven apostles (Ac. 1:21-26).

The number twelve appeared to be important because when "Judas by transgression fell" the disciples elected Matthias to fill the vacancy. Matthew and Mark used the word *apostle* only once each for the twelve (Mt. 10:2 and Mk. 6:30). Luke refers to them as apostles almost exclusively. When speaking of the twelve, Paul employs the term *apostle* in a broader sense, for "messenger" or "agent" (2 Co. 8:23 and Ph. 2:25).

John speaks of false apostles (Re. 2:2).[14] For more on the subject, see commentary on Re. 2:9.

False
Teachers
2101

2:1 ...when the day of Pentecost was fully come...

Some scholars suggest that the church was "born" in the Upper Room on the day of Pentecost. However, to avoid confusion, one may consider those assembled in the Upper Room as believers and, in a sense, already the church. It would be more correct to say that the church was baptized with the Holy Spirit to empower it for world evangelism (Ac. 1:4; 2:4) and to give it inner resources with which to stand up under the forthcoming persecution. Peter is perhaps the outstanding example of the change within a person after he is baptized with the Holy Spirit. It would be correct to say that the church received its commission and authority to witness throughout the world "when the day of Pentecost was fully come."

For more on the day of Pentecost, or Feast of Weeks, see commentary on Ex. 34:22.

Day of
Pentecost
2722

Holy Spirit,
Church
Baptized
With
1605

Feast of
Weeks
1257

2:17 ...I will pour out of my Spirit upon all flesh...

Though in the OT God's Spirit was limited to specially selected leaders, the prophet Joel foresaw the day when the Spirit would be the gift of God to all believers. Dr. Gustave Oehler says, "The NT church of the future...is founded upon the outpouring of the spirit upon all [saved] flesh (Ac. 2:17 ff.)...The direct personal communication with God...is to become the possession of all members of the Church (Nu. 11:29)."[15] For more on the subject, see the essay "The Work of the Holy Spirit in the Old and New Testaments," p. 394.

Holy Spirit
1601-1614
Holy Spirit,
Filling
Saints
1125

2:47 ...the Lord added to the church...

The story of the church is as old as creation, but ever new in its adjustment to each age. A historical perspective of this redemptive institution reveals a progressive development from its pristine origin in Genesis to its full culmination in Revelation. At first, its ritual and form were adapted to the simplicity of nomadic life, but gradually, as society developed in its various complexities, the church made adjustment to developing sociological needs.

Early worship had as its center the altar without benefit of a building; later came the tabernacle, which was followed by the temple; during the exile the synagogue came into existence. All of these places of worship were different in design but were, by purpose and function, similar. In each of these places of worship there was the idea of God meeting man, where sinful man met the condition of salvation.

Thus a progressive element of refinement is to be recognized in the history of worship centers. Five main developments in this area are significant and are the subject of the following chart.

Growth of
the Church
733, 2380

Altars
120
Tabernacle
3528
Temple
3577-3581
Synagogues
3521-3523

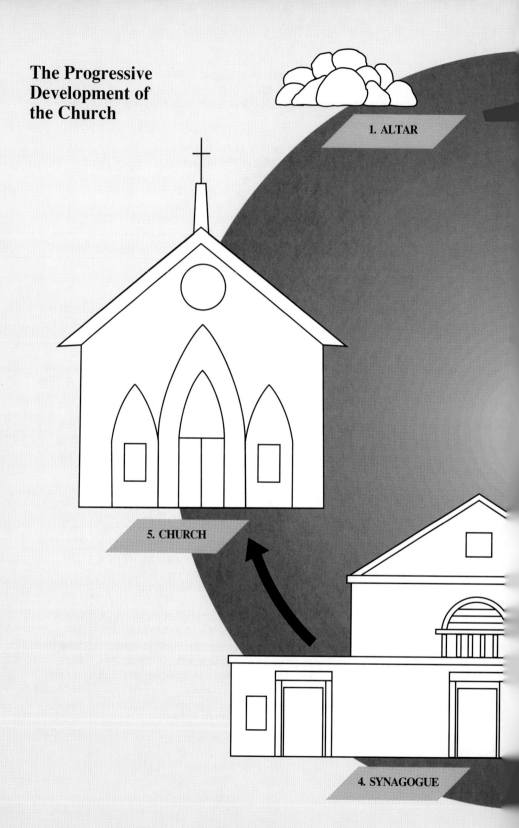

The Progressive Development of the Church

1. ALTAR

5. CHURCH

4. SYNAGOGUE

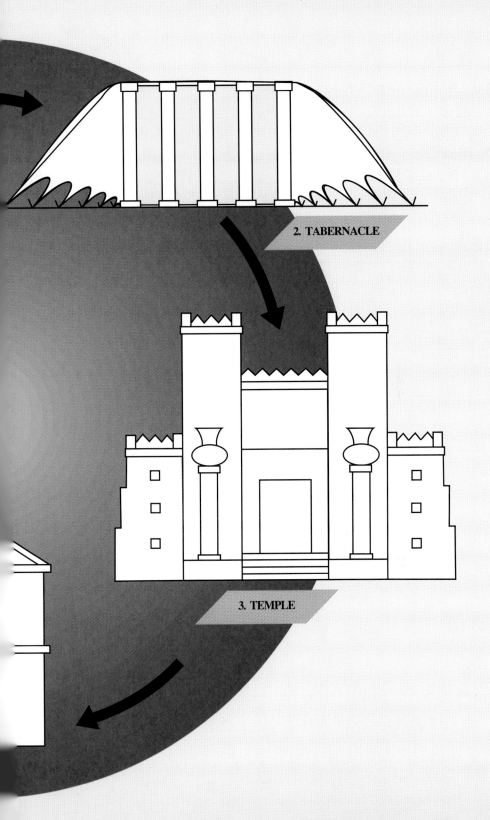

2. TABERNACLE

3. TEMPLE

Development of Worship Centers

Worship Center	Biblical Beginnings	Description
Altar	Cain and Abel offered a sacrifice, but the first mention of an altar is in Ge. 8:20, where Noah built an altar to the Lord.	Any raised structure (not a building) with a marker that would indicate communication with a deity. Usually marked by stones.
Tabernacle	In Ex. 25:9 God's instruction to Moses regarding the Tabernacle begins.	A rather simple, portable structure planned, designed and revealed by God. See Ex. 36.
Temple	1 Chr. 22:7-10. Conceived by David; built by Solomon. Instructions given 1 K. 6.	A permanent, very elaborate, beautiful and expensive structure.
Synagogue	Unknown exactly when first ones began—probably during the exile. Only OT mention: Ps. 74:8.	Generally plain, rectangular buildings, ranging in size from small home unit to special structures where large numbers could gather.
Church	In Mt. 16:18 Jesus said, "...I will build my church and the gates of hell shall not prevail against it."	Does not refer to a structure, but to a body of believers in Christ. Bible contains no reference to church building or denomination. Church began meeting in homes. Later buildings developed in a pattern similar to synagogues.

Sociological Influences Leading to Development	Location of TCRB Helps	For Commentary in This Book, See
The early patriarchs built altars as they desired a site to commune with God. Since they were nomadic, altars were built at many locations.	120 4316 (picture)	Ge. 8:20
A central place of worship for the Israelites. It had to be portable because they were traveling from the Sinai desert to Canaan.	4316 (picture)	Ex. 36
A central, permanent place of worship for the Israelites after they were settled in Canaan.	4316 (sketch) 4319 (plan)	1 K. 6:1
Developed after destruction of the temple and dispersion of the Jews. Since they were scattered there had to be many, smaller worship centers and they were often simply constructed.	3521-3523	Lu. 4:16
The earliest believers in Christ continued to worship in synagogues. However, as the distinction between them and the non-believing Jews sharpened, the early Christians needed to meet separately.	726-761	Phm. 2

The "Street called Straight." After Paul's conversion he entered this street, where God restored his sight through the ministries of Ananias.

Salvation
3116-3128

4:12 Neither is there salvation in any other: for there is none other name under heaven given among men, whereby we must be saved.

Christ's
Name
2516-2517

The words of Peter to the Jewish leaders that it is in the name of Jesus Christ that the lame man was healed and it is in his name alone that man can find salvation. How, then, were people saved before the Advent of Jesus Christ? For commentary on this subject, see the essay "The Mechanics of Salvation in the OT Period," pp. 67-69.

High
Priests
2064
Persecution
3480-3483

5:17-18 Then the high priest rose up, and all they that were with him, (which is the sect of the Sadducees)...and put them [the apostles] in the common prison.

Throughout the book of Acts the religious leaders persecuted the apostles, just as they had persecuted Jesus throughout the Gospels. The ecclesiastical hierarchy of that day, professing themselves to be servants of God, instead served the "synagogue of Satan" (see Re. 2:9 and commentary

Pharisees
3171
Sadducees
3172

there). Jesus had warned, "Take heed and beware of the leaven of the Pharisees and of the Sadducees" (Mt. 16:6). For more on the Sadducees, see commentary on Mk. 12:18; Jn. 8:44.

6:3 "Brothers, choose seven men from among you who are known to be full of the Spirit and wisdom. We will turn this responsibility [of waiting on tables] over to them." (NIV)

The Christian office of deacon is seen in this verse, because the word "deacon" means "to wait upon tables." Though the word is not used in this verse, it is evident that the service transcends the terminology. For more on the office of deacon, see commentary on 1 Ti. 3:10.

7:58...a young man named Saul. (NIV)

In this verse Luke introduces the man who will be the main character of the second half of his book. Saul was an arch enemy of the Christian movement until he met Jesus our Lord on the Damascus Road (Ac. 9:3-9). Soon after his conversion his name was changed from Saul (Hebrew, emphasizing his Jewish background) to Paul (Roman, emphasizing his Hellenistic background). Paul, the Lord tells Ananias, "is my chosen instrument to carry my name before the Gentiles..." (Ac. 9:15). For more on the significance of names in the Bible, see commentary on Mt. 1:21.

After his conversion, Paul went into the Arabian desert (Ga. 1:17) presumably to pray and to study the Scriptures. On his return, he stayed three years in Damascus preaching and teaching that Jesus of Nazareth was indeed the Jewish Messiah, and then went to Jerusalem where he abode for fifteen days with Peter (Ga. 1:18). After this he journeyed to his home, Tarsus.

The city of Tarsus, Saul's boyhood home, is often mentioned with Saul's name throughout the book of Acts. It was here that he received his basic education, though his graduate work was done in the Rabbinical school in Jerusalem. For a closer look at Tarsus, see the essay following.

Spirit-Filled Men
1125
Deacons
753
Spiritual Service
3894-3897
Tree of Paul's Life
4309
Damascus
908, 4360
Names Changed
2518
Journeys of Paul in Early Life
4309b
Preparation for Service
2953
Christ Messiah
695
Tarsus
3551

The City of Tarsus

Tarsus, the boyhood home of Saul of Tarsus, is located about ten miles inland from the Mediterranean Sea, on the Cilician Plain astride the Cyndus River. A super highway through the Cilician Gates connects Tarsus with the coast (Ac. 9:11; 11:25; 21:39).

Tarsus was a dual city. The lower city, only 80 feet above sea level, was separated from the upper city by a series of terraces. The upper city, situated on the higher levels of the Tarsus Mountains, became a popular summer resort.

Tarsus has had a continuous history of 6,000 years. Aramaic cave writings refer to it as *TZR*, probably a contraction of Tarsus. The Assyrians referred to it as *Tarzi*. The Hittites, some of the earliest inhabitants, made Tarsus their capital city. Shalmaneser III captured the city in 832 B.C. and later it was plundered by Sennacherib. Greek merchants established a Greek colony here in the seventh century B.C.

In Roman times Tarsus was the largest, most prominent city in Cilicia, with about 500,000 inhabitants. Saul of Tarsus, a Roman citizen, was born here. Later, when he was known as Paul, he referred to his hometown as "no mean city," a term he apparently borrowed from the writings of Euripides, the Greek poet.

Tarsus was a university town rivaling Athens and Alexandria. It was dignified by the residence of such noted persons as Cicero, the governor (51 B.C.), and Athenodorus (24 B.C.). It was also the seat of the Stoic philosophers.

Today most of the ancient city lies buried under the streets of modern Tarsus and the adjacent farm lands. Archaeological activity has been limited, though several Roman landmarks still remain.

Tarsus 3551

Roman Citizens 772

Hittites 1594

A general view of Tarsus as it appears today. Muslim minarets dominate the scene. Little Christianity remains in this once active Christian city.

10:34-35 "...God does not show favoritism but accepts men from every nation..." (NIV)

It is evident from Peter's statement that the Master's ideas of the kingdom cannot be explained in the framework of the Jewish-pharisaic conception, which assumed that "the choice of Israel" was based upon a superiority of this people. Rather, the "choosing of Israel" conforms to the lowly outward appearance of the divine revelation. Nowhere in the OT is there any approbation of racial exaltation of the unregenerate Jew. On the contrary, it is precisely the OT that is full of direct glowing words of judgment denouncing the holy wrath of God against apostate Israel.[16]

Some Bible scholars interpret the OT to be uniquely and exclusively for the Jews but this position is not tenable. There is evidence to show that "the OT is not the book of Jewish national religion but it is the Book of God and of His revelation. Jewish-Talmudic-Pharisaic moralizing and the OT are not one and the same; the OT purports to be the testimony of the Holy Spirit to the sons of all men, and to the grace of God which pardons the repentant believing sinner. This grace is available to all men alike, Jew or Gentile (see Ro. 2:10ff.)."[17] Perhaps the greatest evangelical appeal recorded in the OT was given to the Gentiles with the preaching of Jonah (3:1ff.). Christ gave recognition of this effort and drew some parallels from the event to illustrate the need of his day. Here is an obvious instance in which Jesus presents his own objectives in the same light as that of an OT preacher. In both cases the urgent business at hand for Jew and Gentile alike was to repent and be saved (Mt. 12:39; Lu. 11:29).

God has no favorites. His grace extends as freely to Gentiles as to Jews (Ac. 15:9; Ro. 2:11,13; 3:22,29; 10:12-13; 1 Co. 12:13; Ga. 3:28; Ep. 2:13, 18; 3:6). Now this truth is evident, but to Peter it was revolutionary. God does not favor a Jew; he has never shown special consideration to an apostate or nonbelieving Jew. Grace always has come by faith and faith alone, to the Jew and to the Gentile alike. In speaking of this matter, Paul raises a question and then answers it in the light of his established premise: "Is he the God of the Jews only? Is he not also of the Gentiles? Yes, of the Gentiles also: seeing it is one God, which shall justify the circumcision by faith, and uncircumcision through faith" (Ro. 3:29-30). Judaism had a dual nature; it was the suspension agent for both the "holy seed" (Ezr. 9:2; Is. 6:13) or the church, and the "congregation of evildoers" (Ps. 26:5). The Jews had the erroneous idea that God would not and did not extend his grace and favor to the Gentiles, and that they were the only ones who enjoyed his speical blessings, even though people were redeemed before the Jewish race was actually founded (through the tribe of Judah).

Apparently for Peter this narrow Pharisaic viewpoint prevailed until he had this heavenly vision at Joppa (Ac. 10:9ff.). He was then convinced that "God was no respecter of persons" (Ac. 10:34), and that "we must all appear before the judgment seat of Christ; that every one may receive the things done in his body..." (2 Co. 5:10); so no one nation, or people or individual could expect to find more preferential favor with God. He is absolutely just and could not ignore the pious prayers, fastings, and benevolent almsgiving of Cornelius. The Biblical record shows that "the noblest spirits (of Israel) did not restrict salvation to Jews but insisted that God wanted Israel to be a light to the nations of the world" (Is. 45:22; 49:6; Zec. 8:20ff.).[18]

Israel, God's Chosen People	1808
Chosen Ones	2725
God's Judgments	1966-1980
God's Impartiality	1979-1980
Universal Father	1247
Divine Grace	1445-1449
Jonah	1909, 4254
Repentance	2706-2712
Whosoever, of Salvation	3828
Faith	1201-1218
One God	2649
Israelites	1807-1829
Jewish Pride	1725
Joppa	4393
Universal Judgment	4123
Universal Worship	2365

So it has always been "whosoever will" may come. This is the truism of the ages. It must be remembered that the redemptive plan was given in its essential form to Adam and Eve and that all nations are included in its spiritual benefits. The Hebrews did not live in a vacuum, but they circulated throughout the heathen nations and scattered abroad the message of salvation. The Diaspora was one of the means by which the message of the Bible spread to many parts of the world.

In his letter to the Romans, Paul presents the basic requirements for salvation: "For therein is the righteousness of God revealed from faith to faith: as it is written, The just shall live by faith" (1:17; see also Hab. 2:4). On the basis of this truth, Abraham, the founder and father of the Jewish people, was justified by faith, even before the Mosaic law was given; trusting in God, Abraham and all his believing descendants have been justified. "And thus the faith of the old covenant led to the faith of the new covenant, which shows that salvation has been by faith…from the beginning. All that were just or righteous in the earth became so by faith, and by this principle alone they were enabled to persevere; as it is written: 'the just shall live by faith.' "[19] This has been the redemptive hope for all men in all ages—Jew or Gentile.

Paul states that "the wrath of God is revealed from heaven against all ungodliness and unrighteousness of men" (Ro. 1:18) whether they be Gentile or Jew. Paul was no longer spiritually blind; his eyes had been opened, and he could see that salvation has always been available to Gentile and Jew alike. This realization is evidenced in these words: "Because that which may be known of God is manifest in them [the Gentiles]; for God hath shewed it unto them. For the invisible things of him from the creation of the world are clearly seen, being understood by the things that are made, even his eternal power and Godhead; so that they are without excuse" (Ro. 1:19-20). Although the Gentiles had no written revelation, yet what could be known of God was everywhere manifest among them (see Ps. 19). The Gentiles were constantly exposed to the Jewish religion; the Court of the Gentiles in the temple provided a teaching medium. It is assumed that the publican prayed in the Court of the Gentiles (Lu. 18:9-14).

When Peter attained the state of grace where he could say, "of a truth I perceive that God is no respecter of persons" (Ac. 10:34), he saw God as he really was and always had been, and Peter realized that Christ is "Lord of all." Both Jew and Gentile have always been eligible for membership in the kingdom, by faith. "There is no other way of obtaining life and salvation…The law condemns all men as being under sin. None therefore is justified by the works of the law."[20]

Therefore justification is by faith and faith alone, and so it has always been since time began.

11:26 …The disciples were called Christians first at Antioch. (NIV)

Antioch in Syria was the city where the first large group of Gentiles was converted to the gospel and it became the center for the Christian movement. Paul's first three missionary journeys were launched from this church (see Ac. 13:1-4; 15:40; 18:23). For more on the city see the following essay.

The City of Antioch, Syria

Antioch, Syria, was a city of about 500,000 people in the days of St. Paul, ranking perhaps second with Alexandria. It was located on the Orontes River at the base of Mt. Siepious, about twenty miles from the Mediterranean Sea and became one of the mighty bastions of the Hellenist Empire under Alexander the Great and his successors. After Antiochus Epiphanes set up a statue of Jupiter in the Holy of Holies and started robbing the Temple treasury in Jerusalem, religious order became confused and disrupted. With the prevailing Hellenistic indignities and Roman suppression the Jews dispersed throughout the Roman Empire. Many fled to Antioch after the martyrdom of Stephen when Christian persecution accelerated; both Jew and Christian found a refuge in this northern city. To the fleeing Jews and Greeks the Gospel evangels opened their arms. Many Jews, separated from the watchful eye of the Temple authorities, responded favorably to the Gospel.

As the center for the Christian movement transferred its base from Jerusalem to Antioch, many of the stronger teachers and prophets, including Barnabas went north to join their brethren (Ac. 11:19-22; 13:1). After some successful crusades in Antioch, the leaders decided to send Barnabas to Tarsus for the purpose of reviving Paul's interest in the Christian movement. The disciples recalled that when the converted Paul returned from Damascus to Jerusalem, the believers were afraid of him and only Barnabas was willing to befriend him. A mighty missionary movement was born when "Saul of Tarsus," now Paul, took charge. The fiery zeal and dedication of the believers won for them the name of Christian. The learned Paul, trained in Old Testament theology and Rabbinics now committed his full energies to proclaiming that Jesus was indeed "he of whom Moses and the prophets spake." They immediately launched three successive missionary campaigns into Asia Minor and the very heart of the Hellenistic Empire. These were followed by Paul's fourth journey, as a prisoner, to Rome itself.

Modern Antakya is now an Islamic stronghold. It is principally a trade and processing center of 60,000 people. The adjacent river valley produces great quantities of citrus fruits, grapes, olives, melons, cotton and tobacco. Only portions of the once high city walls still stand. One tourist attraction is the Grotto of Saint Peter, built by the Crusaders in the 12th and 13th centuries. Also of interest are the ancient catacombs. Few Christians remain in this dominant Muslim culture.

Antioch, Syria, on the banks of the Orontes River with Mt. Siepious in the background.

| Antioch |
| 197, 4330 |

| Paul's Missionary Journeys |
| 2382 |

| Dispersion of Jews |
| 1023 |

| Barnabas |
| 342 |

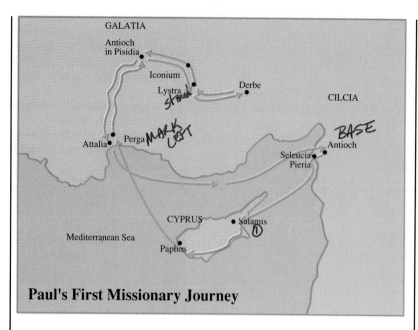

Paul's First Missionary Journey

12:7 And behold the angel of the Lord came upon him...

Angels are mentioned nearly 300 times throughout the Bible. They are often seen as messengers of God to man, either to dispense divine help and grace or to carry out decrees of judgment. They are usually visible only to those whom they address. For more on angels, see commentary on Re. 5:11.

13:2-3 As they ministered to the Lord and fasted, the Holy Ghost said, Separate me Barnabas and Saul for the work whereunto I have called them. And...they sent them away.

The church at Antioch ordained Paul and Barnabas for the first missionary journey into the Gentile world. Apparently young Mark accompanied them. Their first port was Salamis on the Island of Cyprus. A monastery and tomb bearing the name of Barnabas is presently located a few miles west of Salamis. Paul and Barnabas traveled overland to Paphos, on the west coast, where the proconsul Sergius Paulus became a convert and Saul's name was changed to Paul (Ac. 13:4-12).

After the missionary party landed at Perga on the southern coast of Asia Minor, Mark returned to Jerusalem (Ac. 13:13). In Pisidian Antioch Paul preached in the synagogue and was violently opposed by the Jews. The missionary group continued on to Iconium. Strong persecution drove them on to Lystra where Paul was stoned and left for dead (Ac. 14:19).

They traveled as far as Derbe and then, retracing their steps, came to the coastal town of Attalia. By ship they

Cyprus. Monastery of Barnabas, a native of Cyprus and traveling companion of Paul.

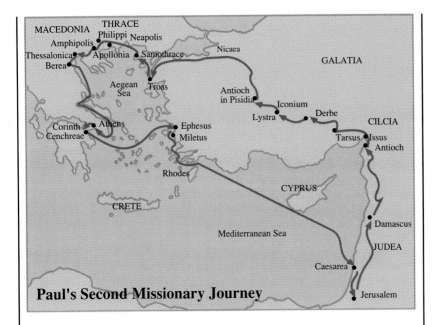

Paul's Second Missionary Journey

returned to the Christian headquarters in Antioch.

14:22 …enter into the kingdom of God.

The message of Paul and Barnabas on their missionary journeys was the central message of Jesus: that through repentance and forgiveness of sins people may enter the kingdom of God. The expression "kingdom of God" was adopted from the language of the OT and Judaism, but Jesus filled it with new expression. For more on the subject, see commentary on Mk. 1:15.

14:23 And when they had ordained them elders in every church…

The official nature of the Christian elders was evidently influenced by that of the Jewish elders because these men were invested with the same kind of authority. According to 1 Ti. 4:14, becoming a Christian elder involved ordination and a formal attestation by the church officials. One of the qualifications for the office was also an aptness to teach. For more on the nature of the office throughout the Bible, see commentary on 1 Ti. 5:17.

15:5 But there rose up certain of the sect of the Pharisees which believed, saying, That it was needful to circumcise them, and to command them to keep the law of Moses.

It is sometimes overlooked that there were Pharisees who did not reject Jesus as the Messiah (though most did; see commentary on Mk. 8:11; Jn. 8:44). These believers, having been steeped

Archaeological excavations at Troas.

Kingdom of God
2011
Repentance
2706-2708
Sin Forgiven
3345
Elders
2078-2079
Christian Elders
754
Christian Teachers
3559
Pharisees
3171
Reversion to Judaism
4092
Legalism
2990

in the Law of Moses, found it difficult to give up their legalistic training. They sought to bring into the Christian church the traditions of Judaism, a subject Paul dealt with specifically in his letter to the Galatians (see Ga. 2:14; 3:3).

Judaizers
1958

15:40 And Paul chose Silas, and departed, being recommended by the brethren unto the grace of God.

Silas
3288
Paul's
Second
Missonary
Journey
4309d
Timothy
3628
Troas
3695, 4444

Paul's second missionary journey was marked by a disagreement with his friend Barnabas. Paul did not want Mark to accompany them; consequently Barnabas and Mark went on independent missionary journeys. Paul chose Silas for his partner, stopping first in Tarsus. From there they traveled to Derbe, Lystra, Iconium, and Pisidian Antioch, all towns which he had visited with Barnabas on his first journey. At Lystra, Timothy, a young man of faith with a Christian background joined Paul and Silas (Ac. 16:1-3). In Galatia, the Holy Spirit urged Paul to proceed to Troas where he received the Macedonian call.

Philippi
2756, 4425
Paul's
Bonds
3479
Thessa-
lonica
3610, 4442
Berea
402
Athens
303, 4336

Sailing to Neapolis, the port city of Philippi, and thence over the coastal mountains, Paul and Silas reached Philippi where, on the Sabbath day, they made contact with some women praying by the river. Opposition to their ministry soon developed, which resulted in the imprisonment of the missionaries and the conversion of the jailer (Ac. 16). Their next ministry was at Thessalonica where again the Jews persecuted Paul and Silas (Ac. 17). In Berea the people were more kindly disposed, searching the Scriptures (the OT) to ascertain if Paul's message was true (Ac. 17). However, when the trouble-making Jews from Thessalonica came to Berea more opposition arose. Paul proceeded to Athens, leaving Silas and Timothy behind to establish and nurture the church.

In Athens, Paul introduced the "unknown god" to the learned men (see the following essay). At Corinth, Silas and Timothy rejoined Paul and there they ministered for eighteen months. Then they began their long journey back to Antioch, stopping briefly in Ephesus, Caesarea, and Jerusalem.

The City of Athens

On his second missionary journey, the apostle Paul brought Greece, the ancient land of the philosophers, under the Christian umbrella. On this journey he established churches in Philippi, Thessalonica, Berea, Athens and Corinth. Upon arrival in Athens, Paul took note of the prevailing heathen idolatry. While Paul was preaching in the marketplace the Epicureans and the Stoics accused him of being a babbler and a teacher of strange gods (Ac. 17:17-18), but after hearing his introductory remarks they were much impressed and invited him to debate his philosophy at the Areopagus, where the venerable council of philosophers met regularly.

Athens
303, 4336

Philosophy
2759

The Areopagus and Mars Hill are the same. Ares was the Greek god of war, while Mars was the Roman god of war. Mars Hill was the official meeting place for the Supreme Court of Athens. The seats of the judges are

still recognizable, and toward the southwest rock-hewn steps still descend to the marketplace. It is here where Paul pleaded his own case and that of Christianity. He was conscious of the fact that he was addressing the most intellectual men in the city known for its learning. Paul soon dem-

Learning
2028

The Parthenon. Paul's debate with the philosophers of Athens took place at the base of this magnificent structure.

onstrated his intellectual skill: First he complimented the learned men on their religiosity and their inscription to a god who might even be unknown to them. He was quick to point out that "The Unknown God" whom they ignorantly worshiped was the very God he represented. This won their attention. Paul began a sermon which included all of the vital elements of the living Lord Jesus Christ. Even though some mocked him, others were so much impressed they said, "We will hear thee again of this matter" (Ac. 17:22-32). It is stated that a few men became followers of Paul and believed, including Dionysius, a member of the Areopagus group, a woman named Damaris, and a number of others (Ac. 17:34). Dionysius was a prominent citizen, being one of the twelve judges forming the highest council. Tradition tells us that he became the first Bishop of Athens and was martyred under Domitian.[21]

Preaching Christ
2089

Martyrs
3488

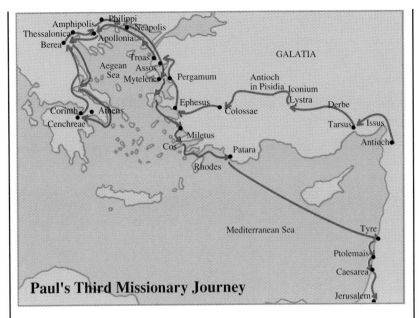

Paul's Third Missionary Journey

18:23 ...he departed, and went over all the country of Galatia and Phrygia in order, strengthening all the disciples.

Paul stayed only a short time in Antioch at the end of his second journey before departing on his third journey, never again to see Antioch. After a visit with the churches in Galatia, he continued to Ephesus. During his second visit in Ephesus the people began to destroy their idols. Demetrius and his fellow silversmiths incited the people to riot because they feared that their sale of idols would be destroyed by the people's conversion to Christianity. From Ephesus, Paul continued his missionary journey northward into Macedonia and Greece where several of Paul's missionary associates joined him.

At Miletus, Paul delivered his notable farewell address to the Ephesian elders who had come to hear him. Despite the elders' warning of danger in Jerusalem at the hand of the Jews, Paul continued on his way to face the wrath of the Jews, stopping briefly at Cos, Rhodes, and Patara as well as Tyre, Ptolemais, and Caesarea. In Jerusalem, Paul related his missionary experiences. While he was at worship in the temple the Jews seized him, but he was rescued by the Roman soldiers. After he appeared before the Sanhedrin, a certain number of Jews made a pact to kill Paul. After a series of charges and defenses before Felix, Festus, and Agrippa in Caesarea, Paul appealed to the court of Caesar in Rome.

Ephesus. This is the theatre where Paul's associates, Gaius and Aristarchus, were taken when the silversmith riot broke out (Ac. 19:29).

The missionary witnesses operating in and out of Antioch were quite impressive. At least sixty missionaries are referred to by name in the Pauline epistles. The greatest number are listed in Acts and the Timothy letters.

20:7 On the first day of the week
we came together to break bread. (NIV)

The origin of the Christian Sunday is not easy to determine. The change from the seventh day to the first day was gradual. To the Christian, the resurrection day was the most important of days, and one can assume that this feeling contributed to the change. Nothing could be more appropriate than to commemorate the resurrection once each week and to link it with the day of rest and worship.

When Christianity was predominantly Jewish, the Sabbath was accepted as the day of rest and worship. However, when Christian congregations finally became predominantly Gentile, the Sabbath was abandoned and Sunday became the official rest day.[22]

The ruler, Constantine, further established the observance of Sunday. After he had a vision of the Cross in the sky (27 Oct. 312) he decided to fight under the banner of Christ. When he won the battle he became a Christian. In his Edict of Toleration in A.D. 313, he legalized Christianity and filled his chief offices with Christians. Constantine had fifty Bibles copied for his churches and by edict made Sunday the official day of rest and worship in his kingdom. When the Roman aristocracy insisted on their pagan religions, Constantine moved his capital to Byzantium and called it Constantinople.

23:5 ...I did not realize that he was the high priest; for it is written: 'Do not speak evil about the ruler of your people.' (NIV)

From the establishment of the levitical priesthood, the priests were the mediators between God and the people. This was a divinely ordained office,

Conversion
836
Rest Enjoined
3010
False Religion
2988-2996
High Priests
2064

The Appian Way. This is the road Paul traversed on his way from Puteoli to Rome (Ac. 28:13).

one that Paul would not have wanted to disparage. For more on the office of priest, see commentary on Ex. 28:1.

27:1 And when it was determined that we should sail into Italy, they delivered Paul and certain other prisoners...

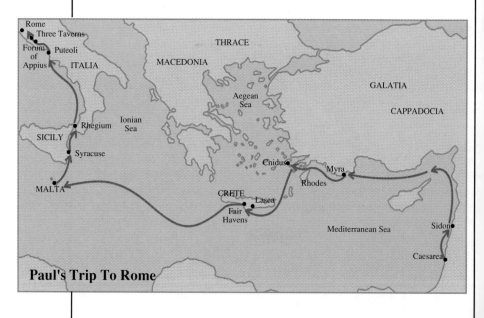

With other prisoners, Paul was delivered to a centurion for the sea voyage to Rome. After some stormy weather and a shipwreck at Malta, Paul was taken overland from Puteoli to Rome. In Rome he continued his ministry without further accusations by the Jews. Tradition holds that Paul ministered about two years in Rome, during which time Luke wrote the book of Acts with Paul's aid, and that eventually Paul died a martyr's death.

Paul's Boat

27:9 ...by now it was after the Fast... (NIV)

"The Fast" refers to the Day of Atonement, the supreme act of national atonement for sin. It took place in the seventh month (Tishri), equivalent to September/October. See commentary on Le. 16:16; Ro. 3:25.

Paul's Trip To Rome

Romans

The Name

The book of Romans takes its name from those to whom the book is addressed. The letter was directed "to all that be in Rome" (Ro. 1:7), and to the Roman church composed of believing Jews, and the heathen who had been converted directly to the Christian faith, some of whom may have been in Jerusalem on the day of Pentecost (Ac. 2:l). From the many people to whom Paul addressed greetings, it would seem that the church was a sizable one at the time Paul wrote the book (Ro. 16:3,23).

Authorship and Date

The book of Romans is one of the few NT books for which Pauline authorship is seldom questioned. Such ancient church fathers as Clement of Rome, Ignatius, Polycarp, and Justin all quote from the book of Romans and assign authorship to Paul the apostle. Even Marcion includes Romans in his list of Pauline Epistles.[1]

The place of writing (Corinth) and the date for this epistle are fixed within narrow limits. This conclusion is organically linked with certain names in the salutation. Phoebe, whom Paul commended to the Romans, was one of the deaconesses at Cenchrea, the port town of Corinth (Ro. 16:1-2). Cenchrea is the location where ships were placed on rollers and pulled by manpower across the narrow isthmus, to avoid the tempestuous waters surrounding Achaia or the Peloponnesian Peninsula.

Gaius, mentioned as an official in the church, provided lodging for Paul in Corinth (Ro. 16:23; 1 Co. 1:14). Erastus is referred to as the chamberlain (treasurer) of the city (Ro. 16:23). Thus it seems that Paul wrote his epistle from Corinth on his third missionary journey during the winter or spring of A.D. 58 following his long residence in Ephesus (Ac. 20:3). The postscript at the end of Romans affirms the place of writing as Corinth and states that the letter was to be sent by Phoebe, a faithful servant of the church at Cenchrea (Ro 16:1).[2]

Background, Purpose, and Content

In the introductory verse of the book of Romans, Paul expresses his desire to go to Rome for the purpose of imparting "some spiritual gifts" and establishing the believers in faith (Ro. 1:10-12). His statement, "I must also see Rome" (Ac. 19:21) apparently implies divine leading (Ac. 23:21). He

Epistle
to the
Romans
4267

Roman
Citizens
772

Rome
3095, 4428

Paul
2697

Corinth
840, 4359

Ships
3273

Gaius
1381

Paul's
Third
Missionary
Journey
**4309e,
4309g**

Spiritual
Gifts
486

had labored in such well-known commercial and religious centers as Ephesus, Corinth, Thessalonica, and Athens. On numerous occasions Paul had expected to go to Rome, but circumstances had prevented him from going (Ro 1:13).

No specific information is available as to when the Christian church in Rome developed; however, on the day of Pentecost, after the Holy Spirit came to those believers assembled in the Upper Room at Jerusalem, there were among the crowd, "strangers of Rome, Jews and proselytes" (Ac. 2:10). Evidently some of the Jews who had gone to Jerusalem to celebrate the Jewish feast day of Pentecost accepted Jesus of Nazareth as their Messiah. It is possible that the Christ-Messiah believers developed from the witness of these believers as well as from those who traveled throughout the Empire and came at times to Rome. The greetings in Ro. 16 indicate that there was a strong Christian group in Rome when Paul wrote his epistle. Apparently those believers were so outstanding that their faith was "spoken of throughout the whole world" (Ro. 1:8).

Rome was opposed to any group which endangered the political tranquility of the empire. Claudius had commanded that all Jews should leave Rome (Ac. 18:1-2). Among the exiles were Priscilla and Aquila, friends of Paul. When he arrived in Corinth, his first contact was with them. Other references to this couple show that they were effective Christians (Ac. 18:18,26). The number of Christian believers in Rome is indicated in the greetings Paul sent; those names include Mary, Andronicus, Junia, Amplias, Urbane, Appeles, the household of Aristobulus, Herodion, the household of Narcissus, Tryphena, Tryphosa, Persis, Rufus, Asyncritus, Phlegon, Hermas, Patrobas, Hermes, Philologus, Julia, Nereus and his sister, and Olympas, "and all the saints which are with them" (Ro. 16:6-15).[3]

Paul suggested that all of these should salute each other with a "holy kiss," and he informed them that the other "churches of Christ salute you" (Ro. 16:16). Paul sent salutations on behalf of the saints with him, including Timotheus, Lucius, Jason and Sosipater, Gaius, Erastus, and Quartus (Ro. 16:21-23), and identified his scribe Tertius as the writer of the epistle (Ro. 16:22). This list of many coworkers is not complete by any means, but it does indicate that there were numerous believers in Rome. Paul indicates the believers were so widespread that some had even penetrated Caesar's household (Ph. 4:22). This roster of believers points out that Paul had remarkable knowledge of and acquaintance with his fellow laborers. It is not surprising that Paul found brothers in the faith waiting for him when he landed at Puteoli (Ac. 28:13-15).

It was Paul's contention, verified by Scripture, that Christianity is the culmination of Judaism and that the Jewish faith came to fulfillment in Jesus Christ. Paul developed the thesis that the true Jews were the ones with spiritual circumcision of the heart (Ro. 2:28-29).

The books of Romans, Galatians, and Hebrews emphasize "justification by faith" (Ro. 1:17; Ga. 3:11; He. 10:38; cf. Hab. 2:4). It is clearly stated that the plan of salvation was the same for both Jew and Gentile as God was no respecter of persons (Ro. 2:10-11). God does not have a double standard— one plan of salvation for the Jew and another for the Gentile (Ro. 3). Paul said that no one is without excuse and that all must come to God by Jesus Christ. No one is saved by the works of the law, but all are saved by faith in Jesus Christ (Ro. 3:22-23; cf. Ro. 3:24-31; Ep. 2:8-9).[4] For more on salvation for the Jew and the Gentile alike, see commentary on Ac. 10:34-35.

Paul described the degenerate state of humanity in Ro. 1:18-32. In these passages one can see the resulting abnormality when there are sexual relationships outside of marriage. The Living Bible describes in modern words the abominable state of this lifestyle:

> Claiming themselves to be wise without God, they became utter fools instead…So God let them go ahead into every sort of sex sin, and do whatever they wanted to—yes, vile and sinful things with each other's bodies…That is why God let go of them and let them do all these evil things, so that even their women turned against God's natural plan for them and indulged in sex sin with each other. And the men, instead of having a normal sex relationship with women, burned with lust for each other, men doing shameful things with other men…(Ro. 1:22,24,26-27).

Many of the NT writers declared that every person—Jew or Gentile—can be delivered from the penalty, power, and pollution of sin through faith in Jesus Christ (Ro. 3:21-31). "The gospel of Christ…is the power of God unto salvation to every one that believeth" (Ro. 1:16; see also Ro. 2:25-29).

Paul explained more clearly the doctrine that no one has an excuse for his sinful conduct because God has given sufficient revelation to direct man's steps into the path of righteousness (Ro. 1:20; 2:1). Paul contended that salvation is not an inheritance but a state attained by faith and that the true spiritual Jew is one who has had circumcision of the heart (the new birth) which gives man a justified relationship with God. Spiritual circumcision also symbolizes the purification of the mind, heart, and will; it gives the believer a status as though he had never committed sin.

In chapter 4 Paul recognized that Abraham and David were justified by faith and not by works of the law (Ro. 4:1-9; cf. Ep. 2:8-9). In this context Abraham is the spiritual father of all who believe and accept God's Messiah (Ro. 4:11-16). To be justified, every individual must appropriate salvation by faith in Christ's atonement. Paul says, "Therefore being justified by faith, we have peace with God through our Lord Jesus Christ" (Ro. 5:1). The high standard of grace and the key to victory over sin is expressed in Ro. 6:1-12. In chs. 6-8 Paul describes the victory through the Spirit and shows that "there is…no condemnation to them which are in Christ Jesus, who walk not after the flesh, but after the Spirit" (Ro. 8:1). It is the dominating Spirit of Christ which frees the sinner from the law of sin and death (Ro. 8:2).

In chapters 9-11 Paul deals with the Jews' rejection of the Messiah, a Jew, and the prophetic revelation of the future Israel in the grace of God. Paul points out that there are two Israels: "For they are not all Israel, which are of Israel" (Ro. 9:6b). He also makes it clear that not all physical descendants of Abraham are his "spiritual seed" (Ro. 9:7-8). Through faith, both the believing Jew and Gentile are made one in Jesus Christ.

Paul gives a theological exposition of the supremacy of God (Ro. 9:15-23) and makes it clear that both Jews and Gentiles are eligible for and included in God's plan of sovereign grace (Ro. 9:24-26; cf. Ro. 9:30-33; 10:4-13). It is evident that God has a long-range design for Israel as a nation because "a remnant shall be saved" (Ro. 9:27b). It is clear that the door of grace is open to the rejecting Jew, for "God hath not cast away his people which he foreknew" (Ro. 11:2a; cf. Ro. 11:2b-32).

Depravity
2545

Fools
3853

Sin's
Shame
1689

Impartiality
1979

Sin
Inexcusable
3347

Regeneration
2154

Spiritual
Circumcision
766

Justification
by Fath
1203, 1985

Works
Insufficient
3904

Atoning
Blood of
Christ
679

Peace
3012-3014

No Condem-
nation
3124

Christ,
Liberator
4009

Messiah
695

Sovereignty
of God
3415

Remnant
1828

Chapters 12-16 deal with personal duties and commitment (Ro. 12:1-2) and individual responsibility to established government (Ro. 13:1-7). As believers, each person has a duty to be charitable (Ro. 14:1-8).

Handley Dunelm presents the doctrinal nature of the book of Romans in the following outline. It is included here to give a perspective of the general content of this book:

1. The Doctrine of Man.
2. The Doctrine of God.
3. The Doctrine of the Son of God.
4. The Doctrine of the Spirit of God.
5. The Doctrine of Duty.
6. The Doctrine of Israel.[5]

When Paul came to Rome, evidently no charges were filed against him by the Jerusalem authorities (Ac. 28:21). Although Paul was "kept" by a soldier in a dwelling, apparently he was free to preach the gospel without religious or political interference (Ac. 28:30-31).

The City of Rome

Rome was founded in the eighth century B.C. and by the time of Christ it had become a great empire. Augustus Caesar was emperor when Jesus was born (Lu. 2:1), though his ministry and death occurred during the reign of Tiberius. Paul's journeys took place during the reigns of Claudius and Nero, the Caesar to whom he appealed. Paul's trip to Rome as a prisoner occurred about A.D. 60

Rome
4428

In A.D. 64 a great fire destroyed much of Rome. To avoid taking the blame personally, the emperor Nero made the Christians his scapegoats, cruelly persecuting and killing many believers. According to tradition Paul and Peter were confined in the Mamertine Prison until they were executed. The Mamertine Prison is located near the site where the famous Colos-

Martyrs
3488

seum was later built (see picture on next page).

Colosseums were large oval-shaped buildings on the order of amphitheaters, whose walls were supported by many joining arches. The arenas themselves were encircled with seats. Similar in construction, but different in detail, were the amphitheater, the Circus Maximus and the Hippodrome. The well-known Colosseum, built by the Roman emperor Vespasian some ten years after Paul's death, seated 87,000 people. Here the Romans were entertained by sporting events, gladiatorial contests, fights by animals among themselves and with human beings as well as by other spectators.

At times the Colosseum was flooded to accommodate several war ships for naval battles. Wild animals were kept in cages underneath the floor in preparation for fights, in

The Roman Forum. The center for private and public assembly, as well as the place where judicial and legal matters were transacted.

which occasionally human beings, including Christians, were thrust into the arena to be mutilated or devoured by the half-starved beasts. The most cruel treatment was imposed upon human beings who did not fit into the Roman political-religious mold. All of the cruel exercises were designed to satisfy sadistic, blood-thirsty people.

Many Christians met their death here by gladiators or wild beasts. But today its galleries are empty, slowly decaying in the dust. Gone are the cries of the vanquished and the shouts of the crowds. The power of imperial Rome and its legions are only a faint memory. Towering over this ruin is a large cross symbolizing Christ's death and sacrifice for sin and the cause for which Paul and many others died.

men heirs of Christ's victory over death, Christianity announced the basic equality of men, and made transiently trivial all differences of earthy degree...Into the moral vacuum of a dying paganism, into the coldness of Stoicism and the corruption of Epicureanism, into a world sick of brutality, cruelty, oppression, and sexual chaos, into a pacified empire that seemed no longer to need the masculine virtues or the gods of war, it brought a new morality of brotherhood, kindliness, decency, and peace.[6]

Today the church circles the globe. Throughout the nations of the world, the gospel has penetrated, either by personal contact or through electronic devices. According to a recent *Information Please Almanac*, the Christians in the world number almost double the number of adherents to any other world religion.[7] In some places the supply of Bibles is not adequate to meet the demand. These develop-

Left: The Colosseum.

The noted historian Will Durant writes:

All in all, no more attractive religion has ever been presented to mankind. It offered itself without restriction to all individuals, classes, and nations; it was not limited to one people, like Judaism, nor to the freemen of one state, like the official cults of Greece and Rome. By making all

Universal Opportunity
3119, 3828, 4189

ments certainly confirm Paul's belief that the cause of Christ would ultimately triumph.

Christ Victor
372

2:11 For there is no respect of persons with God.

The teaching that God does not show favoritism is found throughout the Bible. See commentary on Ac. 10:34-35; see also Introduction to Romans: Backround, Purpose and Content.

2:15 ...the requirements of the law are written on their hearts, their consciences also bearing witness... (NIV)

The word "conscience" does not appear in the OT, but it is used 30 times in the NT. It must be assumed that the essential idea of "conscience" is resident in the OT, perhaps through the Hebrew word for "heart." Some scholars see in the word *reins* a sounding board for the conscience. As the basic natures of God and man have not changed, it is obvious that the NT references to conscience are equally relevant to OT man.

Conscience, as a phase of human intelligence, places a burden of responsibility on man. Conscience is stimulated for good or evil, depending upon the stimuli to which it is exposed. Conscience is the medium through which God can speak to man, but it must be divinely oriented. Although it is the voice of God in the soul, man's conscience can be influenced by experience, reason, intuition, authority, and revelation.

Of course it must be acknowledged that the devil can interfere with God's communication. All of these considerations contribute their share to the reservoir of ethical insight or guiding principles. The NT makes reference to a "conscience seared" (1 Ti. 4:2), which is an unreliable conscience. It is like a dirty contact point in an electric current—it obstructs free transmission. There is also a "convicted conscience" (Jn. 8:9), a "good conscience" (Ac. 23:1), a "conscience void of offense" (Ac. 24:16), a "conscience of the idol" (1 Co. 8:7), "conscience being weak" (1 Co. 8:7b), a "pure conscience" (2 Ti. 1:3), and an "evil conscience" (He. 10:22).

2:29 ...circumcision is circumcision of the heart, by the Spirit, not by the written code... (NIV)

For the OT church the rite of circumcision was the symbol of faith by which believers were distinguished from the heathen. However, it was never meant to be strictly a physical operation, but has always been symbolic of the spiritual change that occurs in the heart of the believer. For more on the significance of circumcision in both Testaments, see commentary on Ge. 17:10.

3:25 God presented him [Christ] as a sacrifice of atonement, through faith in his blood... (NIV)

Paul frequently quotes from and refers to the OT Scriptures. Here the Day of Atonement (Le. 16:16) comes to mind, a holy day which foreshadowed the ultimate day when God would make the sacrifice of his Son to atone for man's sin. For more on the subject of atonement in the Old and New Testaments, see the following essay.

Atonement in the Old and New Testaments

In the Gospels, Christ Jesus himself foretold his anticipated "death on the cross" to be the phase of the Atonement that was provisional from the beginning. Theologians of the early NT Church—such as Iranaeus, Origen, Athanasius, and Augustine—interpreted the death of Christ as a ransom, paid to the devil, and assumed that Christ was the divine Logos Incarnate. Anselm in his book, *Cur Deus Homo?*, argued that the death of Christ, the God-man, was a reparation or satisfaction paid to God for the sins of mankind. Luther and other reformers attested that the suffering of Christ was the divine punishment for the sins of the world.[8] All of these views present segments of the doctrine of the Atonement predicated upon the assumption that man had sinned and that he could regain favor with God only by becoming justified, i.e., restored to a condition as though he had never sinned.

Justification in turn was possible only by faith, a concept stated in the OT and reaffirmed in the New (Hab. 2:4; Ro. 1:17). In the OT, salvation was acquired by faith in Christ, the Messiah, who was foreordained "before the foundation of the world" (1 Pe. 1:20), but was manifest "when the fulness of the time was come" (Ga. 4:4). The OT church had a prophetic look at the cross; the NT church has a backward historical look at the cross to which God committed his Son (see chart on p. 66). Prophets, priests, and holy men of the OT as well as ministers and evangelists in the NT strove to interpret the Atonement God made for man. There is no question that the Lord and all of his NT interpreters present the Atonement as it has existed essentially from the beginning.

> Atonement
> 304-305

> Justification by Faith
> 1203, 1985

Contingent upon repentance, confession, and faith, "He appointed all men in love unto sonship and holiness (Ep. 1:4-5). But therewith 'before all time' He also promised them life (Tit. 1:2), and therefore, from the standpoint of God as above time, His grace is thus given to us 'before the world began' " (2 Ti. 1:9).[9]

> Foreordained Plan
> 4154

It is commonly accepted that "Christianity" had its beginning with the incarnation of Jesus Christ. But provisionally the principle of "Christianity" was a reality when God established a plan for man's redemption. The believers during and before the earthly ministry of Jesus were in fact "Christians" at heart because they exercised saving faith either in the promised or provided Savior. They were Christians in spirit before they were so called at Antioch (Ac. 11:26). By assuming the name "Christians" they did not subscribe to a new religion, they merely accepted a new name. The foundation for salvation has always been rooted in the Atonement made for man: "Jesus Christ was in the divine purpose appointed from the beginning of the world to redeem man by His blood."[10]

Every student of the Bible is aware that in Christ "all the prophets witness, that through his name whosoever believeth in him shall receive remission of sins" (Ac. 10:43). "Christ is the theme of the OT; He said so Himself (Lu. 24:25-27, 46); so His greatest apostle testified (Ac. 26:22-23). It is only from the King of Scripture, that the testimony of His preceding heralds can be understood: it is only from the NT that the question as to the OT solves itself."[11]

> Christ Prophesied
> 2890

Any intelligent interpretation concerning the Atonement must take into consideration the fact that there is only one Atonement—both in the OT and NT, and that the blood of animals in the OT was symbolic of the blood which was shed by the "Lamb of God," which was provisionally, and prophetically, provided before the OT period.[12] "In the NT the initiative is of God, who not only devises and reveals the way of reconciliation but by means of angels, prophets, priests, and ultimately His begotten Son, applies the means of atonement and persuades men to accept the proffered reconciliation…It follows that atonement is fundamental in the nature of God in His relations to men, and that redemption is in the heart of God's dealing in history."[13]

Redemption
2979

The OT contains a counterpart to the various elements recorded in the NT. Sacrificing the animal was a testimony to the fact that the worshiper had truly repented of his sins and that by faith he was trusting in God's promise. The ritual of the Day of Atonement, the "Good Friday of the OT," expresses the very essence of God's plan. Wilhelm Mohler says:

> As the tabernacle, the sacrificial system, the entire law, thus too, the Day of Atonement in particular, contained only the shadow of future good things, but not these things themselves (He. 10:1), and is "the figure of the true" (He. 9:24). Christ himself entered the Holy Place, which was not made with hands, namely, into heaven itself, and has now appeared before God, by once for all giving Himself as a sacrifice for the removal of sin (He. 9:23ff.). By this act the purpose of the OT and its highest development, the Day of Atonement, understood in its typical significance, has been fulfilled…Accord-

Types and Shadows
4121

ingly, our hope, too, like an anchor (He. 6:19), penetrates to the inner part of the veil, i.e., to Heaven.[14]

The Day of Atonement did not make its appearance until the era of tabernacle worship (see commentary on Le. 16:16), but its functional principle was found in the worship system current in earlier days.

Tabernacle
3528

Abraham appropriated the benefits of the Atonement through faith and became a believer in Christ the coming Messiah. The benefits of this faith are reflected in the collective names of the promise (Ro. 4:13) and the blessing (Ga. 3:14), mercy (Lu. 1:54), as well as holiness (Lu. 1:73-75) and the covenant (Ac. 3:25). The way in which Abraham responded to this particular goodness of God makes him the type of the Christian believer. It is declared that he "saw" Messiah's "day" (Jn. 8:56). His faith in the divine promise of the Atonement was for him unsupported by any evidence of the senses: this type of faith led to his justification (Ro. 4:3), and therefore in this sense again he is the "father" of the Christians, as believers (Ro. 4:11-12). For that promise to Abraham was, after all, "preached before the gospel," in that it embraced "all nations" (Ga. 3:8).

By faith Abraham appropriated personal salvation, and he is one with all believers in God's Christ.[15] Even though the formal "Day of Atonement" had not been instituted, Abraham was indeed a kind of spiritual child made possible through the blood Atonement, laid, in principle, in

Abraham
15

the Adamic generation (Ge. 4:4; cf. He. 11:4). Abraham looked ahead 2,000 years and believed what God had promised; today believers look back 2,000 years and believe what God provided.

The Atonement is symbolized in the Passover, which was instituted to commemorate the sparing of the Israelites in Egypt (Ex. 12:3,12,46; 23:15). That night the Angel of the Lord smote all the firstborn in the land of Egypt but passed over the houses of the Israelites where the blood of the Paschal Lamb had been sprinkled. Erich Sauer says:

> The Israelites pleading the blood, mindful of the afflictions from which they awaited deliverance, and putting away wickedness, were the people of the Lord in holy, glad communion before him...Celebrations of the Passover are recorded at Sinai (Nu. 9:1-14), on entering Canaan (Jos. 5:10); under Hezekiah (2 Chr. 30:1-27), with reference to Solomon in v. 26, under Josiah (2 Chr 35:1-19); and in the days of Ezra (Ezr. 6:19-22; Mt. 26:17). The Passover was to be observed as an ordinance forever (Ex. 12:14-24) and the true church has continued this rite to the present time.[16]

Nathan Isaacs adds:

> Naturally the details were impressed on the minds of the people and lent themselves to symbolic and homiletic purposes (1 Co. 5:7), where the Paschal Lamb is made to typify Jesus Christ (He. 11:28). The best known instance of such symbolic use is the institution of the Eucharist [Lord's Supper] on the basis of the paschal meal.[17]

It should be pointed out that the words used in the narratives of the NT institution of the Lord's Supper are

similar to those in connection with the Passover, e.g., "body," "blood," "covenant," "given," "poured out," "for you," "for many," "unto remission of sins," "memorial" (Ex. 24:6-8). The "immediate background of the Lord's Supper is the Passover, and that without prejudice as to whether the Lord Christ was at the paschal meal with His disciples before he instituted the Lord's Supper, as seems most probable (Lu. 22:7-18), or whether he died upon the day of its observance...the Passover was at once a covenant-recalling and a covenant-renewing sacrifice, and the Lord's Supper, as corresponding to it, was instituted at the time of its yearly observance, and of the Immolation of the true paschal lamb, of whose death it interpreted the value and the significance" (Ex. 2:23-28).[18] The use of bread and wine in the Eucharist is suggestive of the accustomed use in the OT (Ex. 29:38-42). Feeding upon the paschal lamb was an expression of faith in God's Paschal Lamb, Jesus Christ.

Information coming from the *Manual of Discipline,* discovered in the Dead Sea Caves, shows that the OT church (of which the Essenes were evidently a part) definitely observed a sacrament similar to the Christian Last Supper. The Lord's Supper or Eucharist confession of this church closely resembles that of the present Christian church. If the records of the OT church strike a frankly Christian note, it is because they proclaim that Christianity is near.

4:9-10 ...We have been saying that Abraham's faith was credited to him as righteousness...Was it after he was circumcised, or before? It was not after, but before! (NIV)

Circumcision
765-766

In Ge. 15:6 it is stated that Abraham "believed in the LORD; and he counted it to him for righteousness." That was 13 years before he was circumcised (Ge. 17:1-14), a fact that lays the groundwork for Paul's message of justification by faith. For more on Paul's message as it relates to Abraham, see commentary on Ge. 15:6.

Justification
by Faith
1985

Law Perfect
436

10:4 For Christ is the end of the law for righteousness to every one that believeth.

Christ's
Mission
684

One of Jesus' first statements was that he had not come to destroy the Law which God had provided in the past, but that he would fulfill or establish the Law. For the three principal ways in which he did this, see commentary on Mt. 5:17.

Sacrifices
3107-3108

12:1 ...offer your bodies as living sacrifices... (NIV)

Though the practice of sacrifice was different in the OT, the true meaning of sacrifice is the same in both Testaments. Just as the OT worshiper brought an animal without spot or blemish, only a person with sins forgiven is a fit subject for consecration at God's altar. The praise of God, evidenced in a life of true holiness by faith in the Lord, the supreme sacrifice which a pure soul offers God, involves a complete, personal dedication.

Consecration
3508-3511

Divine
Mercy
2297, 2299-
2301

The symbolic meaning of the sacrificial system was fulfilled when Jesus Christ died on the cross (see 1 S. 15:22). The whole sacrificial ritual was intended only to point out the infinite mercy of God to fallen man, in his redemption by the blood of the new covenant. God wanted to show his people—his church—that they should look for the mercy and salvation prefigured by the sacrifices. This concept was expressed by many of the OT writers. God touched upon this thought through Hosea: "I desired mercy, and not sacrifice; and the knowledge of God more than burnt offerings" (Ho. 6:6).

Sacrifices
Insufficient
3108

True
Religion
2985

Spiritual
Love
2203-2209

The ultimate end of the levitical ritual was for man to communicate love. The Lord pointed this out when a scribe questioned him about the commandments. Said he: "Thou shalt love the Lord thy God with all thy heart, and with all thy soul, and with all thy mind, and with all thy strength...Thou shalt love thy neighbor as thyself." The scribe replied "[This] is more than all whole burnt offerings and sacrifices," and Jesus said, "Thou art not far from the kingdom of God" (Mk. 12:30-34). "God prefers an act of mercy...to any act of worship to which the person might be called at the time (Mt. 9:13)."[19]

Sacrifices
Insufficient
3108

During the first century B.C. the faithful Jewish believers at Qumran, "the Israel of God," recognized the uselessness of the former sacrifices. In *The Manual of Discipline,* IX 13-15, appear these words: "When these things shall come to pass in Israel, at these destined times, the institution founded by the Holy Spirit for eternal Truth shall make atonement for the guilty, rebellious and sinful infidelities, and to obtain divine Grace without the fat of sacrifices. But the offering of the lips shall be as a fragrance of righteousness and the perfection of my way shall be as the free-will gifts of an acceptable offering."[20]

Offerings
2625-2636

Obedience
2614-2617

The offering of oneself to God as a living sacrifice, obedient to him and merciful to others, is the Christian's response to God's ultimate sacrifice in Jesus Christ.

12:1 ...this is your spiritual act of worship. (NIV)

The word "worship" in the Christian religion means showing respect and honor to God. The first recorded instance in the Bible of a planned worship service was the one in which Abel offered a sacrificial animal. This act of worship was an expression of homage and faith to God.

The essential nature of worship is the same in both the OT and the NT; the cohesive force is love. This is clearly enunciated in a Mosaic address: "Thou shalt love the LORD thy God with all thine heart, and with all thy soul, and with all thy might" (De. 6:5) and "thou shalt love thy neighbor as thyself" (Le. 19:18). Jesus then repeated it as the "great commandment" (Mt. 22:37-40).

13:1 ...the powers that be are ordained of God.

The Bible upholds obedience to the civil authorities (1 Pe. 2:13-14) and illustrates the terrible consequences when a nation forsakes God and turns to unrestrained sin (Eze. 20). The law in all civilized countries reflects the perfect legal code given by God to Moses. For more on the Mosaic Law as a foundation for societies, see the essay, "The Mosaic Law: The Unity of the Legal Structure in Both Testaments," pp. 102-103.

14:17 For the kingdom of God is not a matter of eating and drinking, but of righteousness, peace and joy in the Holy Spirit (NIV)

"The kingdom" was a central message of the Gospels and, before that, of the old covenant. For more on the subject, see commentary on Mk. 1:15.

15:19 ...from Jerusalem, and round about unto Illyricum, I have fully preached the gospel of Christ.

Most impressive are the Christian leaders who were born in the Yugoslavian community known as Illyricum and Dalmatia, where Paul and Titus established early missionary work. Both Jerome and Constantine were natives from this area. Jerome became one of the great Bible scholars and produced the Latin Vulgate Bible.[21] Constantine became the first Roman emperor to embrace Christianity, to legalize it, and to make large donations for its spread.[22]

The controversial Christian persecutor Diocletian was also born in the Illyricum and Dalmatia area. He eventually married Prisca, a Christian woman. We do not know the circumstances of this marriage but we do know that early Christians were mainly of the servant/slave domestic class. Paul states that he had ministered in the palace and that saints were living in Caesar's household (Ph. 1:13; 4:22).[23]

Written to the Romans from Corinthus, and sent by Phebe servant of the church at Cenchrea. (Subscription in KJV)

Many Bible readers discover that the subscriptions in the traditional thirteen Pauline epistles appear only in some English Bibles and not in others. These postscripts give information regarding the traditional place from which each epistle was written, as well as, in some cases, what was believed to be the name of the amanuensis (scribe) writing the letter or the messenger

Worship
3921-3923

Abel
4

Pre-eminence of Love
2209

Love Enjoined
2207

Citizen's Duties
2525

Decalogue
949

Spiritual Kingdom
2007-2013

Paul's Missionary Journeys
2382

Origin of the English Bible
4220

Roman Emperors
611-614

Bond-servants
2138

History of Early Church
4309g

Scribes
3165

delivering the epistle. To give a background for this problem it is necessary to go back to the time when the newly invented Gutenberg printing press produced the first printed copy of Jerome's Latin Vulgate Bible in the mid-fifteenth century. It became the authorized Bible text in the established Church for hundreds of years.[24]

In 1516 Desiderius Erasmus, a Dutch scholar, produced a new Greek text using some of the extant miniscule manuscripts as well as Jerome's Latin Bible. Eventually, the Erasmus text became known as the Textus Receptus and became the basic Greek text for many vernacular translations.

We do not know exactly when these subscriptions were added but we do know that during the first few centuries after the apostolic generation such basic background information was transmitted through oral tradition. To preserve these traditions it became necessary to print them in the Greek texts as explanatory footnotes. Consequently these traditions were passed on to the subsequent English versions including the King James of 1611.

The reason for omission is that some publishers of English Bibles are committed to printing only the Biblical text. However, it is the opinion of some scholars that these subscriptions should be included in contemporary English editions because of their link with ancient authorities.

Manuscripts
4220

Outline
History of
Apostles
4300b
Origin and
Growth of
the English
Bible
4220

1 and 2 Corinthians

The Name

The Epistles to the Corinthians derive their name from the Corinthian church to whom they are addressed.

Authorship and Date

Both epistles to the Corinthians are recognized to be of Pauline authorship. Both the internal and external evidence is such that no critic of note has challenged Paul as the author. Throughout the centuries tradition has insisted that these epistles contain the very *pectus Paulinum,* the mind and heart of the great apostle to the Gentiles, and preserve for the church an impregnable defense of historical Christianity. What has been said of their genuineness applies almost equally to both 1 and 2 Corinthians.[1] In A.D. 95 Clement of Rome made reference to Paul as the writer of the epistles. Ignatius and Polycarp both provide additional external evidence of Pauline authorship. The best information available indicates that Paul wrote his first letter to the Corinthians from Ephesus about three years after his first visit to Corinth,[2] probably about A.D. 55.[3] Most scholars feel that the second epistle was written by Paul from Macedonia, probably in Philippi, during his third missionary journey in about A.D. 57.

Background, Purpose, and Content

Into the morally and spiritually depraved city of Corinth Paul brought the gospel. He intended only a brief stopover, but the Lord commanded him to tarry; Paul had an eighteen-month ministry there (Ac. 18:9-11).

Paul founded the Corinthian church during his first visit on his second missionary journey. His first public ministerial contact was in the synagogue, where he reasoned with the Jews that Jesus was the Christ-Messiah (Ac. 18:4-5). It appears that the church was at first a synagogue congregation. Crispus, the chief ruler of the synagogue, was Paul's first convert (Ac. 18:8). However, it was at Corinth that Jewish hostility and rejection made Paul "shake his raiment" and turn to the Gentiles (Ac. 18:6). When the Jews brought Paul before Gallio, the deputy of Achaia, the Jews were driven out of the Judgment Hall (Ac. 18:12-16). Apparently Sosthenes, one of the chief rulers of the synagogue, was publicly flogged by a Greek mob (Ac. 18:17).

At the end of his ministry in Corinth, Paul took his leave to go to Jerusalem to celebrate Pentecost (Ac. 18:19-21). After a short stay Paul returned to Antioch to begin his third missionary journey. After some meetings in Galatia and Phrygia, he continued on to Ephesus (Ac. 19:1).

First Epistle to the Corinthians	**4268**
Second Epistle to the Corinthians	**4269**
Paul	**2697, 4309**
Gentiles	**2383-2384, 4038**
Ephesus	**1142, 4373**
Paul's Missionary Journeys	**2382**
Corinth	**840, 4359**
Paul's Second Missionary Journey	**4309d**
Opposers	**1567**
Synagogues	**3521-3523**
Paul's Third Missionary Journey	**4309e**

During his stay in Ephesus, travelers from Corinth informed Paul of the difficulties the church was having. Ephesus, an eight-day journey by sea from Corinth, became a kind of relay station for news from Corinth. All the news concerning the Corinthian church was unfavorable.

Chloe, who had come from Corinth, reported serious contentions among church members (1 Co. 1:11). To obtain additional information, Paul sent Timothy to Corinth (4:17). After faithful work in Corinth, Apollos joined Paul in Ephesus (3:5-6; 16:12). Apollos was followed by Stephanus, Fortunatus, and Achaicus (16:17), who supplied Paul with additional information on the conditions in Corinth. According to the reports: "The church had broken into factions, and was distracted by party cries. Some of its members were living openly immoral lives, and discipline was practically in abeyance. Others had quarrels over which they dragged one another into heathen courts. Great differences of opinion had also arisen with regard to marriage, and the social relations generally; with regard to banquets and the eating of food offered to idols; with regard to the behavior of women in the assemblies, to the Lord's Supper and the love-feasts, to the use and the value of spiritual gifts and to the hope of the resurrection."[4]

These gloomy reports distressed Paul greatly. His first impulse was to visit them "with a rod" (1 Co. 4:21), but he decided to write the church a letter instead (1 Corinthians), which was delivered by Titus. Even though the Corinthians deserved the severest rebuke, Paul wrote a masterful letter in which he exercised considerable restraint. He made his appeal to the finer instincts of the church members. With commendation and praise, he fanned the small spark of goodness still remaining. In his appeal "to them that are sanctified in Christ Jesus, called to be saints, with all that in every place call upon the name of Jesus Christ our Lord…" (1 Co. 1:2), he prayed that the grace and peace of God would rest upon them (1:3), and he expressed thanks for the grace of God which had been given to them by Jesus Christ (1:4), "even as the testimony of Christ" had been confirmed by them (1:6). Paul commended them for the gifts which they had so generously given (1:7) and assured them that as they waited for the coming of the Lord, they would be confirmed by the Lord to the end and so they would "be blameless in the day of our Lord Jesus Christ" (1:7-9).

R. Dykes Shaw evaluates the letter of First Corinthians thus: "It moves with firm tread among the commonest themes, but also rises easily into the loftiest spheres of thought and vision, breaking again and again into passages of glowing rhythmical elegance. It rebukes error, exposes and condemns sin, solves doubts, upholds and encourages faith…in a spirit of utmost tenderness and love, full of grace and truth."[5]

In chapter 12 Paul presented his extraordinary insight on spiritual gifts. In chapter 13 he developed a treatise on love, which is truly the greatest statement on love even penned. It is the "high water mark" of all sacred literature.

Shaw says that the First Corinthian letter has three outstanding features:

1. The first is Paul's earnest warning against a factious spirit. The Corinthians were obsessed with a party spirit of Greek democracy and were influenced in their religious activity by the sporting spirit of the athletic games. "They listened to their teachers with itching ears, not as men who wished to learn, but as partisans who sought occasion, either to applaud or to condemn."

2. "The Corinthian letter also made a high ethical contribution in the rules it sets forth for the Christian conscience. Meat offered to idols and then eaten became a serious stumbling block to many Corinthian Christians. Some rationalized that since the idol was a block of wood or stone, the meat was not actually affected. But Paul pointed out that 'Christian liberty must be willing to subject itself to the law of Love.' He recognized that a brother might be weak and would be adversely affected by eating meat offered to idols (1 Co. 8:1-12). For the sake of the brother, Paul took the position that one should refrain from eating meat if it caused another brother to stumble (1 Co. 8:13)." (See Mt. 22:37-39.)

Idolatry
3928-3933

Limitations of Liberty
4056

3. "The exaltation of the cross of Christ is another outstanding feature of this Epistle. To the Apostle, human instrumentality was minimal. It was not what Paul or Apollos or Cephas did, but what resulted from preaching Christ and him crucified (1 Co. 1:18)."[6]

Stumbling Blocks
1565

Paul had spent three years at Ephesus, where he wrote First Corinthians (A.D. 55). Soon after the tumult in Ephesus when Paul nearly lost his life (Ac. 19), he went to Macedonia. While visiting the churches in the Philippi-Thessalonica area (A.D. 57), Paul wrote his second letter to the Corinthians. Somewhere in Macedonia Paul made contact with Titus, who had recently returned from Corinth with good news. Some of the previous problems had been resolved, but now new troubles began to develop. Most serious was the denial by a number of the Corinthians of Paul's apostleship. Had the criticism of the Corinthians been left unchallenged, Paul's authority and influence would have been greatly diminished. Paul immediately wrote the Second Corinthian letter in which he developed a defense of his apostleship. Paul sent this epistle to Corinth by Titus. A few days later Paul continued his journey to Corinth. He reminded the Corinthians that he had founded the church there and that he did have a right in its management.[7] In the introduction to the Second Corinthian letter, Paul once again shows great restraint in his admonition. He is most gracious and benevolent in his solution. Paul chooses to mingle his own sorrows, anxieties and shortcomings with those of the Corinthians. He uses the pronouns "we" and "us" frequently to show that he shares with them their problems.

Cross of Christ
892

Ephesus
1142, 4373

Paul's Apostleship
202

Paul's Care of the Church
732

"Out of much affliction and anguish of heart" he writes to them "with many tears" (2 Co. 2:4). Wick Broomall describes this approach: "In spite of its ruggedness, this letter is as beautiful in his symmetry as a mountain flower—and it carries far more fragrance."[8]

Spiritual Brethren
741

Within the gentleness of his entreaty Paul gives the Corinthians an ultimatum that they must surrender totally to the authority of Christ's apostleship.[9] Paul subtly suggests that his apostleship is evidenced by the Corinthians being living epistles, "known and read of all men...written not with ink, but with the Spirit of the living God; not in tables of stone, but in fleshy tables of the heart" (3:2-3). In chapter 5 Paul assures the Corinthians of immortality: "if our earthly house of this tabernacle were dissolved, we have a building of God, an house not made with hands, eternal in the heavens" (5:1). Regarding readiness for death, Paul says, "Therefore we are always confident, knowing that, whilst we are at home in the body, we are absent from the Lord...we are confident...and willing rather to be absent from the body, and to be present with the Lord" (5:6-8).

Authority of Christ
710

Immortality
2405-2406

Assurance
298

Paul cautions the Corinthian Christians not to be "unequally yoked together with unbelievers" because believers and unbelievers have no communion or fellowship with each other (6:14; cf. De. 22:10). One frequently sees in Palestine a small donkey hitched to a plow with a large cow or ox, or a camel with a cow. It is evident that there could be little compatibility when a long-legged animal and one with short legs are yoked together. The spiritual analogy is clear.

Paul acknowledges the benevolence of the believers in Macedonia and challenges the Corinthians to do likewise (8:1-22). In chapter 10 the apostle continues to discuss the matter of Christian giving, the use of spiritual weapons (10:4-5), and the spiritual discipline necessary in the Christian life (10:6-18).

In chapter 11 Paul affirms his apostleship and follows it with a review of his own sufferings (11:22-33). In the last two chapters Paul has visions of Paradise (12:1), discloses that he has a thorn in his flesh (12:7), and gives disciplinary warnings (13:l-4). He advises the Christians to examine themselves to see whether their conduct and attitude are consistent with the faith (13:5). In the final verses, Paul expresses a heartfelt benediction of love for the Corinthians (13:11-14).

The City of Corinth

The city-state of Corinth, Greece, located about fifty miles west of Athens was already a flourishing center in 1000 B.C. By the time of the Roman conquest it was a city of 400,000 people, superseded only by Rome, Alexandria and Antioch. From early times the Acropolis, or Acro-Corinth, was a fortified bastion encircled by massive walls. It was also a prominent religious center with many temples. Most popular was the temple in honor of Aphrodite, the goddess of love.

| Corinth |
| 840, 4359 |

| Places Devoted to Idolatry |
| 3948-3951 |

Corinth was strategically located on a narrow isthmus, thus forming a buffer zone between the Peloponnesian peninsula and the mainland of Greece. The peninsula was about the size of New Hampshire and formed the greater part of Achaia during Roman times. Before the Corinthian canal was finished in 1893, ships had to sail around the peninsula and face the tempestuous "Euroclydon wind" such as Paul faced when he suffered shipwreck on the way to Rome (Ac. 27:9ff.).

The alternative was to unload a ship on one side of the isthmus and have the cargo carried over the three mile strip by slaves. The boat was then placed on rollers and pushed across, where it was reloaded and sent on its way.

| Ships |
| 3273 |

Since Corinth was a maritime city, it acquired all of the evils peculiar to a dock-side district. Three excellent harbors provided protective facilities for both east and west-bound water traffic as well as loading ports for the land caravans. Because of its strategic location it became the gathering place

Corinth. The seven columns are from the temple of Apollo.

for both the best and the worst in Roman and Greek society. It was a center for arts, crafts, artificers, and tradesmen of every kind, but it also was a place frequented by prostitutes, conmen, gamblers, thieves, adventurers, vagrants, and religious cultists. Its immorality and sensuous pleasures gave the city the title of "sin city." To "act as a Corinthian" was a synonym for the gross immorality of that day. The lowest state of moral corruption was to be "corinthianized."[10] It is referred to as a "renowned and voluptuous city where the vices of East and West met."[11]

Impurity
663-667

St. Paul probably arrived in Corinth in A.D. 52. He supported himself in the tentmaking trade in partnership with Aquila and Priscilla. On his third missionary journey Paul stayed in Corinth for three years, but when the great "silversmith" riot got out of hand, he decided that it was time to return to Jerusalem, through Macedonia with a stop at Ephesus. For a historical background of the Corinthian church it is necessary to consult Ac. 18.

Making of Idols
3932

Archaeological excavations at Corinth are extensive. This city, which once had 500,000 inhabitants, eventually crumbled in the dust. The best preserved part of Old Corinth is the Acro-Corinth—the high city—a stony mountain about 1,800 feet high whose summit is strewn with the remains of old temples and fortifications and is edged with a stone wall around its entire perimeter.

A graphic description of the ruins of Corinth follows:

> More than 30 seasons of patient excavations of ancient Corinth by the American School of Classical Studies [located] in Athens have revealed much of the city known to Paul. Below the conspicuous Doric columns of the archaic temple of Apollo, already six centuries old in his day, and certainly seen by him, there spread the spacious Agora or marketplace—a rectangle bound by an amazing array of small shops shaded by impressive colonnades. The Stoa, largest in all Greece, ran 500 ft. along the south end of the Agora, and was elegantly colonnaded with Doric and Ionic columns. Many of the shops, with their storerooms and wells, from which various treasures and baubles have been excavated, had marble gutters and mosaics. Now visible, north of the Agora, was the 210 ft. long basilica, used for administrative purposes and law courts. The bema where Paul stood trial has been excavated...It was a richly ornamented tribunal, in which the Roman Government sat. It...had three openings between massive piers. Between the piers were benches, where witnesses or prisoners waited to be heard...From the NE corner of the Agora the stately Propylaea Gateway led down to the Lechaeum Road...The "Straight Way" connected Corinth with her W. harbor...the lintel of a Jewish synagogue has been found... The excavation at the Great Theatre—the Radio City of Corinth—revealed an inscription which refers to Erastus...Might this be the "Erastus the city treasurer" whose greetings Paul included in his letter to the Romans (16:23) written from Corinth?...A short walk from ancient Corinth is the nearest ancient equivalent to a general hospital—the healing sanctuary of the Greek god Asklepios. Its dining room, with its sloping stone couches, low stone tables, and hearth where dishes were kept warm, has been excavated. "Ex Volo"—terra cotta "thank offerings," representing hands, legs, feet or organs healed or presented for healing, are now in the Corinth Museum.[12]

Idolatrous Temples
3949

Tree of Paul's Life
4309

Synagogues
3521-3523

In February, 1885, an earthquake destroyed the city.

1 Co. 2:6 ...the wisdom of this age...the rulers of this age...are coming to nothing. (NIV)

The basis of this statement can be found in the very beginning of time, the Garden of Eden. God told Satan, "I will put enmity between thee and the woman, and between thy seed and her seed; it shall bruise thy head, and thou shalt bruise his heel" (Ge. 3:15). Satan is now the "prince of this world" (Jn. 12:31; 16:11) and he "prowls around like a roaring lion looking for someone to devour" (1 Pe. 5:8, NIV). The arch deceiver goes about as an "angel of light" (2 Co. 11:14) trying to deceive even the elect (Mt. 24:24). In this way he continues to bruise the heel of Christ, just as he did on Calvary.

However, his potential defeat was sealed when Christ died on the cross and bruised his head. Satan's power, though active in the world now, will come to an end. In destroying Satan's ultimate power over mankind, God enabled man to turn from the power of Satan unto God (Ac. 26:18). Paul was confident that the powers of this present age would ultimately come to nothing and that God's wisdom would prevail.

1 Co. 4:20 For the kingdom of God is not in word, but in power.

The terms "kingdom of God" and the "kingdom of heaven" are used repeatedly throughout the Gospels. For more on these terms, see commentary on Mk. 1:15.

1 Co. 5:7-8 ...For even Christ our passover is sacrificed for us: Therefore let us keep the feast... with the unleavened bread of sincerity and truth.

The Passover, or Feast of Unleavened Bread, was a reminder to the children of Israel of their deliverance from Egypt on the night when the death angel passed over the homes where blood was sprinkled on the doorposts, but killed the firstborn of the Egyptians. A lamb was slain, roasted whole, and eaten with unleavened bread, accompanied by bitter herbs, to commemorate the Israelites' exit from Egypt in haste, not waiting for their bread to rise (Ex. 12:18).

The powerful Christian implications of the feast are seen in this verse. The Passover lamb was a foreshadowing of Christ, the Son of God. Like the paschal lamb, he was without blemish (Ex. 12:5; 1 Pe. 1:18-19) and not a bone was broken (Ex. 12:46; Jn. 19:36). His blood was presented to the Lord (Ex. 12:13). As the Israelites ate the Passover with each other, so also Jesus ate this memorial meal with his disciples (Lu. 22:1-18).

1 Co. 10:11 Now all these things happened unto them for ensamples: and they are written for our admonition...

The word "ensample" is translated from the Greek word "tupos," meaning literally "a figure, image, or pattern prefiguring a future person or thing." Throughout Scripture there are people or events that prefigure something that will happen later. In this case Paul is calling to mind the exodus from Egypt and tells his readers that they should take warning from the lessons learned there. For more on this subject, see the essay "Salvation Symbolized in the Exodus," pp. 95-99.

Margin references:

Wisdom-Folly
3838-3855

Satan
3148-3155
Deceivers
3707

Enabling Grace
4030

Spiritual Power
3803

Passover
2686

Feast of the Passover
1256
Unleavened Bread
539

Lamb of God
3365

Admonition
799

Salvation Promised
3122

1 Co. 10:16 The cup of blessing which we bless, is it not the communion of the blood of Christ? ...

Atoning
Blood of
Christ
679

The "blood of Christ" is a figurative expression for his atoning death.[13] It is significant that from the very first sacrifices mentioned in the Bible—those of Cain and Abel (Ge. 4:4-5)—it was the blood sacrifice that was accepted as a sin offering. For more on the significance of the blood sacrifice, see commentary on Ge. 4:4-5.

1 Co. 12:13 ...whether Jews or Greeks... (NIV)

Impartiality
of God
1979

This verse, as well as many others in Paul's letters, emphasizes the fact that God has no favorites. See, for example, Ro. 2:11,13; 3:22,29; 10:12-13; Gal. 3:28; Ep. 2:13,18; 3:6. For more on subject of Jews and Gentiles alike before God, see commentary on Ac. 10:34-35. See also the Introduction to Romans: Background, Purpose and Content.

1 Co. 12:28 And God hath set some in the church, first apostles, secondarily prophets...

Apostles
2080-2082
Prophets
2065-2074

Paul uses the term "apostle" in a somewhat broader sense than the writers of the Gospels (see commentary on Ac. 1:26). For more on "prophets" see commentary on Je. 1:5.

1 Co. 15:3-8 For what I received I passed on to you as of first importance... (NIV)

Gospel
1440

These verses spell out the heart of the gospel message, a message transmitted to Paul from other Christians. In this way Paul links himself with early Christian tradition, and these verses could be called his "creed." See the essay "Creeds of the Christian Faith," beginning on the next page.

2 Co. 4:6 For God, who commanded the light to shine out of darkness, hath shined in our hearts...

Light-
Darkness
2165-2180

Christ the
Light
2168
Candlestick
637

Light was the first element God created (Ge. 1:3). Throughout the Bible there are many figures in which light is associated with God. For example, Jesus said, "I am the light of the world: he that followeth me shall not walk in darkness, but shall have the light of life" (Jn. 8:12). In the OT there was the pillar of fire (Ex. 13:21), the burning bush (Ex. 3:2), and the golden candlestick (Ex. 25:31). For more on the candlestick and Christ, the light of the world, see commentary on Ex. 25:31.

2 Co. 10:4 The weapons we fight with are not the weapons of the world... (NIV)

Spiritual
Warfare
358-359
Unworldli-
ness
3918

Ever since the judgment was pronounced that Christ will bruise Satan's head but Satan will bruise his heel (Ge. 3:15), there has been a battle raging. The war is between the forces of righteousness and those of evil (1 Ti. 1:18; 6:12; 2 Ti. 2:4). Paul often uses military terminology to describe the spiritual warfare the Christian must undergo (see Ep. 6:10ff.).

Arch
Deceiver
3153
Satan
3148-3155

2 Co. 11:14 ...Satan himself masquerades as an angel of light. (NIV)

Satan is actually the "prince of darkness." For the association of light with deity, see commentary on 2 Co. 4:6; Ex. 25:31.

Creeds of the Christian Faith

In a religious context the word "creed" means a concise, Biblically based expression of the Christian faith. Creeds were formulated as the church grew and administrative affairs became more complicated. Because heathen philosophies, Gnosticism and Hellenism had crept into the church, it was necessary to make a plain affirmation of the fundamentals of the faith. Learned men of the church convened councils to study the Scriptures and to formulate credal statements. New Testament writers had provided the materials in their clear-cut affirmation of the oneness of God, the unqualified deity of Christ, and the personality of the Holy Spirit.

One God
2649

The Apostles' Creed

The Apostles' Creed is the most widely known statement of faith in the church universal. This creed states clearly all of the basic fundamentals of the Christian faith. Each element in it can be verified by the Scriptures.

The creed arises out of the "mists of antiquity." It originated early in the history of the church when its faith was challenged by many heathen philosophies. It was in use in some form as early A.D. 150. According to tradition each one of the twelve apostles wrote one phrase of the creed, but this is not generally accepted by modern scholars.

Outline History of Apostles
4300b

One early tradition on the origin of the Apostles' Creed was perpetuated by Tyrannius Rufinus (A.D. 345-410), who wrote a commentary on the Apostles' Creed, translated *Church History* by Eusebius, and finally established a monastery on the Mount of Olives in Jerusalem.[14] According to

The Apostles' Creed

I believe in God the Father Almighty,[A] *maker of heaven and earth;*[B]
And in Jesus Christ his only Son our Lord:[C] *who was conceived by the Holy Spirit,*[D] *born of the Virgin Mary,*[E] *suffered under Pontius Pilate,*[F] *was crucified,*[G] *dead,*[H] *and buried,*[I] *the third day he rose from the dead;*[J] *he ascended into heaven,*[K] *and sitteth at the right hand of God the Father Almighty;*[L] *from thence he shall come to judge the quick and the dead.*[M]

I believe in the Holy Spirit,[N] *the holy catholic Church,*[O] *the communion of saints,*[P] *the forgiveness of sins,*[Q] *the resurrection of the body,*[R] *and the life everlasting.*[S] *Amen.*

A. Is. 64:8; Mt. 6:9
B. Ge. 1:1
C. Mt. 17:5; Ac.. 2:36
D. Lu. 1:30-35; Mt. 1:20
E. Mt. 1:18-25
F. Mt. 27:12,24

G. Mt. 27:35; 1 Co. 2:2
H. Lu. 23:46; Jn. 19:33
I. Mt. 27:59-60
J. Lu. 16:9; Jn. 20:9
K. Lu. 24:51; Ac. 1:9
L. Lu. 20:42; Ac. 2:55
M. Ac. 10:42; 2 Ti. 4:1

N. Mt. 1:18; Lu. 1:35
O. Ep. 5:27
P. 2 Co. 13:14
Q. 2 Chr. 7:14; 1 Jn. 1:9
R. 2 Co. 4:14; 1 Th 4:16
S. Jn. 3:16

> *The Nicene Creed*
>
> *I believe in one God: the Father Almighty, maker of heaven and earth, and of all things visible and invisible;*
>
> *And in one Lord Jesus Christ, the only begotten Son of God: begotten of the Father before all worlds, God of God, Light of Light, very God of very God, begotten, not made, being of one substance with the Father, through whom all things were made; who for us men and for our salvation came down from heaven, and was incarnate by the Holy Ghost of the Virgin Mary, and was made man, and was crucified also for us under Pontius Pilate; he suffered and was buried,^A and the third day he rose again according to the Scriptures, and ascended into heaven, and sitteth on the right hand of the Father; and he shall come again with glory, to judge both the quick and the dead; whose kingdom shall have no end.*
>
> *And I believe in the Holy Ghost, the Lord, the giver of life, who proceedeth from the Father and the Son, who with the Father and the Son together is worshipped and glorified, who spake by the prophets. And I believe in one holy catholic and apostolic Church. I acknowledge one baptism for the remission of sins. And I look for the resurrection of the dead, and the life of the world to come. Amen.*
>
> A. Traditional use of this creed includes these words: "He descended into hell."

Rufinus:

> Tradition says...on the eve therefore of departure from one another, they first mutually agreed upon a standard of their future preaching, lest haply, when separated, they might...vary in the statements which they should make to those whom they should invite to believe in Christ. Being all therefore met together, and being filled with the Holy Ghost, they composed...this brief formulatory of their future preaching, each contributing his several sentences to one common summary; and they ordained that the rules thus framed should be given to those who believe.[15]

Inspiration of Prophets and Teachers
1774

Reference is also made to this tradition by Johannes Cassianus (A.D. 360?-435?), an early monk and theologian with extensive travel experience in the Jerusalem-Bethlehem area, as well as by Saint Jerome (Eusebius Hieronymus), translator of the Latin Vulgate.[16]

It is quite likely that the Apostles' Creed, as it is today, underwent many revisions. The Athenian philosopher, Aristides (A.D. 126), wrote a Christian defense to Emperor Hadrian. It contains what is believed to be an approximation of the original Apostles' Creed:

> Now, the Christians trace their origin from the Lord Jesus Christ. And he is acknowledged by the Holy

Tree of Christ's Life
4308

Spirit to be the Son of the Most High God, who came down from heaven for the salvation of men. And being born of a pure virgin, unbegotten and immaculate, he assumed flesh and revealed himself among men that he might recall them to himself from their wandering after many gods. And having accomplished his wonderful dispensation, by a voluntary choice, he tasted death on the cross, fulfilling an august dispensation. After three days he came to life again and ascended into heaven...He had twelve disciples who, after his ascension to heaven, went forth into the provinces of the whole world and declared his greatness.[17]

It is generally agreed that some form of the Apostles' Creed was given to early converts at their baptism. This creed is a common denominator of theology upon which most Christian groups can agree.

The Nicene Creed
As the church developed and questions arose it was necessary to make concise declarations of the basic doctrinal beliefs. "To put these truths together was the great theological achievement of the clear thinking and vigorous debate which led to the Council of Nicaea (A.D. 325) and on to the Council of Chalcedon" (A.D. 451).[18] The Council of Nicaea was called by Emperor Constantine to settle the theological controversy between Arius and Athanasius. Arius of Alexandria argued that Christ was a high creature but that he was not eternal and he was not the nature of God. Athanasius

Christ Eternal
709

"saw clearly that the issue at stake was the distinctiveness of Christianity and the reality of the Incarnation. He recognized that to worship a Christ who is not quite God is an open door to a return to polytheism."[19]

The controversy was settled in Athanasius' favor. The Council adopted a creed which stated in part that God was the Father Almighty and that Jesus Christ the Lord was the only begotten of the Father, who was made flesh, suffered, rose from the dead, and ascended into heaven.

Christ, Oneness with the Father
685

Notwithstanding the victory of Athanasius, the Arian heresy did not die completely. It still appears in some strains of liberal theology. However, the Nicene creed became the "established standard for the normative Christian understanding of Christ throughout the ages."

Other Statements of Faith
The Creed of Athanasius became the third defensive statement of the Christian church. This creed was formulated to explain in detail the Nicene Creed, and dealt mainly with the doctrine of the Trinity and the Incarnation. Even though Athanasius spent many years defending the Nicene Creed, it is generally agreed that he did not write the creed bearing his name. Scholars are of the opinion that the creed, as we have it today, was not formulated in its present form until the time of St. Augustine.

The next theological controversy was over original sin. St. Augustine (A.D. 354-430) challenged the position of Pela-

Origin of Sin
3339

gius, who said that "man was created in a neutral condition, neither sinful or holy and with capacity for good or evil. His will was free and undetermined—each succeeding man is born in the same condition as Adam before the fall and is free from guilt or pollution at birth."[20] In opposition to this view, Augustine contended what is known as the Biblical doctrine of original sin. This controversy resulted in "Augustine establishing, deep in

The Korean Creed

We believe in the one God, maker and ruler of all things, Father of all men, the source of all goodness and beauty, all truth and love.

We believe in Jesus Christ, God manifest in the flesh, our teacher, example, and Redeemer, the Savior of the world.

We believe in the Holy Spirit, God present with us for guidance, for comfort, and for strength.

We believe in the forgiveness of sins, in the life of love and prayer, and in grace equal to every need.

We believe in the Word of God contained in the Old and New Testaments as the sufficient rule both of faith and of practice.

We believe in the Church as the fellowship for worship and for service of all who are united to the living Lord.

We believe in the kingdom of God as the divine rule in human society, and in the brotherhood of man under the fatherhood of God.

We believe in the final triumph of righteousness, and in the life everlasting. Amen.

Christian thought, the conviction that salvation is by faith alone, a grace given to creatures who have inherited a racial predisposition to sin, and who therefore could never in themselves please God."[21]

Statements of faith in the fourth and fifth centuries were called creeds, while similar statements in the sixteenth and seventeenth centuries were called confessions, based mainly on the idea of reconciliation. These confessions were limited in scope and theological range.

The sixteenth-century reformation period produced the Augsburg Confession, setting forth beliefs of the Lutheran movement.

> Reconciliation
> 2971-2972

The Reform movement under Zwingli and Calvin, as distinguished from the Lutheran group, produced the Tetrapolitan Confession by Martin Bucer in 1530 and John Calvin's Consonsus Tigurinus in 1549, both designed to present the Calvinist view.

In 1646 the Westminster Confession was produced to set forth doctrinal articles for the Presbyterians in England and Scotland. During the reign of Henry VIII in England The Articles of 1536 and The King's Book of 1543 were published. Then came the Forty-two Articles showing clearly the Protestant influence on the English Church. The Thirty-Nine Articles reflected the theological posture of the English Church under Queen Elizabeth.[22]

The twentieth century produced several creeds, of which the Korean Creed and A Modern Creed are best known.

The Korean Creed

Henry Gehard Appenzeller and Horace Grant Underwood together were the vanguard of organized missions in Korea.[23] They were both men of letters with unquestioned dedication to the cause of Christ and missions. Under their scholarly leadership the Bible was translated into the native tongue and Tract Societies, Theological Seminaries, and Christian Colleges were founded.

At the time the Korean Methodist Church was organized (1930), it was felt that a supplementary credal statement should be formulated. Bishop Herbert Welch was appointed to make a rough draft of such a statement expressing the basic essentials of the Christian faith in nontechnical language. In consultation with Bishop James C. Baker and the leaders of the Korean church a final draft was made, presented and approved by the first General Conference of the Korean Methodist Church. This creed has been used extensively in the National Church of Korea.[24]

A Modern Creed

Edwin Lewis, the great theologian at Drew Theological Seminary, formulated a Modern Affirmation during the time when the liberal-conservative theological controversy was at its peak, in the mid 1930s. About this time his own theological position was changed to the conservative side.[25] His Affirmation is quoted below.

Examples
of Strife
3734

It is to be acknowledged that this and other newer creeds are limited in scope and content and should not be used exclusively. Bishop Nolan B.

A Modern Affirmation

We believe in God the Father, infinite in wisdom, power, and love, whose mercy is over all his works, and whose will is ever directed to his children's good.

We believe in Jesus Christ, Son of God and Son of man, the gift of the Father's unfailing grace, the ground of our hope, and the promise of our deliverance from sin and death.

We believe in the Holy Spirit as the divine presence in our lives, whereby we are kept in perpetual remembrance of the truth of Christ, and find strength and help in time of need.

We believe that this faith should manifest itself in the service of love as set forth in the example of our blessed Lord, to the end that the kingdom of God may come upon the earth. Amen.

Harmon of the United Methodist Church says,

> No one can object to these modern affirmations being used occasionally as explanations of certain truths of creed, provided—and this is an important proviso—that the one who uses them, and the people who are led to repeat them, know exactly how far they go and do not go...What I object to is to give the impression by the sonorous introduction and the constant use of these affirmations as a church-wide worship that they embody anything like the comprehensive faith of the Christian Church...These 20th century affirmations which sound so lofty and leave out so much. If they supplement, yes; if they supplant, no. Let the Apostles' Creed be used and let its verities be explained and preached—the whole Gospel to the whole world.[26]

Galatians

The Name

The book of Galatians derives its name from the people to whom it was addressed (Gal. 1:2). Galatia was a land-locked sub-division of Asia Minor in which the towns Paul visited were located. The city of Ankara, situated in the heart of the Galatian territory, is the modern capital of Turkey (Asia Minor).

Authorship and Date

There is little opposition to Pauline authorship for the book of Galatians.[1] The literary style, the doctrinal content, the historical background, and the analogies all point to Paul. Such ancient church writers as Clement of Rome, Polycarp, Justin Martyr, Irenaeus, and Tertullian affirm Pauline authorship. Both Marcion (A.D. 139) and the critical Tubingen scholars in Germany accept Paul as the author of Galatians.

The exact date of this book is not known. Scholars estimate that it was written between A.D. 55 and A.D. 60.

Background, Purpose, and Content

The question as to whether Paul evangelized the northern or the southern territory of Galatia has been a matter of some discussion. Since the epistle contains no reference to Paul's having been in the northern cities of Pessinus, Aneyra, and Tavium, the area of travel must have been in the south where Pisidian Antioch, Iconium, Lystra, and Derbe are located. Paul visited these cities on all three of his missionary journeys.

Madeleine Miller concludes that

> the theory that Paul addressed the churches in the southern part of Galatia is supported by the following evidence: (1) Paul and Barnabas had visited the cities of Iconium, Lystra, Derbe, and Pisidian Antioch, all in S. Galatia, and had founded churches there on the First Missionary Journey (Ac. 13:4-14:28). (2) In these cities at this time there were Jews (Ac. 13:14-51;14:1;16:1-3) who might have caused the situation reflected in the Epistle. (3) Familiar reference to Barnabas (Gal. 2:1,9,13) would have been pointless in a letter addressed to N. Galatia, where Barnabas was probably unknown.[2]

In his letter to the Galatians, Paul discusses three major subjects: the authority of his apostleship, the false teaching of the Judaizers, and the doctrine of justification and sanctification by faith. A fourth division concerns the practical application of certain Christian principles.

Sidebar references:

Epistle
to the
Galatians
4270

Paul
2697

Tree of
Paul's Life
4309

Galatia
1382

Antioch
198, 4330

Derbe
4363

Paul's First
Missionary
Journey
4309c

Barnabas
342

Apostleship
of Paul
202

The first two chapters of the letter deal chiefly with Paul's defense of his apostleship. Certain leaders in Galatia taught that before a Gentile could become a Christian he had to be circumcised and submit to ritualistic ordinances of Judaism, but Paul insisted that salvation was obtainable through faith alone (Gal. 2:16). To better promote their teachings, they sought to depreciate Paul's authority by raising questions concerning his apostleship (2:6-9). In answer to these complaints, Paul offered proof that the gospel he preached came by direct revelation from God (1:11-12). Paul also referred to his call (1:1,15); his call independent of the other apostles (1:15-24); his endorsement by the church (2:7-10); and his resistance to the teachings of the Judaizers, including his rebuke of Peter (2:5-14).

A second subject Paul discussed was the teachings of the Judaizers, i.e., salvation by works, the necessity of circumcision, and their effect upon the Galatians. In the introduction of his letter Paul stated the nature of the problem that prompted his discourse. After a brief greeting, he made a statement concerning the atonement, of which the Galatians had been partakers (1:4). He followed this affirmation almost immediately with words of reproof for the Galatians. Paul expressed surprise that they would "so soon" accept "another gospel: which is not another" gospel (1:6-7). He reproved the Galatians who were insisting upon the observance of Mosaic law (3:1-22) and the reinstatement of Jewish festivals and ceremonies (4:8-11).

A prominent theme in the book of Galatians is "justification by faith" without the works of the law, and in this regard the book is a companion to Romans and Hebrews. Each of these books includes the statement of faith made by the prophet Habakkuk (Hab. 2:4; cf. Ro. 1:17; Gal. 3:11; He. 10:38). In Galatians Paul clarified and defended his statement concerning faith, that justification is by faith alone (2:16); faith leads to a union with Christ and identification with the risen Christ (2:20-21); the justified are children of God by faith (3:26); the justified realize their sonship and liberty through faith (3:26-4:7).

Paul further supported his position of justification by faith by showing that Abraham and his seed were justified by faith (3:6-9). Paul pointed out that later the "law" was a means of bringing men to God. The Messianic law did not prevent sin, but was to act as a schoolmaster, "a tutor" (NIV) "to bring us unto Christ, that we might be justified by faith...[and that all believers are] the children of God by faith in Christ Jesus" (3:24-26). Paul emphasized the unity of the faith when he wrote that "there is neither Jew nor Greek, there is neither bond nor free, there is neither male nor female: for ye are all one in Christ Jesus. And if ye be Christ's then are ye Abraham's seed, and heirs according to the promise" (3:28-29).

George H. Findley writes that "The growth of the Christian consciousness has been traced from its germ in Abraham to its flower in the church of all nations. The Mosaic law formed a disciplinary interlude in the process, which has been all along a life of faith."[3] Chapter 5 contains Paul's discussion of liberty through faith. The apostle explained that faith in Christ and the love of God frees the Christian from the "letter of the law ordinances." Findley continues, "The ethical application is contained in the

Apostles
Called
2082

Revelations
2494

Judaizers
1958

Backsliding
993

Justification
by Faith
1985

Union with
Christ
738

Abraham
15, 4290

Purpose of
the Law
4055

Spiritual
Heirs
743

phrase of Ro. 8:2, 'the law of the Spirit of life in Christ Jesus.' (1) Love guards Christian liberty from license; it 'fulfills the whole law in a single word' (Gal. 5:13-15). (2) The Spirit, who imparts freedom, guides the freeman's 'walk...Crucified with Christ' and 'living in the Spirit,' the Christian man keeps God's law without bondage under it (Gal. 5:16-26)."[4]

Pre-eminence of Love **4182**

This formula of love was first expressed by Moses (De. 6:5-6; Le. 19:18) and confirmed by Jesus and Paul (Mt. 22:36-40; Gal. 5:14).

Love Enjoined **2207**

Paul enumerated and amplified the consequences of the Spirit life in terms of "love, joy, peace, long-suffering, gentleness, goodness, faith" (Gal. 5:22). On the other hand, he identifies the works of the flesh with the conditions described in Ro. 1:18-32 (cf. Gal. 5:19-20).

C. Fred Dickason notes that "Paul's purpose, then, is not to prove primarily that justification is by faith. His argument assumes this is true; and building upon the fact that justification has granted them perfect standing with God and full inheritance with Abraham, he seeks to establish that sanctification is in faith, apart from adherence to any part of Mosaic law (Gal. 2:19; 5:18). This is the contention of the whole letter as seen in the key exhortation (Gal. 5:1), the key question (3:3), and the significantly placed illustration of Peter's problem (discussed in 2:11-21)."[5] Paul insists that "the Galatians must recognize that their salvation and early Christian experience were based on faith and not law."[6]

Living Unto God **4062** Sanctifi-cation **3140-3141**

Law Insufficient **4054**

In the final chapter the apostle states that the duty of the believer toward the weak and depressed is to "bear...one another's burdens" (6:2). However, Paul makes a distinction between the external, physical, burdens which can be shared [i.e., interest in the infirmities of others; Greek, *baros*] (6:2) and the inner burdens which only the individual can bear [Greek, *portion*] (6:5).

Personal Respon-sibility **3453** Judaizers **1958**

Paul also presents an important rule in life, the law of input and return: "God is not mocked: for whatsoever a man soweth, that shall he also reap. For he that soweth to his flesh shall of the flesh reap corruption; but he that soweth to the Spirit shall of the Spirit reap life everlasting" (6:7-8).

In the final paragraph of chapter 6 Paul reveals that the objective of the Judaizers was their own self-glorification (6:12-16).

The Province of Galatia
Galatia was a landlocked area in the central part of Asia Minor. The best cartographic information suggests that Iconium, Derbe and Lystra were cities within its boundary. This conclusion would indicate that Paul evangelized this area on his first

missionary journey and made contact with the churches on his second and third journeys (Ac. 14: 5-6, 20, 21-23; 6:6-8).

In Roman times bathtubs in private homes were almost unknown. To satisfy hygenic needs large public bath houses were built where many kinds of baths were available including hot (caldarium), steam (luconarium), warm (tepidarium) and cold (frigidarium), as evidenced by archaeological excavations. These bath houses were social centers where friends and relatives had social contact. They were also places where every kind of sexual immorality including homosexuality was practiced.

This picture shows part of a bath facility in Ankara, near the western edge of Galatia. The small disc pillars supported the floor; hot air was circulated in the space under the floor to keep the baths comfortable in the winter. The space under the floor also provided room for steam as well as hot and cold water pipes.

Black Sea

GALATIA

Antioch

Iconium

Lystra

Derbe

Mediterranean Sea

1:8 ...Though we...preach any other gospel...let him be accursed.

The NT writers regarded the OT as comprising a complete system of revealed religion. Indeed the apostles did not pretend to teach any doctrine, tenet, or truth which they were not ready to prove by the then existing Scriptures. When the word "Scripture" is used in the NT it always refers to the OT. The NT was not canonized until A.D. 397 (see Introduction to the New Testament). If the apostles preached the gospel, they drew it from the OT. They not only preached no other gospel than that contained in the OT, but they repudiated everything contrary to the OT teachings, declaring every addition to it to be false.

A few passages substantiate this claim: "Did ye never read in the scriptures, The stone which the builders rejected, the same is become the head of the corner?" (Mt. 21:42). Here the appeal is made to Ps. 118:22 and Is. 28:16. Jesus himself declared, "I was daily with you in the temple teaching, and ye took me not: but the scriptures must be fulfilled" (Mk. 14:49; Ps. 22:6-8). "And beginning at Moses and all the prophets, he expounded unto them in all the scriptures the things concerning himself" (Lu. 24:27); "Then opened he their understanding, that they might understand the scriptures...Thus it is written [in the Scriptures], and thus it behooved Christ to suffer..." (Lu. 24:45-46). When the Apostle Paul evangelized the Jews he "went in unto them, and three sabbath days reasoned with them out of the scriptures" (Ac. 17:2). The Jews in Berea are commended because they "were more noble than those of Thessalonica, in that they received the word with all readiness of mind, and searched the scriptures daily, whether those things were so" (Ac. 7:11).

OT teachings show that the death of Christ was according to the Scriptures (1 Co. 15:3; see also Ac. 10:43; 26:22-23). The Word states that a man who is not saved in accordance with the OT cannot be saved at all (see Lu. 16:29-31; Is. 8:20). The Holy Scriptures are fully sufficient to make one "wise unto salvation through faith which is in Christ Jesus" (2 Ti. 3:15).

Holiness for Christians is commanded by the OT teachings (Le. 11:44; 1 Pe. 1:16). The Gospels contain the fulfillment of the promises recorded in the OT (Ro. 1:2); these Scriptures reveal the laws, statutes, and judgments of God (Ex. 24:3-4; De. 4:5-14); they testify of Christ (Jn. 5:39; Ac. 10:43; 1 Co. 15:3); they are sufficient for all religious needs and profitable for both doctrine and practice; they were written for instruction (Ro. 15:4); they are not to be added to, nor is anything to be taken from them (De. 4:2); they work effectually in all who believe (1 Th. 2:13); Christ enables the believer to understand them (Lu. 24:45); the Holy Spirit likewise enlightens them (Jn. 16:13; 1 Co. 2:10-14); everything must be tried by them (Ac. 17:11); they are designed for the regeneration of mankind (Ja. 1:18; 1 Pe. 1:23), for converting the soul and making wise the simple (Ps. 19:7), and for sanctifying the soul (Jn. 17:17; Ep. 5:26) as well as producing Christian hope (Ps. 119:49; Ro. 15:4) and obedience (De. 17:19-20). The Scriptures are good for cleansing the heart (Jn. 15:3; Ep. 5:26) and for promoting growth in grace (1 Pe. 4:11).

This examination of many passages indicates that there is no essential doctrine nor teaching known in the NT which is not drawn directly from the

---

Standard of Faith
426
God's Word Sacred
427

Truth of God's Word
436

Fullfillment of Prophecy
2892-2893

Search "The Word"
428

Salvation
3117

Christ's Teaching
3558

Spiritual Enlightenment
2175

Cleansing
965

Preaching of Paul
2087

OT. Paul expressly declared that he preached nothing else, and he instructed Timothy to follow the same rule (2 Ti. 3:15-17; 4:2). However, Paul was accused of preaching false doctrines (Ac. 24:5-6; 25:7). Paul's imprisonment was the result of his commitment to the ancient faith of the OT church, and not to any "new" views, tenets, or practices. "For the hope of Israel," the apostle exclaims, "I am bound with this chain" (Ac. 28:20). "And now I stand and am judged for the hope of the promise made of God unto our fathers: unto which promise our twelve tribes, instantly serving God day and night, hope to come. For which hope's sake, king Agrippa, I am accused of the Jews" (Ac. 26:5-7). The Epistle to the Hebrews is an argument refuting the charges against its author and his associates, that they had imbibed new religious tenets. From the beginning to the end, the writer contends for the unity of Apostolic Christianity with the Judaism of their fathers and the ancient church, but presents Christianity as better than Judaism.

Messianic Hope 4186

Epistle to the Hebrews 4280

At the time of Christ, and for many years previous, the church possessed its Bible, the OT, which was held in the highest veneration. No people ever lived who held their sacred books in greater respect than did the Jews before, and at the coming of, Christ. But there was no printing, and the books were all handwritten. They were few and only in the hands of the learned. Many of the people could not read; indeed, reading and writing were skills attained by only a select group. A knowledge of what the Scriptures contained was communicated to the people through the church by readings on the Sabbath and by means of the sculpture and paintings in the church (see pp. 573-574).

Scriptures 3166

"Word" Read 425

The chief complaint against the apostles was that they preached things new, things not taught in Scriptures and therefore false. To have done this would have been a great offense against revealed religion, and if the apostles or anyone else had taught and preached things not found in the Scriptures, the accusations against them would have been just. But the apostles constantly denied the charges and contended that they were made only by those who did not understand the Scriptures, that they set forth exactly what the OT taught and nothing more. An examination of what the twelve and Paul did teach and a comparison of their teachings with the OT reveal that they did not violate the integrity of the Scripture. They explained and elaborated, but they dared not, nor did they, add to them one new idea.

Apostles 2080-2082

Preaching of Paul 2087

Frequently the "Christian religion" and the "Jewish religion," in these express terms, are "contrasted" with each other, but there is no real contrast—they are the same in Spirit. Of course one must distinguish between the OT teachings and the "traditions of the elders" (Mt. 15:3; Mk. 7:7-8; Col. 2:8; Tit. 1:14; 1 Pe. 1:18).

Character-istics of Christianity 4139

3:24 Wherefore the law was our schoolmaster to bring us unto Christ...

Christ fulfilled the Law, but he did not repudiate it, because its use in past generations had been directed by God (Le. 18:3-4). It was upon the Old Covenant that Christ could establish the meaning of the New. The old Law, observed by use of ritual, was a means, not an end. The Law was to guide God's people, until the time when all the Law would be fulfilled; when Christ, "the end of the law for righteousness" would appear (Ro. 10:4). For more on Christ, the fulfillment of the law, see commentary on Mt. 5:17.

The Law 436-438

Purpose of Law 4055

3:28 There is neither Jew nor Greek...
for ye are all one in Christ Jesus.

Unity in
Christ
3724
Universal
Call
1791

For discussion on the Jew and Gentile alike before God, see commentary on Ac. 10:34-35 and the Introduction to Romans: Background, Purpose and Content.

4:31 ...we are not children of the slave
woman, but of the free woman. (NIV)

Judaizers
1958

Paul uses the story of Sarai and Hagar (Ge. 16:1-21:21) to allegorically reprove the Judaizers in the Galatian church. He emphasizes the message found from Genesis to Revelation: that it is faith, not works, that makes man right with God. See commentary on Ge. 15:6; 16:1.

5:21 ...inherit the kingdom of God.

Spiritual
Kingdom
2007-2013

The "kingdom of God" is a constant expression throughout Scripture. For more on the subject, see commentary on Mk. 1:15.

6:15 ...what counts is a new creation. (NIV)

New Birth
2154

This verse brings to mind Jn. 3:3. "Except a man be born again, he cannot see the kingdom of God." For more on the new birth see the essay "The Nature of the New Birth: Is It Unique to the NT?" pp. 384-386. See also the essay, "The Mechanics of Salvation in the OT Period," pp. 67-69.

Ephesians

The Name

The Epistle to the Ephesians derives its name from the Ephesian church to whom it was addressed.

Authorship and Date

The book of Ephesians has a traditional claim to Pauline authorship. Paul identified himself as the author of the book (1:1). The title was placed on the early manuscripts by the patristic fathers to preserve the integrity of the book. In addition, Paul claimed that he was both an apostle and a prisoner, a statement which is in agreement with Paul's life history (3:1). The literary style, terminology, and theology along with its historical references definitely indicate that the book is Pauline.[1] Church fathers such as Clement of Rome, Ignatius, Polycarp, and Hippolytus, do not hesitate to credit Paul with the authorship. The internal and external evidence is so strong that there is no reasonable objection to Pauline authorship.[2] The entire historical content suggests that Paul wrote the epistle while he was in prison, either in Caesarea or in Rome. The best judgment is that it was composed in Rome toward the end of Paul's imprisonment (A.D. 60-64). In the letter Paul tells the Ephesians that "Tychicus, a beloved brother and faithful minister in the Lord" was to be the messenger. The postscript states that it was written by him from Rome.

Background, Purpose, and Content

The words "in Ephesus" do not occur in the Codex Sinaiticus and the Codex Vaticanus, which has led to speculation that the book was written to the churches in general and not specifically to the church in Ephesus. On the other hand some of the manuscripts such as "Aleph" and "B" include the heading "to Ephesians." The problem of accurately copying manuscripts by hand would make it easy to omit words or phrases.

There is no strong reason for accepting the view that "in Ephesus" was not a part of the autograph when all the evidence is carefully evaluated. It is particularly significant that Paul mentions the designated church in almost all of his letters (1,2 Co., Gal., Ep., Ph., Col., 1,2 Th.). The evidence is strong that the book was for a particular church—most likely the one addressed—namely, the Ephesian.[3] A further reason for assuming that the book was sent to the Ephesians by Paul is his three-year ministry in Ephesus (Ac. 20:31).

The general content of the Ephesian letter is similar to that of Colossians. Both letters were written about the same time and speak of Christ as the Head of the Church (Ep. 1:22; cf. Col. 1:18). In both epistles the people are warned against false teachers (Ep. 5:6; cf. Col. 2:8) and are encouraged to maintain an attitude of love and a state of holiness, both in heart and in conversation.

Paul reaches a high point of revelation when he shows that our Lord is the Head of the whole church and that all believers share a common seat with Christ (Ep. 2:6). All are exhorted to live a life consistent with true holiness and the life and teachings of the Lord.

In the first three chapters of Ephesians, Paul tells the believers that they are in Christ; in the last three chapters the apostle tells them what to do because they are in Christ.[4] The book can be outlined with three words: sitting, walking, and standing. "By position, the believer is seated with Christ in the heavenlies (Ep. 2:6); his responsibility is to walk worthy of the calling wherewith he has been called (Ep. 4:1); and this walk is further seen as a warfare in which he is engaged against Satan and all his hosts and in which he is exhorted to stand against the wiles of the devil (Ep. 6:11)." [5]

One of the purposes of the Ephesian book is to bring unity to the Jewish and Gentile Christians. It is a matter of record that enmity existed between Jew and Gentile. Hostility by the Jews toward the Christians reached its climax in the third quarter of the first century. In this book Paul pleads for a reconciliation and unification of the Jewish and Gentile Christians—not through compromise, but by fusing them together in the Body of Christ through divine love (4:3-6, 11-13).

"The Church is 'in Christ;' it is His Body, and its members have 'put on' the new...life, which is 'Christ in them' (Ep. 2:11-22). Thus the corporate life of Christ is the Fulfiller of the purpose of God. Its ethical practice, down to details, is a working out of that purpose on the level of human experience."[6] Jew and Gentile alike are saved by the blood of Jesus Christ—the middle wall of partition is broken down (2:14), and the veil has been rent in twain, so all now come directly and personally to a common mercy seat. Paul describes this relationship: "For through him [Christ] we both have access by one Spirit unto the Father. Now therefore ye are no more strangers and foreigners, but fellow citizens with the saints, and of the household of God; and are built upon the foundation of the apostles and prophets, Jesus Christ himself being the chief corner stone" (2:18-20).

The book of Ephesians contains an exposition on predestination and election (1:3-12). Paul addresses his readers as the saints—the church, with whom he identifies himself by the use of the personal pronouns "we" and "us."

The predestination here discussed has a direct bearing on the saints—to those who are in Christ "chosen before the foundation of the world." It is the glorious church—the body of Christ—which is here predestined "to be holy and without blame" and to have "an inheritance" in Christ that the believer might " be holy and without blame before him in love" (1:4,11). As to election, God is "not willing that any should perish, but that all should come to repentance" (2 Pe. 3:9). However, man has the power to reject God's will.

Some scholars raise the question whether the epistle refers to the visible or the invisible church. When the term "church" (*ekklesia*) is used in the Scripture it signifies those who are in Christ, the universal body of believers. The visible church consists of the members of local congregations, who should be true Christians. But this visible church is not to be confused with the modern ecumenical movement which sometimes emphasizes form along with liberal theology, without personal, "born again" experience. The visible church also includes a counterfeit element (see commentary on Re. 2:9).

False Religion **2988-2991**

In the book of Revelation the Ephesian church is listed as one of the seven churches of Asia Minor (Re. 2:1-7). This church is commended for its patience and labors but warned of the danger of being self-sufficient and losing its "first love." In Ephesians Paul gives a conclusive statement on salvation by faith and not works: "For by grace are ye saved through faith; and that not of yourselves: it is the gift of God: not of works, lest any man should boast" (2:8-9). "Salvation by works" would eliminate the need for the Savior's death on the cross.

The Seven Churches **762**

Grace **1447**

Works Insufficient **3904**

The book of Ephesians is indeed a practical handbook for believers, setting forth facts on Christian maturity (4:13-32), holy living (5:1-15), Christian truths (5:16-23), sanctification (5:24-33), domestic duties (6:1-10), and the equipment Christians should use for warfare against spiritual wickedness (6:2-19). In his concluding statement Paul indicates he is "an ambassador in bonds" (prison) (6:20).

Spiritual Maturity **997**

Paul's Bonds **3479**

The City of Ephesus

Ephesus, the capital of the Roman Province in Asia Minor, was located on the west coast where the Cayster River enters the Aegean Sea. The Great Temple of Diana, one of the Seven Wonders of the ancient world, made Ephesus the "Vatican City" of the religious world. This great temple has long been dismantled with parts of it on display in the renowned museums of the world, including the Louvre in Paris and the British Museum in London. Some of its massive pillars are standing in the St. Sophia Church in Istanbul, placed there by its leader Constantine. The site of this temple is now a swampy pit with only pieces of marble cherubs protruding from the ground. Historians say that Ephesus had a population of over 300,000; the 25,000-seat amphitheater supports this estimation.

Ephesus was a commercial and industrial center. Overland trade caravans delivered their cargoes to the port, a harbor for ships from all over the known world. Ephesus was the city in which the silversmiths manufactured shrines of the goddess Diana to be sent all over the heathen world. Diana was the mother goddess of the world; the name Diana is the Latinized form of the Greek name Artemis. She may be identified with the Phrygian Cybele, the Cappadocian Ma, the Syrian Mylitta, the Phoenician Astarte, and the Assyrian-Babylonian Ishtar.

Edgar J. Banks says,

> She [Diana] lived in nature; she was everywhere, wherever there was life, the mother of all living things; all offerings of every possible nature were therefore acceptable to her, hence the vast wealth which poured into her Temple. Not only was she worshiped in her temple but in the minute shrines or "naoi" which were sometimes modeled after her temple. More frequently the shrines were

> Ephesus
> 1142, 4373

> Diana
> 3940

> Idolatrous Temples
> 3949

exceedingly crude objects, either of silver, or stone or wood or clay. They were made at Ephesus by dependents of the temple, and carried by the pilgrims throughout the world.[7]

The economy of the area was directly linked to the idol industry. The opposition of the silversmiths to Paul's ministry was based on the decline of idol sales when people were converted to Christ. Banks gives this added insight:

Idolatry
3928-3952

> Though the shrines were sold as sacred dwelling places of the goddess, so that the pilgrims who carried them to their distant homes, or buried them in the graves with their dead, might be assured of her constant presence, their real purpose was to increase the temple revenues by their sale at a price which was many times their cost.[8]

If Ephesus was a center for the "Mother Goddess," it was also a place where many people were exposed and converted to the gospel. The people were inclined toward religions; the very nature of heathendom engendered interest in all the gods. Being religious, many people listened to Paul's preaching and were converted (Ac. 19:18-20). In speaking of Ephesus, Luke states that "all they which dwell in Asia heard the word of the Lord Jesus, both Jews and Greeks" (Ac. 19:10b).

Religious
Awakenings
310-320

For more on the city of Ephesus, see commentary on Re. 2:1.

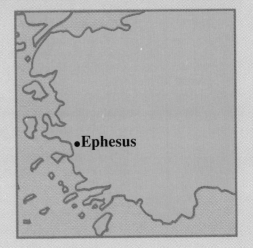

•Ephesus

A general view of Ephesus, showing Marble Street on the right and the library on the left.

1:22-23 ...the church, which is [Christ's] body, the fullness of him who fills everything in every way. (NIV)

It is interesting to study the development of the church throughout the Scriptures. From the beginning, man sought to worship God and built an altar (Ge. 8:20). Through the centuries there was a progression to the tabernacle, the Temple, the synagogue, and finally the culmination, the church. The church was unique in that it did not refer to a physical structure, but instead is the body of believers of which Christ is the head. For more on the development of the church, see commentary and chart at Ac. 2:47.

2:8-9 For by grace are ye saved through faith; and that not of yourselves: it is the gift of God: Not of works, lest any man should boast.

Consistently the Scriptures teach that salvation is without human merit, that redemption is of grace, a free gift entirely by faith. The gospel of the church age was foreshadowed in the covenant with Abraham (Ge. 15:6; 17:4). For more on the nature of salvation in both Testaments, see the essay "The Mechanics of Salvation in the OT Period," pp. 67-69, and "The Nature of the New Birth: Is It Unique to the NT?" pp. 384-386.

2:20 ...built upon the foundation of the apostles and prophets...

There is a difference between "apostles" and "disciples." For a comparison, see commentary on Ac. 1:26. For more on "prophets" see commentary on Je. 1:2.

3:6 ...through the gospel the Gentiles are heirs together with Israel... (NIV)

It was Paul's contention, verified by Scripture, that Christianity is the culmination of Judaism and that the Jewish faith came to fulfillment in Jesus Christ. He made it clear that salvation is not an inheritance restricted to the Jews, but it is a state attained by faith. God does not have a double standard—one plan of salvation for the Jew and another for the Gentile. For more on salvation for the Jew and Gentile alike, see commentary on Ac. 10:34-35.

5:11 Have nothing to do with the fruitless deeds of darkness, but rather expose them (NIV)

Light and darkness are metaphors for the kingdom of God and the kingdom of Satan throughout Scripture. From the very beginning when God said, "Let there be light" (Ge. 1:3), he dispelled darkness. Paul says that the believer in him should also dispel the darkness of the disobedient by living as children of light (5:8). Jesus said, "For every one that doeth evil hateth the light, neither cometh to the light, lest his deeds should be reproved. But he that doeth truth cometh to the light, that his deeds may be made manifest, that they are wrought in God" (Jn. 3:20-21). For more on the symbolism of light, especially in the Tabernacle, see commentary on Ex. 25:31.

Philippians

The Name

The Epistle to the Philippians derives its name from the church at Philippi (Ph. 1:1). The city is named after King Philip, the father of Alexander the Great. Julius Caesar planted a Roman colony in Philippi for retired Roman legionnaires. It became the chief city and capital of Northern Macedonia. The Greek word for Philippi means a "lover of horses."[1]

Epistle to the Philippians
4272

Philippi
2756, 4425

Authorship and Date

The letter to the Philippians was written by Paul after he founded the church on his second missionary journey. From early times tradition has credited Paul with writing this book. He is recognized as the author by such church fathers as Ignatius, Clement of Rome, Polycarp, Irenaeus, Clement of Alexandria, Tertullian, and Marcion.[2] Authorship was never seriously opposed except by the liberal scholars. Ferdinand Christian Baur, professor at the Tubingen school in Germany, objected to Pauline authorship on unsubstantiated grounds. He said that the mention of bishops and deacons in the book was an anachronism, that the Clement referred to was one of a later date, that the letter misrepresented Paul's monetary standards, that the style was un-Pauline and that the reference to the incarnation was Gnostic (Ph. 2:5-11).[3] Evaluation of these objections show them to be based purely on the premise of form criticism and not on Biblical inspiration (for a discussion of form criticism see the Introduction to Acts: Authorship and Date).

If the epistle was written toward the close of Paul's Roman imprisonment, it could be dated A.D. 60-64. If it was written from Ephesus, the date would be about A.D. 54.

Paul's Second Missionary Journey
4309d

Bishops
755

Deacons
753

Paul
2697

Tree of Paul's Life
4309

Background, Purpose, and Content

Though Philippi was a great religious center, as a Roman colony it had few Jews—in fact not enough to have a formal synagogue. For the events leading to Paul's visit to Philippi refer to Ac. 16. The church in Philippi may have been founded on Paul's first visit there (Ac. 16:12-40).

The book of Philippians makes reference to Timothy's being with Paul. This statement is significant. It helps to tie the book in with the passage referring to Timothy in the book of Acts (Ph. 1:1; cf. Ac. 16:1). The book itself is a beautiful personal letter from Paul to the Philippians thanking them for the support they had lovingly given to him while he was in prison (Ph. 4:15-18).

Macedonia
2222

Timothy
3628

Liberality
2115

It was Paul's policy, in order to avoid criticism, not to accept offerings for his own personal need. Paul supported himself with his tent-making trade (Ac. 18:3). According to tradition Paul came from a wealthy family and had means of his own. However, while in prison, he needed help from others.

The people in the church at Philippi were genuinely Christian. Perhaps it was the most devoted congregation among Paul's acquaintances. Their gifts were given in such a spirit of love that Paul could not refuse them.

The immediate purpose for Paul writing the letter to the Philippians was to acknowledge the arrival of Epaphroditus with their love offering. Soon after his arrival this messenger became seriously ill "nigh unto death" (Ph. 2:27), but God miraculously healed him. The situation gave Paul an opportunity to write a personal letter of gratitude to the church at Philippi, to be sent with Epaphroditus on his return. This letter also contained a warning against false teachers and dissension (Ph. 3).

D. Edmond Hiebert says:

> The letter was primarily inspired by friendship matters—Paul's outpouring of love for the church that always stood with him. He wrote to give them the anxiously awaited news about himself...The epistle is distinctly a friendship letter. It is the spontaneous expression of Paul's strong esteem for the readers, wholly devoid of official stateliness. The tone is warmly personal and an undertone of deep joy runs through the whole...Doctrinal formulations are at a minimum and where doctrinal points are touched they have a practical or polemical purpose.[4]

The Epistle to the Philippians expresses a remarkable example of tranquility for a man who is in a Roman prison, momentarily waiting for a hearing before Nero and eventually his execution (Ph. 1:20-23; cf. Ac. 28), possibly in about A.D. 68. Adam Clarke says:

> It is written in a very pleasing style; everywhere bearing evidence of that contented state of mind in which the apostle was, and of his great affection for the people...[He] comforts them in their affliction for the Gospel, returns them thanks for their kindness to him, tells them of his state, and shows a great willingness to be a sacrifice for the faith he had preached to them: this is a Divine unction in this epistle which every serious reader will perceive.[5]

Paul expresses beautifully the spirit and meaning of Ro. 8:28 when he says "that the things which happened unto me have fallen out rather unto the furtherance of the gospel...And many of the brethren in the Lord, waxing confident by my bonds, are much more bold to speak the word without fear: (1:12,14; cf. 4:1-11). Paul's triumphant spirit in this time of crisis is remarkable. He gives them his formula for spiritual health (Ph. 4:8). Solomon once said, "As he [man] thinketh in his heart, so is he" (Pr. 23:7). Throughout the Scriptures the idea is developed that the quality of a man's thoughts affects his physical well being. (See Concordance in TCRB under "think" and "thinketh.")

Merrill C. Tenney gives an overview of this book:

> The theme of "the gospel" runs through Philippians like a current in the ocean. His relation with the church is "the fellowship in the gospel" (1:5). His preaching is "the confirmation of the gospel" (1:7) His career is the "progress of the gospel" (1:12). His conflicts are "the defense of the gospel" (1:17).
>
> Ethical conduct is determined by the standards of the gospel (1:27), and the body of truth that Christians had is "the faith of the gospel" (1:27). The labors in which Paul and

his associates are engaged are "the service of the gospel" (2:22), and he speaks of the women of Philippi "who labored with me in the gospel" (4:3)...In fact, so closely was his entire career bound with this subject that he called the beginning of his campaign in Macedonia and Achaia "the beginning of the gospel" (4:15). Paul used the term in several senses. It denoted his message about Christ, the content of the Christian faith, the sphere of Christian service, and the purpose of his whole career.[6]

Paul concluded his letter with exhortations to maintain unity, to rejoice, to "think on...things" that are good, and with a salutation from "all the saints" to "every saint in Christ Jesus" (Ph. 4:2,4,8,21-22).

Cooperation
3728
Mission of Christ
684
Unity
3724-3727

The City of Philippi

The city of Philippi, a Roman colony, was located in the northern part of Macedonia, north of the port city of Neapolis. It was on the famous Roman road—the Via Ignatia, beginning at Dyrachion on the Adriatic Sea and terminating in Byzantium (modern Istanbul). Parts of the old Roman road are still visible by the side of the modern highway between Philippi and Neapolis (modern Kavalla).

Philippi
2756, 4425

Philippi was an important commercial, medical and religious center. It is probable that St. Luke, the medical doctor, attended the medical school in this Macedonian city, originally called Krenides. The area of eastern Macedonia appeared to be a region to which no organized government gave serious attention. Tradition tells us that this town was once inhabited by colonists from the island of Thaos, who came to work the gold mines. When Philip II of Macedonia became aware of the treasure being taken away he sent a military expedition to annex the territory and left a sizable colony there to hold it (356 B.C.). He then named the territory after himself. Later the Romans conquered Philippi and replaced the Macedonian colony with Roman war veterans.

Luke
2216

When Paul, Silas, Timothy and Dr. Luke arrived at Troas on their second missionary journey Paul heard a voice saying, "Come over into Macedonia, and help us" (Ac. 16:9). They went by boat across the northern end of the Aegean Sea to the city called Neapolis to start their overland journey on the Via Ignatia to Philippi, where they made contact with a group of women who had met to pray on the banks of the Nestos River. Non-rabbinic sources attest the ancient custom of Jews reciting prayers near a river or

seashore.[7] Afterward the missionaries met Lydia, a seller of purple dye or cloth, who became Paul's first convert.

When Paul healed a girl with a strange spirit, the owners of the girl became angered because their income from her divinations dried up. The irate men had Paul and Silas put in prison. While they prayed in prison the angel of the Lord opened the prison gates and set them free. When the authorities discovered that Paul and Silas were Roman citizens, they were frightened because they had confined them without a hearing or a trial. The prisoners were asked to leave Philippi without delay. After a final meeting with Lydia, they departed for Thessalonica.

| Paul's Second Missionary Journey |
| 4309d |

| Roman Citizens |
| 772 |

The archaeological excavations at Philippi are extensive. The work was started by the French School in Athens in 1914. The most commanding discoveries are the double tiered columns marking the site of a fourth century church—an especially important discovery in light of the fact that there were no church buildings until after Constantine was converted to Christianity in the fourth century.

| History of Early Church |
| 4309g |

Philippi

Philippi. The prison where Paul and Silas were detained.

2:17 But even if I am being poured out like a drink offering … (NIV)

Paul's entire life was a sacrifice of thanksgiving to the Lord. For more on the Christian's sacrifice to God in light of the OT sacrifices, see commentary on Ro. 12:1.

3:3 For we are the circumcision, which worship God in the spirit, and rejoice in Christ Jesus, and have no confidence in the flesh.

Paul clarifies once again who the circumcised are—those who worship God, rejoice in Christ, and have no confidence in their own righteousness (v. 9). This is emphasized again and again by the writers of Scripture, for whom the term "circumcision of the heart" is symbolic of the spiritual change brought about by the Holy Spirit (De. 30:6; Ro. 2:25ff.).

For more on the concept of circumcision traced throughout the Bible from its beginning, see commentary on Ge. 17:10.

3:5 …a Hebrew of Hebrews; in regard to the law, a Pharisee…as for legalistic righteousness, faultless. (NIV)

The Pharisees were the strict legalists in Jewish religion. They became known for their self-righteousness and oppressiveness (Lu. 11:46). William Morehead states that "when Pharisaism, with its rigid legalism, with its intolerable burdens, became dominant, all liberty of worship and spontaneous service largely disappeared. The religious life of Israel stiffened into a dreadful monotony."[8]

For more on the Pharisees, see commentary on Mk. 8:11; Jn. 8:44.

4:22 All the saints salute you, chiefly they that are of Caesar's household.

In his letter to the Philippians Paul discloses that Christian converts were so numerous in Rome that they had infiltrated the inner sanctum of Caesar's household (see Ph. 1:13). For further commentary on this subject see Ro. 15:19.

Colossians

The Name

The Epistle derives its name from the church to which it is addressed (Col. 1:2).

Authorship and Date

The book of Colossians, one of the prison epistles, has been accorded Pauline authorship since the days of the church fathers. Paul identifies himself as the author (1:1). Evidence suggests that Paul wrote Colossians because about 25 percent of its content is the same as that in the Ephesian letter. The two churches, only a little over a hundred miles apart, apparently shared some of the same problems.

Some critics, including those at Tubingen,[1] object to Pauline authorship. They claim that the thought patterns do not conform to Romans, Corinthians, and Galatians. However, as each church had its own problems, the letters would understandably be different. These critics also claim that the "Colossian heresy" (combining Judaistic teachings with Gnostic elements) could not have developed in the first century so that the epistle must have been written in the second century by someone other than Paul. Evidence, however, points to Paul writing the letter shortly before his execution in Rome between A.D. 60 and 64.

Background, Purpose, and Content

Theologians differ in opinion as to whether Paul founded the church, or even visited Colosse; nothing in Scripture is said on the subject. Logically and geographically there are several reasons for supporting the assumption that Paul visited Colosse and that he may even have founded the church:

1. Colosse was on the trade route between Mesopotamia and Ephesus. Paul traveled this route on his third missionary journey. Charles F. Pfeiffer and Howard F. Vos say, "The natural route for him [Paul] to have taken on that occasion was from Syria, through the Cilician Gates, then to Derbe, Lystra, Iconium, Antioch of Pisidia, Apamea, Colosse, Laodicea, and down the Menderes river to Ephesus."[2]

2. Paul spent three years in and around Ephesus. Since Colosse is only about 150 miles from Ephesus, it is likely that Paul visited Colosse since he was so near.

3. Paul was in the Phrygian area twice. In this area, where Colosse, Laodicea, and Hierapolis are located, he "went over all the country of Galatia and Phrygia in order, strengthening all the disciples" (Ac. 18:23).

Epistle to the Colossians	**4273**
Paul	**2697**
Epistle to the Ephesians	**4271**
Judaizers	**1958**
Tree of Paul's Life	**4309**
Colosse	**4358**
Paul's Third Missionary Journey	**4309e**
Laodicea	**2050, 4404**
Ephesus	**1142, 4373**

4. Paul's zeal and diligence were so great that all "Asia heard the word" (Ac. 19:10).

5. Paul's close friend, Philemon, lived in the city of Colosse. (See Introduction to Philemon for additional evidence that Paul was a visitor in Colosse.) It is likely that Paul visited him when he came through this area, especially since friendly Christian accommodations were not plentiful in this territory. Also, Philemon had a church in his house (Phm. 2). It is not probable that Paul would entrust to an assistant such an important matter as founding a church.

Among Paul's fellow-laborers at Colosse were Tychicus (Col. 4:18) and Onesimus (4:9). Apparently Aristarchus, Mark, Justus, Luke, and Demas were in prison with Paul or were assisting him in Rome (4:10-11,14). Later Paul wrote that "Demas hath forsaken me, having loved this present world" (2 Ti. 4:10). Archippus and Philemon seem to have been active workers in the Colossian church (Col. 4:17; Phm. 1).

A study of the Colossian letter suggests that Paul had something more than a second-hand knowledge of the situation in Colosse. Paul may have written the letter following a personal visit; the tone of the letter does not leave the impression that Paul was speaking to strangers (1:2,21-25). Its content suggests that he had more than indirect knowledge of the situation.

"The occasion of the epistle was…the information brought by Epaphras that the church in Colosse was subject to the assault of a body of Judaistic…[leaders] who where seeking to overthrow the faith of the Colossians and weaken their regard for St. Paul." This heresy is referred to in theological circles as "the Colossian heresy." [3] It was a peculiar, subtle heresy somewhat different from that in other areas (2:8-23). Gnosticism was indeed a present force in the time of the formation of the early Christian churches. Andrew K. Helmbold writes that Gnosticism "spread throughout the ancient Near East immediately before and after the time of Christ." [4]

Conrad Henry Moehlman says that Adolph von Harnack "termed Christian Gnosticism, the 'acute Hellenization of Christianity'; Gnosticism is now regarded as a 'pre-Christian oriental mysticism.' " [5]

These false teachers were members of a system of metaphysical dualism which mediated through angelic beings for a redemption through knowledge or a "Gnosis." They believed that all religions were a manifestation of one hidden verity and that through knowledge men could find truth. It was not purely a "Gnosis" of the intellect—but rather an enlightenment derived from a mystical experience through contact with angelic beings, along with an allegorical and mythical interpretation of many sacred writings. Through this strange exercise, spiritual enlightenment was supposedly to result in one's redemption from the world of sin and matter.[6]

This Gnostic conception, which regards matter as evil, has no place in the Christian faith. The Gnostic system was actually a syncretism (a mixture) of Greek, Oriental, Jewish, Anatolian, and Egyptian religions with heavy borrowings from Platonism and Stoicism (Col. 2:8,11,16,18). One must remember that in the early days of Christianity, when theological formulas had not yet been established, it would have been easy for new believers out of heathendom to have been deceived and confused, especially when these teachers taught their false doctrines as Christianity. Paul's refutation of this system is positive. He describes what Christ and the church is and does not deal negatively with the problem. Charles Harold Dodd

Epistle to
Philemon
4279

Paul's
Care of the
Church
732

Tychicus
3715

Demas
974

Spiritual
Laborers
3906

Spiritual
Brethren
741

Judaizers
1958

Heresy
1577

History
of Early
Church
4309g

False
Teachers
2101

False
Doctrine
1028

Human
Precepts
2842

Christ,
Head of the
Church
735

presents a scholarly statement on how Paul refuted the "Colossian heresy":

> Paul presents and develops a new and more adequate statement of the position and dignity which Christian experience necessarily assigns to Christ...The outcome of it is to set forth the person and work of Christ as having a cosmic significance. If Christ, known as Savior, were but one among a host of unknowable Powers, the Christian would still be a stranger in the universe. If, however, what we find in Christ is the ultimate Meaning of the Universe, then the salvation he brings is absolute and final. This is the faith that Paul seeks to safeguard by identifying Christ with that divine Wisdom by which the world and all powers controlling it were brought into being, and through which at last, God will fulfill his power in it all...Paul takes up the challenge of the "new thought," by placing his teachings about salvation in Christ upon a more philosophical basis. But in doing so he reasserts with remarkable force and clarity what had always been the core and center of his gospel. Christ died to reconcile men...to the will and purpose of God...it is made plain...that this dying and rising again is an actual moral experience manifesting itself in character and conduct...The Christian's way is, above all, radically ethical, and the "emancipation" it brings is the one sure beginning of a free, progressing and positive morality for men individually and in society.[7]

Paul's approach is very practical: after explaining to the Colossians what he believed, he discussed Christian conduct (4:1-7). Instead of belittling the false teachings, he exalted Christ and the significance of his stature for the believers. As Savior, Jesus is to be their "all in all." Christ is "the head of the body, the church" (1:18,24). E. Earle Ellis says, "To establish the sole sufficiency of Jesus as Lord and Redeemer (in opposition to the gnostic substitution of redeeming disciplines and...meditating powers), Paul stresses both aspects [human and divine] of Christ's character. Important in this regard is the concept of the 'Body of Christ,' with which the Colossians undoubtedly were familiar (Col. 1:18-24; 2:17; 3:15)."[8]

Deceit
3705-3709

Christ our
Savior
3360-3368
Wisdom-
Folly
3838-3855

Reconcili-
ation
2971
Christian
Conduct
808-812
Pre-
eminence
of Christ
716
Christ's
Divinity -
Humanity
701-723

The City of Colosse

Colosse (or Colossae) is a city of Phrygia in the central part of Asia Minor, situated on the lower slopes of Mount Cadmus overlooking the Menderes River to the north. The city is near the great highway traversing the country from Ephesus via Istanbul to the Euphrates Valley. It is 13 miles east of Hierapolis (Holy City) and 10 miles from Laodicea.

| Colosse |
| 4358 |

Soon after the Epistle to the Colossians was written, an earthquake greatly damaged the city along with Laodicea (modern Denizli) and Hierapolis (modern Pamukkule). Chonos or Konos is the inhabited town near the Colossian ruins.[9]

Evidence of earthquake damage remains in all these places, including broken marble columns and a ruined theater at Colosse; Laodicea is still mainly a huge mound where only the viaduct, an old basilica, and two amphitheaters are visible. In Hierapolis massive stones and pillars from the temples, baths, and the church lie strewn over a wide area. The great amphitheater is in relatively good condition. A deep fissure, called "pluto-

| Laodicea |
| 2050, 4404 |

nium," has erupted and still spews poisonous gas (see the essay "The Hot Springs of Hierapolis and the Lukewarmness of Laodicea," pp. 564-565).

Special reference is made here to Laodicea and Hierapolis because they were on the same triangular circuit with Colosse, for whose churches Epaphras labored "fervently...in prayers" and for whom he had "great zeal" (Col. 4:12-13).

| Epaphras |
| 1139 |

Lake Egridir is located near Colosse on the road to Phrygian Antioch over which Paul traveled. The nearness of this road to Colosse gives rise to speculation that Paul visited in this city with his close friend, Philemon.

1:13 Who hath delivered us from the power of darkness, and hath translated us into the kingdom of his dear Son.

Throughout the Bible, the people of God are referred to as members of his kingdom. The term "kingdom" was common in the old covenant and was understood to mean "children of Zion" (Ps. 149:2); "congregation of the saints" (Ps. 89:5), or "those who had faith in the Lord."[10] In the New Testament the central message of Jesus was semantically "the kingdom of God" rather than the church (Mk. 1:14-15).

1:16-17 For by him [Christ] were all things created... and he is before all things, and by him all things consist.

Paul makes it very clear that Jesus Christ is found not only in the NT, but that he has been in existence throughout eternity. The advent of Christ was in no way an afterthought of God's; the redemptive promise and provision were made "from the foundation of the world" (Re. 13:8). Peter indicates this by declaring that we are redeemed "with the precious blood of Christ, as of a lamb without blemish and without spot: who verily was foreordained before the foundation of the world, but was manifest in these last times" (1 Pe. 1:19-20). Moreover in the divine economy of God's redemptive provision, grace "was given us in Christ Jesus before the world began" (2 Ti. 1:8-9). It is therefore evident that the redemptive plan of the NT is basically and substantially the same as that of the OT.

1:24 ...for the sake of his [Christ's] body, which is the church. (NIV)

The church of Jesus Christ, as it developed during the history of worship centers, came to represent a body of believers in him, and did not refer to a structure (as had the Tabernacle, Temple, and synagogues). For more on the development of the church, see commentary and chart at Ac. 2:47; see also commentary on Mt. 16:18; Phm. 2.

2:11 In whom also ye are circumcised with the circumcision made without hands, in putting off the body of the sins of the flesh by the circumcision of Christ.

Physical circumcision was a covenant sign between Abraham and the LORD (Ge. 17:10-11). As a sign, circumcision was never meant to be an end in itself, but instead it was a way of expressing faith in God and his forgiveness of sin. Moses told the children of Israel, "The LORD your God will circumcise your hearts and the hearts of your descendants, so that you may love him with all your heart and with all your soul, and live" (De. 30:6, NIV). The phrase "uncircumcision of heart" is used throughout the Scriptures to describe a lack of receptivity to the things of God (Le. 26:41; Je. 9:25; Eze. 44:7).

Light –
Darkness
2165-2180

Congre-
gation
820-821

Christ,
Creator
680

Christ
Eternal
709

Fore-
ordained
Plan of
Salvation
4154

Church,
Body of
Christ
726

Growth of
the Church
733, 2380

Covenants
877-879

Heart,
The Center
of Life
4162

2:14 ...having canceled the written code, with its regulations, that was against us and that stood opposed to us; he took it away, nailing it to the cross. (NIV)

Bondage
of Law
4092

This verse brings to mind the question of the relationship between the OT laws and Christ's crucifixion. Because of Christ's sacrificial death, the law with all its regulations no longer has power over the Christian. However, does this mean the law no longer has any value? For more on Christ, the fulfillment of the law, see commentary on Mt. 5:17. See also the essay, "The Mosaic Law: The Unity of the Legal Structure in Both Testaments," pp. 102-103.

Mosaic Law
949

Unity of
Believers in
Christ
3724

3:11...there is neither Greek nor Jew, circumcision nor uncircumcision, Barbarian, Scythian, bond nor free: but Christ is all, and in all.

For the teaching that God does not show favoritism, see commentary on Ac. 10:34-35; see also Introduction to Romans: Background, Purpose and Content.

1 and 2 Thessalonians

The Name
The Epistles to the Christians at Thessalonica derive their name from the church to which they are addressed (1 Th. 1:1; 2 Th. 1:1). Tradition says that the city was named Thessalonica, after the daughter of Philip, the King of Macedonia, the father of Alexander the Great.[1]

Authorship and Date
The author of the Thessalonian letters is Paul. He refers to himself by name several times (1 Th. 1:1; 2:18; 2 Th. 1:1; 3:17).

The special significance of 1 Thessalonians is that it is Paul's first letter and the earliest written Christian document dealing with the gospel message, earlier than any of the four Gospels. The epistle was written from Corinth perhaps as early as A.D. 47, but no later than A.D. 53.[2] The second epistle was probably written a few weeks or a few months after the first one.

Pauline authorship of both letters is authenticated by the Muratorian Canon (a list of the NT books used by the church in Rome about A.D. 200), and by such church fathers as Clement of Alexandria, Tertullian, and Polycarp.[3]

Background, Purpose and Content
Paul founded the Christian church in Thessalonica on his second missionary journey. For a historical background of Paul's first visit, see Ac. 17. After his arrival in Thessalonica from Philippi, Paul spent the following three Sabbath days reasoning with the Jews "out of the scriptures" to show that "Christ must needs have suffered, and risen again from the dead" and that Jesus was Christ (Ac. 17:1-4). Some of the Jews responded favorably to the gospel appeal, but another segment of Jews rejected Paul's gospel message. With the assistance of a mob, they "set all the city on an uproar." When Jason, a Christian, befriended Paul and Silas, the Jews assaulted his house, hoping to take the missionaries. When the Jews failed to find Paul and Silas, they "drew Jason and certain brethren" before the city officials, accusing them of treason. When Jason posted a bond, the others were released. During the night the brethren sent Paul, Silas, and Timothy to Berea (Ac. 17:5-10). The Jews in Berea were more open-minded, listened to Paul's message "and searched the scriptures" to determine whether his message was true (Ac. 17:11). Adam Clarke says,

Though the Jews, who were sojourners in this city, rejected the Gospel in general, yet a great multitude of the devout Greeks, i.e., such as were proselytes to Judaism, or the

---

First and
Second
Epistles
to the
Thessa-
lonians
4274-4275
Macedonia
2222
Paul
2697, 4309
Corinth
840, 4359

Paul's
Second
Missionary
Journey
4309d

Jewish
Jealousy
4051

Berea
402

Greeks
1464

descendants of Jewish parents, born and naturalized in Greece, believed and associated with Paul and Silas, and not a few of the chief women of the city embraced the Christian faith. Acts XVII.4.

Gentile
Believers
4038
Persecution
3480
Athens
303, 4336

As the Jews found that, according to the doctrine of the Gospel, the Gentiles were called to enjoy the same privileges with themselves, without being obliged to submit to circumcision and other ordinances of the law, they persecuted that Gospel and those who proclaimed it: for, moved with indignation, they employed "certain lewd fellows of a baser sort"—the beasts of the people, "set the city in an uproar, assaulted the house of Jason," where the apostles lodged, "dragged him" and "certain of the brethren before the rulers" and charged them with seditious designs and treason against the Roman Emperor. The apostles escaped and got to Berea, where they began anew their important evangelical labors: thither the Jews of Thessalonica, pursuing them, raised a fresh tumult; so that the apostle, being counselled by the brethren, made his escape to Athens; Acts XVII 5-15.[4]

Thessa-
lonica
3610, 4442
Idol Altars
3948
Ignorance of
God
2038

Timothy and Silas remained behind to direct the church (Ac. 17:14-15) and then rejoined Paul in Athens. Before Paul left Corinth he sent Timothy back to Thessalonica (1 Th. 3:1- 3).

Upon arrival in Athens, Paul engaged the philosophers on the Areopagus (Mars Hill) in a theological discourse. He noted an altar with an inscription to "the unknown God" and told them that he represented the God who was unknown to them (Ac. 17:23). From Athens Paul went to Corinth where Timothy and Silas met him (Ac. 18:5). From Corinth Paul traveled to Antioch.

Paul's Third
Missionary
Journey
4309e
Persecution
of Paul
3482

When Paul went to Macedonia on his third missionary journey, there is no reference to his journeying to Thessalonica. However, because of Paul's deep interest in the church, it is probable that he made at least a short visit.

In his first epistle Paul commended the saints for the exemplary lives they were living under difficult circumstances (1 Th. 1:1-10) and explained his early departure from Thessalonica because of Jewish hostility. He pointed out his motive for coming to them was to give and not to receive (2:1-14). Paul specifically charged the Jews with killing the Lord Jesus and their own prophets, and with preventing him from presenting the gospel to the Gentiles (2:15-16; cf. Mt. 23:29-35). He told the church he would have returned to Thessalonica but that Satan prevented him (2:17-21).

Satan's
Work
3151

Paul made it clear that tribulation was part of the cost of maintaining the Christian faith, that there would be continued suffering (3:4-5), and that the standard of the Christian life was one of holiness and love (4:4-5).

Holiness
1598
Believers
Walk
3763

The good news from Thessalonica brought by Timothy made the apostle rejoice and he assured his readers that he would be praying for them day and night (3:6-13). In the fifth chapter Paul outlined the personal discipline which all Christians are to practice in their daily walk, using as an armor, faith, love, and hope for their spiritual warfare (5:8). In this letter Paul endeavored to clear up some of the misunderstandings about the Second Coming of Christ. These mistakes were twofold:

Second
Coming of
Christ
1344-1350

1. The saints neglected their daily work because they were expecting the Lord to return momentarily. Paul explained that no one knows the time or the season when the Lord will return, but he will return, and when he does it will be suddenly. Paul amplified the importance of watching and being sober and encouraged them to comfort and edify each other (5:1-11).

Christ's
Kingdom
2012

2. Some had died between the time Paul had visited them and the writing of this letter. The present believers were concerned as to how the deceased saints could be a part of the glories of the kingdom which the returning Lord would establish.[5] Paul told the Thessalonians that when the

Lord did return, he would bring with him the departed saints in their glorified bodies. Those who were still living would be "caught up together with them in the clouds, to meet the Lord in the air" (4:13-18; cf. 1 Co. 15:12-58).

The second coming of Christ is mentioned in every chapter of both 1 and 2 Thessalonians (1 Th. 1:10; 2:19; 3:13; 4:13- 18; 5:1-7; 2 Th. 1:7; 2:1-3; 3:5). The Second Epistle is a continuation and explanation of the First Epistle regarding Christ's second coming. The treatment on the Second Coming in this letter is somewhat different in emotional tone, but this in no way detracts from the book as a genuine Pauline epistle. The subject of Christ's second coming was a relatively new concept for the early church members, and could be easily misunderstood. Up until now the church merely assumed Christ would return but had not had time to work out the mechanical details. Apparently Paul did not feel free to spend more time with the Thessalonians after his first visit; he had no choice but to discuss this misunderstanding in writing.

Paul informed the church at Thessalonica that the Day of the Lord was at hand, that the coming would be sudden, as a thief in the night (1 Th. 5:2), and that the duty of the Christians was to expect it (1 Th. 1:9-10). In the second epistle Paul added that the "Lord Jesus shall be revealed from heaven with his mighty angels, in flaming fire..." (2 Th. 1:7-8).[6] Peter stated in 2 Pe. 3:7,10 that the heavens and the earth are destined to be burned with "fire."[7]

In his second letter, Paul attempted to dispel the idea that the coming of the Lord was imminent. He indicated that before the Lord's return there would be a great apostasy, a falling away from the faith, and that the "man of sin [would] be revealed..." It is generally assumed by the Christians that this "man of sin" is the Antichrist, who will claim that he is God (2 Th. 2:3-6).

There has been controversy in the church from early times with regard to the Antichrist. The church fathers looked for a personal Antichrist in the fall of the Roman Empire. The Protestant Reformers looked upon the Pope as the Antichrist. Two thousand years have now passed and there are still differences of opinion. Many devout scholars believe that the Antichrist will be manifested before the Rapture. Others believe he will come after the Rapture. The Spirit of the Antichrist was already at work in Paul's day (2 Th. 2:7). It is not wise to be dogmatic about the details regarding the Antichrist. We can accept the fact of his coming, but we must let time determine the place and circumstance.[8]

In the last chapter of 2 Thessalonians, Paul deals with such practical things as prayer (2 Th. 3:1-4), patience (3:5), separation from evil associations (3:6-9), the evils of being idle busybodies (3:10-11), and apostolic authority (3:12-15). He ends with a closing benediction (3:16-18).

The City of Thessalonica

Ancient records indicate that Thessalonica was founded in 315 B.C. by Cassander, King of Macedonia (354-287 B.C.). He challenged the sovereignty of Macedonia and captured Olympias, the mother of Alexander the Great, put her to death, and connected himself to the royal family by marrying Thessalonica, the half-sister of Alexander. In 306 B.C. he took the title of king; in 297 he was succeeded by his son, Philip.[9]

After Thessalonica was made the capital, it grew to become the second largest city in that area; only Philippi, a hundred miles to the east, exceeded it. Because of its sheltered harbors, Thessalonica became a commercial and shipping center for the cargoes coming over the Great Highway, the Via Igna-

> Thessalonica
> **3610, 4442**

> Philippi
> **2756, 4425**

tia, from the Adriatic in the west to Byzantium in the east. Because of its position, Thessalonica had some of the same moral problems that characterized Corinth (see "The City of Corinth," pp. 437-439).

Corinth
840, 4359

Christianity has continued to prosper in Thessalonica since its inception there under Paul. It has about fifty active churches today, of which most are Greek Orthodox.[10]

Thessalonica. The main gate in the ancient wall.

1 Th. 2:6 ...As apostles of Christ we could have been a burden to you (NIV)

Apostles
2080-2082

Paul uses the word "apostle" in a somewhat different sense than the writers of the four Gospels. For more on the meaning of the word, see commentary on Ac. 1:26.

1 Th. 4:7 For God hath not called us unto uncleanness, but unto holiness.

Impurity
664-666
Holiness
1598
Sanctifi-
cation
3141

Spiritual
Cleansing
962

Holiness is a theme of both the OT and NT writers. The general theme of the entire book of Leviticus is holiness, both as a description of the nature of God and as a way of life for his subjects. God's command to the people was "Sanctify yourselves therefore, and be ye holy: for I am the LORD your God" (Le. 20:7), a verse that is quoted by Peter in 1 Pe. 1:16. The writer of Hebrews says, "Follow peace with all men, and holiness, without which no man shall see the Lord" (He. 12:14). It was also a subject Paul wrote about to the Corinthian church: "...let us purify ourselves from everything that contaminates body and spirit, perfecting holiness out of reverence for God" (2 Co. 7:1, NIV).

1 Th. 5:5 Ye are all the children of light, and the children of the day: we are not of the night, nor of darkness.

Light
2165-2175
Christ the
Light
2168

Candlestick
637

In Jn. 8:12 Jesus said: "I am the light of the world: he that followeth me shall not walk in darkness, but shall have the light of life." Throughout the Bible, light is associated with God. For examples, God met Moses in a burning bush, he led his children with a pillar of fire, and he guided the Wise Men with a star. For more on the subject, see commentary on Ex. 25:31, where the golden candlestick placed in the tabernacle is shown to symbolize Christ, the light of the world.

2 Th. 1:5 ...that ye may be counted worthy of the kingdom of God, for which ye also suffer.

Spiritual
Kingdom
2007-2011

Jesus announced the nearness of the kingdom of God (Mk. 1:14-15) and his central message was concerned with it. Entering God's kingdom was related to all his ethical demands. For more on this subject, see commentary on Mk. 1:15.

1 and 2 Timothy

The Name

The Epistles to Timothy derive their name from the person to whom they are addressed (1 Ti. 1:2; 2 Ti. 1:2). The name "Timothy" appears nine times in the NT (2 Co. 1:1; 1 Ti. 1:2,18; 6:20; 1 Ti. postscript; 2 Ti. 1:2; Phm. 1; He. 13:23; He. postscript). The name "Timotheus" appears nineteen times (Ac. 16:1;17:14-15; 18:5; 19:22; 20:4; Ro. 16:21; 1 Co. 4:17; 16:10; 1 Co. postscript; 2 Co. 1:19; Ph. 1:1; 2:19; Col. 1:1; 1 Th. 1:1; 3:2; 3:6; 2 Th. 1:1; 2 Ti. postscript). *Timothy* is the Hebrew rendering of the Greek *Timotheus*. It probably appears in these two forms for the sake of both the Jews and the Greeks.

Authorship and Date

The superscription "to Timothy" was placed at the head of the First Book of Timothy by the patristic fathers at an early date to preserve author identity. Such church fathers as Clement I of Rome (A.D. 88-97), Polycarp (A.D. 69-156), and Ignatius (A.D. 67-110) do not hesitate to credit Paul with authorship. However, liberal critics have challenged this book, as they have most NT books. They contend that the book was written by "some unknown author who wrote in Paul's name to promote certain doctrines."[1] Obviously this does violence to the inspiration of the Bible and the integrity of the authors. The three main critical objections are the following:

1. *The Chronological Setting.* Scholars of liberal persuasion insist that the Pastoral Letters, of which 1 Timothy was the first, cannot be fitted into the history of Paul's travels in Acts.

It is true that the content of the Pastoral Epistles cannot be easily fitted into the record of Acts. However, because the Scriptures were not written as history but as religious documents, the authors sometimes omit details (cf. Jn. 21:25). Certain critics do not make allowances for the two imprisonments of Paul and for the events which occurred between them. Jac J. Muller states that:

> The journeys and work of Paul mentioned in the Pastoral Epistles cannot be dated in the period covered by Acts but took place between his "first" and his "second" imprisonment to which II Timothy refers (1:8,16-17).

> That such was the case is borne out by the almost unanimous patristic testimony and tradition. Clemens Romanus, for instance, writing from Rome to Corinth (95 A.D.),

First
Epistle to
Timothy
4276
Second
Epistle to
Timothy
4277
Timothy
3628

Paul
2697

Inspired
"Word"
417
Analysis
of Acts
4266
Paul's
Bonds
3479

Outline
History of
Missionary
Work
4309g

asserts that Paul, after instructing the whole world (Roman Empire) in right-eousness, "had gone to the extremity of the west (was that Spain? Compare with Romans 15:28) before martyrdom." The Canon of Muratori (170 A.D.) alludes to "The Journey of Paul from Rome to Spain"; and Eusebius (beginning of the fourth century) clearly formulates the tradition as follows: "After defending himself successfully, it is currently reported that the Apostle again went forth to proclaim the Gospel, and afterward came to Rome a second time and was martyred by Nero."[2]

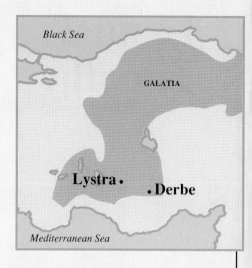

From this discussion it appears that the Pastoral Epistles belong to the period after A.D. 62 and before the apostle's martyrdom, probably A.D. 64-67.

2. *Ecclesiastical Complex.* Some say that the Pastoral Epistles "reveal a more advanced church organization than we find in the rest of the New Testament and presumably too advanced for Paul's day...[based on the] mention of bishops or overseers, and elders or presbyters and deacons in what seems a firmly established church organization of a latter day."[3] However on his first missionary journey Paul ordained elders in every city (Ac. 14:23); another reference indicates the presence of pastors and teachers at Ephesus (Ep. 4:11), while in Philippi bishops and deacons were active (Ph. 1:1). It was a very simple organization in which no sophisticated hierarchy was in-volved.[4]

In these early days the titles of church officials were not clearly defined. Some of them were interchangeable, e.g., overseer for elder (Tit. 1:5-7).

3. *The Linguistic Peculiarities.* Some critics claim that the language of these epistles to Timothy differs from that in Paul's other writings. But it seems plausible that Paul's style and vocabulary would change as he got older. Roy S. Nicholson quotes Ralph Earle as saying: "The difference in the vocabulary of Paul's earlier and later epistles is no greater 'than...[that] between some of the earlier and later works of Shakespeare or Milton.' Another [S. Graham Scroggie] has said that there are 'affinities between these and Paul's other letters...more than sufficient to override the objections which have been raised to their Pauline authorship.' "[5]

Background, Purpose, and Content

To identify Timothy, his history, and some characteristics, one may consult Ac. 16 as well as almost any of the Pauline books. Since the region of Lystra and Derbe was the home of Timothy, his mother Eunice, and his grandmother Lois, it seems certain that Timothy's family had contact with Paul on his first missionary journey. According to Scripture this family was a God-fearing one who looked forward to the coming of the Messiah (2 Ti.

1:5-6). Paul indicates that Timothy had been reared in the fear of God and in the Jewish religion as prophetically revealed in the OT Scriptures (2 Ti. 3:15-17).

When the apostle came to this area on his second journey, he found Timothy, a member of the church, so highly reputed and warmly recommended by the church in that place that Paul could take him to be his companion in his travels (Ac. 16:1-3). Timothy had been taught in the Jewish faith, but, like Gentile believers, he had not been circumcised. Since the head of the household had supreme authority, his Greek father had not permitted Timothy to undergo this Jewish initiation rite.

When Timothy joined Paul's missionary party, the apostle determined that Timothy should be circumcised, not for salvation "but because of the Jews who would neither have heard him nor the Apostle had this not been done...The Gospel testimony they would not have received from Timothy, ...a heathen; and they would have considered the Apostle in the same light..."[6] Timothy's call to be a minister seems to have been confirmed by several prophetic declarations relative to him (1 Ti. 1:18; 4:14). From this time on the name "Timothy" surfaces in most of Paul's epistles. Timothy became Paul's constant traveling companion and comforter. He refers to Timothy in these endearing words, "Unto Timothy, my own son" (1 Ti. 1:2); "To Timothy, my dearly beloved son" (2 Ti. 1:2); "Timotheus, who is my beloved son" (1 Co. 4:17); and "Timotheus our brother" (Col. 1:1; 1 Th. 3:2).

Young Timothy had been appointed to oversee the work of the church in Ephesus (1 Ti. 1:3). Many problems developed in his parish, and Paul counseled his "beloved brother" in prudent church decorum and practices. It is probable that Paul wrote his first letter to Timothy between his first and second imprisonments. It is not certain where Paul was when he wrote this book, but the postscript of 1 Timothy indicates Laodicea. To the very end Paul had hopes of visiting Timothy shortly (1 Ti. 3:14).

These Pastoral Epistles are important to the modern church because the problems discussed in them are still relevant to congregations today. The apostle expressed serious concern that the church should endure sound doctrines (1 Ti. 1:3-4, 6-11; 4:7; 6:3-5). Adam Clarke says that four main errors were about to develop when Paul departed to Macedonia:

> 1. Fables were invented by the Jewish doctors to recommend the observance of the law of Moses as necessary to salvation.
> 2. Uncertain genealogies, by which individuals endeavored to trace their descent from Abraham, in the persuasion that they would be saved, merely because they had Abraham for their father.
> 3. Intricate questions and strifes about some words in the law; perverse disputings of men of corrupt minds, who reckoned that which produced most gain to be the best kind of godliness.
> 4. Oppositions of knowledge, falsely so named.[7]

Paul had a premonition that after he left Timothy in charge at Ephesus, serious problems would arise in the church. Paul said, "I know this, that after my departing shall grievous wolves enter in among you, not sparing the flock. Also of your own selves shall men arise, speaking perverse things, to draw away disciples after them" (Ac. 20:29-30). There is also a personal note of tenderness, as a father writing his son, for to Paul Timothy was his spiritual son. Paul reinforces his plea for diligence by referring to his former expe-

Margin references
Messianic Hope 4186
Good Name 2513
Living Witnesses 3605
Divine Call 1790
Spiritual Relationships 740
Ephesus 1142, 4373
Laodicea 2050
Good Doctrine 1029
Fables 1200
Knowledge-Ignorance 2020-2040
Rapacity 2949
Deceivers 3707

The Emperor Nero ordered the torturous deaths of many Christians, including the Apostle Paul.

rience as a blasphemer, but expresses thanks to Jesus Christ for the change, enabling him to be faithful and to enter the ministry (1 Ti. 1:12-13).

In the second chapter he exhorts Timothy to fervent prayer (2:1) and again asserts his apostleship (1 Ti. 2:7). The irregularities of heathen women prompted the apostle to give some guidelines concerning modesty (2:9ff.). He dealt at length with the qualifications and requirements for bishops or overseers (3:1-7). What he is saying about bishops applies equally to the membership at large. These same standards apply equally to deacons and elders (3:8ff.).

Paul cautions the church to be consistent and to set a good example in daily living, pointing out the danger of hypocrisy (4:1-5). The faithful minister must be "nourished up in the words of faith and of good doctrine" so that he can distinguish between sound and unsound teachings (4:6-11). Paul reminds Timothy that even though he is young, he must not permit his youth to bring reproach upon the church, and exhorts him to "flee…youthful lusts" (2 Ti. 2:22) and to develop the gifts given him (1 Ti. 4:13-14).

The apostle indicated that poor widows are to be cared for by their immediate relatives (1 Ti. 5:3-4, 8,16). He advised the younger widows to marry and bear children (5:14). Paul included advice on bishops and deacons; he then gave instruction for the elders to "rule well" and discreetly (5:17-20).

In the final chapter Paul set forth rules for the servants who were an accepted part of most households (6:1-2). Paul again warned Timothy against false teachers (6:3-8) and about the peril of riches, pointing out that "the love of money is the root of all evil" (6:9-10; cf. 6:17-19); ministers were encouraged to "follow after righteousness, godliness, faith, love, patience, meekness" and to keep themselves unspotted from the world (6:11-14). The first epistle concludes with a personal exhortation to Timothy for stewardship.

Paul must have written the second letter to Timothy soon after he was imprisoned the second time. The city had just been burned by Nero so that, presumably, Nero could realize his plans of building a new "eternal city" from the finest marble in the land.

Of the persecution described in 2 Timothy and 1 Peter Henry H. Halley writes:

> this was "the persecution that brought Paul to his martyrdom, and according to some tradition, Peter also." He (Nero) knew that the Christians did not burn Rome, but someone had to be made the scapegoat for the Emperor's crime. Here was a new and despised sect of people, mostly from humble walks of life, without prestige or influence, many of them slaves. Nero accused them of burning Rome and ordered their punishment. In and around Rome multitudes of Christians were arrested and put to death in the most cruel ways. They were crucified or tied in skins of animals and thrown into the arena to be worried to death by dogs for the entertainment of the people…they were thrown to the wild beasts or tied to stakes in Nero's garden.[8]

The bodies of the Christians were saturated with pitch and ignited to serve as torches to light Nero's gardens while he rode around naked in his chariot to indulge himself and gloat "over the dying agonies of his victims."[9]

Enabling
Grace
4030
Paul's
Apostleship
202

Example
1175-1178
"Word"
as Food
416

Cultivate
Gifts
4016

Elders
754

Earthly
Riches
2805-2811

Stewardship
3453-3458

Persecution
3480-3484

Roman
Emperors
611-614

Martyrdom
3487

Martyrs
3488

During this difficult period Paul was probably apprehended in one of three places: Troas (2 Ti. 4:13), Corinth, or Miletus (2 Ti. 4:20) and brought back to Rome.[10] The charge for which Paul was arrested is not known. Some scholars think that Paul, as the leader of the Christians, may have been accused of instigating the burning of Rome.[11] Phygellus and Hermogenes (2 Ti. 1:15) as well as Demas (2 Ti. 4:10) had forsaken him. Paul had given his life for a cause that was being assailed by both persecution and apostasy. But in the face of all that darkness Paul expressed no regret or doubt. He was still confident that his cause would eventually triumph.

In the center of Rome is the ancient Mamertine prison with its two cells, one on top of the other, cut out of solid rock. The floor of the top compartment has in it a man-sized hole through which prisoners were lowered into the dungeon below. Tradition says that both Peter and Paul were imprisoned here. Today it is a tourist attraction. Nearby is the famous Colosseum, where many early Christians were tortured (see "The City of Rome," pp. 423-425).

Second Timothy indicates that one of Paul's sterling qualities was gratitude (1:1-4). In his old age he remembered his original contact with Timothy and Timothy's family in the Lystra community (1:5). Even as Paul came to the end of his life he encouraged Timothy to follow his steps, to be faithful in his ministry, and not to be ashamed of his old friend now in prison (1:8). Paul reminded Timothy that Jesus Christ gives sufficient grace which was provided before the world began (1:9-10).

Paul recalled how Onesiphorus befriended him in Rome, although some of Paul's friends had deserted him (1:15-18). He outlined for his beloved friend the works of a good soldier of the cross: to be strong to witness and teach, to endure hardships and to receive from God understanding in all things (2:1-7). He told Timothy to "remember that Jesus Christ of the seed of David was raised from the dead" and that this fact was the basis for enduring all things for the sake of those who would yet be saved (2:8-14). Paul encouraged Timothy to study the Word, to avoid "profane and vain babblings [arguments on religion]: for they will increase unto more ungodliness" (2:15-21,23-26). He advised Timothy to flee "youthful lusts" and to be actively involved in God's "righteousness, faith, charity, peace..." (2:22). Paul gave Timothy additional information on the apostasy which he described in his Thessalonian letters (3:1-9; cf. 2:3-17).

Timothy was to be comforted in his sufferings for Christ by reviewing Paul's own experiences. He recited for the young pastor his own longsufferings, persecutions, and afflictions (3:10-17). In the final chapter the apostle charged Timothy to "preach the word" and to be consistent and firm at all times as he reproved, rebuked, and exhorted the people in sound doctrine (4:1-2). Timothy was also alerted to the time when the people would not endure sound doctrine but would follow their own lusts (4:3-5).

Paul had his house in order; he was ready for the executioner. He had no regrets because he had "fought a good fight" and had "kept the faith" (4:7). A crown in heaven was awaiting him. In these last moments Paul desired the company of his "faithful friend" and asked him to bring the coat he had left at Troas. He needed it in his cold, damp cell. Only Luke was with him to comfort him. Paul again urged his friends, Timothy and Mark, to come to him (4:6-13, 21). All the others had either deserted him or had gone on mission assignments (4:10-12).

Preparations for Death
2162
Companion-ship
4013

Deacons
753

Feet-
washing
3404
Spiritual
Service
3894-3897
Officers in
the Church
753-755
Religious
Leaders
2058-2102

1 Ti. 3:10 ...let them serve as deacons. (NIV)

The word *deacon* means "to serve," "to wait upon tables," which suggests a very personal service, a service of love. In Greek tradition the term had demeaning implications, but to Jesus it meant the highest attainment in the kingdom. Jesus demonstrated this at the foot washing (Jn. 13:14-15).

However, in the NT *deacon* is only found four times (Ph. 1:1 and 1 Ti. 3:8,10,13). The word is not employed in Ac. 6:1-3 when the seven men were designated to "serve tables" and to take care of the widows. It is evident that service transcends terminology; Jesus placed much importance on service.

In the church the term *deacon* is associated with a special office. To qualify for the office meant that one must be "proved worthy" (1 Ti. 3:8-9). The historical development of the office, which has a high standard, is linked with that of bishop: "[he must not be] doubletongued, not given to much wine, nor greedy of filthy lucre...being found blameless...the husbands of one wife, ruling their children and their own houses well" (1 Ti. 3:8-16).[12]

1 Ti. 5:17 The elders who direct the affairs of the church well... (NIV)

Elders,
Govern-
mental
2078
Jewish
Elders
2079

The word *elder* could relate to any area in life in which the matter of seniority was concerned. The Bible makes reference to at least three categories of elders: those in government, Jewish religious elders, and officers in the Christian Church. The Biblical definition is an "official, who, so far as can be judged, had, by virtue of his right as firstborn, succeeded to the headship of a father's house, of a tribal family, or of the tribe itself (cf. 1 K. 8:1-3; Jud. 8:14-16)."[13]

Generally, the title indicated an official of the highest rank with great authority (De. 27:1; Ezr. 10:8). The designation "elder" might be synonymous with the chief of a tribe. The word *elder* in Hebrew *(zaqen)* means "one who is bearded," suggesting a man of maturity and distinguishing him as having a certain official rank and position among the people. In the period from Moses to Ezra and on into the intertestamental era, elders were recognized as the highest authoritative body over the people. Their responsibility included both religious and political matters and the settling of intertribal disputes (cf. Jos. 22:13-33).[14]

Tree of
Moses' Life
4307
Holy Spirit
Guides
1611
Atonement
304
Ecclesias-
tical
Government
749-752
Christian
Elders
754

After Ge. 50:7 the next Biblical reference to elders appears in Ex. 3:16-18 where elders were appointed by Moses to be the body of officials to receive the announcement of liberation from Egypt. Later, the covenant was ratified by the seventy elders at Mount Sinai (Ex. 19:7; 24:1,9,14). When Moses' burden of government became too great, the elders were selected and the spirit which was upon Moses was also upon them to govern the people (Nu. 11:16-17). In case of legal infraction, the elders were to represent the people in making an atonement (Le. 4:13-15). While the Jews were in Babylon, the elders were the center of authority in the Jewish community. This prominence continued after the Jews returned to Jerusalem (Ezr. 5:5,9; 6:7-8,14).

In the Greek period the elders developed into the "great assembly" (Knesset) of the Jews. Later the Great Sanhedrin, of seventy elders in number, was the supreme legislative body.[15]

In the Christian church elders became officials and at times seemed to have been interchangeable with presbyters and bishops. By the early period in Acts elders existed in the church at Jerusalem (Ac. 11:30).

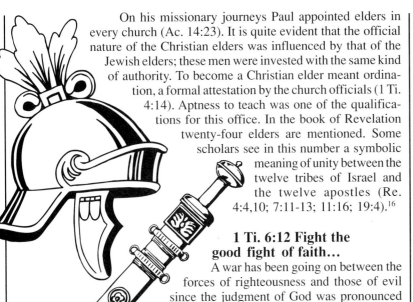

On his missionary journeys Paul appointed elders in every church (Ac. 14:23). It is quite evident that the official nature of the Christian elders was influenced by that of the Jewish elders; these men were invested with the same kind of authority. To become a Christian elder meant ordination, a formal attestation by the church officials (1 Ti. 4:14). Aptness to teach was one of the qualifications for this office. In the book of Revelation twenty-four elders are mentioned. Some scholars see in this number a symbolic meaning of unity between the twelve tribes of Israel and the twelve apostles (Re. 4:4,10; 7:11-13; 11:16; 19:4).[16]

Ordination
1490
Christian
Teachers
3559

1 Ti. 6:12 Fight the good fight of faith...

A war has been going on between the forces of righteousness and those of evil since the judgment of God was pronounced on Satan in the Garden of Eden (Ge. 3:15). Even though Satan is a potentially defeated foe, he is still active as the prince of this world (1 Co. 2:6; 1 Pe. 5:8). The enmity that prevails between the righteous on the one hand and the evil forces on the other is continually manifesting itself, and Paul's letters are filled with exhortations to "fight the good fight." He refers to the "helmet of salvation" and the "sword of the spirit" in Ep. 6:17.

Righteous-
ness—
Unrighteous-
ness
3077-3085
Satan,
Prince of
this World
3155

2 Ti. 3:16 All Scripture is God-breathed... (NIV)

Over a period of many years God spoke to holy men who wrote as they were moved by the Holy Spirit (2 Pe. 1:21). These holy men were early scribes, religious leaders, prophets, wise men and poets. Out of these writings a group of 39 books developed which were certified as Scripture by the Council of Jamnia in about A.D. 90. They did not legislate something new but merely affirmed officially what had been accepted by the covenant community over the years. (See Introduction to the Old Testament: How It Became the Official Canon.)

This written revelation was continued after Jesus, the Messiah, ascended into heaven. "Holy men of God" wrote, organized and formulated the New Testament. Its 27 books were accepted as guidelines for Christian doctrine and conduct and were officially canonized at the Council of Carthage in A.D. 397. (See Introduction to the New Testament: How It Became the Official Canon.) The test of time had now authenticated both Testaments as the Word of God.

An examination of each of the thirty-nine books in the OT and the twenty-seven in the NT discloses that there is complete unity within the books. The thought of Biblical integrity rests on the proposition that the authors of the Bible books had divine illumination. Paul expressed this concept in these words, "All scripture is given by inspiration of God, and is

Divine
Inspiration
1774-1776

God's
Word Sure
430

Holiness
1596
Origin and
Growth of
the English
Bible
4220

"Word"
Inspired
417
Purpose of
"Word"
424

profitable for doctrine, for reproof, for correction, for instruction in righteousness" (2 Ti. 3:16). Peter supports this affirmation: "For the prophecy came not in old time by the will of man: but holy men of God spake as they were moved by the Holy Ghost" (2 Pe. 1:21).

Spirit-filled
Men
1125

Thus it is quite obvious that Bible authority and its veracity are directly connected with the character of the writers. If they were "holy men," they were trustworthy and their character was unquestioned. This being true, the entire Bible is the infallible Word of God. Regardless of any theory of inspiration of how men produced and preserved the Bible, apart from the question of how much is to be interpreted literally and how much figuratively, or what is historical or what may be poetical, we accept the Bible for what it claims to be, the Word of God; it becomes the vehicle unto salvation to all who believe.[17] From Genesis to Revelation the message in the Bible changes the hearts of human beings from a bent to sin to a passion for holiness and love.

"Word"
Purifies
423

"Word"
Despised
2968
Study of
"Word"
428
Perfection
of "Word"
436
Salvation
3116-3128

There is current today a view that the Bible is the record of man's ever upward reach to find God, that God did not really speak, but that men put their ideas about God into written form. Thus some have reduced the Bible to a system based on human speculation or rationalization with only a pretense of it being divine. This idea is vehemently rejected by most conservative Bible scholars who hold that the Bible is the record of God's continual quest for man, even from the time in the Garden when God said to Adam, "Where art thou?" According to scholars, the Bible was written over a fifteen-hundred-year period by more than thirty different writers, and yet the cross reference system shows that unity of thought and purpose remain consistent in all sixty-six books. The promise of salvation can be traced like a scarlet thread through the Bible from Genesis (3:15) to Revelation (7:14).

"Word"
Illuminates
419

The inspiration of the Bible is affirmed by the men who wrote it; they asserted "Thus saith the Lord" and similar expressions; the Word was written in the hearts of men; it has been a source of light and strength to people of all ages; saints have loved it. Internal evidence proves to the devout believer that indeed "holy men of God" wrote the Bible.

Titus

The Name

The Epistle of Paul to Titus derives its name from the person to whom the letter is addressed (Tit. 1:4). The name "Titus" appears several times in the NT (2 Co. 2:13; 7:6, 13-14; 8:6, 16, 23; 12:18; 2 Co. postscript; Gal. 2:1, 3; 2 Ti. 4:10; Tit. 1:4; Tit. postscript).

The Epistle to Titus 4278

Authorship and Date

The traditional view credits Paul with being the author of the book of Titus, in which he identifies himself (1:1). The superscription also recognizes Paul as the author.

Paul 2697

As in the other two Pastoral Epistles, 1 and 2 Timothy, ancient church fathers refer to Paul as the author. For the objections to Pauline authorship see commentary on 1 and 2 Timothy. The letter was probably written about A.D. 63-67 between Paul's two imprisonments.

Paul's Bonds 3479

Background, Purpose, and Content

Titus was a frequent companion of Paul, as evidenced by the many references to him in the Pauline writings, but he is not mentioned in the book of Acts, as were so many of Paul's other companions.[1] Since Titus, a Greek, was apparently converted directly from heathenism, he was not compelled to be circumcised (Gal. 2:3-5). Paul called Titus "mine own son after the common faith" (Tit. 1:4).

Tree of Paul's Life 4309 Circumcision 765 Unity in Christ 3724

Titus was highly and deservedly esteemed by Paul (2 Co. 2:13; 7:6-7, 13, 15; 8:16, 23; 12:18).[2] When Paul, on Crete for only a short time, was unable to stay, he appointed Titus to supervise the affairs of the church on the island (Tit. 1:5). Paul sailed to Judea about A.D. 63, taking Timothy with him. After a few months in Jerusalem Paul proceeded to Antioch, where he set out on his third missionary journey.

Paul's Third Missionary Journey 4309e

It is uncertain where Paul was when he wrote his letter to Titus. Some suggest Nicopolis, where Paul had planned to spend the winter, but others suggest that he wrote the epistle in Corinth.[3] The postscript (an explanatory subscription that appears in some of the ancient Greek texts) gives Nicopolis

Corinth 840, 4359

Paul's
Missionary
Journeys
2382
Govern-
ment and
Discipline
of the
Church
749-752

Good
Doctrine
1029

Chastity-
Impurity
663-667

as the place. In the letter Paul expressed the hope that Titus could meet him in Nicopolis (3:12). Whether Titus was able to accede to Paul's request is not known.

The book indicates that Paul gave Titus some general instructions concerning pastoral work. Apparently Titus had the responsibility of general oversight of the churches, including ordaining church officials and drawing up rules for general church conduct. Paul states that monogamy is the Christian standard for marriage (Tit. 1:6), and that a bishop must be exemplary in all areas of life (1:7-8). False teachers seem to have been as prevalent here as in Ephesus, where Timothy labored. Paul commanded Titus to rebuke the false prophets "sharply" (1:10-16). Paul had advice for "the aged," the "young men," and the "servants,"[4] all of whom were to be dedicated, temperate, chaste, and discreet. Titus is to set a "pattern of good works: in doctrine shewing uncorruptness, gravity, sincerity, sound speech, that cannot be condemned" (2:1-8).

Believers in Christ were to obey magistrates, to speak evil of no man, to be gentle (3:1-2). Paul reminded Titus that "we ourselves also were sometimes foolish, disobedient, deceived, serving divers lusts and pleasures, living in malice and envy, hateful, and hating one another" (3:3). This is a dark picture of their lives before they were committed to Christ. It is evident they were in a position to understand and empathize with those still without salvation.

The setting of the book of Titus.

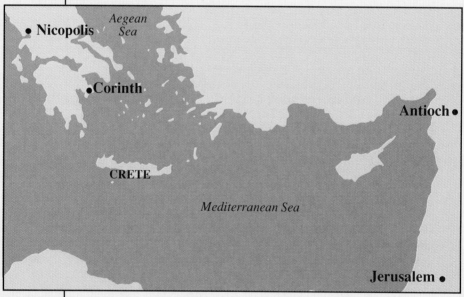

Paul reviewed for Titus the change that had come to them after they accepted by faith "the kindness and love of God our Saviour" (3:4-8). He warned Titus against involvement with "foolish questions, and genealogies, and contentions, and strivings about the law" (3:9). If a man became a heretic, he was to be rejected after he refused the first and second admonition (3:10-11). Paul promised to send some evangelists to Titus in the persons of Artemas and Tychicus. Paul made reference to Zenas the lawyer and Apollos. Nothing is known about Zenas, but Apollos is well known among the missionaries under Paul (Ac. 18:24; 1 Co. 1:12; 3:5-6; 4:6). Apparently Paul was anxious for Titus to help these evangelists with their expenses (3:13).

Characters
Transformed
836
Strife
Forbidden
3732

1:1 Paul, a servant of God and an apostle of Jesus Christ... (NIV)

Apostles
2080-2082
Discipleship
1015-1017

The word "apostle" signifies "one sent forth" as a messenger or ambassador. For more on how the word relates to "disciple," see commentary on Ac. 1:26.

1:5 ...appoint elders in every town, as I directed you. (NIV)

Duties of
Ministers
1060

Jewish
Elders
2079

This instruction to Titus is consistent with Paul's usual practice (see Ac. 14:23). In verse 7 Paul uses the word "bishop" (KJV) or "overseer" (NIV) presumably to describe the same office as "elder." The authority of the Christian elder seems similar to that of the earlier-established Jewish elders. For more on the nature of the office throughout the Bible, see commentary on 1 Ti. 5:17.

1:10 For there are many unruly and vain talkers and deceivers: specially they of the circumcision...

The
Circum-
cision
767
Reversion
to Judaism
4092

This group of troublemakers was similar to the "circumcision group" of Ga. 2:12, who insisted on the observance of the Jewish law for salvation. Some Judaizers had gone so far as to reinstate the Jewish festivals and ceremonies as essential to Christian worship (Ga. 4:8-11). Paul instructs Titus to "rebuke them sharply, so that they will be sound in the faith and will pay no attention to Jewish myths or to the commands of those who reject the truth" (Tit. 1:13-14, NIV).

Justification
by Faith
1203, 1985

Covenants
877-881
Strife
Forbidden
3732

The truth that Paul is referring to is the whole Biblical theme of justification by faith, not by works or outward practices. This message is not by any means unique to the NT, for the groundwork was laid in the case of Abraham, who believed and was counted righteous before he was circumcised (see commentary on Ge. 15:6 and essay following). The "new covenant" is actually the continuation and glorious perfection of the covenant God had made his followers from the beginning.

3:9 But avoid foolish controversies and genealogies and arguments and quarrels about the law, because these are unprofitable and useless. (NIV)

Paul's Care
for Church
732

Paul had also instructed Timothy along these lines because of the divisiveness that existed in the church at Ephesus (1 Ti. 1:3-7). For more on how the law related to both Testaments, see the essay "The Mosaic Law: The Unity of the Legal Structure in Both Testaments," pp. 102-103.

Philemon

The Name

The Epistle of Paul to Philemon derives its name from the person to whom the book is addressed (v. 1).

Authorship and Date

Pauline authorship is self-evident. The name Paul as author is referred to three times in this one-chapter book (vv. 1,9,19). Robert G. Gromacki says, "He [Paul] identified himself twice as 'a prisoner of Jesus Christ' (vv.1,9) and as 'the aged' (v. 9); both of these appellatives would fit into Paul's life history at this time. Its similarity to Colossians (Phm. 1-2, 23-24; cf. Col. 4:10-17) argues for a simultaneous writing from the same place by the same author."[1] Church fathers such as Tertullian, Origen, and Eusebius all attributed authorship of this book to Paul.[2]

This epistle is judged to have been written between Paul's first and second imprisonment, somewhere between A.D. 63 and 67.

Background, Purpose, and Content

It is possible that Philemon was one of Paul's converts at Ephesus. He was probably a man of means as well as a man of hospitality. "Tradition makes Philemon the bishop of Colosse (*Apos. Const.*, vii, 46) and the Greek Martyrology (Menae)...tells us that he, together with his wife and son and Onesimus were martyred by stoning before Androcles, the governor, in the days of Nero."[3]

In the address, it appears that Philemon was an active church member and that a Christian congregation met in his home in Colosse (v. 2). Scholars have assumed that Apphia was Philemon's wife and Archippus was his son (v. 2). The Colossian letter indicates that Archippus held an important office of some kind in Colosse (Col. 4:17), probably that of a presbyter or an evangelist. Paul recognizes him as a "fellow-soldier" of the faith (v. 2).

Paul expressed great spiritual affection for Philemon (vv. 2-9). Apparently Onesimus, Philemon's personal slave, had appropriated some of his master's possessions and made his way to Rome to befriend Paul, who was in prison. After the slave Onesimus arrived in Rome, he was converted (v. 10). Then Paul wrote Philemon that he was sending Onesimus home to make

The Epistle to Philemon 4279

Paul 2697

Tree of Paul's Life 4309

Paul's Bonds 3479

Ephesus 1142, 4373
Onesimus 2650
Martyrdom 3487

The Epistle to The Colossians 4273
Colosse 4358

Conversion 834-836

things right, and he was now a brother in the Lord and no longer "just a slave."

A proper interpretation of the book of Philemon might be as follows: A bond of friendship existed between Paul and Philemon, as described in the introductory verses (1-8). From the comments concerning the Colossians one gathers there are several reasons for assuming that Paul did visit Colosse. It is possible that Paul was a regular visitor in the home of Philemon and that while in his home, Paul befriended Onesimus, the slave who was probably treated in the customary manner and who apparently was hardly worth his room and board (v. 11). Paul may have made a special effort to show Christian love to Onesimus. At any rate, some motivation caused Onesimus to brave the dangers of traveling from Colosse to faraway Rome to be with his friend. The hazards were great. Often a runaway slave, when appre-hended, was placed in the galley of a ship or was subjected to some other harsh employment.

Onesimus was successful in evading the dangers enroute and arrived in Rome, where he sought out Paul. While there, he was converted (vv. 10-11). He was then a new creature in Christ and even his motivation for service changed. Paul appealed to Philemon to receive Onesimus back as a brother in the faith, as he would receive Paul himself should he come (v. 1).

There is evidence to suggest that Philemon was once a slave himself and that Paul bought his freedom. Paul reminded Philemon, "how thou owest unto me even thine own self besides" (v. 19). Could it be that Paul had bought Philemon's freedom and that he had established a tent-making partnership with his friend in Colosse? Paul asked Philemon to charge Onesimus' debts to his own account (vv. 18-19). Possibly Paul was saying: "When you figure our profits at the end of the year." The text could justify this interpretation without its doing theological violence.

It is apparent that Paul was making plans to spend some time with Philemon soon (v. 22). In his closing remarks Paul sent greetings from his fellowprisoner, Epaphras, and his fellowlaborers Marcus, Aristarchus, De-mas, and Lucas (vv. 23-24).

Phm. 2 ...to the church in thy house.

The term "church" is used only three times in the Gospels—once in Mt. 16:18 and twice in Mt. 18:17. The first-century Christian was distinctly Jewish; Christianity was definitely a movement within Judaism (Mt. 13:54; Mk. 6:2). Jesus, as well as his apostles, taught in the temple and in the synagogues (Mt. 13:54; Jn. 6:59; Ac. 13:5). Gradually as the rift widened between the Jews who accepted Jesus as the Messiah and those who did not, the Messianic Christians began to worship in home churches, such as Philemon had in his home. Some sizeable underground chapels give evidence that the early Christians had worship services also in the catacombs.

The importance of the synagogue as a basis from which the Christian Church developed is shown in the commentary on Lu. 4:16. Many parallels can be drawn.

One important difference, however, is that although the quorum required to form a synagogue had been ten heads of families or households, the membership for a Christian church seems to have been reduced by the Lord to "where two or three are gathered in my name" (Mt. 18:20). Also, the Bible contains no reference to a church building as such. The *ekklesia,* the church mentioned in the NT, instead refers to the body of believers in the Lord as Christ, the Messiah. The church was both visible and invisible and was composed of all who were really united to Christ (1 Cor. 1:2; 12:12-13, 27-28; Col. 1:24; 1 Pe. 2:9-10).

This explains the absence of church ruins from the first and second centuries. Extensive church buildings did not come into existence until Constantine made Christianity a state religion (A.D. 275-337). When the Roman aristocracy insisted on adhering to their pagan religions, Constantine moved his capital to Byzantium and called it Constantinople, New Rome, capital of the New Christian Empire. The first historical reference to a church building was made by Alexander Severus, who reigned as Roman emperor A.D. 222-235.[4]

In the third and fourth centuries the word *basilica* took on a Christian tone. The term means a public building ending in a semicircular apse. It was used in Roman times for a court of justice or a public assembly hall. Frequently basilicas were converted into places of worship, especially in the period following Constantine's conversion. This architectural design has been perpetuated throughout the centuries. Even today such basilica terms

---

The
Church
726-761

Synagogues
3521-3523

Judaism
Superseded
1957

Fellowship
in Church
1325

Church,
Body of
Christ
726

Growth of
the Church
733-2380

Unity of
Believers
3724-3727

History
of Early
Church
4309g

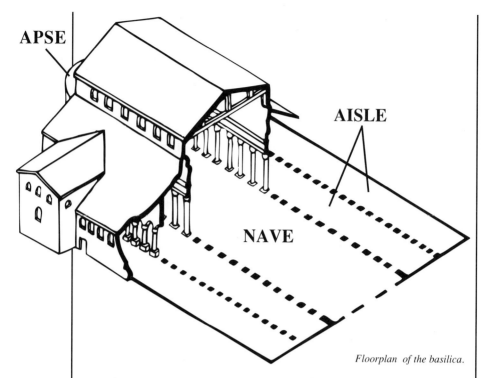

APSE

AISLE

NAVE

Floorplan of the basilica.

as narthex, nave, aisle, apse, and transept are used to describe various parts of a church building.

Worship centers have evolved over the years from the most primitive pile of stones to the modern cathedral with its stained glass, church spires, and pipe organs (see chart on this development at Ac. 2:47).

Hebrews

The Name

The book of Hebrews derives its name from the traditional understanding that the book was written to the Hebrew Christians. The patristic postscript (which appears in some ancient Greek texts, but was not in the original manuscripts) states: "Written to the Hebrews from Italy by Timothy."

Authorship and Date

The book of Hebrews is devoid of any specific reference to authorship. Thomas Rees explains,

> For the purpose of tracing the history and interpreting the meaning of the book…the absence of a title or of any definite historical data, is [a] disadvantage. We are left to infer its historical context from a few fragments of uncertain tradition, and from such general references to historical conditions as the document itself contains. Where no date, name or well-known event is fixed, it becomes impossible to decide, among many possibilities, what known historical conditions, if any, are presupposed.[1]

The name "Paul" was included in the superscription because of the judgment common among the early church fathers that the apostle wrote the book. However, there is no internal evidence to support this position. The Authorized Version and the ERV retain the title: "The Epistle of Paul the Apostle to the Hebrews." Probably it was appended because of the conclusion that Paul was best qualified to write the book.

Stephen S. Smalley says, "All of the existing manuscript copies of this Epistle include the title 'Pros hebraios' (to the Hebrews), which clearly belongs to a very early tradition, even if it is not original, since it is contained in some of the oldest manuscripts."[2] It is difficult to discover a historical clue in Hebrews because no Biblical writers are mentioned by name, although the book contains frequent OT quotations.

Robert G. Gromacki observes that,

> Scholars have suggested several names as possibilities for the authorship of this book. Among them are Apollos, Barnabas, Luke, Priscilla, Silas, and of course, Paul. Generally the debate centers around Paul: Did he or did he not write the book?…Even the early church had problems over the authenticity of the book. The Eastern Church [Constantinople] accepted it as an original Pauline, canonical book, whereas the Western Church [Rome] denied its Pauline authorship [for some time] and excluded it from the canon, namely because of the uncertain authorship.[3]

All of the persons mentioned above have some qualifications for writing the book of Hebrews. An analysis of these names provides the following conclusions:

The Epistle to the Hebrews 4280

Timothy 3628

Study of "Word" 428

Paul 2697, 202

Preaching 2087

Manuscripts 4220

Tree of Paul's Life 4309

Luke
2216

Silas
3288

Barnabas
342

Apollos
200-201

Philip
2754

Aquila and
Priscilla
208

Paul
2697

Paul's
Bonds
3479

Superior-
ity of New
Dispen-
sation
3499-3500
Justification
by Faith
1203,1985

Syna-
gogues
3521-3523
Paul's Care
for the
Church
732

1. Luke was a brilliant scholar with unusual research skill, but he was a Gentile and might not have possessed the intimate knowledge of Judaism which the book reflects.

2. Silas was a constant companion of Paul, but there is no literary tradition to associate authorship with him.

3. Barnabas was a Jew and a Levite with extensive Judaistic insights. He was an intimate friend and companion of Paul who was equally at home with the Jews and Gentiles. However, there is no literary history for Barnabas.

4. Apollos was well versed in the Scriptures and successful in his witness among the Jews. He was closely associated with Paul and was active in the ministry until the end of Paul's life (Tit. 3:13). Nevertheless, tradition for making him the author is lacking.

5. Philip, the Evangelist, was appointed to supervise social services for the Greek widows. He preached the Savior, won many converts (Ac. 8:4-8), and ministered to the Ethiopian eunuch (Ac. 8:26-39). Philip entertained Paul on his last visit to Caesarea (Ac. 21:8), but all of these activities do not constitute proof of his authorship of Hebrews.

6. Prisca (Priscilla), the wife of Aquila, was highly esteemed by Paul (Ac. 18:18-26; Ro. 16:3; 2 Ti. 4:19); there is no indication that she ever wrote a book.

7. Paul's credentials for writing Hebrews seems to have the greatest weight; however, many scholars question his authorship on the basis of style difference, content, and terminology. There is some validity in these objections, and the contenders do have unquestioned qualifications, but there is also some evidence for Pauline authorship.

Some of the reasons for favoring Pauline authorship include the following: The author was a prisoner; Paul was in prison many times (He. 10:34; cf. 2 Co. 11:23). Numerous points of agreement in doctrine are recognizable between Hebrews and other acknowledged writings of Paul. Paul affirmed the preeminence of Christ (He. 1:1-3; cf. Col. 1:14-19) and the humiliation of Christ (He. 2:9-18; cf. Ph. 2:5-11). The apostle referred to the wanderings of Israel as a warning for the Christians (He. 3:7-19); cf. 1 Co. 10:1- 11), and commented on the temporary character of the first covenant (He. 8:1-13; cf. 2 Co. 3:6-18). He dwelt on the principle of faith as expressed in Habakkuk's prophecy, "The just shall live by his faith" (Hab. 2:4), and quoted it in Hebrews 10:38 (cf. Ro. 1:17 and Gal. 3:11). The writer of Hebrews was a close associate of Timothy; so the author could have been Paul (He. 13:23).

Paul made reference to himself as an apostle to the Gentiles (Ro. 11:13), but he usually ministered first in the local synagogue upon arrival in a new preaching place (Ac. 13:14; 17:1-2, 10, 17; 18:4, 8). Paul often visited the church in Jerusalem, showing deep concern for the Jews (Ro. 9:1-5; 10:1-4). His training under Gamaliel in Jerusalem was ample preparation for dealing with Jewish sacrificial and ritualistic complexities. Paul certainly demonstrated his knowledge of the OT and related it to NT theology in his sermon in the synagogue at Antioch (Ac. 13:14-42).[4]

A noted scholar says of Hebrews: "The closing section bears a great resemblance to Pauline concerns. He requested prayer in his behalf (He. 13:18; cf. Ep. 6:18-20), desired a good conscience (He. 13:18; cf. Ac. 24:16; 2 Ti. 1:3), identified the Father as the God of Peace (He. 13:20; cf. Ro. 15:33; Ph. 4:9; 1 Th. 5:23), and pronounced a benediction of grace (He. 13:25; cf. Phm. 25)."[5] "One of the early fathers, Origen, is quoted as saying, 'Only God alone knows who wrote the Epistle.' "[6] This is probably the logical assumption for all scholars to make until new evidence is discovered.

Hebrews must have been written before the destruction of Jerusalem under Titus in A.D. 70. The content strongly suggests it was composed during severe Christian persecution, probably while Nero was the Emperor (A.D. 54-68).[7]

Background, Purpose, and Content

The frequent references to the rituals and ordinances within Judaism suggest that the book of Hebrews was addressed to Jewish Christians. There is constant appeal to the OT, to illustrate that Christianity was the fulfillment of that which was spoken of by the OT prophets (He. 1:1-2; cf. Lu. 24:25-27,44; Ac.. 3:21; Ro. 4:18). In the book there is no reference to Gentile members being in the church. The author emphasizes that "their danger lay in a return, not so much to the law as to the ritual. These allusions best suit the Hebrew Christians of Palestine, and Jewish believers of the East."[8]

The epistle seems to be addressed especially to the believers who were suffering persecution (He. 10:32) and to the faltering Christians who needed to make a complete commitment for inner strength to overcome temptation and to avoid apostasy. The writer speaks to the Christians as brothers in Christ (He. 3:1) and indicates that he had visited with them (He. 13:19). The people addressed in the epistle seem to have been believers for some time (He. 13:7), but apparently they were still "babes in Christ." When

The Wailing Wall (the Western Wall). This is a most sacred worship center for the Jews, especially on the eve of the Sabbath.

they should have been teaching, they needed to be taught. When they should have been taking the meat (of the word) they were still taking milk (He. 5:12-14). Their continued "spiritual infancy" along with the persecution made the danger of apostasy very great. There was the temptation to revert to the ritual of Judaism. To make the situation even more dangerous there were the false teachers with their syncretized heresies. One scholar says,

> The writer of the Epistle to the Hebrews sees the danger of apostasy seriously threatening the community in question, and this causes him to direct his readers' minds to the finality of the Christian revelation: the cruciality of God's work in Christ (10:19), and the supremacy of the new priesthood and covenant (8:6), and of the new, once for all (ephapax) sacrifice (9:12). All of the time he uses theological exposition as the basis for moral exhortation: he is concerned that the readers should "consider Him"—the Person,…(3:1), and the work (12:3) of the Lord Jesus Christ; and on this basis "advance toward maturity."[9]

An important word in Hebrews is the term "better": "the bringing in of a better hope" (7:19); "Jesus made a surety of a better testament" (7:22); "He is the mediator of a better covenant" (8:6); cf. "he is the mediator of the new testament" (9:15). Hebrews also includes the idea of "better" in the sense of "more enduring":

1. A better priest: "Thou art a priest for ever" (7:17; cf. Ps. 110:4); "But this man, because he continueth ever, hath an unchangeable priesthood" (7:24); "he is able…to save them to the uttermost…seeing he ever liveth to make intercession for them" (7:25); "who [Jesus] needeth not daily…to offer up sacrifice…for this he did once, when he offered up himself" [better sacrifice] (7:27; cf. 10:10-12,14).

2. A better offering: "He offered up himself" (7:27); Christ…offered himself without spot" (9:14); "put away sin by the sacrifice of himself" (9:26).

The entire OT religion rests its structure on the foundation of faith. The great notables of faith mentioned in the eleventh chapter of Hebrews were children of God through faith. The book of Hebrews is a counterpart to the book of Romans: both books give emphasis to justification by faith (He. 4:2-3; 10:19-33; 10:38; ch. 11; cf. Ro 1:17; 3:21-22, 26-28; 5:1-2; 10:4-11).

1:1-2 In the past God spoke…at many times and in various ways, but in these last days he has spoken to us by his Son… (NIV)

The writer of Hebrews clearly shows that Christianity was not a new religion but a continuation of a religious system which had its beginning in Genesis. The God who spoke to the OT fathers and prophets had now spoken to the NT apostles through his Son Jesus Christ. The OT and NT are a unity, in that they both speak of a blood-bought salvation by the death of God's Son. In the OT the blood of bulls and goats prefigured the blood of the Lamb of God who did in fact take away the sins of the world.

1:14 Are not all angels ministering spirits sent to serve those who will inherit salvation? (NIV)

Angels are mentioned frequently in both the Old and New Testaments (100 times in the OT and 193 times in the NT). Though they have various functions, in this case it seems they are to supervise men's activities and to dispense divine grace and intelligence. For more on the various types of angels, their function, and the hierarchy of angels mentioned in Scripture, see commentary on Re. 5:11.

2:17 …that he might be a merciful and faithful high priest in things pertaining to God…

In the OT the levitical high priest represented the people before God. Each year, on the Day of Atonement, he ceremonially received a sin offering from the people and transferred their sins to the scapegoat. The high priest, under the law, was a type who foreshadowed the object. The writer of Hebrews presents Jesus Christ as the Great High Priest who now represents the saints and makes intercession for them before God (He. 7:25; cf. Is. 53:12; Ro. 8:27,34).

4:1 Therefore, since the promise of entering his rest still stands, let us be careful that none of you be found to have fallen short of it. (NIV)

The writer of Hebrews uses Israel's apostasy as an object lesson. Wallace Alcorn describes the danger of apostasy thus:

> He [the writer] warns his readers of the inescapable consequences of neglecting salvation (2:1-3), about missing God's rest (3:7-19), about disqualification from the rest (4:1-11), of the impossibility of return from conscious apostasy (6:4-8), and of there being no provision for deliberate sin (10:26-31). Closely related to these are his exhortations: be alert, lest you drift away (2:1-4); be careful, lest you disbelieve (3:7-4:13); go on, lest you walk away (10:19-39); build up, lest you fall apart (12:12-29).[10]

The book was also written to warn the Jewish Christians of the danger that their hearts might also cause them to miss their spiritual Canaan rest (4:11). The Israelites had the gospel preached to them, and they had a deliverance from the bondage of Egypt (cf. 1 Co. 10:1-4), but they were in danger of missing the Promised Land. As the Israelites missed this rest, so the Jewish believers were now in danger of missing their spiritual Canaan—

the experience of sanctification which comes from a complete commitment. One scholar describes this sanctification relationship in Hebrews as follows:

> Sanctification is described in terms highly peculiar to this epistle, and centers around a concept of perfection…the goal of God's rest, which is variously spoken of as arrival at one's destination, as a completion of one's own task, and as peace with God. The rest can be defined as perfect and eternal rest with God.[11]

6:20 …Jesus, made an high priest for ever after the order of Melchisedec.

Melchisedec, the ancient priest of Salem (Jerusalem), stands out in a shroud of mystery, both in the OT and NT. Greatly misunderstood by many people, he is mentioned twice in the OT, by the Hebrew form *Melchizedek* (Ge. 14:18; Ps. 110:4); he is referred to nine times in the NT by the Greek form *Melchisedec* and only in the book of Hebrews (He. 5:6,10; 6:20; 7:1,10,11,15,17,21).

There has been much theological speculation concerning Melchisedec. Some have suggested that he was an appearance of the preincarnate Son of God; others say that he was in some way identified with Christ. Any interpretation of this man should be governed strictly by what the Scriptures disclose; anything beyond that is pure speculation. In Genesis the writer clearly states that Melchizedek was the "king of Salem" and that "he was the priest of the most high God" (Ge. 14:18; cf. He. 7:1-4). He obviously was a high official in the religious hierarchy of that day because "Abraham recognized him as a priest of the True God and publicly testified to sharing the same or kindred faith by paying tithes to him who was representative of God Most High."[12] (See also commentary on Ge. 14:20.)

The reference in the Psalms follows a Messianic prophecy; "Thou art a priest for ever after the order of Melchizedek" (Ps. 110:4). In the Hebrew reference it is stated he was "without father, without mother, without descent, having neither beginning of days, nor end of life; but made like unto the Son of God; abideth a priest continually" (He. 7:3).[13]

John Wesley gives a very reasonable explanation of these passages:

> "Without father, without mother, without pedigree"—Recorded without any account of his descent from any ancestor or the priestly order. "Having neither beginning of days nor of life"…In all these respects, "Made like the Son of God"—who is really "without father," as to His human nature; "without mother," as to His divine; and in this also, "without pedigree"—Neither descended from any ancestors or the priestly order. "Remaineth a priest continually"—Nothing is recorded of the death or successor of Melchisedec. But Christ alone does really remain without death and without successor.[14]

"Keil and Delitzsch nicely summarize the ideas regarding the true identity of Melchizedek: 'We can see in him nothing more than one, perhaps the last, of the witnesses and confessors of the early revelation of God. Coming out into the light of history and the dark night of heathenism.' Herbert C. Leupold adds that 'we are compelled to regard this venerable king-priest as a worshipper and public adherent of the true religion of Yahweh as handed down from the sounder tradition of the times of the Flood.' "[15]

8:5 ...Moses was warned when he was about to build the tabernacle: "See to it that you make everything according to the pattern shown you on the mountain." (NIV)

During the instructions to Moses about building the tabernacle it is stated more than fifty times "As the Lord commanded Moses, so did he."[16] For more on the details of God's instructions to Moses, and how it provided a great object lesson on Christ the Savior, see commentary on Ex. 25:8-9.

Tabernacle
3528

Obedience
2614-2619

Christ our Saviour
3360

8:13 By calling this covenant "new," he has made the first one obsolete... (NIV)

The First Covenant centered around the tabernacle and the Ten Commandments. They had served their purpose. The laws were now written on the tables of the heart (He. 8:10). The First Covenant was temporal; the Second Covenant replaced the First and was Eternal. The First Covenant was sealed with the blood of animals; Christ's Covenant was sealed with his own blood (He. 10:29). It was a better covenant with better promises based on the immutability of God's Word (He. 6:18)..."The New Covenant is called 'The New Testament.' A Testament is a Will, a bequeathment to heirs, effective only after the death of the maker. The New Covenant is the Will which Christ made for His Heirs, which could not become effective till by His Death, He had atoned for their sins."[17]

Covenants
877-881

Covenant-keepers
1232

Spiritual Heirs
743

Candlestick
637

Table
3530

9:2 For there was a tabernacle made; the first, wherein was the candlestick, and the table, and the shewbread; which is called the sanctuary.

The table of shewbread and the candlestick, both found in the Holy Place, are very significant symbols of Christ, who said "I am the bread of life" (Jn. 6:35) and "I am the light of the world" (Jn. 8:12). For a study of these symbols, see commentary on Ex. 25:30 (shewbread) and Ex. 25:31 (candlestick).

Bread of Life
1308

9:11 ...[Christ] went through the greater and more perfect tabernacle that is not man-made... (NIV)

An exposition on Christ and the True Tabernacle, made without hands, is presented in the commentary on Ex. 25:8-30:18. "The High Priest entered once a year; Christ entered once for all (He. 9:7,12). The High Priest obtained annual redemption; Christ obtained Eternal Redemption (He. 9:12)...The High Priest's sacrifices cleansed the flesh; Christ's sacrifice cleanses the conscience (He. 9:13-14)."[18]

Tabernacle
3528

Redemption
2979

9:22 ...without shedding of blood is no remission.

The importance of the blood sacrifice can be seen in the Biblical record as early as the Garden of Eden: Abel's offering, which required shedding of blood, was accepted and Cain's, which was bloodless, was rejected. For more on the subject, see commentary on Ge. 4:4-5. See also the essays, "The Mechanics of Salvation in the OT Period," pp. 67-69, and "The Nature of the New Birth: Is It Unique to the NT?" pp. 384-386.

Blood
516

Remission of Sin
3127

10:1,4 For the law having a shadow of good things to come, and not the very image of the things, can never with those sacrifices which they offered year by year continually make the comers thereunto perfect...For it is not possible that the blood of bulls and of goats should take away sins.

How does Christ, the superior High Priest and the once-for-all sacrifice, relate to the levitical and Mosaic laws? He himself speaks to the subject in Mt. 5:17 when he says, "Do not think that I have come to abolish the Law or the Prophets; I have not come to abolish them but to fulfill them" (NIV). Christ did not repudiate the Law, for its use in past generations had been directed by God (Le. 18:3-4).

If God instituted the Law and if Christ did not repudiate it, does it still have meaning for contemporary Christians? Or, if by Christ's death the law was fulfilled, can it be ignored by believers today? These and other questions about the law and the Christian are dealt with in the essay "The Mosaic Law: The Unity of the Legal Structure in Both Testaments," pp. 102-103; see also commentary on Mt. 5:17.

11:1 Now faith is the substance of things hoped for, the evidence of things not seen.

Hebrews 11 deals in a singular way with the OT heroes of faith. The writer defines faith in this first verse in a way that is not too different from the understanding of the atomic structure of matter. Many of the visible things can be made invisible when the respective elements are separated from the substance; e.g., sodium and chloride are gases but when combined become salt; hydrogen and oxygen are invisible gases but in combination make water.

11:6 But without faith it is impossible to please him: for he that cometh to God must believe that he is, and that he is a rewarder of them that diligently seek him.

This verse highlights the Bible's main redemptive theme: that salvation is by faith and that this has been the case from the creation of the world ("By faith Abel offered unto God a more excellent sacrifice than Cain," v. 4). For more on salvation before the crucifixion, see the essay "The Mechanics of Salvation the the OT Period," pp. 67-69.

12:28 ...we are receiving a kingdom that cannot be shaken... (NIV)

The concept of the kingdom of God has its roots in the OT and was also the central message of Jesus. For more on its meaning throughout Scripture, see commentary on Mk. 1:15.

Sacrifices
Insufficient
3108

Keep the
Law
437
Fulfillment
2892
Purpose
of Law
4055
Law
Perfect
436

Faith
1201-1218

Water
of Life
3789, 4218
Divine
Promises
2878
Justification
by Faith
1203,1985
Salvation
3116-3128

Spiritual
Kingdom
2007-2013

James

The Name

The name James is the English form of the Hebrew *Jacob* and is derived from the Greek word *Iacabos*. The book of James is the first and the oldest of the seven General Epistles addressed to the Christian church at large.

Four men in the NT are named James:

1. James, the son of Zebedee, an apostle and the brother of the apostle John (Mt. 4:21; 10:2).

2. James, the son of Alphaeus, who was also one of the apostles and styled "the less," probably because he was small in stature (Mt. 10:3; Mk. 3:18; 15:40).

3. James, the Lord's brother, who was called "the just" (Mt. 13:55; Mk. 6:3).

4. James, the brother of the apostle Judas (Lu. 6:16; Ac. 1:13).

Authorship and Date

It is commonly assumed that James, the brother of the Lord, was the author of the book of James. Alexander Ross says that "the writer was a Jew, evidenced by the fact that he speaks of Abraham as 'our father' (Ja. 2:21), he applies to a Christian place of worship the word 'synagogue' (Ja. 2:2); the Greek for the term 'assembly' or 'meeting' is the origin of the English word 'synagogue'), he uses the Jewish word 'Gehenna' (Ja. 3:6), and a specifically Jewish name for God in Ja. 5:4."[1] Analysis shows that James, the brother of our Lord, is the only one to be seriously considered as the author. "The disciple of Jesus, James, the son of Alphaeus, seems to have been an obscure person; and James, the son of Zebedee, died early as a martyr in the year 44 (Ac. 12)."[2]

The content suggests that it was written during a time of persecution, affliction, and suffering such as prevailed during Nero's reign of terror (1:3-4), probably A.D. 37-68. It was probably written a few years before James' death.

Background, Purpose and Content

Those who take the position for Mary's perpetual virginity would say that James and his brothers were children of Joseph by a former marriage, which would make them step-brothers or half-brothers of Jesus.[3] However, this position is based merely on conjecture and finds no support in Scripture.

When Jesus went to Nazareth, his work was hampered because of the people's unbelief. James and his brothers did not believe that Jesus was the Messiah; they probably contributed to his difficulties (Jn. 7:5).

The Epistle of James
4281

James
1842-1844

Judas
1959-1963

Abraham
15

Hell
(Gehenna)
1374

Zebedee
3984
Persecution
3480
Suffering
3474-3475

Christ's Brethren
544
Unbelief
1219-1224

Jesus the
Messiah
695
James
1844

Paul
2697
Zealous-
ness
1074
Peter
2746, 4191
John
1902

Prayer
2816

Martyrdom
3487-3488

Sanhedrin
862
Persecution
3480
Forgiveness
2300, 3345

Martyrs
3488

Saints
Scattered
4094

Guidance
1465-1470

Faith
1201-1218
"Word" as a
Standard
426

The brothers may not have attended the crucifixion because they may have been embarrassed by Jesus' claims to Messiahship. The fact that he was crucified as a "malefactor" may have further confirmed their doubts. Apparently, not until after Jesus was crucified and resurrected did James become a believer. Scripture states that the brothers may have been the first to receive the news of Jesus' resurrection (Jn. 20:17). Later, Jesus appeared to James in person (1 Co. 15:7). After Saul of Tarsus (Paul) was converted, he went to Jerusalem and stayed fifteen days with Peter; while there he met "James the Lord's brother" (Gal. 1:18-19). Following his conversion James became a zealous worker in the Christian movement. Shortly after Peter's miraculous deliverance from prison, James became the acknowledged leader of the Jerusalem church (Ac. 15:13; 21:18). He was greatly esteemed by the other apostles; Paul regarded James, along with Cephas (Peter—see Jn. 1:42) and John, as the pillars of the church (Gal. 2:9). The three of them are frequently mentioned, and they worked together as a team.

At the Council of Jerusalem, James took the lead in drafting the letter which was sent to the Gentiles (Ac. 15:13-29).[4] James was very zealous for the cause of Christ. "It is said of him [that] he spent so much time on his knees in prayer that they became hard and calloused like a camel's knees."[5]

James gave his life as a martyr, as did most of the other apostles. Josephus and Hegesippus, both historians in the Christian era, affirm James' martyrdom. In reporting on their statements, Henry H. Halley writes,

> Shortly after Jerusalem was destroyed by the Roman army [under Titus] in 70 A.D....when Jews were, in large numbers, embracing Christianity, Ananus, the High Priest, and the scribes and Pharisees, in about the year 62 A.D. or 66 A.D. assembled the Sanhedrin, and commanded James, "the brother of Jesus who was called Christ," to proclaim from one of the galleries of the Temple that Jesus Was Not the Messiah. But instead, James cried out that Jesus was the Son of God and Judge of the World. Then his enraged enemies hurled him to the ground, and stoned him, till a charitable fuller ended his sufferings with a club, while he was on his knees praying "Father, forgive them, they know not what they do."[6]

James was martyred in about A.D. 62-63.

The book of James is addressed "to the twelve tribes which are scattered abroad" (Ja. 1:1). This is understood to mean that it was addressed to the Christian churches at large (1:2). Similar to the OT book of Proverbs, the book of James contains many short, pithy epigrams especially suited to the growing Christian church. Both the books of Proverbs and James, as well as part of the Sermon on the Mount, are considered to be Wisdom Literature.

Probably James wrote this book during a time of great persecution and uncertainty, and he urged the Christians to "ask of God" for direction (1:5) in genuine faith (1:6-8). He recognized that Christian freedom can be dangerous for those who have been bound by a "letter of the law" legal code. The writer points out that the test of faith for the Christian comes in everyday life. He insisted that faith without works is dead (1:22-25; 2:26). James gave a simple definition for sin in 4:17. He also included directions concerning divine healing in 5:13-16.

"James reminds us of the need for genuine Christian standards...in every area of life. It is...so easy for the world...to squeeze us into its own mold, to convince us that there are no absolutes, no black and white, only gray. The early Christians needed the letter—and so do we."[7]

It is apparent that there are many parallel statements between the message of James and the Sermon on the Mount. James may possibly have heard the sermon, and, if not, he probably talked to some eyewitnesses (Ja. 2:14-26, cf. Mt. 7:21-23; Ja. 1:21, cf. Mt. 7:24-27; Ja. 3:11-12, cf. Mt. 7:16-20; Ja. 4:11-12, cf. Mt. 7:1; Ja. 5:1-6, cf. Mt. 6:19-24; Ja. 5:12, cf. Mt. 5:34-37).[8]

As an overview, Alexander Ross gives this analysis of the book:

> (1) Greeting (1:1); (2) trials from without (1:2-12), (3) trials from within (1:13-18), (4) hearing and doing (1:19-27), (5) respect of persons (2:1-13), (6) relation of faith and works (2:14), (7) sins of the tongue (3:1-12), (8) the false and the true wisdom (3:13-18), (9) mischief caused by strife and evil speaking (4:1-12), (10) the uncertainty and brevity of human life, leading us to humble dependence on the will of God (4:13-17), (11) the terrible doom that the rich oppressors of the church are to meet (5:1-6), (12) final exhortation to the Church to stand firm and to be forbearing in view of the coming of the Lord (5:7-12), (13) various activities of the Church—prayer, praise, visitation of the sick, confession of sins, and the restoration of backsliders (5:13-20).[9]

Sin Defined
3338
Sermon on the Mount
3237

Good Works
3902

Riches Perilous
2806

1:25 ...the perfect law that gives freedom... (NIV)

The law makes the sinner a slave because he cannot obey it by his own strength. However, the perfect law of Christ, based on the moral and ethical teachings of the Old Testament, gives the Christian freedom from the bondage of sin. For more on Christ as the fulfillment of the OT Law, see commentary on Mt. 5:17.

2:1 My brothers, as believers in our glorious
Lord Jesus Christ, don't show favoritism. (NIV)

Though James is speaking here to prejudice against the poor, the same insight about God's impartiality was also shown to Peter in relation to prejudice against the Gentiles. He was shown that "God is no respecter of persons: But in every nation he that feareth him, and worketh righteousness, is accepted with him" (Ac. 10:34-35). From the time of Adam and Eve the Biblical writers tell of only one basic requirement for salvation: faith. There has never been an exclusive group that God favors more than another. Therefore his followers must also not show prejudice. (See commentary on Ac. 10:34-35 and Introduction to Romans: Background, Purpose and Content.)

2:5 ...heirs of the kingdom which he
hath promised to them that love him.

Jesus said that at the coming of the Son of Man in his glory, the King will say to some, "Come, you who are blessed by my Father; take your inheritance, the kingdom prepared for you since the creation of the world" (Mt. 25:34, NIV). The kingdom of God was the central message on Jesus' lips. For more on the kingdom and its OT background see commentary on Mk. 1:15.

2:17 ...faith, if it hath not works, is dead...

How does this passage of Scripture fit into the consistent Biblical teaching that it is faith, not works, that saves? James is speaking here of faith as a mere intellectual affirmation of Christ's existence (see v. 19, for example), but not a genuine experience of faith with the heart. James says that if one has genuine faith (as did Abraham, see v. 23) it will be evidenced by his actions (Abraham offered up Isaac, see v. 21). Still, it is not the actions that save, but it is the kind of faith that produced the actions. Paul affirms this interrelationship between faith and action: "For in Christ Jesus neither circumcision nor uncircumcision has any value. The only thing that counts is faith expressing itself through love" (Gal. 5:6, NIV).

5:14 ...let him call for the elders of the church...

On his missionary journeys Paul had appointed elders in every church, and it is quite evident that the office was influenced by that of Jewish elders before them. For more on the office and its development, see commentary on 1 Ti. 5:17.

1 and 2
Peter

The Name

The Epistles of Peter derive their names from their initial verses, in which the writer identifies himself as the author.

Authorship and Date

From early times the First Epistle of Peter was acknowledged to have been the work of the apostle whose name it bears. By A.D. 200 the epistle had wide circulation in the Roman Empire and was considered to contain authoritative gospel information from an eyewitness.

Peter was diligent in recording and preserving the gospel account, including activities of the founding of the early church. His name appears 146 times in the four Gospels and 57 times in the book of Acts.

Historical evidence for Peter's authorship is plentiful. Polycarp (A.D. 69-156), who was a disciple of John, made references to 1 Peter. Iraneus (A.D. 67-110) quoted from Peter's book frequently; Clement of Alexandria (A.D. 150-216) cited the apostle many times. The internal evidence for Peter's authorship is equally conclusive.

The basic teachings of the Gospels are contained in 1 Peter. Alan W. Stibbs observes that "The Gospel according to Mark was probably a writing of the typical content of Peter's preaching; so 1 Peter may provide a Summary of Peter's customary teaching and exhortation."[1]

The writings also show familiarity with others of the epistles, especially Romans, Ephesians and James, and the content of 1 Peter stands in close relationship with the Apostles' discourses in Acts.[2] The evidence for the authorship of 1 Peter is overwhelming, although his close confidant and scribe, Silvanus, a Greek, may have added the excellent Greek style to Peter's original ideas, as suggested by the phrase, "By Silvanus" (1 Pe. 5:12).

Evidence that Peter wrote 2 Peter is less overwhelming. The external evidence for assigning authorship of 2 Peter to the apostle Peter is very scant, as compared to 1 Peter and some other NT books. Even such fathers of the third century as Origen and Eusebius expressed reservations for assigning authorship to Peter. Origen had doubts as to Peter being the author and Eusebius places the epistle among the disputed books.

On the other hand, such fourth-century writers as Jerome, Athanasius, Augustine, and Ambrose were confident that Peter was the author. The famous church councils at Laodicea (A.D. 372) and Carthage (A.D. 392) affirmed Petrine authorship.[3] Merrill C. Tenney affirms the internal evidence favoring Peter as author in the following quotation:

Old synagogue ruins at Capernaum.

Apostles
2080-2081

The writer claims at the outset to be "Simon Peter, a servant and an apostle of Jesus Christ" (1:1). He announces that the time has come for him to "put off this my tabernacle, even as our Lord Jesus Christ showed me" (1:14), a statement which accords with Jesus' prediction that Peter would die a violent death (Jn. 21:18). He claims to have been present at the Transfiguration when...the divine voice said, "This is my beloved Son, in whom I am well pleased" (1:16-17); cf. Mk. 9:5-7; Mt. 17:4-5)...He identifies himself as one of the apostles of the Lord (3:2).[4]

Beloved
Son
706

Internal evidence for Peter's authorship of both epistles that bear his name is presented in 2 Pe. 3:1: "This second epistle, beloved, I...write unto you..." This verse also indicates that the group addressed in both books is the same.

Those critics who have questioned the authenticity of 2 Peter do so on the grounds that the writer's familiarity with the Pauline epistles, which, together with his reference to the authority of Paul's writings (2 Pe. 3:15-16), is "...an indication that the NT canon had been well established by the time II Peter was written."[5]

Paul
2697

According to this reasoning, the epistle would be too late to have been written by the apostle Peter. An answer to this objection may be that Peter did reach Rome and had fellowship with Paul, perhaps in prison (see Background, Purpose and Content). This visit could have provided opportunities to learn about Paul's epistles.

Rome
3095, 4428
Imprison-
ment
3478

In regard to liberal criticism on 2 Peter, Henry H. Halley comments:

> Some modern critics regard it as a pseudonymous work of the late second century, written by some unknown person who assumed Peter's name, a hundred years after Peter's death. To the

Column's head with "Menorah."

average mind this would be just plain, common forgery, an offense against civil and moral law and ordinary decency. The critics, however, over and over, aver that there is nothing at all unethical in this counterfeiting another's name.[6]

Although there had been hesitancy in admitting the Second Book of Peter into the NT Canon, the epistle was approved and became a part of the Scriptures. Those scholars who accept the superintendency of the Holy Spirit in matters of inspiration and canonization have no difficulty in accepting Peter's authorship for 2 Peter.

From the evidence one might assume that 1 Peter was written shortly before or after Paul's martyrdom, probably about A.D. 63-64. It is thought that 2 Peter was written shortly before Peter was martyred in Rome— between A.D. 64 and 68.

Background, Purpose, and Content: 1 Peter

Simon Peter was a native of Bethsaida, a small fishing village on the northeast shore of Lake Galilee (Jn. 1:44). He was in the fishing business with his father, Jonas, and his brother, Andrew (Mt. 16:17; Jn. 1:40). Later he moved to Capernaum, where local archaeologists claim they have unearthed Peter's house, just south of the old synagogue, resting on the foundations where Jesus is said to have preached.

Ruins of St. Peter's house.

Simon Peter's brother, Andrew, accepted Jesus as the Messiah first and then introduced him to his brother (Jn. 1:41-45). Jesus at once conferred upon Simon Peter the surname Cephas, meaning "rock" (Jn. 1:42).

John W. Davis states, "In common with the earliest followers of Jesus, Peter received three separate calls from his Master: first, to become His disciple (Jn. 1:40 seq.)...secondly, to become His constant companion (Mt. 4:19; Mk. 1:17; Lu. 5:10) and thirdly, to be His Apostle (Mt. 10:2; Mk. 3:14,16; Lu. 6:13-14)."[7]

Falsehood
3702

"Word"
Divinely
Inspired
417

Martyrdom
3487

Bethsaida
411, 4345

Capernaum
641, 4355

Andrew
140
Divine Call
1790
Apostles
Called
2082

It is uncertain whether Peter had a part in founding the church in Rome, or if he ever visited Rome. Some scholars believe that the church began in a synagogue congregation. Upon their return home, those who had been in Jerusalem at the time of Pentecost may have given witness to the effect of the Spirit upon the believers who had been assembled in the upper room when "they were all filled with the Holy Ghost" (Ac. 2:4). In Acts the account states that "strangers of Rome, Jews and Proselytes" were present in Jerusalem (Ac. 2:10b).

According to tradition, near the end of his life, Peter did go to Rome, either because of a summons from Nero or to aid the Christians suffering during the persecution under Nero. Tradition also indicates that Peter was imprisoned and finally executed at Rome in the Mamertine prison which bears his name. "The Quo Vadis Tradition [sic] has it that Peter…was crucified head downward, feeling unworthy to be crucified as the Lord was. This is only a tradition, and we do not know how much of historical fact it may contain."[8] (See Introduction to 1 and 2 Timothy for more on the persecution described in 2 Timothy and 1 Peter, as well as information about the Mamertine prison where both Peter and Paul were apparently imprisoned.)

It had been Roman policy not to interfere with the Christian movement as long as it remained within Judaism, which enjoyed a *Religio Licita*, a religious group allowed by Rome. However, when Christians began to be conspicuous and developed their own identity, causing controversy with established Judaism, Rome began to take measures to restrict them. The persecution of the Christians under Nero, his burning of Rome, and Paul's martyrdom seemed to occur at about the time when Rome began to change from tolerance to hostility. Henry H. Halley says,

> Nero's persecution of Christians (A.D. 64-67) was very severe in and around Rome, but not generally over the Empire. However, the example of the Emperor in Rome encouraged the enemies of Christians everywhere to take advantage of the slightest pretext to persecute…The Church was about 35 years old. It had suffered persecutions in various localities at the hands of local authorities. But now Imperial Rome, which hitherto had been indifferent…had accused the Church of a terrible crime and was undertaking to punish it…The [First] Epistle was born in the atmosphere of suffering shortly before Peter's own martyrdom, while exhorting Christians not to think it strange that they had to suffer, reminding them that Christ did His work by suffering.[9]

The First Epistle of Peter is the second in a series of seven general epistles written to comfort and strengthen the church at large, especially in Asia Minor. First Peter is addressed to the "strangers scattered throughout Pontus, Galatia, Cappadocia, Asia, and Bithynia" (1:1), all provinces in Lesser Asia Minor. In speaking about the "strangers scattered," Stephen W. Payne explains, "The Greek may be rendered, 'to the foreign residents of the dispersion'; these were not strangers to Peter but temporary residents in the Provinces of Asia Minor."[10]

The geographic origin of 1 Peter is uncertain. The reference to "the church that is at Babylon, elected together with you, saluteth you" (5:13) raises as many problems as it solves because three views of Babylon have developed. First, Babylon is a small town in Egypt, too small to be considered. Second, Babylon in Mesopotamia; but since it was almost deserted in NT times, it seems unlikely that Peter would have traveled to it. There is no indication in literature that Peter traveled to Babylon on the Euphrates. The third view is that Babylon is a symbolic name for wickednesses and abominations of every kind as indicated in Re. 17:5; cf. Re. 16:19; 18:2. Rome fitted well into this description of wickedness, and it is probable that the name Babylon was symbolically used to mean Rome. Some scholars have taken the position that intercommunications in the churches frequently employed symbolic language as a kind of code to prevent Roman authorities from identifying places where Christians were active.

The Wicked 3065-3076

Benjamin W. Robinson points out that "Babylon is mentioned repeatedly in Revelation (16:17-21; 17:5; 18:1-3) with reference to Rome. In all probability that is the meaning here. The reference then is to the Church at Rome..."[11]

Rome 3095, 4428

In 1 Peter, during those days of persecution and martyrdom, Peter kept the hope of the resurrection and an inheritance "reserved in heaven" ever before the people. He exhorted them to insure their salvation by resisting temptation to the end. Some, however, had taken the easy way out by renouncing the faith (Jn. 6:66; 1 Ti. 1:20; 2 Pe. 2:15; 3:17; 1 Jn. 2:9). Peter encouraged the Christians by reminding them that the prophets in the OT suffered for their belief (1 Pe. 1:10-12; cf. Da. 3:19; Ja. 5:10; He. 11:32-37). Throughout the book runs the idea that Christians were to prepare for impending persecution and martyrdom (1 Pe. 1:13-14). In the midst of hardships, believers were to be holy in all manner of conversation and conduct (1:15-25).

Resurrection 2407-2416
Resist Temptation 3590
Courage 849

Persecution 3483

Peter uses a different figure in which he designates the believers as "lively stones" to be built into a "spiritual house." Christ is the "chief cornerstone," although he as the "living stone" is rejected by men but chosen of God (NIV). Peter exhorted the believers to "rid yourselves of all malice and all deceit..." and "like newborn babies crave pure spiritual milk, so that by it you may grow up in your salvation" (1 Pe. 2:1-2, NIV).

Christ Cornerstone 692
Spiritual Growth 995

In another comparison, the Christians are likened to a "royal priesthood" giving forth praises unto God (1 Pe. 2:1-10). The believers are to "abstain from fleshly lusts" and to submit themselves "to every ordinance of man for the Lord's sake." They are to "love the brotherhood," to "fear God" and to "honor the king" or established authority (2:11-25). Peter instructs the wives to be modest, to be meek and of a quiet spirit (3:1-6). The husbands are to honor their wives as "the weaker vessel" (3:7). They are to sanctify the Lord in their hearts, to "love as brethren," and to be ready to give a reason for their faith at any time (3:8-15). Peter reminded them of an established principle: It is better to suffer for "well doing, than for evil doing" (3:15-22). They are to cease from sin and follow their great example—Christ (4:8-11). Suffering is to be taken for granted, and they are to rejoice because they are "partakers of Christ's sufferings" (4:12-19).

Holiness Enjoined 1598

Brotherly Love 2200-2202
Christ's Example 1175

In the final chapter the elders are to "feed the flock" (5:1-4); the younger are to obey the elder and to be humble. All are to "be subject one to another," placing their care upon the Lord (5:5-9). In the last few verses Peter pronounces his words of blessing and benediction upon those who are persecuted (5:10-11). In closing, Peter mentions the letter is to be delivered by Silvanus (Silas).

Feeding the Flock 2090
Faith 1201

Background, Purpose, and Content: 2 Peter

The Second Epistle of Peter is addressed "to them that have obtained like precious faith with us through the righteousness of God and our Saviour Jesus Christ" (1:1). These people could have been any Christian group, but the internal evidence suggests that Peter is also speaking to the "strangers scattered" as mentioned in his first epistle (1:1).

In Peter's first letter, the danger to the believers was the ruthless persecution which the Roman Emperor Nero unleashed against them. At the time of the writing of 2 Peter, several years had passed and the political situation possibly had changed or the threatened persecution may not have reached the provinces. Another danger jeopardizing the Christians was the perversion of the moral life of the church (2 Pe. 2:2); greed (2:3); the despising of authority (2:10); boastfulness (2:18, and false liberty (2:19). In this letter Peter endeavored to avert the dangers of the teachings of the deceptive leaders.[12]

Shirley Jackson Case writes:

> The danger that loomed on the author's horizon was a threatened lowering of Christianity's [sic] Moral standards. As the new religion spread to the Gentile lands it had drawn into its membership persons whose ethical ideas were quite different from those cherished by its earlier adherents...The moral life of the Greeks and Romans seemed frightfully low. As a rule Gentile converts lacked the discipline in virtuous living that had been furnished the Jews through attendance upon the services of the synagogue and study of the OT...Even after the adoption of Christianity they were slow in making their conduct conform to the ethical requirements of the new religion.[13]

It is apparent that the writers of 2 Peter and Jude had some similarities. Second Peter 2:1-8 and 3:1-3 incorporate most of Jude 4-18 but omit the references in Jude 9 and 14 from the nonbiblical books of the Assumption of Moses and the Book of Enoch respectively.[14]

Merrill C. Tenney makes this observation:

> The resemblance of II Peter 2 to the Epistle of Jude is so close that the literary relationship between the two books can hardly be accidental. One [author] must have known the work of the other. Although the brevity and compactness of Jude may be used as an argument for its priority, his [the author's] reference to "the apostles of our Lord Jesus Christ" (Jude 17) seems to imply that he was following the lead of some apostolic writer or writers. Since the author of II Peter claims to be an apostle (II Peter 1:1), it is more likely that Jude was stimulated to compose his epistle by Peter's missive than that a pseudonymous document was copied from Jude and published under Peter's name. The fact that II Peter predicts apostasy (2:1), whereas Jude announces that the declension has already begun (Jude 4) may indicate that II Peter belongs to an earlier stage in the history of the apostolic church.[15]

There are two distinct differences between 2 Peter and Jude. Peter's statement about the false teachers is prophetic (2 Pe. 2:1-3,12-13). Note the future tense "shall" in all the verses cited. The author uses the present tense in describing the character of the false prophets (2 Pe. 2:17-18), but he puts their deceptive teachings in the future (2 Pe. 2:13-14). Jude, on the other hand, makes reference to these corrupters as having already come among the people of God and doing their diabolical work (Jude 4,8).[16]

1 Pe. 1:19 ...the precious blood of Christ, as of a lamb without blemish and without spot...

During the Passover observance, which commemorated the deliverance of Israel from bondage in Egypt, an unblemished lamb was slain, roasted whole (no bones broken) and eaten with unleavened bread and bitter herbs. For more on the Christian implications of this holy memorial, see commentary on Ex. 12:17.

Perfection of Christ **2731**
Christ, Lamb of God **3365**

1 Pe. 1:23 For you have been born again, not of perishable seed, but of imperishable... (NIV)

Jesus said, "Except a man be born again, he cannot see the kingdom of God" (Jn. 3:3). Is the "new birth" concept unique to the New Testament? See commentary on Jn. 3:3 and essay following.

New Birth **2154**
God's Kingdom **2009**

1 Pe. 2:13 Submit yourselves to every ordinance of man...

The Bible consistently teaches respect for civil law, unless it violates the law of God. In civilized countries the essential substance of the law is in fact reflective of God's law, based on the Mosaic code, because there is no more perfect legal code on which to base a legal system. Paul states that the law is ordained by God (Ro. 13:1).

Civic Duties **2525-2526**

1 Pe. 5:1 To the elders among you, I appeal as a fellow elder... (NIV)

Elders of Peter's day were faced with the heavy responsibility of providing leadership to the churches during a period of great tribulation. In this verse Peter chose to identify with them and to give them special advice. For more on the office of elder and how it developed throughout the Bible, see commentary on 1 Ti. 5:17.

Jewish Elders **2079**
Tribulation **499**

1 Pe. 5:8 ...your adversary the devil, as a roaring lion, walketh about, seeking whom he may devour...

From the time of God's pronouncement of judgment to Satan in the Garden of Eden (Ge. 3:15) the devil has been waging war against Christ and his followers. The enmity that prevails between the righteous on the one hand the evil forces on the other is continually manifesting itself, and perhaps at no time in history was this more evident than during the persecution that Peter's readers would be facing. Even though Satan is a potentially defeated foe, he is still active (1 Co. 2:6).

Spiritual Warfare **358**
Satan **3148-3155**
Righteousness— Unrighteousness **3077-3085**

2 Pe. 1:3 His divine power... through our knowledge of him... (NIV)

Second Peter contains a key word, knowledge, used seven times (1:2-3,5-6,8; 2:20; 3:18). The apostle is not writing of mere intellectual knowledge, but of the knowledge of God (3:18). This knowledge of Christ is a means of protection against heresy. Through this knowledge of God the Christian receives grace and peace that relate to life and godliness (1:2-3). Knowledge of Christ enables the believer to escape "the pollutions of the world"—the defilement of the flesh (2:20), and makes growth in grace possible (3:18; cf. Ja. 4:4).

Christ's Power **3807**
Heresy **1577**
Spiritual Growth **995**

2 Pe. 1:20-21 …holy men of God spake as they were moved by the Holy Ghost.

Divine
Inspiration
1776
"Word"
Inspired
417

Peter was committed to the belief that Scripture is God's infallible Word and to its integrity and trustworthiness. To Peter, all Scripture is divinely revealed ("God breathed"), but the reader of God's Word also needs God's assistance in the interpretation of it. For more on the subject of the inspiration and infallibility of the Scriptures, see commentary on 2 Ti. 3:16.

2 Pe. 2:1 But there were false prophets also among the people, even as there shall be false teachers among you…

False
Prophets
2100

Deceivers
3707

Adultery
1662

One of the main subjects in this epistle is that of false prophets. In the second chapter Peter gives a description of the false teachers who will deceive the people, whose shameful ways "many will follow" (NIV). Peter speaks of them "as natural brute beasts…[who] speak evil of the things that they understand not…Spots they are and blemishes, sporting themselves with their own deceivings…having eyes full of adultery, and that cannot cease from sin; beguiling unstable souls…they allure…the lusts of the flesh" (2:12-14,18).

2 Pe. 3:10 But the day of the Lord will come like a thief… (NIV)

Day of
the Lord
921
The
Second
Coming
1344-1350
Sudden
Events
3473

Peter was deeply disturbed over the doubt and uncertainty among early Christians concerning the imminent return of the Lord. This belief was based on such words of Jesus as are found in Mk. 9:1,13; Lu. 17:22-37. Belief in the Second Coming was also an article in the apostolic teaching (1 Co. 7:29; 15:51-52; Ph. 4:5; 1 Th. 4:15-17; Ja. 5:8; 1 Pe. 4:7). The early church interpreted these Scriptures to mean that the return of the Lord might be soon, even before the first generation of Christians had passed away.

Divine
Faithfulness
1228
God's
Ways
3796, 4160

Heavens
1551
Diligence
564
Spotless
1760

As time passed, and he did not return, "hope began to give place to doubt, and doubt to impatience, and impatience even to denial."[17] Peter predicted that the false prophets and scoffers would say, "Where is the promise of his coming?" (2 Pe. 3:4). The apostle assures the people that God "the Lord is not slack concerning his promise" (2 Pe. 3:4-9). Peter informed the people that God has a different time schedule than man, "that one day is with the Lord as a thousand years, and a thousand years as one day" (2 Pe. 3:8). Peter reminded the people that the Lord will come suddenly, as "a thief in the night" (2 Pe. 3:10; cf. 1 Th. 5:2), and that his Coming will usher in a cataclysmic destruction of the worldly order. "The heavens shall pass away with a great noise, and the elements shall melt with fervent heat, the earth also and the works that are therein shall be burned up" (2 Pe. 3:10).

The apostle emphasizes the importance of the people maintaining their readiness, that they are to "be diligent that ye may be found of him in peace, without spot, and blameless" (2 Pe. 3:14). In other words, they were not to be merely concerned about the details of the Second Coming. They were to "work…while it is day"; the Second Coming would take care of itself in due time.

1, 2 and
3 John

Name

The Epistles of John derive their names from early tradition, when the patristic fathers added the caption of John to the manuscripts.

Authorship and Date

No specific identification of an author appears in the three Epistles of John. However, early tradition points to John as the writer. Such church fathers as Polycarp, Papias, Iranaeus, Origen, Cyprian, and Eusebius were unanimous in attributing authorship to John the Apostle. The affirmation of Polycarp (A.D. 69-156) and Papias (A.D. 70-155) makes this claim of John being the author even more conclusive because they were pupils of John. Both men held the office of Bishop—Polycarp in Smyrna and Papias in Hierapolis. Both of these episcopal areas were within about a hundred miles of Ephesus.[1]

The question naturally arises: What is the basis of this conclusion when internal evidence of authorship is lacking? Obviously the affirmation of Polycarp and Papias was based on their own association with John. Other traditions were also closely linked with the apostolic generation. Beyond these possible claims one may reach a satisfactory conclusion through analysis.

Eusebius shows that the author of 1 John and the Gospel of John was the same, mainly because of similar idioms, phrases, common themes, and theological agreements distinctive throughout these books.[2] In agreement with this conclusion, John Wesley says, "The great similitude, or rather sameness, both of spirit and expression which runs through St. John's Gospel and all his epistles, is clear evidence of their being written by the same person. In this epistle [1 John] he speaks not to any particular church but to all the Christians of that age; and in them to the whole Christian Church in all succeeding ages."[3]

On the next page a set of comparative tables by B. F. Westcott shows notable parallels between the Gospel of John and the First Epistle of John.[4]

The
Epistles
of John
4284-4286

John
1902
Beloved
Disciple
392

Ephesus
1142, 4373

Outline
History of
Apostles
4300b

Christians
725

1 John	Gospel of John	1 John	Gospel of John
1:2-3	3:11	3:16	10:15
1:4	16:24	3:22	8:29
2:11	12:35	3:23	13:34
2:14	5:38	4:6	8:47
3:5	8:46	4:16	6:69
3:8	8:44	5:9	5:32
3:13	15:18	5:20	17:3
3:14	5:24		

Some scholars agree that 1 and 2 John have the same author because eight of the thirteen verses in the second book match those in the first book. There is also agreement that 2 and 3 John have a single author because they both begin with the designation "the elder" (2 Jn. 1; 3 Jn. 1).[5] Since the Gospel of John and 1 John have a common author, it seems possible to conclude that the four books were written by the same author. As an apostle wrote them, and as John was the only living apostle when the books were written, it seems that John, the apostle, was the author of all four books.

However, in view of the difficulty in compiling canonical books and the lack of internal evidence, especially for the authorship of 2 and 3 John, "it is not surprising that these brief...(epistles) are among the NT writings over which there was a hard struggle for canonical recognition. One is probably, the other certainly, a private letter; and neither had an opportunity or a reason for circulating among the churches as did the other church epistles."[6]

Even such scholars as James Moffatt (1870-1944) said, "We would not have suffered much loss if the second and third epistles of John had been excluded from the New Testament Canon."[7] "On the contrary, we would have suffered very serious spiritual loss if we had never read the subtle rebuke of 'advanced' thinkers in II John 9."[8]

Adam Clarke says:

> When first discovered, all the immediate vouchers were gone; and the Church of Christ, that was always on its guard and restrained by the Holy Spirit against imposture, and especially in relation to writings professing to be the work of Apostles, hesitated to receive them into the number of Canonical Scriptures till it was fully satisfied that they were Divinely inspired. Their extreme caution was of the uttermost consequence to the Christian faith; for had it been otherwise, had any measure of credulity prevailed, the church would have been inundated with spurious writings, and the genuine faith greatly corrupted, if not totally destroyed. The number of apocryphal gospels, acts of apostles and epistles, which were offered to the church in the earliest ages of Christianity is truly astounding.[9]

Regarding the date and place of writing of 1, 2 and 3 John, "First John was probably written as a circular letter from Ephesus about A.D. 85-95, to the believers of the Roman Province of Asia including the churches [addressed] in the book of Revelation (1 Jn. 2, 3)."[10] (All of the other six churches of Asia

Minor are within a radius of about 125 miles from Ephesus.) Both the Second and Third Epistles of John were probably written from Ephesus between A.D. 85 and 95.

From tradition and conjecture, one concludes that John, the sole survivor of the original apostles, may have moved from Jerusalem with Mary, the mother of Jesus, a few years before the Holy City was destroyed in A.D.70. Between A.D. 65 and 70 John probably took Mary to Ephesus, the geographic and numerical center of the Christian community, where he labored among the churches until about A.D. 95, when he was exiled to the Isle of Patmos, about 60 miles southwest from the old harbor of Ephesus. At the time of his exile to Patmos, probably during the Domitianic persecution, John received his vision for the book of Revelation. He returned to Ephesus in about A.D. 97 and died there at the turn of the century.[11] It is not known whether John actually wrote the book of Revelation while on Patmos or after he returned to Ephesus (see Introduction to John: Authorship and Date).

Mary	**2259**
Jerusalem	**1881-1885**
Patmos	**2695**
Visions	**2495**

Background, Purpose, and Content: 1 John

Although it contains no salutation, the First Epistle of John is called a letter. One of its unusual features among "NT books is that it does not contain a single proper name (except Our Lord's), or a single definition allusion, personal, historical, or geographical. It is a composition, however, which a person calling himself 'I' sends to certain other persons whom he calls 'you,' and is, in form at least, a letter."[12]

The First Epistle of John discusses the spiritual welfare of Christians, warning them of certain dangerous views concerning Christ and impressing upon the believers that faith in the Savior manifests itself in love.

By the time Christianity had been in existence for 60-70 years, it had spread throughout the Roman Empire. In this process the Christians had encountered popular philosophical ideas of that day. Some of the heresies in these systems, especially Gnosticism, penetrated the church bodies, causing confusion and apostasy. The Gnostic *(know)* heresy, a combination of Oriental theology, Greek philosophy, and Christian doctrine, was the greatest rival of Christianity in its infancy. "Gnostics" are those who profess to

Letters	**2111**
Spiritual Mind	**2355**
Love	**2200-2209**
Heresy	**1577**

Basilica of St. John at Ephesus. Built in honor of the disciple by this name who spent his declining years here.

Know-
ledge—
Ignorance
2020-2040

have a deeper understanding or wisdom. The Gnostics of the early Christian era were selective in their acceptance of the Christian doctrines. They claimed that all nature, intellectual and material, originated from the deity by successive manifestations, which they called Eons.

Henry H. Halley says,

Origin
of Sin
3339
Incarnation
720
Christ's
Divinity—
Humanity
701-723

> A form of Gnosticism which was disrupting the churches in John's day taught that there is in human nature an irreconcilable principle of Dualism: that the Spirit and Body are two separate entities: that Sin resided in the Flesh only: that the Spirit could have its raptures and the Body could do as it pleased: that lofty mental mystical Piety was entirely consistent with voluptuous sensual life. They denied the Incarnation, that God had in Christ actually become Flesh, and maintained that Christ was a Phantom, a man in appearance only. In Ephesus a man named Cerinthus was leader of this cult. Through-out this Epistle it seems that John must have had these heretics in mind, in insisting that Jesus was the Actual, Material, Authentic Manifestation of God in the Flesh, and that Genuine Knowledge of God must result in Moral Transformation.[13]

The Gnostic heresy could not be reconciled with Christianity. The Gnostic philosophy included dualism (matter is evil, spirit is good) and docetism (the view that the union of Christ with the human Jesus was only apparent). The Gnostics could accept the deity of Jesus but not the humanity.

Christ's
Humanity
719-723
Crucifixion
3495

To some Gnostics, Christ's office was to teach the knowledge or secrets of their system, pertaining to cosmic order. To them the heavenly Christ did not die on the cross, but separated himself from Jesus before death occurred. With this view the Incarnation was impossible, and the human nature of Jesus Christ was considered illusion.

Robert Law writes:

Antichrist
196
Son of God
707
Divine
Care
2911

> It is with this docetic subversion of the truth of the incarnation that the "antichrists" are specially identified (2:22-23; 4:2-3), and against it that St. John directs with wholehearted fervor his central thesis—the complete, permanent, personal identification of the historical Jesus with the Divine Being who is the Word of Life (1:1), the Christ (4:2) and the Son of God (5:5): "Jesus is the Christ, come in the flesh"…To the Gnostic, knowledge was the sum of attainment. "They give no heed to love," says Ignatius, "caring not for the widow, the orphan or the afflicted, neither for those who are in bonds nor for those who are released from bonds, neither for the hungry nor the thirsty." That a religion which banished or neglected love should call itself Christian or claim affinity with Christianity excites St. John's latent indignation; against it he lifts up his supreme truth, God is love, with its immediate consequence that to be without love is to be without capacity for knowing God (4:7-8)…and the crucial test by which we may assure our self-accusing hearts that we are "of the truth" is love, "not love in word, neither with the tongue; but in deed and in truth." (3:18).[14]

God's Love
2206

Incarnation
720
Word
of Life
4126

John's answer then to the Gnostics, as noted above, contained the central message that "Jesus Christ is come in the flesh" (4:2b). The author further affirmed this position: "That which was from the beginning, which we have heard…have seen…have looked upon, and our hands have handled, of the Word of life" (1:1).

By the time of John's writing some of those adhering to the false ideas of the Gnostics had left the church to spread their teachings elsewhere (2:19). John identified and denounced those who denied and opposed Jesus, as antichrists. "And every spirit that confesseth not that Jesus Christ is come in the flesh is not of God: and this is that spirit of antichrist" (4:3; see also 2:18). They were known as "many false prophets" (4:1b). Evidently some still remained within the church for John wrote "concerning them that seduce you" (2:26). Further, "Who is a liar but he that denieth that Jesus is the Christ? He is antichrist…" (2:22).

False
Prophets
2100

The writer urged his readers to "believe not every spirit," but to apply a test to distinguish the false from the true: "…try the spirits whether they are of God" (4:1), "and every spirit that confesseth not that Jesus Christ is come in the flesh is not of God" (4:3). The thought in 1 Jn. 4:7-21 is to oppose the false views of those who deny Jesus to be the Christ. Because of the confusion resulting from the teachings of the Gnostics, John emphasized that the Christian, the true believer, had a knowledge that came, not from speculation, as did that of the Gnostics, but from a spiritual revelation (2:20).

One of the serious problems of that day had to do with the question: Am I saved, and if so, how can I know? In this Epistle, John endeavors to show that the believers can have assurance—that they can know if they are saved. "The phrase 'we know' is used thirteen times to signify the certainty that is achieved through experience, or that is a part of normal spiritual consciousness (2:3,5,29; 3:14,16,19,24; 4:13,16; 5:15,18-19,20)."[15] The epistle of John was written "that ye may know that ye have eternal life" (1 Jn. 5:13).

John understood that to know God is to keep his commandments, to love God and man: "And this commandment have we from him, That he who loveth God love his brother also" (4:21); "and hereby we do know that we know him, if we keep his commandments" (2:3; cf. 4:7-8). Love does not originate with man; man loves God because "he first loved us" (4:19-21). Love, if genuine, comes from the heart and is directed toward man and God (3:18; cf. 4:7-8). John puts love in a proper focus; love of God and love of man are a unity; one cannot love God without loving man (5:2-3).

John said clearly that "love is of God" and that it is the test of true discipleship (4:7-8,12-13,15). "We know that we have passed from death unto life, because we love the brethren" (3:14). God's love within a believer manifests itself not only in man's attitude but love may show itself in compassion for the needy. "If anyone has material possessions and sees his brother in need but has no pity on him, how can the love of God be in him?" (3:17, NIV).

The apostle cautioned the people that their love must not be directed toward "things that are in the world" (1 Jn. 2:15-17). He pointed out that the antidote for fear is love, because "perfect love casteth out fear" (4:18). He declared that the true disciple must "walk in the light" (1:7), keep God's commandments (2:3), and "abide in him" (2:28). John affirmed that God cannot tolerate overt and willful sin because "sin is the transgression of the law" (3:4-5), and that "he that committeth sin is of the devil" (3:8-18; cf. Jn. 8:44). Believers are exhorted to make proper discernment of "the spirits whether they are of God" (4:1-3).

Background, Purpose, and Content: 2 John

At the time John wrote his second epistle, he was probably the active supervisor of the churches in and around Ephesus. His opening words, "the elder," could have referred to his age, he being the last surviving companion of Jesus, or it could have referred to his being a high church officer, an "elder" in the church.

Since early post-apostolic times, scholars have been divided as to the meaning of the expression "the elect lady." Some have understood the phrase to mean that the letter was addressed to an individual, while others have

Truth—
Falsehood
3697-3709

Religion,
True-False
2985-2998

Assurance
298

Eternal Life
2156-2157

Christ's
Commands
790

God's Love
2206

Brotherly
Love
2200

Bene-
volence
2117

Abiding
in Christ
1270, 4130

Prove All
Things
4089

Govern-
ment of
Church
728

Elders
754

The Elect
2724

thought it was addressed to a church group. The views are given below:

Prominent
Women
4300a
Walking
in Truth
3765

1. *To an individual person.* The "elect lady" in v. 1 may have been a prominent woman in a neighboring church to whom John had ministered. The letter speaks of her loyalty to truth in v. 4. Verse 13 contains greetings to the lady and her children from the children of her sister.

Some scholars suggest that the Greek word *Kyria,* translated "lady," should be taken as a proper name.[16]

2. *To a church group.* Another view is that the "elect lady" was used figuratively to designate a church, and "the children," members of that church. "This seems to be a legitimate position to take but neither view can

The
Church
726, 730

be categorically proved. Such scholars as William Barclay, A. E. Brooke, Brooke Foss Westcott, and Amos N. Wilder favor 'the Church' interpretation."[17] On the other hand, Alexander Ross, D. D. Weadon, Albert Barnes, and John Wesley think of the lady as an individual.[18]

Truth
3697-3700

An analysis of 2 John indicates that the word "truth" is one of the leading words, included five times in the first four verses: (1) "I love in the truth," v. 1; (2) "they that have known the truth," v. 1; (3) "for the truth's sake," v. 2; (4) "in truth and love," v. 3; and (5) "walking in truth," v. 4. This reference to truth, which implies that the Person Jesus is the Truth, is in keeping with John's use of this word in the Gospel of John in which Jesus says, "I am the way, the truth, and the life: no man cometh unto the Father, but by me" (Jn. 14:6).

The word "love" as employed in 2 John is in agreement with the writer's use of the word love 22 times in the Gospel of John.

Love
2200-2209

John makes its clear that he is not writing a new commandment (v. 5). He affirms Paul's statement that the faith "was given us in Christ Jesus before the world began" (2 Ti. 1:9b; Tit. 1:2b), and agrees with Jude that the faith "was once delivered unto the saints" (Jude 3). This faith was repeatedly

Faith
1201-1218

identified with the perfection of love referred to by the Master (Mt. 22:36-40).

The Basilica of Serapis Temple at Pergamos.
It later became the church of St. John.

One of the serious dangers facing the church at this time was that there were deceivers circulating among the congregations, who denied the incarnation (2 Jn. 7-9). John urged the believers not to "receive" into their homes these false preachers (2 Jn. 10). They were also warned against bidding these teachers "God speed" or giving encouragement to them, under the peril of identifying themselves with the evil ones (2 Jn. 10-11).

Apparently John wrote this epistle at a time when his duties were strenuous. Even though he had "many things to write," he limited himself to thirteen short verses; he did express his hope that he would be able to visit them soon and speak "face to face" (2 Jn. 12-13). He concluded his letter by sending greetings from his host, or from the church as the case may be.

Deceivers
3707

Evil Associations
276

Saint's Fellowship
1325

Background, Purpose, and Content: 3 John

The Third Epistle of John differs from John's other two epistles in at least one point. It is addressed to a particular person; in the book five other persons are identified.

In this letter John gave a description typical of many modern churches today. Gaius and Demetrius were faithful members in the church, but Diotrephes, who seems to have acted in a manner unbecoming to a Christian, opposed entertaining any of the missionaries. The epistle is addressed to Gaius, a name which commonly refers to Paul's friend who was dragged into the amphitheater during the riot of Ephesus (Ac. 19:29). There was another man named Gaius, from Derbe in the Galatian area, who accompanied Paul on his last journey of Asia (Ac. 20:4). Paul makes mention of a third man by this name whom he baptized in Corinth (Ro. 16:23; 1 Co. 1:14).[19] The Gaius at Ephesus (Ac. 19:29) seems to be the one closest to John's area, but to name any one of the above would be speculation.

Gaius
1381

Christian Graces
1339

Ephesus
1142, 4373

Corinth
840, 4359

The Gaius to whom this letter is addressed was apparently a church officer or the pastor of a church in or near Ephesus. John commended Gaius for his faithful service in the church and for the hospitality he had rendered "the brethren, and to strangers" (3 Jn. 5). John expressed joy over the faithful ministry of Gaius and mentioned that he "has no greater joy than to hear that my children walk in truth" (3 Jn. 4). Because of the charitable treatment and financial help accorded the missionaries, they were able to continue their ministry without taking an offering from the Gentiles (3 Jn. 7-8).

Fidelity
1230

Soul Winners' Joy
4206

There were, however, difficulties existing in this congregation because of Diotrephes, who in a domineering manner tried to control the church. The name Diotrephes appears nowhere else in Scripture.

Strife in Church
734

Apparently John had a desire to conduct a missionary conference in the church where Gaius was a member. John recounted, "I wrote unto the church: but Diotrephes, who loveth to have the preeminence among them, receiveth us not" (3 Jn. 9). It is evident that this man not only opposed missionary activity but even resorted to casting "them out of the church" (3 Jn. 10).

Inhospitality
3401

The third person to whom John addressed himself is Demetrius, a man of "good report of all men" (3 Jn. 12). Only one other Demetrius is listed in the NT, and he was the silversmith in Ephesus who accused Paul of endangering the trade and bringing disrepute upon the goddess Diana (Ac. 19:24ff.). It would be speculation to say that the man at Ephesus was

Good Name
2513

Idol Making
3932

converted and then became a faithful member in the church with Gaius. Since John's ministry was in and around Ephesus, it is at least a possibility, but the answer will have to remain conjecture.

Ephesus
1142, 4373

In this epistle, as in the second letter, John says he has "many things to write," but apparently church affairs prevent him from writing more than this short note. He is also hoping that he will "shortly see" Gaius and Demetrius (3 Jn. 13-14).

Truth
3697-3701
Walking
in Truth
3765

As in both of the other Johannine epistles, the word "truth" is a leading word in 3 John: (1) "I love in the truth," v. 1; (2) "testified of the truth," v. 3; (3) "thou walkest in the truth," v. 3; "fellowhelpers to the truth," v. 8; and (4) "ye know that our record is true," v. 12.

1 Jn. 1:5 …God is light; in him there is no darkness at all. (NIV)

The descriptive metaphors light and darkness are consistently used throughout Scripture to distinguish believers from non-believers. In the Sermon on the Mount, Jesus said, "Ye are the light of the world" (Mt. 5:14). Jesus also said, "I am the light of the world" (Jn. 8:12). Light was created first in the natural world and is essential to existence. Just as physical light dispels darkness, spiritual light dispels spiritual darkness.

The book of Revelation, also written by John, describes the "new Jerusalem"—the ultimate dwelling of God with man— as a city that "does not need the sun or the moon to shine on it, for the glory of God gives it light, and the Lamb is its lamp" (Re. 21:23, NIV). For OT use of light as a symbol, see commentary on Ex. 25:31.

1 Jn. 2:1-2 …Jesus Christ, the Righteous One. He is the atoning sacrifice for our sins… (NIV)

The foundation for salvation has always been rooted in the Atonement made for man by the Righteous One, the only One who was sinless. The question arises: How does this apply to those who came before Christ's incarnation and crucifixion? Did God have a different plan of salvation for them? For more on this subject, see the essay "Atonement in the Old and New Testaments," pp. 427-429.

1 Jn. 5:6 This is he that came by water and blood, even Jesus Christ; not by water only, but by water and blood…

John emphasizes not only water (symbolizing baptism) but also blood (symbolizing death). The importance of a blood sacrifice was evident from the days of Cain and Abel, when Abel offered the acceptable sacrifice because it required the shedding of blood (see commentary on Ge. 4:4-5). Later God gave his people more insight about the importance of the blood sacrifice when he said, "For the life of a creature is in the blood, and I have given it to you to make atonement for yourselves on the altar; it is the blood that makes atonement for one's life" (Le. 17:11, NIV). Finally, the writers of the New Testament explain that Christ, "by his own blood…obtained eternal redemption" (He. 9:12, NIV) and that "without the shedding of blood there is no remission" (He. 9:22).

John's emphasis here on both Jesus' baptism and his death was no doubt prompted by Gnostic heresy, which said that the heavenly Christ joined the man Jesus at his baptism, but then left him before his death. If (as the Gnostics claimed) Jesus was only a man at his death and not God incarnate, then the atonement would have been stripped of its saving power (see 1 Jn. 2:2; 4:10).

2 Jn. 5 …not as though I wrote a new commandment unto thee, but that which we had from the beginning, that we love one another.

This verse is very similar to 1 Jn. 2:7-8, where John speaks of love as both an old and new commandment. It was old in the sense that to love God and to love one's neighbor was a command from the early days of Israel's

---

Light—
Darkness
2165-2180
Christ,
the Light
2168

New
Jerusalem
1886

Atoning
Blood
of Christ
Jesus
679

Salvation
3116-3128

Blood
512-517

Sacrifices
3107-3108

Redemption
through
Christ
2979
Remission
of Sin
3127

Incarna-
tion
720

Love
Enjoined
2207

history (see Le. 19:18; De. 6:5). However, Jesus gave it new depths ("Great-er love hath no man than this, that a man lay down his life for his friends," Jn. 15:13) and new dimensions (see essay "The Mosaic Law: The Unity of the Legal Structure in the Old and New Testaments," pp. 102-103).

Jude

The Name

The General Epistle of Jude derives its name from the first verse in which Jude identifies himself as the author: "Jude, the servant of Jesus Christ, and brother of James, to them that are sanctified by God the Father, and preserved in Jesus Christ" (Jude 1).

The name "Jude" is the English form of the Greek *Judas (Ioudas)* and appears only in the book of Jude. The Greek form *Judas* appears 33 times in the four Gospels and the book of Acts.

Authorship and Date

The question of whether the writer of Jude was the brother of Jesus and whether he was an apostle has been the subject of scholarly debate since the time of the apostolic fathers.[1]

The NT lists "two Judes: Judas, one of the twelve Apostles, Luke 6:16...and Judas, the brother of Jesus, Matthew 13:55. The latter is commonly regarded as the writer of the Epistle."[2]

William C. Morehead says, "Almost from the beginning of the Christian era, men, qualified to speak with authority on the question of genuineness and authenticity, endorsed it [Jude] as entitled to a place in the NT Scriptures."[3]

The church father, Origen, referred to Jude as an epistle with few lines "but full of powerful words of heavenly grace." Clement of Alexandria and Athanasius accepted it as a book written by Jude. The Muratorian Canon, a list of NT books which was probably used in the church in Rome about A.D. 200, includes Jude among the books of Scripture.[4]

There are, however, a few critics who would assign authorship of Jude to "an unknown Jude or to pseudonymity and would place the date near the middle of the second century, but this appears quite unlikely." Objection to the authorship may have been based in part on Jude's reference to fallen angels and the archangel Michael in the book of Enoch. These quotations are from the pseudepigraphal books of The Assumption of Moses and The book of Enoch. Such references do not mean that Jude approved these books in their entirety but that the passages he quoted contained remnants of truth.[5]

Jude's reference to the conflict between the archangel Michael and Satan over Moses' body (v. 9) is from the Assumption of Moses. For the

The
Epistle
of Jude
4287
Jude
1964

Names
of the
Apostles
2081
Judas
1959

Power
of "Word"
421
Rome
3095, 4428

Fallen
Angels
147

Moses
2420-2421

historicity of this book scholars are dependent upon prior references to it by Origen (A.D. 185-254) and Clement of Alexander (A.D. 150-263). "There are several references to the book [Enoch] up to the sixth century but thereafter it disappeared til [A.M.] Ceriani found a fragment of it which is published in the 'Acts Sacra Et Profana.' Vol. I [at Milan in 1874]."[6] This manuscript is full of scribal errors because of the copyists' ignorance of the Greek language. Many of the words are misinterpreted. The fragment did not contain the reference in Jude.

Jude's reference to fallen angels (v. 6) is an allusion to a passage in Enoch (chs. 6-19). The only complete manuscripts of Enoch still extant are written in Ethiopic and copied from Greek originals.[7]

Background, Purpose, and Content

Even though the writer refers to himself as Jude [Judas], "the brother of James," because of modesty, "he refrains from calling himself directly the brother of our Lord. He remembered, may we not believe, that he had been too unworthy a brother to Jesus in the days of His flesh. Brother, though he is, he is content…to be his bond servant."[8]

It is evident that there is a similarity between Jude and 2 Peter and this raises the question: Who copied from whom? However, it need not be that either one copied from the other. They could have been writing to the same people with the same problems, but at different times. Peter may have written before the fall of Jerusalem and Jude afterward. Both writers shared a common concern lest apostasy destroy the Christian heritage.[9]

Jude reveals some information not previously stated in Scripture: i.e., his reference to the fallen angels (v. 6) and Michael's contest with the devil (v. 9), not mentioned in the account of Moses' death and burial at Mount Nebo (cf. De. 34:5-6). The name "Michael" appears fifteen times in the Scriptures but only once in reference to Michael as an archangel, in Jude 9, and once as a leader of the angels in Re. 12:7. It is possible that Daniel's reference to Michael alludes to this angel (10:13,21; 12:1). (For additional information on angels, see commentary on Re. 5:11.)

The books in the pseudepigrapha, which also refer to these incidents, are generally considered to be fanciful and of inferior quality when compared with the canonical books, but Jude shows that there are some elements of truth, even in these non-Biblical books. "There were only five of the fathers between Adam and Enoch (1 Chr. 1:1). The first coming of Christ was revealed to Adam in Ge. 3:15; His second, glorious coming, to Enoch; and the 'seventh from Adam' foretold the things which will conclude the seventh age of the world."[10]

Jude must have had access to the sermon recorded in the book of Enoch, of which he quoted only a small portion. Since Enoch was contemporary with Adam and Eve (v. 14) and the human family lived close together, it may be possible that Adam and Eve and their family heard the sermon of which this segment is a part. Jude went to the other side of the flood for his message and projected it beyond the flood to a future time (v. 23).

In respect to the book(s) of Enoch, "After having been quoted in Jude and noticed by several of the Fathers, this work disappeared from the knowledge of the Christian Church."[11] In the eighteenth century, [James] Bruce, a British explorer, returned from Ethiopia with three copies of the book of Enoch, written in Ethiopic. One copy each was placed in the Kinnard House, the Bodleian Library at Oxford, and the Royal Library in Paris. The book lay there unread until some years later when Sylvester de Sacy translated the first sixteen chapters, and Archbishop Laurence translated and published the entire work for the Bodleian Library. Later, additional copies were found at Magdala. A careful study shows that these Ethiopic copies were all translated from original Greek manuscripts. Some Greek fragments have been found at Giza, near Cairo, Egypt, the seat of the Coptic Church.[12]

Jude's information concerning the book of Enoch, along with his insight into Old Testament history, indicates that he was well-read and a man of culture. "He is forcible and rhetorical, even though his usage of the Greek language suggests that he learnt Greek only late in life, gathering so large a vocabulary that he became encumbered by it."[13]

Regardless of the state of apostasy, Jude approached their problem positively and urged the church to build themselves up in the holy faith and to pray in the Holy Ghost (v. 20). They were to keep themselves "in the love of God" and to look "for the mercy of our Lord Jesus Christ unto eternal life" (v. 21). In the spirit of love, the writer confirmed that "some needed compassionate tenderness because they were close to the fire, some required cautious ministration lest their form of sin contaminate the believers."[14] In a beautiful benediction Jude suggests the Lord's ability to keep Christians "from falling" and to present them (the people of God) "faultless before the presence of his glory with exceeding joy" (v. 24).[15]

Origin and
Growth of
the English
Bible
4220
Study of
"Word"
428

Apostasy
1235-1236
Prayer
Enjoined
2817
Bene-
dictions
395
Joy
Promised
1928

Jude 3 ...although I was very eager to write to you about the salvation we share, I felt I had to write and urge you to contend for the faith... (NIV)

According to this verse Jude intended to write at length about the common salvation, but because of the crisis at hand, he shifted quickly to the perils of apostasy within the church. Because of the rapid influx of members, not fully Christianized, the church body suffered internal turmoil. "There had crept into the church, people who were making the grace of God an excuse for licentiousness, defiant, without reverence, ignorant and sensual; they could not read the lessons of history that showed that upon all such, punishment must fall."[16]

Jude courageously accepted the challenge to rebuke the church, but he did it adroitly and with understanding.

Jude 9 ...Michael the archangel...

Michael is one of only two angels who are mentioned by name in the Bible; the other is Gabriel (Da. 8:16; Lu. 1:19). Michael is referred to as a "prince" (Da. 10:13-21) and he is the only angel with the title "archangel." He appears to be the first in rank among the angels of heaven and is perhaps the presiding angel in the court of heaven. For more on angels see commentary on Re. 5:11.

Jude 17 ...remember what the apostles of our Lord Jesus Christ foretold. (NIV)

The apostle Paul had told the Ephesians, "I know that after I leave, savage wolves will come in among you and will not spare the flock" (Ac. 20:29, NIV). He also warned Timothy, "The Spirit clearly says that in later times some will abandon the faith and follow deceiving spirits and things taught by demons" (1 Ti. 4:1, NIV). For information on the word "apostle" see commentary on Ac. 1:26.

Revelation

The Name

The book of Revelation derives its name from the first verse: "The Revelation of Jesus Christ...unto his servant John." The title in the King James Version reads "The Revelation of Saint John the Divine." The oldest form of the title was probably "Apocalypse of John"; the appended words, "the Divine," were added in about the fourth century.

The Latin background of the word "Revelation" is *revelatio* (from *revelare,* meaning "to reveal or explore that which was previously hidden"). The word "apocalypse" is the Greek title and is the first word in the Greek text—appearing as *Apokalypsis.*

Authorship and Date

The statement concerning the authorship of this book differs from that of any other book in the Bible. All Scripture was given to the prophets and other writers by inspiration of the Holy Spirit (2 Ti. 3:16), but divine disclosure for the book of Revelation was given by God the Father to Jesus Christ, his Son, who communicated the message to "his servant John" by "his angel" (Re. 1:1).

This John was assumed by the church to be the Apostle John. Wilbur M. Smith says, "As early as the first half of the second century, it was the conviction of the church that John was the author. Justin Martyr states that John, one of the apostles of Christ, wrote the book. Eusebius repeatedly assigned the book to John as did Tertullian."[1] The text itself mentions the name of John five times which adds strength to Johannine authorship. In style the language is similar to that of the Gospel of John.

The similarities between John's writings and Revelation are striking. Some of them are listed in the chart on the next page.

The "Logos" (Word) appears only in the Gospel of John and in Revelation (19:13; cf. Jn. 1:1). Merrill C. Tenney states that "there are a number of words and concepts, such as 'Word of God' [used] as a title of Christ, 'Witness,' the concept of the 'Lamb,' and some others that characterize both John and Revelation, and are common to no other writings of the New Testament."[2]

There is, however, some disagreement among scholars concerning the question of the authorship of Revelation. Saint Dionysius, of Alexandria of

The
Book of
Revelation
4288
John
1902
Visions
2495

Divinely
Inspired
417
Christ,
Oracle
of God
2500

The
Gospel of
John
4265

Christ
Jesus, the
"Word"
700

Revelation	Other Johannine Writings	Subject
1:1	Jn. 18:37	Revelation of Jesus
1:5	1 Jn. 1:7	Jesus' blood
1:9	1 Jn. 5:10	Testimony, Witness
2:17	Jn. 6:32	Manna, Bread
3:8	Jn. 17:6; 1 Jn. 2:5	Kept thy word
3:21	1 Jn. 2:13-14; 4:4; 5:5	Overcome
19:13	Jn. 1:1	Word was God
22:8, 10	Jn. 4:23-24	Worship

the third century, asserted that John, the Apostle, did not write the book of Revelation because: (1) author identification is given in Revelation but not in the Gospel, (2) the vocabulary, syntax, and certain theological concepts are different, and (3) the quality of grammar in Revelation is inferior to that in the fourth Gospel. But these objections cannot be sustained in considering the evidence presented supporting Johannine authorship. After all, "Truth…is not made or unmade by the literary form through which it is expressed: and in this case the Apocalypse differs from ordinary Jewish apocalyptic writing…Although it possesses the usual characteristics of Apocalyptic literature…it is not pseudonymous. It was written to seven actual churches in seven well-known cities, and its emphasis on practical ethics is different from the general trend of apocalyptic words."[3]

The first sentence indicates that "God Himself… [gave] it through Jesus Christ, by an angel, to John, who wrote it down and sent the completed book the Seven Churches (Re. 1:1-4)."[4] The final affirmation is that the Holy Spirit approved the book for canonization.

Background, Purpose, and Content

The book of Revelation has always been a difficult book to understand because its content is apocalyptic and its language, in part, figurative and symbolic. However difficult, the book itself is commended to the reader for serious, prayerful study. "Blessed is he that readeth, and they that hear the words of this prophecy, and keep those things which are written therein" (1:3). Certain portions of Revelation are closely related to apocalyptic sections in the OT. Wilbur M. Smith writes,

> It is estimated that of 404 verses in this book [Revelation], 265 contain lines which embrace approximately 550 references to the Old Testament passages: there are 13 references to Genesis, 27 to Exodus, 79 to Isaiah, 53 to Daniel…Many…agree…[that] the eschatology discourse of Jesus (Mt. 24; Mk. 13; Lu. 21) is…the key to the Apocalypse. This book is saturated with Old Testament prophecy, under the guidance of the word of Jesus, and the inspiration of God. It is the climax of the prophecy of the Old and New Testaments.[5]

The book of Daniel is frequently considered to be a companion book to Revelation. Many volumes have been written on the book of Revelation, but this study is limited to the less controversial chapters, especially such chapters as 1-3, 21 and 22. For those who are new students of Revelation, the recommendation is to begin study with the devotional nature of the book in mind. The Holy Spirit will lead the reader into greater depths of truth.

As indicated in the discussion on the Epistles of John, according to tradition the apostle moved from Jerusalem to Ephesus sometime before the fall of Jerusalem. Later, because of his Christian faith he was exiled to the penal settlement on the island of Patmos in the Aegean Sea about A.D. 95. There he remained until about A.D. 97. As understood from the text, John received his vision on the Isle but recorded the Revelation later, perhaps after his return from exile. At the time of writing, John used the past tense: "I…was on the island of Patmos because of the word of God and the testimony of Jesus Christ" (1:9, NIV). Thus the internal evidence points to actual persecution during the time John wrote the book, probably under Domitian (A.D. 81-96), when attack on Christianity reached many areas in the Empire, especially in the year A.D. 95.

John's writings contain a message not only for the Christian's own time, but also for the future when the natural order of the universe will come to an end and Christ will set up his kingdom. Scholars have assumed that much of Revelation was written in figurative language so that the authorities could not understand what the Christians were doing. Three main methods of interpre-

| Daniel |
| 4249 |

| "Spirit" Guides |
| 1611 |
| Jerusalem |
| 1881-1883 |
| Ephesus |
| 1142, 4373 |

| Roman Emperors |
| 611-614 |

For a Further Study of the Apocalyptic Parallels, See:	
Revelation	Compare With:
1:6	Ex. 19:6; 1:7; Da. 7:13-14; Zec. 12:10-12
1:14	Da. 7:9, 13; 10:5
1:16	Is. 2:4; 49:2
1:17	Is. 44:6; 48:12
5:11	Da. 7:10
5:13	Da. 7:13-14
10:7	Da. 12:6-7
11:15	Da. 7:13-14
13:7	Da. 7:21, 25[6]

tation of Revelation have developed:

1. The Preterist view describes the events in the book as having been fulfilled. It emphasizes the historical background and the ethical teachings of the book.

2. The Futurist view suggests that Revelation, beginning with chapter 4, is yet to be fulfilled at the end of time and that parts of the book refer to a period of apostasy (chs. 1-3). Chapters 4-22 describe future events including the Great Tribulation, the second coming of Christ, the Millennium, and the new kingdom under Christ.

3. The Eclectic view teaches that some things have been fulfilled, some things are being fulfilled, and still other events will be fulfilled at the end of the Age.

Furthermore, arising out of the prophetic positions are three aspects of the Millennium:

1. The postmillennial view presupposes that Christ will not return until the church has evangelized the world and has created a general state of peace. Christ will then come from heaven and occupy the throne of peace prepared for him by the church.

2. The amillennial view teaches that Christ could return any moment and immediately set up the Great Judgment seat to be followed by permanent heaven and hell.

3. The premillennial view postpones final judgment until Christ has reigned and ruled on earth with the saints for 1,000 years. Near the end of this period the Great Seven-Year Tribulation is to take place, to be followed by the Final Judgment.[7] The premillennial view is generally accepted by many evangelical Christians.

These three views of the Millennium raise three more questions: Will the Great Tribulation come (a) before, (b) during or (c) after the Second Coming when "the dead in Christ shall rise first...then we which...remain shall be caught up together with them in the clouds, to meet the Lord in the air: and so shall we ever be with the Lord" (1 Th. 4:16-17)? This meeting in the air is frequently referred to as the "Rapture."

In the introduction to the seven churches, John gave an apocalyptic description of the second coming of Christ: "He cometh with clouds; and every eye shall see him, and they also which pierced him: and all kindreds of the earth shall wail because of him. Even so, Amen" (Re. 1:7). Jesus Christ declared, "I am Alpha and Omega, the beginning and the ending, saith the Lord" (1:8). "What thou seest, write in a book, and send it unto the seven churches which are in Asia; unto Ephesus, and unto Smyrna, and unto Pergamos, and unto Thyatira, and unto Sardis, and unto Philadelphia, and unto Laodicea" (1:11). The letters addressed to the seven churches in Asia are applicable to Christians in any age—the body of Christ, the church, as persons joined to Christ.

A Retrospective View of Revelation

After the prologue (1:1-20), which includes the vision of Christ (1:9-20), are the letters to the seven churches (chapters 2 and 3). A study of these messages has value today as they give a cross section of the various conditions of the church in every age. At the beginning of chapter 4 with the view of God's throne and the unusual symbols in a number of visions, the apocalyptic element becomes more evident (chs. 4-20). The final vision of heaven (chs. 21-22) has been a great comfort to believers throughout the ages.

The book contains the seven visions John had on the Isle of Patmos. George Tybout Purvis explains that "these visions are probably not to be understood as representing events which were to follow one another in history in the order of time, but as symbolical portraitures of certain religious truths or principles which were to be realized in the experience of the church. The whole is intended for comfort and warning of the church amid the conflicts of time and in preparation for the second coming of our Lord (1:7-8; 22:7, l0, 17, 20)."[8]

The seven visions may be summarized as follows:

1. The vision of the glorified Christ and His church, followed by seven messages to the seven churches of Asia...
2. The vision of God, presiding over the destinies of the universe and adored by all creation, and the exalted but redeeming Lamb of God, who holds in His hand the sealed book...
3. The vision of the trumpets...
4. The vision of the church under the figure of the woman, bringing forth the Christ against whom the dragon, or Satan, wages war...
5. The vision of the vials, or bowls, containing the last plagues, or judgments of God...
6. The vision of the harlot, the city of Babylon, followed by the victory of Christ over her, ending in the last judgment...
7. The vision of the local church, the bride of Christ, or New Jerusalem, followed by a description of her glory...[9]

The number seven has a peculiar place in Revelation. References in the book refer to seven "churches" (1:4); "Spirits" (1:4); "golden candlesticks" (1:12); "stars" (1:16); "lamps" (4:5); "seals" (5:1); "horns" (5:6); "eyes" (5:6); "angels" (8:2); "trumpets" (8:2); "thunders" (10:3); "thousand" (11:13); "heads" (12:3); "crowns" (12:3); "last plagues" (15:1); "golden vials" (15:7); "mountains" (17:9); and "kings" (17:10).

The
Glorified
Christ
682

Heaven
1356, 1547
Visions
2495

Christ
Comforts
784

Sovereignty
of God
3415-3421

Satan
3148-3149

Babylon
329-331
New
Jerusalem
1886
Seven
3241-3245

Trumpets
2466-2467

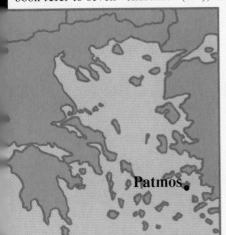

Patmos

Patmos. The city and harbor viewed from the cave where John reportedly wrote the book of Revelation.

Number of Perfection
3241

In addition to the 400 instances in which the number "seven" occurs, the Scripture includes similar expressions; sevenfold, sevens, and seventeen. Henry H. Halley states that "used as often as it is, in the way it is, it must have some significance over and above its numerical value. Symbolically it is thought to stand for completion, a unit of fullness, totality."[10]

Completion
3893

Expositors agree that the presentation of the basic doctrines concerning God, Christ, Holy Spirit, sin, and redemption do not vary in Revelation essentially from those in other parts of Scripture, as illustrated in the chart on the next page. Christology is evident; the Christ in Revelation is definitely equal with God (Re. 1:4-7; 2:8; 5:12-14; 22:13).

"Word" Inspired
417

Redemption Through Christ
2979

There is also a striking similarity in the book to the teaching of Paul and Peter concerning redemption through the blood of Christ (1:5; 5:9; 7:14; 12:11; cf. Ep. 1:7; Col. 1:14; 1 Pe. 3:18-19). Peter signified that the day of the Lord will come as a thief in the night (2 Pe. 3:10a; cf. Re. 3:3; 16:15). In the setting of the new order to come, at the last Judgment "...the earth and the heaven fled away..." (Re. 20:11; 21:1). Peter had written a vivid prophetic description of this sudden (violent) cataclysmic event: "...the heavens shall pass away with a great noise, and the elements shall melt with fervent heat...the heavens being on fire shall be dissolved..." (2 Pe. 3:10,12). These details bear marked resemblance to the potential nuclear disaster generally feared in our day.

Great Day
922

Some scholars suggest that the message in Revelation was entirely historical—that the believers of that period understood the message because they were familiar with the apocalyptic form of writing. The cryptic language is used to reveal to some believers, but to conceal from others. In an effort to interpret the meaning of Revelation, many have shown more enthusiasm than insight.[11] The Revelation of Jesus Christ indicates that God revealed himself to persons and groups in a way so that not only were their lives affected, but the destiny of others altered.

God intervened in the lives of (1) Adam and Eve (Ge. 3:9ff.), (2) Noah (Ge. 7:1ff.), (3) the Hebrews in Egypt and in their journey to Canaan (Ex. 1ff.), (4) the judges (Jud. 1ff.), (5) Esther (Est. 1ff.), (6) Ezra and Nehemiah (Ezr. 1ff.; Ne. 1ff.), (7) Mary (Mt. 1:20ff.), (8) the disciples in the Upper Room (Ac. 1:13ff.).

His future coming will be a final invasion into the lives of men. The book of Revelation deals with the second coming of the Lord Jesus Christ. This has been the blessed hope of the righteous since early times (see Jude 14ff.; Da. 7:9; Jb. 19:25). The twentieth chapter of Revelation contains information concerning events immediately preceding the Second Coming (cf. 1 Co. 15:18-28,50-58; 1 Th. 4:13-18; 5:1-7). The book of Revelation was understood by the church to mean that the Second Coming was near, and in terms of God's time, it is always near. Because cataclysmic disaster is to usher in the kingdom of God, "John wrote to prepare his fellow Christians for these terrors, which he believed were already beginning, and to assure them that the

God:	Re. 1:1 "The Revelation of Jesus Christ, which God gave"
His sovereignty:	Re. 17:14 "Lord of lords, and King of kings"
	Re. 19:6 "God...reigneth"
Christ:	Re. 1:1 "The Revelation of Jesus Christ"
	Re. 7:14b "they...have washed their robes, and made them white in the blood of the Lamb"
Holy Spirit:	Re. 2:7 "...let him hear what the Spirit saith unto the churches"
	Re. 14:13 "...saith the Spirit"
	Re. 22:17 "...the Spirit and the bride say, Come"
Sin:	Re. 22:3 "and there shall be no more curse"
Redemption:	Re. 7:14 "they...have washed their robes and made them white in the blood of the Lamb"
Heaven:	Re. 12:7 "war in heaven"
	Re. 21:1 "I saw a new heaven"
Hell:	Re. 20:14 "death and hell were cast into the lake of fire"
Satan:	Re. 2:9d "synagogue of Satan"
	Re. 20:1-3 "Satan will be bound"

Christ's Revelation
2500
Methods of Revelation
2495-2498

Second Coming of Christ
1344-1350

Imminence
1743

Sovereignty of God
3415-3421

Atoning Blood of Jesus
679
Holy Spirit
1601-1614

Divine Curse
903

Heaven
1356

Hell
1374-1375

Satan
3148-3155

outcome would be the triumph of Christ and His church…His message…was not a message of doom but a call to courage and faith."[12]

A view of the "end of the days" in ch. 20 describes the millennial reign of Christ when Satan will be bound and banished. Chapter 21 contains the vision of a "new heaven and a new earth" and a list of those people who will be excluded (v. 8). In the final chapter, John saw a "pure river of water of life," "the tree of life," and understood "there shall be no more curse" (vv. 1-3). The epilogue (vv. 6-21) emphasizes that Jesus will "come quickly" (translated by some as "suddenly"). The beautiful benediction concludes the book: "The grace of our Lord Jesus Christ be with you all." In Genesis, man's paradise is lost under a tree (Ge. 2:16ff.) and in the Last Book, Paradise is restored under "the tree of life"(Re. 22:2).

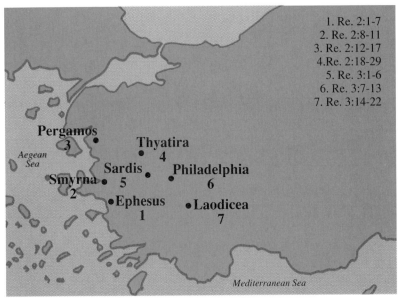

1. Re. 2:1-7
2. Re. 2:8-11
3. Re. 2:12-17
4. Re. 2:18-29
5. Re. 3:1-6
6. Re. 3:7-13
7. Re. 3:14-22

Pergamos 3

Aegean Sea

Thyatira 4

Sardis 5

Philadelphia 6

Smyrna 2

Ephesus 1

Laodicea 7

Mediterranean Sea

The seven churches addressed in the book of Revelation.

1:1 The Revelation of Jesus Christ, which God gave unto him...and he sent...unto his servant John.

The inspiration of the Bible is affirmed by the men who wrote it. They asserted, "I heard a voice from heaven" (see Re. 14:13) or "Thus saith the Lord" or similar expressions to reveal the Source of their writing. For more on the inspiration of Scripture, see commentary on 2 Ti. 3:16.

1:12 ...I saw seven golden candlesticks.

The candlestick is rich with symbolism. According to John Wesley it here represents the faithful Christian believers in the church.[13]

The candlestick made of gold was an important element of the tabernacle—it was the first object that the priest saw as he entered the tabernacle. Symbolically it is an especially apt reminder of Christ, the light of the world. For more on this symbolism see commentary on Ex. 25:31.

2:1 To the angel of the church in Ephesus write...(NIV)

Ephesus was located about 50 miles south of Smyrna (modern Izmir), on the Aegean Sea near the mouth of the Cayster River, sometimes referred to by the natives as the "Little Menderes" river. The other six churches of Revelation were located to the north and east within a radius of about 125 miles.

Ephesus was the capital city of Asia, a seaport town of about 300,000 population, where caravan routes from Europe and the Orient terminated. The dock facilities formerly had been located at the eastern edge of the city, at the foot of Arcadian Avenue, but silting action from the river, erosion in the mountains, and the "dust of the ages" have filled in the old harbor so that the waterfront is now several miles to the west. The modern seaport of Ephesus is now Kusadai, about 20 miles from where the ancient city stood.

The Seven Churches of Asia
762, 4308j

Christ's Revelation
2500
Divine Revelations
2494
Seven
3241
Candlestick
637
Christ the Light
2168
Ephesus
1142, 4373

Archaeological excavations at Ephesus.

Diana
3940
False
Gods and
Goddesses
3935-3940
Mary,
Mother
of Jesus
2259

Greek settlers came to Ephesus in about 1044 B.C.; in 133 B.C. it became part of the Roman Empire. The city was known especially for the Temple of Artemis (Diana), in honor of the Anatolian fertility goddess, who was later Hellenized. Also, Ephesus was a banking center as well as a "city of refuge," where fugitives could find sanctuary in the Great Temple. When Christianity became dominant in Ephesus, another woman replaced Diana, namely the Virgin Mary.

Discovery of the shrine of the Virgin Mary on Mount Coressos came after Anna Emmerich, a nun in Germany, had a vision in 1890 about the home and the tomb of Mary in Ephesus, even though she had never been there. Two priests from Smyrna made a trip in 1891 and found the place on top of the mountain exactly as the nun had described it. Archaeologists, excavating in the area, determined that the ruin was a fourth-century house built over the ruins of a first-century structure. Greek Orthodox Christians in the area confirm the traditional name, *Panaja Kapoulu,* meaning "The most of all." The present reconstructed house was built on the remains of the previous walls—now only 18-30 inches high.

The importance of Ephesus as a religious center is indicated by the number of church councils held here:

Easter
1092
Church
Discipline
750

(a) The Council of A.D. 200 was convened by Polycrates, Bishop of Ephesus, to discuss the date of Easter.

(b) The Council of A.D. 401 gave its attention to restoring clerical discipline in Asia Minor.

(c) The Council of A.D. 431 was called by the Emperor Theodosius II and was presided over by Saint Cyril; 2,000 bishops attended for the purpose of condemning the Gnostic heresy, Nestorianism, prevalent in Asia Minor.

(d) The most spectacular convention was the Robber Council of A.D. 449. Thea B. Van Halsema describes it thus:

> The Council was a rather rough affair in which one bishop died three days after being kicked in the stomach by another. It was called "Robber Council" because one group headed by Mennon of Ephesus and Cyril of Alexandria decided to begin the council before the arrival of the opposing groups led by bishops John of Antioch and Nestorius of Constantinople. The first group excommunicated Nestorius before his group arrived. The second group, upon arrival, met separately and excommunicated their opponents…At issue was the question of Christ's incarnation. Nestorius said that Christ, being God, could not be born of a human mother and he stressed the separation of Christ's manhood and Godhead, so that Mary was to be regarded as mother of Christ—Christokos—but not of God—Theotokos.
>
> Cyril, though unscrupulous in his intrigues, defended the historic position that the two natures of Christ were united in one person, and that the Logos took human nature to himself in Mary's womb. This made her Theotokos, mother of God, opening the way for later Roman Church claims of Mary's sinlessness and bodily assumption, which in our day is leading toward a claim that Mary is co-mediatrix with the Son of God. Both Nestorius and Cyril had large followings. Cyril's group won out at the Ephesus council but the outlawed Nestorians established themselves strongly in Persia, Arabia and China. The ruins of the "double church" of Mary, where the council was held, lie beside the wall, west of the city site.[14]

(e) The Council of A.D. 476 declared the see (bishop's authority) of Ephesus to be independent of the Constantinopolitian Patriarchate.

Three references in the NT suggest the importance of the Ephesus church: the account in Ac. 18:18-19:41, Paul's letter to the Ephesians, and the words of Jesus Christ himself in the book of Revelation (2:1-7). These indicate the prominence of the Ephesian church. This group had once been a witnessing church; but at the time of the Revelation of Jesus the believers had left their "first love." Although Jesus recognized their "works," "labour," "patience," and perseverance (Re. 2:2), he told them to "remember therefore from whence thou art fallen, and repent, and do the first works…" (Re. 2:5), or else he would remove their candlestick (see commentary on Re. 1:12). Christ warned the church leaders that if they did not care for the flock it would be turned over to someone who would.[15]

Jesus acknowledged that the Ephesian believers were true and sound in their disfavor of the Nicolaitan heresy: a system of adulterous lewdness and sacrifices to idols which they condoned in the name of Christian liberty.[16] Those who overcome are to "eat of the tree of life which is in the midst of the paradise of God," which is generally understood to mean "the immortality of the soul and a final state of blessedness."[17]

The excavations of Ephesus are the most extensive of any in the Near-East. Each season Austrian archaeologists continue to uncover more of ancient Ephesus. Marble pillars and arches are visible for miles around. The famous library of Celsus, south of the Mazeus and Mithridates Gates, is under reconstruction; the facade can be seen from a great distance. This two-story library, built by Julius Aquilla, was named for his father, Celsus Poleneanus of Sardis, who was a Roman senator and Governor General of the province of Asia.

For more on the city of Ephesus, see pp. 460-461.

2:8 To the angel of the church in Smyrna write…(NIV)

Pergamos
2736, 4422

Smyrna (modern Izmir), located on the Bay of Smyrna facing the Aegean Sea toward the west, is situated about halfway between Pergamos to the north and Ephesus to the south, both about 50 miles distant. The crescent-shaped city drapes around the 525-foot Mount Pagos, which was at one time the Acropolis of the city.[18]

Smyrna was founded as an Ionian Colony in about 1000 B.C. but was destroyed by the Lydians in 600 B.C.[19] In the third century it came under the control of a loosely knit group of Greeks who made an early association with imperial Rome. The city became a shipping center, with caravan routes from the north and the east terminating at its docks.

Rome
3095, 4428

From early times Smyrna was a religious center. Pilgrims from all over Europe and the East traveled its streets. "In the year 23 A.D. a temple was built in honor of Tiberius and his mother, Julia, and the Golden Street connecting the temples of Zeus and Cybele is said to have been the best in any ancient city."[20]

Idolatrous
Temples
3949

Paul probably introduced Christianity in Smyrna during his extended ministry in nearby Ephesus. Ancient records in Izmir give this ecclesiastical sketch on Smyrna:

Smyrna. Under the Romans, Smyrna became a great shipping and trading center. Pictured here are some of the excavated ruins.

In 105 A.D., a few years after St. John wrote the letter to the Christians at Smyrna, St. Ignatius, the third Bishop of Antioch passed through on his way to Rome, where he was thrown to the beasts in the Roman Colosseum. While waiting for a ship in Troy he [John] wrote the Smyrnaeans and commended them for their "immovable faith as if nailed to the cross of the Lord Jesus Christ." He also wrote to Polycarp, a disciple of John, who became Bishop of Smyrna and linked the apostolic period to the second-century church.

St. Iraenaeus served as an elder in the church of Smyrna. Later (249-251) Pionius the Presbyter and his companions suffered martyrdom in Smyrna.

But Smyrna was also a seat of paganism. Young men flocked to the colleges of Smyrna to learn the philosophies of paganism. In the fifth century, Attila the Hun conquered Smyrna. In 673 the city was occupied by the Arabs for a while but they were unable to take the citadel. The emperor, Leo the Wise (886-912), gave the church at Smyrna one of the major sees in the Byzantine Empire. In 1071 the Selcuk Turks defeated the Byzantine forces. During the later occupation in 1204-1261 several Byzantine emperors took refuge in the region of Smyrna. From the late 1300's until World War I, Turkey was under the dominion of the Ottoman Turks. During this Moslem control the church almost disappeared from the scene. Even today professing Christians in Smyrna are few.[21]

Philosophy **2759**

Edgar J. Banks says, "In Roman times Smyrna was considered the most brilliant city of Asia Minor, successfully rivaling Pergamos and Ephesus. Its streets were wide and paved. Its system of coinage...was from early times, and now about the city are coins of every period. The city was celebrated for its schools of science and medicine, and for its handsome buildings. Among them was Homerium, for Smyrna was one of several places which claimed to be the birth place of the poet."[22]

Rome **3095, 4428**

It seems probable that Smyrna was one of the cities which embraced Christianity at an early date because it already had a flourishing church in John's day. Paul may have stopped there on his third missionary journey. Tradition indicates that many Jews in Smyrna accepted Jesus as the Messiah. Christ commended the church for its faith (Re. 2:8-9). However some Jews did not accept Jesus as their Messiah. They based their hope on their practicing the Jewish ritual and upon being circumcised descendants of Abraham. The question of circumcision and of who were real Jews arose in the church at Rome. Paul puts the meaning of this matter in focus: "A man is not a Jew if he is only one outwardly, nor is circumcision merely outward and physical. No, a man is a Jew if he is one inwardly; and circumcision is circumcision of the heart, by the Spirit..." (Ro. 2:28-29, NIV). Jesus stated that the Jews who claimed to be Jews in spirit, but were not, were committing blasphemy and were of the synagogue of Satan (Re. 2:9). (See commentary on Re. 2:9.)

History of Early Church **4309g** *Christ Rejected* **2965**

Circumcision **765-766** *Blasphemy* **473-474**

It was in Smyrna where "Polycarp, the bishop of Smyrna, was martyred, though without sanction of the Roman government. Apparently the Jews of Smyrna were more antagonistic than were the Romans to the spread of Christianity, for even on Saturday, their sacred day, they brought wood for the fire in which Polycarp was burned. His grave is still shown in a cemetery there."[23] Jesus warned the believers that they would suffer severe tribulation for ten days and would be cast into prison by the devil himself (Re. 1:10). Apparently the persecutions were to last only a short time. The reward for faithfulness was "a crown of life."

Martyrdom **3487**

According to the Greek philosopher, Apallonius of Tyana, the phrase, The "Crown of Smyrna" referred to the appearance of Mount Pagos with the stately public buildings on its rounded top and the city spreading out and down its sloping sides. St. John, on the authority of God, promises the Christians a new crown. The earthly Smyrna wore a crown like that of the patron goddess.

Persecution **3480-3484**

The Smyrnians "faithful unto death" would receive a celestial crown, "a crown of life" (Re. 2:10).

Archaeological activity remains restricted in Smyrna because the modern city of Izmir grew up over the ruins before interest in the preservation of antiquities developed. However, archaeologists have made soundings in several parts of the city and unearthed the remains of NT Smyrna on the eastern rim of the city. They have excavated the Roman Agora in the center of the city and have located a theatre on the slopes of Mount Pagos, the ancient acropolis of Smyrna, with a seating capacity of 20,000 people.

2:9 ...I know the blasphemy of them which say they are Jews, and are not, but are the synagogue of Satan.

In the Scriptures a false, counterfeit religious system is clearly discerned (see chart on p. 66). The conflict between the forces of good and evil in the world is evident on every hand. All means and methods are used by Satan and his angels to frustrate and destroy God's program (see Jb. 1:7ff.; Lu. 4:6; Ac. 26:18; 2 Co. 4:3-4; Ep. 6:12; 2 Th. 2:9). Satan's most effective efforts have been made through imitation, half truths, and counterfeit. Satan has counterfeits for all the good things of God; there is in the world today a counterfeit church made up of people (inside the visible church and out) who are, consciously or unconsciously, motivated by Satan. The "church in the wilderness" (Ac. 7:38) had to contend with this "counterfeit group" known as the "mixed multitude."[24]

Directing this counterfeit church are the false prophets and ministers who perpetuate a counterfeit system, with its seductively beautiful allurements, its ritualistic appeal, its easy religion without repentance or abandonment of sin, and "many there be which go in thereat" (Mt. 7:13).

It is a well-known fact that counterfeits and adulterations are difficult to detect, and many are deceived thereby. The counterfeit church propounds a kind of humanistic, rationalistic salvation which discards "all dependence upon anything outside of man himself for the attainments of the good life...Whatever satisfaction he is to enjoy he must achieve by his ability to control the physical world about him or through his manipulation of social forces which can thus be made to serve him. He is entirely this worldly in his outlook. Science is the key to his hope of a better world."[25]

The counterfeit church consists of people who serve and worship their own self-interests. They are found in the visible church, the denominational groups, with all the appearances of pious saints. They use the forms and terminology of the church, but at the same time are "denying the power thereof" (2 Ti. 3:5). They claim the name "Christian" but are not in union with Christ (Ep. 5:23-27; He. 12:22-23). At times representatives from this group have been able to take control of the visible church and to direct its functions and affairs, while at other times they are associated with other institutions, definitely satanic. They live a kind of "Dr. Jekyll and Mr. Hyde" life. The "mystical body of Satan" and the "mystical body of Christ move along in history, within the framework of the visible Church, sometimes within each other and sometimes parallel to each other. These two lines run through all ages; the ripening of the great 'world' for the tempest of judgment and the preparing of the 'little flock' for deliverance out of misery and distress."[26]

The two will be closely related until the end of time, even as the wheat and tares stay together until harvest. "The attempt to sever the tares from the

Spiritual Crowns 1367
Satan's Power 3150
False Religion 2988-2991
The Arch Deceiver 3153
Mixed Multitude 2388
False Prophets 2100
Salvation of God 3116
Trusting in Works 4120
Union with Christ 738
Satan 3148-3155
Wheat 3822-3823

wheat prematurely has led to many schisms, which have invariably failed to accomplish anything and only generated fresh separations. We must wait till Christ's manifestation for 'the manifestation of the sons of God'" (Ro. 8:19; Col. 3:4).[27] Jesus' parable of the wheat and tares is applicable here (Mt. 13:30). At the judgment "the angels shall come forth, and sever the wicked from among the just" (Mt. 13:49).

Waiting for God 2693
Angels Reapers 142

A very familiar scene in Palestine has always been the mixed flock. The black goats and white sheep pasture together, but there comes a time when the shepherd separates his sheep from his goats. Christ draws an analogy: On the day of judgment a separation will be effected, and to the "sheep on his right hand" he will say "Come, ye blessed of my Father, inherit the kingdom prepared for you from the foundation of the world" (Mt. 25:31ff.). But the goats on his left hand are addressed thus: "Depart from me, ye cursed, into everlasting fire, prepared for the devil and his angels" (Mt. 25:41ff.). Christ further illustrates the physical association of the good and evil until the judgment day: "I tell you, in that night there shall be two men in one bed; the one shall be taken, and the other shall be left. Two women shall be grinding together; the one shall be taken, and the other left. Two men shall be in the field; the one shall be taken, and the other left...Wheresoever the body is, thither will the eagles be gathered together" (Lu. 17:34-37). Obviously, at this point the spiritual wheat and tares, the good and evil, are forever separated.

Last Judgment 1351
End of the World 1126

This division will take place at the judgment. Obviously, political Judaism was the OT agent in which both the true church and the counterfeit church were found. God's plan to redeem man used the shedding of animal blood, which was typical of the "Lamb slain from the foundation of the world" (Re. 13:8b). By offering blood sacrifices as God had commanded, the believers gave evidence of their faith in God's redemptive provision. These early believers expressed faith in the Lord and were thus saved. Favor with God has always depended upon the sinner's acceptance of God's son, Christ the Lord. When the Savior said, "No man cometh unto the Father, but by me" (Jn. 14:6), he clearly revealed that he had always been the way by which sinners obtained favor with the Father.

Final Separation 291
Lamb of God 3365
Salvation Only Through Christ 3117

Abel represents the church; he brought an acceptable blood sacrifice (see commentary on Ge. 4:4-5). Cain, who offered no animal sacrifice, represents the counterfeit church; he brought merely an expression of his own rationalization, falsely assuming that the products of his field could substitute for the blood sacrifice which God required. Thereby he became the prototype of all who dare to approach the sanctuary of God without the shedding of blood (He. 9:22).

Abel 4

Cain must have known the true way since he was reared in the same home with Abel. He was religious but he had a religion of the flesh and he was irreverent and selfish (Ge. 4:9). He was deluded into depending upon his own way; this was the thinking of the first murderer. But on the other hand, the "way of Abel" was to humbly acknowledge that sin necessitates death, and that the guilty rely on the sacrifice appointed by God.

Cain 618
Sin's Penalty 3352-3354

When the Messiah appeared, the degenerate "followers of Cain" put our Lord on a cross (Ac. 3:15) and persecuted his followers (Ac. 4:1-3). By rejecting Christ they proved that they did not know the Father (Ac. 3:14-15,17). They claimed to be the true people of God, but really they were the children of the devil (Jn. 8:44). These God-denying church leaders were also referred to as members in the "synagogue of the Libertines" (Ac. 6:9).

God's People 2723

2:12 And to the angel of the church in Pergamos write...

The city of Pergamos (now Bergama) is situated in western Anatolia (Turkey) and located 50 miles north of Smyrna (Izmir) on the Caicus (Bakir) River, 15 miles above where it empties into the Aegean Sea. The city is built on three terraces with the 1,000-foot high acropolis as its summit.

In historical records Pergamos also appears as Pergamon and Pergamum. The origin of Pergamos is unknown, but the city certainly predates the Greek period. Greek coins discovered here date back to the fifth century B.C.

Frederick C. Grant observes that independent political history of the city began when Lysimachus of Thrace, one of Alexander's bodyguards, deposited here a large part of his treasure of 9,000 gold talents. It was entrusted to Philetaerus, son of Attalus of Tios, who revolted in 283 B.C. and set himself up as a ruler in alliance with the Seleucids. Under Alexander's general the kingdom continued until 133 B.C. when the last ruler, the childless Attalus III, bequeathed it to the Romans."[28] For a time Pergamos was the capital of Asia; however, in 6 B.C. Ephesus became the governor's official headquarters and place of residence. The Golden Age of Pergamos came under Eumenes II in about 190 B.C. During his reign the Menoun library was established.

The city of Pergamos was a thriving religious center from very early times. The acropolis, with its immense altar to Zeus, was the religious focal point of the city. Nearby stood the beautiful temple of Athena. In Roman times a temple to Augustus was also built on the acropolis—the crown of the city. Below was the shrine of Aesculapius, the god of medicine and healing. History does not record the origin of the Christian faith in Pergamos, but the church

Pergamos. The two trees mark the place where archaeologists removed the original Temple of Zeus, now on display in the Pergamos Museum in East Berlin.

was probably founded by Paul, who was in the general area on his missionary journeys. Apparently the church became well established about 30 years later when John began his writing ministry in Ephesus, just 50 miles away. John's transmission of the letter to the believers at Pergamos suggests that he had ministered in their midst.

In the middle of the second century A.D. Pergamos witnessed many martyrdoms (see Re. 2:13). During the Decian persecution (249-251), the martyrs included Carpus, bishop of Thyatira; Papylus, the deacon of Thyatira; Aga Thodoru; and a woman named Aga Thonida, who died, according to Eusebius, "after many glorious confessions." In 347 Eusebius became bishop of Pergamos.

Pergamos was the center of many theological debates. At the Robber Council of Ephesus in 449 Eutropius of Pergamos accepted the Eutychian doctrines, which stated that Christ had only one nature, that of the incarnate Word. In the sixth century the city attracted an ever increasing number of Armenians. When in 716 the city fell to the Arabs, the town never recovered. Soon after 1211 the city came under the control of the Byzantine Empire (fifth and sixth centuries) of Nicaea. Early in the fourteenth century Pergamos fell under Turkish rule. By 1366 the Ottoman Turks seized control of the city and Christian influence began to decline. Churches were converted to mosques, including the Church of St. Sophia, in Constantinople (now Istanbul). When the Moslems converted the Church of St. Sophia into a mosque, they were confronted with the problem of what to do with the icons and mosaics depicting the saints, because to the Muslim all pictures are images or idols—not permitted in a mosque. They decided to paint over the beautiful mosaic pictures. Later when the church became a museum (as it now is), in the restoration process of the use of paint remover brought the pictures back into view. The visitor can now see the beautiful artwork, typical of the period.

Of the seven churches St. John addressed, the two churches of Pergamos and Thyatira were treated with mingled praise and blame. In the opening sentence, he depicted Christ as having the two-edged sword (2:12). To the Roman the sword represented the power of life and death.

In reference to Satan's throne (2:13), some scholars make an allusion to the great altar of Zeus, which was erected on a hill almost 1,000 feet above the lower city. One of the sculptured walls featured a carved frieze 400 feet long, depicting the battle of the gods and the Titans (one of a family of giants born of Uranus and Gaea and rulers of the earth until they were overthrown by the Olympian gods). Many years ago German archaeologists dismantled this beautiful altar and reassembled it in the Pergamum Museum, now in communist East Berlin.

Despite the loyalty to Christ of some believers in the church at Pergamos, there were others holding to the heresy of Balaam, who caused Balak to induce the Israelites to "eat food sacrificed to idols and practice immorality" (2:14, RSV). The main message of Balaam is found in Nu. 22-24. According to Jewish tradition the religion of Balaam was associated with idolatry and temple prostitution. The doctrine of the Nicolaitans was both sensual and idolatrous.

Christ admonished those who held the doctrine of the Nicolaitans to repent (2:15-16). However, the faithful Christians were promised a reward of "hidden manna." Each loyal believer would also receive a white stone and a new name to assure his immortality (2:17).[29]

Paul's Missionary Journeys **2382, 4309c- 4309e** Martyrdom **3487**

Christ's Divinity– Humanity **701-723**

Thyatira **3621** Sword of the Lord **3513**

Idolatrous Altars **3948**

Heresy **1577** Balaam **333**

Repent- ance **2706**

Archaeological excavations in Pergamos are extensive and awe-inspiring. Many of the ancient buildings are now excavated or cleared of rubble and debris. The best known church discovered to date, the so-called Red Basilica, traditionally identified with St. John, stood on the ruins of a temple dedicated to the Egyptian god Serapis. Some materials from the temple were used in building the church. The walls and the tower of the Red Basilica still stand. For centuries this church was a great Christian center. After repeated attempts by the Moslems to convert the Basilica to a mosque, they became discouraged. The minarets kept falling down so the Turks left the building in ruins and named it the Basilica Serapeion (Egyptian Osiris—Apis gods). Little Christian witness is now evident in this once great Christian city.

The library at the Aesculapion in Pergamos was once full of priceless parchments. Parchment was invented here. The visible remains of Pergamos give ample evidence of its once great splendor. The temple of Athena, the foundation of the Zeus altar, the gymnasiums, the baths, and the art galleries are all there to see.

Most outstanding among the archaeological discoveries is the Aesculapion—the ancient medical center dedicated to Aesculapius, the Greek-Roman god of medicine. Pergamos was the medical center of that day. The healing art included both internal and external use of medicine, psychology, art, science, drama, music, hot and cold baths, and water cures. The remains of the uncovered medical center are quite extensive. Immediately outside the entrance is a monument of a serpent wrapped around a pole, the official medical symbol from ancient times (see picture on p. 136). The theater where drama was a part of the process for healing is one of the best preserved small amphitheaters in the world. The diagnostic rooms and treatment rooms now excavated may be viewed by the visitor. The psychological observation tunnel has an interesting feature. The holes in the ceiling enabled the healers to observe the patient secretly.

The Holy Spring, the Holy Passage, the temple of Athena, and the Temple of Serapis indicate that religion had an important part in the healing profession. The large gymnasium complex shows that exercise and gymnastics of all kinds were integral parts of making the body well and keeping it so.

2:18 And unto the angel of the church in Thyatira write...

The city of Thyatira (now Akhisar) was located about 50 miles southeast of Pergamos on the caravan road to Sardis.

Historical information on Thyatira is relatively meager. In his *Letter to the Seven Churches,* William M. Ramsay, the noted historian, writes of the city: "Its history is a blank."

Thyatira was a border outpost, a buffer city between the border of Syria and Pergamos. The images and superscriptions on the coins found in the ruins indicate that the city-state often changed hands. The city was known both as Pelopia and Euhippia in 268 B.C. when Seleucus I (Alexander's general) colonized the area with Greek settlers and changed the name to Thyatira. In 189 B.C. it passed to Roman control. As a garrison outpost, the city had some disadvantages. It had no acropolis or fortification as did Ephesus, Pergamos, and Sardis. Being on the rolling plain, Thyatira was subject to frequent enemy attack. The defenders had to maintain their political integrity by sheer courage

Thyatira. The remains of an ancient Christian church.

and bravery. However, Thyatira's strategic location on a caravan route made it a commercial center. In John's day, Thyatira had more trade guilds than any other city in Asia Minor. Inscriptions in the ruins mention workers in textiles, wool, leather, pottery, and bronze. Each group had its own guild, like the silversmiths in Ephesus.[30]

The city was especially noted for its dyeing industry. Lydia, Paul's first convert in Philippi, was "a seller of purple" from Thyatira (Ac. 16:14). Purple was the color of kings and dignitaries. Purple dye, difficult to make and correspondingly expensive, may have been extracted from a certain kind of shellfish.[31] Ezekiel mentions the isles of Elishah and Syria as sources of purple (Eze. 27:7,16; cf. Ge 10:4-5). Purple, as a distinctive color, is mentioned a number of times in the Bible (cf. Lu. 16:19; Ex. 25:4; Jud. 8:26). Some scholars suggest that the dye was extracted from the madder root, growing in various select places in Asia.[32]

The beginning of Christianity in Thyatira is unknown, but it is quite likely that it was established by Paul or some of his associates. Paul had been martyred about 30 years before John wrote the letter to this church. Apparently the Thyatira church was a well-established congregation at that time. Few historians make reference to the city's pre-Christian religion. Harvey J. S. Blaney observes, "It contains no temple to the Roman emperor, but it did have a temple dedicated to Apollo, Tryimnaios and Artemis."[33]

The church at Thyatira was criticized because of its tolerance for false teachers. The members did have many good qualities such as "love," "service," "faith," "patience," and "zeal" (Re. 2:19), but Christ rebuked them for permitting Jezebel, a prominent and influential woman, to teach their people that conduct had nothing to do with their faith. She may have taught that "worship was a mere form" and was irrelevant to their actions. The influence

Trading
560
Arts and Crafts
224-264
Lydia
2220

Rich Apparel
1043

Paul
4309

False Teachers
2101

Evil
Associates
276-277

Punish-
ment
3047-3048

Jezebel
1893

Revelry
3408

Thyatira
3621

God's
Judgments
1966-1974

History of
Early
Church
4309g

Martyrdom
3487

of Jezebel was so great that the church adopted an attitude of tolerance (v. 20). She taught under the cloak of a prophetess and justified her conduct in the name of broad-mindedness (Re. 2:20-23).[34] The prophetess, warned by God, had refused to repent. "Now her punishment is announced (v. 22). She is to be cast on a bed of suffering and with her those who, misled by her influence, had tried to combine Christianity with paganism: Those who were her spiritual progeny were to perish by the plague."[35]

Adam Clarke suggested that "this bad woman [Jezebel] was the wife of the bishop of the church, and his criminality in suffering [permitting] her was therefore the greater." He pointed out that some manuscripts read "thy wife, Jezebel" instead of "that woman Jezebel" (Re. 2:20).[36] Henry H. Halley says that this false teacher "was called 'Jezebel' because, like Jezebel, the devilish wife of Ahab, who introduced the abominations of Astarte worship in Israel (1 K. 16), she was introducing the same vile practices into the Christian church."[37]

The trade guilds complicated the situation farther. In order to be employed it was necessary to belong to a guild, similar to modern day labor unions. "Eating food offered to idols" and licentious revelry were a part of the guild functions, "What was a Christian to do?" Both one's social and economic life depended on being a guild member.

When the English consul in Smyrna (now Izmir) visited the city of Thyatira in A.D. 1625, he found not more than ten Christians and the name of Thyatira was unknown. The consul reported seeing a small mosque which had been built on an old church foundation. Several times during the building operation, the minarets fell down, and consequently only a token mosque was built. George Wheeler explained that God brought judgment on the mosque because it was built upon the foundations of a church.

J. A. van Egmoat passed through Akhisar (Thyatira) in 1757 but makes no mention of a church. When Richard Chandler traveled the area in 1764, he found a Greek priest. In the eighteenth and nineteenth centuries, Greeks and Armenians settled in Akhisar. Chandler says, "the Greeks maintained one church—a wretchedly poor place below street level so that one had to walk down 5 steps to enter the church." In 1832 the Greeks built the cathedral of St. Nicholas. We are reminded that St. Nicholas—our Santa Claus—has his origin in Myra, Turkey, in the A.D. 300s; he was bishop of Myra. Tradition tells us that Nicholas went out at night and tossed bags of money into the homes of the poor people; subsequently he was called St. Nicholas.

Before World War I, 23,950 people lived in Akhisar (Thyatira); 11,000 Turks, 12,000 Greeks, 800 Armenians, and 150 Jews. In 1922 the Turkish troops occupied Akhisar (Thyatira). An estimated 7000 Christians were killed. There have been few Christians in Akhisar since that time. Today Akhisar is a thriving Turkish town. Its 1973 population was 48,000 with few traces of a Christian community. The church of St. Nicholas has been converted into a movie theater. In the inner court of the Grand Mosque, immediately to the east of the building, are the foundations of a large apse of an early Byzantine church. Local tradition has it that the mosque was built on the site of the church of St. Basil.[38]

As for archaeological interests, the focal point in Thyatira (Akhisar) is a ruined ancient church, built on the foundations of an earlier one. A casual stroll up and down the streets of this city reveals antiquity evident everywhere. Many of the ancient marble carvings, as well as pillars and stones of the ancient city have become building material for the modern city. Capitals of columns are now horse troughs and well tops. Ancient marble columns support some roofs. Stones once in buildings are now used for paving streets.

3:1 And unto the angel of the church in Sardis write...

The ancient city of Sardis (now Sart) was located about 35 miles southeast of Thyatira on the slopes of Mount Tmolus, 1,500 feet high. It overlooked the Hermos River valley (now Gediz). The Pactolus River flowed along the western edge, which in ancient times provided a protective moat. On the eastern flank of the city was the acropolis fort.	Sardis **3147, 4431**
Approaching Sardis, the capital of Lydia, one can see on the horizon massive marble pillars of the Cybel-Artemis temple. On the outer edge of the town flows the Pactolus river, a tributary of the Gediz.	
In contrast to Thyatira, an abundance of historical information is available concerning Sardis. Its history was a rather bloody one. In 700 B.C. King Candaules was assassinated by his favorite palace guard, Gyges, over an incident involving the king's boast about the queen's beauty. Gyges became king, even though the citizens took up arms in the cause of their assassinated king despite the fact that the Delphic oracle spoke in Gyges' favor.	Thyatira **3621**
In about 556 B.C. Croesus, the great king of Lydia, ushered in the Golden Age of Sardis. The wealth he gathered from his gold mines and trade with other countries made the name Croesus a synonym for fabulous wealth, and gave rise to the proverbial expression "as rich as Croesus." He is said to have offered generous contributions for the rebuilding of the Artemisium in Ephesus and to the Greek oracular shrines, especially the one at Delphi, whom he frequently consulted for advice.[39] The great wealth of the nation, along with its "impregnable" outer defense, fostered a false sense of security. The steep rocky fortress was unguarded; and while the soldiers slept at their posts, King Cyrus of Persia and his soldiers scaled the fortress walls and captured the city (546 B.C.). Herodotus describes the attack: "On the fourteenth day of the siege, Cyrus made a proclamation that he would give a reward to the man who should first mount the wall. After this he made an assault but without success...One Hyroeades resolved to approach the citadel and attempt it at a place where no guards were ever set. On this side the rock was so precipitous, and the citadel so impregnable, that no fear was entertained of its being entered at this place...He climbed the rock himself, and other Persians followed until a large number had mounted to the top; thus Sardis was taken."[40]	Riches **2805-2811** Idolatrous Temples **3949** Riches Perilous **2806** Cyrus, King of Persia **907**
In 334 B.C. Sardis surrendered to Alexander the Great, but soon after his death Sardis became a part of the Seleucid Kingdom. Rome gained control of Sardis in 190 B.C. at the battle of Magnesia.	
In A.D. 17 a devastating earthquake destroyed the city, but it was soon rebuilt. "Sardis became an administrative center for Roman-Asia and when, in A.D. 26, the cities of the province contended for the honor of building the second temple for the Caesar-cult, the envoys spoke long and eloquently about the past glory of the place."[41]	Earthquakes **1091** Caesar **611-614**
As with Thyatira, reliable information for the founding of Christianity in Sardis is lacking. It seems probable that Paul and his missionary associates should receive the credit. One may assume that the church of Sardis was	History of Early Church **4309g**

Above: The capital of this column suggests the immensity of the Artemis temple.

Below: The massive marble pillars of the Cybel-Artemis temple at Sardis.

founded in the middle of the first century. According to Menologion, Clement, a disciple of St. Paul (Ph. 4:3), was the first bishop of Sardis. As this city had flourished and then decayed, so the church there prospered and then declined. The letters to Sardis and Ephesus were strikingly similar though the spiritual degeneration was more severe at Sardis. Little is recorded about who the church officials were in Sardis during the first century, but documents show that Meliton was bishop of Sardis in the second century. He wrote the emperor Marcus Aurelius in defense of the Christians' faith. He is the first Christian theologian to provide a list of the OT canonical books.

Sardis was represented at the Council of Nicaea in 325 by Bishop Artemidorus. In 400 the Goths plundered Sardis. In 449 Florentius of Sardis sided with the Monophysite Alexandrian party at the infamous Robber Council of Ephesus. Sardis ranked sixth in the hierarchy of the Orthodox dioceses. By the seventh century it had 27 suffragans (high subordinate church officials under a metropolitan). Sardis became the center of numerous heretical controversies and political intrigues.

The Christian community deteriorated rapidly after the Turks occupied the city in the fourteenth century. In 1346 Sardis was still the See (authoritative seat) of the Metropolitan, but by 1369 the city did not have one high church official. The ecclesiastical affairs were transferred to Philadelphia.

In the first years of the fifteenth century, Tamerlane occupied Sardis and massacred the population as he had in Ephesus, Magnesia, Pergamos, and Philadelphia. Sardis became an abandoned city, but the nearby village of Sart struggled on.

The location of Sardis was never forgotten. In 1670 Jean-Baptiste Tavernier lodged in the park in Sart. He recognized three geographical landmarks familiar to ancient literature and realized he was in Sardis. He made few comments on what he saw. In 1671 Thomas Smith came to Sart and described it as a "beggarly and pitiful village." He alluded to a Christian church with several curious pillars of polished marble at the entrance which had been converted into a mosque. The few Christians who lived there had neither a church nor a priest. In 1698 Edmund Chishull reached the site; his account provides a clear description of the ruins of the great temple of Artemis. Sir Paul Lucas passed through Sardis in 1714, commenting only briefly on the vastness and beauty of the ruins and adding that the little village was called Sart.[42]

When Jesus addressed the Church at Sardis, it was living on its past glory. The believers were alive physically, but many of them were spiritually dead. The letter contains no commendations nor reproofs; it recognizes a faithful remnant, but these show a laxity and a carelessness to the encroaching dangers of heathen philosophies (Re. 3:1).

William H. Ramsay, the historian, draws these conclusions: "It was a city whose history conspicuously and pre-eminently blazoned forth the uncertainty of human fortunes, the weakness of human strength and the shortness of the step which separates our confident might from the sudden and irreparable disaster. It was a city whose name was almost synonymous with pretensions unjustified, promises unfilled, appearance without reality, confidence which heralded ruin."[43]

The introductory exhortations in Revelation revolved around five strong words. They were: to be "watchful" (3:2)—to be alert and to guard

Origin and
Growth of
the English
Bible
4220

Philadel-
phia
2752

Sardis
3147, 4431

Spiritual
Death
2163

Sudden
Destruction
3182

against the subtle encroachment of "the sin which doth so easily beset" (He. 12:1); to "strengthen the things which remain" (Re. 3:2) by inner commitment, prayer and supplications (Ep. 6:18); to "remember" (Re. 3:3)—to be mindful not to trust in their own strength but to put on the spiritual weapons of war," the whole armour of God" (Ep. 6:11-18); to "hold fast" (Re. 3:3) the "profession of (their) faith" (He. 10:23), lest at any time they should let their first love slip away (He. 2:1b); and to "repent" (Re. 3:3)—have a contrite heart and sorrow for their sins (Ac. 22:16).

Watch-fulness 3785

The promise to those who had remained faithful included white raiment and the retention of their names in the book of life (Re. 3:4). Robert G. Gromacki says, "The believer-overcomer was promised a robe of divine righteousness, a guarantee of security and, a heavenly confession. Some identify this church with the Reformation period when individuals tried to strengthen the remaining good points of the Catholic Church."[44]

Weapons and Armor 361-363

White Raiment 53 Robe of Right-eousness 52

There was danger that history would repeat itself in a spiritual way. Prior civilizations had placed presumptuous confidence in their fortified walls (Babylon, Nineveh, Jerusalem); so now the church faced danger because of the people's over-confidence and their permissive attitude toward heathen sensuality.

False Trusts 3183-3186

3:7 To the angel of the church in Philadelphia write... (NIV)

The modern town of Alasehir stands on the ancient ruins of Philadelphia, the city of "brotherly love." It is situated on the Cogamus River at the base of Mount Tmolus, an ancient volcano, dubbed by the Turks as Devitt, meaning "ink wells."[45]

Philadel-phia 2752

Philadelphia. These are the remains of a once-great church, referred to as "Brotherly Love."

Philadelphia was one of the younger cities of Asia-Minor, founded by Attalus II Philadelphus, king of Pergamos. The king acquired the name Philadelphus because of his devotion to his brother, Eumenes — thus the descriptive phrase, "brotherly love."[46]

The city was an outpost of Greek culture, a showplace for Hellenism, on the Roman Post Road, the commercial artery between Rome and the East. In A.D. 17 violent earthquakes almost completely destroyed the city. E. M. Blaiklock reports that "the historian, Tacitus, listed Philadelphia third among the cities of the province that were recipients of earthquake relief from the Roman senate."[47] To acknowledge this generous help, the Philadelphians renamed their city Neo-Caesarea after Tiberias. Sometimes Philadelphia was called "Little Athens" because of the beautiful temples and public buildings which graced its boulevards.[48]

The soil around Philadelphia, enriched by the volcanic residue of ages past, is well suited for certain crops. The area was and still is known for its excellent wine and raisin grapes. In the center of the town, and symbolizing the grape industry, stands a ten-foot monument in the form of a hanging cluster of grapes. A secondary industry is the manufacture of licorice, made from the roots of an Old World perennial plant used medically and in confections.

The existence of a Christian church in Philadelphia is attested in Re. 3:7, but it is not known who founded the church or under what circumstances. As was the case in most cities of Asia Minor, many Jews lived there and had a synagogue. Sometimes the church developed in local synagogues or in homes. The church may have been a result of the witness of the Jews who represented their synagogue at the Feast of Pentecost when the Holy Spirit filled the worshipers in the Upper Room. It is also possible that Paul and his associates initiated a Christian movement among the Jews.

Of the seven churches in Asia Minor, Philadelphia, the city of "brotherly love," had the best Christian testimony. Christian persecutions in this community were not pressed by the heathen world but by the Jews who did not accept Jesus as the Messiah, or by those Jews who had renounced the faith, as defined in Ro. 2:28-29.[49] These unregenerate Jews were designated by Jesus as of the "synagogue of Satan" (Re. 3:9; see commentary at Re. 2:9).

Many attacks were made against Philadelphia in the twelfth century. The massive walled fortifications helped the city to withstand assaults by the Turks and the Sultan of Rum. When hostilities broke out between the Byzantine Empire and the Sultanate of Iconium, the Byzantine Emperor, Manuel I. Comenus (1443), had to take refuge in Philadelphia. The city remained a major center of feudal power even after Constantinople fell in 1204. Despite repeated attacks by the Turks, Philadelphia continued under Byzantine rule until the fourteenth century, when the Ottoman Turks conquered all of Asia Minor.

Following the devastation of Asia Minor by Tamerlane in the fifteenth century, most of the Christians fled to Venice. The Patriarch of Constantinople then sent Severus to Venice with the title of Metropolitan of Philadelphia.

In 1671 Thomas Smith visited Philadelphia and described it as a "city of great strength and beauty, having three strong walls toward the plain, a great part of the inner wall was standing though broken down in several places." Smith found that the great church of St. John had become a dump for the offal of slaughtered beasts by the decision of the Muslim Turks and that they had converted other churches to mosques. He found only four churches surviving. The roster of martyrs in Philadelphia carries the names of Demetrius and Hadji-George.

In 1785 Dr. James Griffiths reported seven or eight active churches in Alasehir. In 1826 the Greek bishop informed Rev. F. V. J. Arundell that the city had 3,000 Turkish families and 300 Greek families. He reported that of the twenty-five churches remaining only five were then in use. Arundell saw the ruins of the church of St. John consisting of "a high stone wall having the remains of a large arch on top." James Emerson visited the city three years later; he returned with high praise for the city "which still survives while her sister cities had crumbled into decay." The number of Christians, estimated between one and two thousand, were chiefly Turkish speaking.

Later travelers report seeing a portion of the wall believed to have been built by the Ottoman-Turks with the bones of the Christians who were massacred while they were worshiping in a nearby church dedicated to St. John. In 1860 A. S. Noroff listed the following five active churches: St. George, The Nativity of the Virgin, St. Theodore, St. Michael, and St. Marina.[50]

F. Bertram Clagg observes that,

> The Christianity of Philadelphia was of high character. This Missionary Church was neither vexed by heresy, nor shamed by heathen practices. Christ is described as "The Holy, par excellence," the true, the genuine Messiah, who has complete authority to admit or to exclude from the city of David. As the prophet (Is. 45:14) anticipated the submission of the Gentiles to Israel, so the Philadelphians are bidden to anticipate that these Jews—who have belied their name and its privileges—will submit to the church, the true Israel of God.[51]

Even though the church of "brotherly love" was small and socially unrecognized, Christ encouraged and assured them that the children of God do not depend on worldly prestige. They were told that persecution would be their lot, but they were also assured that Christ would deliver them from temptation (3:10). All who were faithful to the end would receive a new name by which they would be identified in the "New Jerusalem" (3:12; cf. 21:1ff.).

One of the first objects of antiquity to be observed as one approaches Philadelphia is the remains of the ancient wall. It is broken here and there, but there is enough to show its original fortress-like structure. The effects of the repeated earthquakes are evident in the segmented wall around the city.

The ruins of the once great Christian basilica, built of red brick and still retaining some of the frescoes, are in Ismet Pash Street. The basilica is enclosed with a three-foot-high brick wall. Inside are stumps of massive arches which once were part of a church building.

The Greek Orthodox Church has been active in Turkey for centuries, but with Turkish-Greek political hostility increasing, many of the Greek Orthodox Christians are moving to Greece. There are, however, still some active Christians in Philadelphia, but the number is uncertain. Based on American standards, the church exists at a very low level.

Martyrdom
3487

The
Church
726-761

Christianity
4139
Jesus the
Messiah
695

Children
of God
742
Perse-
verance
3441
New
Jerusalem
1886

Persecution
3480-3484

3:14 To the angel of the church in Laodicea write...(NIV)

The city of Laodicea was a thriving commercial center in the Lycos River valley at the juncture of three trade routes, of which the major one was the east-west highway. One of the spurs connected Laodicea with the Roman Post Road at Philadelphia. Laodicea is about 10 miles west of Colosse, 13 miles south of Hierapolis (see Col. 4:13), and 125 miles east of Ephesus. The ancient mound is now called Eski Hissar, meaning "old castle," probably so-called because of the ancient ruins protruding out of the mound. The modern city of Denizli is located a few miles south of the old ruins.

Laodicea was one of those towns in the Neolithic period (following the Old Stone Age) characterized by new sources of food supply and the development of pottery and weaving. Historical references begin with the ancient name of Diaspolis and Rhoas. The Hellenistic ruler, Antiochus II (261-246 B.C.) rebuilt and renamed the city after his sister-wife, Laodice. Josephus says that his successor, Antiochus III (223-187 B.C.) brought in Jewish settlers to Laodicea from Syria and Babylon (Jos. Ant. XII, 147-149). In his defense of Flocus, Cicero mentions that although the Jews of Asia were forbidden to send money to Jerusalem (pro Flacco, 28) they were guaranteed freedom of worship by the city magistrates (Jos. Ant. XIV, 241).

Evidence points quite definitely to Paul's involvement in establishing the church at Laodicea. It already had a Christian community when Paul wrote to the believers in Colosse (A.D. 60-64). In his letter Paul referred to Epaphras, who "hath a great zeal for you, and them that are in Laodicea, and them in Hierapolis" (Col. 4:12-13). Paul then referred to the "brethren which are in Laodicea, and Nymphas, and the church which is in his house" (Col. 4:5). Paul requested the Colossians to share their letter with "the church of the Laodiceans" and asked that "ye likewise read the epistle from Laodicea" (Col. 4:16).

This, of course, raises the question: What was this letter to the Laodiceans mentioned by Paul, and who wrote it? Since John is communicating the Revelation message from Jesus Christ over 30 years after Paul wrote the Colossian letter, it must have been an epistle which Paul or some of his associates wrote the Laodiceans. Some scholars suggest that this was actually the Ephesian letter. The reference to Laodicea in the epistle by Paul does show that there was a Christian community when he wrote the Colossian letter. This gives credence to the possibility that the Laodicean Church was a result of witness or effort of those who had come from the Jewish community at the Feast of Pentecost in Jerusalem (about A.D. 33) when the Pentecostal outpouring prophesied by Joel was fulfilled (Joel 2:28-32; cf. Ac. 2:16-21).

Both Laodicea, a commercial as well as an industrial city, and the church were affluent. The gold in the river sands, along with its commercial enterprises, made Laodicea the banking center of Asia. Other industries included the minting of gold and silver coins and a textile center which produced and embroidered cloth shipped to many parts of the Near East. It was especially known for its carpets and blankets, made from the black sheep thriving there, its medical school, and a factory for making drugs, especially an eye medicine called "Perygian Powder" for a disease known as "Ophthalmia." These enterprises made Laodicea an industrial center and brought to it the typical immorality of a commercial city. Its abundant wealth tended to make the Laodiceans self-sufficient, exemplified by their rebuilding the city without help from Rome when an earthquake destroyed Laodicea in A.D. 60.

The religious life of the part of the community that worshiped pagan gods revolved around the Temple of Zeus, where human beings were immortalized and the gods were "driven by human moods and passions, plotting against one another and taking sides in human conflicts."[52]

The wealth and worldly prestige of Laodicea led to an increased licentiousness and compromise on moral issues. Jesus' condemnation of the apostate church is direct and positive. What was true of the community was true of the church. F. Bertram Clagg gives this description of the church:

> There was money enough to support its enterprises: it was popular and well supported, for it did not set too high a standard of social and commercial life. Religious enthusiasm was characteristic of Phrygia, but Laodicea was a Greek city and was above that. The church adopted a spirit of accommodation and of broad toleration and was entirely self-satisfied. Proud of its prestige in the city, of its apostate tradition, of its generosity and wealth, it had "need of nothing" (3:17) in its own eyes.[53]

The church was half-hearted, having a "one foot in heaven" attitude which was not accepted by either God or the selfish world. In his *Divine Comedy*, "Dante, at the gate of Hell, hears 'sighs with lamentations and loud moans.' Virgil explains that this was the fate of 'those who lived without... praise or blame,' (Dante, Canto III)...these Laodiceans, neutral souls, were driven forth from heaven and the depth of hell does not receive them."[54]

Of interest is the reference to the lukewarmness of the Christians at Laodicea. They were neither "cold" nor "hot" but "lukewarm." (For an explanation of this analogy, see the essay on pp. 564-565.) Jesus rebuked the affluent and self-centered Laodiceans and counseled them to "buy of me gold tried in the fire." For those who would "repent," listen and "open the door" he would come in and "fellowship" with them. Sitting with Christ on his throne was to be their reward for overcoming (Re. 3:19-20). To each of the seven churches Christ's closing comment refers to overcoming (2:7,11,17, 26; 3:5,12,21).

The church at Laodicea suffered like the other churches of Asia Minor from the persecutions of the second and fourth centuries. In the latter part of the second century Sagaris, Bishop of Laodicea, was martyred and buried there. When Artemon, the Presbyter of Laodicea, destroyed the images in the temples of Diana and Apollo, he was arrested and would have suffered martyrdom had not Sisinius healed the Roman centurion, Patricius, who then embraced the Christian faith.

Bishop Eugenius is credited with building a large and beautiful church in Laodicea during the reign of Constantine the Great. St. Sisinius, Bishop of Laodicea, states that the church was located five "stadia" outside the walls.

Laodicea had representation at the Council of Nicaea in 325, which condemned the Arians as heretics. (The Arians took the theological position that the Son is not of the same substance as the Father but was created as an agent for creating the world.) In 367 the fourth Synod was held in Laodicea. It dealt with such matters as usury and the use of holy places by heretics. The Synod also ruled that priests should not perform marriages involving heretics, that the clergy should not enter taverns, and that beds should not be set up in churches. Other canons prohibited mixed bathing and marriages from taking place during Lent. Bishop Nunechius II of Laodicea participated in the "Robber Council" of Ephesus in 449 (see commentary on Re. 2:1).

Margin references:

Impurity
664-666

Worldly Fullness
2901

Self-confidence
3188

Half-heartedness
1088

Indifference
1083-1088

Overcomers
374

Persecution
3480-3484

Idolatrous Temples
3949

Heresy
1577

Usury
588

Work of Ministers
2087-2094

The city suffered intermittent defeats in the eleventh century and the early part of the twelfth. Late in the twelfth century the Christians built a new city, also called Laodicea, on the site of modern Denizli, for it is described as being located at the foot of a lofty mountain, which would be true of Denizli, but not of the old Laodicea.

In 1190 the German emperor passed through Laodicea on his way to Jerusalem on the third crusade. After that time the city steadily declined. In the late seventeenth century Rev. Thomas Smith reported this of Laodicea: "It was inhabited only by wolves, jackals and foxes." In 1764 Richard Chandler and his party were almost killed by robbers between Denizli and the ruins of Laodicea. The first ruin Chandler saw was the amphitheater, a hollow area

Laodicea
2050, 4404

The cross and other symbols found in this excavation at Laodicea indicates a former Christian church.

about 1,000 feet wide, with many seats remaining. At its western end he identified the vaulted passage as a stable "designed for horses and chariots." He visited the odeum with its remaining seats, and beyond he saw some marble arches standing, the ruins of a gymnasium. No trace of churches or mosques was visible.

The nineteenth century travelers, James Emerson and Charles Fellows, made a similar report: "No wretched outcast dwells in the midst of it. [Laodicea] has long been abandoned to the owl and the fox."[55]

Hierapolis. These magnificent columns were formed by the overflow of the hot mineral springs.

The Hot Springs of Hierapolis and the Lukewarmness of Laodicea

Laodicea had no water supply of its own; so water was piped through a stone conduit from the hot springs in nearby Hierapolis (modern Pamukkale in Western Turkey). By the time the water arrived in Laodicea it was indeed neither hot nor cold, merely lukewarm. Jesus knew about the hot springs at Hierapolis, which provided him with the imagery to describe the lack of spirituality and commitment of the Laodiceans (Re. 3:15-16).

**Laodicea
2050, 4404**

The mound or tell of Laodicea is located only a few miles from the inhabited town of Denizli. The first ruins coming into view from the south are some segments of the massive stone arches of the aqueduct which once carried water from the hot springs in Hierapolis (Pamukkale) to Laodicea. On a more level area the aqueduct funnels into a stone water-pipe about three-feet square with a twelve-inch hole drilled through the center. These stones were joined together with cement to make a continuous conduit. Much of the material in the now partially dismantled water system was used in the construction of buildings.

The hot springs at Pamukkale are one of the principal tourist attractions in Turkey. Several large pools invite the visitors to enjoy the 95-degree water, which contains calcium, carbonate, sulfur, chlorine, and traces of sodium, iron, and magnesium. In the depths of the spring one can see columns and column capitals of ancient Hierapolis. The mound rises about fifty feet above the terrain around it. Marble columns and stones of many shapes protrude from the surface.

Local peasants sow and harvest wheat and barley on the mound in the area between the ruins. A cross carved in a stone identifies one excavated building as a former church.

Two amphitheaters, both reasonably well preserved, are visible in the mound. The remains of a stadium and a colonnade are also exposed to view.

In the seventeenth century archaeologists discovered an area around the ancient city of Hierapolis with several kinds of hydro-pyrogenous emissions. One of the most significant discoveries was made near the amphitheatre built by Alexander the Great—an open mouthed cavern spewing steam, laden with deadly fumes.

The archaeologists in Turkey discovered that the area is riddled with underground streams flowing through beds of calcium carbonate which breaks down to form calcium bicarbonate and carbon dioxide. The carbon dioxide streams, under great underground pressure, reach temperatures of over 460 degrees F. When the hot solution reaches the cave adjacent to the Temple of Apollo its temperature drops to about 95 degrees F. The dissolved carbon dioxide comes out of solution and reverts to a gaseous state. When these deadly carbon dioxide fumes mix with hot water, a deadly vapor results. The cave becomes a death trap for man and beast.

Tradition tells us that the Apollo Temple priests eliminated their enemies by casting them into this murky cavern.

**Idolatrous Temples
3949**

This is evidenced by the many human bones scattered on the floor of the cave. It is referred to locally as the "Temple of Doom."

5:11 Then I looked and heard the voice of many angels... (NIV)

The word "angel" is derived from the Hebrew *Mal'akh* and the Greek *aggelos,* meaning messenger. Angels are mentioned 100 times in the OT and 193 times in the NT. The Scriptures define angels as supernaturally created beings, separated from the creation of man (Ps. 148:2-5; Col. 1:16), who enjoy God-given power (2 K. 19:35). Holy angels comprise "an innumerable com-

pany" (He. 12:22). Jesus makes reference to the legions of angels under his command (Mt. 26:53); their great number is further suggested in Re. 5:11.

The function of the angels is to serve God, to supervise men's activities, and to dispense divine grace and intelligence (Ex. 14:19; Da. 6:22; Ac. 12:7; He. 1:14). They are also commissioned to carry out God's decrees of judgment: death, pestilence, and military defeats (Ge. 19:15-26; Jud. 5:23; 2 K. 19:35; Ac. 12:23). These messengers are spirit beings who usually appear in quasi-anthropomorphic (human) form (Ac. 1:10; He. 1:14; 13:2) and are

usually visible only to those whom they address (Nu. 22:22; 1 Chr. 21:16).

In general, angels are holy and serve Christ or God, but there are some evil angels over whom Satan presides, who defy or challenge God's authority and who inflict harm upon the children of God because of God's temporarily permissive will (Jb. 1:6-12; 2:1-2; Is. 14:12-13). Apparently Satan was once called Lucifer and had heavenly status before he rebelled against God and was

cast out of heaven (Is. 14:12-19). In the book of Revelation Satan is referred to as the dragon, the leader of evil forces in battle against the divine army (Re. 12:7-9). Satan and his followers are represented as being consigned to eternal damnation in hell (2 Pe. 2:4).

As to the general designations given to angels, there are two exceptions. Reference is made to "the angel of the LORD" (Ge. 16:7; 21:17), and the "angel

of his presence" (Is. 63:9). As indicated in the essay on "Theophanies in the Old Testament" (see pp. 72-73), the "angel of the LORD" is not a created being but is the Creator himself—the very Son of God. This "angel of the LORD," considered to be Jesus Christ, was higher than the angels, but when he took on the human body he condescended to become a being "a little lower than the angels" (Ps. 8:5,6; He. 2:7-8). After his earthly humiliation he was exalted above the angels with "glory and honour" (He. 1:4,6; 2:7).

The Scripture refers to a hierarchy of angelic beings:

1. *Cherubim.* These creatures are mentioned 90 times in the OT and once in the NT. Cherubim appeared in Ezekiel's vision by the river Chebar in Babylon (Eze. 10:1-22). He describes these creatures as having wings, hands, and many eyes and being surrounded by spinning wheels (Eze. 10:8-12). These angelic beings once guarded the tree of life in the Garden (Ge. 3:24). Golden cherubim had a place in the tabernacle in the Wilderness (Ex. 25:18-20; 37:7-9) and also in Solomon's temple (1 K. 6:23-28; 8:7; 2 Chr 3:10-13; He. 9:5).

In the Apocalypse John makes reference to creatures similar in appearance to those described in Ezekiel's vision (Eze. 10:16; Re. 4:6). According to the figurative description in the latter reference, cherubim are assumed to have the intellect of man, the strength of an ox, the courage of a lion, and the free movement of an eagle.

2. *Seraphim*. These angelic beings appear twice in a worship service around the Lord's throne (Is. 6:2,6). They had three pairs of wings, which contributes to their unusual appearance (Is. 6:2,3,6).

3. *Beasts*. The term beast usually refers to members of the animal kingdom who have no divine worship instinct, but in Revelation the term is used in connection with heavenly beings who worship around the throne of God and are to be considered to be something more than common beasts of the field. The word beast in Re. 4:6-9 is used in a similar context as that of Isaiah and Ezekiel where they describe cherubim and seraphim (Is. 6:2-6; Eze. 10:1-22).

Both the Hebrew *chay* (Ge. 1:24) and the Greek *zoon* (Re. 4:6) can be translated "beast" or "living creature." Contextual consideration of the heavenly function of the "beasts" in Re. 4:6,9 indicates that "living creatures" or "living beings" would be the better translation.

The RSV renders *zoon* as "living creature' to distinguish it from a beast of the field. The term "clean and unclean" beasts in Ge. 7:2 comes from the Hebrew *behemoth*. The appearance of the creatures in Re. 4:6 may have influenced the "beast" translation.

4. *Holy Angels*. These are referred to frequently, especially at times of important events. They were the "morning stars" and "the sons of God" who shouted for joy at God's creation (Jb. 1:6a; 38:4-7); the angels were present at Jesus' birth (Lu. 2:13-14); they "ministered to him" on the Mount of Temptation (Mt. 4:11); they strengthened him during his agony in Gethsemane (Lu. 22:43); they were present at his resurrection and ascension (Jn. 20:12; Ac. 1:10-11); and they will form the vanguard at his Second Coming. These holy angels serve as "ministering spirits" for the redeemed (He. 1:14; Mt. 18:10; Ps. 34:7). They appear first in Ge. 16:7 and last at the twelve gates of pearl in the Apocalypse (Re. 21:12).

5. *The Angels of the Seven Churches*. A careful study of those passages in the Scriptures referring to angels (messengers), shows that the term does not always imply the same idea. At times the Scripture refers to a heavenly messenger, in others the word applies to man.

The supernatural is suggested in Da. 12:1, Ac. 12:7-10, and Re. 7:1-2. However, the word clearly applies to an ordinary messenger as referred to in 1 S. 11:2, also Lu. 9:52 and Jn. 2:25, to prophets in Is. 42:19, Hag. 1:13, Mal. 3:1a, and to priests in Ec. 5:6 and Mal. 2:7. Under the general sense of messenger, the term "angel" may be applied to Christ as the great angel or messenger of the covenant (Mal. 3:1b), to the ministers of his gospel (Mt. 11:10), the overseers (pastors) and members of his church (2 Co. 8:23).

In Revelation the Seven Angels (messengers) of the Seven Churches received seven letters. It is thought that the seven angels were men—probably the bishops or pastors who presided over these churches (Re. 2:1; 2:8; 2:12; 2:18; 3:1; 3:7; 3:14). The mystery of this figurative language is further intensified by identifying the seven angels with seven stars (Re. 1:20).

Identification of angels by name is limited to two: (1) Gabriel (Man of God) seems to be God's special delivery messenger in both the OT and NT (Da. 8:16; 9:21; Lu. 1:19, 26), (2) Michael (the Archangel who is like God)

Marginal references:

Topic	Reference
God's Throne	3418
Beasts	150
Animals	150-189
Heavenly Joy	4175
Angels Wait Upon Christ	145
God's Messengers	2074
Divine Messenger	694
Ministers	2083-2099
Gabriel	1377
Michael	2335

is referred to as a prince (Da. 10:13-21) and the only angel with the title "arch-angel" (Jude 9). Michael disputed with Satan over the body of Moses (Jude 9) and is mentioned as the commander-in-chief in the heavenly war (Re. 12:7). Michael appears to be first in rank among the angels of heaven and is perhaps the presiding angel in the court of heaven.

11:15 ...The kingdoms of this world are become the kingdoms of our Lord, and of his Christ; and he shall reign for ever and ever.

The central message of Jesus when he was on this earth was the kingdom of God. He announced its nearness (Mt. 3:2), the necessity of being born again to enter it (Jn. 3:3), and the urgency of facing the decision about it (Lu. 14:25-33). The term "kingdom" was also common in the old covenant, meaning "those who had faith in the Lord."[56] The book of Revelation is the grand finale of the theme of the Scriptures, that though there are those who "shall make war with the Lamb...the Lamb shall overcome them: for he is Lord of lords, and King of kings: and they that are with him are called, and chosen, and faithful" (Re. 17:14).

14:8 ...Babylon is fallen, that great city...

For pictures and commentary on the ancient city of Babylon, see pp. 250-251.

21:22 And I saw no temple therein: for the Lord God Almighty and the Lamb are the temple of it.

From the time of man's separation from God by sin, he has needed a place to meet God in worship. In early Genesis the altar was used. In Exodus the tabernacle was instituted by God. Later Solomon built the Temple for worship. When the nation of Israel was in exile synagogues were formed. And finally the Christian church developed (see the chart on pp. 400-403). This verse in Revelation indicates that when man is once again in the presence of God (as he was in creation) there will be no need of finding a place to seek the Lord's presence. God himself and the Lamb, Jesus Christ, will be the temple.

Preservation
of the Bible

What happened to the Sacred Scriptures from the time that they were written until now? What progression has there been in the preserving of God's Holy Word? This section will help the Bible student to understand how the Bible he holds in his hand today has developed through the years, and how its trustworthiness has been protected throughout varying political, social and cultural settings.

God's
Sure Word
430

The Early Languages of the Bible
The Old Testament Scriptures were written in Hebrew, the language of the Israelites before they were exiled from their homeland. When the Jews came back from Babylon they brought with them the Aramaic (Babylonian) language which became the vernacular in the area of Jerusalem. Holy men translated the Hebrew Bible into Aramaic for use by the Babylonian returnees. Thus we see the hand of God moving, keeping up with the need of mankind.

In about 330 B.C. Alexander the Great conquered the eastern part of the Mediterranean world and introduced the common Greek language which became the "Lingua Franca" of the Empire. Jews in the Dispersion and especially Egypt learned Greek but not Hebrew. By 250 B.C. the Hebrew language was no longer known—it was a dead language. Pressure was brought upon Ptolemy Philadelphus, king of Egypt, to authorize translating the Hebrew Bible into Greek. The great scholars of that day were assembled and out of their effort came the Septuagint, the Greek Old Testament. (For more on the Septuagint, see the Intertestamental Period, pp. 303-304.) This was another milestone to make God's Word available to all people.

Latin was the commercial language of Rome and the Roman Catholic Church. Many Latin versions of the Bible had been produced. Confusion reigned because no two were alike. A new linguistic star arose in the man Sophronius Eusebius Hieronymous, better known to us as Jerome from Dalmatia (Yugoslavia). He was one of the best Bible scholars and linguists of that time. His scholarship so impressed Pope Damascus that Jerome was asked to produce a translation of the Bible in Latin which could be used as a standard version in the church. He stayed in Rome until his New Testament was completed and then migrated to a Bethlehem monastery where he produced the Latin Old Testament 15 years later. This work became known as the Latin Vulgate. It was so superior in scholarship that it soon became the standard text in the Roman Catholic Church. Thus God's time table moved on to make a unified Bible available to the Latin-speaking world. God's Word stayed abreast of the time.

Origin and
Growth of
the English
Bible
4220

The Influence of Archaeology on Our Understanding of Biblical Hebrew

The careful work of archaeologists has done much to contribute to the understanding of the customs, culture and language of the people of Biblical times. Two of the most important archaeological discoveries that have contributed to the understanding of the ancient Biblical languages are the findings at Ras Shamra in 1929 and the discovery of the Dead Sea Scrolls in 1947. For more on the Dead Sea Scrolls, see pp. 306-308.

Credit for the discovery of the ancient Phoenician city Ras Shamra, Ugarit, a city on the coast of Syria, can be given to a Syrian farmer whose plow point penetrated an ancient tomb. Excavations have revealed a city whose history dates back to 6000 B.C., and it was found to be one of the main commercial, cultural and religious centers of its day.

In the excavations archaeologists found the oldest alphabet on record. One of the most important finds were the texts dealing with the Baal religion, the one religion which threatened the very survival of Israel as a monotheistic people.

Also among the many important discoveries here was a large number of tablets found in a library under the floor of a Baal temple. These tablets were written in Hurean, Egyptian, Hittite, Cypro-Minonian and a previously unknown Ugarit Semitic text dated from about the 15th to the 14th century B.C. Since these Ugarit epics contain many parallel passages in the

Above: Ras Shamra. This ancient well — uncovered and cleaned out by the archaeologists is still being used by local shepherds.

Right: The coastal gate to this ancient strong-hold of Pre Baal god. There are many parallels between the Ras Shamra writings and the Psalms.

Hebrew Bible, a number of the tablets have provided an excellent backdrop for a better understanding of the Biblical narratives and especially of the Psalms. These parallel passages do not mean that the Ugaritic texts are identical to Biblical record. The differences are much greater than the similarities and the mythological extravagance in these texts set them aside as inferior in quality.

However, these tablets along with the Dead Sea Scrolls have given scholars a new understanding of many Hebrew words, especially the many words in the Hebrew Psalms which are difficult to translate.

Preservation Throughout the Dark Ages

The collapse of the Roman Empire through internal strife and weakness and the invasion by barbaric tribes brought Roman and Greek culture to an end. A period of gloom and despair, called the Dark Ages or Medieval period, was ushered in.

During the Dark Ages (A.D. 476-1000) scarcely any Bible translation work was done. During this time civilization sank to a new low in western Europe. Academic work was limited mainly to a few cathedrals, monasteries, and palace schools. Knowledge of both ancient Hebrew and Greek almost completely disappeared. Few people went to school, and the few writers who remained had little sense of style. In this literary darkness, popular stories and rumors were accepted as true. With the growth of papal power the Bible fell into general disuse, being supplemented by decrees and dogmas of councils and popes.

Organized governments were dissolved and supplanted by myriads of feudal kings and petty political entities. It was an age of opportunism, when ambitious political leaders could find a weak spot in the existing structure and proclaim themselves the ruler. The Vikings, the Crusaders and the Cathedral leaders were all involved in this political fragmentation. Social ferment created a condition in which no one could trust anyone. Even popes and emperors were constantly on the alert to expand their holdings and enrich themselves by invading neighbor territories; they did not hesitate to use bribery, intrigue, and other underhanded ways of gaining their own ends. As a result of these highhanded maneuvers the common people became serfs and slaves.

In an age of such educational and political shortcomings, how did God's redemptive revelation move forward? How did the message of the Holy Scriptures touch the minds and hearts of people? While this literary darkness prevailed, it is significant that God's Holy Message was communicated in new ways. Consideration will be given to seven of these approaches. We must remember that in our modern day, when churches are readily available in every community, when all forms of mass media proclaim the message of the Gospel, and when the Bible is available in many versions and is affordable to all, these symbols and representations may have limited practical value. However, in a day when idolatry, mythology and illiteracy were dominant and the Bible message was locked up in "unknown languages," these means of grace greatly helped to preserve "the faith which was once delivered unto the saints" (Jude 3).

1. **Pilgrimages.** During this dark period most people lived in rural areas isolated from places where formal worship was practiced. The church leaders encouraged its people to go on pilgrimages to churches and Christian shrines where symbols and representations of the Gospel message could be studied. Here trained teachers explained the Bible events and their redemptive message through object lessons based on Bible people and events. Frequently whole feudal communities and villages united in what became a great religious, social and festive event and a respite from the dark and dreary everyday routine. It provided an opportunity for friends and relatives to socialize and at the same time to receive religious instruction.

2. Sculpture and Stained Glass Art. Two thousand years ago under Emperor Tiberias (contemporary with Pilate and Jesus) the people of the river area in what is today Paris, France, built an altar in honor of Jupiter on an island in the Seine. As Christianity spread, the church built shrines near heathen sites such as this one, and in the sixth and succeeding centuries three successive Christian churches were built on the former Jupiter site. In 1210 Philipe Augustus II authorized the completion of the present Notre Dame Cathedral, which had been begun in 1179, on this site.

The Notre Dame Cathedral is typical of other great cathedrals of this time, e.g., St. Mark's in Venice, Cologne Cathedral in Germany, Chartres of France and St. Paul's of London. They played a significant role in the transmission of the Biblical message, because they portrayed the story of the Bible in stone and wood sculpture as well as in stained glass. These tributes to God's Holy Word have ministered to people through many generations from the time they were built in the thirteenth century.

3. Steepled Churches and Their Bells. The crosses on the church steeples and the massive cathedrals rising above the skyline were silent witnesses to redeeming grace. The church steeples pointing toward heaven were constant reminders that this earthly sojourn is only an intermediate station on the pilgrimage to the heavenly city. There are instances in history when people were restrained from committing a crime after hearing the tolling of a church bell. According to tradition, when Armand Louis Couperin was a young man, on his way to rob a store, his mind was changed when the community church bell sent its invitational appeal across the valley. His life was redirected and later he became a great church organist. The inspirational influence of church bells is further evidenced by the Angelus bells which called people to pray four times each day. This is illustrated by Jean Francois Millet's painting, "The Angelus" in which a couple in a field stand in prayer. The church steeple in the distance suggests the occasion.

Prayer Enjoined **2817**

4. Sacred Chants and Other Church Music. Music in church liturgy has been an integral part of worship from the beginning. The Gregorian Chants (590-604) based on Scripture texts are classic examples and did much to lift the souls of men toward God. Worship has been greatly stimulated by such musical masters as Bach, Haydn, Beethoven and Schubert. Among the most significant religious compositions are Handel's *Messiah* and Mendelssohn's *Elijah*.

5. Monasteries. It has been said that during the godless Dark Ages the monasteries served as lightning rods to deflect the wrath of God. Through them, God communicated the Gospel message and provided a refuge for the faith. Despite the ecclesiastical suppression and abuse, the monks prayed, studied the Bible and copied and preserved valuable Bible and other religious manuscripts.

Divine Refuge **370**

The Codex Sinaiticus is a very important ancient manuscript that was preserved in Saint Catherine's Monastery at the foot of Mount Sinai. It is one of the most significant of the Biblical manuscripts and contains the entire NT plus most of the OT Septuagint. Codices Alexandrinus and Vaticanus were preserved under similar circumstances from the barbarian onslaught. Such monastic orders as Benedictine, Dominican and Cistercian provided protective refuge for Christian values and a depository for redemptive oracles. Here the idea of the dignity of honest toil and a holy life were preserved. Religious education and benevolence were made available to the needy.

6. Religious Paintings. It has been said that over half of the subjects in the average art museum are based on the Bible. The great works by Durer, El Greco, Rembrandt and Veronese still lift people's souls to God.

7. Religious Dramas. As the Dark Ages moved on into the Renaissance Period, religious drama began to come into focus. Miracle, mystery and morality plays began to appear in the churches. The devil, salvation and Bible doctrines such as the Seven Deadly Sins were acted out by the priests around the altar. As the plays expanded in scope they were put on in the transept and then in the nave and finally on the church steps where a larger audience could view these spiritual dramatizations.

The Early English Versions

English
Versions
4220

The Dark Ages began to abate gradually in about the 12th and 13th centuries. A Renaissance began to emerge, bringing upon the scene new interest in classical values. Illiteracy began to recede into the darkness out of which it came. Great scholars led the way to a new interest in education and mental stimulation. Translating the Bible from the ancient languages into the vernacular became the challenge of the new social order.

In addition, a major historical event that affected the transmission of the Biblical message was the invention of the printing press. In 1450 Johannes Gutenberg made clay molds in which to form lead type. His first printed book was a Latin Bible completed on August 15, 1456, which came to be known as the "Bible with 42 lines" because it had 42 lines on each page. The Gutenberg Bible is believed to be the first book of importance ever printed with movable type.

1. John Wycliffe (1320-1384). John Wycliffe, a teacher at Oxford, England, preached against the spiritual domination of the priesthood and the authority of the Pope, advocating the people's right to read the Bible in their own language. His followers were called Lollards. Unfortunately the common people had no Bible that they could read since the Scriptures were locked within the Latin, Greek, and Hebrew tongues, which very few people knew. Wycliffe, an outstanding doctor of theology and a master at Oxford, enjoyed great favor with the Pope. He was a learned man, conversant in all the Biblical languages and the theology of the Roman Church. He was sent on several missions to reconcile dissenters but became a dissenter himself through his association with John Gaunt. Wycliffe eventually came to see the inconsistency of the violent struggle between the Pope and clergy on one side, and the kings and nobles on the other. Both were corrupt and were dominated by self-interests.

Corrupt
Priests
2102

In about 1377, Pope Gregory sent several bills to the University of Oxford and to the Archbishop of Canterbury and the Bishop of London, in which he accused Wycliffe of teaching doctrines contrary to the church. The Pope ordered Wycliffe arrested and examined, but the political parties were reluctant to take action against Wycliffe because of the great popularity he enjoyed.

The conditions in Europe gave rise to many questions: Was the Pope lord over kings? Could a civil government punish a wicked bishop? Could the civil government tax the church? Did all laws have to be fair? Wycliffe concluded that "Dominion is found in grace." He applied his ideas to the popes and bishops and was brought to trial several times in church courts, but each time the English royal family saved him from condemnation.

The year 1378 was important in Wycliffe's life. He took a more aggressive stand against certain church abuses and began to question publicly the whole basis of sacerdotalism, or excessive reliance on the priesthood. He shifted his view toward the concept which Luther later expressed in regard to the Mass. Soon he made special appeals to the common people and presented Christianity as a personal faith in Christ rather than as a dogmatic system of the Roman Catholic Church. He began to send out "poor preachers" to the common people and to translate the Latin into the English of his day. Through his lay evangelists the Lollard movement gained great strength and importance. Faith
1201

However, after his death the Lollards suffered severe persecution. Wycliffe had been assisted in his Bible translation work by Nicholas of Hereford. The entire work was taken over and revised by John Purvey when Wycliffe died in 1384. Wycliffe's teachings were soon condemned by the Archbishop of Canterbury at Oxford. As a result many of his followers were excommunicated. Hostility against Wycliffe was so intense that in 1415 the Council of Constance ordered his body exhumed and burned and his ashes thrown into the river Swift.

It is evident that the writings of Wycliffe influenced and encouraged a number of reformers to continue his work. Many credit Wycliffe with being in the vanguard of the Reformation. It is certain that he helped the common people by translating the Bible into a language they could understand sufficiently to teach their children.

2. William Tyndale (1494-1536). William Tyndale was born on the Welsh border near Gloucester about 1494. He received his education at Oxford and taught in Cambridge from 1519 to 1522. A brilliant Greek and Hebrew scholar, he was heavily burdened to make the Bible available to the common people. When he became involved with the reformers, he lost favor with the established church authorities. Later, when the local political climate became too severe, he moved to London with the idea of translating the Bible into English so that "every plow-boy might read it." After his request for help from the Bishop of London was denied, he moved to Hamburg, Germany, where he made contact with Martin Luther.

On May 27, 1524, he registered at the University of Thul and began his translation work. The printing of the Bible was started at Cologne in 1525, but it was stopped by Johann DaBeneck, a churchman who hated the Reformation. Tyndale then fled to Worms, where 6,000 copies of his Bible were printed. In 1525, copies were smuggled into England in grain sacks and various other cargo, but they were sought out and burned by Bishops Worsham and Tousta. Efforts were made to seize Tyndale, but he fled first to Marberg, and then to Antwerp in the Netherlands. Henry VIII tried to seize him for trial in England, but Tyndale escaped. However, he was captured in Antwerp in 1535 by officers of the Emperor and imprisoned at Vilivorde. Despite efforts by Thomas Cromwell to save him he was tried for heresy, condemned, degraded from holy orders, strangled, and his body burned. His last words were, "Lord, open the King of England's eyes." However, Tyndale's influence on England was outstanding and his lifestyle greatly influenced the renderings in the King James Version of the Bible (1611). He was martyred before he completely finished the OT. His work rested upon the ancient versions and the Latin Vulgate. Martyrs
3488

3. Miles Coverdale (1488-1568). Miles Coverdale, born in Yorkshire and educated at Cambridge, carried on the torch of Bible translation which Wycliffe had ignited. Later Coverdale became acquainted with Tyndale on the Continent. He was not as scholarly as Tyndale, but he had great initiative. His translation work depended heavily upon the Latin Vulgate and Luther's German Bible, but mostly upon Tyndale's English version. As a contributor to Bible translation, he was outstanding. He also helped to produce the Great Bible and edited the Coverdale Bible, which was published at Cologne and became the first complete English Bible in print.

In the theological turbulence in England and on the European continent, Coverdale dared to dedicate his 1535 edition to Henry VIII, the king who had tried to apprehend Tyndale. To the amazement of the scholarly world, Coverdale's Bible was given royal license by England.

4. The Matthews Bible, John Rogers (1500-1555). The Matthews Bible was published under a pseudonym, probably in fear of retribution. The author was actually John Rogers, a friend of Tyndale. His published work included the entire translation of Tyndale, for which Tyndale had been burned at the stake as a heretic the year before. Rogers had been educated at Cambridge and was Rector of Trinity and Lees in London. Later he served as a chaplain to the English merchants in Antwerp. Here he met William Tyndale, who influenced him to change his religious commitment. Rogers assumed the pastorate of a Protestant congregation in Wittenberg and prepared for the press the English rendering of the Bible, which included Tyndale's NT and the OT as far as 2 Chronicles.

Rogers' part in the actual translation was minimal, but his marginal notes formed the basis for an early commentary in English on the Scriptures. Three days after Queen Mary arrived in London, Rogers preached against Roman Catholicism. On January 27, 1554, he was imprisoned at Newgate on the insistence of the new Bishop of London. After two examinations he was burned at the stake at Smithfield. Despite the persecution under Mary, Bible translation continued, though not without surveillance and suspicion. Through an act of Parliament, unauthorized persons were forbidden to "read the Bible aloud in a public place. Private reading was forbidden by all artificers, journeymen, servicemen, yeomen, husbandmen and laborers."[1]

5. The Great Bible (1539). The Great Bible was based on the Matthews, the Coverdale, and the Tyndale Bibles. At the prompting of Archbishop Cranmer, Coverdale published the Great Bible without the controversial notes contained in the earlier editions. This Bible "for the use of the church" was the only Bible that could be lawfully used in England. Because of its unusual dimensions, the Bible was chained to the church pulpit where people congregated to hear the reading of God's Word. This Bible was called "great" because of its size and its exclusive use and place in the church.

6. The Geneva Bible (1560). In fifty years the Reformation had swept across Europe. This was a telling blow against the Roman Catholic Church. The Council of Trent (1545-63), in session for eighteen years, abolished some moral abuses of the papacy. However, through the "Counter Reformation" the Roman Church organized for an aggressive onslaught on Protestantism, and under the brilliant leadership of the Jesuits much of the lost territory was regained. During this period many of the Protestant leaders took refuge in Geneva, where the Bible was published in 1560. Based chiefly on

Tyndale's work and on the Great Bible, the new translation was named the Geneva Bible. Included in this version were many notes and annotations concerning those passages with strong Protestant implications. Therefore, it was highly distasteful to the established church in England but received popular support by the common people. Shakespeare used the Geneva Bible as did the Puritans of England as they went to the New World. John Bunyan drew heavily upon it in writing Pilgrim's Progress.

7. The Bishop's Bible (1568). When the Geneva Bible began to crowd out the Great Bible, Archbishop Parker of the Church of England set out to produce a Bible to take the place of the Great Bible. The Bishop's Bible was to be based upon the Great Bible, but actually it incorporated many elements of the Geneva Bible, which it was meant to replace. The Bishop's Bible was used extensively until 1611, when the Authorized Version (KJV) became the dominant version.

8. The Douay Bible (1582-1610). After Elizabeth I became Queen of England many Roman Catholics moved to Florence and Belgium. The English Roman Catholic refugees at the University of Douay in northern France felt a need for an English Bible approved by the Roman Catholic Church. This need resulted in the Rheims-Douay Bible, of which the NT was published at Rheims in 1582 and the OT at Douay in 1610. This version was made mainly from the Latin Vulgate with some slight helps from the Hebrew and Greek originals. The English style and diction were poor compared with some of the Protestant versions, especially in comparison with the King James Version, which appeared soon after the Rheims-Douay version was completed. Eleven books of the Apocrypha were added at the Council of Trent (1545- 63).

9. The King James or Authorized Version (1611). King James Stuart of Scotland and, after A.D. 1603, King of England, convened the Hampton Court Conference in an effort to reconcile the religious parties in his kingdom but failed to bring the Bishops and the Puritan Party together. However, the conference did take action which brought into being a version of the Bible destined to be used for hundreds of years. A resolution was passed at the suggestion of John Reynolds, a Puritan, that translation of the Bible be made from the original Hebrew and Greek into English with no marginal notes or comments. It was suggested that this version should become the state Bible, to be used exclusively in the public worship services of the Church of England. Not all of the conference members favored the move, but King James endorsed it, stating that none of the existing translations was accurate enough for a national Bible. The new version was to be produced by the best scholars in Oxford and Cambridge Universities, then to be reviewed by the Bishops of England and finally approved by the privy council and the king.

King James Version **4220**

Fifty of the greatest Biblical and linguistic scholars were assembled and instructed to divide up into six teams, two at Oxford, two at Cambridge, and two at Westminster, to work on assigned portions of the text. Afterward they were to meet together in one body for critical discussion and then again divide into committees to evaluate the recommendations submitted by the whole group. A final draft was then to be made for further critical examination by cross committees.

At that time the translators had at their disposal the best Hebrew and Greek texts available. The committee used the Tyndale, the Coverdale, and the Geneva versions as helps, and the translators' fidelity to the truth of the Scripture is remarkable. Many years later when the Revised Standard Version was completed, a spokesman for the translation committee stated: "It will be obvious to the careful reader that no doctrine of the Christian faith has been affected by the revision, for the simple reason that, out of the thousands of variant readings in the manuscripts, none has turned up thus far that requires a revision of Christian doctrine." (An Introduction to the Revised Standard Bible of the New Testament by members of the Revision Committee. Luther Weigel, Chairman, 1946.)

Many scholars are agreed that the KJV contains the most beautiful form of English the world has ever known, and that this translation lends itself to memorization. The KJV has been and still is precious to millions of people who have read, studied, memorized, and loved it for its simple, dignified, beautiful presentation of the Word of God.

Excavations at Ur.

10. The Revised Version (1881-1884). By the late nineteenth century almost 275 years had passed since the publication of the KJV. The work of the Biblical scholars since that time, plus the many recently discovered Bible manuscripts, generated a strong feeling within the Church of England that the Bible should be revised. This feeling was shared in America. At the request of the Church of England a group of church leaders convened to consider the matter. As a result fifty scholars from the leading Protestant denominations in the British Isles were brought together. Two committees were formed, one for the OT and the other for the NT. At the same time a committee of thirty Bible scholars was organized in America to collaborate with the English group. It was agreed that a minimum number of changes in the KJV would be made in order to be consistent with the original texts. The basis for the revision was to be the KJV; the alterations would be made only by a two-thirds vote of the main committee. When the American and British committees met to compare notes, their disagreements outweighed

their agreements. By mutual consent the British Revised Version was to be published with the use of a few suggestions from the American committee. These suggestions were to be placed in the appendix, but without the approval of the British as to their content. The American committee agreed not to publish its work until 1901.

11. The American Standard Version (1901). The American committee honored its agreement not to publish for 14 years. In 1901 the ASV came from the press. This version benefited not only from the scholarship of England but also from the added insights of the American scholars. Many of the differences between the two versions were related to "Britishisms" or terms which were not commonly used in America. In addition, the American committee used the term Jehovah instead of LORD as the translation for the Hebrew YHWH, the term Holy Spirit instead of Holy Ghost, and love instead of charity.

The ASV lacked some of the literary beauty of the KJV, but it excelled in accuracy and was based upon a superior Greek text. It has been widely used by scholars as a study Bible, but it has never enjoyed the popularity of the KJV.

English Versions of the Twentieth Century

English
Versions
4220

The preservation of God's Holy Word continues throughout modern day history. At no time has there been such availability of the Sacred Writings in so many versions and editions.

1. Moffatt's Translation (1924-1935). James Moffatt was an outstanding Bible scholar and linguist, but he affirmed that he had "found freedom from the theory of verbal inspiration." This freedom is reflected in passages of both the OT and NT, where doctrinal matters are given a liberal treatment. He incorporated the JEDP Documentary Hypothesis (see Introduction to Genesis, page 37) by italicizing certain portions of the OT text. His liberal bias is further seen in his reference to the Virgin Birth of Christ when he refers to Joseph as "the father of Jesus."

2. The Smith-Goodspeed Version (1923-1931). Edgar Goodspeed completed the translation of the NT in 1923; H. M. Powis Smith, the OT in 1927. The entire Bible was published in 1931. This is the forerunner of the *Bible in Modern English.* Some sections border on paraphrase.

3. The Revised Standard Version (1946-1952). The RSV is a revision of the KJV, 1611, the ERV and the ASV (1881-1885 and 1901). The literary style is similar to that of the KJV. The copyright is owned by the National Council of Churches and it is now used by several of the major Protestant denominations.

4. The Confraternity Version (1948). This is a Roman Catholic Version in Modern English based more on the Latin Vulgate than upon the Hebrew and Greek originals. It also contains the Apocrypha.

5. The Berkeley Version (1945-1959). In this version the NT was originally translated into modern English from the Greek by Gerrit Verkuyl. The OT section was the work of many scholars who carefully preserved the Messianic prophecies. The version contains numerous footnotes on difficult passages. In it the theological emphasis is evangelical, and the Scriptures are treated as the authoritative Word of God.

6. The New American Standard Bible (1960-1971). The NASB is a revision of the ASV supported by the best original Hebrew and Greek texts. This translation represents a ten-year project by leading scholars working in committee. The fourfold aim was (1) to be true to the original language, (2) to be grammatically correct, (3) to be understandable to the lay reader, and (4) to give the Lord Jesus Christ his proper place as accorded in the Word. The marginal cross references and the concordance make this version a useful Bible study tool.

7. The New English Bible (1961-1970). This is a completely new translation from the Hebrew and the Greek texts by leading British scholars from the old-line denominations. Its strong point is its pleasing style and format and its rendering of the Scripture texts into contemporary English. However, it reflects a definite liberal bias. For example, in Isaiah 7:14, the rendering inclines toward a failure to recognize the miraculous. *Almah* is translated "a young woman" whereas the KJV uses the word "virgin" (see Mt. 1:23).

Many of the expressions are "Britishisms" not familiar to the Western mind: e.g., "meal tub" in Mt. 5:15; "midge" in Mt. 23:24; "truckling to no man" in Mt. 22:16; and "who put me in the dock?" in 1 Co. 9:3. The cross is referred to as "gallows" in 1 Pe. 2:24 and as "gibbet" in Ac. 10:30. Some passages border on slang: e.g., "You can take it from me that every man…" (Ga. 5:3) and "they all left me in the lurch" (2 Ti. 4:16). Many of the terms are more philosophical than Biblical.

8. The Amplified Bible (1958-1965). The *AB* is a version in Modern English translated by a committee of qualified Hebrew and Greek scholars. The outstanding feature is the bracketed explanatory words and phrases following places where difficulty might arise. In addition, it contains footnotes to explain the more complicated passages. Thus one has the advantage of several translations in a single text. It is thoroughly orthodox and recognizes the Scriptures as the authoritative Word of God.

9. The Good News Bible (1966-1976). The *GNB* is also known as the *Bible in Today's English* and is published by the American Bible Society. It represents fifteen years of work by leading Hebrew and Greek Biblical scholars. The version claims to be "the most faithful translation possible in vibrant contemporary English," but it has its weak points, as do all other translations. In its attempt to simplify the English language, much of the richness of Biblical thought has been dissipated. Instead of "justify" the *GNB* has "put right"; "different tongues" is rendered "strange sounds." In referring to Christ, "blood" and "death" are frequently used interchangeably (Ep. 1:7; Ac. 20:28).

10. The Jerusalem Bible (1966). The *JB* is a Roman Catholic work produced originally in French by the Dominican Fathers in Jerusalem. The English version, which is the equivalent of the French *"La Bible de Jerusalem,"* was translated from the original Hebrew and Greek texts but supported strongly by the French version when matters of questionable interpretation arose. It is definitely in the direction of the JEDP Documentary Hypothesis (see the Introduction to Genesis, page 37), including the composite authorship of Isaiah and the date, 65 B.C., for Daniel. However, the Messianic prophecies are clearly noted and explained in the documentation.

11. The New International Version (1973-1978). This work was sponsored by the New York Bible Society, Inc., and was produced by over 100 Biblical scholars mainly from the United States, Great Britain, Canada, Australia, and New Zealand. These scholars represent over a dozen main-line denominations. The translation of each book was assigned to a team of scholars. Several committees checked and rechecked each book. From the very beginning the Committee on Bible Translation was concerned that their work would be an accurate translation, clear and scholarly. The translators were committed to "the authority and infallibility of the Bible as God's Word in written form." It is a balanced literary translation, true to the Word, and has been received with great enthusiasm.

12. The New King James Bible (1979-1982). This Bible has been produced by 119 scholars, editors and church leaders representing many denominations. All of its contributors believe in the plenary, verbal inspiration of the original autographs of the Bible.

The scholars made careful comparisons with the Hebrew, Aramaic and Greek texts. They state in the introduction that the NKJB seeks "to produce a revised English edition which will unlock the spiritual treasures found uniquely in the King James Version of the Holy Scriptures."

13. The Living Bible (1962-1971). This paraphrase should not be overlooked in a listing of new versions, though it is not a translation as those listed above. It is the work of Kenneth N. Taylor, who saw the need of a Bible in the simplest modern English. The *LB* has undeniable freshness and clarity that awakens interest. Many difficult passages are qualified by use of interpretive words. For instance, in describing the faith to which James makes reference in James 2:20, the word "real" is added to "faith." The *LB* is referred to as a paraphrase, and in this instance it is faithful to the Biblical doctrine: i.e., paraphrase is "to say something in different words than the author used" or a "restatement of the author's thoughts, using different words than he did." Mr. Taylor is committed to an authoritative, inerrant Bible, and in this undertaking he has made every effort to state as exactly as possible what the writers of Scripture meant. This work has been carefully checked by both Hebrew and Greek scholars and its reception by the Bible-reading public has been phenomenal.

14. New Testament Versions. In conclusion, a few of the modern translations that are limited to the New Testament follow:

a. *The New Testament in Modern Speech*, by R.F. Weymouth (1902).

b. *The Twentieth Century New Testament,* by Mary Higgs and Ernest Malan (1904).

c. *The New Testament in the Language of the People,* by C. S. Williams (1937).

d. *The New Testament in Modern English,* by J.B. Phillips (1958).

e. *The New Testament in the Language of Today,* by William F. Beck (1963).

The work of translation goes on. God's message has always survived and we can be assured that it always will. As Isaiah wrote so many years ago, "The grass withereth, the flower fadeth: but the word of our God shall stand forever" (Is. 40:8).

Dictionary

Aaron (Light). Son of Amran and Jochebed, elder brother of Moses and Miriam (Nu. 26:59). **1**

Ab or **Abba** (Father). An endearing term applied to God the Father by Jesus (Mk. 14:36). **1246-1247**

Abbadon (Destruction). Place of dead; grave. (Jb. 26:6; Ps. 88:11). See Apollyon (Re. 9:11). **1461**

Abarim (Regions beyond). Mountain peak from which Moses viewed promised land (Nu. 27:12). **2424**

Abiathar (Of plenty). Son of Ahimelech, succeeded father as high priest. He was befriended by David (1 S. 22:20-23). **5**

Abib (Green ear of corn). Memorial month for Israel's deliverance from Egypt (Ex. 13:3-4). It is the first month of the Hebrew year. **4451**

Abiezer (Of help). Eldest son of Gilead and descendant of Manasseh (Jos. 17:1-2). **2244-2245**

Abigail (Of exaltation). Wife of Nabal. She befriended David. Upon death of her husband, she married David (1 S. 25:14,38,42). **6**

Abihu (God is my father). Second son of Aaron by Elisheba (Ex. 6:23). **7**

Abijam (Father of Jehovah). Son and successor of King Rehoboam of Judah (1 K. 14:31). **8**

Abishalom or **Absalom** (Father of peace). Third son of King David (2 S. 3:3). **16, 4321**

Abner (Father of light). Son of Ner, the captain of Saul's host (1 S. 14:50). **12**

Abomination of Desolation A sign given by Jesus forshadowing the destruction of Jerusalem (cf. Da. 9:27; Mt. 24:15). **14**

Abram (A high father), or **Abraham** (Father of a great multitude). The father of the Hebrew nation (Ge. 11:26). The change from Abram to Abraham denotes a higher exaltation. **15, 4290, 4306c**

16, 4321   **Absalom** (Father of Peace). Third son of David by Maacha. Rebelled against father. In his effort to escape, his long hair caught in tree limbs and was killed by Joab (2 S. 18:14).

28   **Achan** (Troubler). An Israelite from the tribe of Judah, who created trouble by taking treasure out of Jericho. He was stoned for his sin (Jos. 7:1-26).

29   **Achish** (Angry). Son of Maoch and King of Gath. Befriended David during Saul's persecution (1 S. 21:10-15).

30   **Achor** (Trouble). The valley near Jericho where Achan was stoned (Jos. 7:24-25).

4266   **Acts of the Apostles** The fifth New Testament book, written by Luke, giving an account of the apostles' work after Jesus ascended into heaven.

34   **Adam** (Red). The name given in Scripture to the first man. "Red" probably refers to the color of the ground out of which he was created (Ge. 2:19).

4451   **Adar** or **Addar** (Greatness). A town in southern Judah (Jos. 15:3); also the twelfth month of the Jewish calendar (Ezr. 6:15; Est. 3:7,13; 9:15).

1805   **Adbeel** (Miracle of God). A tribe descended from Ishmael (Ge. 25:13; 1 Chr. 1:29).

42   **Adonijah** (Jehovah is my Lord). The fourth son of David by Haggith (2 S. 3:4).

1199   **Adonikam** (The Lord arises). A prominent Jewish leader returning from Babylon with Zerubbabel and Ezra (Ezr. 2:1,13).

3934-3941   **Adrammelech** (King of fire). A deity to whom the people in Samaria burned their children in the fire (2 K. 17:31).

1662,1814   **Adultery** A term used for every type of unchastity—sexual or religious. Adultery is forbidden in the Ten Commandments (De. 5:18). Worshiping the idols was called spiritual adultery (Je. 3:9; Eze. 23:36ff.).

102   **Ahab** (Uncle). Son of Omri; seventh king of Israel (919-886 B.C.). His wife was Jezebel. He built a temple to Baal (1 K. 16:29-32) and persecuted Elijah (1 K. 17:1-3).

1152   **Ahasuerus** (King). Name of one Median and two Persian kings. Father of Darius (Da. 9:1).

103   **Ahaz** (Possessor). Son of Jotham. Seventh king of Judah; reigned 741-726 B.C. (Is. 7:1; 2 K. 23:12).

104-105   **Ahaziah** (Whom Jehovah upholds). Son of Ahab and Jezebel. Eighth king of Israel; reigned 896-895 B.C. (1 K. 22:51).

108   **Ahimelech** (Brother of the King). Son of Ahitub (1 S. 21:1ff.). The high priest of Nob in the days of Saul.

113   **Alabaster** A marble type of stone used for vessels, jars and jewelry boxes. Mentioned only in the NT (Mt. 26:7).

Alexandria The capital of Egypt founded by Alexander the Great (Ac. 18:24).　114, 4327

Alleluia or **Hallelujah** (Hele). Both mean "Praise be the Lord"(Re. 19:1-6). Alleluia is the expression used in the NT.　1451

Aloes A costly sweet-smelling wood (Ps. 45:8).　3668

Alpha The first letter of the Greek alphabet. Christ expressed his eternity by referring to himself as the Alpha (first) and Omega (last) (Re. 1:8,11).　119

Altar of Burnt Offering (Brazen). Originated in the Tabernacle. It was made of shittim wood and overlaid with brass. A larger model was used in Solomon's Temple (1 K. 8:64).　122

Altar of Incense Also called the "golden altar." The smoke arising from the burning incense symbolized prayer arising to God (Ex. 30:1).　123

Amen Used as an affirmative expression. Literally means "true" and "truth" (1 K. 1:36; Ne. 8:6; Is. 65:16).　128

Ammon (Son of my people). Descended from Ben-ammi, the son of Lot by his younger daughter. Hatred existed between Ammonites and Israel (Ge. 19:38).　129

Amos (Burden). A southern prophet who ministered in the northern kingdom with Hosea about 890 B.C. (Am. 1:1).　132

Amram (Prophecy of the highest). A Levite from the Kohathite family and father of Moses, Aaron and Miriam (Ex. 6:18-20).　4307

Amulets Ornaments, gems or scrolls worn as a safeguard against sorcery, sometimes inscribed with mystical symbols (Ge. 35:4; Is. 3:20).　2230

Anak or **Anakim** (Long necked). A race of giants, descendants of Arba. Goliath was probably one of them (Jos. 15:13).　1410

Ananias Gr. form of *Hananiah*. 1. A high priest (Ac. 23:2-5; 24:1-2). 2. A disciple at Jerusalem, husband of Sapphira. They were stricken because they lied about the sale of their property (Ac. 5:1-11). 3. A Christian in Damascus who healed Paul (Ac. 9:10-18).　135-137

Anathema (Something accursed). As used in the NT, it means a person devoted to destruction (Ro. 9:3; 1 Co. 12:3; 16:22).　1744

Andrew One of the first of the called apostles. He lived in Bethsaida and had been a disciple of John the Baptist (Mt. 10:2).　140

Anna (Grace). A prophetess in Jerusalem when Jesus was presented in the Temple (Lu. 2:36).　4300a

Annas Gr. form of *Hanniah* (Heb.). A high priest in Jerusalem in 7 A.D. (Lu. 3:2).　190

Apollos or **Apollodoris** An eloquent Bible teacher from Alexandria (Ac. 18:24-25).　200-201

Apollyon (One that exterminates). An angel of destruction or the "angel of the bottomless pit" (Re. 9:11).　146

2080-2082　　　**Apostle** (One sent forth). This is the general name of the original twelve disciples (Mt. 10:2-4). It was sometimes used to include other Christians.

208　　　**Aquila** (An eagle). Paul found Aquila and his wife Priscilla in Corinth. They were tent makers who had been expelled from Rome because of their religious faith (Ac. 18:2ff).

1474　　　**Arab** (Ambush). Descendant of the union between Abraham and Hagar, Sarah's maid. Most Arabs are Muslims and live in the Near East. See Jos. 15:52; Ne. 2:19.

2425　　　**Ararat** A mountain 16,946 feet high in eastern Asia Minor (now Turkey) on which Noah's ark came to rest (Ge. 8:4).

211　　　**Archangel** (The chief angel). The angel Michael is called an archangel, or chief angel who is like God. Michael was considered the patron of the Jews (Da. 10:13-21; Jude 9).

213　　　**Aristarchus** (Best ruling). One of the missionaries from Thessalonica who accompanied Paul on several missionary journeys (Ac. 20:4).

216　　　**Ark of the Covenant** The first piece of furniture built for the Tabernacle at Sinai (Ex. 25). It was the depository for the tablets of the Law, Aaron's rod that budded and a pot of manna—all testimonials to God's providential care (Ex. 25:10-22).

2283　　　**Armageddon** (Heights of Megiddo). Megiddo is the prophetic battlefield where the battle of Armageddon is to be fought (Re. 16:16). Scripture cites many battles fought in this area (2 K. 9:27; 23:29; Zec. 12:11).

1199　　　**Artaxerxes** (Honored King). A Persian king. After some hesitation, he finally permitted the Jews to rebuild Jerusalem (Ezr. 4:7; 6:14). In 458 B.C. he allowed Ezra to return to Jerusalem (Ezr. 7:1,11,12,23).

265　　　**Asa** (Physician). Son of Obijah. The third king of Judah (956-916 B.C.). He restored worship in the Temple which idolatrous priests had desecrated (2 Chr. 15:8).

268　　　**Ashdod** or **Azotus** (A strong place). A strong city in southern Judah (Jos. 15:47) where the captured ark caused the idol of Dagon to crumble (1 S. 5:1-6). Philip the evangelist preached here (Ac. 8:40).

3935　　　**Ashtoreth** (She who enriches). The goddess of the Phoenicians called Ishtar by the Assyrians and Ashtarte by the Greeks (1 K. 11:5).

299　　　**Assyria** (The gracious one). A strong military nation on the Tigris River (Ge. 2:14). Nineveh was the capital (Ge. 10:11).

302　　　**Athaliah** (Whom Jehovah made). Daughter of Ahab and Jezebel. She introduced Baal worship in the southern kingdom and was slain by order of the high priest (2 Chr. 23:12-15).

303, 4336　　　**Athens** Seat of learning and civilization during the golden age of Greece. Here Paul matched his intellectual skill with the philosophers on Mars Hill (Ac. 17:14-34).

304-305　　　**Atonement, Day of** The day of national Jewish humiliation commanded by Mosaic law (Le. 23:26-32).

Augustus Caesar (Venerable). First Roman emperor (63 B.C.) (Lu. 2:1). | 611

Baal (Lord, Master). A prominent nature god in the Near Eastern area. The Baal gods were thought to have influence on productivity—human, animal and soil. Its conflict with Jehovah worship came to a head when Elijah contested the Baal priests on Mount Carmel (1 K. 16:31-32; 18:17-40). | 3936 / 102, 1893

Baanah A Benjamite, who with his brother murdered Ish-bosheth. They were both executed by David and their bodies were hung over the pools of Hebron (2 S. 4:2-12). | 1804

Babel (Tower of Confusion). When the people in Shinar tried to erect a tower into heaven, God's displeasure was expressed by confusing their common language (Ge. 11:4-9). | 328

Babylon (Gr. form of *Babel*). The capital of Babylonia. It reached its zenith under Nebuchadnezzar who conquered Judah and took the Jews into a 70-year captivity. The tower of Babel was built nearby on the Shinar plain. | 329-331, 4338

Balaam (Destruction). When the Israelites were passing through Moab, King Balak sent for the prophet Balaam to place a curse on Israel. Jehovah restrained the prophet so that his prophetic office was confused (Nu. 22-24). | 333

Balak or **Balac** (To make empty). The king of Moab who hired Balaam to curse the Israelites (Nu. 22-24). | 334

Baptism The initiatory rite ordained by Christ (Mt. 28:19). It was a water rite expressing an inner work of grace. Jesus was baptized by John, the Baptist. At Pentecost, Christ baptized believers with the Holy Ghost (Mt. 3:1-12; Ac. 2). | 756-760

Barabbas (Son of Abba, or son of the father) (Frequently used). A murderer in prison when Jesus was tried. When Pilate offered to release Barabbas or Jesus, the crowd chose Barabbas (Mt. 27:16-26). | 339

Barak (Lightning). An Israelite who at the command of Deborah the prophetess, gathered 10,000 men of Naphtali and Zebulun, routed Sisera and destroyed his army (Jud. 4:1-24; He. 11:32). | 340

Barbarian By Greek definition, everyone but a Greek was a barbarian (Ac. 28:2-4; 1 Co. 14:11). | 341

Barley A wheat-like grain grown in Palestine for baking bread; especially among the poor (2 K. 4:42; Jn. 6:9-13). It was frequently mixed with wheat, beans, lentils and millet (Eze. 4:9). | 74

Barnabas (Son of prophecy). An early disciple of Christ. In Jerusalem, he introduced the newly converted Paul to the disciples. He was a faithful co-laborer with Paul (Ac. 4:36). | 342

Bartholomew (Son of Talmai). One of the twelve apostles of Christ; also called Nathanael (Mt. 10:3; Mk. 3:18). | 344

Bartimaeus (Son of Timai). A blind beggar on the Jericho road healed by Jesus (Mk. 10:46-52). | 345

354 **Bathsheba** (Daughter of the oath). The wife of Uriah the Hittite with whom David had an adulterous relationship. In order to cover his sin, David sent Uriah to the battle front to be killed in action (2 S. 11ff.).

387 **Beelzebub** or **Baalzebub** (Prince of demons). A heathen deity to whom the Jews ascribed evil spirits (Mt. 10:25; 12:24).

388, 4339 **Beersheba** (Well of seven). The ancient capital in the Negev Desert. Once a camel auction crossroad, it is now a modern city. Ancient home of Abraham (Ge. 28:10).

Bel See **Baal.**

393 **Belshazzar** (Bel protects). The last king of Babylon, slain in the banquet hall as the Persian king Cyrus marched into Babylon (Da. 5:2).

394 **Benaiah** (Whom Jehovah has built). 1. Captain in David's body guard (2 S. 8:18; 23:30). 2. Commander-in-chief of Solomon's army (1 K. 1:36). 3. A priest (1 Chr. 15:18,24). 4. A Levite (2 Chr. 20:14; 31:13).

398-400 **Ben-hadad** (Son of Hadad). A kingly family in Damascus (1 K. 15:18-21; 20:1-4).

401 **Benjamin** (Son of the right hand, fortune). Jacob's youngest son by Rachel (Ge. 35:16-20).

402 **Berea** A city in Macedonia which Paul visited as a missionary (Ac. 17:10-14).

403-409 **Beth** (House). A Hebrew word for "house" frequently used as a prefix; e.g., Bethlehem = house of bread; Bethgader = house of the wall; Bethboglah = the house of the partridge.

404, 4341 **Bethany** (House of dates). A village on the eastern slope of the Mount of Olives. The home of Mary, Martha and Lazarus (Mk. 11:1; Lu. 19:29).

406, 4342 **Bethel** (House of God). A religious shrine where people sought counsel of God (Jud. 20:18,26). The Ark of the Covenant rested here for a season (Jud. 20:26-28; Ge. 28:19).

4343 **Bethesda** (House of Mercy). A reservoir or water cistern in Jerusalem with five porches (Jn. 5:2).

408, 4344 **Bethlehem** (House of bread). A village a few miles south of Jerusalem where David lived. Jesus was born here (Lu. 2:4).

409 **Bethpeor** (Temple of poor). A town east of Jordan dedicated to the god Baal. It was possessed by the tribe of Reuben (De. 4:46; Jos. 13:20).

410 **Bethphage** (House of unripe figs). A town on the Mount of Olives on the road to Jericho. It was close to Bethany (Mt. 21:1).

411, 4345 **Bethsaida** (House of fishing). A town in Galilee—the home of Andrew, Peter and Philip (Jn. 1:44).

632 **Beulah** (Married). The name which Israel shall assume when the land is married to God (Is. 62:4). A Christian hymn refers to Beulah land as heaven.

Bilhah (Modesty). Handmaid of Rachel and concubine of Jacob to whom she bore Dan and Naphtali (Ge. 30:3-8; 46:25). | 1665

Birthright Among the Jews the firstborn enjoyed the right of consecration, great dignity, a double portion and the family estate (De. 21:16-17) and right to royal succession (2 Chr. 21:3). | 1656

Bishop A church official synonymous with elder or presbyter (Ac. 20:17; Tit. 1:5,7; 1 Pe. 5:1-2). | 755

Blasphemy Signifies speaking evil of God (Ps. 74:18; Is. 52:5). This offense was punishable by stoning (Le. 24:11). | 473-479

Blood Revenge The Levitical law stipulated that revenge was not to extend beyond the immediate offender. The involuntary shedder of blood was permitted to enter a city of refuge for trial (Nu. 35:15-28; De. 19:4-10). | 771

Boaz (Fleetness). A wealthy kinsman to Elimelech, husband of Naomi. He married Ruth and redeemed the estate of her deceased husband Mahlon (Ru. 4:1ff). | 520

Brazen Serpent When the Israelites in the desert were bitten by serpents, Moses made a brazen serpent and hung it on a pole. They were told that if any man looked up by faith to the serpent he would be healed (Nu. 21:6-9). Jesus explained the serpent's spiritual significance (Jn. 3:14-15). | 535

Breastplate A square, woven pad made of blue, purple, scarlet and fine twined linen (Ex. 28:15). On it the twelve tribal stones were fastened, each with the engraving of its respective tribe name. Under it the "Urim" and "Thummin" were secured. | 540-541

Bricks Mud bricks were the most commonly-used building materials in ancient times. Bricks made with a straw binder strengthened their durability (Ge. 11:3; Ex. 1:14; Is. 65:3). | 545

Bulrush A water plant growing profusely along a river bank or in the marshy part of a lake. The stems of this plant were used for making baskets and small boats such as was made by Moses' mother in which to hide her baby (Ex. 2:3). | 553

Burial Sepulchres Dead bodies were placed in burial vaults. Sometimes a natural or man-made cave was used, while at other times a stone and plaster vault was built on top of the ground (Ge. 23:6; 2 Chr.16:14). | 936

Burnt Offering This offering was designed to help the Israelites express their undivided devotion to God by presenting their very best—an animal without spot or blemish (Nu. 19:2-5). The total consumption of the animal by fire symbolized the worshiper's total dedication to God. The spiritualization of the burnt offering is expressed in Ro.12:1-2. | 2626

Caesarea A city named after Augustus Caesar, located on the coastal road between Tyre and Egypt. It was Rome's Palestinian capital and the largest city in Palestine in Jesus' day. Pilate had his headquarters here. | 615, 4350

Caesarea Philippi This city, named after Philip the Tetrarch, is mentioned only in the first two Gospels (Mt. 16:13 and Mk. 8:27). | 616, 4351

617   **Caiaphas** (Depression). Joseph Caiaphas was high priest of the Jews under Tiberias (Mt. 26:3, 57; Jn. 11:49; Ac. 4:6) and was the son-in-law of Annas.

618   **Cain** (Possession). The eldest son of Adam and Eve. He was a farmer and had a fit of jealousy toward his brother Abel; when his offering was refused he murdered his brother (Ge. 4:16-17).

638   **Calamus** (Greek, reed or cane). An aromatic, sweet-smelling weed growing in Egypt, Judea and Syria (Song 4:14). It was used in making anointing oil (Ex. 30:23) and to make sacrifices (Eze. 27:19).

3942   **Calf** The calf had significance in both idol and Jehovah worship. It became an idol at Mount Sinai (Ex. 34:4). It was related to the Apis Bull cult in Egypt. Jeroboam instituted calf worship in the Northern Kingdom, Israel (1 K. 12:28).

623, 4353   **Calvary** (Skull). The place where Jesus was crucified (Mt. 27:33). It is also called "Golgotha" (Heb.). Two places in Jerusalem compete for the site: Gordon's Calvary, outside the present wall and the Church of the Holy Sepulchre, inside the wall.

624, 4354   **Cana of Galilee** (Place of reeds). The town where Jesus performed his first miracle at a wedding—changed water into wine (Jn. 2:1-11; 4:46).

624-632   **Canaan** (Low region). The fourth son of Ham (Ge. 10:6) and progenitor of the people west of the Jordan who were called Canaanites (1 Chr. 1:13).

637, 2168   **Candlestick** The seven-pronged candlestick was used in Jehovah worship. See Ex. 25:31-40; 2 Chr. 4:7. It is called the "Menorah" in modern Israel. Christ assumed light as his symbol (Jn. 8:12).

4244   **Canticles** ("Song of Songs"; "Song of Solomon"). Even though sensuous in tone and content, the book was canonized as Scripture and conveys the idea of marital purity.

641, 4355   **Capernaum** (City of consolation or of Nahum). A city on the northeast shore of the Sea of Galilee where Jesus and his disciples carried on much of their ministry (Mt. 9:1; Mk. 1:33). It had a synagogue where our Lord frequently taught (Jn. 6:59; Mk. 1:21).

2428   **Carmel** A mountain ridge about fifteen miles long, jutting into the Mediterranean Sea. This is where Elijah brought the Israelites to a decisive conclusion as to who they should worship—Jehovah or Baal (1 K. 18:38).

1996   **Cedron** or **Kidron** (Dark and turbid). This valley separates Mount Moriah from the Mount of Olives. The Garden of Gethsemane is located at the base of the Olivet Mount (Mt. 26:36ff.).

652   **Censer** A brass vessel fitted to receive burning coals on which ceremonial incense had been sprinkled (Lu. 1:9; Le. 16:12). Those in the Temple were gold (2 Chr. 4:22).

653   **Centurion** (The Latin "centum"—one hundred). A Roman officer who commanded one hundred men (Ac. 21:32; 22:26). Two are mentioned by name: Cornelius in Caesarea to whom Peter ministered (Ac. l0ff.), and Julius who conducted Paul to Rome (Ac. 27:1,3,43).

Chaldea The wide alluvial plain formed by the deposits of the Tigris and Euphrates Rivers. This was the Assyrian, Babylonian and Chaldean area (Je. 50:10; Eze. 1:3). | 329-331

Chamberlain The office of chamberlain was one of trust. He personally supervised the king's personal affairs. He attended to his food, clothing and travel arrangements (Est. 1:10,12,15). | 655

Chebar (Wicker basket or bird cage). A river in Chaldea on whose banks some of the Jewish captives were settled including the prophet Ezekiel (Eze. 3:15).

Cherub, Cherubim (Blessing). Symbolic figures embroidered on the veil for the Tabernacle (Ex. 26:31; 36:35). Solomon made two very large cherubims for the Temple (1 K. 6:23 ff.). | 671-673

Chinnereth or **Gennesaret** (Lyre or harp). A fresh water lake, fed by the Jordan river, in upper Galilee. In more recent years it has been known as the Sea of Galilee. | 1385

Chorazin, Bethsaida and Capernaum Jewish cities near the northern coast of Lake Galilee. Jesus condemned them for rejecting his message (Mt. 11:21-23). Archaeologists have uncovered the ruins of these cities in recent years. | 4345, 4355, 4357

Chronology In Biblical studies a term used to describe the technical and historical development of the Hebrew race. The descendants of Abraham are the only people in history who have kept their social identity from the time they were classified as an ethnic group (Mt. 1:1-17). | 3627

Church The church is composed of a body of individual believers with a common faith in Jesus Christ as Lord and Savior. The New Testament never refers to a church building or a denomination. | 726-752

Cilicia A province in southeast Asia Minor of which Tarsus, the hometown of Saul of Tarsus (Ac. 21:39), was the capital. | 763

Circumcision A Semitic rite by which believers were identified as members of the faith. In the New Testament the rite was changed to water baptism (Ge. 17:10, 21; Ex. 4:25; Col. 2:11). | 765-767

Cities of Refuge Cities to which people could flee after committing an involuntary crime, especially manslaughter, and be protected from an avenger until they could have a fair trial (Nu. 35:9-14; Ex. 21:13). | 771

Claudius The fourth Roman emperor. He reigned from 41 to 51 A.D. (Ac. 11:28). | 613

Cleopas One of the two disciples who encountered the resurrected Christ on the road to Emmaus (Lu. 24:18). | 777

Cloud, Pillar of The pillar of cloud by day and of fire by night led the Hebrew children through the Sinai Wilderness (Nu. 12:5; Ex. 33:9). The cloud was a manifestation of God. | 2501

4358 **Colosse** A city of Phrygia in Asia Minor. It was located in the upper reaches of the Menderes River. Philemon and Onesimus were members of the Christian church in this city (Col. 4:9).

1665 **Concubine** A secondary wife taken from among purchased slaves or captives. This arrangement did not carry the stigma of mistress that is found in our society.

840, 4359 **Corinth** A commercial city in Greece known for immorality of every kind. To be called a "Corinthian" was a great insult. Paul labored here for about eighteen months.

841 **Cornelius** A Roman centurion (a Gentile) stationed at Caesarea, the Roman capital in Palestine. Apparently he was a devout believer and gave evidence that he practiced the Christian religion (Ac. 10:1-5).

692 **Cornerstone** A large stone set at an angle in a corner of a building to help bind two walls together. Tradition says that one of the stones the builders of Solomon's Temple rejected at first became the head of the corner. Quoting Ps. 118:22, Jesus drew an analogy, applying the cornerstone to himself (Mt. 21:42; Mk. 12:10; Lu. 20:17). See also Ac. 4:10-12.

2455 **Cornet** The "shophar" is a loud sounding musical instrument made out of a ram's horn. It was used by the Hebrews to announce the advent of the great Festivals and to warn when an enemy approached (Eze. 33:3,7).

889 **Crete** An island southeast of Greece, which at one time served as her administrative capital. As a superintendent of Crete, Titus was instrumental in winning many converts to Christ (Tit. 1:5; 2 Co. 2:13; 7:6ff; 8:6-16).

891 **Cross** The cross was made of two heavy timbers fastened together in the form of a "T" or an "X." It was an emblem of shame on which criminals were nailed and left to die. (See Mt. 10:38; 16:24; 27:32.)

894-895 **Crown** A head-dress, ususally made of precious metal and stones to symbolize a royal or priestly distinction (Ex. 28:36-38). It also symbolized power, honor and eternal life (1 Pe. 5:4).

3495, 3504 **Crucifixion** An ignominious and disgraceful type of criminal execution in which the body was nailed or fastened to a cross. If the criminal was not dead by sundown the main artery in the leg was cut or his legs were broken so he would quickly bleed to death. Jesus was already dead when the soldiers came to break his legs.

609 **Cupbearer** An officer of high rank who was expected to sample the king's food to make certain it was not poisoned. Nehemiah was a trusted cupbearer to Artaxerxes, the king of Persia (Ne. 1:11; 2:1).

905 **Cyprus** An island south of Asia Minor. It was the native home of Barnabas (Ac. 13:2). Paul and Barnabas encountered Elymais the sorcerer in Paphos on the west coast (Ac. 13:6-12).

907 **Cyrus** The founder and king of the Persian empire (Da. 10:1-13; 2 Chr. 36:22-23). When Cyrus conquered Babylon the Jewish captives were released and given permission to return to Jerusalem to rebuild the Temple and the city (Ezr. 1:1-4; 6:3ff.).

Dagon The national god of the Philistines. He had a temple at Gaza (Jud. 16:21-30) and one at Ashdod (1 S. 5:6; 1 Chr. 10:10). See also 1 S. 5:1-5. | 3939

Damascus Damascus, Syria, is the oldest continuously inhabited city in the Near East. It gained Christian prominence when St. Paul was converted near there and carried on a Christian ministry in the city (Ac. 9:3ff.). | 908, 4360

Dan (A judge). The fifth son of Jacob (Ge. 30:6). The territory of Dan was in the northernmost edge of the promised land, while Beersheba marked the border in the south: thus the expression: "from Dan to Beersheba" (Jud. 20:1). | 909-911, 4361

Daniel Central figure of the book of Daniel. At about age 20 he was taken to Babylon and became elevated to the office of governor. After the captives were liberated by the Persian king Cyrus, Daniel disappeared from the record. He leaves no posterity. | 914, 4300

Daniel, the Book of Conservative scholars assume this book was written by Daniel the prophet. Jesus cited the book several times, thus giving historicity to the Biblical record (Mt. 24:15). | 4249

Darius Three are mentioned in the OT: 1. Darius, founder of the Perso-Arian dynasty, who continued the same liberal policy toward the Jews as that of Cyrus, the liberator of the captives (Ezr. 6:1ff.); 2. Darius, the Mede (Da. 11:1), who assumed the throne when Belshazzar died (Da. 5:31); 3. Darius the Persian (Ne. 12:22), who may be identified with Darius I. | 915-917

David The eighth son of Jesse (1 S. 17:12). He was anointed king to succeed Saul (1 S. 16:13). Under David the twelve tribes were united into one kingdom. Israel had its Golden Age under David and his son Solomon (1 S. 1–1 K. 2). | 919

Dispersion of the Jews The scattering of the Jews into the uttermost parts of the world. Several ways are recorded: 1. Some remained in Babylon after the captivity; 2. Some, for economic, social or political reasons, voluntarily immigrated to other countries; 3. Some went abroad because of persecution. | 1023

Divination A system by which religious and secular leaders sought information, including future events, from the gods, spirits and the dead. But it was against divine law to seek information from anyone other than Jehovah (Ge. 40:8ff; 41:1-4; Mt. 1:20; 2:13). | 2226

Dog The terms "dog," "dead dog" and "dog's head" were considered to be expressions of reproach and humility (1 S. 24:14; 2 S. 3:8; 2 K. 8:13). | 163, 1031

Dothan A town north of Jerusalem, associated with Joseph where his brothers sold him to traders bound for Egypt (Ge. 37:17ff.). It was also the residence of Elisha (2 K. 6:13). | 1034, 4365

Dove A white bird symbolizing peace, beauty and holiness. At Jesus' baptism it is said that "the Spirit of God descended like a dove" (Mt. 3:16). See also Ps. 68:13 and Mt. 10:16. | 456, 469

164 **Dragon** This word is used in reference to a wide variety of animals (Jb. 30:29; Is. 34:13). The dragon is used figuratively to describe the devil (Re. 12:3-17).

1037-1039 **Dreams** In the OT dreams seem to have been a means by which God communicated with man (Jb. 4:13; 7:14; 33:15). However, dreamers are placed below the prophetic office. There were instances when Jehovah refused to reveal himself through dreams (1 S. 28:6).

2627 **Drink Offering** These offerings were given with gifts of meal in connection with sacrificed animals (Ex. 29:40; Nu. 28:7).

3575 **Drink** (Alcoholic). The excessive use of strong drink is expressly forbidden in Scripture (Pr. 20:1; Ep. 5:18; Pr. 23:20). There are instances when a moderate amount of wine seems to be sanctioned and was customary in Biblical days (Jn. 2:1ff; 1 Ti. 5:23).

586 **Earnest** (Pledge). This word was used in Biblical times for "pledge" or "promise" (Ge. 38:17). A cognate word was "surety" (Pr. 17:18).

1091 **Earthquake** Many of the ancient cities in the Near East have been partially or completely destroyed by this natural phenomenon. For general references see 1 S. 14:15; Ac. 16:26-27; Mt. 27:51; Re. 11:19.

2429
1093 **Ebal, Mount** This mountain in Samaria and its sister peak, Mount Gerazim form the narrow mouth of a strategic pass through which land caravans passed on their way north and south. Ebal became known as the Mount of Cursing (De. 27:13-26).

Eben-ezer (The stone of help). This memorial stone was set up by Samuel between Mizpeh and Shen to commemorate the defeat of the Philistines (1 S. 7:11-12).

4243 **Ecclesiastes** An OT book generally ascribed to Solomon. It contains the reflections of a philosopher who has all the carnal enjoyments of life.

1149 **Edom, Idumea** or **Idumaea** (Red). The land which the Lord gave to Esau was called "the country of Edom" (Ge. 32:3). Later it was called "the land of Edom" located in the desert hill country south of the Dead Sea.

1100 **Egypt** A country in northern Africa through which the Nile River flows. Its ancient name was "Mizraim," named after one of Ham's sons (Ge. 10:6).

1101 **Ehud** The son of Gera, of the tribe of Benjamin (Jud. 3:15), and the second judge of the Israelites.

1103 **Elah** The king of Israel (1 K. 16:8-10) who reigned less than two years and who died in a drunken stupor.

2078 **Elder** The title conferred upon older men with deep religious insight and dedication. Later an elder was an ordained officer in the Christian church (Ac. 14:23; 20:17; 1 Ti. 5:17; Tit. 1:5).

1106 **Eleazar** (Whom God aids). The third son of Aaron who was appointed to be chief over the principal Levites (Nu. 3:32). He succeeded Aaron in the office of high priest (Nu. 20:28).

Eli (Height). Eli was a high priest of the line of Ithamar (Le. 10:12). See 1 S. 2:11,22; 1 K. 2:27.

Eliakim (Whom God establishes). The son of Hilkiah and the chief overseer of Hezekiah's household (Is. 36:3; 2 K. 18:18ff.).

Eliezer (My God is help). 1. Abraham's chief servant, called "Eliezer of Damascus" (Ge. 15:2). 2. The second son of Moses by Zipporah (Ex. 18:4).

Elijah (My God is Jehovah). (Gr. *Elias*; see Mt. 17:3). A prophet who challenged Ahab and Jezebel (1 K. 18:17-40; 21:17-24; 2 K. 2; Lu. 9:30).

Eliphaz (To whom God is strength). 1. The son of Esau and Adah, and the father of Teman (Ge. 36:4). 2. The chief of the three friends of Job, a descendant of Teman (Jb. 4:1).

Elisabeth, also **Elisheba** (God is an oath). The wife of Zecharias and mother of John the Baptist. She was herself of a priestly family and a kinsman to our Lord (Lu. 1:36).

Elisha (To whom God is salvation). The successor to Elijah the prophet. Before Elijah ascended into heaven in a chariot of fire, he anointed Elisha to take his place (1 K. 19:15-20; 2 K. 2:8-14; 3:11).

Emmaus The village west of Jerusalem to which two disciples were going when they met the resurrected Lord (Lu. 24:13).

En A prefix to many Hebrew words indicating a spring or fountain; eg., En-gannim, "fountain of gardens," and En-gedi, "well of the wild goat."

En-dor (Fountain of habitation). Held in memory of the Jews as the place of Israel's great victory over Sisera and Jabin. It is here where Saul consulted the witch or soothsayer (1 S. 28:7).

En-gedi (Well of the wild goats). A town in western Jordan below the cliffs facing the Dead Sea (Jos. 15:62). The waters of this fertile oasis are used for agriculture (1 S. 23:29; 1 S. 24).

Enoch (Experienced). 1. The eldest son of Cain (Ge. 4:17) who called the city he built after his son. 2. Son of Jared, father of Methusaleh (Ge. 5:21); he was translated from this life (He. 11:5).

Enon or **Aenon** A place near Salim where John baptized (Jn. 3:23). It was located a few miles north of where the Jordan River flows into the Dead Sea.

En-rogel (A spy's spring). A spring outside the walls of Jerusalem at the junction of the Kidron and Hinnom valleys.

Epaphras or **Epaphroditus** (Handsome). A fellow missionary with Paul mentioned in Col. 1:7. Apparently he had been teaching in the church at Colosse. Later Epaphras was a fellow prisoner with Paul in Rome (Col. 4:12).

Ephesians, Epistle to the Written by Paul during his first imprisonment in Rome (Ac. 28:16). Paul emphasizes that the barriers have been removed between the Jews and the Gentiles.

	1108
	1110
	1111
	1112-1113, 2366, 4298
	1115
	1116
	1117, 2367, 4299
	1119, 4370
	1127-1130
	1127
	1130-1132, 4371
	1135
	1136
	4372
	1139
	4271

1142, 4373   **Ephesus** The capital city of Asia, located on the west coast at the cross-roads of world travel and commerce. At the head of the harbor was the towering temple of Diana (Gr. *Artemis*), one of the Seven Wonders of the ancient world.

1143   **Ephod** (A covering). A sacred garment originally worn by the high priest (Ex. 28:4), but later worn by the ordinary priests (1 S. 22:18) and deemed characteristic of the priestly office (1 S. 2:28; 14:3; Ho. 3:4).

1144-1147   **Ephraim** (Doubly fruitful). 1. The second son of Joseph, who obtained Jacob's blessing (Ge. 48:8-20). 2. A place where Jesus went to rest (Jn. 11:54). 3. A gate of Jerusalem (2 K. 14:13).

4344   **Ephratah** or **Ephrath** (Fruitful). Jesus was born in Bethlehem-Ephra-tah, a political sub-division in Judah, distinguished from Bethlehem in the northern territory of Zebulun (Jos. 19:15). When the prophet Micah prophe-sied the birthplace of the Messiah he was careful to indicate the "Bethlehem Ephratah" (Mi. 5:2).

3201   **Epicureans** The disciples of the Greek philosopher Epicurius, who concluded that the great values in life are determined by the degree of pleasure one derives from an experience. The Epicureans of Athens rejected Paul's teaching but extended the courtesy of hearing him at the court of the Aeropagus (Mars Hill).

1148   **Erastus** (Beloved). 1. One of the deacons at Ephesus who accompanied Timothy into Macedonia while Paul remained in Asia (Ac. 19:21-22). 2. The public treasurer in Corinth who became one of the early converts to Christi-anity (Ro. 16:23).

1803   **Esaias** (Jehovah hath saved). The Greek form of the Hebrew *Isaiah.*

1149   **Esau** (Hairy). The oldest son of Isaac and twin brother of Jacob (Ge. 25:25), also called Edom. The land south of the Dead Sea was named Edom and his descendants were called Edomites (Ge. 26 and 36).

1150   **Eshcol, the Valley** (Cluster). A valley near Hebron where the Hebrew spies went to explore the land (Nu. 13:2-3). In Eshcol they found huge clusters of grapes and other large fruit which they took back to the waiting tribes (Nu. 13:23).

1151   **Eshtaol** A community in the southern part of Judah which was assigned to Dan (Jos. 19:41). This was the boyhood home of Samson to which his body was brought after his death in the Philistine temple (Jud. 16:20ff.).

4362   **Essenes** (Seer). An ascetic Jewish sect whose high ideals and holiness concepts conflicted with the evil hierarchy in the Temple. They finally withdrew to communities of their own. They established a community at Qumram, east of Jerusalem near the Dead Sea.

1152, 4239   **Esther** (Star). While the Jews were dispersed in the Babylon-Persia area, Esther, a Jewish girl, became the queen to the Persian king. As the queen, she saved the Jewish people from extermination by Haman, a petty politician in the Persian Court. See the book of Esther.

Ethiopia The country described by the Greeks and Romans as Aethopia and by the Hebrews as Cush. | 1154

Eunice The mother of Timothy (2 Ti. 1:5). | 1155

Eunuch These men were castrated so that they could be safely employed in Oriental harems without sexual misconduct (Je. 41:16; Est. 1:10). Eunuchs were deprived of many personal privileges including worship in the Temple. Isaiah advocated restoring this privilege (Is. 56:4-5). | 1156

Evangelist An itinerant minister who traveled from place to place preaching the Gospel. Paul tells the Ephesians that God has designated: "...some, evangelists...for the perfecting of the saints, for the work of the ministry, for the edifying of the body of Christ" (Ep. 4:11-12). | 1158

Eve (Life). The name given the first woman. The account of Eve's creation is found in Ge. 2:21-22. This narrative is intended to convey the importance of union between man and wife. | 1159

Exodus, the book of (Going out). The book of Exodus describes the deliverance of the Hebrews under Moses from Egyptian bondage. It can be divided into two parts: 1. Historical (Ch. 1-18) and 2. Legislative (Chs. 19-40). | 4224

Exorcist A person who is thought to have super-occult power to tell fortunes and/or to cast out demons (Ac. 19:13-16). | 3156-3157

Ezekiel (Whom God will strengthen). A prophet-priest exiled from Jerusalem during the Babylonian attack. Many of his prophecies are shrouded in mystical imagery (Eze. 1:1-3; 11:19-20; 18:20-32; 22:30; 33:32-33). | 1197, 4248

Ezra (Help). A famous scribe in Babylon who returned to Jerusalem with the captives. He instigated many reforms and helped to revise the Holy Oracles for canonization. | 1199

Farthing A small Roman brass coin of little value—perhaps a quarter of a cent. Its small value was expressed in the saying "not worth a farthing" (Mt. 5:26). | 1243

Fasts Only one fast was appointed by the law—the Day of Atonement. It appears that while the Jews were in Babylon they fasted and mourned in the fifth and seventh months (Zec. 7:5). They also fasted in the New Testament (Ac. 10:30; Mt. 4:2). | 2710

Felix (Happy). A procurator in Judea, appointed by the Roman emperor, Claudius, under whom Paul was tried in Caesarea (Ac. 21:38). Even though Felix was a cruel despot, he was touched by Paul's testimony (Ac. 24:10-25). | 1263

Fenced Cities Heavily fortified walls in Palestine (2 Chr. 32:5; Je. 5:17). | 770

Festivals Religious celebrations ordained by law. These were times when the people paid special homage to Jehovah through feasts, fasts and | 1256-1261 ritual (De. 16:16; Eze. 45:21; Est. 9:21-28).

1277 **Festus, Porcius** (Joyful). The successor of Felix in Judea (Ac. 24:27).

1286 **Firmament** (Made firm). The overhead expanse or the heavens (Ge. 1:17).

3459 **Firstborn** According to Hebrew law the firstborn received a double portion of his father's inheritance (De. 21:17); the eldest son usually succeeded his father as head of the family. In the royal family the eldest would become the next king (De. 21:17; 1 K. 1:30).

3460 **Firstfruits** The firstfruits were to be offered as a thank offering and always brought a premium price on the market. The adage was, "My best for God."

1289 **Flax** A plant growing in Palestine which was processed into linen cloth. It was used for many purposes including linen for the Temple and the priestly garments (Jos. 2:6; Ho. 2:5,9).

2454 **Flute** (Pipes). A musical pipe made out of cane stalks as well as metal. Shepherd boys were known to play them while tending their flocks. A finer type of flute was used in worship services. It was also used in the palace in Babylon (Da. 3:5,7,10,15).

3001 **Frontlets** or **Phylacteries** Strips of parchment on which Scripture passages were written. They were rolled up in leather containers and worn on the arm or the forehead as a testimony of God's providential care (Ex. 13:2-9; 14-16; De. 6:4-9; 13-23).

1377 **Gabriel** (Man of God). A special messenger from God. The angel Gabriel appeared to Daniel in Babylon (Da. 8:15ff; 9:21ff.); to Zacharias and Elisabeth (Lu. 1:8-20); and to Mary the mother of our Lord (Lu. 1:26-28).

1378-1379 **Gad** (Good fortune). 1. Jacob's seventh son, the firstborn of Zilpah, Leah's maid (Ge. 30:13; 46:16-18). 2. David's seer (1 Chr. 29:29; 2 S. 24:11).

1380 **Gadara** (Gadarenes). One of the cities of the Decapolis south of Lake Galilee (Lu. 8:26). Here the demoniac received healing from Jesus (Mk. 5:1-20).

1382 **Galatia** (Land of the Galli, Gauls). A province in Asia Minor where Paul had missionary contacts (Ac. 16:6; 18:23; 2 Ti. 4:10). He wrote the book of Galatians to believers in this area and emphasized the importance of "justification by faith" (Ro. 1:17).

1384 **Galilee** (Circle). In Jesus' day Galilee was a political sub-division of Palestine. King Hiram of Tyre had given Solomon twenty towns in this area (1 K. 9:11). Non-Jews became the chief settlers and it was dubbed "Galilee of the Gentiles" (Is. 9:1).

1385 **Galilee, the Sea of** (or **Tiberias**). A fresh-water lake into which the Jordan River flows. In ancient times it was known as the "Sea of Chinnereth"

(Nu. 34:11) and later as "Gennesaret" (Lu. 5:1).

Gall (Yellow, bitter). A bitter fluid secreted by the liver (Jb. 16:13; 20:25); it was mixed with vinegar and given to Jesus when he thirsted on the cross (Mt. 27:34). **1386**

Gallio The Roman proconsul of Achaia while Paul was in Corinth (Ac. 18:12). **2870**

Gamaliel (Benefit of God). A Pharisee and a famous doctor of the law, who as a member of the Sanhedrin intervened at the trial of Peter. He made a plea for a more tolerant attitude (Ac. 5:34ff.). **1388**

Garrison A fortified military post located in a strategic place (2 S. 23:14). Sometimes such garrisons were placed on well-traveled roads or in cities of conquered people (2 S. 8:6,14). **1390**

Gates The gate area of a city was a place used for many purposes including: general public meetings (Ge. 19:1; 1 S. 4:18), deliberations and courts of justice (De. 16:18; Jos. 20:4), public secretaries' stands, farmers' produce markets (2 K. 7:1), rest places or inns for overnight sleep and security of the city (Ge. 24:60; De. 12:12; Ru. 4:10). **1391-1394**

Gath (Winepress). One of the five royal cities of the Philistines. It was the native city of the giant Goliath who was slain by David. (1 S. 17:4). **1396**

Gaza The southern-most of the five main cities of the Philistines, near the Egyptian border. **1397, 4376**

Gehazi (Valley of vision). Elisha's servant boy, sent as a messenger to the good Shunammite (2 K. 4). **1399**

Genealogy A biography of a race of people. Only the Jews have a written genealogy tracing their lineage to Abraham. Matthew traces Jesus' line to Joseph, Luke to Mary (Mt. 1:1-17; Lu. 3:23-38). **1400**

Generation In a study of the geneological tables it appears that a generation was computed at 100 years (Ge. 15:16). In later years the length of the generation seems to have been shortened to 30-60 years. **1400**

Genesis (Generation or beginning). The first book of the OT and the record of creation, Adam and Eve and their fall into sin, Noah and the flood, the migration of Abraham from Ur of the Chaldees and the development of the Hebrew nation through the Jacob tribes. **4223**

Gennesaret, Sea of See Galilee, Sea of.

Gentiles In the Old Testament the Gentiles were considered to be the non-Jewish nations. The Jews were God's chosen people for the purpose of receiving and preserving the Laws and revelations of God and to give the Messiah to the world. **2383-2384**

Gershon (Expulsion). The eldest of Levi's three sons, born before the Jacob tribes moved to Egypt (Ex. 6:16). **1405**

Gethsemane (Olive press). A small acreage in the Kidron Valley at the foot of the Mount of Olives. Jesus had the last prayer meeting with his **1408, 4379**

disciples in the garden area.

1409, 1411 **Giants** Reference is made to a race of people of great stature known as the "Nephilim" (Ge. 6:4). Goliath of Gath was six cubits and a span tall or about 9.5 feet (1 S. 17:4).

1412, 4381 **Gibeah** (Hill). 1. A city in the mountain district of Judah. 2. The resting place of the ark from the time it was returned by the Philistines until David reclaimed it (2 S. 6:3ff.).

1413, 4382 **Gibeon** (Pertaining to a hill). One of four Hivite cities who made a covenant with Joshua (Jos. 9:3-15) and thereby escaped the fate of Jericho and Ai.

1414, 4294
4307d **Gideon** (One who cuts down). The youngest son of Joash (Jud. 6:13-19). He was the fifth judge of Israel and probably the most outstanding. He is listed among the men of great faith (He. 11:32).

1415-1416,
4383 **Gihon** (A river). 1. A river in the Garden of Eden area (Ge. 2:13). 2. A place near Jerusalem where Solomon was anointed king (1 K. 1:33).

2432 **Gilboa** (Babbling fountain). A mountain range on the eastern side of the plain of Esdraelon near Jazreel (1 S. 28:4).

1417, 2433 **Gilead** (Hard or firm). The land between the Yarmack and Arnon Rivers east of the Jordon river. Moses permitted Gad and Reuben to stake their claims there (Nu. 32:5-7; 20-22).

1419, 4384 **Gilgal** (A circle). 1. Israel's first camping place after they crossed the Jordan River under Joshua (Jos. 4:19). 2. A distinct place in Gilgal associated with Elijah and Elisha (2 Kings). See also Jos. 15:7.

1420-1421 **Girdle** An essential article of dress, made out of leather or cloth, worn around the waist, over the outer garments to keep them secure. It was fastened with a gold or silver clasp or tied in a knot (Is. 5:27).

1422 **Girgashites** One of the nations in Canaan when the Israelites arrived (Jos. 3:10).

62 **Gleaning** Gleaning was a provision for the poor people who had no fields of their own. They were permitted to follow the harvesters and pick up the grain left behind (Le. 19:9-10).

169 **Goat** A hardy animal able to subsist on very little vegetation. It was valuable for its milk, skin and hair for making cloth (Ex. 25:4; De. 14:4; Pr. 27:27).

884-885
1867-1872 **God** There are two main names for the Creator of the Universe: 1. Elohim, translated God, appears over 2,500 times in the OT. 2. YHWH/ Adonai, variously translated Jehovah, Yahweh and LORD, appears over 6,000 times in the OT.

1430 **Golan** (Exile). A city in an area of ancient Bashan, east of Lake Galilee (De. 4:43). It was designated as one of the Cities of Refuge (Jos. 21:27).

Golgotha The Hebrew name of the place where our Lord was crucified (Mt. 27:33). See Calvary. | 1434

Gomorrah One of the cities of the plain at the southern end of the Dead Sea into which Lot, Abraham's nephew, moved (Ge. 13:12). | 3411, 3412, 4437

Goshen The fertile delta area in Egypt to which the Jacob tribes moved when the Great Famine came to Palestine. It is also called the land of Rameses (Ge. 47:1-11). | 1439

Gospels The record of Jesus' ministry, written by four evangelists: Matthew, Mark, Luke and John. | 1440-1442

Governor A loosely used word in the Bible to designate rulers of different kinds– the head of a family or tribe, an officer with the responsibility to dispense justice in legal matters, or the ruler of a small political subdivision (Ezr. 5:3). | 2540-2544

Hagar (Myrtle). The Egyptian handmaid of Sarah (Ge. 16:1). Sarah gave Hagar to Abraham as a concubine and out of this union, Ismael was born (Ge. 16:2-16). | 1474

Haggai One of the Minor Prophets who prophesied after the captivity. Nothing is known about his tribal ancestry and parentage (Hag. 1:1). | 1475, 4259

Ham (Hot). One of the sons of Noah. He is considered to be the progenitor of the African peopie. Ham's sons were Cush, Mizraim, Put and Canaan. The land of Ham connotes Egypt in Psalms (Ge. 5:32; 10:6; Ps. 78:51). | 1477

Haman The chief counsellor of the Persian king Ahaseurus (Est. 3:1). After his plot to destroy the Jews failed, he was hanged on the gallows he made for Mordecai, Esther's uncle (Est. 7:9). | 1478

Hanani (Whom Jehovah graciously gave). 1. A prophet who rebuked Asa, King of Judah (2 Chr. 16:7). 2. A priest in the time of Ezra who took heathen wives (Ezr. 10:20.) | 1482

Hananiah (Meaning: Same as Hanani). 1. One of the 14 sons of Heman, the counsellor to King Solomon and who wrote Psalm 88. 2. One of King Uzziah's army generals (2 Chr. 26:11). 3. Father of Zedekiah (Je. 36:12). 4. A brother of Nehemiah (Ne. 7:2). | 1483

Hannah (Gracious). One of the wives of Elkanah, an Ephramite, and the mother of Samuel (1 S. 1:2,20). | 1495

Haran (Mountaineer). 1. Youngest brother of Abraham (Ge. 11:26). 2. A Levite of the family of Shimei (1 Chr. 23:9). 3. A son of Caleb (1 Chr. 2:46). 4. A city near the head waters of the Euphrates River (Ge. 11:31). | 1496-1497, 4386

Hebrew Abraham was called a Hebrew the first time in Ge. 14:13. Later the Jews in general were called Hebrews. | 1553-1554

4280   **Hebrews, the Epistle of** The NT book addressed to people who had been converted to Christianity from Judaism. A strong warning is sounded against apostasy and reverting to Judaism.

1555   **Hebron** (Alliance). 1. A son of Kohath (Ex. 6:18). 2. A city in Judah about 20 miles south of Jerusalem (Jos. 15:54). It is one of the oldest continuously inhabited cities, next to Damascus.

1374, 1558   **Hell** The Hebrew *Sheol* is translated "the abode of the dead" or "the grave." In the NT *Hades* and *Gehenna* are translated "Hell" (Mt. 5:29). Implies a place of burning or torture (De. 32:22; Ac. 2:27; Mk. 9:45-46).

1464   **Hellenist** During the formative years of the Christian church, the Greek converts were called Hellenists and the Jewish believers were called Hebrews because of their ethnic signs.

1596   **Hem of Garment** The Jews placed great importance on placing fringes on their garments to remind them that they were to obey the Commandments and to be a holy people unto the Lord (Nu. 15:38-39).

1569-1570   **Heman** (Faithful). 1. One of Solomon's counsellors next to him in wisdom (1 K. 4:31). He is credited with writing a meditative Psalm (Ps. 88). 2. A grandson of Samuel the Prophet (1 Chr. 15:19).

2434, 4415   **Hermon, Mount** (Sacred Mountain). The highest peak in the Anti-Lebanon mountain range at the point where Lebanon, Syria and Israel join. It is called "Sirion" by the Sidonians and "Shenir" by the Amorites (De. 3:9).

1578-1579   **Herod the Great** The first appointed Tetrarch of Judea and the king from 41-4 B.C. He was tyranical and cruel and murdered many people including the children in Bethlehem to protect his throne.(Mt. 2:16).

1582   **Herodias** The granddaughter of Herod the Great. She requested the head of John the Baptist (Mt. 14:6-10).

1584   **Heth** The forefather of the Hittites (Ge. 10:15).

1585   **Hezekiah** (The might of Jehovah). The twelfth King of Judah (726-698 B.C.), who abolished idolatry and built up a strong defense against neighboring nations (2 K. 18-22).

1744   **Hiel** (God liveth). The man from Bethel who rebuilt Jericho in spite of the curse Joshua pronounced upon anyone who would try to rebuild it (Jos. 6:26; 1 K. 16:34). He suffered the curse Joshua predicted.

2050, 4404   **Hierapolis** (A Holy city). A city near Laodicea (Col. 4:13) with hot springs from which water was piped to Laodicea. Upon arrival, the water was neither hot nor cold—only lukewarm. It is thought that this is the basis of Jesus' pronouncement upon the Laodiceans spiritually; they were neither cold nor hot (Re. 3:15-16).

1586-1587, 3950   **High Places** From ancient times it was the custom for religious groups to establish a place of worship on an elevation. This was also a common practice of the Baal nature cults (Nu. 22:41).

High Priest At Mount Sinai, the tribe of Levi was designated to be the priestly tribe. Aaron, a Levite, was distinctly separated and anointed High Priest (Le. 8:12-13).) | **2064**

Hilkiah (Portion of Jehovah). 1. The high priest in the reign of Josiah (2 K. 22:4). 2. A priest in Anathoth, the father of Jeremiah (Je. 1:1). | **1588**

Hind A female deer prominent in the poetical parts of Scripture, emblematic of activity (Ps. 18:33; Hab. 3:19). It is used in connection with gentleness (Pr. 5:19) and feminine modesty (Song. 3:5). | **162**

Hinnom, Valley of Solomon erected a shrine to Molech on the eastern extremity (1 K. 11:7) of this valley, where horrible rites included human sacrifices and burning children in a sacrificial fire (Le. 18:21). | **1590**

Hiram (Noble). The king of Tyre who supplied cedar wood and workmen in connection with building Solomon's temple (1 K. 5:1-12). The king also sent a skilled craftsman named Hiram to assist Solomon (1 K. 7:13-14). | **1591-1592**

Hittites, the (Descendents of Heth). Heth, the second son of Canaan was the progenitor of the Hittites. The Hittite Kingdom extended from northern Palestine to the central part of Asia Minor. | **1594**

Hivites (Villagers). The descendants of Canaan, the son of Ham. Scholars believe that the Horites in Ge. 14:6 are the same as the Hivites in Joshua's day (Jos. 9:1-2). | **1595**

Hophni (Pugulist). One of the sons of Eli the priest. He and his brother Phinehas were judged to be reprobate "sons of Belial" who knew not the Lord (1 S. 2:11-12). | **1700, 2760**

Hor, Mount The mountain near Petra where Aaron died. A memorial marker was built there (Nu. 20:25-29). | **2435**

Horn The word "horn" has a symbolic meaning of strength and honor and authority. The horn was used in Israel to announce certain festive events, and for anointing (Jos. 6:4; 1 K. 1:39). | **1702**

Hornets The hornets are used in Scripture only as weapons of war which Jehovah used in behalf of Israel against the Canaanites (Ex. 23:28; De. 7:20). | **1771**

Hosanna (Save us we pray). This is the song the multitudes sang in our Lord's triumphal procession into Jerusalem (Mt. 21:9,15). | **1703**

Hosea (Salvation). The first of the minor prophets. It is generally assumed that Gomer, his wife, was or became a prostitute and that Hosea continued to love his wife; similarly God continued to love Israel, even when they were unfaithful serving other gods (Ho. 1:1). | **1704, 4250**

Huldah (Weasel). A prophetess. The wife of Shallum, who was the keeper of the wardrobe for King Josiah. When the last Book of the Law was found, Hulda authenticated it as being genuine (2 K. 22:14ff.). | **1713**

1737   **Hyssop** A plant used frequently as a sprinkling device. A hyssop branch was used when the Israelites sprinkled blood on the doorpost when the first passover was celebrated in Egypt (Ex. 12: 22).

3948-3949   **Idol, Idolatry** An idol is an object made by man rather than by the Creator. In the Levitical law idolatry was strictly forbidden (Ex. 20:3-4). God presented himself as a jealous Creator who would not tolerate a division of his creatures' devotion (Ex. 20:5).

1741   **Immanuel** or **Emmanuel** (God is with us). This word is used by Isaiah the Prophet with reference to a child to be born of a virgin (Is. 7 :14). The apostle Matthew identifies the virgin-born Christ as the subject of this prophecy (Mt. 1: 23).

1747   **Incense** A substance used in the ceremonial services of Jehovah worship (Ex. 30:1-9). It was sprinkled on the sacrifices as well as on the hot coals which gave off a rising lazy cloud of smoke, suggestive of communion and prayer with and to Jehovah.

3402   **Inn** The inn of the Near East was a lodging place for the traveler and his animals. Man and beast stayed together, usually on a strawed floor. The better inns provided a second story where the traveler could make his bed (Ex. 4: 24; Lu. 2: 7).

1802   **Isaac** (Laughter). The divinely promised son of Abraham and Sarah. Abraham expressed his great faith in God's providence by his willingness to sacrifice his only son on Mount Moriah (Ge. 17:15-19; 22:1ff.).

1803   **Isaiah** (Salvation of Jehovah). A prophet in Judah in the reigns of Uzziah, Jotham, Ahaz and Hezekiah. He was a great prophet and statesman and has been called the Messianic prophet because of his many prophetic descriptions of the Messiah's suffering and death (Is. 53).

1804   **Ish-bosheth** (Man of shame). The youngest of Saul's sons and his legitimate successor, but his ascension brought an end to Saul's dynasty (2 S. 4:5-8).

1805   **Ishmael** (Whom God hears). The son of Hagar, Abraham's Egyptian concubine, born when Abraham was 86 years old (Ge. 16:15-16). He was the progenitor of the Arab people.

1807-1829, 1882   **Israel** (Soldier of God). The name given to Jacob (Ge. 32:28). It became the name of the Jacob tribe after they revolted from Judah (1 K. 12:16). Eventually taken into Assyrian captivity, they lost their political identity. Those who returned blended in with Judah. This is the name of the modern state of Israel.

1830   **Issachar** (He is hired). The ninth son of Jacob and the fifth of Leah (Ge. 30:17-18).

1835   **Jabbok** (Pouring out). A stream flowing west through the mountains of Gilead into the Jordan River about midway between the Sea of Galilee and the Dead Sea (Jos. 12:2).

1836   **Jabesh** (Dry). 1. Father of Shallum and the 15th king of Israel. 2. A town in Gilead (Jud. 21:8).

Jacob (Supplanter). Son of Isaac and second born twin with Esau. The progenitor of the twelve tribes of Israel (Ge. 32:28). | **1837**

Jair (God enlightens). 1. Jair the Gileadite judged Israel for 22 years (Jud. 10:3-5). 2. A Benjamite, the son of Kish and father of Mordecai (Est. 2:5). 3. Father of Elhanan, a hero in David's army (1 Chr. 20:5-6). | **1839-1840**

Jairus (Gr. form of *Jair*). A ruler of the synagogue, probably at Capernaum, who had a sick daughter that Jesus raised from the dead (Mk. 5:22; Lu. 8:41-42; 51-55). | **1841**

James (English form of *Jacob* in the New Testament). 1. James the Greater was the brother of John (Mk. 1:19ff.). 2. James the Less was another Apostle, the son of Alphaeus (Mt. 10:3). 3. James the brother, or possibly cousin, of Christ is credited with writing the Epistle of James (Mt. 13:55-56). | **1842-1844, 4281**

Japheth (Extension). One of the three sons of Noah (Ge. 5:32). | **1845**

Jasher, Book of (The Book of the Upright). Two places in the OT make reference to this book: Jos. 10:12-1 and 2 S. 1:18. | **1846**

Jasper Stone The last of the twelve stones in the breastplate; it represented the tribe of Naphtali, according to tradition (Ex. 28:20; Re. 21:11,19). | **2855**

Jebus, Jebusite (A place trodden down). An ancient name for Jerusalem in the time when it was a Jebusite city (Jos. 15:8). The Jebusites were descendants of Canaan (Ge. 10:15-16). | **1852**

Jeduthun (Friendship). A Levite who was in charge of the music in the Temple services (1 Chr. 25:1; See also 1 Chr. 16:41-42). | **1853**

Jehoash (Jehovah supports). 1. The uncontracted form of Joash, the eighth king of Judah (2 K. 11:21). 2. The twelfth king in the northern kingdom, son of Jehoahaz (2 K. 13:10). | **1857-1858**

Jehovah (He that is). The Hebrew word for "LORD." This was the most sacred name of the Lord and was never pronounced; Adonai was subsituted (Ge. 28:21; Ps. 83:18: Is. 12:2). | **1867**

Jehovah-jireh (Jehovah will provide). The divine name given by Abraham for the place where he was commanded to offer Isaac (Ge. 22:14). | **1868**

Jehovah-nissi (Jehovah my banner). The name given by Moses to the altar he built to commemorate the victory over the Amalekites by Joshua at Rephidim (Ex. 17:15). | **1869**

Jehovah-shalom (Jehovah is my peace). The title Gideon gave to the altar he built at Ophra in response to the peace message given to him by the Lord (Jud. 6:24). | **1870**

Jehu (Who exists). A prophet of Judah coming in conflict with Jezebel, whom he executed by having her thrown from a tower upon the street where Jehu drove over her body with his chariot (2 K. 9:30-37). | **1874-1875**

1876   **Jephthah** (God opens). The judge in Israel who made a foolish vow with regard to his daughter, resulting in her death (Jud. 11:30ff.).

1877, 4246   **Jeremiah** (Exalted). One of the great prophets of Judah who did his best to warn his people of the impending doom facing the nation. He was subjected to all kinds of indignities by both the secular and the religious leaders (Je. 20:1ff; 37:15ff.).

1878, 4390   **Jericho** (A fragrant place). Judged to be the oldest city in the Palestine area. It was a fortified city guarding the eastern flank of Palestine. Through miraculous divine intervention the Israelites were able to destroy the city under the leadership of Joshua (Jos. 6:lff.).

1879-1880   **Jeroboam** (Whose people are many). The first king of the divided kingdom of Israel. He established two centers of worship: Dan in the north and Bethel in the south and in each he set up a golden calf (1 K. 13:28-34).

1414   **Jerubbaal** (Let Baal plead). The title Gideon acquired when he destroyed the Baal altars while his father defended him from the vengence of the Abiezrites (Jud. 6:32).

1881-1885   **Jerusalem** (Place of Peace). The lofty position of this sacred city made it an ideal worship center down through the ages. At the time of Abraham it was called "Salem." Ancient Egyptian records of the 16th and 19th century refer to "Urusalim" and "Urusalimum."

1886   **Jerusalem, The New** The glorified body of Christ, the church, is referred to as the New Jerusalem in Re. 3:12.

1889   **Jesse** (Gift). The father of David, the son of Obed, referred to as "Jesse the Bethlehemite" (1 S. 16:1,18), but his full title is "The Ephramite of Bethlehem Judah" (1 S. 17:12).

677-723   **Jesus** The Greek form of Joshua or Jeshua. A contraction of Jehoshua which means "help of Jehovah" or "Saviour."

677-723   **Jesus Christ** (Jesus the Saviour). Jesus is his earthly name, Christ is his eternal divine name. The two together mean the God-Man. He was born of the Virgin Mary and died on the cross to save all men from their sins. His universal invitation is —"whosoever will may come."

1892   **Jether** or **Jethro** 1. The father-in-law of Moses (Ex. 4:18); he held the dual offices of priest and prince of Midian. 2. The firstborn of Gideon's seventy sons (Jud. 8:20). 3. The father of Amasa, the general of Absalom's army (1 K. 2:5).

1825-1829,   **Jew** In general terms, a Jew is of the stock of Abraham but specifically
2723, 3482   the word means a descendant from the tribe of Judah. The word "Jew" first appears in Est. 2:5.

1893   **Jezebel** (Unmarried). The wife of King Ahab of Israel and mother of

Queen Athaliah of Judah. Jezebel was a devoted worshipper of the Baal gods. In order to please her, Ahab built a temple and an altar to Baal in Samaria (1 K. 16:32).

Jezreel A city in the Jezreel Valley near Gilboa where Ahab and his son established their chief residence (1 K. 18:45; 2 K. 8:29). | 1894-1896, 4392

Joab (Jehovah is brother). One of the three nephews of David who became a most outstanding leader and general of the army (2 S. 2:13ff.). | 1897

Joash or **Jehoash** (Jehovah is strong). A descendant from the tribe of Manasseh and father of Gideon (Jud. 6:11). Other men by this name are listed in 1 Chr. 4:22; 12:3 and 1 K. 22:26. | 1898

Job A deeply religious and wealthy patriarch of Uz. The OT book by this name is poetical and dramatizes the questions of whether goodness can exist irrespective of reward and why the righteous suffer. | 1899, 4240

Jochebed (Jehovah is glorious). The wife of Amram and the mother of Moses and Aaron (Ex. 6:20). To save her newborn son Moses from execution, she hid him in the bulrushes (Ex. 2:1ff.). | 4307

Joel (Jehovah is might). 1. The eldest son of Samuel the prophet (1 Chr. 6:33; 15:17). 2. A minor prophet who ministered during the reign of Uzziah. He predicted the baptism of the Holy Spirit (Joel 2:28; Ac. 2:16-18). | 1900, 4251

Johanan (Jehovah is gracious). 1. Son of Azariah (1 Chr. 6:9). 2. Son of Elioenai in the line of Zerubbabel (1 Chr. 3:24). 3. The son of Careah in the army of Judah (2 K. 25:23). | 1901

John (Jehovah's gift). A contraction of "Johanan." 1. A man in the council chamber with Annas and Caiaphas (Ac. 4:6). 2. John the Baptist (Lu. 1:5-24). 3. John the Beloved (Mk. 1:19-20). He wrote the Gospel of John, and he is also credited with writing the Epistles of John and Revelation. | 392, 1902, 4265

Jonah, Jona, Jonas (Dove). A prophet of Israel. The book of Jonah tells of his reluctant mission to the Assyrians in Nineveh, the mortal enemies of the Jews. Jonah's prejudice them was so great that he regretted seeing them repent (Jona. 3:10; 4:1ff.). | 1909, 4254

Joppa, Jaffa (Beauty). A town with a sheltered port on the Mediterranean coast in the area of Dan, known in early Biblical days as Japho (Jos. 19:46-47). It became the shipping center for southern Palestine. | 1914, 4393

Jordan River (Flowing Down). The longest river in Palestine. It begins at Mount Hermon in the Ante-Lebanon mountain range, flows south, flows into Lake Galilee and empties into the Dead Sea. | 1915-1916

Joseph (He shall add). 1. The son of Jacob and Rachel who was sold into Egypt (Ge. 37 ff.). 2. The husband of Mary who gave birth to Jesus (Mt. 1:18ff.). | 1917-1921, 4292

Joses 1. A son of Eliezer in the genealogy of Christ (Jose, Lu. 3:29). 2. One of the Lord's brothers (Mt. 13:55). 3. A "son of consolation" and a | 1921

Levite convert of Christ (Ac. 4:35-37).

1922, 4228,   **Joshua** (Saviour). The name "Joshua" has undergone a number of
4293   changes: Jehoshua (Nu. 13:16), Jehoshuah (1 Chr. 7:27), Oshea, (Nu. 13:8),
and in the NT the Grecianized form Jesus appears.

1923   **Josiah** (Whom Jehovah heals). Son of Amon, King of Judah. Josiah is
remembered as the king who brought a great spiritual reform to Judah (2 K.
22:1-20).

1924-1925   **Jotham** (Jehovah is upright). 1. The youngest son of Gideon (Jud. 9:7).
2. The son of King Uzziah (2 K. 15:5).

1953   **Jubilee, the Year of** The fiftieth year, after a succession of seven
Sabbatical years. During this year there was an equalization of land owner-
ship, as well as the liberating of all bondmen of Hebrew blood (Le. 25:8-18).

1955-1956   **Judah** (Praised). 1. The son of Joseph in the genealogy of Christ (Lu.
3:30). 2. Son of Joanna or Hananiah (Lu. 3:27). 3. One of the Lord's brothers
(Mk. 6:3-4). 4. The patriarch Judah (Lu. 3:33).

1959   **Judas Iscariot** The Greek form of the Hebrew proper name *Judah*. In
Bible times, many people carried the name of Judas. The best-known is Judas
Iscariot, the betrayer of our Lord (Mt. 10:4; 26:14-16.)

4287   **Jude, the Epistle** (Abbreviated form of Judas). It contains much of the
material that is in Peter's Second Epistle (Jude 1:1ff; 2 Pe. 2:1-19).

1821-1822   **Judges** Political leaders of Israel after the death of Joshua. A total of
fourteen judges served (see the book of Judges).

1965   **Judgment Hall** The judgement hall in Jerusalem was called the Praetorium. Pilate used this building in which to conduct trials, including that of
Jesus (Mk. 15:1-6).

3930   **Jupiter** The Roman equivalent to the Greek god Zeus. Zeus was the
nationalistic God of the Greeks as well as the ruler of the heathen world and
as such was in direct opposition to Jehovah (Ac. 14:12-13).

1987, 4395   **Kadesh-Barnea, Kadeh** The word "Kadesh" means "holy" or "holiness." Kadesh Barnea was a fertile valley with several springs and became the
focal point for the Israelites as they waited out their forty year judgment (Nu.
32:8).

1992-1993   **Kenite, Kenites** A tribe which was living in Canaan in the time of
Abraham. (Ge. 15:19) A portion of this tribe migrated into the Mount Sinai
area and had integrated with the Midianites by the time of Moses' exile (Jud.
1:16; Nu. 10:29).

         Keturah (Incense). The wife Abraham took after the death of Sarah
(Ge. 25:1). The mention of her as a concubine suggests he may have had her
as a concubine before Sarah died (1 Chr. 1:32).

1996   **Kidron** See Cedron.

1555   **Kirjath-arba** (City of Arba). The early name of Hebron (Jos. 14:15;
Jud. 1:10).

Kirjath-jearim (City of Woods). One of the four cities of the Gibeonites (Jos. 9:17). It later marked the northern boundary (Jos. 15:9). After this, the name was changed to Kirjath-Baal to indicate that they worshiped the Baal gods (Jos. 18:14). | **2014, 4400**

Kish (Bow). A Benjamite, the father of Saul, who became Israel's first king (1 S. 9:3). | **2015**

Kishon, the River (Tortuous). A river in Palestine, in the shadow of Mount Carmel, flowing into the Mediterranean Sea. | **2016**

Laban (White). Father of Leah and Rachel and father-in-law to Jacob (Ge. 29:4ff.). | **2044**

Lachish (Impregnable). A strongly fortified Amorite city. The King of Lachish joined four neighboring kings at the invitation of Adonizedek, King of Jerusalem, to chastise the Gibeonites for making peace with Israel (Jos. 10:3,5). | **2045, 4402**

Lamech or **Lemech** (Destroyer). 1. The fifth descendant from Cain. 2. The father of Noah (Ge. 4:18-24; 5:28-29). | **2047**

Lamentations of Jeremiah A set of poems dealing with the last days under Nebuchednezzar's attack on Jerusalem (See Lam. 1:1). | **1945-1946, 4247**

Laodicea One of the seven churches of Asia Minor which Jesus said he would spew out of his mouth because it was neither hot nor cold (Re. 3:14-16). See Hierapolis for detailed discussion. | **2050, 4404**

Laver A vessel in the Tabernacle filled with water where the priests underwent ceremonial washing before officiating in the sacred principals (Ex. 38:8). In Solomon's Temple, there were ten lavers of brass (1 K. 7:27,30). | **2051**

Law With the article "The," refers to the Levitical or Mosaic Law given to Moses in the Sinai area. Sometimes it means the Pentateuch (Jos. 24:26). | **525, 949**

Lazarus (Gr. *Eleazar*). 1. The Lazarus of Bethany whom Jesus resurrected from the dead (Jn. 11:1). 2. The beggar who laid at the gate for alms, wishing to be fed with the crumbs from the rich man's table (Lu. 16:19ff.). | **2055-2056**

Leah (Languid). The homely daughter of Laban, who was passed off on Jacob instead of her beautiful sister, Rachel (Ge. 29:16ff.). | **2103**

Leaven A substance used to produce fermentation in dough. The use of leaven in any form was forbidden in all offerings made by fire to the Lord (Le. 2:11). | **2104**

Lebanon (The White Mountain). 1. A small country in the Near East. 2. A mountain range (2 Chr. 2:7-10). | **2437, 3674**

2105   **Leeks** (To be green). A large stalked onion usually mentioned with onions and garlic (Nu. 11:5).

2109   **Lentil** A leafy vegetable on the order of spinach, mustard greens and collards (2 S. 23:11).

2112   **Levi** 1. The third son of Jacob by Leah (Ge. 29:34). 2. Two ancestors of Christ—one, the son of Melchi, and the other, Symeon (Lu. 3:24).

2113   **Leviathan** (A water monster). A huge sea monster, generally assumed to be a crocodile (Ps. 74:14; Is. 27:1).

2058   **Levites** (The descendents of Levi). The priestly tribe of Levi were in charge of all religious affairs. They were supported by the tithe of the other tribes (Nu. 35:2).

4225   **Leviticus, the book of** A book dealing with the Levites and priests, enumerating their functional responsibilites, including the sacrifices, the offerings, the festivals and interpreting the Law (Le. 1:1ff.).

2185   **Linen** A white cloth made out of flax. It was used for making priestly vestments. It was also used for the curtains, the veil and doorhangings in the Tabernacle (Ex. 26:1), and later in the Temple.

81   **Locust** An insect from one to several inches long, of the grasshopper family, which ravages vegetation, frequently down to the roots. They sweep across countries by the millions and completely devour all living plants (Ex. 10:4-6).

3102   **Lord's Day, the** In the Old Testament, the Sabbath (seventh day) was set aside for rest and worship. In the New Testament this rest day shifted to the first day of the week or "Sunday" which commemorated the resurrection of our Lord (Jn. 20:1-19).

761   **Lord's Supper, the** This central act of worship in the Christian faith is celebrated by Christian believers around the world. The Lord's Supper is mentioned, as such, only one time in the NT (1 Co. 11:20).

2198   **Lot** (Veil). 1. The son of Haran and the nephew of Abraham (Ge. 11:27, 31). 2. A method by which doubtful questions were settled (Est. 3:7; Jona. 1:7; Mt. 27:35).

3152   **Lucifer** (Lightbearer). The name given the planet Venus as the morning star. The prophet Isaiah likened the glory of the king of Babylon to Lucifer (Is. 14:11-13). Lucifer was Satan's name before his fall (Lu. 10:18).

2216, 4264   **Luke** (Gr. *Loukos*). A Greek physician and fellow-missionary with St. Paul. He is credited with writing the book of Acts and the Gospel of Luke (Lu 1:3; Ac. 1:1).

2220   **Lydia** The first European convert of St. Paul in Philippi (Ac. 16:14-15).

2221, 4406   **Lystra** 1. The house of Timothy (Ac. 16:1). 2. The city in Galatia in which Paul was stoned and dragged to the trash pile outside of the city for dead (Ac. 14:19).

Maath (Small). Son of Mattathias in the genealogy of Jesus (Lu. 3:26) | 1400

Maccabees Originally the surname of Judas, one of the sons of Mattathias, but was afterward extended to the heroic family of which he was a noble representative. The Maccabean revolt resulting from Antiochus Epiphanes II offering a sow on the Jewish altar, led to Jewish independence for about 100 years (167-63 B.C.). | 3042

Macedonia The part of Europe (now Greece) to first receive the Gospel message through St. Paul (Ac. 16:9). | 2222

Magi A religious group in Persia which was influenced by the Jewish Scriptures disseminated in the time of Queen Esther. Their knowledge of the Jewish Oracles enabled them to initiate a journey to Bethlehem to worship the "newborn king." They are referred to as "wise men" in Luke, derived from the Greek *magos* (Mt. 2:1). | 3847

Magic (Magicians). A system manipulating the course of nature by natural or supernatural means, frequently in connection with religious rites. See Divination. | 2226-2232

Magog In Eze. 38:2ff, a country of which Gog was the prince. The prefix "Ma" signified a northern country, hostile to Israel. Some scholars associate this Gog with nations of the north which are to participate in the final war (Re. 20:8-15). | 2889

Makkedah (Place of shepherds). The place where the five confederate kings were executed by hailstones under Joshua (Jos. 10:3, 10:30.) | 2235

Malachi (The message of Jehovah). The last writing prophet who tells about the greatly needed reforms in preparing for the coming Messiah. He accuses his people of robbing God by witholding their tithe (Mal. 3:8-16). | 4261

Mammon (Fullness). A person can have only one supreme devotion and that must be to God. When material wealth obsesses him, there is danger that it may become his God (Mt. 6:24). | 2131-2132

Mamre (Fatness). 1. A town or district of Hebron where Abraham made a covenant with Lot (Ge. 13:6ff.). 2. An Amorite woman who helped Abraham recover property taken by Chedorlaomer (Ge. 14:13,24). | 2236

Manasseh (One who causes to forget). 1. The oldest son of Joseph by his wife Asenath (Ge. 48:1). 2. The thirteenth king of Judah (2 K. 21:1). | 2244-2245

Mandrakes A plant with wavy leaves with violet or blue flowers having roots resembling the human body. They were supposed to act as a love potion and were sometimes called a "Love Apple" (Ge. 30:14-15). | 667

Manna When the Israelites first saw manna in their camp they said, "Man-hu" or "What is this?" Thus it became known as "manna" (Ex. 16:2-31). | 2248

1045   **Mantle** A body covering such as a blanket or a garment, with or without sleeves (Jud. 4:18; 1 S. 15:27; Is. 3:22). Elijah symbolically transferred the prophetic office to Elisha by casting his mantle over Elisha's shoulders (1 K. 19:19).

3097a   **Mara** (Sad or bitter). Elimelech and Naomi went to Moah at the time of the great famine in Bethlehem. While in exile Naomi's husband and her two sons died. Her bitterness over this loss prompted her to take the name "Mara" (Ru. 1:20).

2249   **Marah** (Bitterness). A place in the wilderness where the Israelites found springs of bitter water (Ex. 15:23).

1348   **Maranatha** (Our Lord cometh). A Greek form of the Aramaic word meaning "Our Lord cometh." Negatively, let him be accursed who does not love the coming of the Lord (1 Co. 16:22).

4263   **Mark** (Greek, *Marcos* from Latin, *Marcus*) Early evangelist whose first name was John. He is thought to have written the second Gospel (Ac. 12:12).

2087   **Mars Hill** Better known as the Areopagus in Athens where judges held court and where philosophers debated. Paul was invited to present his case at this place (Ac. 17:22ff.).

2258   **Martha** (Lady). The sister of Mary and of Lazarus, whom Jesus raised from the dead (Lu. 10:38ff.).

2259-2264   **Mary** (Greek form of *Marie* and *Miriam,* meaning rebellious). Six women in the New Testament are called Mary. The most prominent are the Virgin Mary (Lu. 1:26-27) and Mary, Lazarus' sister (Lu. 10:39).

3988   **Mattaniah** (Gift of Jehovah). The original name of Zedekiah, King of Judah (2 K. 24:17). 2. One of the sons of Heman (1 Chr. 25:4). 3. A descendant of Asaph the Levite (2 Chr. 20:14).

2265, 4262   **Matthew** (English form of Heb. *Mattathiah*). The Jewish apostle and evangelist called Levi, the son of Alphaeus, and writer of the Gospel of Matthew (Mk. 2:14)

2266   **Mattias** An early Christian who was elected to fill the place of the traitor, Judas Iscariot (Ac. 1:26). Tradition tells us that he suffered martyrdom in Ethiopia.

2630   **Meat Offering** This offering originally signified a gift from an inferior to a superior, whether God or man. See Le. 2 and 6.

Medes (Inhabitants of Media). A prominent, highly civilized people in Asia. The Medes and Persians were in some way linked politically. Ezra makes reference to both Darius and the Persian king and "the province of the Medes" (Ezr. 6:1-2).

2283, 4411   **Megiddo** (Place of troops). A heavily fortified city in the Jezreel Valley paralleling the Carmel range. It guarded the vital trade route between Egypt and Mesopotamia. Archaeologists have excavated through many strata down to the Canaanite city foundations of 3500 B.C.

Melchizedek (King of righteousness). When Abraham arrived in Salem (Jerusalem) this king was worshiping the same Great High God to whom Abraham was devoted. He showed reverence to the king by giving him his tithe. The writer of the book of Hebrews links a reference to Melchizedek from the book of Psalms (Ps. 110:4) with the Messiah (He. 5:10). | **2284**

Menahem (Comforter). The son of Gadi who slew the usurper Shallum and seized the throne of Israel (2 K. 15:14). | **2290**

Mephibosheth (Destroying shame). 1. The name of Saul's son and grandson (2 S. 21:8). 2. The son of Jonathan, grandson of Saul (2 S. 4:4; 21:8-9). | **2291-2292**

Meraioth (Rebellious). 1. A son of Aaron, a descendent of Eleazar and the head of a priestly house (1 Chr. 6:3,6,7,52). 2. The head of a house of priests represented by Helkai (Ne. 12:15). | **2293**

Merari (Bitter). The third son of Levi and head of the great division of the Merarites (Ge. 46:11; Ex. 6:16). | **2294**

Mercy-Seat The lid of the Ark of the Covenant which was sprinkled annually with blood by the high priest (Ex. 25:17; He. 9:5). | **2303**

Meribah (Water of Strife). The place in the wilderness where the people murmured and where Moses smote the rock. Kadesh is also identified with this name (Ex. 17:6-7; Nu. 20:13,24). | **830**

Merib-baal (Contender against Baal). The son of Jonathan, the son of Saul (1 Chr. 8:34). He is also called "Mephibosheth" who was hanged by the Gibeonites (2 S. 21:8-9). | **2291-2292**

Meroz A city of people who refused to take part in the struggle against Sisera (Jud. 5:23). | **2304**

Meshach One of the three Jews who were cast into the fiery furnace in Babylon (Da. 1:6-7). | **2305**

Mesopotamia The terrain between the Tigris and Euphrates rivers. | **2306**

Messiah (The Anointed One). The Greek equivalent of "Christ" in English. The Greek form is *Messias* (Jn. 1:41; 4:25). | **695**

Methuselah (Man of the Dart?). The son of Enoch and the father of Lamech, the sixth descendent from Seth. He is credited with living longer than any other human being—969 years (Ge. 5:27). | **2332**

Micah A contemporary with the prophets Isaiah and Hosea. He prophesied against the sins of Judah in the rural community of Moresheth while Isaiah condemned the conduct of Judah in Jerusalem. He predicted that the Messiah would be born in Bethlehem-Ephratah (Mi. 5:2). | **2333, 4255**

2335	**Michael** (Who is like unto God). The archangel in the hierarchy of angels. He seems to be the angel who arranged Moses' funeral (Jude 9). Michael also is pictured in a fight against the great dragon, the devil (Re. 12:7-9).
2336	**Michal** (Brook). The youngest of Saul's two daughters (1 S. 14:49).
2338-2340	**Midian** (Strife). A son of Abraham and Keturah, the progenitor of the Midianites (Ge. 25:1-4; 1 Chr. 1:32).
2342	**Migdol** A frontier fortress in Egypt on the route the Israelites traveled in the exodus (Ex. 14:2; Nu. 33:7).
2511	**Milcah** (Counsel). Daughter of Haran and wife of Nahor, Abraham's brother, by whom she had six children (Ge. 11:29; 22:20,23). See also Nu. 26:33.
3941	**Milcom** and **Molech** (King, the reigning one). The "spiritual king" in an abominable system of idolatrous worship. Solomon was drawn into this cult and built an altar to Molech in Jerusalem (1 K. 11:7). Israel, the northern kingdom, became so involved in this worship that God turned them over to the Assyrians for punishment.
2346	**Miletus** A city on the west coast of Asia Minor about 35 miles south of Ephesus. When Paul was enroute to Jerusalem from his third missionary journey he asked the elders at Ephesus to come here for a farewell meeting (Ac. 20:17; 38).
2348	**Millo** (A mound). A fortified area in Jerusalem that David took from the Jebusites (2 S. 5:19). It appears that this was a suburb of Jerusalem, probably Zion (2 K. 13:9-10).
2348	**Millo, the House of** (House on mound). Originally a strongly fortified Jebusite area in Jerusalem, rebuilt by David, reinforced by Solomon and strengthed by Hezekiah (2 S. 5:9; 1 K. 9:15, 24). Here Josiah was murdered by his slaves (2 K. 12:20).
2083-2092	**Minister** A person who renders special services, either good or evil. Priests, public servants and officials were called ministers, as were angels (Ps. 103:20-21). Evildoers were also called priests, prophets and ministers— but of unrighteousness (Je. 5:31; Eze. 22:26; Ho. 5:1).
2454-2469	**Minstrel** A musician playing on a stringed instrument such as the harp and psaltery (2 K. 3:15; 1 S. 16:16).
4069	**Miracle** A sign signifying supernatural or divine power. The miracles of Jesus—healing the leper, raising the dead and making the blind to see— were called signs that confirmed his divinity (Jn. 3:2).
2375	**Miriam** The sister of Moses and Aaron. She first appears in Scripture watching over baby Moses in the Nile bulrushes (Ex. 2:4).
2376	**Mirror** Usually rendered "looking glass" (Ex. 38:8; Jb. 37:18). When

the Tabernacle was built the women gave their treasured possessions, their "looking glasses," with which to make the molten laver.

Mishael (Who is what God is?). 1. A son of Uzziel, the uncle of Aaron and Moses (Ex. 6:22). 2. One of the attendants when Ezra read the newly discovered law to the people (Ne. 8:4-6). 3. Friend of Daniel in captivity, called Meshach (Da. 1:7,19). | 2305

Mite The coin of least value in Jesus' day, yet when the widow cast in her two "mites," making a farthing, Jesus commended her for giving more than the wealthy had given (Mk. 12:42-43). | 2386

Mixed Multitude When the Israelites started leaving Egypt with Moses, there were seekers of fortune and calf worshipers who attached themselves to the Israelites. This was evidenced at Sinai when a mold was produced for the golden calf (Ex. 12:38; Nu. 11:4). | 2388

Mizpah or **Mizpeh** A heap of stones or an altar built by Jacob and Laban to seal their covenant (Ge. 31:44-49). | 2389-2390

Moab 1. The son of Lot. 2. The land on the east side of the Dead Sea made productive by the cooling westerly winds striking the moist air rising from the hot surface of the Sea. God pronounced judgment upon Moab because of its idolatry (Je. 48:1ff; Am. 2:1-2). | 2391

Molech See Milcom. | 3941

Money A substance of value (such as gold or silver jewels) whose worth was determined by its weight. Later precious metal such as gold and silver was used in coinage. Units of measure were the pound, shekel, farthing, mite penny, etc. (Ge. 23:9-16; Zec. 11:12; Mt. 5:26; 26:15). | 2396

Money-changers Worshipers were required to convert their Roman money into Temple coinage, because coins with Caesar's image could not be used. The Temple authorities overcharged the people and sold sacrifical animals at inflated prices. Jesus drove them out of the Temple (Mt. 21:12-13). | 2397

Month The Israelites used the Egyptian calendar at first with its twelve months of thirty days each with five additional days to produce conformity with the solar year of 365 days. Later they appear to have switched over to a lunar year. | 2398

Mordecai The uncle of Esther, the queen of Persia. (See Esther.) | 2401

Moreh (Archer). The first resting place for Abram after entering Canaan (Ge. 12:6). | 2402

Moriah (Provided by Jehovah). A mountain peak in Jerusalem where Abram took Isaac to be sacrificed (Ge. 22:2). Later it became the site of Solomon 's Temple (2 S. 24:18ff; 2 Chr. 2:1ff.). | 2439

Mortar or **Morter** A substance used in the Near East to bind stone and mud brick. This substance was made out of either butumen, common mud, or a compound of sand ashes and lime, sometimes mixed and coated with oil (Ge. 11:3; Ex. 1:14). | 2417-2418

3971-3972   **Mother** The superiority of the Hebrew system is seen in the close family relationship and the high esteem placed on motherhood and fatherhood (Ex. 20:12; Le. 19:3).

180   **Mule** or **Donkey** An inexpensive beast of burden used in plowing, transporting goods and as a vehicle for human transportation.

2449-2451   **Murder** The crime of intentional homicide was defined with strictness (Ge. 9:6; Ex. 20:13). The offender was to be put to death—"an eye for an eye and a tooth for a tooth."

2454, 2477   **Music** Music was not well organized until the period of the prophets, when it became an important part of worship.

2478, 2483   **Mustard** The mustard tree is found in most places in Palestine where sufficient moisture is available to sustain it. The seed is very small. Jesus drews an analogy of the growth of the kingdom by comparing it to a mustard seed which, when planted, grows up into the greatest among the herbs (Mt. 13:31-32).

2485   **Myrrh** A pungent gum in Arabia, Egypt and Abyssinia. It was used for perfume and embalming (Ex. 30:23; Ps. 45:8; Song 3:6).

3681   **Myrtle** A pungent plant used by the Hebrews for perfumes, ointments and spices (Is. 41:19; 55:13; Zec. 1:10).

2505   **Naaman** (Pleasantness). A Syrian army officer who had leprosy. A Jewish slave girl suggested he go to the prophet Elisha for healing. Reluctantly he went and was healed (2 K. 5:1ff.).

2506   **Nabal** A wealthy sheep raiser in Judea whose wife's name was Abigail. After his death, Abigail married David (1 S. 25:1-42).

2507   **Naboth** (Fruits). A man who owned a vineyard which Ahab and Jezebel wanted to possess. After he refused to sell, Jezebel initiated a plot in which Naboth was killed and the property was transferred to the royal couple (1 K. 21:1ff.).

7, 2508   **Nadab** (Liberal) 1. The eldest son of Aaron (Ex. 6:23; Nu. 3:2). 2. King Jeroboam's son and successor to the throne for two years (1 K. 15:25-31).

2509   **Nahash** The king of the Ammonites (1 S. 11:1-11).

2510-2511   **Nahor** Two kinsmen of Abraham: 1. Abraham's grandfather, the son of Serug and the father of Terah (Ge. 11:22-25). 2. Son of Terah and brother of Abraham and Haran (Ge. 11:26-27).

    Nahshon (Enchanted). A prince in the tribe of Judah during the wilderness wandering (Nu. 2:3; 7:12).

4256   **Nahum** (Comforter). Nahum the "Elkoshite" was the seventh minor prophet. Nineveh had repented under Jonah but now apostasy has set in. Nahum describes the bloody carnage which will take place in the streets of Nineveh. See book of Nahum.

Nanea The Persian nature goddess with the attributes of Aphrodite and representing the reproductive power of nature. Sexual orgies were a part of the ritual in this cult. | 3930

Naomi Wife of Elimelech and his wife and mother-in-law of Ruth, who became an ancestress of Christ (Ru. 1:2; 2:1; 4:3). | 2519

Naphtali A son of Jacob born of Bilhah, Rachel's slave (Ge. 30:8). | 2520-2521

Nathan (A giver). One of the leading prophets in Judah during the reign of David and Solomon. Nathan challenged David after his sin with Bathsheba (2 S. 12:1ff.). | 2523-2524

Nathanael (Gift of God). One of Jesus' disciples from Cana of Galilee (Jn. 21:2). | 344

Nazarene A dweller in Nazareth; Jesus was called a Nazarene (Ac. 24:5). This term was applied to Jesus' followers as a term of contempt. | 2570

Nazareth (Branch). A small village separated from the main caravan route from Damascus to the Mediterranean coast. Tradition stated that no prophet would arise out of Nazareth. Since this was Jesus' hometown it was difficult to establish him as the Messiah (Jn. 1:46). | 2571, 4416

Nazarite (One separated). An order that dates back to the early period in the OT. Those who took this vow committed themselves to a separated life. They were to totally abstain from the use of wine or strong drink, and they were not to shave or come near a dead body (Nu. 6:1-11). | 3211

Nebo, Mount The point at which Moses turned over the command of the Israelites to Joshua and where Moses viewed the promised land before he died. Here the angel Michael arranged for Moses' funeral (Jude 9). See also De. 32:49; 34:1. | 2440, 2572, 4417

Nebuchadnezzar (Nebo protect the crown). The Babylonian king who subdued Jerusalem, took the Jews into captivity and kept them enslaved for seventy years. At the end of this time Cyrus, king of Persia, conquered Babylon and set the captives free (2 K. 24; Ezr. 1 ff.). | 2573-2574

Negina, Pl. **Neginoth** (A stringed instrument). A stringed instrument used in Temple worship. The captions of six Psalms indicate they were to be accompanied by a stringed instrument (Ps. 4,6,54,55,67,76). |

Nehemiah (Jehovah hath consoled). A Jew serving as cupbearer to the Persian king, who was granted permission to return to Jerusalem as governor of Judah. Under his leadership the people's spirits were renewed and the city walls were repaired. The book of Nehemiah gives a graphic description of these events. | 2577

Nehiloth (Flutes, wind instruments). The caption of Psalm 5, indicating that wind instruments were to be used to accompany this Psalm in the Temple service. This is the only instance where "Nehiloth" appears. | 2454-2469

Nergal (Lion). A prominent nature deity among the Assyrians and Babylonians; closely related to the Greek god Mars (2 K. 17:30). He was the god of war and pestilence as well as the god of the land of the dead. | 3930

2400   **New Moon** The moon and its phases were very important because they measured time in connection with regulating the Passover and other feasts of the year (Ge. 1:14; Ps. 104:19). Much of the Jewish ritual was determined in relationship to the New Moon.

1028   **Nicolaitans** (Named after Nicholas). Followers of one unidentified Nicholas (Re. 2:6, 14-15), the Nicolaitans were a liberal sect in the churches at Ephesus and Pergamus who taught that the excesses of heathenism and its immorality were not inconsistent with the Christian faith.

753   **Nicolas** or **Nicolaus** (Victor over the people). A dedicated convert in Antioch who was one of the seven (with Philip) elected to serve the neglected widows in the church (Ac. 6:1-6). This man had no relationship to the Nicolaitans.

2591   **Nile-Sihor** The great river of Egypt, 1800 miles long, arising as two forks into the Mediterranean Sea through several branches in the delta area. It is the source of life as it flows through desert mountains and sand hills.

2593, 4418   **Nineveh** (Dwelling). The capital city of Assyria. After becoming one of the largest cities of the world, it was totally destroyed by the Medes. . Its ancient walls, partly crumbled, extend for many miles.

2594   **Nisroch** (Eagle). One of the Assyrian gods whose idol was located in Nineveh. After Sennacherib's utter defeat in Jerusalem he was assassinated by his sons (2 K. 19:37; Is. 37:38).

2597, 4289   **Noah** or **Noe** The tenth descendent in the line of Seth, the son of Lamech and grandson of Methuselah (Ge. 5:28-29). History is silent on Noah until he was 500 years old and had three sons—Shem, Ham and Japheth.

3241   **Number** Some of the significant numbers in Scripture were 3,4,7,10 and 40, all thought to represent completeness. The 3 represented the Trinity, the 4 symbolized the four Gospels, the 7 denoted the seven days in a week while 40 symbolized the forty years in the wilderness.

2607-2611   **Oath** A formal commitment to truth expressed in a few short concise words. Usually an oath made its appeal to God in an attestation of the truth of a statement or the binding character of a promise (Ge. 21:23; He. 6:16).

4253   **Obadiah** (Worshiper of Jehovah). The fourth of the minor prophets. He pronounced judgment upon Edom for its hostile attitude toward Israel. (Obad. 1:10ff.).

2612   **Obed** (Worshiping God). The son of Boaz and Ruth, the Moabitess (Ru. 4:17).

2613   **Obed-edom** (Serving Edom). A Levite in whose care the ark was placed, after the death of Uzziah, for three months (1 Chr. 15:25; 2 S. 6:12).

2637   **Og** (Circle). One of the last kings of Bashan and one of the last giants. It is stated that his iron bedstead was nine cubits long and four cubits wide (13.5 by 6.5 ft.) (De. 3:11).

195, 2638-2641   **Oil** Commonly used for cooking, anointing priests and kings. On days of rejoicing the Hebrews anointed themselves with perfumed oil, and it was used figuratively to express gladness and sadness during mourning (Ps. 45:7; Is. 61:3).

Ointments Ointments made of olive oil, perfumed herbs and unguents were used as body rubs after bathing and for medical purposes, as well as for anointing the dead (Lu. 23:56). | 1532

Olives, the Mount of or **Olivet** A mountain ridge east of Jerusalem, separated from the city by the Kidron Valley. The Garden of Gethsemane is at its base on the Jerusalem side with Bethany on the eastern slopes (2 S. 15:30; Mt. 21:1; Lu. 22:39 and Ac. 1:12). | 2441, 4421

Omri (Impetuous). The commander of Israel's army who became king when Zimri was murdered. He continued the idolatry of his father and earned the reputation of being more wicked than any of his predecessors (1 K. 16:25; Mi. 6:16). | 2646

Onan (Strong). Judah was the father of Onan by a Canaanite woman (Ge. 38:4). | 2648

Onesimus (Profitable). One of Philemon's slaves who fled from his master and became a faithful friend to Paul. Paul entreats Philemon to take him back as a brother in the Lord (Phm. 4). | 2650

Onesiphorus (Bringing profit). One of Paul's converts who rendered fruitful service to Paul, both in Rome and in Ephesus. Paul commends him to Timothy (2 Ti. 1:16-18). | 2651

Onyx Stone A semi-precious stone. Two of these stones, each with the names of six tribes engraved on it, were placed on the High Priest's breastplate. Tradition says the onyx stone was assigned to Asher. | 2856

Ophir A fabled city in India where gold was plentiful (Jb. 22:24; 28:16). | 2654

Orion The stellar constellation known to the Hebrews and the Greeks; the Arabs called it "the giant" (Jb 9:9; 38:31; Am. 5:8). | 2663

Orpha A Moabite woman who became an Israelite by marrying a Jew—Chilon, son of Naomi, from Bethlehem—and thereby she became a sister-in-law to Ruth (Ru. 1:14).

Ospray, Ossifrage and **Ostrich** The first two are named as unclean birds in Le. 11:13 and De. 14:12. The ostrich is described in Jb. 39:13. | 459

Othniel (Powerful man of God). One of the judges of Israel (Jud. 1:13; 3:9). | 2664

Ox An early domesticated animal, used as a beast of burden (Ge. 12:16; 1 K. 19:19) They were used for pulling carts, plows and for treading out grain (De. 25:4) and they were eaten (1 K. 1:25). They were used in religious ceremonies as burnt and peace offerings (Nu. 7:87-88). | 181

Palm trees Palm trees grow in great abundance at the lower, warmer elevations in Palestine, mainly along the coast, and at Tiberias and Jericho where it is tropical and below sea level. Because of the tropical climate, Jericho is called "the city of palm trees." | 3685

1512   **Palsy** A semi-paralyzing, crippling disease accompanied with shaking limbs and hunched-over bodies. The woman who was "bowed together" may have had this disease (Lu. 13:11).

2674   **Pamphylia** A province in the southern part of Asia Minor with Perga for its port city. On his first missionary journey Paul entered at this port (Ac. 13:13).

2677   **Paphos** A town on the west coast of Cyprus, the place where Paul met Elymas, the sorcerer (Ac. 13:6-12).

2678-2679   **Parable** A short, weighty story from which moral and religious truth is extracted. It puts the burden of understanding upon the hearers. Christ used the parable in every phase of his earthly ministry (Mk. 3:23; Lu. 6:39).

2680   **Paradise** An expression used to denote a habitation under ideal conditions. Sometimes it is used in reference to heaven (Lu. 23:43; 2 Co. 12:4; Re. 2:7).

1256, 2686   **Passover** A feast of the Jews commemorating the time when God smote the firstborn in every Egyptian household where the blood was not applied on the doorpost and lintel.

2695   **Patmos** A bleak, rugged island in the Aegean Sea, where John received the Revelation (Re. 1:9-10).

732, 1178, **2087, 2371,** **2382, 2697**   **Paul** (Saul of Tarsus) The great apostle of Christ, who spread the faith and established churches throughout Asia Minor and Macedonia (Ac. 12:24ff.). Tradition tells us that he died as a martyr in Rome.

2703   **Pekah** (Open eyed). A military officer in the Israeli army under Pekahiah; he killed the king and assumed the throne of Israel (2 K. 15:25-28).

4291   **Peniel** (The face of God). The place where Jacob wrestled with an angel and where his name was changed to Israel. Jacob named the place Peniel because he had "seen God face to face" (Ge. 32:24-30).

2720, 3537   **Penny** A silver Roman coin worth about seventeen cents in the time of Christ. It was considered to be a day's pay for an agricultural worker (Mt. 22:19).

949   **Pentateuch** The Greek name for the first five Old Testament Books, called the "Books of Moses." In Hebrew it was called the Torah, "The Law."

1257, 2722   **Pentecost** The Hebrew harvest festival, observed on the fiftieth day from Passover (Ex. 23:16; 34:22; Le. 23:15-22). In the Christian Church, Pentecost is celebrated seven weeks after Easter to commemorate the baptism of the Holy Spirit on the Day of Pentecost (Ac. 2:1-4).

2726   **Peor** The mountain in Moab to which Balak took Balaam for his final conjurations (Nu. 23:28).

Perga The port city of Pamphylia, a southern province in Asia Minor (Ac. 13:14; 14:26). See Pamphylia.   2735

Pergamos or **Pergamum** (Citadel). A city in northwest Asia Minor in the province of Mysia on the Caicus river. Nearby, a temple and medical center to Aesculapius, the god of medicine, was built. The church in Pergamum is addressed in the book of Revelation (Re. 2:12ff.).   2736, 4422

Perizzites (Dwellers in unwalled villages). One of the Canaanite villages which Joshua never fully conquered (Jos. 9:1ff.). The earliest reference to these people is in Ge. 13:7.   2742

Persia A country around the Persian Gulf. Persia was influenced by the Jehovah religion during the reign of the Jewish queen Esther.   2744

Peter, Simon The son of Jonas (Jn. 1:42). Peter is always named first in the lists of the apostles (Mt. 10:2; Mk. 3:16). He was the natural spokesman among the disciples (Ac. 2:10, 38) and was the first to confess Jesus as the Christ-Messiah (Mt. 16:16; Mk. 8:29). Peter wrote two general epistles.   4191, 4282, 4305

Pharaoh (The sun). The title of the supreme ruler of Egypt. Sometimes his personal name was added, as Pharaoh-hophra (Je. 44:30) and Pharaoh-echoh (Je. 46:2). It is generally assumed that Ramesses II was the pharaoh of the exodus.   2747-2748

Pharisees One of the very early sects among the Israelites who adopted a rigid way of life including fasting and the exactitude of the Law; they were strict legalists. They studied the Law and made outer pretensions of being more holy than others.   2750, 3171

Philadelphia (Brotherly love). A city of Lydia in Asia Minor founded by Ptolemy Philadelphus and the location of one of the seven churches in the book of Revelation (Re. 1:11; 3:7-13).   2752

Philemon (Affectionate). The Christian, presumably residing in Colosse, to whom Paul addressed his epistle by that name. Paul urges him to take his runaway slave Onesimus back as a brother in Christ (Phm. 10ff.).   4279

Philip (Lover of horses). Several men named Philip are mentioned in the Bible. Philip, the apostle, is the most prominent. See Mt. 10:3; 14:3; Ac. 8:26ff.   2753-2755

Philippi (Named after Philip of Macedonia). The city of Philippi lies about twelve miles from the port city of Neapolis. Paul landed here and began his Macedonian ministry (Ac. 16:12ff.).   2756, 4425

Philistines (Wanderers). The power of these people endangered Israel during the reign of Saul (1 S. 14:52). After much prayer and repentance David broke the backbone of Philistine power by killing Goliath, a giant and leader of the enemy army (1 S. 17:38 ff.).   2758

Phinehas (Serpent's mouth). 1. A grandson of Aaron (Ex. 6:25). 2. A second son of Eli, the priest (1 S. 1:3, 21, 34; 4:4-19). Both sons, Phinehas and Hophni, were so wicked they were called "sons of Belial" (1 S. 2:12).   2760

2751	**Phoebe** (Servant). A saint in Rome whom Paul commends highly (Ro. 16:1-2).
2761	**Phoenicia** A small country on the coast in Palestine, a province of Syria. It was called Canaan by the ancient Hebrews (Is. 23:11). When Jesus visited Tyre and Sidon he visited in the territory of Phoenicia (Mt. 15:21; Mk. 7:24,31).
2762	**Phrygia** A large province in western Asia Minor, embracing all of the Seven Churches of Revelation. Paul traveled extensively in this area on his second and third missionary journeys.
3001	**Phylacteries.** See Frontlets.
3315-3316	**Pieces of Silver** Could mean bars or coins used as a medium of exchange. The Greek "drachma" and the Roman "denarius" were the most common coins in Palestine. The most notable instance of the use of silver was when Judas sold the Lord for "thirty pieces of silver" (Mt. 26:14-15).
2763	**Pilate, Pontius** (Armed with a javelin). The sixth procurator of Judea. Contrary to Jewish law and scruples, he brought the imperial insignia and standards into the Holy City (Ex. 20:4). He used the military to quell disorder over some of his indiscretions and was under such pressure that he accomodated the Jews by having Jesus crucified.
2461	**Pipe** This word signifies "bored through" and suggests an instrument with holes like a bamboo flute (1 S. 10:5; 1 K. 1:40).
2442	**Pisgah, Mount** (A boundary). The highest point in the Pisgah mountain range is Mount Nebo, the place where Moses was permitted to view the promised land but was not permitted to enter it (De. 34:1,5,6).
2769	**Pisidia** A small land-locked province in central Asia Minor north of Pamphylia, through which Paul traveled on his first missionary journey (Ac. 13:13 ff.).
2771	**Pitch** A petroleum substance rising to the ground; it is now called asphalt. It was used for sealing boats to make them watertight (Ex. 2:3). In Babylon it was mixed with sand and used as mortar (Ge. 6:14). See Is. 34:9.
1973-1974	**Plagues, the Ten** Imposed by God upon the Egyptians when Pharaoh refused to let the Hebrews leave the country. The tenth plague, the death of the firstborn, included the king's own son and forced Pharaoh to release the people (Ex. chs. 3-12).
2777	**Pleiades** A beautiful cluster of stars sometimes called "the seven stars," although there are only six of them (Jb. 9:9; 38:31; Am. 5:8)
2783	**Pontus** A coastal province on the Black Sea in Asia Minor. Under Roman rule, it merged with Bithynia and is so named on most Bible maps. Pliny, the historian, became one of its proconsuls.
4292	**Potiphar** (Belonging to the sun). An officer in Pharoah's household who bought Joseph from the Midianites (Ge. 37:36). Later Potiphar's wife falsely accused Joseph and had him put in prison (Ge. 39:19ff.).
2058-2063	**Priest** The leader of a religious group. All of the heathen religions had

a priesthood. The Jewish priesthood was passed from the patriarchs to the tribe of Levi at Mount Sinai, where Aaron became their first high priest (Ex. 28:1ff.).

Proconsul Political leader over a small political sub-division appointed by the Roman Senate. His function was purely political. Sometimes they are referred to as "deputies" (Ac. 13:7; 19:38).　　　　2870

Procurator This was a regional officer of high rank in the provinces, appointed by the head of State (as opposed to the Senate, as in the case of the Proconsul).　　　　2541

Prophet Briefly stated, one who foretold the future and warned of approaching judgment, explained obscure passages of Scripture, or made known the truths of the Bible and urged men to obedience (1 Co. 14:29).　　　　2065-2074

Proselyte This word means "stranger," or a heathen person who has been converted to the true faith (Ac. 2:10; Ezr. 6:21; Jn. 12:20ff; Ac. 6:5).　　　　2895-2896

Pruning Hooks Cutting instruments used to prune grapes and other vines (Is. 18:5).　　　　93

Psalms The Hebrew title is *Sepher Tehillim* meaning "Book of Praises." These sacred poems were used in many aspects of Temple worship, both as hymns and responses. For 1,500 years they were used exclusively by the Christian church as its hymnody.　　　　4241

Psaltery The Hebrew word *Nobel* from which the word "Psaltery" is derived indicates that it was a musical instrument of Sidonian origin. The body of the instrument was made of wood (2 S. 6:5; 2 Chr. 9:11). The Psalmist suggests it had ten strings (Ps. 33:2).　　　　2462

Publican The publican was not a duly appointed tax collector but one who made the highest bid at a tax collecting auction sale. This opened the door to many abuses including excessive taxing.　　　　2926

Rachel (Ewe). The younger and more attractive daughter of Laban. Jacob contracted to marry her, but on the night of the wedding Laban substituted Leah. Jacob agreed to work seven more years for Rachel (Ge. 29:16ff.).　　　　2941

Rahab or **Rachab** (Broad, roomy). A woman living in Jericho, who befriended Joshua's spies and hid them while the authorities made a search (Jos. 2:1 ff.). She is included in the genealogy of David as well as of our Lord (Mt. 1:5).　　　　2942

Ram The male of the sheep (Eze. 34:17) which was used for food (Ge. 31:38), as a burnt-offering or peace-offering (Ge. 22:13; Le. 1:10) and as a trespass-offering (Le. 5:15; 6:6).　　　　183

Ramah (A hill). 1. A city in Benjamin's territory (Jos. 18:25). 2. The birthplace, residence and burial place of Samuel (1 S. 1:19).　　　　2945

Rameses or **Raamses** A city and a district of Goshen in lower Egypt where the Hebrew tribes first settled (Ge. 47:11). Another town by this name was built on the eastern border where grain was stored for the lean years.　　　　2946

2959	**Rebekah** (A noose). The daughter of Bethuel and sister of Laban who married Isaac, her father's cousin (Ge. 22:23).
2969	**Rechab, Rechabites** (Horseman). 1. One of the two "captains of bands" whom Ishbosheth took into his service and who conspired to murder him (2 S. 4:2ff.). 2. A kinsman of Jehonadab (2 K. 10:15, 23; 1 Chr. 2:55).
253, 496	**Refiner** The refiner took the raw metal ore and by a fire or water process extracted the pure gold, silver, copper lead, tin or other metals (Is. 1:25; Je. 6:29).
2983	**Rehoboam** (Who enlarges the people). The son of Solomon, successor to the throne. Reigned seventeen years (1 K. 12:1ff.).
4307	**Rephidim** The camp site in the wilderness where there was no water and the Israelites protested and chided with Moses. He met the emergency by striking a rock and making water come rushing out (Ex. 17:1-7).
3029	**Reuben** (Behold a son). Jacob's first son by Leah (Ge. 29:32).
4288	**Revelation of Saint John** The last of five books written by the apostle John. John had this special revelation of the Isle of Patmos and either wrote it there or moved to Ephesus to write down what he had envisioned on the Isle (Re. 1:1ff.).
3052	**Riblah** The military outpost between Jerusalem and Babylon where Nebuchadnezzar and his army staff established headquarters while their soldiers attacked Palestine and Phoenicia (2 K. 25:1-6).
3095, 4428	**Rome** Called the "eternal city" because of its religious background and also because of its stone columns and buildings. The years between 63 B.C. and 638 A.D. are known as the Empire period, when Rome controlled all the countries bordering on the Mediterranean Sea.
4267	**Romans, the Epistles of** Paul wrote this epistle from Corinth when he was 60 years old, with the Christians in Rome in mind.
2857	**Ruby** The precious stone assigned as a tribal symbol to the tribe of Judah. The Saviour came from this tribe so the red color of this stone symbolized the Saviour's blood.
3097, 4230	**Ruth** A native of Moab, who embraced the Jewish religion, married Boaz, and became an ancestress of Christ (Mt. 1:5; Ru. 1:1 ff.). Her story is told in the book of Ruth.
3098-3102, 3927	**Sabbath** God created the world in six daily stages and set aside the seventh day for rest. This was to be a pattern for man. Christians changed their rest day to the first day of the week, the day of Christ's resurrection and named it Sunday.
3103, 3533	**Sabbath Day's Journey** The law of a Sabbath Day's Journey has no Scriptural validity. It was invented by the rabbis to protect the Sabbath and keep the people in close proximity of the worship center on the Sabbath.

Sabbatical Year This Holy Year was the "Sabbath among years," e.g. it was a week of Sabbaths coming once in every seven years. It was a general year of rest for the land, animal and man (Ex. 23:10ff; De. 15:1ff.). | 3104

Sackcloth A coarse, cheaply made cloth, used for sacking commodities such as potatoes and commercial goods. A garment made from this material was donned in time of mourning and sorrow (2 S. 3:31). It was also a sign of repentance and sorrow for sins (1 K. 21:27-29). | 1950

Sacrifice In the Hebrew ritual, provision was made for dramatic expression of sorrow, gladness, repentance for sin, restitution, thanksgiving and devotion toward God. The many offerings were systematized and organized when the laws were given at Mount Sinai (Le. chs. 1-7). | 3107-3111

Sadducees A sect of liberal Jews who denied the existence of angels and spirits, the immortality of the soul and the resurrection of the body (Antiq. XIII; Mt. 22:23ff; Ac. 23:8). | 3172

Salome The wife of Zebedee (cf. Mt. 27:56 with Mk. 15:40). Salome petitioned Jesus to give her sons the most honored places in the kingdom of heaven (Mt. 20:20). | 3113

Salt A most important substance in human as well as animal diets, symbolizing hospitality, durability, fidelity, purity and cleanliness (Le. 2:13; Nu. 18:19; 2 Chr. 13:5). | 281, 3114-3115

Salutation It was customary among the Hebrews to give each other God-related greetings: "God be gracious unto thee" (Ge. 43:29), "Blessed be thou of the Lord" (Ru. 3:10), "The Lord be with you" (1 S. 15:13), etc. | 3409-3410

Samaria A noted city in Israel founded by Omri, King of Israel (1 K. 16:22-24). | 3133-3134, 4430

Samaritans To the natives of Judah the Samaritans were ceremonially unclean and were shunned. Jesus disputed this concept when he visited with the Samaritan woman at the well (Jn. 4:4ff.). | 3135-3136

Samaritan Pentateuch The Samaritans possessed an ancient Hebrew Torah or Pentateuch which they claimed dated back to ancient times, but scholars have concluded it dates back only to the tenth century A.D. It differs in some aspects from the Hebrew Mesoretic text. | 4220

Samuel A faithful prophet, born in Ramah of the tribe of Ephraim, who was dedicated by his mother to the Lord's service from birth (1 S. 1:11; 3:1). He is credited with writing 1 Samuel and the books of Judges and Ruth. | 3138, 4231-4232

Sanballat An influential Samaritan (Ne. 2:10) who was opposed to rebuilding the walls of Jerusalem after the Jews returned from Babylon (Ne. 4:7-8). Sanballat founded and promoted the Samaritan religion and built a temple at Gerazim (Antiq. XIII, 9,1). | 3139

Sanhedrin The Supreme Council or Court of the Jews in Jesus' day. The Sanhedrin ceased to function when Jerusalem fell to the Roman Titus in 90 A.D. | 862

2858	**Sapphire** A precious blue stone, which according to tradition was the tribal stone of Simeon. It also had a place in the breastplate of the high priest.
3145	**Sarah** The wife of Abraham and mother of Isaac (Ge. 11:29).
3147, 4431	**Sardis** Sardis was conquered by king Cyrus of Persia in 546 B.C. It is one of the seven churches of Asia Minor (Re. 3:1-6).
	Sargon One of the great kings of Assyria (772-705 B.C.), Sargon is credited with conquering and taking the nation of Israel into captivity (2 K. 17:5-6).
3158, 4307e	**Saul** The first king of Israel. When the Spirit of the Lord departed from Saul he sought assurance from the Witch of Endor (1 S. 28:8 ff.), which was a direct violation of God's law, and ended with Saul committing suicide (1 S. 31:3 ff.).
3160	**Scapegoat** After the high priest made an atonement for himself and his house he was presented with two goats (Le. 16:6 ff.). Lots were cast to determine the scapegoat, after which the high priest prayed and transferred the sins of the people upon the head of the scapegoat which in turn was led into the wilderness to perish. Here is seen the pattern of the innocent perishing for the guilty in the same way that Christ the innocent Lamb of God died for guilty sinners.
2561	**Scourge** or **Whip** Inflicted upon one who transgressed certain laws such as adultery and social sins (Le. 19:20; De. 25:1-3). Criminals were frequently scourged before they were executed, as was the case with our Lord (John 19).
3165	**Scribe** An educated man with the ability to write and copy important documents. Many scribes hand-copied sacred manuscripts. Some scribes had seats in the Sanhedrin (Mt. 16:21; Lu. 22:66).
3166	**Scriptures** The word "Scripture" is used only one time in the Old Testament (Da. 10:21). All New Testament references to "Scripture" have the Old Testament in mind.
3094	**Scroll** or **Roll** Ancient books were in the form of a roll of paper, papyrus or an animal skin. The writings were placed on sheets which were glued or sewed together to make long strips which was then rolled in a single roll. Sometimes two rollers were used to facilitate moving the text forward or backward.
2443	**Seir, Mount** (Hairy, shaggy). Originally inhabited by the Horites (Ge. 14:6), but later Edom occupied this territory and drove the Horites out (De. 2:12).
2474	**Selah** (Forte?).Generally assumed to be some sort of notation in the worship service. It probably means a response, a pause, a repetition or orchestral interlude, or it could be a signal for some instrumental intervention (Ps. 3:8; 9:20; 46:11; Hab. 3:3,9,13).

Seleucia (Called after Seleucus). A city on the extreme northern coast of Syria; the port city of Antioch, 20 miles up the river (Ac. 13:4). | 4330

Sennacherib (The moon). The king who sent an ultimatum to Hezekiah, King of Judah (2 Chr. 32:9ff.), but after the Angel of the Lord put 185,000 of Sennacherib's soldiers to death he retreated to Nineveh. There his two sons assassinated him (2 K. 19:37; 2 Chr. 32:20ff.). | 3235

Septuagint The Greek version of the Old Testament.

Seraphims (Burning ones). An order of celestial beings Isaiah saw standing before the enthroned Lord, in the year King Uzziah died (Is. 6:2-3). | 3236

Sergius Paulos The proconsul of Cyprus who was residing in Paphos when Paul and Barnabas came through on their first missionary journey. When he saw Paul perform a miracle, he was astonished and believed (Ac. 13:6-12). | 2382

Serpent An animal with head, tail and body which creeps upon the ground. The serpent tempted Adam and Eve to eat the forbidden fruit (Ge. 3:1, 14). The devil was incarnate in the snake. See Brazen Serpent. | 3148-3155

Seth A son born to Adam and Eve after the murder of Abel. In some respects he became a substitute in the ascendency of righteousness. He became the father of Enos and died at the age of 912 (Ge. 5:6,8). | 34

Shaddai An ancient name of God rendered "Almighty." By this name God was known to the patriarchs before the name Jehovah was revealed (Ex. 6:3). | 1868-1872

Shadrach One of the three Hebrew children who were thrown into the fiery furnace in Babylon (Da. 1:7). | 3247

Shallum The fifteenth king of Israel who brought the dynasty of Jehu to a close by murdering Zechariah, the son of Jeroboam II. After only one month on the throne, he was dethroned and killed (2 K. 15:8-15). | 3248

Shalmaneser The Assyrian king who ruled before Saigon and immediately after Tiglath-Pileser (2 K. 17:3ff.). | 3249

Shamgar A son of Anath and judge of Israel. With an ox-goad he assaulted the Philistines, killed 600 of them and delivered Israel (Jud. 3:31). | 3251

Sharon A triangular coastal area between Joppa, Carmel and the hills of Samaria. It was fertile (Is. 35:2) and a pasture land for flocks (1 Chr. 27:29). The most common flower in this area is the Rose of Sharon (Song 2:1; Is. 65:10). | 3253

Sheba (A man). A country in southwest Arabia ruled over by a queen who visited Solomon and was quite impressed with his political power and wealth (1 K. 10:10 ff.). | 3256

Shechem or **Sichem** A walled city near Mount Gerizim (Jud. 9:7). God gave Abraham a special revelation and told him that he and his descendents would inherit this land, so he built an altar (Ge. 12:7). | 3258-3259, 4432

3261   **Shekel** (To weigh). A weight originally coming from Babylon, dealing in fractional parts of an ounce. Eventually the Jews used this measurement in their coinage (Ge. 24:22; 23:15-16; 1 S. 17 :5,7).

3262   **Shem** The oldest son of Noah; born after his father was 500 years old (Ge. 5:32).

Sheminith Denotes a certain musical quality. Scholars present three views: It was the pitch of an octave, the name of a tune or the number of strings in a musical instrument (1 Chr. 15:21; Ps. 6 and 12).

2090, 2099, 3268   **Shepherd** An honorable occupation (Ge. 4:2; 13:1-6; 29:6; Ex. 2:16-22), but dangerous because of snakes and wild animals, exposure to the elements, thieves and robbers, and no medical facilities.

3269, 3530   **Shewbread** The twelve loaves of bread on the Tabernacle table. The term meant "Bread of Faces" because it was always on display before the face of Jehovah (Ex. 25:30; Le. 24:5ff; Jn. 6:48-51).

3271, 4433   **Shiloh** (Peaceable or rest). A town on the road between Jerusalem and Bethel near Shechem (Jud. 21:19). The Tabernacle ark was administered here by Eli the priest (1 S. 2:12-17) and finally by Samuel the prophet (1 S. 3:20).

3272   **Shinar** Another name for the area between the Tigris and Euphrates rivers, known as Chaldaea. The towns of Babel, Erech, Accad and Calneh were in its boundaries (Ge. 10; 11:2; Da. 1:2).

3274   **Shishak** (Illustrious). A king of Egypt known for his many monuments. He conquered the fenced cities of Judah and came to Jerusalem and took away the treasures from the House of the Lord (2 Chr. 12:2-9; and 1 K. 14:25-26).

24   **Shittah** or **Shittim** (Acacia). A tree associated with the acacia tree. It is a very durable wood and was used in building the Tabernacle and its furniture (Ex. 25:5,10,13,23; 26:15 ff.).

2455   **Shofar.** See Cornet.

Shuite or **Shuah** A son of Abraham by Keturah (Ge. 25:2). An Arab tribe which settled in the land of Uz (Jb. 2:11), identified wlth the Assyrian Suhu. One of Job's comforters was a Shuhite (Jb. 8:1ff.).

3279   **Shunamite, the** (Descendent of Shua). This name is related to two persons: 1. King David's nurse (1 K. 1:3,15; 2:17,21,23). 2. An obscure woman that rendered good service to Elisha, who assured her that she would have a son (2 K. 4:8-17).

3282, 4435   **Sidon** or **Zidon** (Fishing). An ancient city on the Mediterranean Sea 22 miles north of Tyre. It was the northern border of the Canaanites (Ge. 10:19). The Baal nature gods were dominant in this region (1 K. 16:31). Tyre was closely linked politically with the city of Sidon.

3286   **Sihon** (Brush). Sihon was king of the Amorites when the Hebrew tribes arrived in the promised land under the leadership of Joshua (Nu. 21:21).

3288   **Silas** or **Silvanus** Silas was one of the early Christian leaders in the Jerusalem area and an associate of Paul (Ac. 15:22,32).

Siloam (Outlet of water). A spring rising out of the foot of Mount Zion whose gates were repaired by Shallum (Ne. 3:15).

3314, 4436

Silver A precious white metal used as a medium of exchange, either in bars or coins (Ge. 20:16; Ac. 3:4; 1 Pe. 1:18). Abraham brought a burial ground from Heth for four hundred shekels of silver (Ge. 23:15-16).

3315-3319

Simeon (A heartening). 1. The second son of Jacob by his wife Leah (Ge. 29:33). 2. An aged saint who embraced the baby Jesus (Lu. 2:25-34). 3. A Christian convert in Antioch (Ac. 13:1).

3320-3323

Simon (A heartening). A very common name in Bible times. Some of the most familiar are: 1. Simon Peter (Mt. 10:2). 2. The tanner at Joppa (Ac. 9:43ff). 3. One of the twelve, a Canaanite (Mt. 10:4). 4. A brother of Jesus (Mt. 13:55). 5. The man from Cyrene (Mk. 15:21). 6. The sorcerer (Ac 8:9,18).

3324-3331

Sinai (Pointed). A triangular peninsula jutting into the north end of the Red Sea. The terrain is desert sand, bleak sandstone and granite mountains.

3369

Sion, Mount or **Mount Zion** (Lifted up). In early OT times Mount Hermon was called Mount Sion (De. 4:48). Later Mount Moriah was given the secondary name of Zion where Solomon built Israel's first Temple (1 K. 5:1ff.).

3996

Sisera (Binding in chains). A Canaanite king who held Israel in subjection. Israel gained the upper hand in the Kishon Valley and as Sisera fled, he sought refuge with Heber the Kenite. Heber's wife invited him into her tent where she killed him while he slept (Jud. 4:21).

3371

Sling An instrument made of an oval piece of leather to which two cords were attached. David used a sling to kill Goliath, the giant (1 S. 17:40).

3383

Smyrna (Myrrh). A city of great antiquity in the western part of Asia Minor. The church was one of the seven addressed by St. John in the book of Revelation (Re. 2:8ff.).

4308j

Sodom (Burning). One of the five great cities of the Canaanites in the Dead Sea area. When Abraham and Lot separated, Lot moved to Sodom. God gave Lot and his family an opportunity to escape before he rained brimstone and fire upon Sodom and Gomorrah. (Ge. 19:24ff.).

3411, 4437

Sodomite The term refers to a repulsive act of sexual immorality (Ge. 19:5; Is. 3:9).

3412

Solomon (Peaceable). The son of David by Bathsheba; he succeeded his father as king. During the reign of David and Solomon Israel had its Golden Age. Under Solomon the great Temple was constructed (1 K. 4:34; 10:23-25).

3414, 4297, 4307g

Spain A country at the opposite end of the Mediterranean Sea from Palestine. Paul had made plans to visit this country but whether he went or not is uncertain (Ro. 15:24).

2382

3430	**Spikenard** A highly aromatic plant from which extracts and ungents were obtained for making perfumes to be used after bathing and for enbalming (Mk. 14:3; Jn. 12:3).
3450	**Stephen** (Crowned). The chief of the seven deacons elected to oversee the social needs of the widows in Jerusalem (Ac. 6:5). He was the first Christian martyr and died by stoning (Ac. 7:58-60).
2141	**Stocks** A wooden frame in which a person's neck and arms could be clamped and put on public display. Job makes reference to being put in stocks (Jb. 13:27). It is stated in Acts that Paul and Silas were flogged and put in stocks (Ac. 16:23-24).
3462	**Stoic** A Greek philosophy with emphasis on logic, physics and ethics. The heart of this philosophy is that the supreme goal of life is happiness and man attains this by conforming to the laws of nature, purely on humanistic grounds. Paul encounters this philosophy at the Areopagus in Athens (Ac. 17:18ff.).
3467	**Streets** City streets were narrow and winding and were lined with display shops where food, commodities and sundries were displayed in sacks and trays. Perhaps the best-known street in the Near East is the "Street Called Straight" in Damascus (Ac. 9:11).
3471-3472	**Succoth** (Booths). An ancient town east of Jordan near the Jabbock (Ge. 33:17) where Jacob stopped to build some "booths for his cattle" on his way back from Padanaram; he called it Succoth.
185	**Swine, Pig, Hog** A ceremonially unclean animal (Le. 11:7; De. 14:8). Those that tended swine were social outcasts;to feed swine was the most despicable occupation. The pig was the emblem of filth (Pr. 11:22; Mt. 7:6; 2 Pe. 2:22). This puts the Prodigal Son in the social perspective of his day (Lu. 15:15).
3664-3691	**Sycamine tree** A type of mulberry and distinct from the sycamore (Lu. 17:6).
3689	**Sycamore** A type of wild fig tree abounding in Palestine, especially in the more humid coastal area and around Jericho. The Zaccheus fig tree in Jericho is about 50 feet high and has a trunk about three feet in diameter (Lu. 19:4ff.).
3521-3523	**Synagogue** (Place of prayer). When the Jews returned to Jerusalem from Babylonian exile they brought with them the synagogue. Jesus spoke in synagogues on several occasions (Lu. 4:15-16).
3525	**Syrophoenician** (A Phoenician living in Syria). The woman who came asking Jesus to cast the devil out of her daughter. She was probably of mixed race—Phoenician and Syrian (Mk. 7:26).
3528	**Tabernacle** A tent type portable structure in which the Israelites worshiped in the wilderness. Specific instructions for its construction were given to Moses (Ex. 25:8ff.).
2445	**Tabor, Mount** (Height). A round topped mountain in Galilee a few miles southeast of Nazareth with an elevation of 1843 feet above sea level.

Many Christians believe that Mount Hebron is the place.

Tadmor (Latin, **Palmyra**) (City of Palms). A desert town in Syria, northeast of Damascus (2 Chr. 8:4), fortified by Solomon. (1 K. 9:18) Extensive ruins, one and a half miles long testify to the greatness of this once important crossroads city. | **3544, 4439**

Talmud (learning). The depository for Jewish laws and doctrines. It contains parts of both the Mishna, tradition and oral law, and the Gamara (Commentary). It provides the theological and doctrinal guidelines for Judaism. | **1957**

Tammuz (Son of Life). The chief Babylonian deity who provided the name of the fourth Jewish month. He is mentioned only once in the Scripture (Eze. 8:14) but the heart of this religion is expressed in the Baal religion (Nu. 22:41; Jud. 2:13; 1 K. 16:31, 32; 2 K. 10:18ff.). | **3936**

Tares A kind of thorny weed, perhaps darnel, which grew abundantly in the midst of the crops (Mt. 13:29-30). | **291**

Tarshish or **Tarsus** Several places carried this name: 1. Tarsus of Cilicia where Saul was from (Ac. 9:11; 21:39). 2. A city in Spain to which Jonah tried to flee (Jona. 1:3; Ps. 72:10). | **3550**

Tartak One of the gods worshiped by the Avites in Samaria, similar to Molech, to whom children were burned in the fire (1 K. 17:31). | **3552**

Taxing Under the judges the Israelites were required to pay a religious tax or tithe for support of the priests and the Tabernacle. Produce of the field was taxed by Solomon (1 K. 4:7ff.). Tribute was paid by subject people (2 S. 8:6-14). | **2529, 2530, 2926**

Tekoa or **Tekoah** (Sound of trumpet). A small town in Judah south of Jerusalem near Bethlehem, the hometown of Amos (Am. 1:1). | **3565**

Temple A permanent worship center built by Solomon after the twelve tribes were united as a single nation (1 K. 5:3ff.). | **3577**

Ten Commandments, the The Articles of the Law given to Moses on Mount Sinai (Ex. 20:1ff.). | **949**

Tent See Tabernacle. | **3528**

Terah The father of Abraham (Ge. 11:24-32). | **3597**

Teraphim (Nourishes) Images connected with magical rites, kept in homes, small enough to be carried in hasty flight (Ge. 31:19). See also Jud. 17:5; 1 S. 19:13; Eze. 21:21; Ho. 3:4. It is apparent that these idols were used freely by the Hebrews. | **3945**

Tetrarch The Romans granted this title to a ruler over a small territory. Three NT tetrarchs are named: Herod of Galilee, Philip of Iturea and Lysanias of Abilene (Lu. 3:1). | **4428**

Thaddeus This man is listed in Mark's catalog of apostles (Mk. 3:18). The three names of Judas, Lebbaeus and Thaddeus were borne by the same person. | **3609**

2633   **Thank Offering** Given at a time when the community could express praise and thanksgiving to the Lord for his goodness and mercy. The spirit of such an event is given in Je. 33:11. See also Le. 7:12; 2 Chr. 29:31; and Ps. 116:17.

4264, 4266   **Theophilus** (Friend of God). The man to whom Luke addresses the book of Acts and the Gospel of Luke (Lu. 1:3; Ac. 1:1). Many believe that this man was a Gentile convert. Apparently he had an important position— possibly the chairman of a Christian body.

3610, 4274-4275   **Thessalonians, the Books of** Two books written by Paul to the church he had founded in Thessalonica, Macedonia (Ac. 17:1ff.). The first letter encourages the church to be faithful and to look for the coming of Christ. The second letter is a further explanation of the second coming.

3614   **Thomas** (A twin). One of the twelve apostles, also called "Didymus," the twin (Mt. 10:3).

3621   **Thyatira** A city in Asia Minor where one of the seven churches in the book of Revelation is located (Re. 2:18). It was situated on an elevation near the Lycus river, a few miles from Pergamum. It was the home of Lydia, a seller of purple in Philippi, Paul's first convert in this city (Ac. 16:14).

3622   **Tiberias, the Sea of** or **the Sea of Galilee** A harp-shaped fresh water lake into which the Jordan River flows (Mt. 4:18; Jn. 6:1).

3625, 4352   **Tiglath Pileser III** The second Assyrian king who came in contact with the Israelites (745-727 B.C.). Ahaz paid him tribute of silver and gold from the Temple (2 K. 16:8).

1096   **Tigris** One of the four rivers which watered the Garden of Eden. It joins the Euphrates River at Korenah, near the Persian Gulf (Ge. 2:14; Da. 10:4).

3628   **Timothy** or **Timotheus** (Honoring God). A native of Lystra. His father was a Greek and his mother and grandmother were Hebrews who taught him the knowledge of the Scriptures (Ac. 16:1ff.).

4276-4277   **Timothy, Books of** Two books written by Paul to Timothy (see entry on Timothy).

2123   **Tithes** The giving of ten percent of one's income. This principle seems to have been practiced by the Phoenicians and Carthagenians, sometimes voluntarily and sometimes by law. Under Moses at Sinai, their tithe was developed for support of the tribe of Levi who did not receive a regular land allotment (Nu. 28:21-24). In addition to money, the produce of the fields and herbs were acceptable in the tithe formula (Mal. 3:8-10; Mt. 23:23; He. 7:5).

3643   **Tola** (Worm). A judge of Israel after Abimelech who served for 23 years (Jud. 10:1-2).

3646-3647   **Tongues, Gift of** The gift of new tongues was promised to the disciples by our Lord (Mk. 16:17) and fulfilled on the day of Pentecost (Ac. 2:4).

2860   **Topaz** A precious stone, the topaz was the second stone in the first row of the high priest's breastplate (Ex. 28:17). This was the stone assigned to Issachar.

Towers Built on a building or a wall so that guards could view the countryside. Vineyards had watchtowers from which to watch for thieves and marauders (2 K. 9:17; 2 Chr. 26:10). | 3651

Townclerk The title ascribed to the magistrate in Ephesus who appeased the mob in the theatre when Paul was being attacked (Ac. 19:35).

Tribute Money Tribute money was paid by the Jews both to the Temple and the Roman government (Mt. 17:24-25; 22:17). | 2529-2530

Troas The city at which Paul had his "Macedonian call" to carry the Gospel to Europe (Ac. 16:8, 11). | 3695, 4444

Trumpets, Feast of The first new moon of Tishri; "the seventh month in the first day of the month shall ye have a Sabbath, a memorial of blowing of trumpets, a holy convocation" (Le. 23:24). | 1258

Tubal (Production). This man is reckoned with Javan and Meshech to be the sons of Japheth (Ge. 10:2; 1 Chr. 1:5). | 3710-3711

Turtledove Turtledoves were plentiful, inexpensive and readily trapped so poor people could offer them as burnt offerings instead of a more expensive animal (Le. 1:14). | 469

Tychicus and **Trophimus**, **Fortuitous** Fellow laborers with Paul in Corinth. When Paul was informed that the Jews had set a death trap for him he decided to leave for Asia. Several of the brethren including Tychicus and Trophimus decided to go with Paul (Ac. 20:3-6). | 3696, 3715

Tyre An ancient Phoenician city on the Mediterranean coast a few miles south of Sidon (Is. 23:7). | 3716, 4445

Unclean A doctrine that distinguishes between edible and non-edible animals (Le. 11:3-4, 27; De. 14:4-5). It was also determined that non-Jews were unclean and this is seen in Jonah's racial prejudice (book of Jonah) and the Jewish prejudice toward the Samaritans (Jn. 4:9). | 150, 1297

Ur (Light). A city in the land of the Chaldees from which the Abraham tribes came into Canaan (Ge. 11:31-32). From Haran, Abraham went on into Canaan (Ge. 12:1ff.). | 3738, 4446

Uriah (Light of Jehovah). One of the soldiers in David's army. David had an adulterous relationship with his wife, Bathsheba (2 S. 11:1ff.). In order to cover up his sin, he had Uriah killed in battle (2 S. 11:24). Psalm 51 gives an account of David's repentance and sorrow. | 3739

Urim and **Thummim** (Light and Perfection). This was an object or device of some kind which the high priest wore over his heart under the breastplate to determine the will of God in difficult cases (Ex. 28:30; Le. 8:8). | 2497

Usury The law of usury related to charging a fellow Jew excessive interest or interest beyond the legal rate (Ex. 22:25). It also required the lender to return a pledged garment by sundown (Ex. 22:26). | 588

Uz (Fertile). The country east of Palestine bordering the Euphrates River where Job lived (Jb. 1:1). | 3742

Uzza (Strength). The place where Manasseh king of Judah and his son Amon are buried (2 K. 21:18-26).

3743   **Uzzah** (Strength). The son of Abinadab, who was hauling the ark in his cart, and when he placed his hand on the ark to steady it God struck him dead (2 S. 6:7). The place was called Perez-uzzah, "to this day" (2 S. 6:8).

3744   **Uzziah** or **Azariah** (Might of Jehovah). The alternate Hebrew name (Azariah) is found in 2 K. 1:21; 15:1, 6-8, 17. After Amaziah the father of Uzziah was murdered, the son ascended to the throne. He was a godly king and ruled for fifty-two years.

3749   **Vashti** (Beautiful). The queen of King Ahasuerus who refused to come into the banquet hall to present herself. This displeased the king and consequently the Jewish girl Esther was chosen as the new queen (Est. 1:10ff.).

3745-3746   **Veil** In the Near East it was customary, in most cases, for a woman to wear a veil in public (Ge. 24:65; 38:14).

94   **Vineyard** Raising grapes was a very important enterprise in Near Eastern economy. They were eaten fresh, eaten as raisins, and used for making wine (Jud. 15:5; 1 K. 21:1).

187   **Viper** A very poisonous serpent or snake whose bite was usually fatal (Jb. 20:16; Mt. 3:7). John the Baptist refers to the corrupt Temple leaders as vipers.

882-883   **Vow** A solemn and voluntary promise made to God to refrain from some action or to do some special thing (Ge. 28:20-22; Nu. 21:2; 1 S. 1:11; Jona. 1:16).

4220   **Vulgate** The many Latin versions of the Bible had created confusion. Bishop Damascus of Rome requested a noted Biblical scholar and linguist, Jerome of Dalmatia, to produce a Latin Bible which could be used as a semi-official version. The result was the Vulgate Latin Bible.

3831, 3995   **Wilderness** The kind of wilderness to which the Bible refers is a barren, desert area—granite or sandstone mountains with little vegetation. Specific wilderness areas through which the Hebrews traveled are mentioned in Nu. 33:6, 11, 15, 36.

3847   **Wise Men** See Magi.

3855a-3857   **Witness** A witness could be a memorial stone (Ge. 31:46-52), or a statement by someone who was eyewitness to an event. It could also be a written document such as a letter, deed, bond, or ledger (De. 24:1-3), or the testimony of two persons (Nu. 35:30; De. 17:6).

189   **Wolf** A wild and fierce carnivorous animal that kills sheep (Jn. 10:12). Violent men who prey on the helpless are likened to wolves (Eze. 22:27), as are false teachers (Mt. 7:15) and enemies of God (Mt. 10:16).

3859-3861   **Woman** God made the woman to be the counterpart of man and to be his helpmate (Ge. 2:21-24). The capable and virtuous woman was highly praised (Pr. 31:10-31). Both man and woman shared in receiving the grace of God.

Wool and **Linen** Materials used for making clothing. Combining wool and linen, however, was forbidden (Le. 19:19; De. 22:11). — 3884

Wormwood This word occurs frequently in the Bible and is usually used metaphorically to denote an end, as in Pr. 5:3-4. It is also used symbolically to mean bitter calamity and sorrow (Re. 8:11). — 3920

Writing The first mention of writing in the Bible appears in Ex. 17:14, where Moses is commanded to write a memorial. Writing materials were soft clay tablets, stone, skins and papyrus paper (Da. 7:1; Re. 5:1). — 3961-3962

Year The Hebrews had two years—a sacred and a civil one. The sacred year began with the month Abib (April) and the civil one with Tishri (October). The months were lunar, twelve in number with adjustments every three years. — 4451

Yoke Basically a wooden or leather collar placed around the neck of a beast of burden. It was frequently used metaphorically for "devotion" or "subjection." — 2525

Zabulon See Zebulun. — 3985-3986

Zacchaeus (Pure). A tax collector in Jericho whom Jesus called (Lu. 19:1-10). — 3977

Zacharias (Whom Jehovah remembers). The father of John the Baptist (Lu. 1:5). — 1903

Zarephath The place where Elijah lived at the latter part of the drought (1 K. 17:9-10). — 3982, 4447

Zebedee (Full form of). The senior fisherman on Lake Galilee, the father of John and James the Great, and the husband of Salome (Mt. 27:56). — 3984

Zebulun One of the sons of Jacob (Ge. 30:20; 35:23; 1 Chr. 2:1). — 3985-3986

Zechariah 1. Son of Jeroboam II, the fourteenth king of Israel (2 K. 15:10). 2. One of the minor prophets and a contemporary of Haggai. They worked together to get the walls rebuilt. — 3979, 3987-4260

Zedekiah The last king of Judah before the Babylonian captivity. He was forced to see his sons killed, then blinded and taken to Babylon (2 K. 24:17-25; 25:1-7; 2 Chr. 36:11-21). — 3988-3989

Zephaniah (Whom Jehovah hid). One of the minor prophets and priest related to Hezekiah. (Zep. 1:1) — 3990

Zerubbabel (Born at Babel). He is also called Shealtiel, appointed to be governor over the Jews who returned to Jerusalem (Ne. 7:6ff.). — 3991

Zilpah (Dropping). Zilpah was a Syrian, given by Laban to his daughter Leah as an attendant (Ge. 29:24), and by Leah to her husband Jacob as a concubine. She was the mother of Gad and Asher (Ge. 30:9-13). — 2103

Zimri (Celebrated). The fifth king of the northern kingdom (Israel). He was slain at Shittim for worshiping the Midianite idols (Nu. 25:14-15). — 1823

Ziphron (Sweet smell). The northern boundary of the promised land as defined by Moses "and the border shall go to Ziphron" (Nu. 34:9). — 627

3997   **Zipporah** (Bird). The daughter of Jethro, the priest of Midian at Mount Sinai who married Moses. She became the mother of his two sons, Gershon and Eliezer (Ex. 2:21).

3999   **Zoar** (Smallness). One of the cities of the Dead Sea plain near Sodom when Lot was kidnapped by the five kings of that area (Ge. 14:2).

4000   **Zophar** (Chatterer). One of Job's three comforters (Jb. 2:11; 11:1).

Notes

Preface
1. Gustave Oehler, *Theology of the Old Testament* (Grand Rapids: Zondervan Publishing House, 1883), p. l.

Old Testament Introduction
1. Benjamin Breckenridge Warfield, "Inspiration," *ISBE* (Grand Rapids: Wm. B. Eerdmans Co., 1959), III, p. 1473.
2. Millar Burrows, *The Dead Sea Scrolls* (New York: Viking Press, 1955), p. 314.
3. Norman L. Geisler, "Bible Manuscripts," *WBE* (Chicago: Moody Press, 1975), I, p. 252.

Genesis
1. Herbert C. Leupold, "Genesis," *ZPEB* (Grand Rapids: Zondervan Publishing House, 1975), I, p. 678
2. R. Laird Harris, "Genesis," *WBE* (Chicago: Moody Press, 1975), I, p. 665.
3. W. T. Purkiser, *Exploring the Old Testament* (Kansas City: Beacon Hill Press, 1967), p. 67.
4. Nathan J. Stone, *Names of God* (Chicago: Moody Press, 1944), p. 10ff.
5. Elmer B. Smick, "Pentateuch," *WBE* (Chicago: Moody Press, 1975), I, p. 675.
6. For a definition of *demiurge* see Shirley Jackson Case, "Demiurge," *ER,* (New York: The Philosophical Library, 1945), p. 222.
7. Gustave Oehler, *Theology of the Old Testament* (Grand Rapids: Zondervan Publishing House, 1883), p. 2.
8. Ibid, p. 30.
9. Grace Saxe, *Studies in Hebrews* (Chicago: Moody Press, n.d.), p. 49.
10. Erich Sauer, *The Dawn of World Redemption* (Grand Rapids, Wm. B. Eerdmans Co., 1952), p. 21.
11. Harris, p. 668.
12. Henry H. Halley, "Genesis," *HBH,* (Grand Rapids: Zondervan Publishing House, 1962), p. 60.
13. Charles Darwin, *The Autobiography of Charles Darwin, 1809-1882,* ed. Nora Barlow (New York: W. W. Norton and Co., 1958), p. 85-87. Omissions are restored in this edition. The editor, who also added an appendix and notes, is Darwin's granddaughter.
14. Ibid.
15. R. Laird Harris, "The Bible and Cosmology," *Bulletin of the Evangelical Theological Society* (March, 1962), p. 11.
16. James D. Bales, "The Relevance of Scriptural Interpretation," *Bulletin of the Evangelical heological Society* (December, 1961), p. 127.
17. Howard A. Hanke, *The Validity of the Virgin Birth* (Grand Rapids: Zondervan Publishing House, 1963), p. 78ff.
18. Franz Julius Delitzsch, *The Old Testament History of Redemption* (Edinburgh: T. and T. Clark Publishers, 1881), p. 26.
19. Ibid, p. 27.
20. Sauer, p. 62.
21. Jasper Huffman, *The Messianic Hope in Both Testaments* (Butler, Ind.: The Higley Press, 1945), p. 75.
22. Ibid, p. 76.
23. John D. Davis, "Blood," *DDB* (Grand Rapids: Baker Book House, 1973), p. 77.

24. Sauer, p. 63.
25. Adam Clarke, "Genesis," *CBC* (New York: Abingdon-Cokesbury, n.d.), I, p. 77.
26. Delitzsch, p. 50.
27. *TSB* (New York: William H. Wise and Co., 1952), I, p. 94.
28. Lee Haines, "Genesis," *TWBC* (Grand Rapids: Wm. B. Eerdmans Co., 1967; reprinted Grand Rapids: Baker Book House, 1978), I, p. 65.
29. Stone, p. 98.
30. Raissa Maritan, "Abraham and the Ascent of Conscience," *The Bridge,* ed. John M. Oesterreicher (New York: Pantheon Books, 1955), p. 35.
31. Huffman, p.75.
32. Sauer, p.156.
33. Thomas Rees, "God," *ISBE* (Grand Rapids: Wm. B. Eerdmans Co., 1959), II, p. 1253.
34. James A. Borland, *Christ in the Old Testament* (Chicago: Moody Press, 1978), p. 34.
35. Ibid, p. 10.
36. Ibid, p. 21.
37. Stone, p. 98.
38. Walter Gellen Clippenter, "Blood," *ISBE* (Grand Rapids: Wm. B. Eerdmans Co., 1959), I, p. 188.
39. Ibid
40. R. Allan Killen, "Baptism," *WBE* (Chicago: Moody Press, 1975), I, p. 194.
41. John Nuelsen, "Regeneration," *ISBE* (Grand Rapids: Wm. B. Eerdmans Co., 1959), IV, p. 2547
42. Charles W. Slemming, *These Are the Garments* (London: Marshall, Morgan and Scott, Ltd., n.d.), p. 53.

Exodus

1. John Rea, "The Book of Exodus," *WBC*, I, p. 566.
2. Allan A. MacRae, "The Book of Exodus," *ZPED*, II, p. 437.
3. Erich Sauer, *The Dawn of World Redemption* (Grand Rapids: Wm. B. Eerdmans Co., 1952), p. 156.
4. R. Allen Killen, "Names and Titles of God," *WBE*, I, p. 695.
5. Harold B. Kuhn, "God, His Names and Nature," *Fundamentals of the Faith* (Christianity Today, 1014 Washington Blvd., Washington, D.C., n.d.), p.13.
6. Elmer Smick, *Wycliffe Bible Encyclopedia,* pp. 287-290.
7. Grace Saxe, *Studies in Hebrews* (Chicago: Moody Press, n.d.), p. 1.
8. A.M. Hodgkin, *Christ in All the Scriptures* (London: Pickering and Ingals, 1907), p. 20.
9. Ibid.
10. Saxe, p. 45.
11. W. S. Hottel, *Typical Truth in the Tabernacle* (Cleveland: Union Gospel Press, n.d.), p. 161.
12. Ibid., p. 199.
13. Charles Slemming, *Made According to Pattern* (London: Marshall, Morgan and Scott, n.d.), p. 109.
14. Hottel, p. 180.
15. Slemming, p. 87.
16. A. B. Simpson, *Christ in the Tabernacle* (Harrisburg: Christian Publications, Inc., n.d.), p. 98.
17. Ibid., p. 70.
18. Slemming, p. 96.
19. Iris McCord, *The Tabernacle* (Chicago: Moody Press, n.d.), p. 34.
20. Saxe, p. 44.
21. Slemming, p. 61.
22. Saxe, p. 44
23. John D. Davis, "Day of Atonement," *DDB,* p. 65.
24. McCord, p. 59.
25. Simpson, p. 118ff.
26. McCord, p. 61.
27. Slemming, p. 94.
28. Simpson, p. 106.
29. McCord, p. 30.

Leviticus

1. Robert H. Pfeiffer, *Introduction to the Old Testament* (New York: Harper and Brothers, 1941), p.188.
2. Bruce K. Waltke, "Leviticus," *ZPEB* III, p. 915.
3. Robert O. Coleman, "Leviticus, *WBC*, p. 87.
4. Wilhelm Moller, "Day of Atonement," *ISBE*, I, p. 324ff.
5. Madeleine S. Miller and J. Lane Miller, "Festivals, Feasts and Fasts," *HBD*, p. 52.
6. Nathan J. Stone, *Names of God* (Chicago: Moody Press, 1944), p. 151.
7. Miller and Miller, p. 190; W.T. Purkiser, *Exploring the Old Testament* (Kansas City: Beacon Hill Press, 1967), p.127.
8. Hobart E. Freeman, "Festivals," *WBE*, I, p. 501ff.

Numbers

1. Thomas Whitelaw, "Book of Numbers," *ISBE*, IV, p. 2169.

Deuteronomy

1. Howard A. Hanke, "The Book of Deuteronomy," *TWBC*, vol. I, part I, p. 471.
2. Howard Vos, *Religion in a Changing World* (Chicago: Moody Press, 1959), p. 44.

Joshua

1. John Rea, "Joshua," *ZPEB*, III, p. 698.
2. Ibid.
3. Charles R. Wilson, "Joshua," *TWBC*, vol. I, part I, p. 11.
4. Ferm, *Encyclopedia of Religion*, Philosophical Library.

Judges

1. Adam Clarke, "The Book of Judges," *CBC*, II, p. 99.
2. F. F. Bruce, "The Book of Judges," *NBC*, p. 237.
3. Charles R. Wilson, "The Book of Judges," *TWBC*, vol. I., part II, p. 64.
4. Clarke, p. 98.

Ruth

1. Madeleine S. Miller and J. Lane Miller, "The Book of Ruth," *HBD*, p. 630.
2. Adam Clarke, "The Book of Ruth," *CBC*, II, p. 190.
3. Arthur E. Cundall, "The Book of Ruth," *ZPEB*, V, p. 176ff.

1 and 2 Samuel

1. Herbert W. Wolf, "Samuel 1 and 2," *ZPEB*, V, p. 256.
2. Elmer B. Smick, "Books of Samuel," *WBE*, II, p. 1515.
3. Charles R. Wilson,"The First Book of Samuel," *WBC*, vol. I., part II. p. 138.
4. Ibid.

1 and 2 Kings

1. Samuel J. Schultz, "Books of Kings," *ZPEB*, III, p. 812.
2. "1 and 2 Kings," *EHB*, p. 251.
3. Schultz, p. 812.

1 and 2 Chronicles

1. Adam Clarke, "The Two Books of Chronicles," *CBC*, II, p. 572.
2. Ibid.
3. Ibid., p. 573.
4. Ibid., p. 574.
5. J. Barton Payne, "The Books of Chronicles," *WBE*, I, p. 338.

Ezra

1. Henry H. Halley, "Ezra," *HBH*, p. 218.
2. Charles R. Wilson, "The Book of Ezra," *TWBC*, II, p. 435.
3. Adam Clarke, "The Book of Ezra," *CBC*, II, p. 716.
4. Halley, p. 218.
5. Clarke, p. 716.

Nehemiah

1. Henry H. Halley, "Nehemiah," *HBH*, p. 220
2. Ibid.
3. Ibid.
4. Charles R. Wilson, "The Book of Nehemiah," *WBC*, vol. I. part II, p. 436.

Esther

1. Robert B. Demsey, "Book of Esther," *WBE*, I, p. 549.
2. Henry H. Halley, "Esther," *HBH*, p. 222.
3. Demsey, p. 549.
4. Charles R. Wilson, "The Book of Esther," *TWBC*, vol. I, part II, p. 483.
5. Demsey, p. 551.

Job

1. Stephen Barabas, "The Book of Job," *ZPEB*, III, p. 600.
2. M.G.K., "Job," *WBE*, I, p. 931.
3. Madeleine S. Miller and J. Lane Miller, "The Book of Job," *HBD*, p. 337.
4. Henry H. Halley, "Job," *HBH*, p. 225.
5. Adam Clarke, "The Book of Job," *CBC*, III, pp. 6-7.
6. Halley, p. 225.
7. Ibid.
8. John D. Davis, "The Book of Job," *DDB*, p. 722.

Psalms

1. J. Barton Payne, "The Book of Psalms," *ZPED*, IV, p. 937.
2. Henry H. Halley, "Psalms," *HBH*, p. 230ff.
3. Ralph L. Smith, "Book of Psalms," *WBE*, II, p. 1425.
4. Payne, p. 936ff.
5. W. T. Purkiser, *Exploring the Old Testament* (Kansas City: Beacon Hill Press, 1967), p. 221.
6. Payne, pp. 939-940.
7. Halley, p. 239.
8. Payne, p. 939.
9. William Smith, "The Book of Psalms," *SBD*, p. 551.
10. C. S. Lewis, *Reflection on the Psalms* (New York: Harcourt Brace and Co., 1958), p. 120.
11. Martin J. Wyngaarden, "Psalms in the Christian Liturgy," *ISBE*, IV, p. 2494A.
12. John R. Sampey, "Book of Psalms," *ISBE*, IV, 2494.
13. The Book of Psalms was the hymn book of the Christian church for the first 1500 years of its history. The Psalms are still used exclusively by several Christian groups, including certain Presbyterian and Reformed denominations. A hymnal containing all of the Psalms in metrical form, set to familiar tunes, is currently published by Wm. B. Eerdmans Co., Grand Rapids, Michigan, under the title *The Psalter*. The Christian use of the Psalter is irrefutable proof that the Book of Psalms has extensive Christological content.
14. "Christ in the Psalms," *EHB*, p.329.

Proverbs

1. W.O.E. Oesterley, "Proverbs," *TSB*, II, p. 614.
2. Purkiser, *Exploring the Old Testament*, p. 239.
3. W.T. Purkiser, *Know Your Old Testament* (Kansas City: Beacon Hill Press, 1947), p. 141.

Ecclesiastes

1. Dennis Kinlaw, "The Book of Ecclesiastes," *TWBC*
2. Henry H. Halley, "Ecclesiastes," *HBH*, p. 255.

Song of Solomon

1. John Richard Sampey, "Song of Songs," *ISBE*, V, p. 2833.
2. N. H. Snaith, "Solomon and the Rose of Sharon: A Springtime Idyll," *TSB*, II, p. 646
3. Ibid.
4. John D. Davis, "The Song of Songs," *DDB*, p. 777.

Isaiah

1. George L. Robinson, "Isaiah," *ISBE*, III, p. 1504.
2. Robert H. Pfeiffer, *Introduction to the Old Testament* (New York: Harper and Brothers, 1941), p. 453ff.
3. R. Laird Harris, "Isaiah," *ZPEB*, III, pp. 313-321.
4. Allan A. MacRae, "Prophets and Prophecy," *ZPEB*, IV, p. 879.
5. Henry H. Halley, "Isaiah," *HBH*, p. 262.
6. Robinson, "Isaiah," p. 1495ff.

7. G. Frederick Owen, "4362, Dead Sea Scrolls," *TCRB*, p. 1742.
8. Robinson, "Isaiah," p. 1505.
9. Karl S. Sabiers, *The Virgin Birth* (Los Angeles: Robertson Publishing Co., l943), p. 58.
10. J. Gresham Machen, *The Virgin Birth of Christ* (New York: Harper and Brothers, l930), p. 29ff.
11. Adam Clarke, "Isaiah," *CBC*, IV, p. 56.

Jeremiah
1. Adam Clarke, "Jeremiah," *CBC*, IV, p. 249.
2. Henry H. Halley, "Jeremiah," *HBH*, p. 284.
3. Samuel J. Schultz, "Jeremiah the Prophet," *ZPEB*, III, p. 435.
4. Halley, p. 282.
5. D.D. Deere, "The Book of Jeremiah," *WBE*, I, p. 899
6. Edward J. Young, "Prophets," *WBE*, II, p. 1412ff.
7. Madeleine S. Miller and J. Lane Miller, "Prophets," *HBD*, pp. 582ff.

Lamentations
1. Bruce K. Waltke, "The Book of Lamentations," *ZPEB*, III, p. 863.
2. Adam Clarke, "The Lamentations of Jeremiah," *CBC*, IV, p. 398.

Ezekiel
1. Wilhelm Moeler, "Ezekiel," *ISBE*, XIX, p. 445.
2. Henry H. Halley, "Ezekiel," *HBH*, p. 298.
3. Lewis L. Orlin, "Tyre," *TWBE*, XIX, p. 445.
4. Halley, p. 303.
5. Nathan J. Stone, *Names of God* (Chicago: Moody Press, 1944), p. 155.

Daniel
1. John D. Davis, "Daniel," *DDB*, pp. 155ff.
2. Edward J. Young, *The Prophecies of Daniel* (Grand Rapids: Wm. B. Eerdmans Co., 1955), p. 318.
3. A. H. McDonald, "Porphyrius," *TME*, p. 931.
4. Gleason L. Archer, Jr., trans., *Jerome's Commentary on Daniel* (Grand Rapids: Baker Book House, 1958), pp. 15-16.
5. Clyde J. Hurst, "Book of Daniel," *WBE*, I, p. 422.
6. Bert Harold Hall, "The Book of Daniel," *TWBC*, III, p. 503.
7. William Smith, "The Book of Daniel," *SBD*, p. 130.
8. W.T. Purkiser, *Exploring the Old Testament* (Kansas City: Beacon Hill Press, 1967). pp. 377-78.
9. Henry H. Halley, "Gensis," *HBH*, p. 308.

Hosea
1. Henry H. Halley, "Hosea," *HBH*, p. 324.
2. John Davis, "Jezebel," *DDB*, p. 414.
3. Halley, p. 325.
4. P. D. F., "Book of Hosea," *WBE*, I, p. 814

Joel
1. Allan A. MacRae, "Prophets and Prophecy," *ZPED*, IV, p. 879.
2. John D. Davis, "Joel," *DDB*, pp. 419-20.
3. James Robertson, "Joel," *ISBE*, III, p. 1688ff.
4. "Joel," *EHB*, p. 442.

Amos
1. Henry H. Halley, "Amos," *HBH*, p. 329.
2. Ibid., p. 330.
3. Adam Clarke, "Amos," *CBC*, IV, p. 691.

Obadiah
1. John Richard Sampey, "Obadiah," *ISBE*, IV, p. 2173.
2. G. Herbert Livingston, "Obadiah," *WBC*, p. 839.

Jonah
1. Pfeiffer, *Introduction to the Old Testament*, p. 587.
2. G. Herbert Livingston, "Jonah," *WBC*, p. 844.
3. Henry H. Halley, "Jonah," *HBH*, p. 333.

4. Wallace A. Alcorn, "Book of Jonah," *WBE*, I, p. 845.
5. Ibid.
6. M. Rowton, "Nineveh," *EA*, XV, p. 368.
7. Livingston, p. 844.
8. Ibid.

Micah

1. Andrew K. Helmbold, "Micah," *ZPEB*, V, 215.
2. "Micah," *EHB*, p. 449.
3. Claude A Ries, "The Book of Micah," *TWBC*, III, p. 677.
4. Henry H. Halley, "Micah," *HBH*, p. 337.
5. Ibid.

Nahum

1. Frederick Carl Eiselen, "The Book of Nahum," *ISBE*, IV, p. 2100.
2. William C. Graham, "Nahum," *ABC*, p. 799.
3. Henry H. Halley, "Nahum," *HBH*, p. 340; Joseph F. Free, *Archaeology and Bible History* (Wheaton: Van Kampen Press, 1950), p. 28.

Habakkuk

1. Claude A. Ries, "The Book of Habakkuk," *TWBC*, III, p. 711.
2. Henry H. Halley, "Habakkuk," *HBH*, p. 342.

Zephaniah

1. Allan A. MacRae, "Prophets and Prophecy," *ZPED*, IV, p. 879.
2. Howard A. Hanke, "Zephaniah," *WBC*, p. 883.
3. Frederick Carl Eiselen, "Book of Zephaniah," *ISBE*, V, p. 3145.
4. Madeleine S. Miller and J. Lane Miller, ed., "Zephaniah," *HBD*, p. 838.
5. Eiselen, p. 3145.
6. Ibid.
7. Henry H. Halley, "Zephaniah," *HBH*, p. 343.

Haggai

1. R.K. Harrison, "Haggai," *ZPEB*, III, p. 11.
2. Charles L. Feinberg, "Haggai," *WBC*, p. 895.

Zechariah

1. George L. Robinson, "Book of Zechariah," *ISBE*, V, p. 3136.
2. Ibid.
3. John D. Davis, "Zechariah," *DDB*, p. 878.
4. Henry H. Halley, "Zechariah," *HBH*, p. 346.
5. Ibid., p. 347.
6. R. K. Harrison, "Book of Zechariah," *ZPEB*, V, pp. 1045-46.
7. Halley, p. 349.
8. J. Kenneth Grider, "The Book of Zechariah," *TWBC*, III, p. 757.

Malachi

1. Burton L. Goddard, "Malachi," *WBC*, p. 913.
2. Hobart E. Freeman, "Malachi," *WBE*, II, p. 1071.
3. "Malachi," *EHB*, p. 459.
4. Henry H. Halley, "Malachi," *HBH*, p. 353.

The Intertestamental Period

1. Madeleine S. Miller and J. Lane Miller "Medes," *HBD*, p. 431.
2. Howard Clark Kee, Franklin W. Young, and Karlfried Froehlich, *Understanding the New Testament* (Englewood Cliffs, N.J.: Prentice-Hall, 1973), p. 34.
3. Ibid., p. 43.
4. Ibid.
5. Robert Pfeiffer, "The Apocrypha," *EA*, III, p. 650.
6. Millar Burrows, *The Dead Sea Scrolls* (New York: The Viking Press, 1955), p. 327.
7. Ibid., p. 329.
8. Ibid., p. 328.
9. Gaster, p. 12ff.
10. Alvin B. Rogers, *The Land of Jesus* (Minneapolis: Augsburg Publishing House, 1974), p. 8.

11. Theodore Gaster, *The Dead Sea Scriptures* (New York: Doubleday and Co., 1956), p. 5; Père de Vaux, "Dead Sea Jewels," *Time Magazine* (September 5, 1955), p. 34.
12. Gaster, p. 10ff.
13. Père de Vaux, "Dead Sea Jewels," *Time Magazine* (September 5, 1955), pp. 33-34.
14. J. E. H. Thompson, "The Essenes," *ISBE,* I, p. 163.
15. Herman Hausheer, "Peter Waldo and Waldenses," *ER,* p. 817.
16. Morton Scott Enslin, "Therapeutae," *ER,* p. 784.
17. Thompson, II, p. 998.
18. Frank M. Cross, "The American Schools of Oriental Research in Jerusalem," *Time Magazine* (September 5, 1955), p. 34.
19. Père de Vaux, pp. 33-34.
20. Will Durant, *Caesar and Christ* (New York: Simon and Schuster,1944) III, p. 560
21. Thompson, II, p. 998.
22. The Methodist Hymnal (New York: The Methodist Book Concern, 1939).
    No. 5, Daniel Ben Judah "The God of Abraham Praise"
    No. 85, James Montgomery, "Hail to the Lord's Anointed"
    No. 150, William J. Irons, "Sing with All the Sons of Glory"
    No. 193, John M. Neale, "Art Thou Weary, Art Thou Troubled"
    No. 199, John Chennick, "Jesus My All, to Heaven is Gone"
    No. 390, Percy Dearmer, "Book of Books, Our People's Strength...Poets, Prophets, Scholars, Saints"
    No. 488, Thomas Hastings, "Hail to the Brightness..."
    No. 543, William P. Merrill, "Not Alone for Mighty Empire"
23. Fenton John Anthony Hort,*The Ecclesia* (London: Macmillan Co. 1828-1829), p. 1.
24. Ibid., p. 8.

Introduction to the New Testament

1. James Iverach, "The Synoptic Gospels," *ISBE,* II, p. 1281.
2. Madeleine S. Miller and J. Lane Miller, "Canon," *HBD,* p. 91.
3. Miller and Miller, pp. 520-521.
4. J. Harold Greenlee, "Texts and Manuscripts of the New Testament," *ZPED,* V, p. 708.
5. W. L. Walker, "Name," *ISBE,* IV, p. 2112.
6. James Orr, "The Bible," *ISBE,* I, p. 460.

Matthew

1. Robert McL. Wilson, "Gospel of Matthew," *ZPEB,* IV, p. 122.
2. George Henry Schodde, "The Gospel of Matthew," *ISBE,* III, p. 380.
3. Wilson, p. 136.
4. Howard Clark Kee, Franklin W. Young, and Karlfried Froehlich, *Understanding the New Testament* (Englewood Cliffs, N.J.:Prentice-Hall, l973), p. 315.
5. Henry H. Halley, "Matthew," *HBH,* p. 380.
6. *Exploring New Testament Backgrounds, A Special Survey of the New Testament Books* (Washington, D.C.: Christianity Today, n.d.), p. 7
7. Robert H. Gundry, *A Survey of the New Testament* (Grand Rapids: Zondervan Publishing House, l970), p. 86ff.
8. Clark H. Pinnock, "Gospels," *ZPEB,* II, p. 788.
9. Gundry, p. 84; Ward W. Gasque, "Pseudepigrapha," *ZPED,* IV, p. 949ff.
10. Clarence T. Craig, "The Church of the New Testament," *The Universal Church of God's Design* (New York: Harper and Brothers, n.d.), p. 31.
11. Ibid, p. 32.
12. Ibid.
13. Ibid., p. 33.
14. Erich Sauer, *The Dawn of World Redemption* (Grand Rapids: Wm. B. Eerdmans Co., 1948), p. 21.
15. John Davis, "Church," *DDB,* p. 146.
16. A. R. Fausset, "Church," *Bible Encyclopedia and Dictionary* (Grand Rapids: Zondervan Publishing House, n.d.), p. 150.

Mark

1. Canon R. J. Campbell,"Mark," *TSB,* III, p. 1052.
2. Ralph Earl, "The Gospel According to Mark," *TWBC,* IV, p. 131.
3. Henry H. Halley, "Mark," *HBH,* p. 418ff.
4. Adam Clarke, "St. Mark," *CBC,* V, p. 287.

5. Donald W. Burdick, "Mark," *WBE*, II, p. 1078.
6. Robert H. Gundry, *A Survey of the New Testament* (Grand Rapids: Zondervan Publishing House, 1970), p. 68ff.
7. Weldon O. Klopfenstein, "Gospel of Mark," *ZPEB*, IV, pp. 80-81
8. J. Newton Davies, "Mark," *ABC*, p. 998.
9. A. R. Fausset, "Church," *Bible Encyclopedia and Dictionary* (Grand Rapids: Zondervan Publishing House, n.d.), p. 23.
10. J. C. Lambert, "Church," *ISBE*, I, p. 651.
11. Erich Sauer, *The Triumph of the Crucified* (Grand Rapids: Wm. B. Eerdmans Co., 1952), p. 22.
12. William Whiston, *Josephus' Complete Works* (Grand Rapids: Kregel Publications, 1963), Wars, II, VIII, 14; Antiquities, XIII. X. 6.
13. William Whiston, *Josephus' Complete Works* (Grand Rapids: Kregel Publications, 1963), Antiquities, XIII. X. 6; Louis Goldberg, "Sadducees," *WBE*, II, p. 1500.

Luke

1. A.T. Robertson, "The Evangelist Luke" and "The Gospel of Luke," *ISBE*, III, p. 1935.
2. Robert G. Gromacki, *New Testament Survey* (Grand Rapids: Baker Book House, 1974), p. 110ff.
3. Adam Clarke, "St. Luke," *CBC*, V, p. 352.
4. Henry H. Halley, "Luke," *HBH*, p. 444.
5. A. R. Fausset, "Church," *Bible Encyclopedia and Dictionary* (Grand Rapids: Zondervan Publishing House, n.d.), p. 131
6. Ibid, p. 130

John

1. Henry H. Halley, "John," *HBH*, p. 485.
2. Ibid.
3 . Everett F. Harrison, "The Gospel of John," *WBC*, p. 1118.
4. Robert G. Gromacki, *New Testament Survey* (Grand Rapids: Baker Book House, 1974), p. 130.
5. Halley, p. 484.
6. George A. Turner, "The Gospel of John," *ZPEB*, III, p. 673.
7. William Smith, "Salome," *SBD*, p. 595.
8. Conrad Henry Muehlman, "Gnosticism," *ER*, p. 301.
9. Ibid, p. 300.
10. Paul H. Halsel, "Logos," *ER*, p. 449.
11. Ibid.
12. George A. Turner, "Logos," *ZPEB*, p. 953.
13. Halsel, p. 449.
14. John Nuelsen, "Regeneration," *ISBE*, IV, p. 2546.
15. Adam Clarke, "John," *CBC*, V, p. 532.
16. R. Allan Killen, "Baptism," *WBE*, I, p. 200.
17. Nuelsen, p. 2548.
18. Ibid, p. 2544.
19. Andri Dupont-Sommer, *The Jewish Sect of Qumran and the Essenes* (New York: Macmillan Co., 1955), V, pp. 134ff.
20. Millar Burrows, *The Dead Sea Scrolls* (New York: The Viking Press, 1955), p. 245.
21. J. E. H. Thompson, "The Essenes" *ISBE*, II, pp. 997ff.
22. William G. Morehead, "Priesthood," *ISBE*, IV, p. 2444.
23. James Orr, "Jesus," *ISBE*, III, p. 1627.
24. Hobart E. Freeman, "Festivals," *WBE*, I, p. 605.
25. Thomas Rees, "God," *ISBE*, II, p. 1253.
26. Gustave Oehler, *Theology of the Old Testament* (Grand Rapids: Zondervan Publishing House, 1883), p. 124.
27. Ibid., p. 508.

Acts

1. Adam Clarke, "The Acts of the Apostles," *CBC*, V, p. 679.
2. A.T. Robinson, "The Acts of the Apostles," *ISBE*, I, p. 39.
3. Joseph S. Exell, "The Acts of the Apostles," *The Pulpit Commentary* (New York: Anson D. F. Randolph & Co., n.d.), I, p. iv.
4. Ibid., p. ix.
5. Ibid.

6. Ibid.
7. Ibid., p. x.
8. Ibid.
9. Charles W. Carter, "The Acts of the Apostles," *TWBC,* IV, p. 489.
10. Merrill C. Tenney, "The Book of Acts,"*WBE*, I, p. 22
11. F. F. Bruce, "The Acts of the Apostles," *Exploring New Testament Backgrounds* (Washington, D.C.: Christianity Today, n.d.).
12. Exell, p. iii.
13. G. Henry Waterman, "The Lord's Day," *ZPEB,* III, p. 962.
14. Edwin Lueker, "Apostle," *WBE,* I, p. 116; "Apostle," *HBD,* p. 116.
15. Gustave Oehler, *Theology of the Old Testament* (Grand Rapids: Zondervan Publishing House, 1883), p. 508.
16. Sauer, *Triumph of the Crucified*, p. 32.
17. F. F. Bruce, "The Acts of the Apostles," *NBC*, ed. F. Davison (Grand Rapids: Wm. B. Eerdmans Co., 1953), p. 913.
18. Clarence T. Craig, "The Church of the New Testament," *The Universal Church of God's Design* (New York: Harper and Brothers, n.d.), p. 32.
19. Adam Clarke, "Romans," *CBC*, VI, p. 40.
20. John Wesley, *Wesley's Explanatory Notes on the New Testament* (London: Epworth Press, 1966), pp. 435,520.
21. *WBE,* p. 458ff.
22. R. Allen Killen, "Sabbath Day's Journey," *WBE,* II, p. 1494.

Romans
1. Handley Dunelm, "Epistle to the Romans," *ISBE*, IV, p. 2614.
2. Joseph S. Exell, "The Epistle of Paul to the Romans, *The Pulpit Commentary* (New York: Anson D. F. Randolph & Co., n.d.), I, p. iff.
3. "Romans," *EHB,* p. 588.
4. John Wesley, "Romans," *Explanatory Notes upon the New Testament* (Napierville, Ill.: Alec R. Allenson, l966), p. 515.
5. Dunelm, p. 2616ff.
6. Will Durant, *Caesar and Christ* (New York: Simon and Schuster), III, 602, 1944.
7. Adelaide L. Lewis, "Religion," *Information Please Almanac* (New York: Information Please Publishing Co., 1979), p. 430.
8. Wilhelm Pauck, "Atonement in Christianity," *ER,* p. 54.
9. Erich Sauer, *The Dawn of World Redemption* (Grand Rapids: Wm. B. Eerdmans Co., 1952), p. 21.
10. Adam Clarke, "Revelation," *CBC,* VI, p. 1019.
11. Sauer, p. 155.
12. Jasper Huffman, *The Messianic Hope in Both Testaments* (Butler, Ind.: The Higley Press, 1945), p. 29.
13. William Owen Carver, "Atonement," *ISBE,* I, p. 323.
14. Wilhelm Mohler, "Day of Atonement," *ISBE,* I, p. 326.
15. Ibid., p. 324.
16. Erich Sauer, *Dawn of World Redemption* (Grand Rapids: Eerdmans Publishing Co., 1952), p. 21.
17. Nathan Isaacs, "Passover," *ISBE,* IV, p. 2257.
18. Henry Riley Gummy, "Lord's Supper," *ISBE,* III, p. 1922.
19. Adam Clarke, "Matthew," *CBC,* V, p. 110.
20. Andri Dupont-Sommer, *The Jewish Sect of Qumran and the Essenes* (New York: Macmillan Co., 1955), V, p. 134.
21. *TWBE,* V, p. 796.
22. *TWBE,* XI, p. 75.
23. *HCC,* p. 85ff.
24. Bruce M. Metzger, *The Text of the New Testament* (New York: Oxford University Press, 1964), p. 206. See also Metzger, *A Textual Commentary on the Greek New Testament* (New York: United Bible Societies, 1971) and Colvin Brown, Gen. Ed., *New Testament Theology* (Grand Rapids: Zondervan Publishing House, 1962).

1 and 2 Corinthians
1. R. Dykes Shaw, "First Epistle of the Corinthians," *ISBE,* II, p. 711.
2. John Wesley, "I Corinthians," *Explanatory Notes upon the New Testament* (Naperville, Ill.: Alec R. Allenson, l966), p. 584.

3. S. Lewis Johnson, "The First Epistle to the Corinthians," *WBC,* p. 1228; Shaw, p. 713.
4. Shaw, p. 714.
5. Ibid.
6. Ibid., p. 715.
7. Henry H. Halley, "II Corinthians," *HBH,* p. 552
8. Wick Broomall, "The Second Epistle to the Corinthians," *WBC,* p. 1261.
9. Ibid.
10. John D. Davis, "Corinth," *DDB,* p. 152; Joseph Edward Harry, "Corinth," *ISBE,* II, p. 711.
11. Halley, p. 593.
12. Madeleine S. Miller and J. Lane Miller, "Corinth," HBD, p. 113.
13. John D. Davis, "Blood," *DDB,* p. 77.
14. "Tyrannus Rufinus," *EA,* XXIII, p. 755.
15. Henry Wheeler, *The Apostles Creed* (New York: Eaton and Main, 1912), p. 13.
16. Ibid.
17. Ibid., p. 21; see also Solomon J. Schepps (Foreword), "The Apostles' Creed," in *The Lost Books of the Bible* (New York: Bell Publishing Co., 1979 Ed.) p. 91.
18. W. T. Purkiser, *Exploring the Christian Faith* (Kansas City: Beacon Hill Press, 1960), p. 88.
19. Ibid.
20. R. Allen Killen, "Pelagianism," *WBE,* II, p. 1303.
21. Purkiser, p. 89.
22. "Creeds and Confessions," *EA,* VIII, p. 174ff.
23. "Henry Gerhard Appenzeller," *EA,* II, p. 81; "Horace Grant Underwood," *EA,* XXVII, p. 275.
24. Herbert Welch, "The Story of the Creed," *The Christian Advocate* (August 1, 1946), p. 973.
25. Ibid.
26. Nolan B. Harmon, "The Apostles Creed Says it Best," *The Christian Advocate* (August 22, 1968), pp. 11-12.

Galatians
1. Lorman M. Peterson, "Epistle to Galatians," *ZPEB,* II, p. 627
2. Madeleine S. Miller and J. Lane Miller, "The Epistle of Paul the Apostle to the Galatians," *HBD,* p. 211
3. George G. Findley, "Epistle to the Galatians," *ISBE,* II, p. 1157.
4. Ibid.
5. C. Fred Dickason, "Epistle to the Galatians," *WBE,* I, p. 648
6. Ibid.

Ephesians
1. Robert G. Gromacki, *New Testament Survey* (Grand Rapids: Baker Book House, 1974), p. 241
2. Charles Smith Lewis, "Epistle to the Ephesians," *ISBE,* II, p. 956.
3. Alfred Martin, "The Epistle to the Ephesians," *WBC,* p. 1301.
4. Ibid.
5. Ibid.
6. Charles Harold Dodd, "Ephesians," *ABC,* p. 1223
7. Edgar J. Banks, "Diana," *ISBE,* II, p. 843
8. Ibid.

Philippians
1. Robert G. Gromacki, *New Testament Survey* (Grand Rapids: Baker Book House, 1974), p. 256.
2. Ibid.
3. James Alex Robinson, "Philippians," *ABC,* p. 1238.
4. D. Edmond Hiebert, "Letter to the Philippians," *ZPEB,* IV, p. 766.
5. Adam Clarke, "The Epistle of Paul the Apostle to the Philippians," *CBC,* VI, p. 488.
6. Merrill C. Tenney, "Philippians," *Exploring New Testament Backgrounds* (Washington, D.C.: Christianity Today, n.d.).
7. Philo Flaceus, 14; Josephus, *Antiquities,* XIV, X. p. 23.
8. William G. Morehead, "Priesthood," *ISBE,* IV, p. 2444.

Colossians

1. Charles Smith Lewis, "Epistle to the Colossians," *ISBE*, II, p. 617
2. Charles F. Pfeiffer and Howard F. Vos, "Other Pauline Cities," *The Wycliffe Historical Geography of the Bible Lands* (Chicago: Moody Press, 1967), p. 376.
3. Lewis, "Colossians," p. 677.
4. Andrew R. Helmbold, "Gnosticism" *WBE*, I, p. 687; E. Earle Ellis, "The Epistle to the Colossians," *WBC*, p. 1334.
5. Conrad Henry Moehlman, "Gnosticism," *EBH*, p. 300.
6. Ellis, p. 1333.
7. Charles Harold Dodd, "Colossians," *ABC*, p. 1250ff.
8. Ellis, p. 1334.
9. Edward M. Blaiklock, "Colosse, "*ZPEB*, I, p. 914; Adam Clarke, "The Epistle of Paul the Apostle to the Colossians," *CBC*, VI, p. 510.
10. A. R. Fausset, "Church," *Bible Encyclopedia and Dictionary* (Grand Rapids: Zondervan Publishing House, n.d.), p. 23.

1 and 2 Thessalonians

1. Adam Clarke, "The First Epistle of Paul the Apostle to the Thessalonians," *CBC*, VI, p. 537.
2. Rollin Hough Walker, "The First Epistle of Paul to the Thessalonians," *ISBE*, V, p. 2966.
3. John D. Davis, "The Second Epistle to the Thessalonians," *DDB*, p. 818.
4. Clarke, "Thessalonians," p. 537.
5. Davis, p. 817.
6. Henry H. Halley, "II Thessalonians," *HBH*, p. 578.
7. Ibid.
8. Ibid.
9. "Cassander," *EA*, V, p. 706.
10. Clarke, Thessalonians," p. 537.

1 and 2 Timothy

1. Henry H. Halley, "I Timothy," *HBH*, p. 580.
2. Jac J. Muller, "I Timothy," *Exploring New Testament Backgrounds* (Washington, D.C.: Christianity Today, n.d.). p. 39.
3. Ibid.
4. Ibid.
5. Roy S. Nicholson, "I Timothy," *TWBC*, V, p. 567.
6. Adam Clarke, "The Epistle of Paul the Apostle to Timothy," *CBC*, VI, p. 580.
7. Ibid.
8. Henry H. Halley, "II Timothy," *HBH*, p. 584.
9. Ibid.
10. John Rutherford, "The Pastoral Epistles," *ISBE*, IV, p. 2260.
11. Robert G. Gromacki, "Second Timothy," *New Testament Survey* (Grand Rapids: Baker Book House, 1974), p. 302.
12. Walter M. Dunnett, "Deacon," *WBE*, I, p. 430; "Deacon," *DDB*, p.175.
13. John D. Davis, "Elder," *DDB*, pp. 211ff.
14. John Rea, "Elder," *WBE*, I, p. 509.
15. Ibid.
16. Davis, "Elder," pp. 211ff.
17. Henry H. Halley, "The Bible is the Word of God," *HBH*, p. 26.

Titus

1. Walter W. Wessel, "Titus," *Exploring New Testament Backgrounds* (Washington, D.C.: Christianity Today, n.d.), p. 43.
2. Adam Clarke, "The Epistle of Paul the Apostle to Titus," *CBC*, VI, 642.
3. Wessel, p. 43.
4. Henry H. Halley, "Titus," *HBH*, pp. 588ff.

Philemon

1. Robert G. Gromacki, "Philemon" *New Testament Survey* (Grand Rapids: Baker Book House, 1974), p. 314.
2. John Rutherford, "Philemon," *ISBE*, IV, p. 2367.
3. Ibid, p. 2366.
4. W. T. Purkiser, *Exploring the Christian Faith* (Kansas City: Beacon Hill Press, 1966), p. 448; "Alexander Severius," *EA*, I, p. 367.

Hebrews

1. Thomas Rees, "Epistle to the Hebrews," *ISBE*, II, p. 1355.
2. Stephen J. Smalley, "Hebrews," *Exploring New Testament Backgrounds* (Washington, D.C.: Christianity Today, n.d.) p. 49.
3. Robert G. Gromacki, *New Testament Survey* (Grand Rapids: Baker Book House, 1947), p. 319.
4. Ibid.
5. Ibid.
6. Smalley, p. 49.
7. "Hebrews," *EBH*, p. 626.
8. John B. Davis, "Epistle to the Hebrews," *DDB*, p. 309.
9. Smalley, p. 49.
10. Wallace A. Alcorn, "Epistle to the Hebrews," *WBE*, I, p. 775.
11. Ibid, p. 776.
12. James D. Borland, *Christ in the Old Testament* (Chicago: Moody Press, 1978), p. 164ff.
13. Davis, p. 511.
14. John Wesley, "Hebrews," *Explanatory Notes upon the New Testament* (Naperville, Ill.: Alec R. Allenson Inc., 1960), p. 827.
15. Borland, pp. 171-72.
16. A. M. Hodgkin, *Christ in All the Scriptures* (London: Pickering and Ingals, 1907), p. 20.
17. Henry H. Halley, "Hebrews," *HBH*, p. 598.
18. Ibid.

James

1. Alexander Ross, "The Epistle of James," *Exploring New Testament Backgrounds* (Washington, D.C.: Christianity Today, n.d.), p. 51.
2. Ibid.
3. Merrill C. Tenney, *New Testament Survey* (Grand Rapids: Wm. B. Eerdmans Co., 1953), p. 262.
4. Doremus Almy Hays, "Epistle of James," *ISBE*, III, p. 1567.
5. Henry H. Halley, "James," *HBH*, p. 602
6. Ibid.
7. "James," *EHB*, p. 663.
8. Gromacki, p. 340
9. Ross, p. 52.

1 and 2 Peter

1. Alan M. Stibbs, "1 Peter," *Exploring New Testament Backgrounds* (Washington, D.C.: Christianity Today, n.d.), p. 53.
2. William G. Moorehead, "The First Epistle of Peter," *ISBE*, IV, p. 2352.
3. Robert G. Gromacki, *New Testament Survey* (Grand Rapids: Baker Book House, 1974), p. 359.
4. Merrill C. Tenney, "II Peter," *Exploring New Testament Backgrounds* (Washington, D.C.: Christianity Today, n.d.), p. 55.
5. Stephen W. Payne, "The Second Epistle of Peter," *WBC*, p. 1453.
6. Henry H. Halley, "II Peter," *HBH*, p. 610.
7. John D. Davis, "Peter," *DDB*, p. 624ff.
8. Henry H. Halley, "I Peter," *HBH*, p. 606.
9. Halley, "I Peter," p. 607.
10. Stephen W. Payne, "The First Epistle of Peter," *WBC*, p. 1444.
11. Benjamin W. Robinson, "First Peter," *ABC*, p. 1344.
12. Merrill C. Tenney, "The Second Epistle of Peter," *WBE*, II, p. 1321.
13. Shirley Jackson Case, "Second Peter," *ABC*, p. 1345.
14. Madeleine S. Miller and J. Lane Miller, "The Second Epistle of Peter," *HBD*, p. 544.
15. Tenney, "Second Epistle of Peter," p. 1321.
16. William G. Moorehead, "The Second Epistle of Peter," *ISBE*, IV, p. 2356.
17. D. Russell Scott, "Second Peter," *TSB*, IV, p. 1539ff

1, 2 and 3 John

1. Henry H. Halley, "I John," *HBH*, p. 614.
2. Huber L. Drumwright, Jr., "The Epistles of John," *ZPEB*, III, p. 650.
3. John Wesley, "I John," *Explanatory Notes upon the New Testament* (Naperville, Ill: Alec R. Allenson, 1966), p. 902.

4. Drumwright, p. 650.
5. Alexander Ross, "The Johannine Epistles," *Exploring New Testament Backgrounds* (Washington, D.C.: Christianity Today, n.d.), p. 57.
6. Robert Law, "The Epistles of John," *ISBE*, III, p. 1718.
7. Ross, p. 56.
8. Ibid., p. 58.
9. Adam Clarke, "The Second Epistle of John," *CBC*, V, p. 934.
10. Robert G. Gromacki, *New Testament Survey* (Grand Rapids: Baker Book House, 1974), p. 370.
11. Drumwright, p. 469.
12. Robert Law, "The First Epistle of John," *"ISBE*, III, p. 1711.
13. Halley, "I John," p. 614.
14. Law, "First Epistle of John," p. 1713.
15. Merrill C. Tenney, "First John," *New Testament Survey* (Grand Rapids: Wm. B. Eerdmans Co., 1953), p. 370.
16. John Wesley, "The Second Epistle of St. John, *Explanatory Notes upon the New Testament* (Naperville, Ill.: Alec R. Allenson, 1966), p. 921; Drumwright, p. 656.
17. Leo G. Cox, "Second John," *TWBC*, VI, p. 315.
18. Ibid.
19. Drumwright, p. 657.

Jude
1. Adam Clarke, "The Epistle General of Jude," *CBC*, VI, p. 944ff.
2. Henry H. Halley, "Jude," *HBH*, p. 620.
3. William C. Morehead, Jr., "The Epistle of Jude," *ISBE*, III, p. 1768.
4. Ibid.
5. S. Maxwell Coder, "Epistle of Jude," *WBE*, I, p. 968.
6. J. E. H. Thompson, "Apocalyptic Literature," *ISBE*, I, p. 169.
7. Ibid.
8. D. Russell Scott, "Jude," *TSB*, IV, p. 1545.
9. Coder, p. 968.
10. John Wesley, "The Epistle General of St. Jude," *Explanatory Notes upon the New Testament* (Naperville, Ill.: Alec R. Allenson, 1966) p. 929.
11. Thompson, p. 164.
12. Ibid.
13. Scott, p. 1549.
14. Coder, p. 969.
15. Ibid.
16. R. Duane Thompson, "Jude," *TWBC*, VI, p. 389.

Revelation
1. Wilbur M. Smith, "Revelation," *WBC*, p. 1493.
2. Merrill C. Tenney, "Revelation," *Exploring New Testament Backgrounds* (Washington, D.C.: Christianity Today, n.d.), p. 61.
3. Ibid.
4. Henry H. Halley, "Revelation," *HBH*, p. 622.
5. W. M. Smith, p. 1495.
6. Merrill C. Tenney, *Interpreting Revelation* (Grand Rapids: Wm. B. Eerdmans Co., 1957), p. 101ff.
7. Halley, p. 623; Robert G. Gromacki, *New Testament Survey* (Grand Rapids: Baker Book House, 1974), p. 393ff.
8. George Tybout Purvis, "Revelation," *DBD*, p. 687.
9. Ibid.
10. Halley, p. 627.
11. Madeleine S. Miller and J. Lane Miller, "Thyatira," *HBD*, p. 615.
12. Ibid.
13. John Wesley, "Revelation," *Explanatory Notes upon the New Testament* (Naperville, Ill.: Alec R. Allenson, 1966), p. 944.
14. Thea B. van Halsema, *Safari for Seven* (Grand Rapids: Baker Book House, 1967), p. 100.
15. Wesley, p. 944.
16 Ibid.
17. Adam Clarke, "Revelation," *CBC*, VI, p. 977.

18. Howard F. Voss, "Revelation," *WBE*, II, p. 1601.
19. Harvey J. S. Blaney, "Revelation," *TWBC*, VI, p. 430.
20. Edgar J. Banks, "Smyrna," *ISBE*, IV, p. 2319.
21. Based on research data obtained at Pergamum and the Department of Antiquities in Izmir.
22. Banks, "Smyrna," p. 2819.
23. Ibid, p. 2818.
24. Gustave Frederick Oehler, *Theology of the Old Testament* (Grand Rapids: Zondervan Publishing House,1950), p. 159.
25. Charles S. Browden, "Religious Humanism," *ER*, p. 349.
26. Erich Sauer, *The Dawn of World Redemption* (Grand Rapids: Wm. B. Eerdman's Co., 1952), p. 52.
27. A. R. Fausset, "Church," *Bible Encyclopedia and Dictionary* (Grand Rapids: Zondervan Publishing House, n.d.), p. 130.
28. Frederick C. Grant, "Pergamum," *EA*, XXI, p. 582.
29. Based on research data obtained at Pergamum and the Department of Antiquities at Izmir.
30. Edward M. Blaiklock, "Thyatira," *ZPEB*, V, p. 743.
31. Miller and Miller, "Thyatira," *HBD*, p. 594; John D. Davis, "Thyatira," *DBD*, p. 672.
32. Edgar J. Banks, "Thyatira," *ISBE*, IV, p. 2977.
33. Blaney, p. 434.
34. E. Bertram Clagg, "Revelation," *ABC*, p. 1374.
35. Ibid.
36. Clarke, p. 980.
37. Halley, p. 638.
38. Based on research data obtained at Thyatira and the Department of Antiquities at Izmir.
39. Editors, *EA*, 1957, VIII, p. 219ff.
40. Edward M. Blaiklock, "Sardis," *ZPEB*, V, p. 278.
41. Ibid.
42. Based on research data obtained in Sart and at the Department of Antiquities at Izmir.
43. William H. Ramsey, *The Letters to the Seven Churches*, 4th ed. (London: Hodder and Stoughton, 1895), p. 85.
44. Robert G. Gromacki, "Revelation," *New Testament Survey* (Grand Rapids: Baker Book House, 1974), p. 402ff.
45. Robert J. Banks, "Philadelphia," *ISBE*, IV, p. 2366.
46. Edward M. Blaiklock. "Philadelphia," *ZPEB*, IV, p. 755.
47. Ibid.
48. Charles Lewis Smith, Philadelphia," *ISBE*, IV, p. 2366.
49. Blaney, p. 439.
50. Based on research data obtained at Philadelphia and the Department of Antiquities at Izmir.
51. Clagg, p. 1375.
52. Robert H. Pfeiffer, "Greek Religion," *ER*, p. 311.
53. Clagg, p. 1376.
54. Ibid.
55. Based on research data obtained in Laodicea and the Department of Antiquities at Izmir.
56. A. R. Fausset, "Church," *Bible Encyclopedia and Dictionary* (Grand Rapids: Zondervan Publishing House, n.d.), p. 23.

Preservation of the Bible
1. W. Russell Bowie, "History of the English Bible," *EA*, III, p. 671d.

Bibliography

Adams, J. McKee. *Ancient Records and the Bible*. Nashville: Broadman Press, 1946.
____. *Biblical Backgrounds*. Rev. ed. Nashville: Broadman Press, 1938.
Aharoni, Yohanan. *The Land of the Bible: A Historical Geography*. Translated by A. F. Rainey. London: Burns & Oates, 1967.
Aharoni, Yohanan, and Avi-Yonah, Michael. *The Macmillan Bible Atlas*. Prepared by Carta, Jerusalem. New York: Macmillan Co., 1968.
Albright, William F. *Archaeology and the Religion of Israel*, 2nd ed. Baltimore: Johns Hopkins Press, 1946.
____. *The Archeology of Palestine*. Rev. ed. Baltimore: Penguin Books, 1961.
____. *From the Stone Age to Christianity*. Baltimore: Johns Hopkins Press, 1940.
Allenby, E. H. H. *The Advance of the Egyptian Expeditionary Force, July, 1917 to October, 1918*. London: His Majesty's Stationery Office, 1919.
Amiran, David H. K.; Elster, Joseph; Gilead, Mordeha; Rosenan, Naftali; Kadmon, Naftali; and Paran, Uzi, eds. *Atlas of Israel*. Jerusalem: Survey of Israel, Ministry of Labour; Amsterdam: Elsevier Publishing Co., 1970.
Anati, Emmanuel. *Palestine Before the Hebrews: A History from the Earliest Arrival of Man to the Conquest of Canaan*. New York: Alfred A. Knopf, 1963.
Anderson, Bernhard W. *Rediscovering the Bible*. New York: Association Press, 1951.
____. *Understanding the Old Testament*. 2nd ed. Englewood Cliffs, N.J.: Prentice-Hall, 1966.
Anderson, George W. *A Critical Introduction to the Old Testament*. London: Gerald Duckworth & Co., 1959.
Angus, S. *The Environment of Early Christianity*. New York: Charles Scribner's Sons, 1920.
Archer, John Clark. *Faiths Men Live By*. New York: Thomas Nelson and Sons, 1934.
Arminius, James. *The Writings of Arminius*. Edited by James Nichols and W. R. Bagnall. Reprint. Grand Rapids, Mich.: Baker Book House, 1956.
Ashbed, C. R., ed. *Jerusalem*. London: John Murray, 1920, 1924.
Auerbach, Joseph, *The Bible and Modern Life*. New York: Harper and Brothers, 1914.
Aulen, Gustaf. *Christus Victor*. Translated by A. G. Hebert. New York: Macmillan Co., 1931.
Avi-Yonah, Michael. *The Holy Land*. Grand Rapids: Baker Book House, 1966.
Baab, Otto J. *The Theology of the Old Testament*. New York: Abingdon-Cokesbury, 1949.
Bacher, Wilhelm. "Synagogue." In *Jewish Encyclopedia*. New York: Funk and Wagnalls, 1912, XI, 619-628.
Baikie, James. *The English Bible and Its Story*. London: Seeley, Service and Co., Ltd., 1928.
Bailey, Cyril, ed. *The Legacy of Rome*. Oxford: Clarendon Press, 1924.
Baillie, Donald M. *The Theology of the Sacraments*. New York: Charles Scribner's Sons, 1957.
Baillie, John. *The Idea of Revelation in Recent Thought*. New York: Columbia University Press, 1956.
Bainton, Roland H. *Here I Stand: A Life of Martin Luther*. New York: Abingdon-Cokesbury, 1950.
Bales, James D. "The Relevance of Scriptural Interpretation to Scientific Thought." *Bulletin of the Evangelical Theology Society*, Dec. 1961.
Baly, Denis. *The Geography of the Bible: A Study in Historical Geography*. New York: Harper & Row, 1957.
Baly, Denis, and Tushingham, A. D. *Atlas of the Biblical World*. New York: World Publishing Co., 1971.

Banks, Edgar J. *The Bible and the Spade*. New York: Association Press, 1913.

Barbour, Clarence A. *The Bible in the World of Today*. New York: Association Press, 1911.

Barnes, Albert. *Barnes' Notes on the New Testament*. Grand Rapids: Baker Book House, 1949-50.

Baron, Salo Untermeyer. *A Social and Religious History of the Jews*. 2nd ed., rev. 2 vols. New York: Columbia University Press, 1952.

Barth, Karl. *The Doctrine of the Word of God. Prolegomena to Church Dogmatics*. Vol. I, Part I. Translated by G. T. Thompson. New York: Charles Scribner's Sons, 1936.

Bartlet, James Vernon. *The Apostolic Age in Ten Epochs of Church History*. Vol. I. New York: Charles Scribner's Sons, 1900.

Barton, George A. *Archaeology and the Bible*. 7th ed. Philadelphia: American Sunday School Union, 1937.

Batten, Samuel Z. *The Social Task of Christianity*. New York: Fleming H. Revell, 1911.

Battenfield, James R. "An Exegetical Study of the YHWH Mal'ak in the Old Testament." Postgraduate seminar paper, January 1971, Grace Theological Seminary, Winona Lake, Ind.

Bavinck, Hermann. *Our Reasonable Faith*. Grand Rapids, Mich.: Wm. B. Eerdmans Co., 1956.

Baxter, J. Sidlow. *Explore the Book*. 6 vols. Grand Rapids: Zondervan Publishing House, 1960.

Beach, Waldo, and Niebuhr, Reinhold, eds. *Christian Ethics*. New York: Ronald Press Co., 1955.

Beavan, Albert W. *The Local Church*. New York: Abingdon-Cokesbury, 1937.

Bentzen, Aage. *Introduction to the Old Testament*. Reprint (2 vols. in 1). Copenhagen: G.E.C. Gad, 1952.

Berkhof, Louis. *The History of Christian Doctrines*. Grand Rapids, Mich.: Wm. B. Eerdmans Co., 1949.

____. *The Kindgom of God*. Grand Rapids, Mich.: Wm. B. Eerdmans Co., 1951.

____. *Systematic Theology*. 4th ed., rev. Grand Rapids, Mich.: Wm. B. Eerdmans Co., 1949.

Berkouwer, G. C. *Faith and Sanctification*. Grand Rapids, Mich.: Wm. B. Eerdmans Co., 1952.

____. *The Person of Christ*. Grand Rapids, Mich.: Wm. B. Eerdmans Co., 1954.

Bewer, Julius. *The Literature of the Old Testament*. Revised by Emil G. Kraeling. 3rd ed. New York: Columbia University Press, 1962.

Biederwolf, William Edward. *The Visible God: or The Nature of Christ, A Study in Theophany*. Reading, Pa.: Boyer, n.d.

Birch, W. Grayson. *Veritas and The Virgin or The Son of God and the Children of Joseph and Mary*. Berne, Ind.: Berne Witness, Inc., 1960

Black, M., and Rowley, H. H., eds. *Peake's Commentary on the Bible*. Rev. ed. . New York: Thomas Nelson and Sons, 1962.

Blaikie, William G., and Matthews, Charles D. *A. Manual of Bible History*. Rev. New York: Ronald Press Co., 1940.

Blaiklock. E. M. *The Archaeology of the New Testament*. Grand Rapids: Zondervan Publishing House, 1970.

____. *Out of the Earth*. Rev. ed. Grand Rapids, Mich.: Wm. B. Eerdmans Co., 1961.

____. *The Zondervan Pictorial Bible Atlas*. Grand Rapids, Mich.: Zondervan Publishing House, 1969.

Blair, J. Allen. *Living Faithfully*. Neptune, N.J.: Loizeaux Bros. 1961.

Boak, A. E. R. *A History of Rome to 565 A.D.* New York: Macmillan Co., 1921.

Bogardus, Emory S. *Fundamentals of Social Psychology*. New York: The Century Co., 1924.

Booth, Henry K. *The World of Jesus*. New York: Charles Scribner's Sons, 1933.

Boslooper, Thomas. *The Virgin Birth*. Philadelphia: Westminster Press, 1962.

Boulanger, Robert. *Hatchette World Guides: The Middle East, Lebanon, Syria, Jordan, Iraq, Iran*. Translated by J. S. Hardman. Paris: Hatchette, 1966.

Bowne, Borden Parker. *Metaphysics*. Rev. ed. Boston: Boston University Press, 1898.

____. *Theory of Thought and Knowledge*. New York: American Book Co., 1897.

Boyer, James L. *Chart of the Period Between the Testaments*. Winona Lake, Ind.: Bible Charts, n.d.

____. *New Testament Chronological Chart* Winona Lake, Ind.: Bible Charts, n.d.

Braden, Charles S. "Anglo-Israel." In *Twentieth Century Encyclopedia of Religious Knowledge*. Grand Rapids, Mich.: Baker Book House, 1955, I. 44.

Breasted, James H. *A History of Egypt*. 2nd ed., rev. New York: Charles Scribner's Sons, 1945.

Brew, William Thomas. "A Study of the Process of Revelation in the Pentateuch." Th. M. thesis, Dallas Theological Seminary, 1963.

Bright, John. *Early Israel in Recent History Writing*. London: S. C. M. Press, 1956.

_____. *A History of Israel,* Philadelphia: Westminster Press, 1959.

_____. *The Kingdom of God.* New York: Abingdon-Cokesbury, 1953.

Brightman, Edgar Sheffield. *Moral Laws.* New York: Abingdon Press, 1933.

_____. *Person and Reality.* New York: Ronald Press Co., 1958.

_____. *A Philosophy of Religion.* New York: Prentice-Hall, 1940.

_____. *Religious Values.* New York: Abingdon Press, 1925.

Brockett, Henry E. *Scriptural Freedom from Sin.* Kansas City, Mo.: Beacon Hill Press, 1941.

Brown, Charles Ewing. *The Meaning of Salvation.* Anderson, Ind.: The Warner Press, 1944.

_____. *The Meaning of Sanctification.* Anderson, Ind.: The Warner Press, 1945.

_____. *The Reign of Christ.* Anderson, Ind.: Gospel Trumpet Co., 1950.

Brown, Francis; Driver, Samuel Rolles; and Briggs, Charles A. *A Hebrew and English Lexicon on the Old Testament.* Oxford: Clarendon Press, 1907.

Brown, William Adams. *Christian Theology in Outline.* New York: Charles Scribner's Sons, 1906.

Bruce, F. F. *The Books and the Parchments.* Old Tappan, N.J.: Fleming H. Revell, 1953.

_____. *The Spreading Flame: The Rise and Progress of Christianity.* Grand Rapids, Mich.: Wm. B. Eerdmans Co., 1953.

Bruce, W. S., *The Wisdom Literature of the Old Testament.* London: James Clark and Co., 1904.

Brunner, Emil. *The Christian Doctrine of God: Dogmatics.* Vol. I. Philadelphia: Westminster Press, 1950.

_____. *The Divine Imperative.* Translated by Olive Wyon. Philadelphia: Westminster Press, 1947.

_____. *Eternal Hope.* Translated by Harold Knight. Philadelphia: Westminster Press, 1954.

_____. *The Scandal of Christianity.* Philadelphia: Westminster Press, 1951.

Buck, Harry M. *People of the Lord.* New York: Macmillan Co., 1965.

Buis, Harry. *The Doctrine of Eternal Punishment.* Philadelphia: Presbyterian and Reformed Publishing Co., 1957.

Bullock, William Thomas. "Melchizedek." In *Dr. William Smith's Dictionary of the Bible.* Edited and revised by Horatio B. Hackett. 4 vols. Reprint. Grand Rapids: Baker, 1971.

Bultmann, Rudolf. *Theology of the New Testament.* New York: Charles Scribner's Sons, 2 vols. 1951, 1955.

Burrows, Millar. *The Dead Sea Scrolls.* New York: Viking Press, 1955.

_____. *An Outline of Biblical Theology.* Philadelphia: Westminster Press, 1946.

_____. *What Mean These Stones?* New Haven, Conn.: American Schools of Oriental Research, 1941.

Burtner, Robert W., and Chiles, Robert E. *A Compend of Wesley's Theology.* New York: Abingdon Press, 1954.

Burton, Ernest D. *The Records and Letters of the Apostolic Age.* New York: Charles Scribner's Sons, 1923.

Busch, Fritz-Otto. *The Five Herods.* Translated by E. W. Dickes. London: Robert Hale, Ltd., 1958.

Bush, George. *Notes, Critical and Practical on the Book of Exodus.* 2 vols. New York: Newman, 1844.

Buttrick, George A. *Prayer.* New York: Abingdon-Cokesbury, 1942.

Caiger, S. L. *Bible and Spade.* Oxford: Oxford University Press, 1936.

Calloway, T. W. *Christ in the Old Testament.* New York: Loizeaux Bros., 1950.

Calvin, John. *Institutes of the Christian Religion.* Translated by Henry Beveridge. 2 vols. Grand Rapids, Mich.: Wm. B. Eerdmans Co., 1953.

_____. Calvin's New Testament Commentaries. Edited by T. F. Torrance and D. W. Torrance. 12 vols. Grand Rapids: Wm. B. Eerdmans Co., 1960.

Cannon, William. *The Theology of John Wesley.* New York: Abingdon-Cokesbury, 1946.

_____. *The Redeemer: The Work and Person of Jesus Christ.* New York: Abingdon-Cokesbury, 1951.

Carmichael, P. H. *Understanding the Books of the Old Testament.* Richmond, Va.: John Knox Press, 1950.

Carter, Charles W., ed. *The Wesleyan Bible Commentary.* 6 vols. Grand Rapids: Wm. B Eerdmans Co., 1965-69.

Carter, John Franklin. *A Layman's Harmony of the Gospels.* Nashville, Tenn.: Broadman Press, 1961.

Cartledge, Samuel A. *A Conservative Introduction to the Old Testament* 2nd ed. Athens, Ga.: University of Georgia Press, 1944.

Casola, Pietro (1427-1507). *Canon P. Casola's Pilgrimage to Jerusalem.* Translated by M. M. Newett. Manchester, Eng.: University Press, 1907.

Cawood, John. *Let's Know the Bible.* Old Tappan, N.J.: Fleming H. Revell, 1971.

Ceram, C. W. *The March of Archaeology.* New York: Alfred A Knopf, 1970.

Chadwick, Samuel. *The Gospel of the Cross.* Kansas City, Mo.: Beacon Hill Press, 1949.

Chafer, Lewis Sperry. *Systematic Theology.* 8 vols. Dallas, Tex.: Dallas Seminary Press, 1947.

Charlier, C. *The Christian Approach to the Bible.* Translated by H. J. Richards and B. Peters. Westminster: Newman, 1958.

Cheney, Johnston M., and Ellisen, Stanley A. *The Life of Christ in Stereo.* Portland: Western Baptist Seminary Press, 1969.

Cherbonnier, Edmund LaB. *Hardness of Heart.* Garden City, N.Y.: Doubleday and Co., 1955.

Churchill, Randolph S., and Churchill, Winston S. *The Six Day War.* Boston: Houghton Miffin Co., 1967.

Clark, Elmer T. *The Small Sects in America.* New York: Abingdon-Cokesbury, 1949.

Clark, Neville. *An Approach to the Theology of the Sacraments.* Chicago: Alec R. Allenson, 1956.

Clarke, Adam, ed. *Clarke's Bible Concordance.* Grand Rapids: Baker Book House, 1968.

Clarke, William Newton. *An Outline of Christian Theology.* New York: Charles Scribner's Sons, 1898.

Collett, Sidney. *All About the Bible.* 3rd ed. Chicago: Christian Witness Co., n.d.

Conner, C. R., and Kitchener, H. H. *The Survey of Western Palestine.* 8 vols. London: Palestine Exploratory Fund, 1883.

Cook, Thomas C. *New Testament Holiness.* London: Epworth Press, 1952.

Cooke, Richard J. *Did Paul Know of the Virgin Birth?* New York: Macmillan Co., 1926.

Cooper, David L. *Messiah: His Nature and Person.* Los Angeles: David L. Cooper, 1933.

Coppens, J. *The Old Testament and the Critics.* Translated by E. A. Ryan, S.J., and E. W. Tribbe, S. J. Paterson, N. J.: Guild Press, 1942.

Corlett, Lewis T. *Holiness in Practical Living.* Kansas City, Mo.: Beacon Hill Press, 1948.

_____. *Holiness, the Harmonizing Experience.* Kansas City, Mo.: Beacon Hill Press, 1951.

Couch, Herbert N., and Geer, Russell M. *Classical Civilization: Rome.* Edited by Russell M. Geer. 2nd ed. New York: Prentice-Hall, 1950.

Couriet, A. La Prise *De Jerusalem Par Les Perses en 614 A.D.* Orleans, 1896.

Cowan, Henry. *Landmarks of Church History to the Reformation.* Rev. ed. New York: Fleming H. Revell, n.d.

Craig, Clarence T. "The Church of the New Testament." In *The Universal Church in God's Design.* New York: Harper and Brothers, 1948.

Crain, Orville E. *The Credibility of the Virgin Birth.* New York: Abingdon Press, 1925.

Cross, Frank Moore, Jr. *The Ancient Library of Qumran and Modern Biblical Studies.* Garden City, N.Y.: Doubleday & Co., 1958.

Cunliffe-Jones, H. *The Authority of the Biblical Revelation.* Boston: Pilgrim Press, 1948.

Curtis, Olin A. *The Christian Faith.* New York: Methodist Book Concern, 1903; Grand Rapids, Mich.: Kregel Book Store, reprint, 1956.

Daiches, David. *The King James Version of the English Bible.* Chicago: University of Chicago Press, 1941.

Dalman, Gustaf. *Sacred Sites and Ways: Studies in the Topgraphy of the Gospels.* Translated by Paul P. Levertoff. London: Society for Promotion of Christian Knowledge; New York: Macmillan Co., 1935.

Daniel-Rops, Henry. *Sacred History.* New York: Longmans, Green and Co., 1949.

Daugherty, John J. "The One God." In *The Bridge.* Edited by John M. Oesterreicher. New York: Pantheon Books, 1955.

David, M., and Van Groningen, B. A. *Papyrological Primer.* 2nd ed. Leyden: E. J. Brill, 1946.

Davidson, A. B. *The Theology of the Old Testament.* Edinburgh: T. and T. Clarke, 1904.

Davidson, Robert F. *The Old Testament.* London: Hodder and Stoughton, 1964.

Davies, D. R. *Secular Illusion or Christian Realism.* London: Latimer House, 1942.

Davis, Jerome. *Contemporary Social Movements.* New York: The Century Co., 1930.

Davis, John D. *Davis Dictionary of the Bible.* Grand Rapids, Mich.: Baker Book House, 1972.

Davison, W. T. *The Praises of Israel.* London: Charles H. Kelly, 1902.

_____. *The Wisdom Literature of the Old Testament.* London: Charles H. Kelly, 1894.

Deal, William S. *Baker's Pictorial Introduction to the Bible.* Grand Rapids, Mich.: Baker Book House, 1967.

Deane, William J. "David, His Life and Times," *Men of the Bible.* New York: Fleming H. Revell, n.d.

_____. "Samuel and Saul: Their Lives and Times," *Men of the Bible.* New York: Fleming H. Revell, n.d.

Dearden, Robert R., Jr. *The Guiding Light on the Great Highway.* Philadelphia: John C. Winston Co., 1929.

De Joinville, Lord John, comp. *Chronicles of the Crusades: Contemporary Narratives of the Crusade of Richard Coeur de Lion, by Richard of Devizes and Geoffrey de Vinsauf, and of the Crusade of Saint Louis.* London: Bell and Daldy, 1870.

Demaray, Donald E. *Basic Beliefs: An Introductory Guide to Christian Theology.* Grand Rapids, Mich.: Baker Book House, 1958.

Denney, James. *The Atonement and the Modern Mind.* New York: A. C. Armstrong and Son, 1903.

____. *The Christian Doctrine of Reconciliation.* New York: George H. Doran Co., 1918.

DeVaux, Roland, et al. "Method in the Study of Early Hebrew History." In *The Bible in Modern Scholarship.* Edited by J. Philip Hyatt. Nashville: Abingdon Press, 1965.

Dewey, John. *Democracy and Education.* New York: Macmillan Co., 1939.

DeWolf, L. Harold. *A Theology of the Living Church.* New York: Harper and Brothers, 1953.

Dinsmore, C. A. *The English Bible as Literature.* New York: Houghton Mifflin Co., 1931.

Dodd, C. H. *According to the Scripture.* New York: Charles Scribner's Sons, 1953.

____. *The Bible Today.* New York: Macmillan Co., 1947.

____. *The Epistle of Paul to the Romans: Moffatt New Testament Commentary.* New York: Charles Scribner's Sons, 1932.

____. *The Parables of the Kingdom.* London: Nisbet and Co., 1936.

Donovan, Robert J. *Israel's Fight for Survival: Six Days in June.* New York: The New American Library; London: The New English Library, A Signet Book, 1967.

Douglas, J. D., ed. *The New Bible Dictionary.* Grand Rapids, Mich.: Wm. B. Eerdmans Co., 1962.

Driver, S. R. *Introduction to the Literature of the Old Testament.* Rev. ed. New York: Charles Scribner's Sons, 1913.

Duckworth, H. T. F. "The Roman Provincial System." In *Beginnings of Christianity.* Part I, Vol. I, pp. 171-207. Edited by F. J. Foakes-Jackson and Kirsopp Lake. London: Macmillan & Co., Ltd., 1920.

Dummelow, J. R., ed. *A Commentary on the Holy Bible.* London: Macmillan Company, 1909.

Dunnett, Walter. *Outline of New Testament Survey.* Chicago: Moody Press, 1963.

Dupont-Sommer, A. *The Jewish Sect of Qumran and the Essenes.* New York: Macmillan Co., 1955.

Eason, J. Lawrence. *The New Bible Survey.* Grand Rapids: Zondervan Publishing House, 1963.

Easton, W. Burton, Jr. *Basic Christian Beliefs.* Philadelphia: Westminster Press, 1957.

Edersheim, Alfred. *The Bible History: Old Testament.* Grand Rapids: Wm. B. Eerdmans Co., 1949.

Edwards, Douglas. *The Virgin Birth in History and Faith.* London: Faber and Faber, Ltd., 1941.

Ehrlich, Ernst Ludwig. *A Concise History of Israel.* Translated by James Barr. London: Darton, Longman and Todd, 1962.

____. *Man in the Old Testament.* Studies in Biblical Theology, no. 4. Translated by K. and R. Gregor Smith. London: S.C.M. Press, 1956.

Eichrodt, Walther. *Theology of the Old Testament.* Vol. 1. Translated by J. A. Baker. Philadelphia: Westminster Press, 1961.

Eiselen, F. C., ed. *Abingdon Bible Commentary.* New York: Abingdon Press, 1929.

Eissfeldt, Otto. *The Old Testament: An Introduction.* Translated by Peter R. Ackroyd. New York: Harper & Row, 1965.

Ellis, Peter F. *The Men and the Message of the Old Testament.* Collegeville, Minn.: The Liturgical Press, 1962.

Ellison, H. L. *Jesus and the Pharisees.* Edited by Jakob Jocz. London: The Victoria Institute, 1953.

Ellwood, Charles. *The Reconstruction of Religion.* New York: Macmillan Co., 1922.

Ellyson, E. P. *Ye Must.* Marshalltown, Iowa: Christian Messenger Publishing Co., 1904.

Erdman, Charles R. *An Exposition of the New Testament.* 17 vols. Philadelphia: Westminster Press, 1948.

Eusebius. *The Ecclesiastical History.* 2 vols. Translated by J. E. L. Oulton. London: William Heinemann; New York: G. P. Putnam's Sons, 1932.

Everett, Walter G. *Moral Values.* New York: Henry Holt and Co., 1918.

Farrar, F. W. *The Life of Lives.* Cleveland: F. M. Barton, 1900.

____. *Solomon, His Life and Times.* New York: Fleming H. Revell, 1895.

Ferm, Vergilius. *Living Schools of Religion.* Ames, Iowa: Littlefield, Adams and Co., 1956

(originally published as *Religion in the Twentieth Century*. New York: The Philosophical Library, 1948)

Ferrar, William J. *The Uncanonical Jewish Books*. London: Society for Promoting Christian Knowledge, 1925.

Ferre, Nels F. S. *The Christian Understanding of God*. New York: Harper and Brothers, 1951.

____. *Evil and the Christian Faith*. New York: Harper and Brothers, 1947.

____. *Strengthening the Spiritual Life*. New York: Harper and Brothers, 1951.

Field, Benjamin. *The Student's Handbook of Christian Theology*. New York: Eaton and Mains, n.d.

Filson, Floyd V. *The New Testament Against Its Environment*. Chicago: Henry Regnery Co., 1950.

____. *One Lord, One Faith*. Philadelphia: Westminster Press, 1943.

Finegan, Jack. *Light from the Ancient Past*. 2nd ed. Princeton, N.J.: Princeton University Press, 1960.

Finkelstein, Louis, ed. *The Jews, Their History, Culture, and Religion*. New York: Harper and Brothers, 1949.

____. *The Pharisees*. 2 vols. Philadelphia: The Jewish Publication Society of America, 1938.

Fisher, George Park. *History of Christian Doctrine*. New York: Charles Scribner's Sons, 1911.

Fison, J. E. *The Christian Hope*. London: Longmans, Green and Co., 1954.

Flanders, H. K.; Crapps, R. W.; and Smith, D.A. *People of the Covenant: An Introduction to the Old Testament*. New York: Ronald Press Co., 1963.

Flew, R. N. *Jesus and His Church*. London: The Epworth Press, 1943.

Flewelling, Ralph Tyler. *Personalism and the Problems of Philosophy*. New York: The Methodist Book Concern, 1915.

____. *The Things That Matter Most*. New York: Ronald Press Co., 1946.

Fodor, Eugene, and Fodor, William, eds. *Fodor's Modern Guides: Israel 1967-68*. New York: David McKay Co., 1967.

Ford, Jack. *What the Holiness People Believe*. Birkenhead, Cheshire: Emmanuel Bible College, n.d.

Forster, Arnold. *Report from Israel*. New York: Anti-Defamation League of B'nai B'rith, n.d.

Forsyth, Peter Taylor. *The Person and Place Of Jesus Christ*. London: Independent Press, 1951.

____. *Positive Preaching and the Modern Mind*. New York: George H. Doran Co., 1907.

Francisco, Clyde T. *Introducing the Old Testament*. Nashville: Broadman Press, 1950.

Free, Joseph, *Archaeology and Bible History*. Wheaton, Ill.: Scripture Press, 1956.

Free, Joseph P. *Archaeology and Bible History*. Wheaton, Ill.: Van Kampen Press, 1950.

Freedman, David Noel, and Greenfield, Jonas C., eds. *New Directions in Biblical Archaeology*. Garden City, N. Y.: Doubleday, 1969.

Freeman, John D. *More than Money*. Nashville: Sunday School Board of the Southern Baptist Convention, 1935.

Friedlander, L. *Roman Life and Manners Under the Early Empire*. 4 vols. Authorized translation of the 7th enlarged and revised edition of the *Sittengeschichte Roms* by L. A. Magnus. 2nd ed. New York: Dutton, n.d.

Fulcher of Chartres. *A History of the Expedition to Jerusalem, 1095-1127*. Translated by Frances Rita Ryan (Sisters of Saint Joseph). Edited by Harold S. Fink. Knoxville: University of Tennessee Press, 1969.

Fuller, R. H. *The Mission and Achievement of Jesus*. London: S.C.M. Press, 1953.

Gaebelein, Arno C. *The Annotated Bible*. Neptune, N.J.: Loizeaux Bros., 1970.

Gaebelein, Frank. *Exploring the Bible*. Reprint; Wheaton, Ill.: Van Kampen Press, 1950.

Garstang, John. *Joshua, Judges*. London: Constable and Co., 1931.

Gaster, Theodore H. *The Dead Sea Scriptures*. New York: Doubleday and Company, Inc., 1956.

Geikie, Cunningham. *Hours with the Bible*. New York: John B. Alden, n.d.

Gelin, Albert. *The Key Concepts of the Old Testament*. New York: Sheed and Ward, 1955.

____. "The Religion of Israel." *Twentieth Century Encyclopedia of Catholicism*. J. R. Foster, tr. New York: Hawthorne Books, 1959.

Genung, John F., *The Epic of the Inner Life*. New York: Houghton Mifflin Co., 1891.

Glueck, Nelson. *The Other Side of the Jordan*. New Haven, Conn.: American Schools of Oriental Research, 1940.

____. *Rivers in the Desert: A History of the Negeb*. New York: Farrar, Straus, and Cudahy, 1959.

Godet, Frederick C. *Commentary on the Epistle to the Romans*. Translated by A. Cusin, revised by T. W. Chambers. Grand Rapids, Mich.: Zondervan Publishing House, reprint, 1956.

Goodspeed, C. "The Angel of Jehovah." *Bibliotheca Sacra* 36 (1879): 593-615.

Gordon, Alex R. *Early Traditions of Genesis*. Edinburgh: Clark, 1907.

_____. _Poets of the Old Testament_. New York: Hodder and Stoughton, 1912.

Gordis, Robert, Koheleth, _The Man and His World_. New York: Jewish Theological Seminary of America, 1951.

Gordon, Cyrus H. _Introduction to Old Testament Times_. Ventnor, New Jer.: Ventnor Publishers, Inc., 1953.

Gore, Charles. _Dissertation on the Incarnation_. London: John Murray and Co., 1907.

_____. _The Holy Spirit and the Church_. New York: Charles Scribner's Sons, 1924.

_____. _The Incarnation of the Son of God_. New York: Charles Scribner's Sons, 1891.

Gould, J. Glenn. _The Precious Blood of Christ_. Kansas City, Mo.: Beacon Hill Press, 1959.

Gottwald, Norman, _A Light to the Nations_. New York: Harper and Row, 1959.

Graetz, H. _Popular History of the Jews_. Translated by Rabbi A. B. Rhine. Six volumes. Fifth Edition. New York: Hebrew Publishing Co., 1937. See vol. II, pp. 1-232.

Grant, Elihu, ed., _Haverford Symposium on Archaeology and the Bible_. New Haven: American Schools of Oriental Research, 1938.

Grant, F. W. _The Numerical Bible_. Neptune, N.J.: Loizeaux Bros., 1944-53.

Grant, Frederick C. _Introduction to New Testament Thought_. New York: Abingdon-Cokesbury Press, 1950.

Grant, Michael. _The Climax of Rome_. London: Weidenfeld & Nicolson, 1968.

Gray, Albert F. _Christian Theology_. Anderson, Ind.: The Warner Press, 1944.

Gray, James M. _Synthetic Bible Studies_. Old Tappan, N. J.: Fleming H. Revell, 1923.

Gray, John. _Archaeology and the Old Testament_ World. New York: Thomas Nelson and Sons, 1962.

_____. _A History of Jerusalem_. London: Robert Hale, 1969.

Greathouse, William M. _The Fullness of the Spirit_. Kansas City, Mo.: Nazarene Publishing House, 1958.

Green, Thomas Sheldon. _A Greek-English Lexicon to the New Testament_. New York: Macmillan Co., 1890.

Greenleaf, Simon. _The Testimony of the Evangelists_. Grand Rapids: Baker Book House, 1965.

Greenway, Leonard. _Basic Questions About the Bible_. Grand Rapids, Mich.: Zondervan Publishing House, 1948.

Gregory, Caspar R. _Canon and Text of the New Testament_ in _International Theological Library_. New York: Charles Scribner's Sons, 1907.

Griffith-Thomas, W. H. _The Holy Spirit of God_. Grand Rapids, Mich.: Wm. B. Eerdmans Co., 1955.

Grimes, Howard. _The Church Redemptive_. New York: Abingdon Press, 1958.

Grollenberg, L. H., comp. _Nelson's Atlas of the Bible_. New York: Thomas Nelson and Sons, 1956.

Groves, John A. _A Greek and English Dictionary_. Philadelphia: J. B. Lippincott and Co., 1861.

Grutzmacher, Richard H. _The Virgin Birth_. New York: Eaton and Mains, 1907.

Guthrie, D., et al. _The New Bible Commentary: Revised_. Grand Rapids: Wm. B. Eerdmans Co., 1970.

_____. _New Testament Introduction_. Downers Grove, Ill.: Inter-Varsity Press, 1961.

Hadjiantoniou, George A. _New Testament Introduction_. Chicago: Moody Press, 1957.

Halderman, I. M. "Does It Make Any Difference? or The Question of the Virgin Birth." _Book Bulletin_. Malverne, N. Y.: The Christian Evidence League.

Halley, Henry H. _Halley's Bible Handbook_. Grand Rapids: Zondervan Publishing House, 1964.

Halverson, Marvin, and Cohen, Arthur A., eds. _A Handbook of Christian Theology_. New York: Meridian Books, Inc., 1958.

Hamilton, Floyd E. _The Basis of Christian Faith_. 3rd ed., rev. New York: Harper and Brothers, 1946.

Hamlin, Howard H. _From Here to Maturity_. Kansas City, Mo.: Beacon Hill Press, 1955.

Hanke, Howard A. _Christ and the Church in the Old Testament_. Grand Rapids, Mich.: Zondervan Publishing House, 1957.

_____. _From Eden to Eternity_. Grand Rapids, Mich.: Wm. B. Eerdmans Co., 1960.

_____. "The Origin and Development of the Baal Religion," Th.D. dissertation, Iliff School of Theology, Denver, Colo., 1949.

_____. _The Tabernacle in the Wilderness_. Grand Rapids, Mich.: Wm B. Eerdmans Co. , 1952.

_____. _The Virgin Birth of Christ_. Grand Rapids, Mich.: Wm. B. Eerdmans Co., 1953.

Harkness, Georgia. _Christian Ethics_. New York: Abingdon Press, 1957.

Harper, Robert F. _The Code of Hammurabi_. Chicago: The University of Chicago Press, 1904.

Harrelson, Walter. _From Fertility Cult to Worship_. Garden City, N.Y.: Doubleday Anchor Books, 1970.

_____. *Interpreting the Old Testament.* New York: Holt, Rinehart and Winston, 1964.

Harrington, John B. *Essentials in Christian Faith.* New York: Harper and Brothers, 1958.

Harris, Laird. "The Bible and Cosmology." *Bulletin of the Evangelical Theological Society.* March, 1962.

Harrison, Everett F., ed. *Baker's Dictionary of Theology.* Grand Rapids, Mich.: Baker Book House, 1960.

_____. *Introduction to the New Testament.* Grand Rapids, Mich.: Wm. B. Eerdmans Co., 1964.

Harrison, R. K. *The Archaeology of the Old Testament.* London: The English Universities Press, 1963.

_____. *Old Testament Times.* Grand Rapids, Mich.: Wm. B. Eerdmans Co., 1970.

Hastings, James, ed. "Prayer." *Great Christian Doctrines.* New York: Charles Scribner's Sons, 1915.

Hazelton, Roger. "On Proving God." *A Handbook in Christian Conversation.* New York: Harper and Brothers, 1952.

_____. *Renewing the Mind.* New York: Macmillan Co., 1949.

Hedenquist, Gote. *The Church and the Jewish People.* London: Edinburgh House Press, 1954.

Hedley, George. *The Christian Heritage in America.* New York: Macmillan Co., 1946.

Heidt, William George. *Angelology of the Old Testament: A Study in Biblical Theology.* Washington, D.C.: Catholic University of America, 1949.

Heinisch, Paul. *Theology of the Old Testament.* Collegeville, Minn.: The Liturgical Press, 1950.

Henry, Carl F. H., ed. *The Biblical Expositor.* Vol. 3. Philadelphia: A. J. Holman Co., 1960.

_____. *Christian Personal Ethics.* Grand Rapids, Mich.: Wm. B. Eerdmans Co., 1957.

Hessert, Paul. *Introduction to Christianity.* Englewood Cliffs, N. J.: Prentice-Hall, 1958..

Hiebert D. Edmond. *Introduction to the Non-Pauline Epistles.* Chicago: Moody Press, 1962.

_____. *Introduction to the Pauline Epistles.* Chicago: Moody Press, 1954.

Hills, A. M. *Fundamental Christian Theology.* 2 vols. Pasadena, Calif.: Pasadena College, 1931. Abridged edition, C. J. Kinne, 1932.

Hindson, Edward E. *The Philistines and the Old Testament.* Grand Rapids, Mich.: Baker Book House, 1971.

Hoade, Eugene. *Guide to the Holy Land.* 4th ed., rev. Jerusalem: Franciscan Press, 1962.

Hocking, William Ernest. *The Meaning of God in Human Experience.* New Haven: Yale University Press, 1912.

Hodge, A. A. *The Atonement.* Grand Rapids, Mich.: Wm. B. Eerdmans Co., 1953.

Hodge, Charles. *Systematic Theology.* 3 vols. New York: Charles Scribner's Sons, 1893.

Hodges, J. W. *Christ's Kingdom and Coming.* Grand Rapids, Mich.: Wm. B. Eerdmans Co., 1957.

Hodgkin, A. M. *Christ in All the Scriptures.* London: Pickering and Inglis, Ltd., 1943.

Hort, Fenton. *The Christian Ecclesia.* New York: Macmillan Co., 1898.

Horton, Walter Marshall. *Christian Theology: An Ecumenical Approach.* New York: Harper and Brothers, 1955.

Howley, G. C. G.; Bruce, F. F.; and Ellison, H. L., eds. *A New Testament Commentary.* Grand Rapids, Mich.: Zondervan Publishing House, 1969.

Huffman, J. A. *The Meaning of Things.* Winonna Lake, Ind.: The Standard Press, 1953.

_____. *Voices from Rocks and Dust Heaps of Bible Lands.* Rev. Marion, Ind.: The Standard Press, 1943.

Hunter, Archibald M. *Introducing New Testament Theology.* Philadelphia: Westminster Press, 1957.

_____. *The Message of the New Testament.* Philadelphia: Westminster Press, 1944.

_____. *The Work and Words of Jesus.* London: S. C. M. Press, 1950.

Hyatt, J. Philip, ed. *The Bible in Modern Scholarship.* Nashville: Abingdon Press, 1965.

Hyde, Walter Woodburn. *Paganism to Christianity in the Roman Empire.* Philadelphia: University of Pennsylvania Press, 1946.

Hyde, William DeWitt. *The Five Great Philosophies of Life.* New York: Macmillan Co., 1923.

Ironside, H. A. *In the Heavenlies.* Neptune. N.J.: Loizeaux Bros., 1937.

Irwin, W. A. *The Old Testament: Keystone of Human Culture.* New York: Henry Schuman, 1952.

Jacob, Edmond. *Theology of the Old Testament.* Translated by A. W. Heathcote and P. J. Allcock. New York: Harper and Brothers, 1958.

Jastrow, Morris. *The Song of Songs.* Philadelphia: J. B. Lippincott and Co., 1921.

Jauncey, James H. *Science Returns to God.* Grand Rapids, Mich.: Zondervan Publishing House, 1961.

Jeans, Sir James. *This Mysterious Universe.* Rev. New York: Macmillan Co., 1937.

Jenkins, Daniel. *The Strangeness of the Church*. Garden City: Doubleday and Co., 1955.

Jensen, Joseph, O.S.B. *God's Word to Israel*. Boston: Allyn and Bacon, 1968.

Jeremias, Joachim. *Jerusalem in the Time of Jesus*. Translated by F. H. Cave and C. H. Cave. London: S.C.M. Press, 1962, 1967.

Jessop, T. E., et al. *The Christian Understanding of Man*. London: George Allen and Unwin Ltd., 1938.

Jirku, Anton. *The World of the Bible*. Translated by Ann E. Kepp. London: Weidenfeld and Nicholson, 1967.

Johns, C. N. *Palestine of the Crusades*. Jaffa: 1938.

Johnson, Aubrey. *The Vitality of the Individual in the Thought of Ancient Israel*. Cardiff: University of Wales Press, 1949.

Johnson, Paul E. *Psychology of Religion*. New York: Abingdon-Cokesbury, 1945.

Join-Lambert, Michael. *Jerusalem*. Translated by Charlotte Haldane. London: Elek Books, 1958.

Jones, E. Stanley. *Christ and Human Suffering*. New York: Abingdon Press, 1933.

Josephus. *Josephus: Complete Works*. Translated by William Whiston. Grand Rapids, Mich.: Kregel Publications, 1964.

Jurji, Edward J., ed. *The Great Religions of the Modern World*. Princeton, N.J.: Princeton University Press, 1946.

Kantonen, T. A. *The Christian Hope*. Philadelphia: Muhlenberg Press, 1954.

Kaufmann, Yehezkel. *The Religion of Israel*. Translated by Moshe Greenberg. Chicago: University of Chicago Press, 1960.

Kautzsch, Emil Friedrich. "Theophany." In *The New Schaff-Herzog Encyclopedia of Religious Knowledge*. Edited by S. M. Jackson. 13 vols. Grand Rapids, Mich.: Baker Book House, 1957.

Kay, James. *The Nature of Christian Worship*. New York: Philosophical Library, 1954.

Keil, Carl Frederick, and Delitzsch, Franz. *The Pentateuch*. Vols. 1-3. Translated by James Martin. *Biblical Commentary on the Old Testament*. Grand Rapids, Mich.: Wm. B. Eerdmans Co., n.d.

Kelchner, John Wesley. *A Description of Solomon's Temple and the Tabernacle in the Wilderness*. New York: A. J. Holman, 1925.

Kelly, Howard A. *A. Scientific Man and the Bible*. Philadelphia: The Sunday School Times Co., 1925.

Kennedy, Gerald. *God's Good News*. New York: Harper and Brothers, 1955.

Kennedy, H. A. A. *St Paul and the Mystery Religions*. London: Hodder & Stoughton, 1913.

Kent, Charles Foster. *A History of the Jewish People During the Babylonian, Persian, and Greek Periods*. 5th ed. New York: Charles Scribner's Sons, 1902.

____. *The Kings and Prophets of Israel and Judah*. New York: Charles Scribner's Sons, 1913.

Kent, Hormer A., Jr. *Jerusalem to Rome*. Grand Rapids, Mich.: Baker Book House, 1972.

Kenyon, Kathleen M. *Archaeology in the Holy Land*. New York: Praeger, Publishers, 1960.

____. *Jerusalem: Excavating 3000 Years of History*. New York: McGraw-Hill Book Co.; London: Thames & Hudson, 1967.

Kenyon, Sir Frederic. *Our Bible and the Ancient Manuscripts*. 4th ed. New York: Harper and Brothers, 1939.

Kepler, Thomas S., ed. *The Fellowship of the Saints*. New York: Abingdon-Cokesbury, 1948.

Kerr, Hugh Thompson, Jr., ed. *A Compend of the Institutes of the Christian Religion by John Calvin*. Philadelphia: Presbyterian Board of Christian Education, 1939.

Kerr, John H. *A Harmony of the Gospels*. Old Tappan, N.J.: Fleming H. Revell, 1903.

Kierkegaard, Soren. *Works of Love*. Translated by David and Lillian Swenson. Princeton. N.J.: Princeton University Press, 1946.

King. Albion R. *The Problem of Evil*. New York: Ronald Press Co., 1952.

Kirk, Thomas. *Solomon: His Life and Works*. Edinburgh: Andrew Elliot, 1915.

Kitchen, J. Howard. *Holy Fields: An Introduction to the Historical Geography of the Holy Land*. Grand Rapids, Mich.: Wm. B. Eerdmans Co., 1955.

Kittel, Gerhard, ed. *Theological Dictionary of the New Testament*. Translated by Geoffrey W. Bromiley, 9 vols. Grand Rapids, Mich.: Wm. B. Eerdmans Co., 1964-74.

Knight, George A. F. *A Christian Theology of the Old Testament*. London: S. C. M. Press, 1959.

Knopf, Carl S. *The Old Testament Speaks*. New York: Thomas Nelson and Sons, 1934.

Knott, Laura A. *Student's History of the Hebrews*. New York: Abingdon Press, 1922.

Knudson, Albert C. *The Principles of Christian Ethics*. New York: Abingdon-Cokesbury, 1943.

____. *The Religious Teaching of the Old Testament*. New York: Abingdon-Cokesbury, 1918.

Köhler, Ludwig. *Old Testament Theology.* Translated by A. S. Todd. Philadelphia: Westminster Press, 1957.

Kollek, Teddy, and Pearlman, Moshe. *Jerusalem: A History of Forty Centuries.* New York: Random House, 1968.

Kopp, Clemens. *The Holy Places of the Gospel.* New York: Herder & Herder, 1963.

Kraeling, Emil G. *The Old Testament Since the Reformation.* New York: Harper and Row, 1955.

_____.,ed. *Rand McNally Historical Atlas of the Holy Land.* Chicago: Rand McNally & Co., 1959.

Kuhl, Curt. *The Old Testament: Its Origins and Composition.* Translated by C.T. M. Herriott. Richmond: John Knox Press, 1961.

Kunkel, Fritz. *In Search of Maturity.* New York: Charles Scribner's Sons, 1946.

Kuntz, John Kenneth. *The Self-Revelation of God.* Philadelphia: Westminster Press, 1967.

Kurtz, Johann Heinrich. *History of the Old Covenant.* Translated by Alfred Edersheim and James Martin. 3 vols. Clark's Foreign Theological Library. 3d ser. Edinburgh: Clark, 1859.

Ladd, G. H. *Crucial Questions About the Kingdom of God.* Grand Rapids, Mich.: Wm. B. Eerdmans Co., 1952.

Lake, Kirsopp. *The Text of the New Testament.* 6th ed. Revised by Silva New, A. B. London: Rivingtons, 1933.

Landau, Eli. *Jerusalem the Eternal: The Paratroopers' Battle for the City of David.* Translated by R. Lev. Edited by Murray Roston. Tel-Aviv: Otpaz, 1968.

Lange, John Peter. "Genesis." Translated by Tayler Lewis and A. Gosman. In *Commentary on the Holy Scriptures.* Vol. 1. Edited by Philip Schaff. 12 vols. Grand Rapids. Mich.: Zondervan, 1960.

Larue, Gerald A. *Old Testament Life and Literature.* Boston: Allyn and Bacon, Inc., 1968.

Latimer, Elizabeth W. *Judea from Syrus to Titus 537 B.C.-70 A.D.* Chicago: A. C. McClurg & Co., 1899.

Latourette, Kenneth Scott. *A History of Christianity.* New York: Harper and Brothers, 1953.

Laurin, Roy L. *John: Life Eternal.* Chicago: Moody Press, 1972.

Lawrence, T. E. *Crusader Castles.* London: Golden Cockerel Press, 1936.

Lawson, John. *The Biblical Theology of Saint Irenaeus.* London: Epworth Press, 1948.

Leavell, Roland Q. *Evangelism.* Nashville: Broadman Press, 1951.

Leighton, J. A. *Man and the Cosmos.* New York: D. Appleton and Co., 1922.

Lenski, R. C. H. *Interpretation of the New Testament.* 12 vols. Minneapolis: Augsburg Publishing House, 1933-46.

Levie, Jean, S. J. *The Bible, Word of God in Words of Men.* New York: Kenedy, 1961.

Levison, Nahum. *The Jewish Background of Christianity.* Edinburgh: T. & T. Clark, 1932.

Lewis, C. S. *The Case for Christianity.* New York: Macmillan Co., 1944.

_____. *The Great Divorce.* New York: Macmillan Co., 1946.

_____. *Miracles.* New York. Macmillan Co., 1947.

Lewis, Edwin. *The Creator and the Adversary.* New York: Abingdon-Cokesbury, 1948.

_____. *A Manual of Christian Beliefs.* New York: Charles Scribner's Sons, 1927.

_____. *A Philosophy of the Christian Revelation.* New York: Harper and Brothers, 1940.

Liddell, Henry George, and Scott, Robert. *A Greek- English Lexicon.* Oxford: Oxford University Press, 1940.

Liddon, Henry Parry. *The Divinity of Our Lord and Savior Jesus Christ.* 18th Ed. London: Longmans & Green, 1897.

Lloyd-Jones, D. Martyn. *God's Way of Reconciliation.* Grand Rapids, Mich.: Baker Book House, 1972.

Lockyer, Herbert. *All the Prayers of the Bible.* Grand Rapids, Mich.: Zondervan Publishing House, 1959.

Louvish, Misha, ed. *Facts About Israel, 1970.* Jerusalem: Keter Books, 1970.

Luck, G. Coleman. *The Bible Book by Book.* Chicago: Moody Press, 1955.

McClain, Alva J. *Romans: The Gospel of God's Grace.* Edited by Herman A. Hoyt. Chicago: Moody Press, 1973.

McCown, C.C. *The Ladder of Progress in Palestine.* New York: Harper and Brothers, 1943.

MacDonald, William Graham. "Christology and 'The Angel of the Lord.' " In *Current Issues in Biblical and Patristic Interpretation.* Edited by Gerald F. Hawthorne. Grand Rapids, Mich.: Wm. B. Eerdmans Co., 1975.

McFayden, John E. *The Wisdom Books.* London: James Clarke and Co., n.d.

McGiffert, A.C. *A History of Christian Thought.* 2 vols. New York: Charles Scribner's Sons, 1932.

McGregor, G.H.C. *Jew and Greek: Tutors unto Christ. The Jewish and Hellenistic Background of the New Testament.* New York: Charles Scribner's Sons, 1936.

McKibben, Frank M. *Christian Education Through the Church.* New York: Abingdon-Cokesbury, 1947.

McKenzie, John L. *The Two-Edged Sword.* Milwaukee: Bruce Publishing Co., 1960.

Machen, J. Gresham. *The Origin of Paul's Religion.* Grand Rapids, Mich.: Wm. B. Eerdmans Co., 1947.

_____. *The Virgin Birth of Christ.* New York: Harper and Brothers, 1930.

Macintosh, Robert. *Historic Theories of the Atonement.* London: Hodder and Stoughton, 1920.

Maclaren, Alexander. *Expositions of Holy Scripture.* 11 vols. Grand Rapids, Mich.: Wm. B. Eerdmans Co., 1944.

Manley, G.T. *The New Bible Handbook.* Chicago: The Inter-Varsity Christian Fellowship, 1949.

Marsh, Frank Burr. *The Reign of Tiberius.* Oxford: University Press, 1931.

Marston, Leslie R. *From Chaos to Character.* Winona Lake, Ind.: Light and Life Press, 1944.

Martin, Ralph P. *Mark: Evangelist and Theologian.* Grand Rapids, Mich.: Zondervan Publishing House, 1973.

Matson, G. Olaf. *The Palestinian Guide, Including Trans-Jordan.* Jerusalem: Joshua Simon, 1946.

Matthews, C.E. *Every Christian's Job.* Nashville: Broadman Press, 1955.

Mattingly, Harold. *Roman Imperial Civilization.* London: Edwin Arnold Ltd., 1957.

Mazzolani, L.S. *The Idea of the City in Roman Thought (from walled city to spiritual commonwealth).* Translated by S. O'Donnell. Toronto: Hollis & Carter, 1967, 1970.

Meistermann, P. Barnabe. *Guide de Terre Sainte.* Paris: Editions Franciscaines; Librarie Letouzey & Ané, 1936.

Mendenhall, George E. "Biblical History in Transition." In *The Bible and the Ancient Near East.* Edited by G. Ernest Wright. New York: Doubleday Anchor Books, 1965.

_____. *Law and Covenant in Israel and the Ancient Near East.* Pittsburgh: Biblical Colloquium, 1955.

Metzger, Bruce M. *An Introduction to the Apocrypha.* New York: Oxford University Press, 1957.

Meysels, Theodor F. *Israeli in Your Pocket.* Tel Aviv: Ben-Dor Israel Publishing Co., 1956.

Michaud, Joseph Francis. *History of the Crusades.* Translated by W. Robson. New York: Redfield, 1853.

Miley, John. *The Atonement in Christ.* New York: Phillips and Hunt, 1879.

Miller, Dorothy Ruth. *A Handbook of Ancient History in Bible Light.* New York: Fleming H. Revell, 1937.

Miller, H. S. *General Biblical Introduction.* 2nd ed. Houghton, N.Y.: The Wood-bearer Press, 1940.

Miller, H. V. *The Sin Problem.* Kansas City, Mo.: Nazarene Publishing House, 1947.

_____. *When He Is Come.* Kansas City, Mo.: Nazarene Publishing House, 1941.

Miller, M. S. and J. L., eds. *Harper's Bible Dictionary.* New York: Harper and Brothers, 1952.

Miller, Park Hays. *How to Study and Use the Bible.* Boston: W. A. Wilde Co., 1949.

Mills, Sanford C. *A Hebrew Christian Looks at Romans.* Grand Rapids, Mich.: Zondervan Publishing House, 1968.

Minear, Paul S. *The Eyes of Faith.* Philadelphia: Westminster Press, 1946.

Mitchell, T. Crichton. *Mr. Wesley.* Kansas City, Mo.: Beacon Hill Press, 1957.

Moore, Elinor A. *The Ancient Churches of Jerusalem: The Evidence of the Pilgrims.* London: Constable, 1961.

Moore, George Foot. *Judaism.* 2 vols. Cambridge: Harvard University Press, 1927.

Morgan, G. Campbell. *The Analyzed Bible.* Old Tappan, N.J.: Fleming H. Revell, 1971.

_____. *Hosea, the Heart and Holiness of God.* New York: Fleming H. Revell, 1934.

_____. *Living Messages of the Books of the Bible.* New York: Fleming H. Revell, 1912.

Morgenstern, Julian. *The Fire upon the Altar.* Chicago: Quadrangle Books, 1903.

Moriarty, Frederick L. *Introducing the Old Testament.* Milwaukee: Bruce Publishing Co., 1960.

Morris, Leon. The Apostolic Preaching of the Cross. London: Tyndale Press, 1955.

_____. *The Epistles of Paul to the Thessalonians.* The Tyndale New Testament Commentaries. Grand Rapids, Mich.: Wm. B. Eerdmans Co., 1957.

Mott, John R. *The Larger Evangelism.* New York: Abingdon-Cokesbury, 1944.

Mould, Elmer K. *Essentials of Bible History.* Rev. New York: Ronald Press Co., 1951.

Moule, H. C. G. *Veni Creator.* London: Hodder and Stoughton, 1895.

Moulton, James H. *A Grammar of New Testament Greek.* Vol. I: *Prolegomena.* 3rd ed. Edinburgh: T. & T. Clark, 1908.

Moulton, James Hope, and Milligan, George. *The Vocabulary of the Greek Testament.* Grand Rapids, Mich.: Wm. B. Eerdmans Co., 1952.

Mowinckel, Sigmund. *He That Cometh.* Translated by G. W. Anderson. New York: Abingdon Press, 1956.

Mozley, J. K. *The Doctrine of the Atonement.* New York: Charles Scribner's Sons, 1916.

Muilenburg, James. "The History of the Religion of Israel." In *The Interpreter's Bible.* Vol. I. New York: Abingdon Press, 1952.

____. *The Way of Israel.* New York: Harper and Row, 1961.

Muir, James C. *His Truth Endureth.* Philadelphia: National Publishing Co., 1937.

Nash. Arnold. S., ed. *Protestant Thought in the Twentieth Century.* New York: Macmillan Co., 1951.

Nease, Orval J. *Heroes of Temptation.* Kansas City, Mo.: Beacon Hill Press, 1950.

Needler, Winifred. *Palestine Ancient and Modern.* Toronto: Royal Ontario Museum of Archaeology, 1949.

Neil, William. *Harper's Bible Commentary.* New York: Harper & Row, 1963.

Nelson, Lawrence E. *Our Roving Bible.* New York: Abingdon-Cokesbury, 1945.

Neve, J. L. *A History of Christian Thought.* 2 vols. Philadelphia: Muhlenberg Press, 1946.

Nevius, Warren N. *The Old Testament: Its Story and Religious Message.* Philadelphia: The Westminster Press, 1942.

Newman, Murray. *The People of the Covenant.* New York, 1962.

Newton, A. P., ed. *Travel and Travellers in the Middle Ages.* London: 1930; Freeport, N. Y.: Brooklyn Libraries Press, 1967.

Nicholson, Ernest W. "The Interpretation of Exodus XXIV 9-11." *Vetus Testamentum* 24 (1974): 77-97.

Nicoll, W. Robertson, *The Expositor's Greek Testament.* Grand Rapids, Mich." Wm. B. Eerdmans Co., 1961.

Niebuhr, Reinhold. *Beyond Tragedy.* New York: Charles Scribner's Sons, 1948.

____. *The Nature and Destiny of Man.* 2 vols. New York: Charles Scribner's Sons, 1943.

Niles, Daniel T. *The Preacher's Task and the Stone of Stumbling.* New York: Harper and Brothers, 1958.

Noth, Martin. *The History of Israel.* Translated by S. Godman. Revised by P. R. Ackroyd. 2nd ed. New York: Harper & Row, 1960.

Nygren, Anders. *Agape and Eros.* Translated by Philip S. Watson. Philadelphia: Westminster Press, 1953.

Oehler, Gustav. *Theology of the Old Testament.* Grand Rapids, Mich.: Zondervan Publishing House, 1950.

Oesterley, W. O. E. *A History of Israel.* Vol. II: *From the Fall of Jerusalem to the Bar-Kokhba Revolt, A.D. 135.* Oxford; Clarendon Press, 1939.

____. *An Introduction to the Books of the Apocrypha.* New York: Macmillan Co., 1935.

Oldenbourg, Zoe. *The Crusades.* Translated by Anne Carter. London: Weidenfeld and Nicolson, 1966.

Oman, W. W. C. *A History of the Art of War in the Middle Ages.* 2nd ed., rev. 2 vols. London, 1934.

Orchard, B.; Sutcliffe, E. F.; and Russell, R., eds. *A Catholic Commentary on Holy Scripture.* Edinburgh: Thomas Nelson and Sons, 1953.

Orlinsky, Harry M. *Ancient Israel.* Ithaca, N. Y.: Cornell University Press, 1964.

Orni, Efriam, and Efrat, Elisha. *Geography of Israel.* Jerusalem: Israel Program for Scientific Translations, 1964.

Orr, James. *International Standard Bible Encyclopedia.* 5 vols. Grand Rapids, Mich.: Wm. B. Eerdmans Co., 1939.

____. *The Virgin Birth of Christ.* New York: Charles Scribner's Sons, 1907.

Ottley, R. L. *A Short History of the Hebrews to the Roman Period.* New York: Macmillan Co., 1940.

Otto, Rudolf. *The Kingdom of God and the Son of Man.* Grand Rapids, Mich.: Zondervan Publishing House, 1938.

____. *The Idea of the Holy.* Translated by J. W. Harvey. London: Oxford University Press, 1957.

Owen, G. Frederick. *Abraham to Allenby.* 2nd ed. Grand Rapids, Mich.: Wm. B. Eerdmans Co., 1941.

Parker, DeWitt H. *The Principles of Aesthetics.* New York: Appleton-Century-Crofts, 1920.

Parkes, James. *A History of Palestine from 135 A.D. to Modern Times.* New York: Oxford University Press, 1949.

Paxson, Ruth. *Wealth, Walk, and Warfare of the Christian.* Old Tappan, N.J.: Fleming H. Revell, 1939.

Pearlman, Moshe, and Yannai, Yaacov. *Historical Sites in Israel.* New York: Vanguard Press, 1964.

Perowne, J.J.S. The Book of Psalms. 7th ed., rev. Boston: Bradley and Woodruff, n.d.

Perowne, Stewart. *Jerusalem—Bethlehem.* South Brunswick, N.Y.: A. S. Barnes Co., 1965.

____. *The Life and Times of Herod the Great.* London: Hodder & Stoughton, 1956.

Peters, John. *Christian Perfection and American Methodism.* New York: Abingdon Press 1956.

Pfeiffer, Charles F. *Baker's Bible Atlas,* Grand Rapids: Baker Book House, 1961.

____. *The Biblical World.* Grand Rapids, Mich.: Baker Book House, 1972.

____. ,ed. *The Biblical World: A Dictionary of Biblical Archaeology.* Grand Rapids, Mich.: Baker Book House, 1966.

____. and Vos, Howard F. *The Wycliffe Historical Geography of the Holy Lands.* Chicago: Moody Press, 1967.

Power, A. D. *The Proverbs of Solomon.* New York: Longmans, Green and Co., 1949.

Price, Ira M. *The Ancestry of Our English Bible.* 2nd ed., rev. New York: Harper and Brothers, 1949.

____. *The Dramatic Story of Old Testament History.* 4th ed. New York: Fleming H. Revell, 1945.

____. *The Monuments and the Old Testament.* 17th ed. Philadelphia: The Judson Press, 1946.

____. *A Syllabus of Old Testament History.* 8th ed. New York: Fleming H. Revell. 1912.

Pritchard, James B., ed. *The Ancient Near East: An Anthology of Texts and Pictures.* Princeton: Princeton University Press; London: Oxford University Press, 1958.

____. *Archaeology and the Old Testament.* Princeton, N.J.: Princeton University Press, 1958.

Purkiser, W. T. *Conflicting Concepts of Holiness.* Kansas City, Mo.: Beacon Hill Press, 1953.

Qualben, Lars Pederson. *A History of the Christian Church.* Rev. New York: Thomas Nelson and Sons, 1936.

Rad, Gerhard, von. *Old Testament Theology.* Vol. I: *The Theology of Israel's Historical Traditions.* Translated by D. M. G. Stalker, Vol. II: *The Theology of Israel's Prophetic Traditions.* New York: Harper and Row, 1962, 1965.

Ralston, Thomas N. *The Elements of Divinity.* Nashville: Publishing House of the M. E. Church, South, 1919.

Ramm. Bernard. *The Christian View of Science and Scripture.* Grand Rapids, Mich.: Wm. B. Eerdmans Co., 1954.

Ramsay, W. M. *The Church in the Roman Empire Before A.D. 170.* New York and London: G. P. Putnam's Sons, n.d.

Ramsey, Paul. *Basic Christian Ethics.* New York: Charles Scribner's Sons, 1950.

Rappoport, A. S. *The Psalms,* London: The Centenary Press, 1935.

Rashdall, Hastings. *The Idea of Atonement in Christian Theology.* London: Macmillan Co., 1920.

Rauschenbusch, Walter. *Christianity and the Social Crisis.* New York: Macmillan Co., 1920.

____. *The Gospel for the Social Awakening.* New York: Association Press, 1950.

____. *The Social Principles of Jesus.* New York: Association Press, 1916.

Raven, John H. *Old Testament Introduction, General and Special.* New York: Fleming H. Revell, 1910.

Read, David H. C. *The Christian Faith.* London: English Universities Press, 1955.

Redford, M. E. *The Rise of the Church of the Nazarene.* Kansas City, Mo.: Nazarene Publishing House, 1948.

Rees, Paul S. *Stir Up the Gift.* Grand Rapids, Mich.: Zondervan Publishing House, 1952.

Reid, J. K. S. *The Authority of Scripture.* London: Methuen and Co., 1957.

Renckens, Henry. *The Religion of Israel.* Translated by N. B. Smith. New York: Sheed and Ward, 1966.

Reno, Cora. *Evolution: Fact or Theory?* Chicago: The Moody Press, 1953.

Rice, John M. *The Old Testament in the Life of Today.* New York: Macmillan Co., 1920.

Richardson, Alan, ed. *Theological Word Book of the Bible.* London: S.C.M. Press, 1950; New York: Macmillan Co., 1955.

Richardson, Cyril C. *The Church Through the Centuries.* New York: Charles Scribner's Sons, 1938.

Riggs, James Stevenson. *A History of the Jewish People During the Maccabean and Roman Periods.* New York: Charles Scribner's Sons, 1908.

Ringenberg, Loyal R. *The Word of God in History.* Butler, Ind.: The Higley Press, 1953.

Ringgren, Helmer. *Israelite Religion.* Philadelphia: Fortress Press, 1966.

_____. *The Messiah in the Old Testament*. Studies in Biblical Theology, No. 18. Chicago: Alec R. Allenson, 1956.

Robertson, A. T. *The Pharisees and Jesus*. New York: Charles Scribner's Sons, 1920.

Robinson, Edward. *Biblical Researches in Palestine and in the Adjacent Regions*. Boston: Crocker and Brewster, 1856.

_____. *Later Biblical Researches in Palestine and in the Adjacent Regions*. Boston: Crocker and Brewster, 1868.

Robinson, H. Wheeler, *The History of Israel,* Studies in Theology, No. 42. London: Duckworth Press, 1957.

_____. *The Old Testament, Its Making and Meaning*. Nashville: Cokesbury Press, 1932.

_____. *The Religious Ideas of the Old Testament*. New York: Charles Scribner's Sons, 1913.

Robinson, Theodore. *The Poetry of the Old Testament*. London: Duckworth, 1947.

Rogers, A. K. *A Student's History of Philosophy*. 3rd ed. New York: Macmillan Co., 1932.

Romanoff, Paul. *Onomasticon of Palestine*. New York: American Academy of Jewish Research, 1937.

Roop, Hervin U. *Christian Ethics*. New York: Fleming H. Revell, 1926.

Rowley, Harold H. *The Biblical Doctrine of Election*. London: Lutterworth Press, 1950.

_____. *The Faith of Israel*. Philadelphia: Westminster Press, 1956.

_____. ed. *The Old Testament and Modern Study*. New York: Oxford University Press, 1951.

_____. *The Rediscovery of the Old Testament*. London: James Clarke and Co., 1945.

_____. *The Unity of the Bible*. Philadelphia: Westminster Press, 1953.

_____. *Worship in Ancient Israel: Its Forms and Meaning*. Philadelphia: Fortress Press, 1967.

Rose, Herbert J. *Ancient Roman Religion*. London: Hutchinson's University Library, n.d.

Rosenau, William. *Jewish Ceremonial Institutions and Customs*. New York: Bloch Publishing Co., 1929.

Rostovtzeff, M. *A History of the Ancient World*. Vol. II: *Rome*. Translated by J. D. Duff. Oxford: Clarendon Press, 1928.

_____. *The Social and Economic History of the Hellenistic World*. 3 vols. Oxford: Clarendon Press, 1941.

Roth, Cecil. *The Casale Pilgrim*. London: Soncino Press, 1919.

Rowley, Harold. H. "Israel, History of" In *Interpreter's Dictionary of the Bible*. New York: Abingdon Press, 1962. vol. II, pp. 750-765.

_____. *From Joseph to Joshua*. London: Oxford University Press, 1950.

_____. *From Moses to Qumran: Studies in the Old Testament*. London: Lutterworth Press, 1963.

_____. *The Rediscovery of the Old Testament*. Philadelphia: Westminster Press, 1946.

_____. *The Zadokite Fragments and the Dead Sea Scrolls*. Oxford: Basil Blackwell, 1952.

Runciman, Steven. *A History of the Crusades*. Cambridge: University Press, 1951.

Sachar, Abram Leon. *A History of the Jews*. 2nd ed., rev. New York: Alfred A. Knopf, 1940.

Salmon, Edward T. *A History of the Roman World from 30 B.C. to A.D. 138*. New York: Macmillan Company, 1944.

Salmon, F. J. *Palestine of the Crusades*. Jaffa, 1937.

Sampey, John R. *The Heart of the Old Testament*. Rev. Nashville: Broadman Press, 1922.

_____. *Syllabus for Old Testament Study*. New York: George H. Doran Co., 1924.

Sanday, William. *Sacred Sites of the Gospels*. Oxford; Oxford University Press, 1903.

Sandmel, Samuel. *Herod: Profile of a Tyrant*. Philadelphia: J. B. Lippincott Co., 1967.

Sangster, W. E. *The Path to Perfection*. New York: Abingdon-Cokesbury, 1943.

Sauer, Erich. *The Dawn of World Redemption*. Grand Rapids, Mich.: Wm. B. Eerdmans Co., 1952.

_____. *From Eternity to Eternity*. Grand Rapids, Mich.: Wm. B. Eerdmans Co., 1954.

_____. *The Triumph of the Crucified*. Grand Rapids, Mich.: Wm. B. Eerdmans Co., 1952.

Sawtelle, Henry A. "The Angel of Jehovah." *Bibliotheca Sacra and Biblical Expository* 16 (1859): 805-35.

Sayce, A. H. *Babylonians and Assyrians, Life and Customs*. New York: Charles Scribner's Sons, 1909.

_____. *Fresh Light from Ancient Monuments*. New York: Fleming H. Revell, 1895.

Scholer, David M. *A Basic Bibliographic Guide for New Testament Exegesis*. Grand Rapids, Mich.: Wm. B. Eerdmans Co., 1973.

Schroeder, Fredrick W. *Preaching the Word with Authority*. Philadelphia: Westminster Press, 1954.

Shubert, Kurt. *The Dead Sea Community: Its Origin and Teachings*. Translated by J. W. Doberstein. London: Adam and Charles Black, 1959.

Schweitzer, Albert. *The Quest of the Historical Jesus.* New York: Macmillan Co., 1922.

Scroggie, W. Graham. *A Guide to the Gospels.* London: Pickering and Inglis, 1948.

____. *Know Your Bible.* 2 vols. London: Pickering & Inglis, 1940.

____. *The Unfolding Drama of Redemption.* Grand Rapids, Mich.: Zondervan Publishing House, 1970.

Segal, J. B. *Edessa: The Blessed City.* Oxford: Clarendon Press, 1970.

Serao, Matilda. *In the Company of Jesus.* Translated by Richard Davey. London: Thomas Nelson and Sons, n.d.

Sheldon, Henry Clay. *History of Christian Doctrine.* 2 vols. New York: Harper, 1886.

Shelton, O. L. *The Church Functioning Effectively.* St. Louis: Christian Board of Publication, 1946.

Shepard, J. W. *The Life and Letters of St. Paul.* Grand Rapids, Mich.: Wm. B. Erdmans. Co., 1950.

____. *Basic Introduction to the New Testament.* Grand Rapids, Mich.: Wm. B. Erdmans Co., 1964.

Shield Bible Study Series. 18 vols. Grand Rapids, Mich.: Baker Book House, 1957.

Simons, J. *Jerusalem in the Old Testament.* Leiden: E. J. Brill, 1952.

Simpson, John E. *Faithful Also in Much.* New York: Fleming H. Revell, 1948.

Skeel C. A. J. *Travel in the First Century.* Cambridge: University Press, 1901.

Souter, Alexander. *The Text and Canon of the New Testament.* New York: Charles Scribner's Sons, 1923.

Smail, R. *Crusading Warfare, 1097 and 1193.* Cambridge: University Press, 1956.

Smart, W. A. *Still the Bible Speaks.* New York: Abingdon-Cokesbury, 1948.

Smith, C. Ryder. *The Bible Doctrine of Man.* London: Epworth Press, 1951.

____. *The Bible Doctrine of Sin.* London: Epworth Press, 1953.

Smith, David. *The Days of His Flesh.* New York: George H. Doran Co., n.d.

Smith, George Adam. *The Historical Geography of the Holy Land.* 15th ed. New York: A. C. Armstrong & Son, 1909.

____. *Jerusalem: The Topography, Economics and History from the Earliest Times to A.D. 70.* 2 vols. New York: A. C. Armstrong & Son, 1908.

Smith, George D., ed. *The Teaching of the Catholic Church.* 2 vols. New York: Macmillan Co., 1955.

Smith, Hannah Whitall. *The Christian's Secret of a Happy Life.* Rev. Boston: The Christian Witness Company, 1885.

Smith, Henry P. *Old Testament History.* New York: Charles Scribner's Sons, 1915.

Smith, Timothy L. *Revivalism and Social Reform.* New York: Abingdon Press, 1957.

Smith, Wilbur M. *Profitable Bible Study.* Boston: W. A. Wilde Co., 1939.

Smith, William. *Old Testament History.* New York: American Book Company, n.d.

Smyth, J. Patterson. *How to Read the Bible.* New York: James Pott and Co., 1925.

Snaith, Norman H. *The Distinctive Ideas of the Old Testament.* Philadelphia: Westminster Press, 1946.

____. *The Jews from Cyrus to Herod.* New York: Abingdon Press, 1956.

Speer, Robert E. *The Finality of Jesus Christ.* New York: Fleming H. Revell, 1933.

Spence, H. D. M., and Exell, Joseph S. *The Pulpit Commentary.* 8 vols. Grand Rapids, Mich.: Wm. B. Eerdmans Co., 1959.

Sperry, Willard L. *Religion in America.* New York: Macmillan Co., 1947.

Spurrier, William A. *Guide to the Christian Faith.* New York: Charles Scribner's Sons, 1952.

Stanton, V. H. "New Testament Canon." In *Hastings' Dictionary of the Bible,* III, 529b-542b. New York: Charles Scribner's Sons, 1902.

Stearns, O. S. *Introduction to the Books of the Old Testament.* New York: Silver Burdett and Co., 1892.

Stevenson, William B. *The Poem of Job.* London: Oxford University Press, 1947.

Stewart, James S. *A Faith to Proclaim.* New York: Charles Scribner's Sons, 1953.

____. *The Life and Teaching of Jesus Christ.* New York: Abingdon Press, n.d.

____. *A Man in Christ.* New York: Harper and Brothers, n.d.

Stinson, Ernest C. *The Temple of King Solomon.* No publisher given, 1934.

Stoffel, E. L. *His Kingdom Is Forever.* Richmond: John Knox Press, 1956.

Stone, John Timothy. *Winning Men.* New York: Fleming H. Revell, 1940.

Stott, John R. W. *Basic Christianity.* Grand Rapids, Mich.: Wm. B. Eerdmans Co., 1958.

Strong, James. *Exhaustive Concordance of the Bible.* New York: Abingdon Press, 1890.

Stuart, Moses. *A Commentary on the Epistle to the Hebrews.* Edited by R. D. C. Robbins. 4th ed. Andover: Draper, 1864.

Stump, Joseph. *The Christian Faith: A System of Dogmatics.* Philadelphia: The Muhlenberg Press, 1942.

Sweet, William Warren. *Revivalism in America.* New York: Charles Scribner's Sons, 1944.

Sykes, Percy H. *A Brief History of King Solomon's Reign.* Philadelphia: Hiram Abibb, 1929.

Tarn, W. W. *Alexander the Great.* Vol. I: *Narrative.* Cambridge: University Press, 1948.

Tasker, R. V. G. *The Old Testament in the New Testament.* Grand Rapids, Mich.: Wm. B. Eerdmans Co., 1954.

Taylor, Richard S. *A Right Conception of Sin.* Kansas City, Mo.: Beacon Hill Press, 1945.

Taylor, Vincent. *The Atonement in New Testament Teaching.* London: Epworth Press, 1941.

____. *The Gospel According to St. Mark.* London: Macmillan Company, 1953.

____. *The Person of Christ in New Testament Teaching.* New York: Macmillan Co., 1958.

Taylor, William M. *David, King of Israel.* New York: Harper and Brothers, 1874.

Temple, William. *Foundations.* London: Macmillan and Co., 1912.

____. *Nature, Man and God.* London: Macmillan and Co., 1934.

Tenney, Merrill C. *New Testament Survey.* Grand Rapids, Mich.: Wm. B. Eerdmans Co., 1961.

____. *New Testament Times.* Grand Rapids, Mich.: Wm. B. Eerdmans Co., 1965.

____. ,ed. *The Zondervan Pictorial Bible Dictionary.* Grand Rapids, Mich.: Zondervan Publishing House, 1963.

Terrien, Samuel. "History of the Interpretation of the Bible; Modern Period," *Interpreter's Bible,* vol. I. New York: Abingdon Press, 1952. pp. 127-141.

____. *The Psalms and Their Meaning for Today.* New York: Bobbs-Merrill Co., 1952.

Thelen, Mary F. *Man as Sinner.* New York: King's Crown Press, 1946.

Thiessen, Henry C. *Introduction to the New Testament.* Grand Rapids, Mich.: Wm. B. Eerdmans Co., 1943.

Thomas, D. Winton, ed. *Archaelogy and Old Testament Study.* Oxford: Clarendon Press, 1967.

Thompson, Edward. *Crusaders Coast.* London: Ernest Benn, 1929.

Thompson, J. A. *The Bible and Archaeology.* Grand Rapids, Mich.: Wm. B. Eerdmans Co., 1962.

Thompson, William M. *Central Palestine and Phoenicia. The Land and the Book,* vol. 2 Hartford, Conn.: S. S. Scranton Co., 1908.

Tillett, Wilbur F. *Personal Salvation.* Nashville: Cokesbury Press,1930.

Titus, Harold H. *Ethics for Today.* New York: American Book Co., 1947.

Torrey, Reuben A. *The Person and Work of the Holy Spirit.* New York: Fleming H. Revell, 1910.

Toynbee, Arnold, ed., *The Crucible of Christianity: Judaism, Hellenism and the Historical Background to the Christian Faith.* London: Thames and Hudson, 1969.

Tristram, H. B. *The Land of Israel: A Journal of Travels in Palestine.* London: Society for Promoting Christian Knowledge, 1865.

Trueblood, D. Elton. *The Logic of Belief.* New York: Harper and Brothers, 1942.

____. *Philosophy of Religion.* New York: Harper and Brothers, 1957.

____. *The Trustworthiness of Religious Experience.* London: George Allen and Unwin, 1939.

Trueblood, D. Elton, and Trueblood, Pauline. *The Recovery of Family Life.* New York: Harper and Brothers, 1953.

Tsanoff, R. A. *The Moral Ideals of Our Civilization.* New York: E. P. Dutton and Co., 1942.

____. *Ethics.* Rev. New York: Harper and Brothers, 1955.

Tucker, T. G. *Life in the Roman World of Nero and St. Paul.* New York: Macmillan Company, 1924.

Turner, George A. *Historical Geography of the Holy Land.* Grand Rapids, Mich.: Baker Book House, 1973.

____. *The More Excellent Way.* Winona Lake, Ind.: Light and Life Press, 1952.

Turnowsky, W., ed. *Tour Guide to Israel.* Tel Aviv: Litour, 1952.

Turretin, Francis. *The Atonement.* New York: Board of Publication of the Reformed Protestant Dutch Church, 1859.

Uhlhorn, Herhard. *The Conflict of Christianity and Heathenism.* Edited and translated by Egbert C. Smyth and C. J. H. Ropes. Rev. New York: Charles Scribner's Sons, 1901.

____. *Archaeology and the New Testament.* Grand Rapids, Mich.: Zondervan Publishing House, 1964.

Unger, Merrill F. *Archaeology and the Old Testament.* Grand Rapids: Zondervan Publishing House, 1954.

____. *Introductory Guide to the Old Testament.* Grand Rapids, Mich.: Zondervan Publishing House, 1951.

____. *Unger's Bible Dictionary.* Chicago: Moody Press, 1957.

____. *Unger's Bible Handbook*. Chicago: Moody Press, 1966.

Van Diest, John W. "A Study of the Theophanies of the Old Testament." Th.M. thesis, Dallas Theological Seminary, 1966.

Vilnay, Zev. *The Guide to Israel,* Jerusalem: Ahiever, 1968.

____. *New Israel Atlas: Bible to Present Day.* Jerusalem: Israel University Press, 1968.

Vincent, L. H. *Jerusalem de L'Ancien Testament: Recherches d'Archeologie et d'Historie.* Paris: Librarie Lecoffre, 1954.

Vincent, Marvin R. *Word Studies in the New Testament.* 4 vols. Grand Rapids, Mich.: Wm. B. Eerdmans Co., 1957.

Vine, W. E. *Expository Dictionary of New Testament Words.* 4 vols. London: Oliphants, Ltd., 1939-41.

____. *An Expository Dictionary of New Testament Words.* Old Tappan, N. J.; Fleming H. Revell, 1956.

Von Allmen, J.J., ed. *A Companion to the Bible.* New York: The Oxford Press, 1958.

____. *Biblical Theology.* Grand Rapids, Mich.: Wm. B. Eerdmans Co., 1954.

Vos, Geerhardus. *The Teaching of Jesus Concerning the Kingdom of God and His Church.* New York: American Tract Society, 1903.

Vos, Howard F. *Beginnings in the New Testament.* Chicago: Moody Press, 1973.

____. *Religions in a Changing World.* Chicago: Moody Press, 1959.

Vriezen, Thomas. *An Outline of Old Testament Theology.* Translated by S. Neuijen. Oxford: Brasil Blackwell, 1958.

Walvoord, John F. *Jesus Christ Our Lord.* Chicago: Moody, 1969.

____. ,ed. *Inspiration and Interpretation.* Grand Rapids, Mich.: Wm. B. Eerdmans Co., 1957.

Warren, C., and Conder, C. R. *Survey of Western Palestine and Jerusalem.* London: Palestine Exploration Fund, 1884.

Waterman, Leroy. *The Song of Songs.* Ann Arbor: University of Michigan Press, 1948.

Watson, George D. *Spiritual Feasts.* Cincinnati: Revivalist Office, 1904.

Watson, J. B., ed. *The Church.* London: Pickering and Inglis, Ltd., 1949.

Weatherhead, Leslie D. *The Will of God.* New York: Abingdon-Cokesbury, 1944.

Welch, Claude. *In This Name.* New York: Charles Scribner's Sons, 1952.

Wesley, John. *Explanatory Notes upon the New Testament.* London: The Epworth Press. 1950.

____. *The Plain Account of Christian Perfection.* Boston: The Christian Witness Co., n.d.

____. *Sermons.* 2 vols. New York: Lane and Scott, 1852.

____. *Works.* 14 vols. Kansas City, Mo.: Nazarene Publishing House, 1958.

Wesley, John, et al. *New Testament Commentary.* Grand Rapids, Mich.: Baker Book House, 1972.

Westcott. B. F. *General Survey of the History of the Canon of the New Testament.* 7th ed. London: Macmillan & Co., 1896.

Westermann, Claus, ed., *Essays on Old Testament Hermeneutics.* Translated and edited by James Luther Mays. Richmond, Va.: John Knox Press, 1963.

Whale, J. S. *Christian Doctrine.* New York: Macmillan Co., 1945.

White, Stephen S. *Essential Christian Beliefs.* Kansas City, Mo.: Beacon Hill Press, n.d.

Whitehead, John. *The Life of the Rev. John Wesley,* M. A. New York: The United States Book Company, n.d.

Whitesell, Faris D. *Basic New Testament Evangelism.* Grand Rapids, Mich.: Zondervan Publishing House, 1959.

Wieand, Albert Cassel. *A New Harmony of the Gospels.* Grand Rapids, Mich.: Wm. B. Eerdmans Co., 1953.

Wiener, Harold M. "The Rama of Samuel." *Journal of the Palestine Oriental Society,* 1927.

Wiley, H. Orton. *Christian Theology.* 3 vols. Kansas City, Mo.: Beacon Hill Press, 1940.

____. and Culbertson, Paul T. *Introduction to Christian Theology.* Kansas City, Mo.: Nazarene Publishing House, 1945.

Wilkes, A. Paget. *The Dynamic of Redemption.* Kansas City, Mo.: Beacon Hill Press, 1946.

Willett, Herbert L. *Our Bible: Its Origin, Character, and Value.* Chicago: The Christian Century Press, 1917.

William, Archbishop of Tyre. *A History of Deeds Beyond the Sea.* Vol. 2. Translated by E. A. Babcock and A. C. Krey. New York: Columbia University Press, 1943.

Williams, Daniel Day. *God's Grace and Man's Hope.* New York: Harper and Brothers, 1949.

Williams, George. *The Student's Commentary on the Holy Scriptures.* Grand Rapids, Mich.: Kregal Publications, 1971.

Williams. R. T. *Temptation: A Neglected Theme.* Kansas City, Mo.: Nazarene Publishing House, 1920.

Williams, Walter G. *Archaeology in Biblical Research*. New York: Abingdon Press, 1965.

Wilson, Edmund. *The Scrolls from the Dead Sea*. New York: Oxford University Press, 1955.

Wilson, Capt. Warren. *The Recovery of Jerusalem: A Narrative of Exploration and Discovery in the City and the Holy Land*. Edited by Walter Morrison. New York: D. Appleton & Co., 1871.

Winchester, Olive M., and Price, Ross E. *Crisis Experiences in the Greek New Testament* Kansas City, Mo.: Beacon Hill Press, 1953.

Wiseman, Donald J. *Illustrations from Biblical Archaeology*. Grand Rapids, Mich: Wm. B. Eerdmans Co., 1958.

Wittek, P. *The Rise of the Ottoman Empire*. London, 1938.

Wood, J. A. *Perfect Love*. Chicago: Christian Witness Co., 1905.

Wood, Nathan R. *The Secret of the Universe*. Grand Rapids, Mich.: Wm. B. Eerdmans Co., 1936.

Wright, G. Ernest, ed. *The Bible and the Ancient Near East*. Garden City, N. Y.: Doubleday and Co., 1961.

_____. *Biblical Archaeology*. 2nd ed. Philadelphia: Westminster Press, 1962.

_____. *The Challenge of Israel's Faith*. Chicago: The University of Chicago Press, 1944.

_____. *God Who Acts*, Studies in Biblical Theology, no. 8. London: S.C.M. Press, 1952.

_____. *The Old Testament Against Its Environment*, Studies in Biblical Theology, no. 2. London: S.C.M. Press, 1950.

_____. *The Old Testament and Theology*. New York: Harper & Row, 1969.

Wright, G. Ernest, and Filson, Floyd Vivian, eds. *The Westminster Historical Atlas to the Bible*. Philadelphia: Westminster Press, 1945.

Wright, G. Ernest, and Freedman, D. N. eds. *The Biblical Archaeologist Reader*. Garden City, N.Y.: Doubleday Anchor Books, 1961.

Wright, Sara Margaret. *A Brief Survey of the Bible*. Neptune, N.J.: Loizeaux Bros., 1958.

Wright, Thomas, ed. *Early Travels in Palestine*. New York: KTAV Publishing House, 1948, 1968.

Wuest, Kenneth S. *Word Studies in the Greek New Testament*. 4 vols. Grand Rapids, Mich.: Wm. B. Eerdmans Co., 1966.

Yates, Kyle M. *Preaching from the Prophets*. New York: Harper and Brothers, 1942.

_____. *Preaching from the Psalms*. New York: Harper and Brothers, 1948.

_____. *Studies in Psalms*. Nashville: Broadman Press, 1953.

Yohn, David Waite. *The Christian Reader's Guide to the New Testament*. Grand Rapids, Mich.: Wm. B. Eerdmans Co., 1973.

Young, Edward J. *An Introduction to the Old Testament*. Grand Rapids, Mich.: Wm. B. Eerdmans Co., 1949.

_____. *The Study of Old Testament Theology Today*. Westwood, N.J.: Fleming H. Revell, 1959.

Young, Kimball. *Personality and the Problems of Adjustment*. New York: F. S. Crofts and Co., 1940.

Young, Robert. *Analytical Concordance to the Bible*. Grand Rapids, Mich.: Wm. B. Eerdmans Co., 1955.

Young, Warren C. *A Christian Approach to Philosophy*. Wheaton, Ill.: Van Kampen Press, 1954.

Zahn, Theodor. *Introduction to the New Testament*. 3 vols. Grand Rapids, Mich.: Kregel Publications, 1953.

Zenos, Andrew C. *Compendium of Church History*. Philadelphia: Presbyterian Board of Publication, 1896.

Zwemer, Samuel M. *The Moslem Doctrine of God*. New York: Young People's Missionary Movement, 1905.

Index

Aristarchus 370, 470, 496, 586
Aristeas 303, 306
Ark
   Noah's 53
Ark of the Covenant 106, 107, 203, 586
   Contents of 27, 134
Armageddon 586
Artaxerxes 586
Artemis 460, 542
Asa 586
Asceticism and mysticism 388
Ashdod 586
Asher
   Character study of 81
Ashtoreth 586
Assurance of salvation 523
Assyria 586
Assyrians
   Defeated by Jerusalem 171, 180
Athaliah 586
Athanasius 326, 427, 445
Athens 413, 586
   "Unknown god" 412
Atonement 69, 123
   Christ's 230, 428
   Day of 123, 586
   In OT-NT 427
Augsburg Confession 446
Augustus Caesar 302, 423, 587
Authenticity of the Bible 28
Avarice 354
Azariah 634
Azotus 586

B
Baal 157, 587
   Compound Names 137
      Gad 137
      Jerub 137, 158
      Peor 137
      Zebub 137
      Zephon 137
   Description of 136, 137
   God of fertility 139
Baalbeck 138, 139
Baalzebub 588
Baanah 587
Babel 587
Babylon 93, 182, 233, 250, 515, 587
Babylonian Calendar 93
Backsliding 450
Balaam 133, 136, 587
Balac 587

Balak 136, 587
Baptism 587
   And circumcision 320
   John's 75, 343, 344
Barabbas 587
Barak 587
Barbarian 587
Barley 587
Barnabas 410, 500, 587
Bartholomew 587
Bartimaeus 587
Basilica 497
Bath House, Roman 453
Bathsheba 588
Beelzebub 588
Beersheba 588
Bel (See Baal)
Bells, Church
   Witness 573
Belshazzar 588
Ben-hadad 588
Benaiah 588
Benjamin 588
   Character study 82
Berea 412, 588
Bereshith 35
Berkeley Version 580
Beth 588
Bethany 588
Bethel 76, 262, 588
Bethesda 588
Bethlehem 58, 588
Bethpeor 588
Bethphage 588
Bethsaida 346, 513, 588, 591
Beulah 588
Bible
   And science 41
   And theory of evolution 42
   Authenticity of 28, 29
   Development of canon 28
   Doctrines in OT/NT 32
   Doctrines in Revelation 539
   English versions 37
   Inspired by Holy Spirit 489, 490
   Integrity of 29
   Its authority 38
   Its origin 26
   Its practicality 30
   Its preservation 27
   Mss trustworthy 26
   Test of time 30
   Thematic unity of 70
   Unique 32
   Written by holy men of God 27, 29, 175, 228, 235
   Written by honest men 29
Bible names 341

Bible preserved
   Early English versions 574
   Early languages 569
   English versions of the twentieth century 580
   Throughout Dark Ages by Monasteries 573
      Religious Dramas 574
      Religious Paintings 574
      Sacred Chants and Other Church Music 573
      Sculpture and Stained Glass Art 573
      Steepled Churches and Their Bells 573
Bible, writing of
   Conservative position 490
Bildad 196
Bilhah 589
Birthright 589
Bishop 482, 589
Bishop of Athens 414
Bishop's Bible, The 577
Bishops, qualifications 485
Blasphemy 589
Blessing of Jacob 78
Blessings of the Exile and Dispersion of the Jews 285
Blood
   Of Christ 442, 527
Blood redemption 74
Blood Revenge 589
Blood sacrifice
   And Cain and Abel 51
   In both Testaments 34
Boat, the Jesus 365
Boaz 153, 160, 589
Bondage, Spiritual 70
Born again 74, 384, 458
Brazen altar 111 (See also Altar of Burnt Offering)
Brazen laver 116
Brazen Serpent 589
Bread
   Physical 144
   Spiritual 144
Breastplate 589
   Of the High Priest 78, 114
Bricks 589
   With straw 97
Bridges (Links) Between OT-NT
   Ekklesia 316
   Essenes 309, 312, 313, 314, 315
   Hymnody 315
   Liturgy 316
   Sacraments 320
Bulrush 589

Confraternity Version 580
Congregation of the righteous 385, 389
Conscience 426
Consecration 124, 430
Constantine 329, 417, 431, 467
Contend for faith 532
Conversion
In OT-NT 64, 129, 386
Convocation 129
Corinth 437, 592
Depraved city 433
Persecution 433
Synagogue church 433
Vice and crime 437
Corinthian church
Factions 435
Immorality 434
Corinthians, the epistles to 433
Authorship 433
Christian liberty 435
Cross exalted 435
Love chapter 434
Cornelius 592
Cornerstone 352, 592
Cornet 592
Council of A.D. 200 542
Council of A.D. 401 542
Council of A.D. 431 542
Council of A.D. 476 543
Council of Jerusalem 508
Council of Nicaea 556, 561
Counterfeit church 132, 141, 546
Court of the Gentiles 170, 408
Covenant 142
With Abraham 63
Coverdale, Miles 576
Creation
"After their kind" 43
Days 41
Of man 43
Creed of Athanasius 445
Creeds of the Christian Faith 443
Crete 592
Cross 40, 592
Crown 592
Crucifixion 592
Crusader Castle 350
Cupbearer 592
Curtain (See Veil)
Cybel-Artemis temple 553
Cyprus 592
Cyrus, King of Persia 592
Conquers Babylon 296

Defeated at Salamis 297
Diverts Euphrates 296
Jews return to Jerusalem 296
Liberates Jews 176, 182, 296
Returns Temple Vessels 296
Rebuilds Jerusalem 296
Supplies Finances 296

D
Dagon 593
Dalmatia 431
Damascus document 312
Damascus, Syria 593
Dan 593
Character study of 80
Daniel 239, 593
And Joseph 249
Biographical Sketch 245
Devout, prayerful 245
Dreams 248
Fiery furnace 248
Visions 249
Daniel, the book of 245, 593
Analysis of 248
Authorship 245
Historicity of 247
Liberal view 247
Writing hand 248
Darius 593
Dark Ages 572
Darwin, Charles
Biographical sketch 42
David 593
King 164, 217
Musical instruments 204
Day of
Atonement 123, 170, 428
Creation 41
The Lord 477, 518
Wrath 282
Deacon
Office of 488
Meaning of word 488
Dead Sea Scrolls 306, 307
Confirm the ancient MSS 28
Forerunners of the Gospels 307
Isaiah scroll 28, 29, 226
Similar to the Gospels 308
Death 48
Universal 47
Vanquished 47, 50
Decalogue 33, 62

Decapolis 344
Dedication, Feast of 392
Demas 370, 496
Despondency
In Moses 216
In David 216
In Elijah 216
In Jeremiah 216
In Job 216
In Joshua 216
In the Bible 216
In The Disciples 216
Deutero-Isaiah 223
Deuteronomic laws 27, 30
Deuteronomy, the book of 141
Mosaic authorship of 141
Diana, Temple of 542
Diaspora 408
Diocletian 431
Dionysius 414
Disaster, total 193
Disciple
Meaning of word 398
Disobedience 154, 205
Dispersion of the Jews 57, 182, 593
Word defined 286
Dissension 464
Divination 593
Divine
Appearances 72, 73
Image 43, 203
Names 74, 90
Presence 118, 227
Revelation 34, 135
Divorce 145
Documentary Hypothesis 36
Documents, Link OT/NT 303
Dog 593
Dome of the Rock 54
Domitian 414
Donkey 616
Door
Christ 112
Of grace 282
Dothan 593
Douai (See Douay)
Douay Bible 305
Dove 593
Dragon 594
Dreams 594
Drink Offering 594
Drink, Alcoholic 594
Drunkenness 56
Dunamis (power) 360

And the Lord's Supper 320, 322
Lamb 94, 98, 322
Past Tense Salvation 68
Pastoral Epistles 483
Patmos 620
Patriarchal Period 193
Paul 65, 620
Defense of his apostleship 450
Facing death 487
Pekah 620
Penalty for sin 32
Peniel 620
Penny 620
Pentateuch 30, 35, 36, 38, 83, 620
Pentecost 399, 620
Pentecost, Day of 99, 117
Peor 620
Perga 621
Pergamos 548, 621
Pergamum (See Pergamos)
Perizzites 621
Persecution of Christians 424, 485, 501, 508, 515, 561
Persecution of the Jews 189
Persia 126, 187, 248, 286, 296, 297, 621
Defeated at Salamis 297
Peter, James and John 69, 379
Peter, Simon 360, 407, 621
Biographical sketch 513
Peter, the epistles of 511
Authorship 511
Petra 266
Pharaoh 87, 621
Pharisees 184, 365, 389, 390, 392, 621
Believing 411
Legalists 365
Some Believers 366
Philadelphia 557, 621
Christianity of 559
City of brotherly love 558
Philemon 621
Biographical sketch 495
Philemon, epistle to 495
Authorship 495
Interpretation of 496
Philip 621
Philip, the Evangelist 500
Philippi 412, 466, 478, 621
Founding of church 463
Philippi, church in 464
Philippians, the book of 463
Authorship 463
Friendship 464

Theme of "the gospel" 464
Philistines 621
Philosophers vs. wise men 214
Phinehas 621
Phoebe 419, 622
Phoenicia 622
Phoenician Calendar 93
Phrygia 622
Phylacteries 598
Pieces of Silver 622
Pig 630
Pilate, Pontius 622
Pillar of cloud 98, 118
Pillar of fire 110
Pipe 622
Pisgah, Mount 622
Pisidia 622
Pitch 622
Place of the Skull, the 368
Plagues, the Ten 622
Pleasure, sensual is empty 217
Pleiades 622
Pliny the Elder 312
Polycarp 511, 545
Polycrates 542
Pontus 622
Pool of Siloam 180
Pope
Relationship to King 574
Porphyry 246, 247
Potiphar 622
Prayer
Effectiveness of 115
Predestination 458
Presbyter 380, 482
Priest 622
Priesthood 32
Levitical 85, 120
Of believers 110
Of Christ 110
Priests
Garments of 113
High 123
Pre-levitical 113
Prince of demons 137
Prisca (Priscilla) 500
Proconsul 623
Procurator 302, 623
Progressive Development of the Church 400
Promised Land 205
Proof of God 41
Prophet 623
Prophets 32
Duty of 235
Major 235
Minor 235

Nebhiim 30, 31
Women 235
Proselyte 623
Prostitutes 153
Proverbs
Deuteronomic influence 213
Sanctified common sense 213
Teaching device 211
Wise sayings 211
Proverbs, the book of 211
Authorship 211
Pruning Hooks 623
Psalms 623
Christ in the 209
Christian Hymns 204
Christological 209
Degrees 201
Devotional 202
Hallel 208
Hallelujah 208
Historic or National 201
Historical bridge of NT 202
Imprecatory 201
Jesus quotes 209
Joy 203
Levitical singers 203
Messianic 202
Nature 201
OT-NT hymnal 64
Penitential 201
Praise 201
Sin in 203
Singing 203
Social 201
Psalms, the book of 199
Authorship 199
Book of praises 200
Psaltery 623
Pseudepigrapha 305, 530
Ptolemies 298
Ptolemy Philadelphus III 304
Publican 623
Publicans 346
Pure language 282
Purim, Feast of 187, 192
Purple dye 551
Pyramids 59
Of Giza 60

Q
Qahal
OT Church 32, 318, 319, 321
Quail 135
Qumran 93, 306, 307, 309, 313, 388

R

Rabbinical Council 30
Rachab 623
Rachel 623
Rahab 152, 623
Ram 623
Ramah 623
Rameses or Raamses 83, 623
Ramesses II 86
Rapture 477, 537
Ras Shamra 139
Rebekah 624
Rechab 624
Rechabites 624
Red Sea 98
Redemption
    For Adam and Eve 50
    From Genesis to Revelation 26
    In OT-NT 34, 39, 67, 68, 473
    Plan of, same for all time 49
    Symbolism 33
    Through Christ 40
Refiner 624
Refuge, Cities of 142
Regeneration 136, 385
Rehoboam 624
Rejected stone 65
Religion
    True and false 97
    Jehovah unique 32
Remnant
    Of Israel 226
    To be saved 282
Renaissance 574
Repentance
    In OT 384
Rephidim 624
Rest, Essential 48
Resurrection 50
Retribution 282
Reuben 624
    Character study of 79
Revelation
    Methods of 43
Revelation of Saint John 624
Revelation, Divine
    OT/NT Unity of 34
Revelation, redemptive 103
Revelation, the book of 533
    A Retrospective View 537
    And other Johannine writings 534
    And the book of Daniel 535
    And the OT 534
    Apocalytic parallels with OT 535

Authorship 533
Methods of interpretation
    Eclectic 536
    Preterist 536
Revised Standard Version 580
Revised Version 579
Rheims-Douay Bible 577
Riblah 624
Riches 366
Robber Council 549
Rock, Divine 351
Rod
    Of Aaron 106
    Of Moses 100
Rogers, John 576
Roman Period 299
Romans
    Engineers 362
Romans, the book of 419, 624
    Authorship 419
Rome 420, 423, 624
    Church in 420
    Conquers Carthage 299
    Jews Expelled 299
    The church in 514
Ruach, 32
Ruby 80, 624
Ruth, the book of 159, 624
    Authorship 159
    The Moabites 159

S

Sabbath 398, 624
    Day of rest 48, 143
    From the creation 48
    Holy day 101
    Observed 117
    Rest for the believer 109
    Therapeutic 49
Sabbath day's journey 398, 624
Sabbatical year 92, 104, 121, 130, 625
Sackcloth 625
Sacraments, the 320
    Christ our Passover 323
    Passover-Lord's Supper 322
Sacrifice 625
    Abel's 34
    Christ's 50
    Essential to worship 54
    Evidence of Faith 120
    Expresses love 164
    Foreshadows Christ 64
    Inadequate 120
    Meaning of 164
    Meaning of in OT-NT 430
    Prefigured Christ 52, 54
    Symbolizes faith 33

Sacrifice, blood
    And Cain and Abel 51
    Of Christ 52
Sadducees 184, 312, 366, 389, 625
Saint Catherine's Monastery 573
Salome 625
Salt 625
Salutation 625
Salvation 26, 50
    Basic Bible doctrine 65
    By Christ exclusively 68
    By faith 65
    From the foundation of the world 39, 40
    In OT period 39, 64, 65, 66, 67, 385
    Pre-creation 39
    Pre-crucifixion 68
Stand-by atonement 39
Symbolized in the exodus 95
Samaria 625
Samaritan Pentateuch 625
Samaritans 387, 625
Samuel 625
    Judge and prophet 162
Samuel, the books of 161
    Authorship 161
    Historical content 162
Sanballat 625
Sanctification 505
    By Holy Spirit 99
    In OT, Conditions of 55,124
Sanhedrin 625
Sapphire 626
Sarah 626
Sarai (Sarah) 70
Sardis 553, 556, 626
Sargon 626
Satan 136, 196
    Angel of Light 50
    Prince of this world 50
    Ultimate Defeat 50
Saul 626
    Disobedience 162
    First king 162, 163
    Suicide 162
    Witch at Endor 162
Saul (Paul)
    Biographical sketch 405
Saved by faith, through grace 33
Scapegoat 124, 626
Scarlet cord 108
Scientific dogmatism 42
Scientific truth 41
Scourge 626

Scribe 626
    Description of 183, 184
    Accuracy 27, 184, 329
    Honored profession 184
    Members of Sanhedrin 184
    Teachers 184
Scriptures 626
Scroll or Roll 626
Sea of Galilee (See Chinnereth)
Second Coming of Christ 41, 476, 477, 578
Seed
    Foreshadows Christ 50
    The Woman's 50
Seir, Mount 626
Selah 626
Seleucia 627
Seleucids 298
Selfishness 62
Semite 26
Sennacherib 627
Septuagint 35, 303, 569, 627
How written 304
Seraphims 627
Sergius Paulos 627
Sermon on the Mount
    And the OT 33
Serpent of Brass (See Brazen Serpent)
Serpents 133, 627
Seth 627
Seven, the number 537, 538
Shaddai (See El Shaddai)
Shadrach 248, 627
Shallum 627
Shalmanezer 347, 627
Shamgar 627
Sharon 627
Sheba 627
Shechem 627
Shekel 628
Shem 628
Sheminith 628
Sheol (See Hell)
Shepherds 628
    False 112
Shewbread 130, 628
    Christ 108, 109
    Twelve loaves 109
Shiloh 628
Shinar 57, 628
Shishak 628
Shittah 628
Shittim 628
Shofar horn 129 (See also Cornet)
Shuah 628

Shuite 628
Shunamite, the 628
Sichem 627
Sidon 347, 349, 350, 628
    And Tyre 350
Sihon 628
Sila 628
Silas 412, 476
Silas (Silvanus) 65
Siloam 629
Silvanus 628
Silver 629
Simeon 629
    Character study of 79
Simon 629
Sin 47
    Defined 102
    Destructive nature of 102
    Historical beginning of 52
    In penitential Psalms 206
    Misery of 238
    Of adultery 125
    Origin of 119
    Penalty of 32
    Remedy for 52
    The first 49
Sinai, Mount 33, 100, 101, 113, 117
Singing (See also Music)
Sion, Mount 629
Sling 629
Smith-Goodspeed Version 580
Smyrna 544, 545, 629
Sodom 629
Sodomite 629
Solomon 166, 167, 629
    Age of properity 168
    Author of Ecclesiastes 215
    Biographical sketch 168
    Jehovah covenant 168
    Temple of 169, 170
    Wisdom 168
    Wrote proverbs 211
Son of man, the 136
Song of redemption 64
Song of victory 98
Sopherim 30, 184
Sovereignty of God 189
Spain 629
Sphinx 61
Spikenard 630
Spirit of God (See Holy Spirit)
Spiritual
    Cleansing 115
    Ignorance 42
    Kingdom 40
St. Augustine 445
Stephen 630
Stocks 630

Stoic 630
Stone, Cut 139
Streets 630
Subscriptions in KJV 431
Succoth 630
Suffer
    The righteous 195
Suffering 195
Sunday 416
Swine, 630
Sycamine tree 630
Sycamore tree 630
Symbol of Sin 133
Synagogue 303, 312, 319, 402, 630
    In the NT 373, 376
    Synoptic Problem, the 337
    Mutual Use Theory 337
    Oral Tradition 337
Source Theory 338
Syrophoenician 630

T
Tabernacle 85, 402, 630
    Blueprint 106
    Christological study 105
    Constuction 105
    In NT 105
    Portable 105
Table of shewbread 108
Tablets, Clay 58
Tabor, Mount 630
Tadmor (See Palmyra) 631
Talmud 184, 222, 224, 384, 631
Tammuz 631
Tares 631
Tarshish 268, 631
Tarsus 406, 631
Tartak 631
Tax collector 346
Taxing 631
Tekoa 259, 631
Tekoah 631
Temple 402, 631
    Desecrated 298
    Destroyed 303
Temple leaders 29
    Apostasy 312
Temple of Diana 460
Temples
    Jupiter 140
Ten Commandments 27, 30, 62, 85, 101, 102, 142, 631
Ten Generations, the 36, 38
Tent (See Tabernacle)
Tent of Meeting 134

Z

Zabulon (See Zebulun)
Zacchaeus 346, 371, 386, 635
Zacharias 635
Zarephath 635
Zealots 342
Zebedee 635
Zebulun 635
    Character study of 81
Zechariah 635
Zedekiah 240, 635
Zeno 350
Zephaniah 635
    Prophet 281
Zephaniah, the book of 281
    Authorship 281
Zerubbabel 183, 635
Zeus 548
Zidon 628
Zimri 635
Zin, wilderness of 99
Zion, Mount 205, 258, 629
Ziphron 635
Zipporah 636
Zoar 636
Zophar 636